DIVERSE VOICES IN HEALTH LAW AND ETHICS

Diverse Voices

Series Editors: **Se-shauna Wheatle**, Durham University and **Jonathan Herring**, University of Oxford

---

Diverse Voices presents a ground-breaking platform for critiquing the law from the perspective of minoritized and marginalized groups and debating and understanding the impact of the law on these different groups. Each book brings together an inclusive group of authors to explore a range of underexplored perspectives on the law and amplify voices that remain underrepresented in the field.

Find out more about the new and forthcoming titles in the series:

bristoluniversitypress.co.uk/diverse-voices

DIVERSE VOICES IN HEALTH LAW AND ETHICS

Important Perspectives

Edited by
Elizabeth Chloe Romanis, Sabrina Germain, and
Jonathan Herring

BRISTOL
UNIVERSITY
PRESS

First published in Great Britain in 2025 by

Bristol University Press
University of Bristol
1–9 Old Park Hill
Bristol
BS2 8BB
UK
t: +44 (0)117 374 6645
e: bup-info@bristol.ac.uk

Details of international sales and distribution partners are available at bristoluniversitypress.co.uk

British Library Cataloguing in Publication Data
A catalogue record for this book is available from the British Library

ISBN 978-1-5292-3653-8 hardcover
ISBN 978-1-5292-3654-5 paperback
ISBN 978-1-5292-3655-2 ePub
ISBN 978-1-5292-3656-9 ePdf

Cover design: Nicky Borowiec
Front cover image: Adobe Stock/Dedraw Studio
Bristol University Press uses environmentally responsible print partners.
Printed and bound in Great Britain by CPI Group (UK) Ltd, Croydon, CR0 4YY

FSC
www.fsc.org
MIX
Paper | Supporting responsible forestry
FSC® C013604

For anyone who has ever felt unheard

Contents

PART II The Body of Health Law

Series Editors' Preface

Law is dominated by a select range of actors: the wealthy, the white, the male, and the enabled. Their prevalence among those who appear before the courts, whether as litigants or legal representatives, and those who judge the cases, is inescapable.

This is true in much academic discourse too. The privileged dominate the practice of law, the law reports, and the professorati. *Diverse Voices* is an attempt to engage with a wider range of voices and perspectives than are typically encountered within the legal academy and legal studies. What are the stories which are not told in traditional law courses? Whose values are permitted and who is ignored? Who is rendered visible and who subjected to the legal gaze? Who is controlled and who is empowered by the law?

Inevitably this series will not capture all the voices that need to be heard. It cannot capture the depth of nuance that a deep intersectional analysis requires. What the series does do is to disrupt the dominant discourse, to highlight those marginalised, silenced, or misrepresented by the law. It seeks to start a listening process and begin a journey. It is certainly not the last word or the final destination. It is a beginning.

List of Figures, Tables, and Boxes

Figures

Tables

Boxes

Table of Cases

AB v CD [2013] EWHC 1418 (Fam)
Aintree University Hospital NHS Foundation Trust v James [2013] UKSC 67
Airedale NHS Trust v Bland [1993] AC 789 (Fam)
Ampthill Peerage Case [1977] AC 547
Andrews v DPP [1937] AC 576
Ashworth Security Hospital v MGN Limited [2000] 1 WLR 515
Attorney-General's Reference (No. 3 of 1994) [1997] 3 WLR 42
B v C (Surrogacy: Adoption) [2015] EWFC 17
Barking, Havering and Redbridge University Hospitals NHS Trust v X (A Child), Mrs W (Mother) [2020] EWHC 1630 (Fam)
Barnett v Chelsea and Kensington Hospital Management Committee [1969] 1 QB 428
Bawa-Garba v GMC [2018] EWCA Civ 1879
Bell v Tavistock [2020] EWHC 3274 (Admin)
Bell v Tavistock and Portman NHS Foundation Trust [2021] EWCA Civ 1363
Blyth v Bloomsbury Health Authority (1993) 4 Med LR 15
Bolam v Friern Hospital Management Committee [1957] 1 WLR 582
Bolitho City v Hackney Health Authority [1998] AC 232
Briody v St Helens and Knowsley Area Health Authority [2001] EWCA Civ 1010
Briggs v Briggs [2016] EWCOP 48
Burton v Islington Health Authority [1993] QB 204
Campbell v Mirror Group Newspapers [2004] UKHL 22
Chatterton v Gerson [1981] QB 432
Chester v Afshar [2004] UKHL 41
CP (A Child) v Criminal Injuries Compensation Authority [2015] QB 459
Crowter v Secretary of State for Health and Social Care [2021] EWHC 2536
Crowter v Secretary of State for Health and Social Care [2022] EWCA Civ 1559
Darnley v Croydon Health Services NHS Trust [2018] UKSC 50
Diamond v Royal Devon and Exeter NHS Foundation Trust [2019] EWCA Civ 585
Evans v Amicus Healthcare Ltd; Hadley v Midland Fertility Services Ltd [2003] EWHC 2161
F v West Berkshire HA [1989] 2 All ER 545
General Dental Council v Savery and Others [2011] EWHC 3011
General Medical Council v Bawa-Garba [2018] EWHC 76 (Admin)
Gillick v West Norfolk & Wisbeck Area Health Authority [1986] AC 112
Glass v UK [2004] 1 FCR 553

Goodwill v British Pregnancy Advisory Service [1996] 2 All ER 161
Greater Glasgow Health Board v Doogan [2014] UKSC 68
Guys and St Thomas NHS Foundation Trust (GSTT) & South London and Maudsley NHS Foundation Trust (SLAM) v R [2020] EWCOP 4
Janaway v Salford Health Authority [1988] UKHL 17
Jepson v Chief Constable of West Mercia [2003] EWHC 3318 (Admin)
Khan v Meadows [2021] UKSC 21
Kings College v C [2015] EWCOP 59
Leeds Teaching Hospital NHS Trust v A [2003] 1 FLR 412
Manchester University NHS Foundation Trust v Fixsler [2021] EWHC 1426 (Fam)
McCulloch v Forth Valley Health Board [2023] UKSC 26
McFarlane v Tayside Health Board [2000] 2 AC 59
McGhee v National Coal Board [1973] 1 WLR 1
The Mental Health Trust, The Acute Trust, The Council v DD [2014] EWCOP 11
Montgomery v Lanarkshire Health Board [2015] UKSC 11
Muller v King's College Hospital NHS Trust [2017] QB 987
An NHS Foundation Trust v AB & Ors [2019] EWCOP 26
NHS Trust v CX (Medical Treatment: Gillick Competence: Consent to Treatment) [2019] EWHC 3033 (Fam)
NHS Trust & Ors v FG [2014] EWCOP 30
An NHS Trust v ST [2023] EWCOP 40
Northern Health and Social Services Board v A and Others [1994] NIJB 1
Nottingham University Hospitals NHS Trust v M (by His Children's Guardian, Leonie Cobham) [2021] EWHC 3380
Oliver v Williams [2013] EWHC 600
Parkinson v St James and Seacroft University Hospital NHS Trust [2001] EWCA Civ 530
Paton v British Pregnancy Advisory Service Trustees [1979] QB 276
Paul and Another v Royal Wolverhampton NHS Trust; Polymear v Royal Cornwall Hospitals NHS Trust; Purchase v Ahmed [2024] UKSC 1
PC, NC v City of York Council [2013] EWCA Civ 478
Pearce v United Bristol Healthcare NHS Trust [1999] ECC 167
R (A and Another) v Secretary of State for Health [2017] UKSC 41
R (Axon) v Secretary of State for Health [2006] EWHC 37
R (Burke) v General Medical Council [2005] EWCA Civ 1003
R (McConnell and YY) v Registrar General and Secretary of State for Health and Social Care and Others [2020] EWCA Civ 559.
R (Nicklinson) v Ministry of Justice [2014] UKSC 38
R (Purdy) v DPP [2009] UKHL 45
R (YA) v Secretary of State for Health [2009] EWCA Civ 225
R v Adomako [1995] 1 AC 171
R v Bateman (1925) 19 Cr App R 8
R v Bawa-Garba [2016] EWCA Crim 1841
R v Bourne [1938] 3 All ER 615

R v Catt [Sentencing Remarks] (12 September 2012)
R v Cornish (Errol) [2016] EWHC 779
R v Department of Health ex p Source Informatics Ltd [2000] 1 All ER 786
R v Foster [Sentencing Remarks] (12 June 2023)
R v Foster [Summary of the Decision of the Court of Appeal, Criminal Division] (18 July 2023)
R v Garg [2012] EWCA Crim 2520
R v Kovvali [2013] EWCA Crim 1056
R v Misra [2005] 1 Cr App R 21
R v Pora [2016] 1 Cr App R 3
R v Prentice, Sullman, Adomako, Holloway [1994] QB 302
R v Rose [2018] QB 328
R v Rudling [2016] EWCA Crim 741
R v Sellu [2016] EWCA Crim 1716
R v Woollin [1998] 1 AC 82
RE (a Minor) and Others v Calderdale & Huddersfield NHS Foundation Trust [2017] EWHC 824
Re A [1992] 3 Med LR 303
R (A and Another) v Secretary of State for Health [2017] UKSC 41
Re AB (Termination of Pregnancy) [2019] EWCA Civ 1215
Re B (Adult Refusal of Medical Treatment) [2002] EWHC 429 (Fam)
Re B (a Minor) (Wardship: Sterilisation) [1988] AC 199
Re E (a Minor) (Wardship: Medical Treatment) [1993] 1 FLR 386
Re DD (No. 4) (Sterilisation) [2015] EWCOP 4
Re F (Mental Patient: Sterilisation) [1990] 2 AC 1
Re the Human Fertilisation and Embryology Act 2008 (Case G) [2016] EWHC 729
Re JA (a Minor) (Medical Treatment Child Diagnosed with HIV) [2014] EWHC 1135
Re JB [2014] EWHC 342 (COP)
Re L (Medical Treatment: Gillick Competency) [1998] 2 FLR 810
Re M (Medical Treatment: Consent) [1999] 2 FLR
Re MB (Medical Treatment) [1997] 2 FLR 426 (CA)
Re N (a Child) [2021] EWHC 2517 (Fam)
Re P (Sexual Relations and Contraception) [2018] EWCOP 10
Re R (a Minor) [1991] WL 837976
Re S (Child as Parent: Adoption: Consent) [2017] EWHC 2729 (Fam)
Re T (Adult: Refusal of Treatment) [1993] Fam 95
Re W (a Minor) (Medical Treatment: Court's Jurisdiction) [1993] Fam 64
Re X (a Child) (No. 2) [2021] EWHC 65 (Fam)
Re Z [2020] EWCOP 20
Rees v Darlington Memorial Hospital NHS Trust [2003] UKHL 52
RK v Oldham NHS Trust [2003] Lloyd's Rep Med 1 (QB)
Salford Royal NHS Foundation Trust v Mrs P and Q [2017] EWCOP 23 (Fam)
Sidaway v Board of Governors of the Bethlem Royal Hospital and the Maudsley Hospital [1985] AC 871

Smeaton v Secretary of State for Health [2002] EWHC 610
St George's Healthcare NHS Trust v S [1998] 3 All ER 673
United Lincolnshire NHS Hospitals Trust v CD [2019] EWCOP 24
University Hospital Plymouth NHS Trust v B (a Minor) [2019] EWHC 1670
W v Edgell [1990] 1 All ER 835
The Wagon Mound [1961] AC 388
Western Health and Social Services Board v CMB and the Official Solicitor (NI High Ct, 1995)
Wilsher v Essex Area Health Authority [1988] AC 1074
Wyatt v Curtis [2003] EWCA Civ 1779
Wye Valley NHS Trust v Mr B [2015] EWCOP 60
Z v Finland [1997] 25 EHRR 371

Table of Statutes

Abortion Act 1967
Brexit in the European Union (Withdrawal) Act 2018
Care Act 2014
Children Act 1989
Civil Partnership Act 2004
Congenital Disabilities (Civil Liability) Act 1976
Coronavirus Act 2020
Counter-Terrorism and Security Act 2015
Criminal Justice (NI) Act 1945
Data Protection Act 2018
Equality Act 2010
Family Law Reform Act 1969
Gender Recognition Act 2004
Genital Mutilation Act 2003
Government of Wales Act 2006
Health Act 2009
Heath and Social Care Act 2008
Health and Social Care Act 2012
Health and Social Care Act 2022
Homicide Act 1957
Human Fertilisation and Embryology Act 1990
Human Fertilisation and Embryology Act 2008
Human Rights Act 1998
Human Tissue Act 2004
Human Tissue (Authorisation) (Scotland) Act 2019
Infant Life (Preservation) Act 1929
Marriage and Civil Partnership (Scotland) Act 2014
Marriage (Same-Sex Couples) Act 2013
Mental Capacity Act 2005
Mental Health Act 1959
Mental Health Act 1983
Mental Health Act 2007
Mental Health Units (Use of Force) Act 2018
National Health Service Act 2006
National Health Service Reorganisation Act 1973

NHS and Community Care Act 1990
NHS Family Planning Act 1967
NHS Redress Act 2006
Northern Ireland Act 1998
Northern Ireland (Executive Formations) Act 2019
Offences Against the Person Act 1861
Organ Donation (Deemed Consent) Act 2019
Organ and Tissue Donation (Deemed Consent) Act (Northern Ireland) 2022
Public Health (Control of Disease) Act 1984
Road Traffic Act 1998
Scotland Act 1998
Serious Crime Act 2015
Sexual Offences Act 2003
Suicide Act 1961
Terrorism Act 2000

Notes on Contributors

Amel Alghrani (she/her)
Professor of Law, University of Liverpool
Motivated by my identity as a Black, Asian, Minority Ethnic (BAME) academic specialising in the regulation of healthcare, my involvement in this collection exploring the prosecution of doctors for gross negligence manslaughter (GNM) stems from an awareness of the disparate impact of laws on BAME individuals. With approximately 46 per cent of NHS doctors being of BAME background, our chapter wanted to highlight their heightened vulnerability to prosecution and regulatory referrals and harsher sanctions. My chapter with Hannah Saad aims to address unexplored diverse voices at the intersection of healthcare and criminal law, specifically within the context of GNM. Our commitment to highlighting these disparities underscores the importance of diverse perspectives in understanding and reforming healthcare practices.

Dunja Begović (she/her)
Research Associate, Lancaster University
Coming from a background of bioethics and medical jurisprudence, and more recently working on research projects about palliative care, I have found myself fascinated by the end-of-life context and the important, though sometimes neglected, ethico-legal challenges raised by it. I hope that the chapter I have contributed to will help students expand their thinking about death and dying and provide insight into an area of medicine – and life – that is often not talked about openly but is nevertheless of high significance to societies and individual humans alike.

Zareen Bheekhun (she/her)
Clinical Research Nurse/PhD Student, King's College London
I qualified as an adult nurse in 2006 and my career as a clinical research nurse began in 2012. Before that, I wasn't aware nurses have a key role in research. As a research nurse, I was faced with questions about the justifications behind research. I got in contact with Silvia Camporesi in the hopes of starting a PhD in this area. Silvia has since then been my mentor through thick and thin. What Silvia and I find permanently interesting about clinical research ethics is its ability to generate perpetual debate; for example, the role humans have played in the search for the 'greater good'.

Philip Bremner (he/him)
Lecturer in Law, King's College London
My research has focused on legal parenthood in the context of diverse families. Assisted reproductive technology is a central part of family formation for many same-sex families. I was, therefore, interested in reflecting on how considerations about who is recognised as a parent in these families forms part of the context surrounding the legal regulation of assisted reproductive technologies.

Silvia Camporesi (she/her)
Professor of Bioethics and Sports Integrity and Ethics, KU Leuven
I've been writing on clinical research ethics since my PhD at the European Institute of Oncology in 2010, and over the years I have retained deep interest in the 'ethical knot' at the centre of it. What motivated me the most to join this project was the opportunity to work again with Zareen Bheekhun. Zareen, a clinical research nurse originally from Mauritius, with an MSc in Anthropology from University College London (UCL), was my graduate teaching assistant at King's College London for the Ethics of Clinical Research course. Zareen is one of the most gifted teachers and researchers I have ever met. If you find our chapter interesting, genuine, or captivating, you'll know it's because of her!

Beverley Clough (she/her)
Professor in Law and Social Justice, Manchester Law School, Manchester Metropolitan University
Whilst ideas of mental capacity and decision-making are core aspects of medical and health law textbooks, these tend to take central assumptions around capacity/incapacity and disability for granted. I have been keen to explore what disability studies offers to medical law. It can highlight the ways in which medicine has traditionally focused on diagnosis and cure, and the problematic consequences of this in terms of the denial of legal agency and the harms of non-consensual treatments. A shift in emphasis towards societal structural barriers offers the tools for radically rethinking law and legal responses in this context.

John Coggon (he/him)
Professor of Law, University of Bristol
Health law is an important field of study. But it is complex and controversial: in part because the very ways that we choose to look at law and health at once open up insights and understanding while also hiding or skewing points that matter. In jargonistic terms, critical analysis in health law works through simplifying assumptions; for instance, that a person has 'full autonomy' or has straightforward access to services. I am pleased to contribute to a foundational text in health law that explores and challenges different simplifying assumptions and represents ranging perspectives, including marginalised voices, on multiple practical topics.

Rita D'Alton-Harrison (she/her)
Professor of Law, Royal Holloway, University of London
The principles and values of the NHS Constitution enshrine the belief that 'everyone counts' and that a comprehensive service should be provided to all. This serves as an important reminder that equality in access to healthcare should be a protected right. To understand if this protection exists it is important to critically examine all aspects of healthcare and its impact on particular groups within our society. As both a practitioner and an academic I believe that only through challenge and accountability can we ensure that equitable treatment becomes a reality for all. Education is the stage from which we can view the improvements and change society can and should make for a sustainable and harmonious future in the field of health law.

Thana C. de Campos-Rudinsky
Associate Professor of Ethics, Law, and Global Public Policy, Pontifical Catholic University of Chile
My work examines our ethical responsibility to care for one another in moments of great vulnerability, especially within the contexts of structural poverty, illnesses, disabilities, loneliness, pregnancy, and early motherhood. Conventional wisdom grounds this responsibility on the moral value of justice. Few scholars acknowledge, and in actuality several dismiss, the power of love as a robust practical principle. As a Global South scholar, I offer an interpretation of our ethical responsibility to care for one another, grounded in a decolonial perspective of love, where love is a practical reason/directive for individual and institutional deliberation, grounding a responsibility to accompany, in a non-intrusive way, those experiencing medical suffering.

Aileen Editha (she/her)
PhD Candidate and Robert Sutherland Fellow in Law, Queen's University Canada
I am honoured to be part of this endeavour to increase and encourage representation in health and medical law discourse. In addition to highlighting the disparate outcomes of health policy, my chapter aims to explore the perspectives of the marginalised 'others' that are seldom included in textbooks and mandatory reading lists. This book is an opportunity for learners and educators to engage with other perspectives as well as broaden and reflect on their own.

Magdalena Furgalska (she/her)
Lecturer in Law, University of York
It is easy to see mental health law as a complex and technical area and to justify coercive measures based on our perceptions and misunderstandings about mental ill-health and who a mental health patient is; 'we fear what we don't know' comes to mind. My work aims to demonstrate how the law affects people's everyday lives in the hope of challenging the status quo. The chapter is designed to allow students to reflect on the law of psychiatric detention and the implicit biases that

exist about mental health, and to approach these topics not only as future lawyers but also as human beings.

Sabrina Germain (she/her)
Reader in Healthcare Law and Policy, The City Law School, City St George's, University of London
The structural inequalities that affect vulnerable and marginalised groups are not often featured in currently available health law textbooks. However, health disparities scholars like me want to bring into the classroom conversations around the role of the law in creating or sustaining barriers affecting these groups. It was important for me to supply chapters that would help colleagues ignite these discussions, providing them with an alternative perspective and original and accessible materials as a useful starting point. Recently I have also been reflecting on my identity and race and my role as a writer. I feel compelled to bring to the fore more meaningfully the experiences of racialised and vulnerable groups in healthcare.

Jonathan Herring (he/him)
Professor of Law, University of Oxford
Law students are well trained to deal with businesspeople and the issues that trouble them. They are required to read many cases involving disputes between rich people, who are using the law to get richer. The boardroom, the solicitor's office, and the construction site are regularly visited. The nursing home, the asylum centre, and the childcare centre are rarely visited. I want to hear the voice of those marginalised by mainstream society; to see those places where the privileged don't want to look; and to explore the power imbalances within society.

Harleen Kaur Johal (she/her)
PhD Candidate and National Institute for Health Research Academic Clinical Fellow, University of Bristol
Understanding and addressing health disparities is of great importance to me as a doctor and researcher. Through my work, I explore how power structures in academic and healthcare institutions impact on healthcare policy and practice, thus disadvantaging marginalised groups. Although this has long been an interest of mine, given my identity as a third-generation immigrant and woman of colour, it was through working in an adult intensive care unit during the COVID-19 pandemic that I experienced at first hand the impact that inequitable access to healthcare has on vulnerable groups and their outcomes, which I discuss in my chapter with Sabrina Germain.

Naomi Jones (she/her)
Honorary Clinical Lecturer, UCL Medical School
Paediatric Registrar, London
As a paediatrician, I am a passionate advocate for the health and wellbeing of children, young people, and families, particularly those from vulnerable or marginalised groups. My intention in contributing to this book was to enable

students of healthcare law, of any professional background, to consider the structures within society, healthcare, and the law that impact diverse groups. I have sought to explore how the law affects clinicians and patients, and to reflect the dilemmas faced in real-life practice. I hope this book is valuable for students to better empower patients in their healthcare journey.

Beth W. Kamunge-Kpodo (she/her)
Lecturer in Law, University of Leicester
I was motivated to participate in this project as it aligns with my personal and professional social justice values. I am aware of the ways in which the erasure, exclusion, or token/unethical 'inclusion' of marginalised communities in research and practice can have harmful effects. I would like to see a world in which marginalisation is no longer possible.

Rebecca Limb (she/her)
Lecturer in Law, University of Southampton
Child patients face many challenges as they navigate their medical treatment; however, their voices are often unheard. My scholarship, informed and inspired by my experiences as a child patient, is concerned with capturing, recording, and sharing the lived experiences of children who undergo medical treatment with the academic community and using their experiences as a lens through which to analyse child medical law. I was therefore excited to contribute a chapter that has a child's voice at its core and encourages its readers to analyse the law from the child's perspective.

Zaina Mahmoud (she/her)
Lecturer in Law, University of Liverpool
It always struck me as odd that diversity in academic research is seen as an afterthought or optional. As an Arab woman, my identity shapes every aspect of my daily interactions and cannot be ignored or removed. Participating in a textbook that recognises this reality was important to me, as it contributes to diversifying reading lists, allowing students to feel seen and heard, and ideally, prompts other academics and researchers to adopt an intersectional approach to their work.

Cynthia Mbugua (she/her)
PhD Student, Royal Holloway, University of London
When navigating the use of and access to fertility treatments, it is crucial to acknowledge that there are various external factors that have become impediments in accessing assisted reproduction, beyond the emotional and financial facets. In the chapter to which I have contributed, the goal was to scrutinise and engage with these factors – namely, age, ethnicity, and sexual orientation – encouraging a thoughtful examination of the broader personal, societal, and legal implications inherent in this deeply personal journey. This in turn provides valuable insights into the dynamic and evolving nature of health law, while

encouraging a deeper understanding of the need for legal reform and advocacy in the realm of assisted reproduction.

Caterina Milo

Lecturer in Law, School of Law, University of Sheffield

Dialogue and inclusion of diverse voices are at the heart of my academic engagement. I feel called to foster teaching environments where no voice is silenced, but students find the opportunity to respectfully, truthfully, and critically develop and share their own ideas. Such an approach is also reflected in my writings. In my chapter, together with Thana C. de Campos-Rudinsky, I highlight the importance of seeking a more holistic account of patients' rights, one that doesn't silence but listens and values patients' needs in a person-centred way. It is, ultimately, a desire to foster bridges of dialogue, rather than walls of silence and division, that motivated me to take part in this textbook.

Anna Nelson (she/her)

Research Associate, University of Sheffield

Through my research and teaching about issues around reproductive technology, childbirth, and the law I have come to believe it is important to approach new issues by asking: who (or what views) does the dominant framing of this issue serve? I was therefore delighted to be asked to contribute to this textbook, which offers a vital tool to help think through this question across a wide range of health law issues. With my chapter, I hope to encourage readers to think critically about 'everyday' concepts in health law and to interrogate the role that (problematic) norms play in constructing these.

Joshua Parker (he/him)

PhD Candidate in Bioethics, Lancaster University

Healthcare seems to be falling short of its goal of promoting social justice. In spite of all the advances of modern medicine, vast health inequalities exist and healthcare is facing various challenges of sustainability, including economic and environmental issues. This concerns me both as a doctor and an academic. By focusing on the broad issues of justice raised by the intersection between health, healthcare, and climate change, my hope is to demonstrate not just the significant scholarly interest of this underexplored topic, but its practical relevance.

Jordan A. Parsons (he/him)

Assistant Professor in Medical Ethics and Law, University of Birmingham

Through my research, it has become increasingly apparent to me the extent to which various marginalised groups are disproportionately negatively affected by many of the structures and systems in healthcare. This was an issue that was largely absent from my undergraduate studies, so I now make a point of highlighting these sometimes challenging perspectives when I am teaching. In doing so, I am currently limited in the readings I can set that are pitched at the appropriate level. As such, I was keen to be part of this textbook and hope that its uptake will encourage students' critical reflection on healthcare law.

Sheila Payne (she/her)
Emeritus Professor in Palliative Care, International Observatory on End of Life Care, Lancaster University
I have been undertaking research and policy development to promote service innovation in global palliative care for many years. Raising awareness of needs to access equitable and affordable services and medicines for people in the final phase of life is essential. Working closely with colleagues in large international collaborative research programmes has helped to highlight what constitutes best practice and enabled the development of free massive open online courses to improve access to educational resources. I have worked with international non-governmental organisations such as the World Health Organization and the European Association for Palliative Care to implement change.

Elizabeth Chloe Romanis (she/her)
Associate Professor in Biolaw, Durham Law School, Durham University
Examining how the deployment of power in social structures, like law and medicine, impacts people is at the heart of my scholarship (feminist reflections on reproductive law and ethics). This is a critique relevant to all areas of health law and so I try to place it at the centre of my teaching. Yet, of the mainstream textbooks, few acknowledge, and none place at the centre, the ways in which law and medicine themselves can marginalise users of healthcare, especially women, people with chronic illness, and people with the physiology to become pregnant. In the chapters to which I contribute, my intention was to make the power dynamics in doctor–patient relationships more visible so that students can reflect on these.

Hannah Saad
Paralegal, UK Covid-19 Public Inquiry
As a daughter of two doctors who emigrated from Egypt to work in the NHS, I am acutely aware of the monumental task faced by public health sector workers. Studying medical law at both undergraduate and postgraduate level further highlighted how laws can impact BAME individuals differently and was a topic I would have liked to explore in more depth when I was a student. I was particularly interested in looking at this specifically in the medical law context, given the diversity of the NHS and the fears many health professionals feel following high-profile GNM cases. My chapter explores some of the factors that may be undermining equality of legal and professional regulation in the NHS and seeks to advance this dialogue further.

Yakubu Salifu (he/him)
Lecturer in Palliative Care, International Observatory on End of Life Care, Lancaster University and CEO COMPASS-GhanaCharity

I am motivated to contribute to this textbook a chapter on death and dying due to my passion for enhancing compassionate end-of-life care. Exploring the intersection of legal and ethical frameworks from a palliative care perspective is crucial. Addressing evolving needs demands adaptability in guidelines to ensure patient-centred care, respecting individual choices and promoting dignity in the context of death and dying. My contribution aims to shed light on aligning legal and ethical considerations with the empathetic principles of palliative care for a more holistic and compassionate approach to end-of-life challenges, especially in resource-limited settings.

Zoe L. Tongue (she/they)

Lecturer in Law, University of Leeds

My scholarship focuses on feminist perspectives on reproductive rights and the structural inequalities that shape access to and experiences of reproductive healthcare. In my teaching, I try to bring in gender, race, class, and disability-based perspectives to highlight how healthcare law (and especially abortion law) marginalises some groups of people more than others. We need to weave these issues throughout textbooks on healthcare law, rather than treating these perspectives as an afterthought. The chapters I contribute use a feminist standpoint to explore the impacts on pregnant people of law, medical practice, and broader societal structures.

Marisha Wickremsinhe (she/her)

Honorary Research Fellow, London School of Hygiene & Tropical Medicine

I was eager to contribute to this volume because its orientation and content support health law's ongoing reckoning with structural injustice and the ways in which the law sometimes works to harm, not help, wellbeing. Legal frameworks – for example, those that tell us which drugs (and, by extension, which people who use drugs) – are 'acceptable' in mainstream society, shape our views on whether and how certain groups can access healthcare. Encouraging students who represent the future of the field to critically engage with the normative assumptions underlying these frameworks is a key step in the road towards health equity.

1

Introduction

Elizabeth Chloe Romanis, Sabrina Germain, and Jonathan Herring

Healthcare law is an intimate subject. In talking about our reproductive choices, our bodies, our pain, and our deaths we are reflecting on things that affect many or all of us. Some of our personal beliefs related to the subjects of this book are based on deep-seated intuitions and strongly held moral beliefs and opinions that speak to who we are, our cultures, and how we have been socialised. With this in mind, there should be space in healthcare law for different perspectives. Healthcare law, however, has traditionally had just one voice: that of the 'medical profession'. Few would claim that today. The way we teach and learn about the law and medicine makes little space for diversity and critical perspectives, revealing some of the power dynamics that have made the law (and medicine) what it is. In this book, we create space for different voices and perspectives. It is important to us that this book is seen as an opportunity for dialogue – what is presented should not be treated as the final word. Readers are invited to add their voice to the conversation. Sometimes the quietest voice is the most convincing. Sometimes the 'taken-for-granted truth' is an error.

This book contains what you would expect to find in a healthcare law textbook – it covers medical negligence, confidentiality, abortion, organ donation, and so on. However, the authors of each chapter use different approaches to examine the issues. Some use literature and storytelling. Some use empirical data detailing lived experiences. Some employ underused theoretical frameworks. What all the chapters have in common is a focus other than the archetype example and acknowledgement of the fact that law and medicine are not politically neutral institutions. Most consider the experience of a group that is often marginalised as a user of healthcare (in the given context). The book features many groups that are 'otherised' in healthcare: intravenous drug users, women, racialised people, domestic abuse victims, mental health inpatients, terminally ill people, and intersex people (among others). There are also chapters that represent areas that should be core content in a healthcare law course but never have been treated as such; for example, climate change, health disparities and the broader social implications of healthcare, and even what we mean by 'health'.

This book is designed for teachers and students of healthcare law and ethics, whatever their disciplinary background. A reader will gain a comprehensive understanding of the key legal and ethical issues, but they will do so with a richer, more well-rounded perspective, with insight into how different groups, especially those who are less often heard, could experience these.

Why diverse voices?

In compiling this text, we sought to develop a method for *inclusivity* in teaching and learning. There is increasingly, and rightly so, a call to change the way we teach and learn healthcare law, to be more mindful of the differing impacts of the law and of medicine on different groups of people and to make space for a diversity of voices that can tell their stories. During the pandemic, and following Black Lives Matter, the 'WhyIsMyCurriculumWhite' movement took centre stage.[1] At the time of writing, there is also a movement for decolonisation of knowledge and institutions. The elephant in the room is that often attempts to diversify curriculums result in only small changes (adjusting the reading list) that do not result in meaningful overhaul (changing the approach and mindset of educators and students). However, the healthcare law and ethics curriculum needs an overhaul, and that overhaul must make space for a multitude of different voices and recognition of their complexity. We take up the mantle in the book of starting the *ongoing* process of '*inclusifying*' (bringing inclusivity to) healthcare law.

This is not a textbook that should be read as a complete or uncriticisable authority. This book welcomes different perspectives and voices into the field of health law by showcasing them. In presenting some diversity, we invite a broader range of voices to be a part of the conversation that occurs in our classrooms beyond these pages. The method that sits behind this project is multifaceted. First, we embarked on critical reflection about whose voices are centred in what we are teaching and the materials that we are using. We sought to create materials that include a broader range of perspectives. We wanted to show teachers *how* we can teach the classic topics and key content but in ways that better reflect diversity. It is not about changing the content of healthcare law (though there is space for additional content), but about teaching this content in a different way. There is, in UK law schools, much nervousness and fear about how to begin changing the way we teach and learn when it comes to diversifying and inclusifying. We have created a tool that offers a clear starting point. We hope teachers of healthcare law will take ownership of this material and take it further in different ways and directions.

1 E.g., Julia Parris, 'Why Is My Uni So White?' (2020) https://decolonisinglse.wordpress.com/2020/06/26/why-is-my-uni-so-white/, accessed 13 December 2023.

The second aspect of our method is thinking critically about how teaching is received by students. Law and medical schools are sites of power.[2] As Adébísí explains, law schools are 'centres for incubation of new legal minds … crucibles of research, revolving around new strands of legal knowledge and thoughts'.[3] How students are taught has a huge impact on their futures, the future of the professions, and on future clients/patients. These schools have the power, where it is appropriately harnessed, to create positive change. In teaching and learning about healthcare law without a conscious focus on diversity we miss this opportunity to create and participate in a future where more voices and perspectives are recognised in the social structures of medicine and law. It is much easier to learn, and to learn with enthusiasm, where the content speaks to our experience. For some students, their experiences, and that of those around them with whom they share a history and/or culture, have been overlooked or subject to violence in medicine and law.[4] This book acknowledges the truth of these experiences in the perspectives that it offers. Who is presented as someone that matters, or who has an authoritative voice, or who is missing affects students' perceptions of other people and of themselves.

'Diverse Voices' is the name of the series in which this book appears. We want to stress, however, that the authors in this collection offer perspectives of marginalised groups – but not (necessarily) their voices. Diversity is complex and requires looking at and beyond protected groups. It is also important to remember that diversity exists in a multitude of ways, not all of which are (immediately) visible. This book is not just about presenting diverse perspectives, but also about speaking to people with different perspectives. In order for us to do so we needed to find a 'common language' and common ground on how we unpack each issue. We were mindful to write in an accessible manner. All contributors have made a conscious effort to share their expertise using simple language and varied mediums of communication to unpack complex concepts and suggesting non-traditional materials for further reflection. It recommends to students that they engage with sources that present the impact the law has on people's life beyond the formal setting of a court room or a clinical space – films, documentaries, podcasts – that show the realities of healthcare law beyond academic canon. If we are *only* learning by reading academic articles, we get only a limited sense of how health(care) law affects people in the real world.

This book covers the core material that features in any healthcare law course so that the book can function as a standalone textbook. It features chapters with a focus on health*care* law – that is, the legal issues that arise in the interactions between healthcare professionals and patients – *and* others that have addressed matters of health law – that being the legal issues that arise around our health

[2] Malika Sharma, 'Applying Feminist Theory to Medical Education' (2019) 393 Lancet 570.

[3] Folúké Adébísí, *Decolonisation and Legal Knowledge* (Bristol University Press 2023) 1.

[4] Amna Akbar, 'Law's Exposure: The Movement and the Legal Academy' (2015) 65 J Leg Educ 352, 355.

and wellbeing beyond individual encounters with healthcare professionals. On health(care) law courses what is taught, outside of some core concepts, varies considerably between institutions. We wanted to cover the range of applied topics that are often featured on these courses in law and medical schools. However, due to space limitations, there are some subjects that are missing that we would be keen to include in future editions: genetics, artificial intelligence in healthcare, and the intersection between health and social care, to name a few.

Our commitment as researchers in this area, thinking about the needs of marginalised healthcare users, is how we became the editors of this collection: we were frustrated that health(care) ethics and law textbooks infrequently acknowledge *what is missing*. Deciding who to invite to contribute was a difficult process. You will find authors' own reflections on why they wanted to contribute to this project in the 'Notes on Contributors' section of this book. Their reflections exemplify the range of different commitments to diversity that exist amongst academic health(care) lawyers and ethicists. There are many voices and perspectives that we wanted to see in this book that are not featured. Relatedly, it was challenging for contributors to address key information and intersectional marginalisation within short chapters. The limitations of space mean that authors have focused on some group(s) more than others within their particular topic area. We encourage readers to think beyond what is written and recommended about what voices remain hidden and/or marginalised. This book is only a starting point in changing approaches to health(care) law to diversify who is centred in discussions of health, healthcare, and the law.

Some key theories and methods

This section outlines some of the key approaches that you will come across in this book, all of which are good jumping-off points, but are not an exhaustive list. These theories (feminism, critical race theory (CRT), and intersectionality) and methods (socio-legal method) make up the foundation of the perspectives across all the chapters in this book.

Feminism

While one can't (and shouldn't) 'squeeze' the variety of feminist ways of thinking 'into a single way of thinking',[5] feminist perspectives share a commitment to 'calling attention to and eradicating gender-based oppression'.[6] Feminism examines how social structures create and perpetuate sources of gendered and sexist oppression. There are several critical tools from feminism that can be used

5 Caroline Ramazanoglu and Janet Holland, *Feminist Methodology: Challenges and Choices* (SAGE 2002) 62.

6 Iris Marion Young, *Throwing Like a Girl and Other Essays in Feminist Philosophy and Social Theory* (Indiana University Press 1990) 85.

to critique the institutions of medicine and law and understand the power they can deploy to marginalise people on the grounds of gender.

Engaging with lived experience

Asking the question, 'how are women and gender minorities affected by the law',[7] is the first step in considering the *effect* of the law and uncovering what structural gendered injustices it may create or perpetuate. We can ask the same question about medical practices to understand their effects and any structural gendered injustices they can perpetuate. There may be places where the two questions need to be asked together to get a full picture of what is at play.

Relationships between doctors and patients have the potential for oppression because of knowledge imbalance. This can also happen at a broader policy level when it is decided who can have access to what treatment. The reality of the oppression is revealed when we hear from and centre the people affected. Standpoint theory suggests that in a potentially oppressive relationship the person/group who is disempowered can have a much better understanding of what is at play because of how they are affected. For example, a doctor may believe they are recommending a treatment to a patient, but the patient may perceive this as being told what they must do because they lack the power to disagree with the doctor or are fearful of what will happen if they do. We must listen to, and/or put ourselves in the shoes of, people who are most impacted. This way of thinking renders visible the experiences of people who are often marginalised because they, for example, have not been involved in, or thought about, in the process of law-making. Or their needs have been neglected or misinterpreted in medicine.

Individuals are different and thus have varying experiences of the law and of medicine. Sometimes these experiences will be contradictory – and we must make space for this.[8] Feminism rejects the notion, perpetuated in some moral theories, that there is such a thing as a 'universal' way of thinking and being,[9] and thus we should not generalise nor dismiss stories that do not fit with a majority viewpoint.

Social context

Law and medicine do not exist in a vacuum. Given the kinds of issues, and their intimate nature, that arise in healthcare (law), context is crucial.[10] A person's

---

7 This is adapted from the 'woman question': Katherine Bartlett, 'Feminist Legal Methods' (1990) 103 Harv Law Rev 829.

8 Ibid.

9 Catherine MacKinnon, 'Feminism, Marxism, Method and the State: An Agenda for Theory' (1982) 7 Signs 515, 537.

10 Elizabeth Chloe Romanis, 'Legal Method and Health Law in Feminist Perspective' in Jean McHale and Atina Krajewska (eds), *Reimagining Health Law: From Medical to Health and Social Care Law* (Edward Elgar, forthcoming).

social circumstances and their history (and that of their family, their community, and others around them) may affect how they feel about healthcare and the law and whether they will resort to medicine and/or law in the event that they need help. Whether a patient feels they can disagree with a doctor may depend on their education, social status, and so on. Feminist approaches foreground thinking about how social forces impact on healthcare and thus healthcare law. Patriarchy (the system in which men and assumed masculine characteristics dominate and are afforded privilege and women, gender minorities, and perceived feminine attributes are marginalised and thought less valuable) has pervaded into social consciousness in the West over centuries. It affects how we are all socialised and how individuals perceive and react to each other and who is treated as having a voice that matters. Dhairyawan describes how women, particularly racialised women, are treated as 'unreliable narrators' and systematically ignored and silenced in healthcare.[11] Patriarchy has concrete impacts in terms of outcomes. A recent study concluded that female patients are 32 per cent more likely to die when their surgical procedure is performed by a male (as opposed to a female) surgeon.[12] Patriarchy affects healthcare professionals as well as their patients. Many female doctors experience gendered micro-aggressions, including patients assuming they are not doctors but other health professionals traditionally gendered female (e.g., nurses).[13] A recent survey of surgeons working in the NHS found that 63.3 per cent of women experienced sexual harassment and 29.9 per cent had been sexually assaulted (they experienced this harassment and assault at a much higher rate than their male colleagues).[14]

Questioning sources of authority

Law and medical knowledge are often seen as 'neutral'. This, however, is a fallacy. Both law and medicine are professions that have historically been dominated by men, implemented by men, and thought of as an instrument for men. As a result, law and medicine are unsurprisingly androcentric – and this is deeply ingrained in their fabric.[15] An obvious example is how we define health itself (see Chapter 3). The history of medicine is replete with examples of where minoritised groups were presented as 'ill'. For example, it was not until 1973 that the American

---

11 Rageshiri Dhairyawan, 'The Medical Practice of Silencing' (2021) 398 Lancet 382.

12 Christopher Wallis and others, 'Association of Surgeon–Patient Sex Concordance with Postoperative Outcomes' (2022) 157 JAMA Surg 146.

13 Sarah Ahmed and others, 'Are You Really the Doctor? Physician Experiences with Gendered Microaggressions from Patients' (2022) 31 J Women's Health 521.

14 Christopher Begeny and others, 'Sexual Harassment, Sexual Assault and Rape by Colleagues in the Surgical Workforce, and How Women and Men are Living Different Realities: Observational Study using NHS Population-Derived Weights' (2023) 110 Br J Surg 1518.

15 Romanis (n10).

Psychiatric Association removed 'homosexuality' from its internationally relied-upon list of pathologies.[16] When we look closely, asking questions of the way the law or medicine work in reality, we can see this sexism in practice in places that are presented as neutral.[17] We can see disparities in what conditions, affecting what people, are prioritised in medical research,[18] as well as in what bodies are used as the archetype for collecting information about signs and symptoms.[19] Similarly, sexism is evident in the stereotypes of women that are written into the law around abortion.[20]

Representation is only one aspect of how bias is baked into these professions and instruments.[21] Diversity has improved in medicine and law.[22] The changing make-up of the profession does not necessarily result in a shift away from long-entrenched biases. In law, for example, the importance of consistency and uniformity in decision-making (a trait of common law) means an emphasis is put on the 'neutrality' of legal decisions and this can implicitly perpetuate biased thinking and result in decisions that disadvantage marginalised people irrespective of the gender or any other characteristics of the judge.

Inclusivity

Feminist approaches, especially those deemed 'radical', can make the mistake of assuming that '"woman" is a unitary category, and in so doing installs … white, straight, middle class experience as the norm'.[23] Some schools of thought, expressly or implicitly, encompass hostility towards trans persons.[24] In legal theory, much of the transphobia that is evident results from biological

---

16 Jack Drescher, 'Out of DSM: Depathologizing Homosexuality' (2015) 5 Behav Sci 565.

17 Martha Minow, 'Feminist Reason: Getting It and Losing It' in Katherine Bartlett and Rosanne Kennedy (eds), *Feminist Legal Theory: Readings in Law and Gender* (Westview Press 1991) 357.

18 Annabel Sowemimo, *Divided: Racism, Medicine and Why We Need to Decolonise Healthcare* (Profile Books 2023).

19 Ibid.

20 Sally Sheldon, *Beyond Control: Medical Power and Abortion Law* (Pluto Press 1997).

21 See Romanis (n10).

22 NHS England, 'NHS Workforce More Diverse than Any Point in Its History, as Health Service Commits to More Action on Representation' (2021) Available from: https://www.england.nhs.uk/2021/07/nhs-workforce-more-diverse-than-any-point-in-its-history-as-health-service-commits-to-more-action-on-representation, accessed 13 December 2021. E.g., Solicitors Regulatory Authority, 'Diversity in Law Firms' (2024) Available from: https://www.sra.org.uk/sra/equality-diversity/diversity-profession/diverse-legal-profession/, accessed 15 August 2024.

23 Victoria Margree, *Neglected or Misunderstood: The Radical Feminism of Shulamith Firestone* (Zero Books 2017) 5.

24 Sexualised misogyny and anti-transgender bigotry are mutually reinforcing: Catherine MacKinnon and others, 'Exploring Transgender Law and Politics' (2023) https://signsjournal.org/exploring-transgender-law-and-politics/, accessed 13 December 2023.

essentialism: the way that some scholars describe who women are and what their relationship to the law is like is reductive and lacks recognition of diversity.[25] Transphobia is unacceptable. Trans people exist and their lives and experiences matter. Indeed, trans people, often having hostile experiences with healthcare, are an important group whose voices and perspectives must be amplified rather than silenced or ridiculed. As such, we reject transphobia and embrace inclusive feminisms. As a part of this commitment to inclusive feminism we also stress the importance of feminism that is class and race aware. We address this when we explain intersectionality and its role in diversification in healthcare law later in this chapter. Before this we outline the relevance of perspectives informed by CRT.

Critical race theory

CRT organically emerged as a movement in the 1980s, with activists, lawyers, and scholars reflecting on the limitations of the civil rights movement in addressing more subtle forms of racism in American society. Building on the insights of critical legal studies and radical feminism, academic work began to highlight the dynamics of power, oppression, and the role of patriarchy and racism in the construction of social roles and hidden patterns of marginalisation.[26] Looking beyond the law, CRT seeks to include elements of economics, history, and science to critique and analyse how white elites have been able to consolidate their interests over time.[27]

Law as an instrument to establish and sustain white privilege

CRT provides an important reading grid to approach complex issues, including how the law is designed, implemented, and discussed. Law is often presented as a politically neutral instrument to achieve collective goals. However, CRT exposes how legislators and policy makers have used their positions of power to serve and protect the interests of a distinct group by directly helping white elite prosper and the white working class to establish itself as physically superior to other segments of society.[28]

CRT highlights how the law's arbitrariness and subjectivity support other aspects of white dominance. In particular, legal indeterminacy, the idea that a

25 E.g., Robin West, 'Jurisprudence and Gender' (1988) 55 U Chi L Rev 1–72. Judith Baer, 'Feminist Theory and Law' in Robert Goodin (ed), *The Oxford Handbook of Political Science* (OUP 2011) 309.

26 E.g., Richard Delgado, Derrick A. Bell, and Hass Konig, *Critical Race Feminism: A Reader* (NYU Press 1997); Richard Delgado and Jean Stefancic, *Critical Race Theory: The Cutting Edge* (Temple University Press 1999).

27 Richard Degado and Jean Stefancic, *Critical Race Theory: An Introduction* (4th edn, NYU Press 2017).

28 Ibid.

legal case can have multiple outcomes based on the weight and interpretation given to authorities and facts, which often are unfavourable to a racialised or a marginalised party. Claims of 'colour blindness' and formal equality upholding the judicial system – insisting that everyone be treated the same across the board – often mask layers of inequalities that translate into unjust outcomes that perpetuate discrimination.

The law normalises patterns of dominance and discrimination to favour the dominant group's need and becomes a self-serving system in which legal institutions that comprise of a mostly white group help legitimise their interest. Legal storytelling, diverse narratives, and perspectives must be intentionally invited into our analysis of legislation, its impact, and its outcomes in specific cases. Bringing forward the accounts of Black and Brown people (and other racialised and marginalised groups) and their experiences with the legal system is key in bringing into focus less explicit forms of racism. One important way of doing this is by asking how Black and Brown people are impacted by social structures. There are ways in which structures of power try to avoid addressing the realities of inequalities along the axes of race. In an ethnographic study of premature birth in the US, Davis (an anthropologist) reflects on how some doctors choose to use class as a proxy for race (analysing disparities with a focus on factors like low income or low educational attainment) in place of race to explain disparities in pregnancy and birth outcomes.[29] In so doing, she explains, these doctors who do not want to talk about race render invisible the way in which structural racism has perpetuated disparities and thus they fail to address this racism.[30]

Race as a social construct

CRT aims to expose racism in all aspects of society, which includes, but is not limited to, the legal sphere. Race is a product of social thought and relations that have been instrumentalised to establish and sustain white privilege in all areas of ordinary life, including healthcare.[31] The CRT approach has gained significant traction in bioethics since the start of the SARS-Cov2 pandemic, partly because the public emergency has brought into sharp focus the structural inequalities and ethno-racialised differences in health outcomes (see Chapter 5).[32] The NHS Confederation confirmed that 'Black males are 4.2 times more likely to die from

29 Dána-Ain Davis, *Reproductive Justice: Racism, Pregnancy, and Premature Birth* (NYU Press 2019) 60.
30 Ibid.
31 Kalwant Bhopal, *White Privilege: The Myth of a Post-Racial Society* (Policy Press 2018).
32 This term encompasses both ethnic and racial groups' characteristics, emphasising the interconnectedness of these aspects of identity.

a COVID-19-related death and black females are 4.3 times more likely than white ethnicity males and females.'[33]

CRT scholars have explicitly unpacked race as a social construct and debunked the idea that this concept was based on no valid scientific evidence. It has now been scientifically demonstrated that we are, as humans, more genetically similar than different.[34] However, physical attributes such as skin colour, physique, or hair textures have been taken as arbitrary benchmarks to create categories to organise society, rank the worthiness of humans, and help justify the violence inflicted on Black and Brown bodies for the benefit of non-racialised groups.[35] As highlighted in several chapters in this book, these physical attributes were used to show just cause for unethical 'medical' experiments on Black women and men for many years. In some respect, even though less explicitly, these arbitrary traits continue to justify, consciously or unconsciously, treating racialised patients differently than their white counterparts. Black British feminist scholar Sowemimo, similarly to her American predecessors Davis and Roberts,[36] links colonialism, slavery, and healthcare in her work, unpacking the deep-rooted history of exploitation and racism in medicine and the current experiences of Black patients who see their pain and illness undermined or even ignored.[37]

Engaging with lived experience

CRT's lens in bioethics has been crucial in elevating and centring marginalised and racialised groups' voices and experiences in health, when often non-white bodies have been treated as less than human and subject to violence. However, the approach is often criticised for focusing on anecdotal evidence of discrimination or personal accounts that cannot be generalised or simply undermine the law and the work of legal institutions. CRT is also attacked for framing issues around racial binaries of white *versus* non-white groups rather than seeking a more nuanced understanding of inequality and marginalisation.[38] Yet, the wealth of information offered by lived experiences is too often hidden

---

33 NHS Confederation, 'ONS Data on COVID-19-Related Deaths by Ethnicity in England and Wales' (2020) https://www.nhsconfed.org/publications/ons-data-covid-19-related-deaths-ethnicity-england-and-wales, accessed 13 December 2023.

34 Vivian Chou, 'How Science and Genetics are Reshaping the Race Debate of the 21st Century' (2017) https://sitn.hms.harvard.edu/flash/2017/science-genetics-reshaping-race-debate-21st-century/, accessed 4 December 2023.

35 Keisha Ray, *Black Health: The Social, Political, and Cultural Determinants of Black People's Health* (OUP 2023).

36 Angela Davis, *Women, Race and Class* (Women's Press 1982). Dorothy Roberts, *Killing the Black Body: Race, Reproduction and the Meaning of Liberty* (Pantheon Books Penguin 1997).

37 Sowemimo (n18).

38 A. Javier Treviño, Michelle A. Harris, and Derron Wallace, 'What's So Critical about Critical Race Theory?' (2008) 11 Contemp Justice Rev 7.

in the mainstream narrative. Recognising that racialised groups' voices are being silenced, ignored, and distorted must be part of any transformational and reparative project.

Ray points to racial medical bias and the American Black community's cultural fatalism to explain health inequities. Black Americans need to be recognised as a group, not because of the colour of their skin, but because of the lived experiences of sub-standard care, where their pain is ignored and for the most part not adequately managed.[39] However, the racism impacting Black Americans' health goes beyond the clinical setting. Along with environmental determinants, for many, poor housing conditions and 'colour-blind' public health interventions (or lack thereof) are deepening social inequities that lead to poor health. Race as a social construct thereby becomes pivotal to our understanding, not just of power dynamics, but of the engrained structural inequalities that have a detrimental effect on racialised groups.[40] Parallels can be drawn between the lived experiences of Black patients in the US and the UK.[41]

Highlighting this is not to say that the other side of the doctor–patient relationship is unaffected by racial bias. Many racialised medical professionals at all levels in the NHS have experienced racism in the workplace.[42] Most common are micro-aggressions and subtle interpersonal racism which they think their employer is not addressing or appropriately dealing with and, they believe, has an indirect negative impact on patient care and might even be hindering their career progression. Junior doctors also find themselves most vulnerable to patients' racist attacks, which often deeply affects their mental health and wellbeing.[43]

Disability approaches

Disability is a good example of the exercise of power within medicine. Bodies that do not conform to the expected norm are labelled disabled. They are seen as needing to be corrected so they can be returned to how they 'should be'. Disabled bodies are seen as 'misfits' that need to be 'enabled' to fit within society. This way of presenting disability is surprisingly common. It is striking how, when disabilities are discussed in medical literature, they are presented in negative terms, with no acknowledgement of the benefits that misfitting bodies or mind

39 Ray (n35).

40 Ibid.

41 Sabrina Germain and Keisha Ray, 'Book Review: *Shedding Light on Racial Inequity in Health, in Conversation with the Author: Black Health: The Social, Political, and Cultural Determinants of Black People's Health*' (2023) 24 Med Law Inter 151–8 https://journals.sagepub.com/doi.org/10.1177/09685332231211914, accessed 1 July 2024.

42 Gareth Iacobucci, 'Foreign NHS Doctors Face Persistent Racism at Work, Survey Finds' (2023) 383 BMJ 2637.

43 BMA (British Medical Association), 'Racism an Issue in NHS, Finds Survey' (2022) https://www.bma.org.uk/news-and-opinion/racism-an-issue-in-nhs-finds-survey, accessed 7 December 2023.

can bring.[44] Some philosophers are willing to argue that people with severe intellectual disabilities have less moral status than other people and should be ranked, in moral terms, with non-human animals of a similar capability. The impact of such remarks on the disability community seems to go unnoticed.[45] This status quo, reflecting the medical model of disability in action, is in striking contrast to the social model of disability. This views disability as caused by social conditions, which can render some things disabilities and others not.[46] Social spaces, services, and provisions are modelled around certain kinds of bodies and minds, privileging some and disadvantaging others.

This approach highlights that although it may be seen as 'natural' or 'scientific' that a certain body or mind is seen as disabled, this is, in fact, largely or wholly a societal decision. Certain conditions were seen in the past as a disability, which would now certainly not be.[47] The Supreme Court in *Khan v Meadows* described autism as a disability, without debate.[48] But that designation is controversial. Certainly, there is now increasing acceptance that a disability may be a difference, rather than necessarily a disadvantage; and that many disabilities come with benefits as well as challenges.[49] Perhaps the biggest challenge here is to neuro-normativity. Academic discourse tends to privilege certain forms of thinking and expression: rationality, coherence, logic, and the like. This can downplay neuro-diverse forms of thinking and engaging with the world and its problems.

Intersectionality

Feminist approaches, approaches grounded in CRT, and approaches centred in the social model of disability are rich, but they sometimes do not allow sufficient space for recognition of the multiple axes along which some people experience oppression. As hooks explains it, Black men and white women 'have it both ways' in some contexts: there are ways in which they are oppressed but there are also ways in which they have privilege over others.[50] Individuals experience multiple forms of advantage and disadvantage tied to a person's complex and layered identities:[51] white women are structurally disadvantaged by patriarchy but

---

44 Heloise Robinson and Jonathan Herring, 'Naming and Describing Disability in Law and Medicine' (2024) Camb Q Healthc Ethics https://doi.org/10.1017/S0963180123000609, accessed 1 July 2024.

45 Eva Feder Kittay, 'The Personal is Philosophical is Political: A Philosopher and Mother of a Cognitively Disabled Person Sends Notes from the Battlefield' (2009) 40 Metaphilosophy 606.

46 See Tom Shakespeare, *Disability Rights and Wrongs* (Routledge 2006).

47 Rosemarie Garland-Thomson, 'Feminist Disabilities Studies' (2005) 30 Signs 1557.

48 [2021] UKSC 21.

49 Robinson and Herring (n44).

50 bell hooks, *Feminist Theory: From Margin to Center* (South End Press 1984), 15.

51 The City Law School Law and Society Podcast, 'Episode 6: Feminist Legal Theory & Intersectionality' 3 March 2022 https://soundcloud.com/cls-law-society-podcast/episode-6-adrienne-yong, accessed 1 July 2024.

benefit from white supremacy; Black men may experience some advantage from the operation of patriarchy but are systemically oppressed by white supremacy. Of feminism, hooks observed that 'A central tenant of modern feminist thought has been the assertion that "all women are oppressed".[52] But this assertion implies that women share a common lot, that factors like class, race, religion, sexual preference etc. do not create a diversity of experience that determines the extent to which sexism will be an oppressive force in the lives of individual women.'[53] However, 'there is much evidence substantiating the reality that race and class identity creates differences in quality of life, social status and lifestyle that take precedence over the common experience women share – differences that are rarely transcended'.[54] What hooks is explaining is that different aspects of our identities are consistently interacting with each other, affecting how we see ourselves and how others and institutions see us and treat us in complex ways and with compounding effects.[55]

Crenshaw coined the concept of 'intersectionality'[56] in an attempt to address the ways in which some experiences, those marginalised by both race, gender, disability, class, and other attributes, remain silenced at times by anti-racist and feminist perspectives.[57] As Crenshaw's scholarship makes clear, consideration of a single identity attribute or axis will never be sufficient to understand and interrogate the complexities of individual experience.[58] We must try to avoid one-dimensional thinking and adopt a way of thinking that focuses on the intersections of experience and on where there is 'sameness and difference [between persons] and its relation to power' that individuals both experience as oppression and that they can wield in different contexts.[59] Thinking this way allows a much better understanding of inequalities in society because systems that perpetuate inequality are not isolated from each other.[60] Intersectionality is an analytical lens that places this fact – that oppressive institutions co-construct each other – centre stage to make visible how multiple forms of discrimination, oppression, and sometimes relative privilege, overlapping and interlocking, are impacting on individuals in society.[61] Intersectional approaches are especially able to produce useful understandings of the world by straddling the traditions

52 hooks (n50) 5.

53 Ibid.

54 Ibid 4.

55 Kimberlé Crenshaw, 'Demarginalizing the Intersection of Race and Sex: A Black Feminist Critique of Antidiscrimination Doctrine, Feminist Theory and Antiracist Politics' (1989) 1 U Chi Leg F 139.

56 Ibid.

57 Patricia Hill Collins, *Intersectionality as Critical Social Theory* (Duke University Press 2019).

58 Patricia Hill Collins and Sirma Bilge, *Intersectionality* (2nd edn, Polity Press 2020) 2.

59 Collins (n57) 795.

60 Bhopal (n31).

61 Collins and Bilge (n58) 2–4.

of social justice and activism and academic scholarship.[62] As many scholars have emphasised, solving social problems at a local, national, or even global context will always require an intersectional analysis of the problem.[63]

The struggle for equality is traditionally focused on gender and race, but intersectional analyses can bring in other important dimensions of experience including age, sexuality, disability, language, and religion.[64] Patriarchy, white supremacy, cis-heteronormativity, ableism (among other harmful sources of social stereotypes) co-construct each other and reinforce the stereotypes each can perpetuate to marginalise and exclude individuals and groups. Women with a disability, for example, can experience, in multiple health settings, both the oppressive effect of disablism and patriarchy.[65] Disabled women are not only treated as lacking in credibility because of their gender,[66] but also because they are reduced to their disability – they are dismissed when they want to discuss health matters beyond the condition that means that they are (identified as) disabled.[67] In narrative accounts, some women with disabilities have explained that they were treated by doctors in a particular way *because* they were a *woman with a disability*.[68] Some doctors have described feeling harassed, bullied, or made to feel embarrassed by colleagues because they wear a hijab:[69] a practice that is specific to their intersecting identities as a woman, a religious person, and, for some, their ethnicity.

Socio-legal approaches

In the approaches just described, emphasis is placed on contextualising the law: looking at how the law plays out rather than just looking at what the law says. What the law says, and how it says it, matters, but it cannot be understood in isolation. We must think about how law is experienced by those who have lived it. How can we get a picture of people's lived experiences? Some researchers will use socio-legal methods to collect this information directly.[70] Indeed, there has been a

62 Collins (n57); Sabrina Germain and Adrienne Yong, 'COVID-19 Highlighting Inequalities in Access to Healthcare in England: a Case Study of Ethnic Minority and Migrant Women' (2020) 28 Fem Leg Stud 301.

63 Ibid.

64 Bhopal (n31).

65 Carol Thomas, 'Medicine, Gender, and Disability: Disabled Women's Healthcare Encounters' (2001) 22 Health Care Women Int 245.

66 See Elizabeth Barnes, 'The Hysteria Accusation' (2020) https://aeon.co/essays/womens-pain-it-seems-is-hysterical-until-proven-otherwise, accessed 13 December 2023.

67 Thomas (n65) 253.

68 Ibid 254.

69 Abida Malik and others, '"I Decided Not To Go Into Surgery Due To Dress Code": A Cross-Sectional Study within the UK Investigating Experiences of Female Muslim Medical Health Professionals on Bare Below the Elbows (BBE) Policy and Wearing Headscarves (Hijabs) in Theatre' (2019) 9 BMJ Open e019954.

70 See Chapter 11.

significant empirical turn in focus of health(care) law scholarship in recent years – something that has yet to translate into the classroom. However, empirical work is not always possible (you must be properly trained and equipped, you must have ethical approval, and you must have the necessary resources). Where this is not an option, published empirical work can be drawn upon to inform your analysis of the impact of the law. You can also use informal sources like newspaper articles and similar sources can assist. A doctrinal approach that considers how the law, and the language of the law, might impact on marginalised people's experiences and which tries to consider it from their perspective (while recognising one's limitations sometimes in being able to do this) is an approach that better centres marginalised people.[71] This is often described as 'law in context'.

On language

Language matters – it 'is always in flux. It reflects socio-cultural norms, which necessarily means that language and power intersect.'[72] In the chapters of this book, choice of language has been conscious. There is diversity in the various ways that authors have each used language to describe marginalised groups. We raise here some important points in how people or groups are described for reflection.

Gender-inclusive language

When talking about biological functions like menstruation and pregnancy, there remains a tendency within healthcare law for scholars to use gendered language. However, to do so often erases and undermines the experiences of those whose bodies can and do perform these functions but who do not identify as women.[73] Many scholars, therefore, will use additive language, 'women and people who can become pregnant', to avoid obfuscating that most people who get pregnant and birth are women, whilst also avoiding erasing the experience of trans masculine and non-binary people.[74] Other scholars choose to use gender-neutral language in recognition of the fact that there are women who cannot become pregnant and men and non-binary people who can. They remain explicit about where and how gender norms around activities like pregnancy and menstruation have come to impact on persons who become pregnant and menstruate because, historically, these have been considered gendered activities. You will see both approaches in this book – both are about ensuring inclusivity.

---

71 Romanis (n10).

72 Alicita Rodriguez, 'Is the B in Black Capitalized? Yes' (2021) https://news.ucdenver.edu/is-the-b-in-black-capitalized-yes/, accessed 13 December 2023.

73 Ruth Kamau and others, 'Inclusivity Starts with Language' (2022) 399 Lancet 434, 435.

74 Alys Einion, 'Embracing the Power of "And"' (2021) https://www.all4maternity.com/embracing-the-power-of-and/?sfw=pass1702487115, accessed 13 December 2023.

Capitalising the words 'Black' and 'Brown', but not 'white'

The UK government's guidance on writing style and ethnicity is explicit that ethnic and racial groups should not be capitalised unless the name of the group is a geographic place (e.g., 'Asian' or 'black Caribbean').[75] However, contrary to this position, throughout this book you will notice that 'Black' is capitalised and 'white' is not. In this, we follow the decision made by many individuals, groups, and institutions (like newspapers) in the US. In these decisions, there is a recognition that the capital 'B' in Black denotes a culture and shared history that is tied up in the legacy of enslavement. Capitalisation is about recognising that people lost their ancestral lineage and connection to other nations to the transatlantic slave trade and may consider themselves ethnically Black (as a result of this culture-shattering and creating experience) rather than racially Black (identified as such on the basis of physical characteristics). There are some concerns about capitalisation of Black in the UK. Some have questioned it on the ground that the 'American experience is simply cut and pasted' into the UK and erases some of the specifics of the Black British experience.[76] Other UK commentators, however, have emphasised the importance of recognising that capitalisation affirms the identity and dignity of Black people and can draw attention to the ways in which Black British people are marginalised.[77] Similarly, we have chosen to capitalise 'Brown' to point to the common colonial past experienced by this group, even though we are aware of the heterogeneity of this group and the range of cultures it encompasses.

While Black and Brown people are often presented as minority groups in much UK and US literature, in fact they are the majority populations in many countries worldwide, albeit impacted by empire and colonialism. It is easy to lose sight of the 'Majority World' as so much of the promoted academic literature comes from the US and the UK.

The choice to capitalise throughout this book to us was about how language reflects history, highlighting the enduring harmful legacy of British colonialism and recognising the role of enslavement (the slave trade) in creating contemporary social injustices. We believe this to be particularly pertinent in the context of health and healthcare. We have not, in contrast, capitalised 'white' because

---

75 UK Government, 'Writing about Ethnicity' https://www.ethnicity-facts-figures.service.gov.uk/style-guide/writing-about-ethnicity/, accessed 13 December 2023.

76 Minna Salami, 'Why I Don't Believe the Word "Black" Should Always Have a Capital "B"' (2021) https://www.theguardian.com/commentisfree/2021/jun/03/word-black-capital-letter-blackness, accessed 13 December 2023.

77 Abi Adamson, 'Seeing Black Written with a Capital B Means More Than You Think It Does' (2022) https://metro.co.uk/2022/10/01/seeing-black-written-with-a-capital-b-means-more-than-you-think-it-does-2-17480271/, accessed 13 December 2023.

doing so perpetuates the centring of whiteness and follows 'the lead of white supremacists'.[78]

Person-forward or identity-forward language

Person-forward language describes individuals in a way that centres their personhood first and the attribute we are describing second. This means it is inappropriate to talk about, for example, 'the disabled', because doing so means we can lose sight of the fact we are talking about real people. People take different approaches as to how to centre personhood. Taking the example of disability, some prefer the language of 'people with a disability' to make it clear that individuals are people first and foremost and not defined by disability. On the other hand, some prefer 'disabled people' to communicate the fact that people have been disabled by the way society is structured. We left such issues to individual contributors to approach as they preferred.

We will not have always got our choice of language and expression correct, but we have thought about our language choices. We encourage students and teachers of health(care) law to do the same. How we describe people in the course of healthcare law matters and should be a pertinent point of the conversations we have in our classrooms.

Synopsis

This textbook is structured in three parts. Part I covers introductory aspects of health law and ethics in England and Wales, including reflection about the general principles that underpin it, how we understand health, and how we do, and should, organise healthcare. Part II covers some of the 'body of health law'; that is, the key overarching bodies of law within health law. Part III covers some of the applied topic areas in health law that are most commonly taught in law and medical schools in England and Wales.

Part I

Chapter 2, 'Ethical Principles in Health', by Marisha Wickremsinhe opens up space for reflection on how interpretations of ethical theories that underlie health law and ethics in practice shape our understandings about what is 'right' in the face of ethical dilemmas in healthcare. Using the case study of caring for people who use heroin as inpatients in hospital, Wickremsinhe illustrates how we can challenge assumptions about what is often decided to be 'right' and 'wrong' in

78 Mike Laws, 'Why We Capitalize "Black" (and Not "White")' (2020) https://www.cjr.org/analysis/capital-b-black-styleguide.php, accessed 13 December 2023.

healthcare. This chapter makes for important context for much of the content in this book.

In Chapter 3, Anna Nelson takes up a difficult task of exploring what health is. She sets some important parameters for understanding health, critiquing how narrow conceptions of health have come to impact marginalised groups in different ways. Using three case studies (intersex infants, sufferers of menstrual pain, and racialised people) Nelson illustrates how marginalised groups are problematically labelled as unhealthy unnecessarily, while, simultaneously, others struggle to have their pain or symptoms recognised by healthcare professionals. In Chapter 4, 'Health Inequalities, Law and Society', John Coggon and Beth W. Kamunge-Kpodo highlight that although the law in the UK formally supports equal healthcare opportunities for all, in reality there are multiple practical and principled challenges to equal healthcare opportunities. In particular, they showcase how some are excluded from healthcare in this jurisdiction, how there remains unequal access to healthcare, and how causes of ill health and inequalities are often related to the environment. Social and health justice are intertwined. Chapter 5 by Harleen Kaur Johal and Sabrina Germain, 'Health Disparities, Equity, and Pandemic Ethics', delves into the distinction between equality and equity in healthcare and why it matters, using the pandemic as a case study. Johal and Germain illustrate how healthcare law and policy and clinical guidance – as it has been developed and implemented in the UK – is steeped in inequity and how the fault lines, specifically of systemic racism, were made more visible during the SARS-Cov2 pandemic.

A final addition to Part I of the book is Chapter 6, 'Ethics, Health(care) and Climate Change', by Joshua Parker. We placed this chapter in the introductory section of this book in recognition of the fact that the way in which the provision of healthcare poses ethical dilemmas in light of the climate crisis is an issue that deserves more prominence – being, as it is, in the backdrop of all the other issues discussed in this book. Parker provides an overview of the ethical questions raised when we examine the relationship between health, the provision of healthcare, and climate change, as well as what patients, policy makers, and doctors should do to address the climate crisis.

Part II

Part II begins with an examination of errors in healthcare. In Chapter 7, 'Medical Negligence', Zoe L. Tongue, Elizabeth Chloe Romanis, and Sabrina Germain present the different avenues for complaints and compensation for errors that cause injury to patients. It illustrates how the NHS complaints system and the tort of negligence can exclude marginalised groups from recourse as a result of gendered and racialised norms. In Chapter 8, 'Medical Manslaughter', Amel Alghrani and Hannah Saad examine cases where negligence is considered so severe it becomes a criminal matter. They highlight the recurring problems around the definition of the offence of gross negligence manslaughter and the disproportionate impact the law in this area has on Black, Asian, and Minority Ethnic (BAME) doctors.

Moving on from errors, the rest of the part turns to some of the legal obligations of doctors that affect everyday practice. In Chapter 9, 'Consent to Treatment', Caterina Milo and Thana C. de Campos-Rudinsky analyse the landmark Supreme Court case of *Montgomery v Lanarkshire Health Board*, arguing that the case signals a shift in perception, where patients are no longer recipients of medical advice but consumers. They propose an alternative view, calling on the Ethics of Love as a holistic approach to informed consent. In Chapter 10, 'Mental Capacity and Decision-Making', Beverley Clough takes a disability studies perspective to examining the Mental Capacity Act 2005, emphasising the need for a social model critique, and challenges how the legislation deals with cognitive impairments when assessing capacity and best-interests decision-making. In Chapter 11, 'Mental Health: Inpatient Care', Magdalena Furgalska provides an outline of English mental health law on inpatient care and offers a rights-based approach to understanding its impact. Furgalska draws from her empirical work to illustrate how mental health law (as it relates to inpatient care) is experienced in real life. This part closes with Chapter 12, 'Confidentiality', in which Elizabeth Chloe Romanis, Jordan A. Parsons, and Naomi Jones outline healthcare professionals' legal obligations relating to confidentiality and the importance of confidentiality to maintain trust between professionals and diverse patient groups. They then use two case studies – safeguarding and abortion data collection – to illustrate the complexities of confidentiality and how its importance can sometimes go unrecognised.

Part III

Part III begins with issues related to reproduction. In Chapter 13, 'Assisted Reproduction', Rita D'Alton-Harrison, Philip Bremner, and Cynthia Mbugua examine how access to fertility treatment is limited along the axes of ethnicity, sexual orientation, and age. In Chapter 14, 'Abortion and Contraception', Zoe L. Tongue introduces feminist ethical perspectives and outlines the regulation of and access to abortion and contraception in the UK. Tongue then considers two big future challenges for abortion regulation: decriminalisation and abortion on the grounds of fetal disability. In Chapter 15, 'Pregnancy and Birth', Elizabeth Chloe Romanis and Zaina Mahmoud outline the systemic problems in the NHS of obstetric violence and obstetric racism, limitations on access to choices in and about birth, and how medical, social, and legal regulation can control pregnant people's behaviour, with the greatest impact on those marginalised in society across a number of axes including gender, race, and socio-economics.

Moving on from reproduction, Chapter 16 by Rebecca Limb explores 'Capable Children's Medical Treatment'. Limb uses a fictional case study from a popular book to showcase the complex, unique, and often unacknowledged challenges that capable children face when making decisions about their healthcare. In

Chapter 17, 'Organ Donation: Deceased Donation', Aileen Editha presents the organ scarcity issue against the increasing need for transplants and how this particularly impacts on ethnic minorities. She examines whether and what law and regulation can help solve the organ scarcity issue for ethnic minority communities, with special attention paid to the recent introduction of an opt-out system in England. In Chapter 18, 'Clinical Research Ethics', Zareen Bheekhun and Silvia Camporesi provide a much-needed historical contextualisation of the foundations of clinical research ethics and highlight three fundamental principles in clinical research ethics: vulnerability, clinical equipoise, and therapeutic misconception. They illustrate the application of these principles in contemporary clinical research and critique how, at times, this application is unsatisfactory or even harmful. Finally, they reflect on whether these principles could be subject to a reinterpretation since the COVID-19 pandemic. In the final chapter, 'Death and Dying', Dunja Begović, Yakubu Salifu, and Sheila Payne outline the ethical and legal dilemmas in palliative care – noting that the focus in death in healthcare law is often about the (absence of a) right to die, rather than on quality-of-life healthcare that can be offered to dying people. They also explore inequalities in access to palliative care within societies and on a global scale.

Bibliography

Adamson A, 'Seeing Black Written with a Capital b Means More Than You Think It Does' (2022) https://metro.co.uk/2022/10/01/seeing-black-written-with-a-capital-b-means-more-than-you-think-it-does-2-17480271/, accessed 13 December 2023

Adébísí F, *Decolonisation and Legal Knowledge* (Bristol University Press 2023)

Ahmed S and others, 'Are You Really the Doctor? Physician Experiences with Gendered Microaggressions from Patients' (2022) 31 J Women's Health 521

Akbar A, 'Law's Exposure: The Movement and the Legal Academy' (2015) 65 J Leg Educ 352

Baer J, 'Feminist Theory and Law' in R Goodin (ed), *The Oxford Handbook of Political Science* (OUP 2011)

Barnes E, 'The Hysteria Accusation' (2020) Available from: https://aeon.co/essays/womens-pain-it-seems-is-hysterical-until-proven-otherwise, accessed 13 December 2023

Bartlett K, 'Feminist Legal Methods' (1990) 103 Harv Law Rev 829

Begeny C and others, 'Sexual Harassment, Sexual Assault and Rape by Colleagues in the Surgical Workforce, and How Women and Men are Living Different Realities: Observational Study using NHS Population-Derived Weights' (2023) 110 Br J Surg 1518.

Bhopal K, *White Privilege: The Myth of a Post-Racial Society* (Policy Press 2018).

BMA (British Medical Association), 'Racism an Issue in NHS, Finds Survey' (2022) https://www.bma.org.uk/news-and-opinion/racism-an-issue-in-nhs-finds-survey, accessed 7 December 2023

Chou V, 'How Science and Genetics are Reshaping the Race Debate of the 21st Century' (2017) https://sitn.hms.harvard.edu/flash/2017/science-genetics-reshaping-race-debate-21st-century/, accessed 4 December 2023

City Law School Law and Society Podcast, 'Episode 6: Feminist Legal Theory & Intersectionality' 3 March 2022. https://soundcloud.com/cls-law-society-podcast/episode-6-adrienne-yong, accessed 1 July 2024

Crenshaw K, 'Demarginalizing the Intersection of Race and Sex: A Black Feminist Critique of Antidiscrimination Doctrine, Feminist Theory and Antiracist Politics' (1989) 1 U Chi Leg F 139

Davis A, *Women, Race and Class* (Women's Press 1982)

Davis D-A, *Reproductive Justice: Racism, Pregnancy, and Premature Birth* (NYU Press 2019)

Delgado R and Stefancic J, *Critical Race Theory: The Cutting Edge* (Temple University Press 1999)

Delgado R and Stefancic J, *Critical Race Theory: An Introduction* (4th edn, NYU Press 2017)

Delgado R, Bell DA and Konig H, *Critical Race Feminism: A Reader* (NYU Press 1997)

Dhairyawan R, 'The Medical Practice of Silencing' (2021) 398 Lancet 382

Drescher J, 'Out of DSM: Depathologizing Homosexuality' (2015) 5 Behav Sci 565

Einion A, 'Embracing the Power of "And"' (2021) https://www.all4maternity.com/embracing-the-power-of-and/?sfw=pass1702487115, accessed 13 December 2023

Garland-Thomson R, 'Feminist Disabilities Studies' (2005) 30 Signs 1557

Germain S and Ray K, 'Book Review: *Shedding Light on Racial Inequity in Heath, in Conversation with the Author: Black Health: The Social, Political, and Cultural Determinants of Black People's Health*' (2023) 24 Med Law Inter 151–8 https://journals.sagepub.com/doi.org/10.1177/09685332231211914, accessed 1 July 2024

Germain S and Yong A, 'COVID-19 Highlighting Inequalities in Access to Healthcare in England: A Case Study of Ethnic Minority and Migrant Women' (2020) 28 Fem Leg Stud 301

Hill Collins P and Bilge S, *Intersectionality* (2nd edn, Polity Press 2020)

hooks b, *Feminist Theory: From Margin to Center* (South End Press 1984)

Iacobucci G, 'Foreign NHS Doctors Face Persistent Racism at Work, Survey Finds' (2023) 383 BMJ 2637

Kamau R and others, 'Inclusivity Starts with Language' (2022) 399 Lancet 434

Kittay FE, 'The Personal is Philosophical is Political: A Philosopher and Mother of a Cognitively Disabled Person Sends Notes from the Battlefield' (2009) 40 Metaphilosophy 606

Laws M, 'Why We Capitalize "Black" (and Not "White")' (2020) https://www.cjr.org/analysis/capital-b-black-styleguide.php, accessed 13 December 2023

MacKinnon C, 'Feminism, Marxism, Method and the State: An Agenda for Theory' (1982) 7 Signs 515, 537.

NHS Confederation, 'ONS Data on COVID-19-Related Deaths by Ethnicity in England and Wales' (2020) https://www.nhsconfed.org/publications/ons-data-covid-19-related-deaths-ethnicity-england-and-wales, accessed 13 December 2023

NHS England, 'NHS Workforce More Diverse than Any Point in Its History, as Health Service Commits to More Action on Representation' (2021) https://www.england.nhs.uk/2021/07/nhs-workforce-more-diverse-than-any-point-in-its-history-as-health-service-commits-to-more-action-on-representation, accessed 13 December 2021

MacKinnon CA and others, 'Exploring Transgender Law and Politics' (2023) https://signsjournal.org/exploring-transgender-law-and-politics/, accessed 13 December 2023

Malik A and others, '"I Decided Not To Go Into Surgery Due To Dress Code": A Cross-Sectional Study within the UK Investigating Experiences of Female Muslim Medical Health Professionals on Bare Below the Elbows (BBE) Policy and Wearing Headscarves (Hijabs) in Theatre' (2019) 9 BMJ Open e019954

Margree V, *Neglected or Misunderstood: The Radical Feminism of Shulamith Firestone* (Zero Books 2017)

Minow M, 'Feminist Reason: Getting It and Losing It' in K Bartlett and R Kennedy (eds), *Feminist Legal Theory: Readings in Law and Gender* (Westview Press 1991), 357

Parris J, 'Why is My Uni So White?' (2020) https://decolonisinglse.wordpress.com/2020/06/26/why-is-my-uni-so-white/, accessed 13 December 2023

Ramazanoglu C and Holland J, *Feminist Methodology: Challenges and Choices* (SAGE 2002)

Ray K, *Black Health: The Social, Political, and Cultural Determinants of Black People's Health* (OUP 2023)

Roberts D, *Killing the Black Body: Race, Reproduction and the Meaning of Liberty* (Pantheon Books Penguin 1997)

Robinson H and Herring J, 'Naming and Describing Disability in Law and Medicine' (2024) Camb Q Healthc Ethics https://doi.org/10.1017/S0963180123000609, accessed 1 July 2024

Rodriguez A, 'Is the B in Black Capitalized? Yes' (2021) https://news.ucdenver.edu/is-the-b-in-black-capitalized-yes/, accessed 13 December 2023

Romanis EC, 'Legal Method and Health Law in Feminist Perspective' in J McHale and A Krajewska (eds), *Reimagining Health Law from Medical to Health and Social Care Law* (Edward Elgar, forthcoming)

Salami M, 'Why I Don't Believe the Word "Black" Should Always Have a Capital "B"' (2021) https://www.theguardian.com/commentisfree/2021/jun/03/word-black-capital-letter-blackness, accessed 13 December 2023

Shakespeare T, *Disability Rights and Wrongs* (Routledge 2006)

Sharma M, 'Applying Feminist Theory to Medical Education' (2019) 393 Lancet 570

Sheldon S, *Beyond Control: Medical Power and Abortion Law* (Pluto Press 1997)

Solicitors Regulatory Authority, 'Diversity in Law Firms' Workforce' (2024) https://www.sra.org.uk/sra/equality-diversity/diversity-profession/diverse-legal-profession/, accessed 15 August 2024

Sowemimo A, *Divided: Racism, Medicine and Why We Need to Decolonise Healthcare* (Profile Books 2023)

Thomas C, 'Medicine, Gender, and Disability: Disabled Women's Healthcare Encounters' (2001) 22 Health Care Women Int 245

Treviño AJ, Harris MA and Wallace D, 'What's So Critical about Critical Race Theory?' (2008) 11 Contemp Justice Rev 7

UK Government, 'Writing about Ethnicity', https://www.ethnicity-facts-figures.service.gov.uk/style-guide/writing-about-ethnicity/, accessed 13 December 2023

Wallis C and others, 'Association of Surgeon–Patient Sex Concordance with Postoperative Outcomes' (2022) 157 JAMA Surg 146

West R, 'Jurisprudence and Gender' (1988) 55 U Chi L Rev 1–72

Young IM, *Throwing Like a Girl and Other Essays in Feminist Philosophy and Social Theory* (Indiana University Press 1990)

PART I

General Principles of Health Law and Ethics

2

Ethical Principles in Health

Marisha Wickremsinhe

Clinicians and healthcare workers – as well as professionals working in clinical research, public health, and other affiliated fields – are constantly making decisions, whether choosing which course of treatment to recommend to the patient sitting before them or how to respond to an infectious disease outbreak affecting a whole community. While these decisions turn on the available scientific evidence, they are also subject to ethical analysis to ensure that the right decision has been made.

But defining what is 'right' in a given context is often contested. How should we decide which 'right' is, indeed, *right*?

Philosophers search for the answer to this question through the field of normative ethics, where their reflections are guided by various ethical theories based on, for example, making 'right' decisions according to their outcomes (consequentialist ethics), or as guided by a set of defined ethical rules or duties (deontological ethics), or even in alignment with the character traits of a virtuous person (virtue ethics). Critically, determining what is truly 'right' turns on the decision-maker's own view on which ethical theory should be applied to distinguish right from wrong.

Consequentialist ethics, deontological ethics, and virtue ethics are themselves the subject of vast philosophical debate, with each theory both commended and critiqued according to various benchmarks. One aspect of these debates relates to challenges in applying ethical theories to real-world ethical decision-making. Application is complicated for two reasons. Firstly, applying ethical theory in practice requires some sort of broader justification as to why a particular 'yardstick' for measuring right and wrong should be used (i.e., justification of the use of a specific theory itself). Secondly, in practice, applying a particular theory does not always yield direct 'answers' on how to act in the real world. This second complication can be especially challenging for decision-makers like clinicians, who need to determine an ethically defensible course of action to take (not just debate it!).

This chapter explores the four-principles approach, an ethical framework for decision-making developed by two American philosophers in the 1970s with an eye towards overcoming these complications in applying consequentialism, deontological, and virtue ethics in practice. While I focus on the four-principles approach, there are a range of principles that are relevant to health, especially public health, over and above these four principles. Indeed, the development of the four-principles approach stems primarily from debates in clinical ethics – that is, the ethics of providing direct care to patients. The principles of the four-principles approach are also closely related to principles derived for the purposes of guiding the ethical conduct of medical research, which is why I have included illustrative examples from both clinical and research ethics throughout this chapter.

While the four-principles approach is widely adopted in healthcare ethics, it has also been widely critiqued. This chapter's focus on the four-principles approach is not a comment on its superiority, or, indeed, inferiority. Rather, this chapter seeks to take the approach seriously – in large part *because of* its widespread use across healthcare and healthcare ethics – and begin to explore how we might apply the four-principles approach in practice. This chapter offers a framing to ensure that application of the four-principles approach in context is practically and ethically useful, with due attention to context-specific considerations and influences.

Firstly, I offer a brief background to the development of the four-principles approach and describe each of the principles. Secondly, I explore a few prominent critiques of the widespread use of the four-principles approach and review defences of the framework. Thirdly, I use a case example – providing hospital care to people who use heroin – to explore how the four-principles approach may be differentially interpreted in practice. In conclusion, I offer a discussion on the importance of reflexivity – critically examining our own assumptions, feelings, and intuitions – in ethical analysis. Reflexivity, as conceptualised in this chapter, asks us to examine not just our moral intuitions or 'gut feelings', but also social and political norms, where relevant, in the application of any ethical approach, including the four-principles approach.

While reading, I invite you to reflect on the ways in which interpretations of ethical principles in medical decision-making, often narrowly biomedical in focus, inevitably shape interpretations of what is 'right' in healthcare. These reflections challenge assumptions about how healthcare ethics and law should distinguish right from wrong in health.

Introducing the four-principles approach

The four-principles approach was born from the need to develop a 'systematic account' of the principles of bioethics.[1] American philosophers Beauchamp

1 Tom Beauchamp and James Childress, *Principles of Biomedical Ethics* (4th edn, OUP 1994) 23.

and Childress refined the four-principles approach alongside publication of the Belmont Report in 1979, authored by the US National Commission for the Protection of Human Subjects of Biomedical and Behavioural Research.[2] The Belmont Report described three ethical principles to govern medical research – respect for persons, beneficence, and justice – derived through extensive deliberations by the 11-person Commission.[3] Beauchamp and Childress, who also gave papers on relevant topics for consideration in the Commission's deliberations,[4] wrote the core text of their four-principles approach in 1976, and published their book, *The Principles of Biomedical Ethics*, in 1979.[5]

Beauchamp and Childress define four core principles of biomedical ethics: respect for autonomy, non-maleficence, beneficence, and justice. Critically, these principles are non-absolute. That is, none of these principles takes precedence over the others, and weighing these principles in practice necessitates moral judgements:

> Principles do not function as precise action guides that inform us in each circumstance how to act in the way more detailed rules do. Principles are general guides that leave considerable room for judgment in specific cases and that provide substantive guidance for the development of more detailed rules and policies.[6]

Beauchamp and Childress offer detailed explanation of how each of the four principles may be understood in context. The following subsections provide a brief overview of these discussions.

Respect for autonomy

Put simply, respect for autonomy describes the ethical norm of respect for individuals' 'self-rule', or decision-making capacity with respect to matters of their own life and personal goals. In biomedical ethics, respect for autonomy

2 National Commission for the Protection of Human Subjects of Biomedical and Behavioral Research, 'The Belmont Report' (1978) https://www.hhs.gov/ohrp/regulations-and-policy/belmont-report/index.html, accessed 6 December 2023.

3 Ibid. The Commission was convened following a series of national and international research ethics scandals including the 'Tuskegee Study of Untreated Syphilis in the Negro Male', where US researchers withheld diagnosis and treatment from 399 Black American men enrolled in the study. The study, which ran from 1932 to 1972, was conducted by the United States Public Health Service and the Centers for Disease Control and Prevention. See Susan Reverby, *Examining Tuskegee: The Infamous Syphilis Study and Its Legacy* (University of North Carolina Press 2009).

4 National Commission (n2), Appendix 1.

5 Tom Beauchamp, 'The "Four Principles" Approach to Health Care Ethics' in Richard Ashcroft and others (eds), *Principles of Health Care Ethics* (2nd edn, John Wiley & Sons 2007).

6 Beauchamp and Childress (n1) 38.

generally refers to respect for the right of the individual to hold their own views and to make decisions, usually about treatment or research participation, based on those views.

This principle can be understood as a response to historical patterns and norms of medical decision-making. Historically, medical decision-making followed a more paternalistic model, where, for example, a doctor decided *for* the patient which treatment to pursue,[7] or even whether or not to inform the patient of their diagnosis or prognosis.[8] The principle of respect for autonomy, applied to counter medical paternalism, would instead demand that the doctor explain the risks and benefits of various treatment options and support the patient to identify which treatment option might best align with their own aims.[9] Respect for autonomy may also demand that the doctor offer clear, easily comprehensible information about the patient's health status.

In modern medicine and clinical research, respect for autonomy has entered clinical protocol through the informed consent process, where the patient is: (a) provided with sufficient detail on the risks and benefits of a particular intervention or course of treatment in order to weigh that information in line with their own views and preferences; and (b) empowered to voluntarily make a treatment decision based on that knowledge. In some specific cases, respect for autonomy can be overridden by a 'best interests' standard where the individual lacks decision-making capacity, for example, in an emergency.[10]

In general, the principle of respect for autonomy seeks to centre the patient/research participant as a rational agent (a person able to make optimum decisions rationally) whose own wishes and views should be honoured as part of medical decision-making. As such, autonomous agents should be enabled to make their own choices freely and voluntarily with respect to healthcare/research participation.[11] This orientation also challenges the notion of the patient as an 'object' to be acted upon by clinicians, or the research participant as an

7 Mark Siegler, 'From Physician Paternalism to Patient Autonomy to Bureaucratic Parsimony' (1985) 145 Arch Intern Med 713.

8 Bryan Sisk and others, 'The Truth about Truth-Telling in American Medicine: A Brief History' (2016) 20 Perm J 15.

9 The respect afforded to autonomy is a matter of law: *Montgomery v Lanarkshire Health Board* [2015] UKSC 11.

10 People living with psychosocial disabilities such as schizophrenia have historically also been included in this designation of lacking decision-making capacity, wherein a 'best interests' standard would ordinarily be applied to treatment decisions. Recently, though, advocacy through disability rights movements, including publication of the United Nations Convention on the Rights of Persons with Disabilities (adopted 13 December 2006, entered into force 3 May 2008) 2515 UNTS 3 has sought to challenge this notion. See Chapter 9.

11 As a non-absolute principle, respect for autonomy may be outweighed by other principles (discussed later) in certain situations. For example, the implementation of population-wide public health interventions may be justified based on justice and beneficence, even where respect for autonomy may be infringed upon, e.g., vaccination mandates. A rich literature on public health ethics explores these tensions. E.g., Ruth Faden, Sirine Shebaya, and Andrew

experimental site to be studied by researchers, by acknowledging the 'humanness' of individuals – that is, by acknowledging the innate worth of all individuals.

Non-maleficence

Non-maleficence describes the ethical norm of refraining from causing harm. Distinct from beneficence (described shortly), this principle seeks to ensure that actions taken do not cause undue pain or suffering to an individual. In biomedical ethics, non-maleficence demands that physicians (and researchers) avoid *causing* harm. Very simply, non-maleficence begins from the basic premise of 'do not kill' and extends from there to incorporate a range of simple moral rules that call for moral actors to avoid causing pain or suffering to others.[12]

From a legal standpoint, non-maleficence is most easily understood in the context of medical negligence, where clinicians are held responsible for taking actions (or failing to take actions) that cause harm.[13] For a harm to be classed as professional malpractice as a form of negligence, the clinician's actions (or lack thereof) must represent a breach of professional duty, wherein that breach of duty directly causes a specific harm to the patient.[14]

Many perceive non-maleficence to be the pre-eminent principle within the 'four-principles' approach in practice, at least insofar as the maxim *primum non nocere* ('first, do no harm') has long been upheld in medical traditions. Indeed, upholding the principle of non-maleficence may sound rather straightforward at first, but a case example makes clear that the demands of non-maleficence can be more complex when applied in practice.

Consider ethical questions surrounding assisted dying[15] – where a physician 'brings about' the patient's death in some way. On the face of it, the principle of non-maleficence demands that the physician *never*, under any circumstance, hasten the death of a patient, as death is a demonstrable harm. However, Beauchamp and Childress defend a view of non-maleficence that centres quality-of-life judgements, whereby clinicians are also responsible for ensuring that patients are not unjustifiably left to suffer, for example, where assisted dying would eliminate suffering.[16]

Beauchamp and Childress argue that, where specific conditions are met – with focus on respect for the patient's autonomy – the act of assisting a patient in dying represents a scenario in which the principle of non-maleficence is non-absolute when considered alongside the principle of beneficence. Moral

Siegal, 'Distinctive Challenges of Public Health Ethics' in Anna Mastroianni, Jeffrey Kahn, and Nancy Kass (eds), *The Oxford Handbook of Public Health Ethics* (OUP 2019).

12 Beauchamp and Childress (n1).

13 See Chapter 7.

14 Beauchamp and Childress (n1).

15 See Chapter 19.

16 Beauchamp and Childress (n1).

actors such as clinicians have a negative obligation not to cause harm, but also a positive obligation to actively support the patient's welfare (e.g., eliminating suffering), which may, under specific circumstances, include bringing about death. Here, a 'negative' obligation refers to the duty to refrain from causing harm (e.g., refraining from actively pushing someone to the ground), while a 'positive' obligation refers to the duty to take active steps towards supporting others' wellbeing (e.g., making the effort to help someone who has fallen get up off the ground).

Beneficence

In biomedical ethics, the principle of beneficence demands that moral actors act in ways that *actively promote* the patient's wellbeing – not just by preventing harm or avoiding harm, but by taking positive steps to promote welfare. Indeed, Beauchamp and Childress distinguish between simply *refraining from* causing harm, as in the principle of non-maleficence, and taking proactive steps to help others, as in the principle of beneficence.

Put simply, the principle of beneficence requires that medical practitioners act to promote 'good', generally by preventing, removing, or alleviating a harm such as pain. In the context of medicine and clinical research, the principle of beneficence also acknowledges that many medical interventions themselves pose harm – but that the benefits of these interventions should outweigh these harms.[17]

As a simple example, a clinician might offer a vaccine to reduce the risk of fatal illness. At first, the principle of non-maleficence would demand that the clinician *avoid* the harm of the injection required to administer the vaccine itself – and any directly consequent harms, like muscle soreness at the injection site. The principle of beneficence, however, balanced alongside the principle of non-maleficence, suggests that the benefit of preventing fatal illness, a significant harm, far outweighs the minor harm of inflicting a small amount of pain to give the injection. In this case, the benefit of the antibodies justifies the harm of the injection/muscle soreness.

In balancing non-maleficence against beneficence, ethicists weigh the probability and magnitude of the risk of harm associated with a particular intervention/course of treatment alongside the likelihood and scale of the possible benefit of the intervention/course of treatment. In many cases, the decision is fairly straightforward: the potential harms of chemotherapy – fatigue, hair loss, nausea, and so on – are widely considered to be more than justified by the benefits of chemotherapy – eliminating or slowing the growth of a cancerous tumour.

In other cases, the decision is more complex and reasonable people may disagree about whether the benefits of a particular intervention outweigh the harms. For example, debates still rage about whether electroconvulsive therapy

17 Ibid.

(sending electrical currents through the brain to induce a brief seizure under general anaesthetic) to treat refractory depression is ever 'beneficial' given the risks of the procedure.

In either instance, balancing beneficence with respect for autonomy in clinical care also demands that the patient's own views of what constitutes a 'benefit' and a 'harm' are incorporated into decision-making. As a stark example of this point (and for illustrative purposes only, without medical context): a patient with a fatal condition may have their own view of the relative 'benefit' of a treatment that prolongs quantity of life but worsens quality of life in comparison with a treatment that shortens quantity of life but improves quality of life. Imagine, for example, someone with a terminal illness who wants to live longer, even with a poorer *quality* of life, in order to see their child graduate university in six months, as compared to someone with the same terminal illness who would rather have a higher quality of life, even if the quantity of that life is shorter, say three months, in order to be able to fulfil a life dream of travelling abroad.

At its core, beneficence may seem the most obvious principle. Indeed, historical practices of Western medicine have largely prioritised beneficence above any other principle. Clinicians tend to be entrusted, by virtue of their knowledge but also their moral standing, with near-absolute power over the care of their patients – where 'doctor knows best'. However, this model of medicine has been problematised by the fact that any 'benefit' of care received was interpreted and defined solely by clinicians, and often through a narrow biomedical lens. Per Beauchamp and Childress, the principles of respect for autonomy and non-maleficence work to balance this unlimited power of clinicians to determine what is best for the patient by calling on the former to support patients to make their own treatment decisions in line with their views and aims.

Justice

Writing about the Belmont Report, Beauchamp remarks:

> The [US] National Commission noted that, historically, the burdens of research were placed heavily on the economically disadvantaged, the very sick, and the vulnerable, owing to their ready availability. [...] The overutilization of readily available, often compromised, segments of the US population was a matter of deep moral concern to the National Commission.[18]

In the context of research ethics, the principle of justice captures the ethical norm of fair distribution of benefits and risks across a population. Where each of the

---

[18] Tom Beauchamp, 'The Belmont Report' in Ezekiel Emanuel and others, *The Oxford Textbook of Clinical Research Ethics* (OUP 2008).

previously described principles focus rather narrowly on the particular individual in the context of clinical research, the principle of justice broadens the scope of the ethical calculus of decision-making by ensuring that benefits are maximised and harms are minimised at the population level. Justice demands that the burdens associated with a social good such as medical research are evenly distributed across the population slated to benefit from that social good. Specific populations, especially marginalised or otherwise disadvantaged populations, should not be overburdened with the risks of clinical research.

In the context of the clinical encounter, the principle of justice demands that people (or patients) are treated equitably. Resource constraints aside, if two clinically identical patients requiring ventilators are admitted in hospital, both should be offered ventilators – that is, 'like cases should be treated alike'.[19]

Disagreements, of course, may arise, especially with respect to determining what characteristics or qualities should be factored into determinations of what constitutes equal treatment. Few would argue that social characteristics, such as socio-economic status, should be used to discriminate between otherwise 'like' cases in general, but should more subjective medical concepts, say current kidney function, or body mass index, be used to differentiate treatment?

This question illustrates an important feature of the four-principles approach: each of these principles is subject to interpretation and application *in context*. Importantly, our understanding of the contours of 'justice', or indeed of any of the four principles, may change according to medical advancements and social norms.[20]

Drawing from common morality

Beauchamp and Childress root their four-principles approach in *common morality*, drawing 'directly from the morality shared in common by the members of a society – that is, unsophisticated common sense and tradition'.[21] Put simply, 'common morality' refers to the broad intuitive beliefs we all hold about right and wrong – for example, that lying is wrong.[22] An appeal to common morality assumes that all humans have, at least at a foundational level, the same kinds of intuitions and moral instincts.

Per Beauchamp and Childress, rooting the four-principles approach in common morality then allows for wide agreement across individuals, without predicating consensus on a shared view of which specific ethical theory, and its interpretation in context, should be applied. For example, reasonable people disagree over

19 Beauchamp (n5) 6; see Chapter 5.

20 For further discussion see: Anna Mastroianni and Jeffrey Kahn, 'Swinging on the Pendulum: Shifting Views of Justice in Human Subjects Research' (2001) 31 Hastings Cent Rep 21.

21 Beauchamp and Childress (n1) 100.

22 Robert Veatch, 'Is There a Common Morality?' (2003) 13 Kennedy Inst Ethics 189.

whether to establish ethical norms on the basis of obligation, for example, acting according to moral duty (deontological theory); outcomes, for example, acting according to the action's consequences (consequentialist theory); or virtue, for example, acting according to good character (virtue-based theory). Beauchamp and Childress argue that 'far more social consensus exists about principles and rules drawn from the common morality (for example, our four principles) than about theories'.[23]

Having argued for their universality, Beauchamp and Childress acknowledge that common morality and its derived principles are not immune to revision and alteration. However, they suggest that this revision would stem not from revision to broad and widely agreed norms themselves (e.g., 'justice'), but rather to how those are specified and interpreted in context.

Critiques of the four-principles approach

Though widely referenced, the four-principles approach has also been widely critiqued. I offer an overview of a few of these critiques, drawing heavily on Shahvisi's summary of critiques of the four-principles approach as part of a broader call towards decolonial feminist bioethics.[24]

Anti-coloniality: common morality is not 'common' to all

The four-principles approach can be critiqued for assuming that common morality is truly 'universal'. This critique holds that applications of each of the four principles, especially the principle of respect for autonomy in relation to the principle of justice, rely on Western ideals. Many non-Western societies do not prioritise individualistic conceptions of freedom to the same extent, focusing instead on concepts like the common good, which necessarily requires that individuals see themselves not as single autonomous beings but as part of a community. This communitarian ethic prioritises the collective, positioning the individual as a member of their community first and foremost, not merely an individual operating independently and of their own accord.

By this critique, the principle of respect for autonomy centres what could be perceived, ultimately, as a completely irrelevant concept. Behrens argues against 'respect for autonomy' in favour of 'respect for persons', contending that the individualistic notion of autonomy does not align with African accounts of interdependence, where 'individuals are bound up with their communities'.[25] Even where the broadest sense of this communitarian ethic may not apply, many

---

23 Beauchamp and Childress (n1) 102.

24 Arianne Shahvisi, 'Towards an Anticolonial Feminist Bioethics' in Wendy Rodgers and others (eds), *The Routledge Handbook of Feminist Bioethics* (Routledge 2022).

25 Kevin Behrens, 'A Critique of the Principle of "Respect for Autonomy", Grounded in African Thought' (2017) 18 Dev World Bioeth 128.

cultures prioritise group decision-making, such as family decision-making, over individual decision-making. Chen and Fan argue that the central role of the family in Chinese bioethics renders the *family*, not the individual, the 'basic autonomous unit'.[26] Such an account challenges the claim that the principle of respect for (individual) autonomy is part of a common, that is, universal, morality.

Defenders of the four-principles approach, and specifically the principle of respect for autonomy, suggest that the implied dichotomy between community and individual is false – indeed, Beauchamp and Childress make this very argument,[27]quoting Feinburg:

> It is impossible to think of human beings except as part of ongoing communities, defined by reciprocal bonds of obligation, common traditions, and institutions. ... The idea [in liberals' accounts] of the autonomous person is that of an authentic individual whose self-determination is as complete as is consistent with the requirement that he [sic] is, of course, a member of a community.[28]

Beauchamp and Childress also lodge a more general defence with respect to the 'commonness' of common morality by clarifying that even where 'common morality provides the starting point and the constraining framework', the principles and their applications in practice will continue to evolve.[29] While the principles themselves are universal at their core, Beauchamp and Childress claim, the ways in which stakeholders interpret and balance their applications in practice are open to challenge and revision.

The extent to which the four principles are, indeed, universal remains an important point of disagreement.

Feminism: the impossibility of abstraction

Wolf argues that 'top-down ethics' – for example, ethics structured according to principles or norms – favours what is often considered to be a 'neutral' standpoint for analysis. However, Wolf argues, 'One's standpoint (including one's gender) can affect what is perceived as a problem in the first place, and then each step of the analysis.'[30] Moreover, 'reasoning from abstract rules and principles governed by requirements of universality and impartiality overlooks the importance of

26 Xiaoyang Chen and Ruiping Fan, 'The Family and Harmonious Medical Decision Making: Cherishing an Appropriate Confucian Moral Balance' (2010) 35 J Med Philosophy 579.

27 Beauchamp and Childress (n1) 84.

28 Joel Feinburg, *The Moral Limits of the Criminal Law: Harm to Others* (OUP 1986) 47.

29 Beauchamp and Childress (n1) 102.

30 Susan Wolf, 'Introduction: Gender and Feminism in Bioethics' in Susan Wolf (ed), *Feminism and Bioethics: Beyond Reproduction* (OUP 1996) 15.

partiality, context, and relational bonds in moral life'.[31] The implied neutrality of a principles-based approach to ethics – with a 'top-down' rather than 'bottom-up' approach to determining the right course of action – obscures the importance of context.

Critics argue that principles like those invoked in the four-principles approach – hypothesised in relation to a 'generic' person – necessarily erase substantive markers of moral significance, such as gender, race, class, and sexuality.[32] For example, as Wolf notes, even understanding the historic (and still fairly common) practice of categorically excluding 'women of reproductive age' from clinical trials – to avoid any potential risk to a potential fetus – as a 'problem' may depend on one's standpoint. Initially, a universal appeal to non-maleficence – preventing a potential adverse effect to a potential fetus – seems reasonable, especially where the potential benefits are uncertain. However, to anyone who is excluded or subsequently left without adequate data to guide health decisions as a consequence, this narrow interpretation and application of non-maleficence is surely inadequate and unjustifiable.

Feminist philosophers also challenge the notion of autonomy as individualistic,[33] aligning with critiques from non-Western scholars, as described when exploring the critiques of principlism from the perspective of anti-coloniality.

Theory: no way to resolve conflict between principles

Some philosophers critique the four-principles approach for its lack of a unifying ethical theory. Clouser and Gert explain:

> By 'applying' the 'principles' of autonomy, beneficence, and justice, the agent [decision-maker] is unwittingly using several diverse and conflicting accounts rather than simply applying a well-developed unified theory.[34]

The result of Beauchamp and Childress choosing to draw principles from a breadth of normative theories (primarily consequentialism, deontology, and virtue ethics), Clouser and Gert argue, is that the approach therefore lacks any method for reconciling conflicting principles in practice. Moreover, the meaning of each individual principle is itself conflicting:

---

31 Ibid 15.

32 Ibid.

33 E.g., Catriona MacKenzie and Natalie Stoljar (eds), *Relational Autonomy: Feminist Perspectives on Autonomy, Agency, and the Social Self* (OUP 2000).

34 K. Danner Clouser and Bernard Gert, 'A Critique of Principlism' (1990) 15 J Medicine Philosophy 219.

> When, for example, we are told that a particular case calls for the application of the principle of beneficence, this can mean that the case involves either (1) the utilitarian ideal of promoting some good, or (2) the moral ideal of preventing some harm or removing some harm, or (3) some duty which is morally required.[35]

With respect to the first critique, Beauchamp and Childress acknowledge this limitation of their approach and challenge whether ethics could ever be rooted in a unified theory. Beauchamp and Childress developed their principles from the starting point of disagreement over theory and identified the four principles of respect for autonomy, non-maleficence, beneficence, and justice as points of convergence across competing ethical theories.[36]

With respect to the second critique lodged by Clouser and Gert, Beauchamp and Childress argue that 'no system of guidelines could reasonably anticipate the full range of conflicts' one might encounter in ethical decision-making.[37] Indeed, the four-principles approach demands specification – for example, tailoring an abstract concept, such as respect for autonomy, to a particular context – as *over*specification of a principle at the outset could render its application 'too rigid and insensitive to circumstances'.[38] Beauchamp and Childress give the example of understanding the demands of 'respect for autonomy' for people living with severe cognitive disabilities in an institutional setting. Overspecification of 'respect for autonomy' at the outset could inadvertently miss necessary considerations for justifiably applying 'respect for autonomy' in practice in these settings; for example, by failing to acknowledge institutional norms or resource constraints.

Applying principles in practice: caring for people who use heroin in hospital

Despite its challenges, this section aims to engage meaningfully with the application of the four-principles approach in the context of providing care for a marginalised and criminalised group: people who use drugs, specifically heroin (an opioid drug derived from the opium poppy plant).

This case study draws from the work of the Improving Hospital Opioid Substitution Therapy (iHOST) study, funded by the UK National Institute of Health and Care Research, which aims to decrease rates of self-discharge and its consequences (primarily readmission within 28 days) among people who use opioids who are admitted to hospital. The iHOST study was sparked by evidence of long delays in accessing healthcare among the population of people

35 Ibid 221.

36 Beauchamp and Childress (n1).

37 Ibid 107.

38 Ibid 107.

who use opioids living in London.[39] Through qualitative interviews with people who use opioids, Harris explored reasons for delaying care-seeking. Participants highlighted stigmatising treatment in hospital and past experiences of intolerable withdrawal symptoms during admission.

Following on from this work, Harris and others investigated guidelines for managing opioid withdrawal symptoms across 86 NHS trusts, given participants' testimonies of going into withdrawal in hospital due to a lack of access to opioid agonist therapy, such as methadone, to treat withdrawal symptoms. The team identified several procedural barriers in hospital guidelines, including mandatory urinalysis screenings, even where the patient is clearly experiencing symptoms of opioid withdrawal, and restrictive low initial dosing of methadone or buprenorphine.[40]

Background

Regular and sustained use of opioids such as heroin can lead to physical dependence – where the body relies on external opioids to function and therefore endures withdrawal symptoms if these external opioids are not available in the bloodstream. People who have experienced opioid withdrawal describe a range of painful and intolerable symptoms, including joint and bone aches, tremors, chills, nausea, and vomiting, which can generally only be fully alleviated by a dose of opioids.

Heroin has a relatively short duration of action, with withdrawal symptoms typically occurring four to six hours after each dose. Once a person becomes dependent on heroin, regular use of the drug is therefore needed to prevent withdrawal symptoms.[41] Withdrawal symptoms can also be prevented through prescription of opioid agonist treatment; for example, taking a daily dose of synthetic opioid.[42]

When people who use heroin are admitted to hospital to treat a presenting condition, prevention of withdrawal symptoms becomes a time-sensitive and critical aspect of providing care. However, many hospital settings restrict access to opioid agonist therapy; indeed, some hospitals refuse to offer opioid agonist therapy to people who use heroin.[43] In many cases, people who use heroin are

39 Magdalena Harris, 'Normalised Pain and Severe Health Care Delay among People Who Inject Drugs in London: Adapting Cultural Safety Principles to Promote Care' (2020) 260 Soc Sci Med 113183.

40 Magdalena Harris and others, 'Barriers to Management of Opioid Withdrawal in Hospitals in England: A Document Analysis of Hospital Policies on the Management of Substance Dependence' (2022) 20 BMC Med 1.

41 While individuals may wish to decrease use of opioids in their lifetime, opioid intake should not be stopped suddenly, but decreased in dose over a period of time to prevent withdrawal.

42 Heroin-assisted treatment – the prescription of medical-grade heroin to prevent withdrawal symptoms – is available in some settings.

43 Harris and others (n40).

prescribed only symptomatic relief, such as anti-nausea medication for vomiting or over-the-counter medications such as ibuprofen for joint pain.

People who use heroin highlight the irony of this state of affairs: healthcare settings are perceived as some of the *least* caring settings by people who use drugs.[44] Moreover, restrictive policies for opioid substitution treatment (OST) provision mean that admitted patients must *leave* hospital to address a pressing health need – preventing withdrawal symptoms. This lived reality of people who use drugs seeking access to care sets the backdrop for our case example: how should hospitals reorient clinical guidelines on access to OST in hospital?

Applying the four-principles approach

Tackling this question using the four-principles approach firstly requires a clear diagnosis of the ethical challenge at hand. People who use heroin will often leave hospital, despite high medical need to treat a presenting condition, such as injury or infection, to self-medicate their withdrawal symptoms in the absence of access to opioid agonist therapy during admission.

Secondly, we must acknowledge relevant clinical considerations:

1. Opioid tolerance cannot be directly calculated or measured. Clinicians and patients alike are not easily able to estimate tolerance, even based on accurate reports of the patient's usual heroin intake. Also, given the unregulated supply of heroin, clinicians and patients cannot safely assume that the quantity of heroin bought is equivalent to the quantity of heroin consumed, as many street drugs are cut with adulterants.
2. Determining the dose of methadone or buprenorphine equivalent to a patient's usual heroin intake, even assuming a regulated supply, is not straightforward. It requires a degree of caution to avoid the risk of opioid toxicity – where too much opioid agonist therapy is prescribed relative to the patient's tolerance.
3. As methadone and buprenorphine are controlled drugs in the UK, clinicians may be reticent to prescribe them, especially if they are non-specialists, given the potential risks of toxicity (note, however, that opioid toxicity, if monitored and quickly acted upon, is not fatal).
4. Opioid withdrawal symptoms are widely considered to be severely painful, but opioid withdrawal *itself* rarely causes death (unlike, say, benzodiazepine withdrawal). However, available evidence suggests that people who use heroin have a high risk of fatal overdose during hospital admission and the days following discharge.[45] This is likely due to no or insufficient opioid withdrawal management in hospital.

---

44 Harris (n39).

45 Dan Lewer and others, 'Opioid-Related Deaths during Hospital Admissions or Shortly after Discharge in the United Kingdom: A Thematic Framework Analysis of Coroner Reports' (2023) PLoS One e0283549.

Thirdly, any analysis of this kind must take account of social and political context. The UK government deems heroin a Class A drug, where possession is punishable by 'up to 7 years in prison, an unlimited fine or both' and distribution is punishable by 'up to life in prison, an unlimited fine or both'.[46] At the time of writing (2023), government efforts to curb drug use have taken shape, including the Home Office U-turn banning drug-checking at festivals in June 2023,[47] and publication of the 2022 Home Office White Paper,[48] outlining a range of penalties for 'recreational' drug users. At the same time, the Taliban's 2022 ban on opium production has created a gap in the UK heroin supply, such that distributors have started cutting heroin with powerful synthetic opioids.[49]

Socially, intravenous drug use is widely stigmatised.[50] This stigma in turn influences scientific inquiry and medical practice: even experts disagree on the aetiology of drug dependence, while debates rage over the best ways to support people who use heroin – ranging from detoxification and abstinence to legalisation and safe supply.

I will now briefly describe competing views of the principles of respect for autonomy, non-maleficence, and beneficence, as well as an initial exploration of how these principles might be balanced in context.

Respect for autonomy

As discussed, autonomy is a contested concept in and of itself. How should respect for autonomy apply in this particular case? Some might argue that heroin use is an autonomous decision[51] – one that any individual can freely make – and that therefore clinicians should simply prescribe opioid agonist therapy and not interfere with the patient's prior decision to use heroin. Conversely, others

46 UK Government, 'Drug Penalties' https://www.gov.uk/penalties-drug-possession-dealing, accessed 5 September 2023.

47 Rajeev Syal, 'Home Office U-turn on Festival Drug Tests "Puts People at Risk"' https://www.theguardian.com/politics/2023/jun/14/home-office-u-turn-on-festival-drug-tests-puts-people-at-risk, accessed 22 December 2023.

48 Home Office, 'Swift, Certain, Tough: New Consequences for Drug Possession' (2022) https://www.gov.uk/government/consultations/swift-certain-tough-new-consequences-for-drug-possession-white-paper/swift-certain-tough-new-consequences-for-drug-possession-accessible-version, accessed 22 December 2023.

49 These are more dangerous – there has been an increase in overdoses since the increase in synthetic opioids: Cranstoun, 'Synthetic Opioids: A Whole System Response to a Public Health Emergency' (2023) https://cranstoun.org/wp-content/uploads/2023/10/Cranstoun-Contaminated-Drugs-Report-Final.pdf, accessed 22 December 2023.

50 UK Drug Policy Commission, 'Getting Serious about Stigma: The Problem with Stigmatising Drug Users' https://www.ukdpc.org.uk/wp-content/uploads/Policy%20report%20-%20Getting%20serious%20about%20stigma_%20the%20problem%20with%20stigmatising%20drug%20users.pdf, accessed 22 December 2023.

51 Bennett Foddy and Julian Savulescu, 'A Liberal Account of Addiction' (2010) 17 Philos Psychi Psychol 1.

might argue that opioid dependence is necessarily autonomy-limiting,[52] and that therefore clinicians are justified in withholding opioid agonist therapy, as prescribing would *itself* constitute an infringement of autonomy by 'continuing' the patient's drug dependence.

Take a minute to reflect on your own views. How should clinicians respect the autonomy of patients experiencing opioid withdrawal?

Non-maleficence

As explained, non-maleficence generally refers to *refraining* from causing harm. The principle describes a negative obligation, distinct from the positive obligation(s) associated with beneficence. Some might argue that heroin dependence is, itself, a harm, and that prescribing opioid agonist therapy could constitute a harmful action insofar as such therapy effectively 'maintains' the patient's dependence. Others might argue that withholding treatment in this case is a clear-cut violation of the principle of non-maleficence, whereby the clinician is actively causing the patient's suffering by refusing to prescribe. Others still might hold that prescribing any opioid agonist therapy could be harmful in the event of opioid toxicity – especially where clinicians aren't experienced prescribers and a patient's tolerance to opioids is unknown.

Take a minute to reflect on your own views. How should clinicians uphold the principle of non-maleficence in caring for patients experiencing opioid withdrawal?

Beneficence

Some might argue that the clinician is obliged to alleviate the patient's suffering (e.g., opioid withdrawal symptoms). Drawing on the notion of drug use as a harm in and of itself, others might argue that clinicians should not prescribe opioid agonist therapy and instead support the patient in detoxification – for example, attempting to stop a patient's drug use through symptomatic treatment of withdrawal symptoms (e.g., by prescribing anti-emetics to treat nausea and vomiting, or ibuprofen to treat pain).[53] One might argue that in maximising benefits and minimising harms, continued drug use constitutes a worse harm than experience of withdrawal symptoms.

Analysing the case from a different standpoint entirely, others might suggest that, given the high risks of discharge against medical advice and fatal overdose following hospital discharge, clinicians should prescribe opioid agonist therapy in hospital to enable patients to stay in hospital to receive treatment for their presenting condition (to maximise benefit) and to prevent lost tolerance over

52 See Neil Levy, 'Autonomy and Addiction' (2006) 36 Can J Philos 427.

53 Withdrawal symptoms from short-acting opioids like heroin can last for up to ten days.

the course of the patient's hospital stay, where lost tolerance can lead to a fatal overdose.

Take a minute to reflect on your own views. How should clinicians weigh the principle of beneficence in caring for patients experiencing opioid withdrawal?

Balancing principles

As no principle is absolute in the four-principles approach, decision-makers must further determine how to balance these competing principles to arrive at a solution. A clinician may take seriously the risk (however small) of opioid toxicity that accompanies prescription of opioid agonist therapy – drawing on the principle of non-maleficence. The clinician may also wish to prevent the downstream harm of *not* prescribing, which could increase the likelihood that the patient leaves hospital against medical advice and therefore does not receive treatment for their health condition – drawing on the principle of beneficence. Abiding by the principle of non-maleficence, prescribing methadone or buprenorphine could cause harm; abiding by the principle of beneficence, prescribing methadone or buprenorphine could prevent harm.

This reality points to a common critique lodged against the four-principles approach, as discussed, with respect to the lack of a unifying ethical theory to guide disagreement between these principles. A related critique recognises that the decision-maker's unique interpretation of each principle, and that principle's relative importance in comparison to other principles, can yield multiple 'solutions' to the ethical challenge analysed.[54] Indeed, a decision-maker could derive a range of solutions to the question of whether or not to prescribe opioid agonist therapy in hospital and why – a range of solutions which some might argue *over*-rely on the decision-maker's intuition or 'gut feeling'.

Discussion

In this brief analysis, views of drug use – arguably socially and politically constructed – hold a critical place in assessments of 'benefit' and 'harm' and in interpretations of autonomy and agency. The takeaway of the analysis as presented is to recognise the ways in which personal beliefs, dominant social perceptions, and political landscapes collide to influence applications of principles in practice. One's views of the moral, social, economic, or other benefits and harms of drug use will, without careful reflection, necessarily seep into ethical analysis.

How should ethical analyses account for – and systematically document – engagement with the social and political determinants of health, especially with respect to subjective assessments of 'benefit' and 'harm' in context? This question relates to an even greater – though not insurmountable – challenge in applying

54 Raanan Gillon, 'Four Scenarios' (2003) 29 J Med Ethics 267.

principlism (or, indeed, any) approach: the application of principles depends on the inclusion and assessment of the particular 'moral presuppositions and empirical assumptions'[55] deemed relevant to analysis, which in turn can radically shift the outcome of the analysis. For example, weighing up 'benefit' can be complicated by determinations of direct and indirect benefit: for example, in the selected case, should clinicians summarily exclude any mitigation of the risk of fatal overdose following hospital discharge in their analysis insofar as their decision to prescribe or withhold opioid agonist therapy does not *directly* cause someone to overdose after leaving hospital?

In the case example of prescribing opioid agonist therapy to inpatients who use heroin, a range of perspectives may inflect ethical analysis without systematic documentation of these socially and politically shaped 'intuitions'. Especially with respect to contentious topics such as drug use, personal convictions can work to alter the ways in which certain principles are defined or interpreted in context. Some would argue that the view of drug dependence as autonomy-limiting at all (or at least any more than any other drug dependence, e.g., on a prescribed drug such as beta-blockers) is fundamentally flawed. This view may be challenged by drawing distinctions between 'physical dependence' and 'addiction', but note that the term 'addiction', in and of itself, is widely perceived to be infused with moral judgement. Surely, then, these subtle shifts in how drug use itself might be conceived of in the analysis will impact the kind of solution a decision-maker may discern.

Avoiding pitfalls through reflexivity

Irrespective of the derived ethical solution in this example, note that a number of 'judgements' that sit beyond the narrow conceptions of each principle, as defined by Beauchamp and Childress, also weigh on the analysis. Indeed, moving beyond critiques of the principles themselves, or even how the principles should be balanced in different circumstances, reveals another challenge: their interpretation in context is subject to a range of other factors – including not just the empirical facts at hand, and moral judgements about how and whether those empirical facts are relevant to analysis, but also social and political factors that might influence deeply held convictions/relevant 'moral' intuitions.

How, then, might we 'save' the four-principles approach from these criticisms? Transparency in ethical analysis – noting which empirical facts matter when and why; noting whether and how initial moral judgements influence the calculus; and, as exemplified by our case example, carefully accounting for any socially or politically driven preconceived notions of the patient or the patient's health needs – could go a long way in protecting the approach from misuse and misinterpretation. Systematically documenting and accounting for one's own

55 Ruth Macklin, 'Applying the Four Principles' (2003) 29 J Med Ethics 276.

moral intuitions in analysis, the practice of *reflexivity*, has been promoted as a strategy for mitigating, or at least acknowledging, the role that one's own views might play.[56] Drawing from the practice of reflexivity may also allow us to account for the socially and politically infused norms that affect analysis – thereby offering a more rigorous and defensible application of the four-principles approach.

Summary

- Beauchamp and Childress championed the four-principles approach, which centres consideration of the principles of respect for autonomy, non-maleficence, beneficence, and justice in medical decision-making.
- The application of these principles to cases in practice can yield differing 'solutions' to ethical challenges, largely dependent on how the principle is specified in context. How the principle is specified in context in turn depends on not only available evidence and patient values, but also social and political influences.
- Engaging in the practice of reflexivity in bioethical analysis offers the opportunity to document the ways in which moral intuitions may impact our analysis of a particular moral quandary.

Questions for reflection

1. How would you decide what to do in the case example, and how would you justify your decision using the four-principles approach?
2. Is the four-principles approach fit for purpose, or at least a useful starting point, for ethical analysis in healthcare?
3. How, if at all, should social norms and political landscape be factored into analysis using the four-principles approach?

Recommended resources

- Tom Beauchamp, 'The "Four Principles" Approach to Health Care Ethics' in Richard Ashcroft and others (eds), *Principles of Health Care Ethics* (2nd edn, John Wiley & Sons 2007) 3–10.
- Raanan Gillon, 'Four Scenarios' (2003) 29 J Med Ethics 267.
- Ruth Macklin, 'Applying the Four Principles' (2003) 29 J Med Ethics 275.
- Jon Ives and Michael Dunn, 'Who's Arguing? A Call for Reflexivity in Bioethics' (2010) 24 Bioeth 256.
- Arianne Shahvisi, 'Towards an Anticolonial Feminist Bioethics' in Wendy Rodgers and others (eds), *The Routledge Handbook of Feminist Bioethics* (Routledge 2022).

56 Jon Ives and Michael Dunn, 'Who's Arguing? A Call for Reflexivity in Bioethics' (2010) 24 Bioeth 256.

Bibliography

Beauchamp T, 'The "Four Principles" Approach to Health Care Ethics' in R Ashcroft and others (eds), *Principles of Health Care Ethics* (2nd edn, John Wiley & Sons 2007)

Beauchamp T, 'The Belmont Report', in E Emanuel and others, *The Oxford Textbook of Clinical Research Ethics* (OUP 2008)

Beauchamp T and Childress J, *Principles of Biomedical Ethics* (4th edn, OUP 1994)

Behrens K, 'A Critique of the Principle of "Respect for Autonomy", Grounded in African Thought' (2017) 18 Dev World Bioeth 128

Chen X and Fan R, 'The Family and Harmonious Medical Decision Making: Cherishing an Appropriate Confucian Moral Balance' (2010) 35 J Med Philos 579

Clouser KD and Gert B, 'A Critique of Principlism' (1990) 15 J Med Philos 219

Cranstoun, 'Synthetic Opioids: A Whole System Response to a Public Health Emergency' (2023) https://cranstoun.org/wp-content/uploads/2023/10/Cranstoun-Contaminated-Drugs-Report-Final.pdf, accessed 22 December 2023

Faden R, Shebaya S and Siegal A, 'Distinctive Challenges of Public Health Ethics' in A Mastroianni, J Kahn, and N Kass (eds), *The Oxford Handbook of Public Health Ethics* (OUP 2019)

Feinburg J, *The Moral Limits of the Criminal Law: Harm to Others* (OUP 1986)

Foddy B and Savulescu J, 'A Liberal Account of Addiction' (2010) 17 Philos Psychi Psychol 1

Gillon R, 'Four Scenarios' (2003) 29 J Med Ethics 267

Harris M, 'Normalised Pain and Severe Health Care Delay among People Who Inject Drugs in London: Adapting Cultural Safety Principles to Promote Care' (2020) 260 Soc Sci Med 113183

Harris M and others, 'Barriers to Management of Opioid Withdrawal in Hospitals in England: A Document Analysis of Hospital Policies on the Management of Substance Dependence' (2022) 20 BMC Med 1

Home Office, 'Swift, Certain, Tough: New Consequences for Drug Possession' (2022) https://www.gov.uk/government/consultations/swift-certain-tough-new-consequences-for-drug-possession-white-paper/swift-certain-tough-new-consequences-for-drug-possession-accessible-version, accessed 22 December 2023

Ives J and Dunn M, 'Who's Arguing? A Call for Reflexivity in Bioethics' (2010) 24 Bioeth 256

Levy N, 'Autonomy and Addiction' (2006) 36 Can J Philos 427

Lewer D and others, 'Opioid-Related Deaths during Hospital Admissions or Shortly after Discharge in the United Kingdom: A Thematic Framework Analysis of Coroner Reports' (2023) PLoS One e0283549

MacKenzie C and Stoljar N (eds), *Relational Autonomy: Feminist Perspectives on Autonomy, Agency, and the Social Self* (OUP 2000)

Macklin R, 'Applying the Four Principles' (2003) 29 J Med Ethics 276
Mastroianni A and Kahn J, 'Swinging on the Pendulum: Shifting Views of Justice in Human Subjects Research' (2001) 31 Hastings Cent Rep 21
National Commission for the Protection of Human Subjects of Biomedical and Behavioral Research, 'The Belmont Report' (1978) https://www.hhs.gov/ohrp/regulations-and-policy/belmont-report/index.html, accessed 6 December 2023
Reverby S, *Examining Tuskegee: The Infamous Syphilis Study and Its Legacy* (University of North Carolina Press 2009)
Siegler M, 'From Physician Paternalism to Patient Autonomy to Bureaucratic Parsimony' (1985) 145 Arch Intern Med 713
Shahvisi A, 'Towards an Anticolonial Feminist Bioethics', in W Rodgers and others (eds), *The Routledge Handbook of Feminist Bioethics* (Routledge 2022)
Sisk B and others, 'The Truth about Truth-Telling in American Medicine: A Brief History' (2016) 20 Perm J 15
Syal R, 'Home Office U-turn on Festival Drug Tests "Puts People at Risk"' https://www.theguardian.com/politics/2023/jun/14/home-office-u-turn-on-festival-drug-tests-puts-people-at-risk, accessed 22 December 2023
UK Drug Policy Commission, 'Getting Serious about Stigma: The Problem with Stigmatising Drug Users' https://www.ukdpc.org.uk/wp-content/uploads/Policy%20report%20-%20Getting%20serious%20about%20stigma_%20the%20problem%20with%20stigmatising%20drug%20users.pdf, accessed 22 December 2023
UK Government, 'Drug Penalties' https://www.gov.uk/penalties-drug-possession-dealing, accessed 5 September 2023
Veatch R, 'Is There a Common Morality?' (2003) 13 Kennedy Inst Ethics 189
Wolf S, 'Introduction: Gender and Feminism in Bioethics' in S Wolf (ed), *Feminism and Bioethics: Beyond Reproduction* (OUP 1996)

3

Defining and Understanding 'Health' in Health Law

Anna Nelson

Despite the widespread use of the term health, the task of pinning down an exact and universally acceptable definition of health is extremely tricky and has been the subject of much academic debate. This chapter starts by explaining why definitions matter in law and by exposing the complexity of the attempt to define 'health' through the example of the World Health Organization's (WHO's) 1948 definition and subsequent critique.

The rest of the chapter considers how health should be understood or, more specifically, how health should *not* be understood. Rather than attempting to defend one fixed and universally applicable definition of health, I instead focus on creating a set of parameters within which the task of defining health can take place. This seeks to avoid the risk of creating a reductive approach to understanding what it is to be healthy, while also offering some guidance to ensure that 'health' is defined in a manner that appropriately protects all patients. In particular, emphasis is placed on the need to avoid defining health in relation to 'norms', to avoid perpetuating stigma, biases, and systemic racism.

In writing this chapter, I recognise that everyone who writes and thinks about health will do so with different perspectives, experiences, and underpinning assumptions and biases – including myself.

Why bother defining health at all?

In its everyday usage *good health* or being *healthy* can mean different things to different people. People's perception of health is contingent upon the cultural contexts within which they live, their particular circumstances, and their stage of life.[1] As Jadad and O'Grady aptly note, 'health is in the eye of the

1 Jackie Leach Scully, 'What is Disease?' (2004) 5 EMBO Rep 650.

beholder'.[2] Given this subjectivity, the obvious starting point for this chapter is to ask: why bother defining health at all?

The answer lies in the fact that we are concerned with the meaning of health *in law*. Definitions matter significantly because 'our law is a law of words'.[3] Within the law, definitions are 'authoritative' rather than merely descriptive;[4] the way that terms are used and defined is the basis upon which rights and obligations are afforded and assigned. We need to understand what the words used in law mean, in order for the law to have effect.[5] Therefore, legally speaking, the definition of health matters significantly and impacts 'practice, policy, health services, and health promotion'.[6] It is also important for determining what comes within the scope of state-based healthcare systems such as the NHS.

Both national and international law provide citizens with health-related rights and states with obligations to respect and fulfil these rights.[7] For example, Article 12 of the International Covenant on Economic, Social and Cultural Rights, to which the UK is a signatory, affords people the right 'to the enjoyment of the highest attainable standard of physical and mental health', while the National Health Service Act 2006 imposes a duty on the Secretary of State to 'continue the promotion in England of a comprehensive health service designed to secure improvement … in the physical and mental health of the people of England' (s 1(a)). The definition afforded to health is constitutive of the nature of such obligations.

Narrow definitions of health, which centre only on the provision of clinical or pharmaceutical treatment to alleviate or manage symptoms, limit governmental obligations to the provision of specific health services to promote the health of their citizens. Broader, more holistic definitions of health, which require states to see issues such as access to quality housing and combatting climate change as key components of good health, impose more extensive obligations – creating greater impetus (and potentially greater political will) to fund the tools to support these.

The definition of health also matters on the individual patient level. The way that 'health' is framed and understood impacts the kind of medical interventions which are seen as desirable, justifiable, and/or worthy of funding.

---

2 Alejandro Jadad and Laura O'Grady, 'Editorial: How Should Health Be Defined?' (2008) 10 BMJ 337.

3 Perer Tiersma, *Legal Language* (University of Chicago Press 2000) 1.

4 Yaniv Roznai, '"A Bird is Known by its Feathers": On the Importance and Complexities of Definitions in Legislation' (2014) 2 TPLeg 145, 147.

5 Zsolt Zödi, 'The Limits of Plain Legal Language: Understanding the Comprehensible Style in Law' (2019) 15 Int J Law Context 246, 256.

6 Fabio Leonardi, 'The Definition of Health: Towards New Perspectives' (2018) 48 Int J Health Serv 735, 736.

7 OHCHR (Office of the United Nations High Commissioner for Human Rights), 'The Right to Health: Fact Sheet No. 31' (2008) https://www.ohchr.org/sites/default/files/Documents/Publications/Factsheet31.pdf, accessed 2 July 2023.

The WHO definition of health: contested and confusing?

Defining health is a complex but necessary endeavour. A good place to start is by examining the most widely known definition of health, which is contained within the WHO Constitution. Drafted in 1948, this states: 'Health is a state of complete physical, mental, and social well-being and not merely the absence of disease or infirmity.'

At the time it was written, this definition was considered ground-breaking due to its 'breadth and ambition'.[8] It played a useful role in 'broadening of the lens through which we consider health'[9] and in pushing states to think beyond negative conceptions of health as merely the absence of disease.

Though it persists, the WHO definition has faced considerable criticism in more recent times. Concerns have been raised that the definition's width undermines its utility, legally and practically speaking. Some scholars have argued that the inclusion of the word 'complete' sets a standard that is hard to measure,[10] while others have focused on the fact that this definition conceptualises health in overly 'aspirational terms', rendering attainment 'near impossible':[11]

> To declare health a state of complete physical, mental, and social well-being, leaves a great deal of people out from having health. Anyone with a chronic illness or disability, for example, is left out of that definition; our friend in a wheelchair; our colleague who is HIV positive. Anyone living with a mental illness, or without a support network of family and friends, are left out of that definition; our aunt with anxiety; our neighbor who doesn't have a support system.[12]

Others have critiqued this definition for failing to serve disabled and chronically ill communities – as the inclusion of the phrase 'not merely' seems to necessarily 'imply that having a disease or infirmity would preclude good health'.[13] Given the medical advances that have occurred since WHO drafted their constitution, the number of people living for many years, and in many cases living *well*, with chronic diseases has increased significantly.[14] These concerns are compounded

8 Machteld Huber and others, 'How Should We Define Health?' (2011) 343 BMJ 1, 1.

9 Alan Card, 'Moving beyond the WHO Definition of Health: A New Perspective for an Aging World and the Emerging Era of Value-Based Care' (2017) 9 World Med Health Policy 127, 130.

10 Gloria Krahn and others, 'It's Time to Reconsider How We Define Health: Perspective from Disability and Chronic Condition' (2021) 14 Disability Health J 1, 4.

11 Gerard McCartney and others, 'Defining Health and Health Inequalities' (2019) 172 Public Health 22, 23.

12 Jennifer Lee and Cat Pausé, 'Stigma in Practice: Barriers to Health for Fat Women' (2016) 7 Front Psychol 1, 4.

13 Krahn and others (n10) 2.

14 Huber and others (n8).

by the fact that in an increasingly ageing population, more people will have (multiple) chronic health conditions.[15]

A final strand of criticism is that this definition perpetuates a falsely black-and-white perception of health as something one either does or does not have. Some have argued that it is more accurate and useful to define health as a continuum, rather than as a 'static' binary state.[16]

This represents just one of a number of attempts that have been made to define health in the sphere of law and policy. It is included here by way of introduction to the complexity associated with trying to reach an authoritative definition of health.

Exploring the definition of health: setting some parameters

In this chapter I do not defend any specific definition of health or articulate a new definition.[17] Rather, I aim to provide some core parameters within which one can develop a contextually appropriate definition of health.

Hervey and McHale have argued that 'the context-specific nature of "health" precludes an all-embracing, fixed definition'.[18] Taking a broader approach to the meaning of health recognises that it may be useful to define health differently depending on the specific purpose for which, or context within which, the term is being used. It acknowledges that there may be value in understanding health differently 'in the context of different kinds of projects and goals'.[19] It allows space for the fact that aspects of health may depend on time and geographical location.[20] For example, when the term 'health' is used to make policy or create obligations upon states at a macrolevel, it may make sense to include within this concept considerations about housing or workplace protection – given the impact that we know these have upon people's health. However, such a broad-strokes approach to health might not serve the purposes of a more technical piece of policy or legislation aimed at a particular aspect of healthcare provision through the NHS.

---

15 Card (n9). Carla Kiernan Fallon and Jason Karlawish, 'Is the WHO Definition of Health Aging Well? Frameworks for "Health" after Three Score and Ten' (2019) 109 Am J Public Health 1104, 1104.

16 Krahn and others (n10) 3.

17 Though many have attempted this task: Leonardi (n6); Huber and others (n8); Obinna Ositadimma Oleribe and others, 'Health: Redefined' (2018) 30 Pan Afr Med J 1.

18 Tamara Hervey and Jean McHale, *European Union Health Law: Themes and Implications* (CUP 2015) 13.

19 Rebecca Kukla, 'Medicalization, "Normal Function", and the Definition of Health' in John D. Arras, Elizabeth Fenton, and Rebecca Kukla (eds), *The Routledge Companion to Bioethics* (Routledge 2014) 515.

20 Hervey and McHale (n18) 13.

Health is not just physical

For a long time, the primary focus of healthcare was the physical health of the population. The closure of asylums from the 1970s and the deinstitutionalisation of mental healthcare brought mental illness into the orbit of 'mainstream' medicine, from which it had previously been set apart.[21] This also brought mental illness, and the treatment of those experiencing mental ill-health, into the public eye.

There has been increasing recognition of the importance of mental health, and there is now widespread acceptance that 'health' needs to be understood as including *both* mental and physical health. This has seen legislative recognition in the UK. Section 1 of the Health and Social Care Act 2012 enshrined the principle of 'parity of esteem' into law.[22] This principle requires that mental and physical health be valued equally in the operation of the NHS.[23] Furthermore, the Health and Social Care Act 2022 updated the statutory definition of health to include 'mental health'.[24] Though it is clear that the obligation to read 'health' as including mental health predated this Act, it can be argued that the explicit adoption of this definition carries important signalling power as the law is considered an influential tool that can send powerful and authoritative social messages.

When evaluating health law, it is important to look beyond the letter of the law to its application in practice. Identifying gaps between what the law says and what actually happens in the world creates space for critical reflection about what needs to change in order for the law to meet its purported aims.

In 2018/19, Clinical Commissioning Groups in England (bodies that are responsible for deciding what services are commissioned in regional areas) spent only 13.8 per cent of their total budget on mental health services,[25] despite the fact that mental health amounts for around 23 per cent of the burden of disease in the UK.[26] The British Medical Association (BMA)

---

21 Barbara Taylor, 'The Demise of the Asylum in Later Twentieth-Century Britain: A Personal History' (2011) 21 Trans R Hist Soc 193, 194.

22 Sue Bailey, 'Parity of Esteem for Mental Health' in Richard Williams and others (eds), *Social Scaffolding Applying the Lessons of Contemporary Social Science to Health and Healthcare* (CUP 2019) 67.

23 Royal College of Psychiatrists, 'Whole-Person Care: From Rhetoric to Reality. Achieving Parity between Mental and Physical Health' (2013) https://www.ucl.ac.uk/core-study/sites/core-study/files/lester.pdf, accessed 8 July 2023, 20.

24 National Health Service Act 2006 s275(1).

25 BMA (British Medical Association), 'Beyond Parity of Esteem: Achieving Parity of Resource, Access and Outcome for Mental Health in England' (2020) https://www.bma.org.uk/media/2099/mental-health-parity-of-esteem-report-jan-2020-2.pdf, accessed 10 July 2023, 3.

26 House of Lords Select Committee on the Long-Term Sustainability of the NHS, 'The Long-Term Sustainability of the NHS and Adult Social Care' (2017) https://publications.parliament.uk/pa/ld201617/ldselect/ldnhssus/151/151.pdf, accessed 1 September 2023, 77.

criticised this 'modest' level of funding allocation, stating that it 'does not go far enough in reversing the historical underinvestment in mental health compared to physical health services'.[27] Despite such criticisms, it was reported that in 2022/23 some local NHS areas in England still plan to spend 13.8% of their total spend on mental health, learning disability, and dementia services.[28]

This continued underinvestment in mental health services seems to imply that, despite legislative and policy statements to the contrary, mental health is still seen by some as secondary to physical health.

Health is not 'merely' the absence of disease

One conception of health, most famously articulated by Boorse, defines health as simply absence of disease.[29] This approach may initially look appealing due to its seeming simplicity. However, such appeal falls away once you realise that it merely shifts the definitional challenges to the concept of 'disease' – a term which is itself contested and hard to define.[30]

This alone does not provide a sufficient reason to reject this approach to defining health. However, there are other potential concerns. Defining health as the absence of disease has been criticised for unduly excluding too many people from being considered healthy. Bluhm, for example, has argued that 'this account would leave many people unhealthy who would consider themselves to be in robust health. Anyone who wears eyeglasses for near-sightedness, for example, would be diseased on Boorse's account and therefore unhealthy. Similar for anyone with well-controlled asthma or hypothyroidism.'[31] As medical science innovates to develop more sophisticated tests that can detect a greater range of health problems, however minimal their actual impact upon patients' lives, this critique is only going to gain traction. Furthermore, a definition of health that is tied to the absence of disease seems ill-suited to the realities of an ageing population, within which the incidence of chronic disease is increasing.[32]

---

27 BMA (n25) 3.

28 Carl Barker and Esme Kirk-Wade 'Mental Health Statistics: Prevalence, Services and Funding in England' (2023) https://researchbriefings.files.parliament.uk/documents/SN06988/SN06988.pdf, accessed 5 July 2023, 42.

29 Christopher Boorse, 'Health as a Theoretical Concept' (1977) 44 Philos Sci 542.

30 Havi Carel and Rachel Cooper 'Introduction' in Havi Carel and Rachel Cooper (eds), *Health, Illness and Disease: Philosophical Essays* (Routledge 2014).

31 Robyn Bluhm, 'Connecting Philosophy of Medicine with Feminist Bioethics: Health, Illness and Disease' in Wendy Rogers and others (eds) *The Routledge Handbook of Feminist Bioethics* (Routledge 2022), 326. Hypothyroidism is a condition where the thyroid gland does not produce enough thyroid hormone. It is easily treated with medication.

32 Huber and others (n8) 2.

At the same time as excluding too many people from being healthy, this Boorsian approach can also be criticised for implying that a person who *does not* have a disease is inherently and necessarily healthy.[33] In reality, a person who shows no evidence of 'any objectively verifiable disease' may nonetheless 'feel and/or act sick'.[34] It is suggested that despite the lack of 'disease' status, it is clear that the health of such a person is diminished.

Given these criticisms, I suggest that the absence of disease is neither necessary nor sufficient to determine a person's health status. A person may live a healthy life with a well-managed disease, or may experience substantial harms to their wellbeing that render them lacking in health without having a disease. The approach to 'health' articulated by scholars such as Boorse can be criticised for being simultaneously overly inclusive *and* overly restrictive.

Health is not an all-or-nothing matter

Defining health solely in relation to disease is also problematic as it enforces a binary understanding of health: either a person has a disease or they do not, thus they are either healthy or not. Such stringent boundaries are unrealistic and unfair and create a situation within which too great a percentage of the population are framed as missing out on health – even while living and feeling well. Conversely, these boundaries also exclude those who feel unwell but lack a diagnosis to explain this. This critique is not unique to the Boorsian understanding of health; the same can be said for the WHO definition, which sits on the opposite end of the spectrum!

Chronic disease is becoming increasingly prevalent,[35] and the world's population is 'rapidly aging'.[36] The reality is that 'disease and disability can and often do co-exist with wellness' and a workable contemporary conception of health must be able to account for this.[37] Therefore, it is more realistic and more useful to think of health in less absolute terms – as a spectrum. Nordenfelt, for example, suggests that health be understood as more of 'a dimension ranging from a state of complete health to a state of complete illness', with ill-health occurring only when a person is within the 'negative half of that scale'.[38]

---

33 Fran Baum, *The New Public Health* (4th edn, OUP 2016) 4.

34 Ellen Lidler, 'Definitions of Health and Illness and Medical Sociology' (1979) 13 Soc Sci Med 723, 723.

35 Machteld Huber and others, 'Towards a "Patient-Centred' Operationalisation of the New Dynamic Concept of Health: A Mixed Methods Study' (2016) 5 BMJ Open 1, 1–2.

36 Card (n9), 128.

37 Yevdokiia Streltsova and others, 'The Evolving Idea of "Health" in the Legal Landscape: An Attempt to Identify Critical Aspects' (2021) 74 Wiadomości Lekarskie 2954, 2956.

38 Lennart Nordenfelt, 'The Opposition between Naturalistic and Holistic Theories of Health and Disease' in Havi Carel and Rachel Cooper (eds), *Health, Illness and Disease: Philosophical Essays* (Routledge 2014) 29; Bluhm (n31) 327.

'Health(y)' does not equal 'normal'

Some accounts of health tether their definitions to conformity or divergence from norms (standards that are considered socially or culturally normal).[39] However, where health is too closely and uncritically tethered to socio-medical norms, this can enable harm to be done in the name of preserving health. Alternatively, it can impede upon identifying developments and improvements that are necessary to ensure that *all people* are able to benefit from health services equally and in a manner that promotes their physical and psychological wellbeing.

Simply because something is considered a 'norm' or 'normal' at a particular point in time does not mean that it is 'right' in any objective sense. Rather, norms are socially constructed[40] – they are contextual and contingent upon social biases and expectations. Medical structures, medical professionals, and medical knowledge are no more immune to such biases than the rest of society, and indeed can play a significant role in perpetuating these given the authority afforded to medical voices.

We must ask who gets to construct the 'norms' against which health is to be defined and measured? What prejudices, preconceptions, and knowledge gaps do these people have? Whose experiences and embodied realities are validated and whose are hidden? In healthcare and medical science, as in other parts of our society, the voices that historically have (and largely continue to) prevail as authoritative in constructing norms belong to people that are white, male, cis-gendered, able-bodied, middle class, and whose circumstances have them afforded good educational opportunities. This is perhaps most obvious when the norms that we are dealing with are socio-cultural in nature. However, doubt can also be legitimately cast upon the objectivity of norms that appear to be predicated on the basis of scientific fact.

Scientific research and knowledge are not value free. They are shaped by the way research questions are framed, by which questions are asked (and which are not), and by which kinds of people are invited to participate in the research. For example, if I design a research project exploring the question 'why do women have a lower pain threshold?', my research and the results will be impacted by the inherent assumption that women are less able to tolerate pain. This is likely to obscure any findings that could indicate the women may actually be experiencing

39 Understanding the relationship between 'health' and 'norms' is also vital for our comprehension of disability. The (increasingly contested) medical model of disability frames disabled people as being in need of medical intervention to 'restore normal functioning'. Important concerns have been raised about what counts as 'normal functioning' and who gets to define which bodily variations are negative, stigmatised, and in need of correction. For a more detailed discussion see: Rosemarie Garland-Thomson, 'Integrating Disability, Transforming Feminist Theory' (2003) 14 NWSA J 1.

40 Hervey and McHale (n18) 11.

more intense pain.[41] Research agendas are set, results interpreted, and findings communicated by people who have their own experiential and socio-political assumptions and biases.

To highlight the problem with uncritically accepting the use of norms to ascribe meaning to 'health', Foster and Herring invite us to consider a historical perspectives: 'look at what was considered "unhealthy" in the past: it included the wish of the [enslaved person] to be free, to sexual desire in women'.[42] This is reflected, too, when we remember that in fairly recent history homosexuality was considered an unhealthy divergence from the norm.[43] It was not until 1973 that the American Psychiatric Association voted to remove 'homosexuality' from the influential *Diagnostic and Statistical Manual of Mental Disorders*.[44]

Defining 'health' in relation to the norms of the day serves not only to obscure, but also to legitimise and compound, biases in our healthcare system. This, in turn, undermines the efficacy of health law as a means through which *all* patients can be protected.

I illustrate this point using three examples; however, these are far from exhaustive. Many other problematic norms, which construct barriers to adequate understandings of health – and thus barriers to adequate healthcare – such as those associated with weight and neurotypicality, exist.[45]

The 'binary norm': intersex infants and gender-'normalising' surgery

Intersex is an umbrella term 'referring to a diverse range of congenital bodily variations that at the chromosomal, gonadal, hormonal and/or anatomical level do not neatly fit into the binary categories of male or female'.[46] For a number of reasons, including 'inconsistencies in reporting' and ongoing debate about which bodily variations beyond the male/female binary fall under the

---

41 E.g., Naomi Elster, 'How an Objective Measure of Pain Could Counter Bias in Medicine' (2023) https://www.bbc.com/future/article/20230414-the-search-for-an-objective-measure-of-pain, accessed 3 October 2023.

42 Charles Foster and Jonathan Herring, 'What is Health?' in Michael Freeman, Sarah Hawkes, and Belinda Bennett (eds), *Law and Global Health: Current Legal Issues*, vol 16 (OUP 2014), 27.

43 Marc Ereshefsky, 'Defining "Health" and "Disease"' (2009) 40 Stud Hist Philos Biolog Biomed Sci 221, 225.

44 Sarah Baughey-Gill, 'When Gay Was Not Okay with the APA: A Historical Overview of Homosexuality and its Status as Mental Disorder' (2011) 1 Occam's Razor 5, 14.

45 Lee and Pausé (n12); Adrian Brown, Stuart Flint, and Rachel Batterham, 'Pervasiveness, Impact and Implications of Weight Stigma' (2022) 47 eClinicalMed 1. Thomas Armstrong, 'The Myth of the Normal Brain: Embracing Neurodiversity' (2015) 17 AMA J Ethics 348.

46 The language used to describe intersex variations and intersex individuals remains contested, and not all people are comfortable with the same terms: Tove Lundberg and others, 'Making Sense of "Intersex" and "DSD": How Laypeople Understand and Use Terminology' (2017) 9 Psychol Sex 161.

definitional umbrella,[47] it is hard to provide a clear picture of what proportion of the population have an intersex variation:[48] estimates range from 0.018 per cent to 1.7 per cent.[49]

In most instances the intersex variations themselves are clinically benign, including a number that result in the appearance of 'ambiguous internal and external reproductive organs'.[50] The genital divergence from binary 'norms' is almost always aesthetic in nature; it does not impact upon the health of the child nor the functioning of the genitalia. Therefore, it does not give rise to a clinical necessity to intervene.

However, 'over the past century … the medical profession has increasingly claimed "intersex" within its jurisdictional remit "in the name of correcting nature's mistakes"'.[51] The typical response to ambiguous genitalia resulting from intersex variations is to perform surgical (and/or hormonal) interventions with the purpose of 'normalising' the appearance of the genitalia, such that the bodies of intersex infants 'aesthetically fit the male/female binary'.[52] In the UK it remains commonplace for these surgeries to take place within the first year of an infant's life, despite there being no clinical necessity to conduct this procedure at an early age.

Unlike the ambiguous appearance of the genitalia, the impact of clinical interventions is not always benign: 'these medical interventions lack any evidence regarding the success of long-term outcomes and instead are leading to an array of lifelong negative consequences both physically (including sterilisation and vaginal stenosis) and psychosocially'.[53]

When ideas of 'norm' and health are collapsed together, it can result in harm being done in the name of legitimate clinical intervention. If intersex bodies, in their difference from the norm, are perceived as *lacking* in heath then there comes expectation and pressure (on the parents) to consent to clinical interventions aimed at returning these bodies (and specifically genitals) as close to the norm as possible, under the false premise that this is in the child's best interests. In reality, rather than enhancing the health of intersex individuals, this exposes them to clinical interventions that are, at best, unnecessary and, at worst, actively harmful.[54] This clearly exposes the risks associated with defining

---

47 Fae Garland and others, 'Management of "Disorders of Sex Development"/Intersex Variations in Children: Results from a Freedom of Information Exercise' (2021) 21 Med Law Int 116.

48 Ibid 120.

49 Leonard Sax, 'How Common Is Intersex? A Response to Anne Fausto-Sterling' (2002) 39 J Sex Res 174. Anne Fausto-Sterling, *Sexing the Body: Gender Politics and the Construction of Sexuality* (Basic Books 2000) 51.

50 Fae Garland and Mitchell Travis, 'Making the State Responsible: Intersex Embodiment, Medical Jurisdiction, and State Responsibility' (2020) 47 J Law Soc 298, 304.

51 Ibid.

52 Fae Garland, Kay Lalor, and Mitchell Travis, 'Intersex Activism, Medical Power/Knowledge and the Scalar Limitations of the United Nations' (2022) 22 Hum Rights Law Rev 1, 3.

53 Ibid.

54 Garland and Travis (n50).

health in relation to prevailing socio-medical norms. Where accounts of health (on which our understanding of 'best interests' that determine what it is lawful for doctors to do are often based)[55] fail to make space for the diversity of human bodies (and the human beings that inhabit them), we risk creating conditions that inhibit the law from serving its purpose of protecting the bodily integrity and rights of all patients.

The 'menstrual norm': pain and 'hysterical' women

In this section I use gendered language to reflect specific socio-cultural perceptions of women. However, it is vital to acknowledge that others, such as transgender men and non-binary people, also menstruate and will experience specific barriers to accessing care for menstrual pain. Menstrual pain has been constructed as a normal part of 'womanhood' and of menstruation,[56] a perception shored up by culture and the media. In research conducted with women with gynaecological and reproductive health conditions 'all participants understood pain to be part and parcel of being a woman'.[57] Those who work in healthcare are not immune to this 'deeply-rooted sociocultural belief'.[58] For this reason, many menstruating patients still have their pain dismissed as 'merely "women's problems", which therefore warrant[ed] no further investigation, or as normal menstruation pain, and therefore was to be expected'.[59]

Alongside this sits the pervasive stereotyping of women as weak and overly emotional[60] – particularly when it comes to matters of the womb. This creates a situation within which complaints about severe menstrual pain are not correctly interpreted as indicating physiological health issues, but rather are often seen to suggest some form of mental infirmity or weakness on the part of the 'complainer':[61] 'nearly all of the women in the collected narratives experienced denial from relational others and medical professionals surrounding the severity of their pain. Instead, these women were told that their complaints were rooted in their inability to cope in effective (that is,

55 *Re F (Mental Patient: Sterilisation)* [1990] 2 AC 1.

56 Mike Armour and others, 'Self-Care Strategies and Sources of Knowledge on Menstruation in 12,526 Young Women with Dysmenorrhea: A Systematic Review and Meta-Analysis' (2019) 14 PLoS One 1, 2; Maya Dusenbery, *Doing Harm: The Truth about How Bad Medicine and Lazy Science Leave Women Dismissed, Misdiagnosed, and Sick* (HarperOne 2018) 221–2.

57 Lenore Manderson and others, 'Circuit Breaking: Pathways of Treatment Seeking for Women with Endometriosis in Australia' (2008) 18 Qual Health Res 522, 526.

58 Emily Krebs and Kelsea V. Schoenbauer, 'Hysterics and Heresy: Using Dialogism to Explore the Problematics of Endometriosis Diagnosis' (2019) 35 Health Commun 1013, 1018.

59 Elaine Denny, '"I Never Know From One Day to Another How I Will Feel": Pain and Uncertainty in Women with Endometriosis' (2009) 19 Qual Health Res 985, 989.

60 Krebs and Schoenbauer (n58) 1017.

61 Nicole Fernley, 'That One Doctor … Qualitative Thematic Analysis of 49 Women's Written Accounts of their Endometriosis Diagnosis' (2021) 13 J Endometr Pelvic Pain Disord 3, 41.

"normal") ways'[62] or that their symptoms are 'all in the head' (and thus do not have a 'biological cause').[63]

Operating in tandem, these 'norms' have obscured the physical health needs of many menstruating women, while conversely assigning them a false status as mentally unhealthy. Dusenbery has noted that this long-term perception of 'female problems' as 'alternately normal or psyschogenic' has not only operated as a barrier to individual healthcare, but has also led to a wider failure to conduct the research needed to understand the cause of such problems – and consequently how to treat them.[64] This is clearly illustrated using the experience of those with endometriosis: a 'condition where cells similar to the ones lining the womb (the endometrium) are found elsewhere in the body'.[65] Endometriosis can cause inflammation and scarring, and symptoms include severe pain during menstruation, pain during sex, and difficulty conceiving. It is experienced by many as 'debilitating'.[66] Despite the fact that around one in ten women of reproductive age have endometriosis,[67] those with this condition have 'long described journeys characterized by ignorance, disbelief, and lack of knowledge on the part of their doctors and the public', regularly encountering the assumption that they have 'exaggerated or imagined their symptoms or [have] low pain thresholds',[68] alongside insinuations that their symptoms are 'enhanced' by 'psychological factors'.[69]

Where the health of menstruating women (and others who menstruate) is understood in relation to norms constructed on the basis of hundreds of years of incorrect patriarchal assumptions about the female body and female pain, this poses a barrier to efficacious care and treatment. The example of menstrual pain also clearly illustrates that norms which are constructed as barometers for health ought not to be assumed to be neutral or value free. Instead, these reflect historical biases and assumptions upon which existing medical knowledge is constructed.[70]

---

62 Krebs and Schoenbauer (n58) 1017.

63 Fernley (n61) 41.

64 Dusenbery (n56) 216.

65 AAPG on Endometriosis, 'Endometriosis in the UK: Time for Change' (2020) https://www.endometriosis-uk.org/sites/default/files/files/Endometriosis%20APPG%20Report%20Oct%202020.pdf, accessed 31 August 2023, 12.

66 Ibid 4.

67 Endometriosis UK, 'Endometriosis Facts and Figures' (nd) https://www.endometriosis-uk.org/endometriosis-facts-and-figures, accessed 31 August 2023. Gendered terms reflect existing statistics.

68 Heather Guidone, 'The Womb Wanders Not: Enhancing Endometriosis Education in a Culture of Menstrual Misinformation' in Chris Bobel and others (eds), *The Palgrave Handbook of Critical Menstruation Studies* (Palgrave Macmillan 2020) 273.

69 Hanna Grundström and others, 'The Double-Edged Experience of Healthcare Encounters among Women with Endometriosis: A Qualitative Study' (2018) 27 J Clin Nurs 205, 207.

70 Dusenbery (n56).

The 'white norm': medical textbooks and systemic racism

Bray and Lemore argue that:

> The myth of a default human posits that white people are the natural reference group for all others when designing scientific studies, reporting scientific findings, allocating human, money and time resources. ... Demolishing this myth starts with acknowledging that Black people are not the architects of their own destruction: the default standard of whiteness is.[71]

The focus upon the presentation of symptoms in white bodies within medical education entrenches a perception that Black and Brown patients exist 'outside the parameters of "normal"', by positioning 'whiteness as the standard' upon which normal is based.[72] This positioning of whiteness as the default creates a situation in which blame and judgement for ill-health is placed at the feet of Black and Brown patients, rather than in the system that has failed them.

Visual cues are routinely used to assess a person's state of health. Looking red, flushed, pale, or gaunt, or showing signs of bruising or rashes may all be used to indicate ill-health: 'blue-tinged fingertips are a harbinger of dangerously low oxygen levels; the yellow stain of jaundice can be an early warning sign of irreversible liver damage; and a patient who is bleeding internally might be saved by a doctor who knows to look for pallor not in the cheeks, but under the eyes and inside the mouth'.[73]

Conversely, the absence of an 'expected' visual symptom can make it harder to gain a diagnosis and access treatment. While visual cues can operate as useful diagnostic tools, harm occurs when the white body is used as the standard against which a person's health status is determined. Where students only learn how symptoms present on white skin, they are ill-equipped to recognise – and therefore treat – symptoms experienced by Black and Brown patients, as 'skin changes are easy to miss if you don't know what you are looking for'.[74]

This was powerfully illustrated in a report examining systemic racism in UK maternity care. One participant shared the challenges she experienced when seeking care for her jaundiced baby as the 'white staff did not recognise jaundice

71 Stephanie Bray and Monica McLemore, 'Demolishing the Myth of the Default Human That Is Killing Black Mothers' (2021) 9 Front Public Health 1.

72 Robin DiAngelo, *White Fragility: Why It's So Hard for White People to Talk about Racism* (Beacon Press 2018) 25.

73 Neil Singh, 'Decolonising Dermatology: Why Black and Brown Skin Need Better Treatment' (2020) https://www.theguardian.com/society/2020/aug/13/decolonising-dermatology-why-black-and-brown-skin-need-better-treatment, accessed 1 September 2023.

74 Ibid.

in a Black baby'.[75] Her health visitor was initially reluctant to take her concerns about the appearance of her child seriously, and when test results indicated high levels of bilirubin (an indicator of jaundice) it was suggested that the 'machine must be broken'. When a hospital referral was eventually made, the family faced similar challenges. While accepting that the baby's test results were concerning, the doctor nonetheless insisted there was 'nothing to [visually] suggest he was severely jaundiced, just a "slight" yellowing of his eyes'. By this stage, the jaundice was readily apparent to the mother, who reported that the baby 'looked neon' to her. When further tests were carried out, jaundice was eventually diagnosed and the child was 'hospitalised for several weeks'.[76]

Positioning the white body as the norm obscures the very real issue of systemic racism in health research commissioning,[77] medical education, and healthcare,[78] and the impact this has upon the health of Black and Brown patients. This is not only unjust but also dangerously misplaces the responsibility for improving the health of Black and Brown patients – responsibility that should lie with the state and with the institutions that deliver healthcare and educate healthcare professionals.

Western understandings of health should not be assumed to be universal

Predominant narratives in legal literature frame 'health' through a Western lens. However, alternative conceptions exist, and it is important to question the tendency to 'universalise' this particular approach to health. Here, I briefly introduce the idea that there are different components to health in different communities, rather than providing a comprehensive overview of such approaches.

Many African perspectives on health centre an approach which is more community-centric and spiritually engaged than that held by their Euro-American counterparts:[79]

> Good health for the African consists of mental, physical, spiritual, and emotional stability for oneself, family members, and community; this integrated view of health is based on the African unitary view of reality. … Good health is usually understood in terms of one's relationship

75 Birthrights, 'Systemic Racism, Not Broken Bodies: An Inquiry into Racial Injustice and Human Rights in UK Maternity Care' (2022) https://www.birthrights.org.uk/wp-content/uploads/2022/05/Birthrights-inquiry-systemic-racism_exec-summary_May-22-web.pdf, accessed 28 November 2023, 48.

76 Ibid 48.

77 Richard Powell and others, 'Tackling Racism in UK Health Research' (2022) 376 BMJ 1.

78 Victor Adebowale and Mala Rao, 'It's Time to Act on Racism in the NHS' (2020) 368 BMJ 1.

79 There are, of course, cultural differences between and within countries in Africa, and different communities may understand health in different ways.

> with his ancestors ... it is of paramount importance that the ancestors stay healthy so that they can protect the living.[80]

The definition of 'Aboriginal health' adopted by the National Aboriginal Community Controlled Health Organisation also encompasses more than just the 'physical well-being' of the individual. Rather, it refers to 'the social, emotional and cultural well-being of the whole Community in which each individual is able to achieve their full potential as a human being thereby bringing about the total well-being of their Community'.[81]

Comprehending how health is understood by different communities is important both as a matter of respect and also practically. Health interventions and initiatives that are not responsive to people's health needs and understandings are likely to fail.[82] This is perhaps most significant when thinking about health (law) in the international context, such as through the operation of international law and treaties; however, Britain has a culturally diverse society and different communities will have different health needs – meaning different steps may need to be taken to fulfil their health-related rights.

Summary

- The concept of health is challenging to define and there are a variety of opinions about what it means to be healthy.
- Definitions matter in law because these help us to understand the nature of rights and obligations.
- The appropriate definition of health can differ depending on the context and purpose for which it is being used.
- Defining health is relation to what is considered 'normal' is problematic, because 'norms' can perpetuate biases.
- Western understandings of health should not be assumed to be universal.

Questions for reflection

1. Imagine that you have been tasked with writing a definition of health to be included within the NHS Constitution. Make sure you are able to explain your reasoning.

---

80 Peter Omonzejele, 'African Concepts of Health, Disease, and Treatment: An Ethical Inquiry' (2008) 4 Explore 120.

81 National Aboriginal Community Controlled Health Organisation (nd) https://www.naccho.org.au/, accessed 5 July 2023.

82 On the importance of culturally sensitive health services see: O. Pearson and others, 'Aboriginal Community Controlled Health Organisations Address Health Equity through Action on the Social Determinants of Health of Aboriginal and Torres Strait Islander Peoples in Australia' (2020) 20 BMC Public Health 1.

2. Should we aim towards one universal definition of health?
3. Can a person be healthy while living with a disease? And can a person be unhealthy, even if they do not have a disease?

Recommended resources

- Fabio Leonardi, 'The Definition of Health: Towards New Perspectives' (2018) 48 Int J Health Serv 735.
- Fran Baum, *The New Public Health*, 4th edn (OUP 2016), chapter 1.
- Robyn Bluhm, 'Connecting Philosophy of Medicine with Feminist Bioethics: Health, Illness and Disease' in Wendy Rogers and others (eds), *The Routledge Handbook of Feminist Bioethics* (Routledge 2022).
- Ed Horowicz, 'Intersex Children: Who Are We Really Treating?' (2017) 17 Med Law Int 1.
- Neil Singh, 'Decolonising Dermatology: Why Black and Brown Skin Need Better Treatment' (2020) https://www.theguardian.com/society/2020/aug/13/decolonising-dermatology-why-black-and-brown-skin-need-better-treatment, accessed 28 November 2023.
- Elinor Cleghorn, *Unwell Women: A Journey through Medicine and Myth in a Man-Made World* (Weidenfeld & Nicolson 2021).
- Maya Dusenbery, 'Endometriosis is Going Undiagnosed Due to the Normalization of Menstrual Pain' (2018) https://www.teenvogue.com/story/endometriosis-period-pain-book-excerpt, accessed 28 November 2023.
- Nancy Jecker and Caesar Atuire, 'Bioethics in Africa: A Contextually Enlightened Analysis of Three Cases' (2021) 22 Dev World Bioeth 112.
- Ministry of Health – Manatū Hauora, 'Māori Health Models' (nd) New Zealand Government https://www.health.govt.nz/our-work/populations/maori-health/maori-health-models, accessed 28 November 2023.

Bibliography

AAPG on Endometriosis, 'Inquiry Report; Endometriosis in the UK: Time for Change' (2020) https://www.endometriosis-uk.org/sites/default/files/files/Endometriosis%20APPG%20Report%20Oct%202020.pdf, accessed 31 August 2023

Adebowale V and Rao M, 'It's Time to Act on Racism in the NHS' (2020) 368 (m568) BMJ 1

Armour M and others, 'Self-Care Strategies and Sources of Knowledge on Menstruation in 12,526 Young Women with Dysmenorrhea: A Systematic Review and Meta-Analysis' (2019) 14(7) PLoS One 1

Armstrong T, 'The Myth of the Normal Brain: Embracing Neurodiversity' (2015) 17(4) AMA J Ethics 348

Bailey S, 'Parity of Esteem for Mental Health' in R Williams and others (eds), *Social Scaffolding Applying the Lessons of Contemporary Social Science to Health and Healthcare* (CUP 2019)

Barker C and Kirk-Wade E, 'Mental Health Statistics: Prevalence, Services and Funding in England' (2023) 'Commons Library Research Briefing', 13 March https://researchbriefings.files.parliament.uk/documents/SN06988/SN06988.pdf, accessed 5 July 2023

Baughey-Gill S, 'When Gay Was Not Okay with the APA: A Historical Overview of Homosexuality and its Status as Mental Disorder' (2011) 1(2) Occam's Razor 5

Baum F, *The New Public Health* (4th edn, OUP 2016)

Birthrights, 'Systemic Racism, Not Broken Bodies: An Inquiry into Racial Injustice and Human Rights in UK Maternity Care' (2022) https://www.birthrights.org.uk/wp-content/uploads/2022/05/Birthrights-inquiry-systemic-racism_exec-summary_May-22-web.pdf, accessed 13 December 2023

Bluhm R, 'Connecting Philosophy of Medicine with Feminist Bioethics: Health, Illness and Disease' in WA Rogers and others (eds), *The Routledge Handbook of Feminist Bioethics* (Routledge 2022)

BMA (British Medical Association), 'Beyond Parity of Esteem: Achieving Parity of Resource, Access and Outcome for Mental Health in England' (2020) https://www.bma.org.uk/media/2099/mental-health-parity-of-esteem-report-jan-2020-2.pdf, accessed 10 July 2023

Boorse C, 'Health as a Theoretical Concept' (1977) 44(4) Philos Sci 542

Brown A, Flint SW, and Batterham RL, 'Pervasiveness, Impact and Implications of Weight Stigma' (2022) 47(101408) eClinicalMed 1

Card AJ, 'Moving beyond the WHO Definition of Health: A New Perspective for an Aging World and the Emerging Era of Value-Based Care' (2017) 9(1) World Med Health Policy 127

Carel H and Cooper R, 'Introduction' in H Carel and R Cooper (eds), *Health, Illness and Disease: Philosophical Essays* (Routledge 2014)

D'Angelo R, *White Fragility: Why it's So Hard for White People to Talk about Racism* (Beacon Press 2018)

Denny E, '"I Never Know From One Day to Another How I Will Feel": Pain and Uncertainty in Women With Endometriosis' (2009) 19(7) Qual Health Res 985

Dusenbery M, *Doing Harm: The Truth about How Bad Medicine and Lazy Science Leave Women Dismissed, Misdiagnosed, and Sick* (HarperOne 2018)

Elster N, 'How an Objective Measure of Pain could Counter Bias in Medicine' (2023) https://www.bbc.com/future/article/20230414-the-search-for-an-objective-measure-of-pain, accessed 3 October 2023

Endometriosis UK (nd), 'Endometriosis Facts and Figures' https://www.endometriosis-uk.org/endometriosis-facts-and-figures, accessed 31 August 2023

Ereshefsky M, 'Defining "Health" and "Disease"' (2009) 40(3) Stud Hist Philos Biolog Biomed Sci 221

Fausto-Sterling A, *Sexing the Body: Gender Politics and the Construction of Sexuality* (Basic Books 2000)

Fernley N, 'That One Doctor… Qualitative Thematic Analysis of 49 Women's Written Accounts of their Endometriosis Diagnosis' (2021) 13(1) J Endometr Pelvic Pain Disord 3

Foster C and Herring J, 'What is Health?' in M Freeman, S Hawkes, and B Bennett (eds), *Law and Global Health: Current Legal Issues*, vol 16 (OUP 2014)

Garland F and Travis M, 'Making the State Responsible: Intersex Embodiment, Medical Jurisdiction, and State Responsibility' (2020) 47(2) J Law Soc 298

Garland F, Lalor K, and Travis M, 'Intersex Activism, Medical Power/Knowledge and the Scalar Limitations of the United Nations' (2022) 22(3) Hum Rights Law Rev 1

Garland F and others, 'Management of "Disorders of Sex Development"/Intersex Variations in Children: Results from a Freedom of Information Exercise' (2021) 21(2) Med Law Int 116

Garland-Thomson R, 'Integrating Disability, Transforming Feminist Theory' (2003) 14(3) NWSA J 1

Grundström H and others, 'The Double-Edged Experience of Healthcare Encounters among Women with Endometriosis: A Qualitative Study' (2018) 27(1) J Clin Nurs 205

Guidone H, 'The Womb Wanders Not: Enhancing Endometriosis Education in a Culture of Menstrual Misinformation' in C Bobel and others (eds), *The Palgrave Handbook of Critical Menstruation Studies* (Palgrave Macmillan 2020)

Hervey T and McHale J, *European Union Health Law: Themes and Implications* (CUP 2015)

House of Lords Select Committee on the Long-Term Sustainability of the NHS, 'The Long-Term Sustainability of the NHS and Adult Social Care' (2017) https://publications.parliament.uk/pa/ld201617/ldselect/ldnhssus/151/151.pdf, accessed 1 September 2023

Huber M and others, 'How Should We Define Health?' (2011) 343 BMJ 1

Huber M and others, 'Towards a "Patient-Centred" Operationalisation of the New Dynamic Concept of Health: A Mixed Methods Study' (2016) 5 BMJ Open 1

Jadad AR and O'Grady L, 'Editorial: How Should Health Be Defined?' (2008) 10 BMJ 337

Kiernan Fallon C and Karlawish J, 'Is the WHO Definition of Health Aging Well? Frameworks for "Health" after Three Score and Ten' (2019) 109(8) Am J Public Health 1104

Krahn GL and others, 'It's Time to Reconsider How We Define Health: Perspective from Disability and Chronic Condition' (2021) 14(4) Disability Health J 1

Krebs E and Schoenbauer KV, 'Hysterics and Heresy: Using Dialogism to Explore the Problematics of Endometriosis Diagnosis' (2019) 35(8) Health Comm 1

Kukla R, 'Medicalization, "Normal Function", and the Definition of Health' in JD Arras, E Fenton, and R Kukla (eds), *The Routledge Companion to Bioethics* (Routledge 2014)

Leach Scully J, 'What Is Disease?' (2004) 5(7) EMBO Reports 650

Lee JA and Pausé CJ, 'Stigma in Practice: Barriers to Health for Fat Women' (2016) 7(2063) Frontiers Psychol 1

Leonardi F, 'The Definition of Health: Towards New Perspectives' (2018) 48(4) Int J Health Serv 735

Lidler E, 'Definitions of Health and Illness and Medical Sociology' (1979) 13(A) Social Sci Med 723

Lundberg T and others, 'Making Sense of "Intersex" and "DSD": How Laypeople Understand and Use Terminology' (2017) 9(2) Psychol Sex 161

Manderson L and others, 'Circuit Breaking: Pathways of Treatment Seeking for Women with Endometriosis in Australia' (2008) 18(4) Qual Health Res 522

McCartney G and others, 'Defining Health and Health Inequalities' (2019) 172 Public Health 22

National Aboriginal Community Controlled Health Organisation https://www.naccho.org.au/, accessed 5 July 2023

Nordenfelt L, 'The Opposition between Naturalistic and Holistic Theories of Health and Disease' in H Carel and R Cooper (eds), *Health, Illness and Disease: Philosophical Essays* (Routledge 2014)

OHCHR (Office of the United Nations High Commissioner for Human Rights), 'The Right to Health: Fact Sheet No. 31' (UNHCR, June, 2008) https://www.ohchr.org/sites/default/files/Documents/Publications/Factsheet31.pdf, accessed 2 July 2023

Oleribe OO and others, 'Health: Redefined' (2018) 30(292) Pan Afr Med J 1

Omonzejele PF, 'African Concepts of Health, Disease, and Treatment: An Ethical Inquiry' (2008) 4(2) Explore 120

Pearson O and others, 'Aboriginal Community Controlled Health Organisations Address Health Equity through Action on the Social Determinants of Health of Aboriginal and Torres Strait Islander Peoples in Australia' (2020) 20(1859) BMC Public Health 1

Powell RA and others, 'Tackling Racism in UK Health Research' (2022) 376 BMJ 376 1

Royal College of Psychiatrists, 'Whole-Person Care: From Rhetoric to Reality. Achieving Parity between Mental and Physical Health' (2013) https://www.ucl.ac.uk/core-study/sites/core-study/files/lester.pdf, accessed 8 July 2023

Roznai Y, '"A Bird is Known by its Feathers": On the Importance and Complexities of Definitions in Legislation' (2014) 2(2) TPLeg 145

Sax L, 'How Common is Intersex? A Response to Anne Fausto-Sterling' (2002) 39(3) J Sex Res 174

Singh N, (2020) 'Decolonising Dermatology: Why Black and Brown Skin Need Better Treatment', *The Guardian* (2020) https://www.theguardian.com/society/2020/aug/13/decolonising-dermatology-why-black-and-brown-skin-need-better-treatment, accessed 20 July 2023

Streltsova Y, Streltsov Y and Kuzmin E, 'The Evolving Idea of "Health" in the Legal Landscape: An Attempt to Identify Critical Aspects' (2021) 74(11) Wiadomości Lekarskie 2954

Taylor B, 'The Demise of the Asylum in Later Twentieth-Century Britain: A Personal History' (2011) 21 Trans R Hist Soc 193

Tiersma PM, *Legal Language* (University of Chicago Press 2000)
Zödi Z, 'The Limits of Plain Legal Language: Understanding the Comprehensible Style in Law' (2019) 15(3) Int J Law Context 246

4

Health Inequalities, Law, and Society

John Coggon and Beth W. Kamunge-Kpodo

This chapter presents and addresses some foundational questions for legal studies of health inequalities. It adopts a broad understanding of health and explains how health opportunities and outcomes are subject in large part to determinants created by social structures and systems, including legal and political decisions and norms. We will explain how we understand problematic health inequalities to refer to avoidable, unfair, and systemic health disparities. Even whilst there is wide recognition of the existence of health inequalities across the UK, to give real meaning to health inequalities as a question for law and policy, much work has to be done. It is necessary to explain what health means and which group(s) is/are being identified as suffering unfair inequality. And it is necessary to identify how law, policy, and social structures more widely are part of the problem and what might be done to make them part of the solution.

The chapter works by asking four questions:

- What is health?
- What are health inequalities?
- Doesn't a legal right to equal healthcare secure health equality?
- How might a diverse range of voices contribute to fairness?

Our aim is to present ideas that are applicable across the UK. However, noting that health is a devolved area of law and policy, as explained in Chapter 5 by Johal and Germain, the predominant focus is on laws in England. We expand on the points made by reference to various practical examples, aimed at helping us to consider more broadly why diverse voices are necessary for a better understanding of health and health justice. We make particular reference to some of the lived experiences of Black communities more generally and Black girls and women in particular. We recognise that the term 'Black' has been used in different ways in the UK, including the political usage of 'Black' as a collective reference for all ethnic minority groups who have been racialised as deviating from the white norm.[1] A full reflection on the contested nature of various terminologies for racialised peoples is outside the scope of this chapter. In this chapter, the term Black will be used to refer to people of African or Caribbean descent, as tends to be the norm within anti-racist feminist work more broadly. Our focused practical discussions allow more general reflections on how the inclusion of marginalised and/or previously suppressed voices contributes to shifting how we know and understand various phenomena.

Where we provide the focus on Black communities more generally, and the lived experiences of Black girls and women more specifically, this is based on the historical and ongoing recognition of ways in which racialised and gendered systems collude to erase particular perspectives. For example, feminist epistemic (in)justice scholars have already highlighted the ways in which social locations such as race and gender can be used to discredit a person's testimony. In other words, sometimes people are not believed,[2] or are not allowed to contribute to common pools of knowledge, simply because of who they are.[3] This does not mean that people within marginalised communities do not continue to try and make sense of experiences that matter to them.[4] Our focus on Black communities more generally or Black girls and women is not to suggest that they are a monolithic category who all face erasure in exactly the same way,[5] and/or that there are no other historically marginalised groups whose voices need to be heard. Rather, the chapter invites readers to take our discussion further by considering how other underserved groups may shape our understanding of health inequalities and social justice and prompt analysis of what the law does, can, and should do in the face of that understanding.[6]

What is health?

People are often very light on the detail of what they mean by 'health'. This is challenging because, in practice, it does not take long to see that 'health' does not mean just one thing. To explain the point, we can refer to the broadest definition of which we are aware, which comes from the World Health Organization (WHO) Constitution:

1 Heidi Safia Mirza (ed), *Black British Feminism: A Reader* (Taylor & Francis 1997) 3.

2 Miranda Fricker, *Epistemic Injustice: Power and the Ethics of Knowing* (OUP 2007) 9–30.

3 Ibid 147–75.

4 Kristie Dotson, 'A Cautionary Tale: On Limiting Epistemic Oppression' (2012) 33 Front J Women Stud 24.

5 Kimberlé Crenshaw, 'Demarginalizating the Intersection of Race and Sex: A Black Feminist Critique of Antidiscrimination Doctrine, Feminist Theory, and Antiracist Politics' (1989) 140 U Chi Leg F 139.

6 See also Fricker (n2). Note that we are not specifically focused in this chapter on an epistemic injustice framing, but more broadly on distinct questions of social justice and law.

> Health is a state of complete physical, mental and social well-being and not merely the absence of disease or infirmity.[7]

You may or may not think this is a good definition. But just reflect on what it captures and how it tells us 'health' means several things at once. The term covers three different domains: physical, mental, and social. Emphatically it concerns 'disease' and 'infirmity'; matters that fall within the 'jurisdiction' of the health and social care sector and the expertise of the health sciences and caring professions (including, but not limited to, medicine). But it also indicates broader ideas of 'well-being'; positive states that are something and somewhere beyond simply not being unwell.

When we focus on 'health', we need to be aware that it could refer to an expansive, varied cluster of matters, such as we find in the WHO definition. Or it may denote just one or some of them. Clarity is thus important, as Anna Nelson explains in Chapter 3, so that it is sufficiently clear what is meant in a given instance when we identify a health aim or decide to protect or promote good health or address ill health. This is important simply because clarity is important. But it is also important because we are often presented with conflicts; for instance, of health *versus* autonomy or health *versus* the economy. But we can also see here how 'health' may even conflict with 'health': for instance, something that promotes an aspect of physical health (say a measure that protects us from a virus) may cause other health harms (say disregarding other physical health conditions or causing or worsening mental health conditions); or something that in the short term is benign may harm health in the future, or a health benefit now may come with future health costs.[8]

A further point is that we need to be able explain why a question regarding health makes it a *shared* value; a matter that is the business of law and policy, as opposed to a matter that should just be left to individuals and the market. As well as exploring what health is and why it matters, we need to be able to understand *how* health and health-affecting decisions exist as something to be governed through public institutions and mechanisms, including the law.[9] It is thus important, when looking at the ways that health features in law and legal studies, to make sure that it is clear what is being discussed, why it matters, and how its value exists as one value that is shared across society and properly subject to governance through policy and law.

In this chapter, we are focused on broad definitions of health, reflective of the characterisations found in the National Health Service Act 2006 (the NHS

---

7 WHO (World Health Organization), 'Constitution' https://www.who.int/about/governance/constitution, accessed 11 January 2024.

8 John Coggon, 'Living and Dying with COVID: Ethical Complexity and Health/Health Trade-Offs' (2021) https://ukpandemicethics.org/living-and-dying-with-covid-ethical-complexity-and-health-health-trade-offs/, accessed 11 January 2024.

9 John Coggon, *What Makes Health Public? A critical evaluation of moral legal, and political claims in public health* (Cambridge: Cambridge University Press, 2012).

Act 2006), which we look at in detail shortly. Our focus embraces both physical and mental health, and it looks both to the absence or diminution of disease and illness and to positive states of wellbeing. In approaching health, we note its normative dimensions; that it is a concept which carries value judgements. But we emphasise too that it is not a single issue, or the only value of concern. In approaching health as we conceive it here, we argue that it covers a range of things that matter, but that other 'non-health' issues matter too.

What are health inequalities?

When looking at inequalities, we again need to focus on identifying and explaining what matters, why, and how. 'Equality of what?' is an important question, and the 'what' here is health, broadly conceived. But do all inequalities in health matter?

The best answers to the question of identifying problematic health inequalities engage three criteria: health inequalities matter when they are *avoidable*, *unfair*, and *systemic*.[10] The first criterion asks an empirical question: we look at two groups or more groups, or at people's situations at different points along socio-economic gradients, and we then ask if there is a cause of relatively worse health outcomes that can be removed or ameliorated for socially marginalised groups or for people who are less well-off socio-economically. If the answer is yes, we can then move to the question of unfairness. And this is answered by reference to ideas of justice, responsibility, power, and social positionality. Who, within current structures, does and can shape the influences of (ill) health, and how might those influences be changed for the better?[11]

In unpacking critical questions regarding health inequalities, we have to look at how we identify different groups. As indicated, we might do so by reference to socio-economic position and/or to characteristics such as age, disability, ethnicity, gender, nationality, race, or sexuality.[12] And we might pay special attention to health inequalities where there are overlaps across these; that is, in the jargon, and as explained in more detail in Johan and Germain's chapter the book, Chapter 5, where we find *intersectionality*.[13] For instance, we might find a compounding of disadvantage for Black, immigrant women in low-paid, precarious employment.

---

10 For overview and analysis, see Ethan Williams and others, 'What Are Health Inequalities?' https://www.kingsfund.org.uk/publications/what-are-health-inequalities, accessed 11 January 2024.

11 Katherine E. Smith, Clare Bambra, and Sarah E. Hill (eds), *Health Inequalities: Critical Perspectives* (OUP 2015).

12 Beth Wangarĩ Kamunge, 'Which Inequalities Should We Focus on in Evaluating Health Policy Before, During, and Following COVID-19?' (2021) https://ukpandemicethics.org/wp-content/uploads/2021/12/Intersectionality-Framework.pdf, accessed 11 January 2024.

13 Crenshaw (n5).

The questions of whether and how unequal health opportunities and outcomes materialise may be explored by reference to *structural determinants*; by studying social, professional, and political norms and practices, including legal rules and principles, which create an environment that is conducive to worse health. Where those structures are understood, we can then ask who, practically, is empowered to change things to address the unfair inequalities, and how they might do so.

Such a project draws from social epidemiology,[14] which explains cause and effect in what are labelled the *social determinants of health*.[15] Social determinants capture how the very ways that our societies are configured influence health, for better and for worse. And researchers in this field then look at different sources of influence within social determinants, including commercial determinants,[16] political determinants,[17] and – of particular interest in this chapter – *legal determinants of health*.[18] Works in social (including legal) epidemiology allow us to show how laws create, entrench, and worsen health outcomes, and how burdens of ill health may be spread unequally across society. And they allow us to see how laws may have the opposite effect.

Case study on unfair health inequalities

The health inequalities we are concerned with are those that are unfair, avoidable, and systemic. In order to flesh this out, we will begin from the lived experiences of Black girls and women by explaining in what ways Black female perspectives have tended to be marginalised historically.

Black girls and women have historically faced erasures of their perspectives. In the 1980s various Black feminist scholars pointed to how Black female voices and experiences tended to fall through the cracks of society, including in social justice spaces.[19] These scholars explained that, on the one hand, when people talked

---

14 Michael Marmot and others, 'Fair Society, Healthy Lives: The Marmot Review' (2010) https://www.instituteofhealthequity.org/resources-reports/fair-society-healthy-lives-the-marmot-review/fair-society-healthy-lives-full-report-pdf.pdf, accessed 11 January 2024; Michael Marmot and others, 'Health Equity in England: The Marmot Review 10 Years On' (2020) https://www.health.org.uk/publications/reports/the-marmot-review-10-years-on, accessed 11 January 2024.

15 WHO (World Health Organization), 'Closing the Gap in a Generation: Health Equity through Action on the Social Determinants of Health: Commission on Social Determinants of Health Final Report' (2008) https://www.who.int/publications/i/item/WHO-IER-CSDH-08.1, accessed 11 January 2024.

16 Anna Gilmore and others, 'Defining and Conceptualising the Commercial Determinants of Health' (2023) 401 Lancet 1194.

17 Ole Petter Ottersen and others, 'The Political Origins of Health Inequity: Prospects for Change' (2014) 383 Lancet 630.

18 Lawrence O. Gostin and others, 'The Legal Determinants of Health: Harnessing the Power of Law for Global Health and Sustainable Development' (2019) 393 Lancet 1857.

19 E.g., see bell hooks, *Ain't I a Woman: Black Women and Feminism* (Pluto 1982); Crenshaw (n5); Patricia Hill Collins, *Black Feminist Thought: Knowledge, Consciousness, and the Politics of Empowerment* (Routledge 1990); Hazel Carby, 'White Woman Listen! Black Feminism

about Black people's lived experiences of racism, they centred Black male voices. On the other hand, when the discussion was on women's lived experiences of sexism and patriarchy, the discussions centred white women's experiences.[20] This meant that Black female perspectives often went unheard.[21]

It continues to be the case that Black female perspectives continue to be vulnerable to erasure.[22] For example, Black women tend to be under-represented in decision-making spaces, as noted by the House of Commons Women and Equalities Committee 2023 report, which said that: 'Black women are regularly underrepresented in research or data and therefore in policymaking.'[23] An approach that starts from marginalised lives can illuminate the unfair, avoidable, and systemic nature of health inequalities.

One such approach is to tell the story of Ella Adoo-Kissi-Debrah, a nine-year-old Black British girl who died in 2013. Her death was formally recorded as a consequence of air pollution-induced asthma. Ella lived 25 metres from the heavily congested South Circular Road in Lewisham, London, and had been hospitalised 27 times for asthma-related incidents, before suffering a fatal asthma attack in February 2013.[24] The initial inquest found the cause of death to be asthma not air pollution. However, Ella's mother, Rosamund Adoo-Kissi-Debrah petitioned the court in July 2018 for the inquest to be reopened and for exposure to excessive air pollution to be acknowledged as having contributed to Ella's death. In May 2019 the court granted permission to reopen the inquest.[25] It was reopened on 17 December 2019 and concluded with the inquest on 16 December 2020. In the report to prevent future deaths,[26] Philip Barlow, the assistant coroner for inner South London, recorded the medical cause of death as follows: '(1a) acute respiratory failure, (1b) severe asthma, and (1c) air pollution

---

and the Boundaries of Sisterhood' in Centre for Contemporary Cultural Studies (ed), *The Empire Strikes Back: Race and Racism in 70's Britain* (Routledge 1982); Audre Lorde, *Sister Outsider: Essays and Speeches* (The Crossing Press 1984).

20 Ibid; Crenshaw (n5).

21 See also Kristie Dotson, 'Tracking Epistemic Violence, Tracking Practices of Silencing' (2011) 26 Hypatia 236.

22 E.g., Christen A. Smith and others, 'Cite Black Women: A Critical Praxis (a Statement)' (2021) 2 Fem Anthropol 10; Brittney Cooper, 'Love No Limit: Towards a Black Feminist Future (in Theory)' (2015) 45 Black Scholar 7.

23 House of Commons Women and Equalities Committee, 'Black Maternal Health' (2023) https://committees.parliament.uk/publications/38989/documents/191706/default/, accessed 8 January 2024.

24 Learn more at the Ella Roberta Foundation https://www.ellaroberta.org/about-ella, accessed 5 January 2024.

25 Sandra Laville, 'Ella Kissi-Debrah: New Inquest Granted into "Air Pollution" Death' (2019) https://www.theguardian.com/uk-news/2019/may/02/ella-kissi-debrah-new-inquest-granted-into-air-pollution-death, accessed 5 January 2024.

26 Philip Barlow, 'Regulation 28: Report to Prevent Future Deaths (1)' (2020) https://www.judiciary.uk/wp-content/uploads/2021/04/Ella-Kissi-Debrah-2021-0113-1.pdf, accessed 5 January 2024.

exposure', and concluded that Ella 'died of asthma contributed to by exposure to excessive air pollution'.[27] Ella's story can help us flesh out the three criteria for problematic health inequalities discussed (*avoidable*, *unfair*, and *systemic*).

The first question is whether Ella's death from air pollution-induced asthma was avoidable. In other words, was there a cause for worse life expectancy outcomes for Ella that could have been removed? The answer here appears to be yes. As explained in Philip Barlow's inquest report:

> [A]ir pollution was a significant contributory factor to both the induction and exacerbations of her asthma. During the course of [Ella's] illness between 2010 and 2013 she was exposed to levels of nitrogen dioxide and particulate matter in excess of World Health Organization Guidelines. The principal source of her exposure was traffic emissions.[28]

Air pollution levels from road traffic are not set in stone and can be improved through collective human efforts to improve outdoor air quality, which could include, but are not limited to, for example, traffic-calming measures in residential areas.

Moreover, Ella's untimely death could have potentially been prevented had her mother been given information about the adverse effects of air pollution on health; information which, at the time, was not being routinely communicated to parents by medical professionals. To be clear, we are not then placing responsibility on Ella's parents/caregivers to have moved to an area with less air pollution, nor suggesting that would have been a straightforward and realistic option for them. In fact, suggesting this is one of the unfair responsibilities placed on people from lower income backgrounds – to take 'personal responsibility' to fix systemic problems.[29] Indeed, the Royal College of Paediatrics and Child Health, in their formal response to the report, noted, on the basis of two major previous pieces of research that they had conducted, that avoidable illnesses, disability, and death from air pollution are 'strongly associated with deprivation' and 'that the responsibility for clean air cannot solely rest with individuals'.[30] As one of us has argued more fully elsewhere,[31] it is unfair that

27 Ibid [3].

28 Ibid [4].

29 See Townsend Centre for International Poverty Research 'Alternative Top Ten Tips for Health' www.bristol.ac.uk/poverty/healthinequalities.html, accessed 11 January 2024.

30 Royal College of Paediatrics and Child Health, 'Reg 28 Ella Adoo Kissi-Debrah RCPH Response' (2021) https://www.rcpch.ac.uk/sites/default/files/2021-06/RCPCH-response-Reg-28-assistant-coroner-report-EAKD.pdf, accessed 9 January 2024.

31 Beth Kamunge, 'Place and Health Inequalities: An Ethical Framework for Evaluating and Developing Policy' (2022) https://ukpandemicethics.org/wp-content/uploads/2022/04/Place-IF.pdf, accessed 11 January 2023.

a person's postcode should serve as an indicator of their life expectancy.[32] Yet that is what we see exemplified in Ella's case. And at a more general level, the COVID-19 pandemic served as a reminder that Black communities are amongst those disproportionately represented in neighbourhoods and housing conditions associated with premature death.[33] As argued elsewhere,[34] these are avoidable, systematised conditions, which are unfair. They are created by market structures that disproportionately segment particular groups of people towards the dirty, hazardous, precarious, and poorly paid parts of the labour market.[35] These racialised, gendered, and classed income and wealth inequities in turn contribute to the reality of being more likely to live in a highly polluted area, and to subsequent ill health and even premature death.

In conclusion, this practical case study has considered how diverse lived experiences can help make visible problematic health inequalities. Stories such as Ella Adoo-Kissi-Debrah's contribute to fleshing out avoidable and unfair health disparities. Social-structural determinants of (ill) health raise questions of social justice.[36] A focus primarily or solely on more privileged narratives, such as those of people living in areas with (lower than) average levels of air pollution, may skew understandings, for example by placing a greater focus on 'personal responsibility' and individual efforts over collective action and systemic reforms.

Doesn't a legal right to equal healthcare secure health equality?

The discussion so far has indicated that our health is not simply defined by healthcare. But we might question why we need to talk about health inequalities in the UK, where healthcare is freely available to all, with access based on need. As a question in health law, we might respond through four stages. The initial two involve analysis of *formal* (in)equality, and the latter two analysis of *substantive* (in)equality: in other words, we will explore two questions about what the law, on the face of it, formally 'says' about (in)equality, and then two questions about the substantive reality – that is, real-world effects – that people experience in practice.

32 For a fuller discussion on the role of place in health outcomes see Clare Bambra, *Health Divides: Where You Live Can Kill You* (Policy Press 2016).

33 House of Commons Women and Equalities Committee, 'Unequal Impact? Coronavirus and BAME People. Third Report of Session 2019–21' (2020) https://committees.parliament.uk/publications/3965/documents/39887/default/, accessed 9 January 2024.

34 Beth Kamunge, 'An Equal Recovery? Written Evidence Submitted to the UK Parliament's Treasury Committee' (2021) https://committees.parliament.uk/writtenevidence/37923/pdf/, accessed 11 January 2024.

35 Ibid 3.

36 Sridhar Venkatapuram, 'Global Justice and the Social Determinants of Health' (2010) 24 Ethics Int Aff 119.

Healthcare services and formal equality for all

Within legal studies, we may explore formal equality by looking to the letter of the law; by asking, 'does the law say the same for everyone?' In England, the NHS Constitution spells out seven core principles or values (see Box 4.1).[37] The first two are explained as follows:

Box 4.1: Key text: the NHS Constitution

1. The NHS provides a comprehensive service available to all

It is available to all irrespective of gender, race, disability, age, sexual orientation, belief, gender reassignment, pregnancy, and maternity or marital or civil partnership status. The service is designed to improve, prevent, diagnose, and treat both physical and mental health problems with equal regard. It has a duty to each and every individual that it serves and must respect their human rights. At the same time, it has a wider social duty to promote equality through the services it provides and to pay particular attention to groups or sections of society where improvements in health and life expectancy are not keeping pace with the rest of the population.

2. Access to NHS services is based on clinical need, not an individual's ability to pay

NHS services are free of charge, except in limited circumstances sanctioned by parliament.

To be clear, the NHS Constitution itself is not a foundational source of legal rights. However, the Secretary of State is legally bound to 'have regard' for it,[38] as are bodies such as NHS trusts, NHS England, local authorities, and the National Institute for Health and Care Excellence.[39] And the two principles just listed give us a firm view of the principled foundations on which legal rights within the NHS sit: they capture 'the philosophy' of the NHS.

More firmly as a legal starting point, for the NHS in England, section 1 of the NHS Act 2006 provides that:

---

[37] Department of Health and Social Care, 'The NHS Constitution for England' (2021) https://www.gov.uk/government/publications/the-nhs-constitution-for-england/the-nhs-constitution-for-england, accessed 11 January 2024.

[38] National Health Service Act 2006, s 1B(1).

[39] Health Act 2009, s 2(2).

(1) The Secretary of State must continue the promotion in England of a comprehensive health service designed to secure improvement –
  (a) in the physical and mental health of the people of England, and
  (b) in the prevention, diagnosis, and treatment of physical and mental illness.

The section goes on to list a number of further duties that fall on the Secretary of State. These include the duty, when

> exercising functions in relation to the health service … [to] have regard to the need to reduce inequalities between the people of England with respect to the benefits that they can obtain from the health service.[40]

So, in law, we find duties to provide a *comprehensive* health service, with a focus on physical and mental health, and a view to the promotion of positive states of health, as well as the prevention and remediation of ill health. These duties are circumscribed by express attention to health inequalities. Furthermore, the Minister, and the actors and organisations that make up the NHS, are bound by equality laws such as (in England, Scotland, and Wales) the public sector equality duty provided in the Equality Act 2010,[41] and (across the UK) the protection against discrimination in the enjoyment of rights enumerated in the European Convention on Human Rights (ECHR).[42] However, this formal equality may be challenged if we drill into its legal meaning and reach.

Formally, does 'all' mean 'everyone'?

On its face, the NHS provides equal rights for *all*. However, even formally, terms do not always mean what they seem. And in relation to healthcare in the UK, 'all' does not mean 'everyone'. In 2009, the Court of Appeal heard the case of a Palestinian-born man who had a chronic liver condition.[43] He was living in the UK but had failed to successfully apply for asylum. The questions for the court concerned the lawfulness of NHS trusts withholding treatment from him if he could not pay, and of guidance issued by the Secretary of State, which explained what treatments could be charged for. The case addressed the meaning of being 'ordinarily resident' and – of particular interest in this chapter – provided the following approach to interpreting the NHS Act 2006. Ward LJ, with whom Lloyd and Rimer LJJ agreed, held:

---

40 National Health Service Act 2006, s 1(1C).

41 See Equality Act 2010, s 149. In relation to Northern Ireland, see https://www.equalityni.org/Legislation, accessed 3 July 2024.

42 ECHR, Article 14.

43 *R (YA) v Secretary of State for Health* [2009] EWCA Civ 225.

> [T]he Secretary of State's duty prescribed by section 1 [of the NHS Act 2006] is to continue the promotion in England of a comprehensive health service designed to secure improvement in the health 'of the people of England'. Note that it is the people *of* England, not the people *in* England, which suggests that the beneficiaries of this free health service are to be those with some link to England so as to be part and parcel of the fabric of the place. It connotes a legitimate connection with the country. The exclusion from this free service of non-residents and the right ... to charge such persons as are not ordinarily resident reinforces this notion of segregation between them and us. This strongly suggests that, as a rule, the benefits were not intended by Parliament to be bestowed on those who ought not to be here.[44]

The law, then, expressly and directly applies 'them and us' reasoning and invites legally sanctioned 'segregation' – discrimination – in the reading of the duties conferred by the NHS Act 2006.

This approach to understanding 'all' has since been affirmed and applied in the Supreme Court, in the case of *R (A and another) v Secretary of State for Health*[45] (albeit with dissenting judgments from Lady Hale and Lord Kerr). That case concerned charges for a person travelling to England from another part of the UK; specifically, a 15-year-old girl who lived in Northern Ireland, coming to England for the termination of her pregnancy (a procedure that could not lawfully be provided at the time in Northern Ireland). Lord Wilson (with whom Lords Reed and Hughes agreed) reasoned that each of the four nations of the UK provides its own respective duty on its own health authorities. He thus re-emphasised Ward LJ's point that 'the 2006 Act refers not to the people in England but the people of England',[46] before going on to state that:

> [A]rticle 4(a) of the Health and Personal Social Services (Northern Ireland) Order 1972 (SI No 1972/1265) (NI 14), requires the Department of Health, Social Services and Public Safety in Northern Ireland to provide services designed to promote the health of the 'people of Northern Ireland'. The general scheme is therefore that the health service for the people who live in Northern Ireland is to be provided for them by the Northern Irish authority.[47]

At a formal level, we may therefore conclude that while the UK's healthcare systems aim to provide equal access to all, 'all' does not mean 'everyone'. Next,

44 Ibid [55].

45 *R (A and Another) v Secretary of State for Health* [2017] UKSC 41.

46 Ibid [10].

47 Ibid.

however, we examine the point that even where formal equality does exist, it does not translate into substantive equality.

Substantive inequality: what is the 'inverse care law' and how can healthcare providers respond to real-world health inequalities?

Having looked at what the law says, and its underpinning principles, should we not expect to see equality in healthcare at least for the 'everyone' entitled to it? Perhaps we should. But it does not happen. And this is not a new phenomenon or a novel realisation. Julian Tudor Hart, a general practitioner who worked in Port Talbot, captured the reality of substantive inequalities within NHS care over fifty years ago. He expressed this through his concept of *the inverse care law* (see Box 4.2):

Box 4.2: Key concept: the inverse care law

In areas with the most sickness and death, general practitioners have more work, larger lists, less hospital support, and inherit more clinically ineffective traditions of consultation, than in the healthiest areas; and hospital doctors shoulder heavier case-loads with less staff and equipment, more obsolete buildings, and suffer recurrent crises in the availability of beds and replacement staff. These trends can be summed as up *the inverse care law*: that *the availability of good medical care tends to vary inversely with the need of the population served*.[48]

The inverse care law has received considerable attention since its publication, and, in the words of Michael Marmot, a leading authority on health inequalities within England and globally, 'remains as relevant as ever'.[49] In short, even where healthcare is formally available equally to all, in practice people enjoy, or suffer, different real-world healthcare opportunities and outcomes. And this is something that is recognised expressly within the healthcare service, as evidenced by the statutory duties relating to health inequalities and wider policy responses. We will again focus on England to explain.

The NHS in England expresses the priority it aims to give to hearing diverse voices. In explaining 'our approach to reducing healthcare inequalities', it states:

> The NHS Long Term Plan placed tackling health inequalities at the heart of NHS goals for this decade [i.e., the 2020s]. The big

48 Julian Tudor Hart, 'The Inverse Care Law' (1971) 297 Lancet 405, 412 (emphasis added).
49 Michael Marmot, 'An Inverse Care Law for Our Time' (2018) 363 BMJ k3216.

> population health improvement goals can only be met through far better engagement with those least likely to present at NHS services now.[50]

In relation to addressing inequalities that arise in healthcare, there is a focus on the need to tackle 'relative disparities in access to services, patient experience and healthcare outcomes'.[51] However, this is not a straightforward task.

To understand the practical and political challenges of the inverse care law as it manifests today, we refer to a paper by Jasmine Olivera and colleagues. They highlight these challenges through analysis of policy response documents of local healthcare systems in England, which outline plans to address health inequalities.[52] Olivera and colleagues' analysis presents problems of vagueness and variation, which they attribute to three things: a lack of clarity on what health inequalities actually means; the place of (political) value judgements in the identification of causes of ill health and the groups to be addressed who suffer unfair health inequality; and a lack of clear, concrete aims and markers of success. We will look at their paper in some detail to exemplify the material issues that they argue need to be addressed.

The problems of vagueness that Olivera and colleagues identify include 'ambitions for the future' that are 'undefined and non-specific, lacking metrics, time frames or a clear description of the populations being discussed or inequalities being targeted'.[53] As regards variation, they find 'variation in definitions of terms, groups being compared and the use of metrics and indicators'.[54] These problems of vagueness and variation, as already indicated, are attributed to three factors. Regarding the first of these, where the authors identify a 'lack of prior conceptualisation and approach', this means, for instance, that healthcare systems lacked 'awareness of what inequalities are present'.[55]

Where, secondly, Olivera and colleagues identify the place of value judgements, they note a:

> [F]ocus on self-management of lifestyle and behavioural practices as a means of reducing health inequalities, without mentioning a need to address the systematic political, social and environmental origins of health inequalities.[56]

---

50 NHS England, 'Our Approach to Reducing Healthcare Equalities' (nd) www.england.nhs.uk/about/equality/equality-hub/national-healthcare-inequalities-improvement-programme/our-approach-to-reducing-healthcare-inequalities/, accessed 11 January 2024.

51 Ibid.

52 Jasmine N. Olivera and others, 'Conceptualisation of Health Inequalities by Local Healthcare Systems: A Document Analysis' (2022) 30 Health Soc Care Comm e3977.

53 Ibid e3980.

54 Ibid.

55 Ibid e3981.

56 Ibid.

They also identify how value judgements apply in the ways that different populations are identified as (not) requiring attention; again, inviting a politicised framing. Across the materials that they reviewed, they found these typically focused on populations such as 'children, people of old age, mothers, the mentally ill, physically disabled and those with autism or learning disabilities'.[57] By contrast, they found consistent omission of populations such as 'immigrants, minority ethnic groups, criminals and LGBTQ+ groups', and unpaid carers.[58] And in relation to the final theme, a lack of concrete aims, Olivera and colleagues identify a failure to match the headline commitment to addressing health inequalities with meaningful, specific commitments reflected in 'concrete and accountable targets or actions'.[59]

Health inequalities, law, and society: why is it insufficient just to look at healthcare and patients?

If we are concerned about health inequalities, it is insufficient simply to focus on formal and substantive inequalities within the healthcare system. This is what Olivera and colleagues are driving at, for instance, where they discern political value judgements in measures that focus on self-management and lifestyle, with no regard to political and social determinants of health opportunities and outcomes. And it is why, when Marmot speaks to the relevance of the inverse care law today, he notes the continued relevance of Tudor Hart's concerns about the effects of a market system within healthcare and real-world differences in the provision of healthcare across the country. But first and foremost, Marmot emphasises that the core message of Tudor Hart's paper concerns determinants *beyond* the healthcare system.[60] He repeats Tudor Hart's words from the original paper on the inverse care law:

> Medical services are not the main determinant of mortality and morbidity; these depend most upon standards of nutrition, housing, working environment, and education, and the presence or absence of war.[61]

In short, our understandings from population health sciences show that the greater causes of ill health, and lack of opportunity to enjoy good health, are not reducible to questions of *patients*' rights. This is certainly not to diminish the importance or value of healthcare. It is rather to ensure that studies in health law do not fail to see the bigger picture; the crucial reality, as explained, that

57 Ibid.
58 Ibid.
59 Ibid.
60 Marmot (n49).
61 Hart (n48) 409.

health opportunities and outcomes are defined in the main by socially generated determinants of health and structural and institutional norms and realities. In seeking constructively to hear diverse voices in relation to health inequalities, we therefore need to look to wide-reaching structural determinants of ill health – for instance, how housing policy, or education policy, or transport policy generate health inequalities – rather than just inequalities within the healthcare system. We must not forget healthcare. But the greatest part of health law is not about healthcare or *patients*' rights, and the questions of ethics that arise are not (limited to) healthcare ethics.

How might a diverse range of voices contribute to fairness?

In this closing section we reflect further on how the inclusion of diverse voices may contribute to greater fairness in society. We begin by noting that it is itself a matter of justice to ensure that as many perspectives and social locations as possible are represented in discussions of health (and justice). Health affects everyone, whether or not they care about 'being healthy' or would understand 'health' differently from others. So, it is a matter of justice that diverse voices are heard and engaged with, even if not necessarily always agreed with.

Engaging with under-represented communities can lead to better understandings of the socio-political context in which health and health justice are conceptualised. What 'health' is has changed over space and time in ways that have had an impact on marginalised communities. For example, Black people who were fleeing slavery were once pathologised as having a disease known as 'drapetomania', which was defined by Dr Samuel Cartwright as the disease of slaves running away from their slave masters and slavery conditions.[62] Another example is how same-sex attraction was once understood as an endocrine disturbance, then later as a mental disorder, before finally being depathologised after the American Psychiatric Association removed it from the listed disease states in the *Diagnostic and Statistical Manual IV*. Starting our inquiry from the perspective of marginalised communities contributes to dispelling the notion that concepts such as 'health' have always been understood in ways that contribute to the flourishing of all. Paying attention to who benefits and loses from particular understandings of concepts puts us on the path towards fairness.

Moreover, the inclusion of diverse voices is itself generative of new knowledge, concepts, language, and ideas.[63] As mentioned in the introduction of this chapter, a vulnerability to erasure does not then mean that marginalised communities do not continue to share and create knowledges about their life experience.

---

62 Christopher Willoughby, 'Running Away from Drapetomania: Samuel A. Cartwright, Medicine, and Race in the Antebellum South' (2018) 84 J S Hist 579.

63 Sandra Harding, *Whose Science? Whose Knowledge? Thinking from Women's Lives* (Cornell University Press 1991).

For example, LGBTQ+ communities, and communities of people living with mental health conditions, are good examples of communities in which new language, concepts, and ideas are generated as people try and make sense of what matters to them. It is from within LGBTQ+ communities that the concept of being 'agender' was produced for example.[64] Or one can think about how the concept of 'sexual harassment' was coined within the context of feminist-informed women coming together to make sense of problematic experiences they had gone through in workspaces.[65] Not including diverse voices can result in wilful ignorance amongst more dominant groups, leading to further injustice.

The inclusion of diverse voices is thus essential to better/improved health practices and outcomes. We close with an example where a change in practices has been recommended as a result of engaging with marginalised experiences in the context of maternal healthcare in the UK. In the UK, Black women are at least four times more likely than white women to die during childbirth.[66] The disproportionate rates of Black female death in childbirth have been a long-standing problem that was recognised as requiring 'urgent explanation'.[67] Death in childbirth is undeniably a complex, multidimensional issue. However, one of the issues that has arisen through engagement with Black female childbirth experiences is the issue of systematised failings in care. For example, a review of the death records by MBRRACE-UK assessors (who were medical professionals themselves)[68] found evidence of myths related to Black women's experience of pain, leading to pain mismanagement, micro-aggressions, and unconscious bias.[69] This has been affirmed as more pregnant Black women in the UK have raised the concern that when they try to communicate their experiences of pain to healthcare providers, their experiences are treated as unintelligible or false.[70] Black women in those situations report then facing the conundrum of

64 Trystan Goetze, 'Hermeneutical Dissent and the Species of Hermeneutical Injustice' (2018) 33 Hypatia 73.

65 Fricker (n2) 153–5.

66 MBRRACE-UK, 'Saving Lives, Improving Mothers' Care: Lessons Learned to Inform Maternity Care from the UK and Ireland Confidential Enquiries into Maternal Deaths and Morbidity 2014–2016' (2018) https://www.npeu.ox.ac.uk/mbrrace-uk/presentations/saving-lives-improving-mothers-care, accessed 11 January 2024, vi.

67 Ibid.

68 MBRRACE-UK stands for Mothers and Babies: Reducing Risk through Audit and Confidential Enquiries. It is the national body responsible for investigating the causes of maternal deaths, stillbirths, and infant deaths in the UK.

69 House of Commons Women and Equalities Committee (n33); more broadly, see discussions on racialised (mis)management of pain, e.g., Karen Aderson and others, 'Racial and Ethnic Disparities in Pain: Causes and Consequences of Unequal Care' (2009) 10 J Pain 1187; Eseosa T. Ighodaro and others, 'Giving Voice to Black Women in Science and Medicine' (2021) 27 Nat Med 1316.

70 Birthrights, 'Systemic Racism, Not Broken Bodies' (2022) https://www.birthrights.org.uk/wp-content/uploads/2022/05/Birthrights-inquiry-systemic-racism_exec-summary_May-22-web.pdf, accessed 11 January 2024.

not wanting to advocate for themselves as firmly as they should be able to do, for fear of being further dismissed as an 'angry black woman' – a particularly painful stereotype that usually leads to the concerns of the person in question being further dismissed. Engaging with marginalised experiences can therefore shed greater light on why problematic health inequalities occur and what changes in practice and policy are required to respond to these when they are unfair, avoidable, and systemic.

Summary

- To address health inequalities, we must be clear on what we mean by health, and which groups we identify as suffering health inequalities.
- UK laws formally support a system that offers equal healthcare opportunities to all.
- However, there are various practical and principled challenges to address:
  - The 'all' in 'healthcare for all' does not mean everyone.
  - Even for those with equal entitlement to healthcare, we see unequal health opportunities and outcomes: a phenomenon known as the inverse care law.
  - Most significantly, the greater causes of health inequalities are not about healthcare, but about our broader natural, built, and social environments.
- Legal studies of health inequalities need to look both at and far beyond healthcare, generating understanding of how laws can and do influence health within different social contexts, and with a critical view to how laws may help better achievement of social justice.

Questions for reflection

1. How would you define which health inequalities should be addressed through law and policy?
2. What are the social determinants of health, and how do legal determinants of health fit within these?
3. Do the current and/or proposed NHS-related laws, policies, and practices successfully address health inequalities within the UK? Why or why not?
4. With reference to the cases discussed within the chapter, do you think that NHS services should only be to 'people of England' or 'people in England'? Which approach do you think leads to greater fairness in society? If you had to write definitions of the terms 'people of England' and 'people in England' to guide decision-makers, what would your definitions be and why?
5. Which communities can you think of whose voices have historically been marginalised in discussions about health and society? What impact do you think this has had on the (un)equal protection and promotion of health?
6. What areas of law and policy beyond healthcare need to be considered if we are to address avoidable, unfair, systemic health inequalities?

Recommended resources

- Moya Bailey, 'A Black Feminist Disability Framework' https://www.youtube.com/watch?v=mIBD1g-fQB8, accessed 11 January 2024.
- John Coggon and Beth Kamunge-Kpodo, 'The Legal Determinants of Health (In)justice' (2022) 30 Med Law Rev 705.
- Crunk Feminist Collective: https://www.crunkfeministcollective.com/, accessed 11 January 2024.
- Lawrence O. Gostin and others, 'The Legal Determinants of Health: Harnessing the Power of Law for Global Health and Sustainable Development' (2019) 393 Lancet 1857.
- Michael Marmot, 'An Inverse Care Law for Our Time' (2018) 362 BMJ k3216.
- Jasmine N. Olivera and others, 'Conceptualisation of Health Inequalities by Local Healthcare Systems: A Document Analysis' (2022) 30 Health Soc Care Comm e3977.
- Katherine E. Smith, Clare Bambra, and Sarah E. Hill (eds), *Health Inequalities: Critical Perspectives* (OUP 2015).
- Sridhar Venkatapuram, 'Global Justice and the Social Determinants of Health' (2010) 24 Ethics Int Aff 119.
- Sridhar Venkatapuram, 'First Principles of Health Justice: A Human Right to Be Healthy' https://www.youtube.com/watch?v=Ex1AqnM6U9Y, accessed 11 January 2024.

Bibliography

Aderson K and others, 'Racial and Ethnic Disparities in Pain: Causes and Consequences of Unequal Care' (2009) 10 J Pain 1187

Bambra C, *Health Divides: Where You Live Can Kill You* (Policy Press 2016)

Barlow P, 'Regulation 28: Report to Prevent Future Deaths (1)' (2020) https://www.judiciary.uk/wp-content/uploads/2021/04/Ella-Kissi-Debrah-2021-0113-1.pdf, accessed 5 January 2024

Birthrights, 'Systemic Racism, Not Broken Bodies' (2022) https://www.birthrights.org.uk/wp-content/uploads/2022/05/Birthrights-inquiry-systemic-racism_exec-summary_May-22-web.pdf, accessed 11 January 2024

Carby H, 'White Woman Listen! Black Feminism and the Boundaries of Sisterhood' in Centre for Contemporary Cultural Studies (ed), *The Empire Strikes Back: Race and Racism in 70's Britain* (Routledge 1982)

Coggon J, *What Makes Health Public? A critical evaluation of moral legal, and political claims in public health* (Cambridge University Press 2012).

Coggon J, 'Living and Dying with COVID: Ethical Complexity and Health/Health Trade-Offs' (2021) https://ukpandemicethics.org/living-and-dying-with-covid-ethical-complexity-and-health-health-trade-offs/, accessed 11 January 2024

Cooper B, 'Love No Limit: Towards a Black Feminist Future (In Theory)' (2015) 45 Black Scholar 7

Crenshaw K, 'Demarginalizating the Intersection of Race and Sex: A Black Feminist Critique of Antidiscrimination Doctrine, Feminist Theory, and Antiracist Politics' (1989) 140 U Chi Leg F 139

DHSC (Department of Health and Social Care), 'The NHS Constitution for England' (2021) https://www.gov.uk/government/publications/the-nhs-constitution-for-england/the-nhs-constitution-for-england, accessed 11 January 2024

Dotson K, 'Tracking Epistemic Violence, Tracking Practices of Silencing' (2011) 26 Hypatia 236

Dotson K, 'A Cautionary Tale: On Limiting Epistemic Oppression' (2012) 33 Front J Women Stud 24

Ella Roberta Foundation, https://www.ellaroberta.org/about-ella, accessed 5 January 2024

Fricker M, *Epistemic Injustice: Power and the Ethics of Knowing* (OUP 2007)

Gilmore A and others, 'Defining and Conceptualising the Commercial Determinants of Health' (2023) 401 Lancet 1194

Goetze T, 'Hermeneutical Dissent and the Species of Hermeneutical Injustice' (2018) 33 Hypatia 73

Gostin LO and others, 'The Legal Determinants of Health: Harnessing the Power of Law for Global Health and Sustainable Development' (2019) 393 Lancet 1857

Harding S, *Whose Science? Whose Knowledge? Thinking from Women's Lives* (Cornell University Press 1991)

Hart JT, 'The Inverse Care Law' (1971) 297 Lancet 405

Hill Collins P, *Black Feminist Thought: Knowledge, Consciousness, and the Politics of Empowerment* (Routledge 1990)

hooks b, *Ain't I a Woman: Black Women and Feminism* (Pluto 1982)

House of Commons Women and Equalities Committee, 'Unequal Impact? Coronavirus and BAME People. Third Report of Session 2019–21' (2020) https://committees.parliament.uk/publications/3965/documents/39887/default/, accessed 9 January 2024

House of Commons Women and Equalities Committee, 'Black Maternal Health' (2023) https://committees.parliament.uk/publications/38989/documents/191706/default/, accessed on 8 January 2024

Ighodaro ET and others, 'Giving Voice to Black Women in Science and Medicine' (2021) 27 Nat Med 1316

Kamunge BW, 'An Equal Recovery? Written Evidence Submitted to the UK Parliament's Treasury Committee' (2022) https://committees.parliament.uk/writtenevidence/37923/pdf/, accessed 11 January 2024

Kamunge BW, 'Which Inequalities Should We Focus on in Evaluating Health Policy Before, During, and Following COVID-19?' (2021) https://ukpandemicethics.org/wp-content/uploads/2021/12/Intersectionality-Framework.pdf, accessed 11 January 2024

Kamunge BW, 'Place and Health Inequalities: An Ethical Framework for Evaluating and Developing Policy' (2022) https://ukpandemicethics.org/wp-content/uploads/2022/04/Place-IF.pdf, accessed 11 January 2023

Laville S, 'Ella Kissi-Debrah: New Inquest Granted into "Air Pollution" Death' (2019) https://www.theguardian.com/uk-news/2019/may/02/ella-kissi-debrah-new-inquest-granted-into-air-pollution-death, accessed 5 January 2024

Lorde A, *Sister Outsider: Essays and Speeches* (The Crossing Press 1984)

Marmot M, 'An Inverse Care Law for Our Time' (2018) 363 BMJ k3216

Marmot M and others, 'Fair Society, Healthy Lives: The Marmot Review' (2010) https://www.instituteofhealthequity.org/resources-reports/fair-society-healthy-lives-the-marmot-review/fair-society-healthy-lives-full-report-pdf.pdf, accessed 11 January 2024

Marmot M, 'Health Equity in England: The Marmot Review 10 Years On' (2020) https://www.health.org.uk/publications/reports/the-marmot-review-10-years-on, accessed 11 January 2024

MBRRACE-UK, 'Saving Lives, Improving Mothers' Care: Lessons Learned to Inform Maternity Care from the UK and Ireland Confidential Enquiries into Maternal Deaths and Morbidity 2014–2016' (2018) https://www.npeu.ox.ac.uk/mbrrace-uk/presentations/saving-lives-improving-mothers-care, accessed 11 January 2024

MBRRACE-UK, 'Saving Lives, Improving Mothers' Care: Lessons Learned to Inform Maternity Care from the UK and Ireland Confidential Enquiries into Maternal Deaths and Morbidity 2017–18' (2020) https://www.npeu.ox.ac.uk/mbrrace-uk/presentations/saving-lives-improving-mothers-care, accessed 11 January 2024

Mirza HS (ed), *Black British Feminism: A Reader* (Taylor & Francis 1997)

NHS England, 'Our Approach to Reducing Healthcare Equalities' (nd) england.nhs.uk/about/equality/equality-hub/national-healthcare-inequalities-improvement-programme/our-approach-to-reducing-healthcare-inequalities/, accessed 11 January 2024

Olivera JN and others, 'Conceptualisation of Health Inequalities by Local Healthcare Systems: A Document Analysis' (2022) 30 Health Soc Care Comm e3977

Ottersen OP and others, 'The Political Origins of Health Inequity: Prospects for Change' (2014) 383 Lancet 630

Royal College of Paediatrics and Child Health, 'Reg 28 Ella Adoo Kissi-Debrah RCPH Response' (2021) https://www.rcpch.ac.uk/sites/default/files/2021-06/RCPCH-response-Reg-28-assistant-coroner-report-EAKD.pdf, accessed 9 January 2024

Smith CA and others, 'Cite Black Women: A Critical Praxis (A Statement)' (2021) 2 Fem Anthropol 10

Smith KE, Bambra C and Hill SE (eds), *Health Inequalities: Critical Perspectives* (OUP 2015)

Townsend Centre for International Poverty Research, 'Alternative Top Ten Tips for Health' www.bristol.ac.uk/poverty/healthinequalities.html, accessed 11 January 2024

Venkatapuram S, 'Global Justice and the Social Determinants of Health' (2010) 24 Ethics Int Aff 119

WHO (World Health Organization), 'Closing the Gap in a Generation: Health Equity through Action on the Social Determinants of Health: Commission on Social Determinants of Health Final Report' (2008) https://www.who.int/publications/i/item/WHO-IER-CSDH-08.1

WHO 'Constitution' (nd) https://www.who.int/about/governance/constitution, accessed 11 January 2024

Williams E and others, 'What Are Health Inequalities?' https://www.kingsfund.org.uk/publications/what-are-health-inequalities, accessed 11 January 2024

Willoughby C, 'Running Away from Drapetomania: Samuel A. Cartwright, Medicine, and Race in the Antebellum South' (2018) 84 J S Hist 579

5

Health Disparities, Equity, and Pandemic Ethics

Harleen Kaur Johal and Sabrina Germain

The COVID-19 pandemic did not create new disparities in health – it exacerbated the long-standing inequity affecting historically disadvantaged groups of people.[1] In this chapter we explore how vulnerable groups were disproportionately impacted by the burden of disease, and how healthcare policy may have worsened health disparities for marginalised members of society who struggle to engage with healthcare services because of various barriers to access that uniquely affect them. We use the COVID-19 pandemic as a case study to evaluate how healthcare policy, from national public health measures to triage guidance, indirectly discriminated against people from ethnic minorities, women, and people with cognitive impairment.

First, we must distinguish 'equity' – a key term that will be used throughout this chapter – from 'equality'. These terms are used interchangeably but there are important distinctions between the two. 'Equality' can be thought of as 'sameness',[2] or formal equality.[3] A policy that promotes equality will treat everyone in the same way. This might mean that resources are distributed equally – that is, everyone is given the same (amount of a) resource. By contrast, 'equity' can be described as promoting 'fairness'[4] or 'substantial equality',[5] and an equitable policy will distribute resources in a way that meets individual

1 COVID-19 refers to coronavirus disease – the infectious disease caused by the SARS-CoV-2 virus. Sabrina Germain and Adrienne Yong (eds), *Beyond the Virus: Multidisciplinary and International Perspectives on Inequalities Raised by COVID-19* (Bristol University Press 2023).

2 Conversely, 'inequality' recognises that differences exist.

3 Both equality and equity are concerned with equality in treatment; these concepts are often used interchangeably.

4 By contrast, 'inequity' acknowledges that any differences that exist are unfair. Though there is much philosophical debate around the meaning of 'fairness', which in itself is sometimes taken to mean 'sameness', engaging with these debates is beyond the scope of this chapter.

5 Both equity and substantial equality are concerned with equality of outcomes; these concepts are often used interchangeably.

Figure 5.1: 'Equal' distribution of resources to individuals versus 'equitable' distribution of resources (based on individual need)

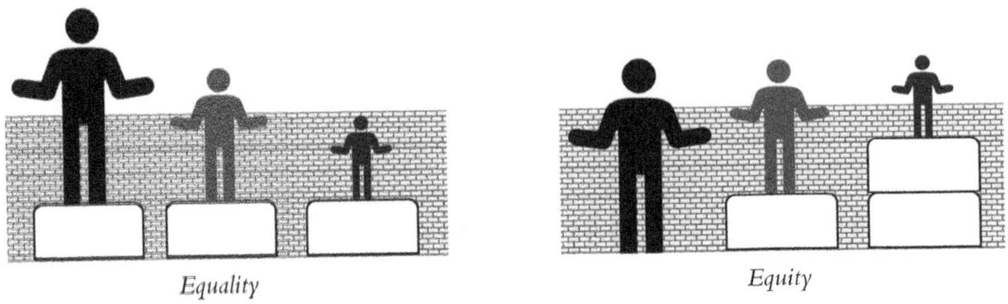

needs.[6] Equality is based on the assumption that everyone needs the same amount of resource in order to benefit; however, equity recognises that different people have different needs and will therefore require different (amounts of) resources in order to achieve an equal outcome (see Figure 5.1). Equity therefore naturally aligns with social justice. Working towards 'health equity' requires resources to be distributed in a way that meets individual needs, so that all people can achieve the best health.[7]

In this chapter, we first consider how healthcare law and policy is developed and implemented in the UK. This will improve our understanding of how healthcare systems are structured, how policy makers operate, and who puts policy into practice. Following this discussion, we demonstrate how intersectionality, as an analytical framework, provides insight into how health disparities occur and how and why healthcare law and policy is inequitable. We then unpack the health disparities that were exacerbated by the COVID-19 pandemic, before analysing the reasons for these disparities, by discussing how various members of society are affected differently by the same law and policy (using COVID-19-related policy as an example). Finally, we consider how the restructuring of the delivery of healthcare services following the pandemic may improve health inequity.

Healthcare law and policy development and implementation

UK healthcare services are publicly funded through general taxation and provided free at the point of use. All 'ordinary residents'[8] have access to the NHS based

6 David Takeuchi and others, 'Equality and Equity: Expanding Opportunities to Remedy Disadvantage' (2018) 42 Generations 13.

7 Paula Braveman, 'What are Health Disparities and Health Equity? We Need To Be Clear' (2014) 129 Public Health Rep 5.

8 DHSC (Department of Health and Social Care), 'Guidance on Implementing the Overseas Visitor Charging Regulations' (2018) https://assets.publishing.service.gov.uk/government/uploads/system/uploads/attachment_data/file/767905/guidance-on-implementing-the-overseas-visitor-charging-regulations.pdf, accessed 29 August 2023.

Figure 5.2: Healthcare policy in England

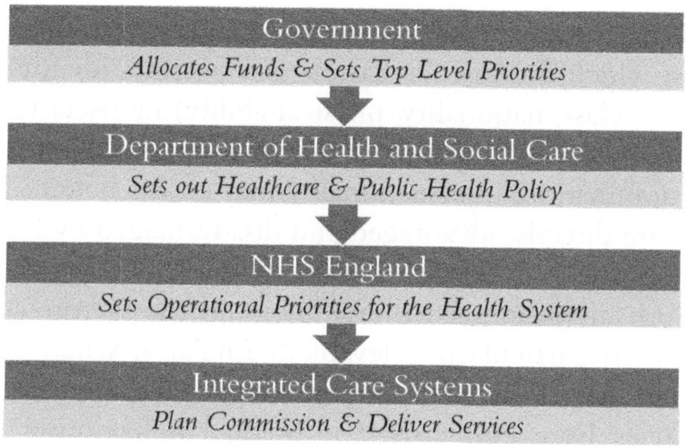

on need rather than ability to pay, 'irrespective of gender, race, disability sexual orientation, religion, belief, gender reassignment, pregnancy, and maternity or marital or civil partnership status'.[9]

The devolved governments of Scotland, Wales, and Northern Ireland each have responsibility for the organisation and delivery of healthcare services within their territory.[10] In England, the government sets top-level priorities and, through parliament, allocates a budget to the Department of Health and Social Care (DHSC), which is overseen by a senior minister appointed as the Secretary of State for Health and Social Care. In turn, the Secretary of State is accountable to parliament for the performance and the central planning policy objectives for NHS England.

The majority of the DHSC's budget is dedicated to resourcing NHS England. With these resources in hand, NHS England sets operational priorities for Integrated Care Systems, the entities responsible for the planning and delivery of healthcare services in a set geographical area.[11] See Figure 5.2 for how this all fits together.

Rules outside the legislative sphere, enclosed in ethical guidance and regulations formulated by professional medical bodies also have a substantial impact on individual experiences in healthcare and inequalities in accessing healthcare services.

With an improved understanding of the process of healthcare law and policy development, we can discuss how intersectionality is a useful analytical framework for critically analysing policy.

---

9 Ibid.

10 Gwyn Bevan, 'The impacts of asymmetric devolution on health care in the four countries of the UK', (2014) https://www.health.org.uk/sites/default/files/TheImpactsOf AsymmetricDevolutionOnHealthCareInFourCountriesUK.pdf, accessed 29 November 2023.

11 NHS England, 'What Are Integrated Care Systems?' (nd) https://www.england.nhs.uk/integratedcare/what-is-integrated-care/, accessed 1 September 2023.

Intersectionality in healthcare law and policy

As discussed in the introduction of this book, intersectionality recognises the different ways in which the various aspects of a person's identity (e.g., gender, ethnicity, sexuality, class, nationality, physical ability) intersect to create unique forms of privilege and discrimination.[12] Through this recognition of structural oppression and domination, intersectionality may enable better identification of individuals who are directly advantaged and disadvantaged by healthcare policy in diverse populations.[13]

Identifying both disadvantaged individuals and the factors contributing to inequitable health is particularly relevant in England, where national health promotion policies have long been criticised for having limited success. Health promotion policies have emphasised individual behavioural changes (e.g., smoking cessation and improved diet) and focused on politics of blame,[14] without adequately addressing the 'upstream' social determinants of health (e.g., having sufficient income to purchase healthy food or having the education and resources needed to make decisions about health).[15] Intersectionality conversely scrutinises how systems of power, which oppress certain groups, limit access to these social determinants of health and thus worsen health inequity. As a framework, intersectionality has the potential to inform policy makers where the greatest health vulnerability is in society, what resources are needed, and where these resources ought to be focused.[16]

Employing intersectionality in healthcare law and policy development could help identify and address health inequity. More detailed frameworks – such as the Intersectionality-Based Policy Analysis Framework – have been proposed by academics, but these have not been widely implemented.[17] This lack of traction could be attributed to critics' concerns about the theoretical foundations of intersectionality. Its focus on unique experience and individual narratives perhaps makes intersectionality unworkable when developing population-level policy.[18]

12 Kimberlé Crenshaw, 'Demarginalizating the Intersection of Race and Sex: A Black Feminist Critique of Antidiscrimination Doctrine, Feminist Theory, and Antiracist Politics' (1989) 140 U Chi Leg F 139.

13 Olena Hankivsky and others, 'An Intersectionality-Based Policy Analysis Framework: Critical Reflections on a Methodology for Advancing Equity' (2014) 13 Int J Equity Health 119.

14 Robert Crawford, 'You are Dangerous to Your Health: The Ideology and Politics of Victim Blaming' (1977) 7 Int J Health Serv 663.

15 Fran Baum and Matthew Fisher, 'Why Behavioural Health Promotion Endures Despite its Failure to Reduce Health Inequities' (2014) 36 Soc Health Illn 213.

16 Gita Sen, Aditi Iyer, and Chandan Mukherjee, 'A Methodology to Analyse the Intersections of Social Inequalities in Health' (2009) 10 J Hum Dev Capabil 397.

17 Hankivsky and others (n13).

18 Daniel Holman and others, 'Can Intersectionality Help with Understanding and Tackling Health Inequalities? Perspectives of Professional Stakeholders' (2021) 19 Health Res Policy and Syst 97.

Irrespective of these concerns, our objective is to critically analyse COVID-19 healthcare law and policy retrospectively through an intersectional lens, rather than using intersectionality as a tool to propose or develop new law or policy.

We now have an overview of the processes through which healthcare law and policy have historically been developed within the UK and a relevant tool to identify the issues within these processes. We can therefore shift our attention towards the health disparities that were arguably exacerbated by healthcare law and policy implemented during the COVID-19 pandemic.

Health disparities unmasked by COVID-19

Early in the COVID-19 pandemic, reports emerged that certain groups had poorer outcomes from SARS-CoV-2 infection. In the UK, the greatest disparity was caused by age; however, notable disparities pertaining to ethnicity, occupation, and location were also identified. A Public Health England (PHE) report confirmed that people from racialised groups were most likely to be diagnosed with COVID-19.[19] Mortality rates were highest among Black and then Asian ethnic minority groups,[20] with the risk of mortality estimated as being 10–50 per cent higher than among people of white ethnicity. Occupational risk of mortality from COVID-19 was highest among taxi drivers, bus and coach drivers, construction workers, and workers in social care. Geographically, the highest COVID-19 death rates were in deprived, urban areas.[21]

The correlation between socio-economic disadvantage and poorer COVID-19 outcomes was evident; however, the reasons for this association were nuanced. A second PHE report, looking at the disproportionate impact on ethnic minorities, suggested that the overrepresentation of ethnic minorities in 'low-skilled' jobs and their reliance on public transport increased their risk of exposure to SARS-CoV-2. Living in intergenerational households or in crowded housing conditions further increased this risk. Higher rates of underlying cardiometabolic disease, caused by smoking and poor diet, also contributed to the likelihood of contacting more severe disease.[22] The British Medical Association (BMA) – the

19 PHE (Public Health England), 'Disparities in the Risk and Outcomes of COVID-19' (2020) https://assets.publishing.service.gov.uk/government/uploads/system/uploads/attachment_data/file/908434/Disparities_in_the_risk_and_outcomes_of_COVID_August_2020_update.pdf, accessed 1 September 2023.

20 The language used to write about race and ethnicity is constantly changing. We have chosen to use the term 'ethnic minorities', as per national recommendations at the time of writing this chapter, though we recognise that 'ethnic minorities' within the UK may be part of the global ethnic majority.

21 PHE (n19).

22 PHE (Public Health England), 'Beyond the Data: Understanding the Impact of COVID-19 on BAME Groups' (2020) https://assets.publishing.service.gov.uk/government/uploads/system/uploads/attachment_data/file/892376/COVID_stakeholder_engagement_synthesis_beyond_the_data.pdf, accessed 1 September 2023.

leading trade union for doctors in the UK – observed that of the healthcare workers that had died from COVID-19, the vast majority were from ethnic minority backgrounds.[23] While the PHE report acknowledged that fear of racial discrimination within the NHS might have prevented healthcare workers from voicing their concerns about occupational exposure to SARS-CoV-2,[24] the report was widely criticised as it made no recommendations on how these issues or disparities should be tackled.[25]

If we view these disparities through an intersectional lens, we can see that individuals who experienced multiple forms of disadvantage were disproportionately impacted by COVID-19. However, it was not just COVID-19 that exacerbated health disparities. The pandemic saw exceptional circumstances arise for healthcare policy making, which impacted the allocation of NHS resources.[26] The system had always aimed to provide equal access to services for all; however, it was destabilised as the public health emergency mandated that resources be distributed based on chances of survival of patients rather than need. Non-COVID-19-related healthcare interventions were immensely affected, mostly in the areas of preventive and acute care, which saw many of their activities suspended.[27] The consequences continue to be felt, with growing waiting lists for non-urgent planned care. In 2022, over six million patients in England were waiting for an intervention.[28]

In the following sections, we explore why healthcare law and policies (and guidance)[29] implemented during COVID-19 were inequitable. The discussion spotlights two of the most contentious pandemic policy issues: lockdown and triage.

The impact of COVID-19 public health measures on vulnerable groups

The UK government, like others around the world, imposed public health interventions in March 2020 to limit the spread of COVID-19. At the time of the first wave, no effective treatments or vaccines had been discovered, and thus

23 Sakkaf Ahmed Aftab, 'Tackling COVID-19's Effect on BAME Doctors' (2020) https://www.bma.org.uk/news-and-opinion/tackling-covid-19-s-effect-on-bame-doctors, accessed 18 June 2023.

24 PHE (n22).

25 Gareth Iacobucci, 'COVID-19: PHE Review Has Failed Ethnic Minorities, Leaders Tell BMJ' (2020) 369 BMJ m2264.

26 Sabrina Germain, 'The Role of Medical Professionals in Shaping Healthcare Law during COVID-19' (2021) 3 Amicus Curiae 33.

27 Sabrina Germain, 'Will COVID-19 Mark the End of an Egalitarian National Health Service?' (2020) 11 Eur J Risk Regul 358.

28 Michael Anderson and others, 'United Kingdom: Health System Review' (2022) 24 Health Syst Transit 1.

29 National policy on triage decisions was not developed and multiple forms of ethical guidance emerged.

social distancing measures were introduced to prevent spread.[30] These emergency measures were set out in the Coronavirus Act 2020. The Act enabled a radical reallocation of healthcare resources to support the frontline NHS response to COVID-19.

As soon as the Coronavirus Bill was introduced in parliament, advocacy groups began raising alarms over the reallocation of healthcare resources and the infringement of civil liberties as a result of lockdown.[31] Disability rights' activists worried about the implications of suspending the Care Act 2014, which temporarily released local authorities from their legal duty to provide social care and support to vulnerable people.[32] Mental health advocates pushed back against the modifications to the Mental Health Act 1983 (MHA 1983), which would require only one doctor (rather than two) to detain someone for diagnosis or treatment in a mental health hospital.[33] As advocacy groups typically focus on specific issues affecting particular groups of people, press releases and articles written by different advocacy groups highlighted concerns with the Coronavirus Bill and presented these problems as a single-axis issue. This arguably promoted the interests of majority narratives within disadvantaged groups, rather than identifying the subgroups of people that were most likely to be disadvantaged by these policies.[34] For instance, articles authored by Liberty,[35] Disability Rights UK,[36] and the British Institute of Human Rights acknowledged the greater risk of inappropriate detention under the MHA 1983.[37] Yet, there was no acknowledgement of how this might disproportionately impact racially minoritised groups, despite national datasets demonstrating that Black people are most likely to be detained.[38] By contrast, the Synergi Collaborative Centre, which aims to tackle the multiple forms of disadvantage experienced by people from ethnic minorities with severe

30 WHO (World Health Organization), 'Coronavirus Disease (COVID-19)' (2023) https://www.who.int/health-topics/coronavirus, accessed 1 June 2023.

31 Liberty, 'Coronavirus Bill: Liberty Responds to "Drastic Reimagining of State Powers"' (2020) https://www.libertyhumanrights.org.uk/issue/coronavirus-bill-liberty-responds-to-drastic-reimagining-of-state-powers/, accessed 18 June 2023.

32 Disability Rights UK, 'Suspension of the Care Act – Act Immediately' (2020) https://www.disabilityrightsuk.org/news/2020/march/suspension-care-act-act-immediately, accessed 18 June 2023.

33 Katrin McEntee, 'What The Coronavirus Bill Could Mean For Mental Health' (2020) https://eachother.org.uk/what-the-coronavirus-bill-could-mean-for-mental-health/, accessed 18 June 2023.

34 Silke Roth, 'Intersectionality and Coalitions in Social Movement Research: A Survey and Outlook' (2021) 15 Sociol Compass e12885.

35 Liberty, 'Coronavirus: Mental Health and Social Care' (2020) https://www.libertyhumanrights.org.uk/issue/coronavirus-mental-health/, accessed 18 June 2023.

36 Disability Rights UK (n32).

37 McEntee (n33).

38 UK Government, 'Detentions under the Mental Health Act' (2023) https://www.ethnicity-facts-figures.service.gov.uk/health/mental-health/detentions-under-the-mental-health-act/latest, accessed 18 June 2023.

mental illness, published an article acknowledging the risk at this intersection.[39] This suggested that policy makers were failing to protect the rights of people affected by multiple forms of disadvantage, and advocacy groups – focusing on single-axis issues – were also unsuccessful in promoting their interests.

This phenomenon can be described as 'intersectional invisibility', where 'possessing multiple subordinate-group identities renders a person "invisible" relative to those with a single subordinate-group identity'.[40] The consequences of intersectional invisibility became more evident as the COVID-19 pandemic progressed. While women had better survival rates following SARS-CoV-2 infection overall,[41] they were disproportionately impacted by the effects of lockdown. As schools had closed to most children, the persistence of gendered cultural norms caused childcare responsibilities to largely fall on women, which increased their levels of psychological distress. This effect became more pronounced among single mothers.[42] The temporary suspension of national cancer-screening programmes in the UK may have also disproportionately affected women, with the number of breast cancer diagnoses having seen the most significant decline.[43] Women and birthing people's experiences of maternity services during the pandemic were also largely negative.[44] Yet as Germain and Yong note, ethnicity and migrant status amplified and exacerbated these issues.[45] Institutional barriers, such as legal concerns about migrant status and the inaccessibility of patient-facing literature for non-English speaking patients, persisted. Language barriers became more harmful in the context of ever-changing public health messages regarding the developing COVID-19 situation.[46] This could partly explain why SARS CoV-2 infection affected ethnic minority pregnant people more severely. Despite recommendations from the Royal College of Obstetricians and Gynaecologists that eligible pregnant people should be vaccinated, ~98 per cent of women admitted to hospital from February to

---

39 J. Nazroo and K. Bhui, 'New Coronavirus Act May Increase the Mental Health Detention of Ethnic Minority People' (2020) https://legacy.synergicollaborativecentre.co.uk/new-coronavirus-act-may-increase-the-mental-health-detention-of-ethnic-minority-people/, accessed 18 June 2023.

40 Valerie Purdie-Vaughns and Richard Eibach, 'Intersectional Invisibility: The Distinctive Advantages and Disadvantages of Multiple Subordinate-Group Identities' (2008) 59 Sex Roles 377.

41 PHE (n22).

42 Sonia Oreffice and Climent Quintana-Domeque, 'Gender Inequality in COVID-19 Times: Evidence from UK Prolific Participants' (2021) 87 J Demogr Econ 261.

43 Stephen Duffy and others, 'The Projected Impact of the COVID-19 Lockdown on Breast Cancer Deaths in England due to the Cessation of Population Screening: A National Estimation' (2022) 126 Brit J Cancer 1355

44 Anna Nelson and Elizabeth Chloe Romanis, 'The Medicalisation of Childbirth and Access to Homebirth in the UK: COVID-19 and Beyond' (2021) 29 Med Law Rev 661.

45 Germain and Yong (n1).

46 Adrienne Yong and Sabrina Germain, 'Ethnic Minority and Migrant Women's Struggles in Accessing Healthcare during COVID-19: An Intersectional Analysis' (2022) 26 J Cult Res 65.

September 2021 with COVID-19 had not been vaccinated, and over half of the pregnant people admitted were from ethnic minority backgrounds.[47] Looking beyond inequity in women's health, the impact of lockdown on young people was noted. Higher rates of depressive and anxious symptoms were recorded among young people, as compared to pre-pandemic rates. Poorer mental health outcomes were also noted in young people who experienced additional forms of disadvantage, such as having a chronic illness or being neurodiverse.[48]

Neutrality at policy level during the pandemic – on issues pertaining to children, neurodivergence, ethnicity, migrant status, and gender – has since been widely criticised.[49] A failure to acknowledge potential obstacles faced by vulnerable groups resulted in the development and implementation of 'one-size-fits-all' national policy that did not meet the differing needs of vulnerable populations. These policy issues were identified early, as human rights organisations called for 'the most vulnerable to be put first', having recognised that 'some groups [were] underserved' by the Coronavirus Bill.[50] Where policy changes were suggested, they focused on single-axis issues (e.g., the effect on women or migrant workers), in keeping with Strolovitch's observation that advocacy groups commonly prioritise the welfare of their most advantaged members.[51] It is possible that policy makers and advocates exacerbated health disparities by best serving individuals who were already comparatively advantaged by their socio-political characteristics.

Indirect discrimination in triage guidance

Despite the unprecedented nature of the public health crisis, a national ethical framework, outlining rules for the triaging of finite resources like critical care, was not provided by NHS England.[52] This normative vacuum was filled by professional bodies – ranging from the National Institute for Health and Care Excellence (NICE) to the BMA and academic groups – who produced guidance out of necessity. Yet, in the rush to produce guidance that could support clinicians making difficult decisions, the impact of these ethical recommendations on vulnerable individuals was arguably overlooked, leading to indirect discrimination against the already disadvantaged.

---

47 Sanaa Zayyan and Charlotte Frise, 'COVID-19 in Pregnancy: A UK Perspective' (2022) 15 Obstet Med 216.

48 Hasina Samji and others, 'Review: Mental Health Impacts of the COVID-19 Pandemic on Children and Youth: A Systematic Review' (2022) 27 Child Adolesc Ment Health 173.

49 Gabriela Lotta and others, 'Gender, Race, and Health Workers in the COVID-19 Pandemic' (2021) 397 Lancet 1264; Rakhee Shah and Michael Absoud, 'The Failure of Provision for Neurodiverse Children during the COVID-19 Pandemic' (2021) 375 BMJ n2711.

50 Amnesty International UK, 'UK: Government's Coronavirus Bill Explained' (2020) https://www.amnesty.org.uk/coronavirus/uk-coronavirus-bill-explained, accessed 10 July 2023.

51 Dara Strolovitch, *Affirmative Advocacy: Race, Class, and Gender in Interest Group Politics* (University of Chicago Press 2007).

52 Zoe Fritz and others, 'Ethical Road Map through the COVID-19 Pandemic' (2020) 369 BMJ m2033.

The first iteration of the NICE guideline for critical care in adults, published in March 2020, was amended following the threat of judicial review from disability groups.[53] NICE had initially recommended the use of the Clinical Frailty Scale – a judgement-based scoring system adopted by clinicians to screen for frailty in older people[54] – to help identify patients to whom it may not have been appropriate to offer hospital treatment (see Box 5.1). The guideline suggested a cut-off score of 5 or more (which indicated 'mild frailty'), though critics suggested that this discriminated against adults with chronic cognitive impairment caused by learning disabilities or neurodivergence.[55] Subsequent versions of the guideline declared the Clinical Frailty Scale to be inappropriate for assessing frailty in 'younger people, people with stable long-term disability ... learning disabilities, or autism'.[56] However, Paton also raised concerns about the NICE guideline's weighting of underlying health conditions, such as cardiovascular disease, as factors that could help determine whether escalation to critical care was appropriate for patients with COVID-19.[57] Notwithstanding their clinical relevance, conditions such as cardiovascular disease and diabetes are particularly prevalent among Black and South Asian groups.[58] Yet these conditions are preventable, as they are associated with modifiable risk factors (e.g., diet, smoking, physical activity). The ability to prevent these diseases is, however, contingent on addressing 'upstream' determinants such as health illiteracy and language barriers.[59]

Box 5.1: Key text: Admission to critical care – COVID-19 rapid guideline: critical care (NG159)

Involve critical care teams in discussions about admission to critical care for a patient where:

53 Hodge Jones & Allen, 'NICE Amends COVID-19 Critical Care Guideline after Judicial Review Challenge' (2020) https://www.hja.net/expert-comments/blog/personal-injury/nice-amends-covid-19-critical-care-guideline-after-judicial-review-challenge/, accessed 10 July 2023.

54 Kenneth Rockwood and others, 'A Global Clinical Measure of Fitness and Frailty in Elderly People' (2005) 173 Can Med Assoc J 495.

55 Jordan A. Parsons and Harleen Kaur Johal, 'Best Interests versus Resource Allocation: Could COVID-19 Cloud Decision-Making for the Cognitively Impaired?' (2020) 46 J Med Ethics 447.

56 NICE (National Institute for Health and Care Excellence), 'COVID-19 Rapid Guideline: Managing COVID-19' (2021) https://www.nice.org.uk/guidance/ng191, accessed 10 July 2023.

57 Alexis Paton, 'Fairness, Ethnicity, and COVID-19 Ethics' (2020) 17 J Bioeth Inq 595.

58 Veena Raleigh, 'The Health of People from Ethnic Minority Groups in England' (2023) https://www.kingsfund.org.uk/publications/health-people-ethnic-minority-groups-england, accessed 10 July 2023.

59 Ibid.

- the Clinical Frailty Scale score suggests the person is less frail (for example the score is less than 5), they are likely to benefit from critical care organ support, and they want critical care treatment; or
- the Clinical Frailty Scale score suggests the person is more frail (for example the score is 5 or more), there is uncertainty regarding the likely benefit of critical care organ support, and critical care advice is needed to help the decision about treatment.

Take into account the impact of underlying pathologies, comorbidities, and severity of acute illness on the likelihood of critical care treatment achieving the desired outcome.

Several inferences can be drawn from the NICE example. The first is that the use of standardised scoring systems in triage guidance could have propagated discrimination against already disadvantaged groups. A second conclusion is – as per Paton's argument[60] – that clinical guidelines do not sufficiently acknowledge health disparities or the social determinants of health. A final observation is that, in its original version, the NICE guideline inadvertently discriminated against people with stable cognitive impairment *and* people with underlying health conditions that are more prevalent among Black and South Asian ethnic minorities. This could have resulted in, for example, ethnic minority patients with a learning disability (that might increase dependency) and/or stable cardiovascular disease (that is described as a severe comorbidity) being excluded from critical care. Though the NICE guideline was quickly amended and is unlikely to have been utilised in practice, data from the Intensive Care National Audit and Research Centre (ICNARC) report on COVID-19 until July 2020 indicated that the patients from ethnic minority backgrounds admitted to critical care had lower incidence of severe comorbidity (excluding renal disease) and lower dependency prior to admission than the white patients who were also admitted.[61] As the white patients who were admitted to ICU had more severe underlying health conditions, this could indicate that, occasionally, patients from ethnic minority groups may have been excluded from critical care when white patients with similar (or worse) health conditions were admitted.[62]

---

60 Paton (n57).

61 ICNARC (Intensive Care National Audit and Research Centre), 'ICNARC Report on COVID-19 in Critical Care' (2020) https://www.icnarc.org/Our-Audit/Audits/Cmp/Reports, accessed 22 May 2023.

62 Harleen Kaur Johal, Rachel Prout, and Marianne Tinkler, 'Indirect Racial Discrimination in COVID-19 Ethical Guidance' (2020) https://blogs.bmj.com/medical-ethics/2020/08/14/indirect-racial-discrimination-in-covid-19-ethical-guidance/, accessed 12 July 2023.

Although direct racial discrimination is unlawful per the Equality Act 2010,[63] racial biases have been shown to exist amongst healthcare professionals.[64] Indeed, racism,[65] sexism,[66] and ableism have all been identified as prevalent issues in the NHS.[67] If ethical guidance emphasises the prioritisation of resources for COVID-19 patients with high chances of survival or a 'capacity to benefit quickly',[68] and vulnerable groups (e.g., the elderly, ethnic minorities) have been identified as being at greater risk of death from COVID-19, this is arguably problematic. It becomes even more problematic when guidance is then interpreted and implemented in ways that perpetuate the biases of individual healthcare professionals regarding who is likely to benefit from these resources. In the UK, this may well have contributed to the introduction of blanket 'do not attempt resuscitation' orders in care homes.[69]

Critiquing utilitarian approaches to pandemic ethics

Throughout the pandemic, public health policy and guidance focused on maximising population survival. Ethical guidance suggested that indirect discrimination may have been justifiable, if 'more lives and more years of life' were saved.[70] This focus, on maximising population outcomes, aligned with the ethical theory of utilitarianism, which seeks to maximise the wellbeing of the greatest number of people (see Figure 5.3). It also arguably reflected non-utilitarian views, which intrinsically value human life.[71]

Defenders of utilitarian ethics suggest that utilitarianism seeks to avoid the influence of individual biases, emotions, and assumptions that may prevent the maximisation of utility, in favour of considering more objective criteria such as probability of survival, likely duration of treatment, and efficacy of available

63 Race and ethnicity are protected characteristics.

64 Chloë FitzGerald and Samia Hurst, 'Implicit Bias in Healthcare Professionals: A Systematic Review' (2017) 18 BMC Med Ethics 19.

65 Tim Tonkin, 'Racism an Issue in NHS, Finds Survey' (2022) https://www.bma.org.uk/news-and-opinion/racism-an-issue-in-nhs-finds-survey, accessed 16 July 2023.

66 BMA (British Medical Association), 'A Joint Pledge to End Sexism in Medicine' (2023) https://www.bma.org.uk/end-sexism, accessed 20 August 2023.

67 Deborah Fenney, 'Tackling Ableism in Health Care: The Role of Primary Care' (2023) https://www.kingsfund.org.uk/blog/2023/06/tackling-ableism-health-care-role-primary-care, accessed 20 August 2023.

68 BM,A (British Medical Association), 'COVID-19 – Ethical Issues: A Guidance Note' (2020) https://www.bma.org.uk/media/2226/bma-covid-19-ethics-guidance.pdf, accessed 16 July 2023.

69 Hannah Bows and Jonathan Herring, 'DNACPR Decisions during COVID-19: An Empirical and Ethical Study' (2022) 30 Med Law Rev 60.

70 Ezekiel Emanuel and others, 'Fair Allocation of Scarce Medical Resources in the Time of COVID-19' (2020) 382 N Engl J Med 2049.

71 Ibid.

Figure 5.3: Utilitarianism: the morally right course is when a person or a group of people (e.g., an organisation or government) creates rules ('rule' utilitarianism) or perform an action ('act' utilitarianism) that produces the greatest good for the greatest number of people

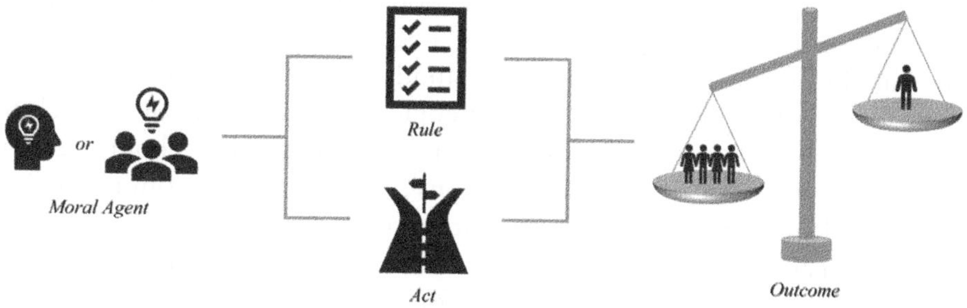

resources.[72] Further, utilitarianism emphasises impartiality and equality,[73] which seem relevant to addressing inequity. However, the theory does not sufficiently consider questions of distributive justice – that is, how resources should be fairly distributed for *equity*. This is significant, as treating all people impartially or equally, without considering their individual differences and needs, could result in the worst off becoming more disadvantaged (see Figure 5.1). Whether impartiality can truly be achieved has long been challenged, as it requires healthcare professionals to separate themselves from their relationships, including their obligations to care for the patients directly in front of them.[74] Indeed, overvaluing impartiality may create a bias towards agents (e.g., racially privileged, adult men), who are less oppressed in society and therefore more likely to be able to be able to maintain impartiality, as their decisions are less influenced by relationships where there is unequal power.[75]

Moreover, the idea that using objective criteria counters the influence of individual biases on decision-making is limited by the observation that seemingly objective criteria (e.g., trajectory of illness, severity of disease) are inherently subjective or biased. Physicians have been shown to vary considerably in how they estimate and communicate what should be expected over the course of illness in other conditions, which in turn affects their subsequent treatment recommendations.[76] Further, established diagnostic techniques – such as pulse

72 Julian Savulescu, Ingmar Persson, and Dominic Wilkinson, 'Utilitarianism and the Pandemic' (2020) 34 Bioethics 620.

73 Ibid.

74 Margaret Urban Walker, *Moral Contexts* (Rowman & Littlefield 2003).

75 Eva Feder Kittay, *Love's Labor: Essays on Women, Equality, and Dependency* (Routledge 2019).

76 Darin Zahuranec and others, 'Variability in Physician Prognosis and Recommendations after Intracerebral Hemorrhage' (2016) 86 Neurology 1864.

oximetry (i.e., a non-invasive test for monitoring the oxygen saturation levels in a person's blood) – have been found to inaccurately measure oxygen saturation levels in people with darker skin, resulting in underestimation of the severity of COVID-19 among ethnic minorities, who were already disproportionately more likely to develop severe SARS-CoV-2 infection. A failure to adequately recruit ethnic minorities into the initial studies investigating pulse oximetry likely contributed to this diagnostic inaccuracy and bias.[77] On the issue of research, Emanuel and colleagues suggested that 'people who participate in research to prove the safety and effectiveness of vaccines and therapeutics should receive some priority for COVID-19 interventions'.[78] Again, this recommendation is influenced by utilitarianism, as this prioritisation is regarded as a reward for research participation, to encourage others to participate in research. Yet this recommendation does not account for the lasting issues of mistrust in the research process that the historic maltreatment of ethnic minorities and people with disabilities through medical research has created,[79] nor does it take into consideration that research studies often have strict eligibility criteria pertaining to underlying health conditions. Potential research participants are therefore less likely to be from ethnic minority backgrounds or have chronic conditions,[80] thus the recommendation that research participants should have some priority may have once again led to the systematic deprioritisation of disadvantaged individuals.

The application of abstract ethical theory, such as utilitarianism, is not sufficiently sensitive to the social, economic, and political realities of our world. A review of non-utilitarian approaches to triage suggests that alternatives to utilitarianism (e.g., systems based on: egalitarianism, a first-come-first-served basis, or giving priority to the most in need or worst off) also fail to overcome issues of racial or socio-economic bias.[81] Even outwardly attractive options, such as Rawls' difference principle, which suggests that policies should most benefit the least-advantaged members of society, creates potential social, economic, and political contention in defining who the least advantaged members of society are.[82] Daniels contends that in Rawls' account, health justice requires the fair distribution of the social

77 Ashraf Fawzy and others, 'Racial and Ethnic Discrepancy in Pulse Oximetry and Delayed Identification of Treatment Eligibility among Patients with COVID-19' (2022) 182 JAMA Int Med 730.

78 Emanuel and others (n70).

79 Harriet Washington, *Medical Apartheid: The Dark History of Medical Experimentation on Black Americans from Colonial Times to the Present* (Doubleday 2008).

80 Mahvash Hussain-Gambles, Karl Atkin, and Brenda Leese, 'Why Ethnic Minority Groups are Under-Represented in Clinical Trials: A Review of the Literature' (2004) 12 Health Soc Care Comm 382.

81 Benjamin Tolchin, Sarah Hull, and Katherine Kraschel, 'Triage and Justice in an Unjust Pandemic: Ethical Allocation of Scarce Medical Resources in the Setting of Racial and Socioeconomic Disparities' (2021) 47 J Med Ethics 200.

82 John Rawls, *A Theory of Justice* (Harvard University Press 1971).

determinants of health.[83] In view of our reflections on health inequity aggravated by the COVID-19 pandemic, it is imperative that healthcare law, policy, and guidance shift towards addressing what we know to be the wider causative factors of poor health. How this will be achieved is beyond the scope of our discussion, though greater emphasis on relational ties and fostering social networks may improve health outcomes. The latest redesign of the health and social care systems seems to acknowledge the importance of social connection and local networks, but details around the implementation of this reform are yet to come. Nevertheless, it is worth examining this new law and policy in greater detail.

Future delivery of healthcare services in England

In November 2020, the Conservative government published its plans to change the structure of the health and social care system with the introduction of new legislation. The reform proposition was put forward in an effort to increase integration of services, improve the management of resources, and increase quality of care.[84] As the policy was in preparation, the backdrop of the pandemic highlighted the urgency for the NHS to better address needs of marginalised, vulnerable, and local populations.

In July 2022, the implementation of the reform was initiated. The Health and Care Act 2022 dictated that all 135 existing Clinical Commissioning Groups, which had been responsible for the purchasing of healthcare services, be abolished and replaced by 42 Integrated Care Systems (ICSs), which were now in charge of healthcare commissioning and strategy for the allocation of healthcare resources across the entire territory.[85] Although some ICSs had formed organically as early as 2016, they had a new statutory footing and the official mandate to plan and deliver health and social care services for populations ranging from 500,000 to 3 million people in a set geographical area.[86] Emphasis was put on collaboration, with the aims to 'improve outcomes in population health and health care; tackle inequalities in outcomes, experiences, and access to services; enhance productivity and value for money; and help the NHS support broader social and economic development'.[87]

---

83 Norman Daniels, *Just Health Care* (CUP 1985).

84 NHS England, 'Integrating Care: Next Steps to Building Strong and Effective Integrated Care Systems across England' (2021) https://www.england.nhs.uk/wp-content/uploads/2021/01/integrating-care-next-steps-to-building-strong-and-effective-integrated-care-systems.pdf, accessed 1 September 2023.

85 Anna Charles, 'Integrated Care Systems Explained: Making Sense of Systems, Places and Neighbourhoods' (2022) https://www.kingsfund.org.uk/publications/integrated-care-systems-explained, accessed 1 September 2023.

86 Pheobe Dunn and others, 'Integrated Care Systems: What Do They Look Like?' (2022) https://www.health.org.uk/publications/long-reads/integrated-care-systems-what-do-they-look-like, accessed 29 November 2023.

87 NHS England (n84).

Figure 5.4: The functions of Integrated Care Systems

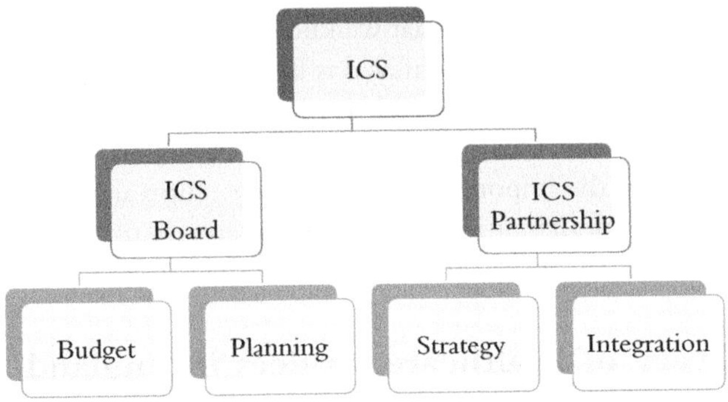

ICSs have been designed with the expectation that they could more accurately identify and more efficiently tackle health inequalities.[88] ICSs' functions are twofold. Firstly, they handle the planning and commissioning of services with their Integrated Care Boards (ICBs). Secondly, they develop strategy for integration for the delivery of health and social care with local government and other agencies through the Integrated Care Partnerships.[89] Figure 5.4 illustrates the functions of Integrated Care Systems.

Other organisations at lower and more local tiers also support ICSs in finding joined-up solutions for a more integrated approach between commissioners and providers.[90] GP surgeries are coming together in Neighbourhoods to form Primary Care Networks.[91] They are encouraged to work collaboratively with other community stakeholders to offer a wider range of services than individual primary care providers would if working in isolation (see later in this chapter). ICS Places are the wider areas hosting Neighbourhoods; they provide a space for NHS organisations to engage with local government, residents, charities, and NHS partners to articulate strategies and work more widely on socio-economic health determinants (see Figure 5.5 for a visual representation of ICS structures).

The benefits of integrated care have already been observed (see Box 5.2). In Slough (a town characterised by its ethnic diversity), efforts to identify deprivation and, accordingly, the local population's needs, have resulted in more targeted

88 NHS England, '2022/23 Priorities and Operational Planning Guidance' (2022) https://www.england.nhs.uk/wp-content/uploads/2022/02/20211223-B1160-2022-23-priorities-and-operational-planning-guidance-v3.2.pdf, accessed 1 September 2023.

89 NHS England, 'Integrated Care Systems: Design Framework' (2021) https://www.england.nhs.uk/wp-content/uploads/2021/06/B0642-ics-design-framework-june-2021.pdf, accessed 1 September 2023.

90 Charles (n85).

91 NHS England, 'Working Together at Scale: Guidance on Provider Collaboratives' (2021) https://www.england.nhs.uk/wp-content/uploads/2021/06/B0754-working-together-at-scale-guidance-on-provider-collaboratives.pdf, accessed 1 September 2023.

Figure 5.5: The structures of Integrated Care Systems

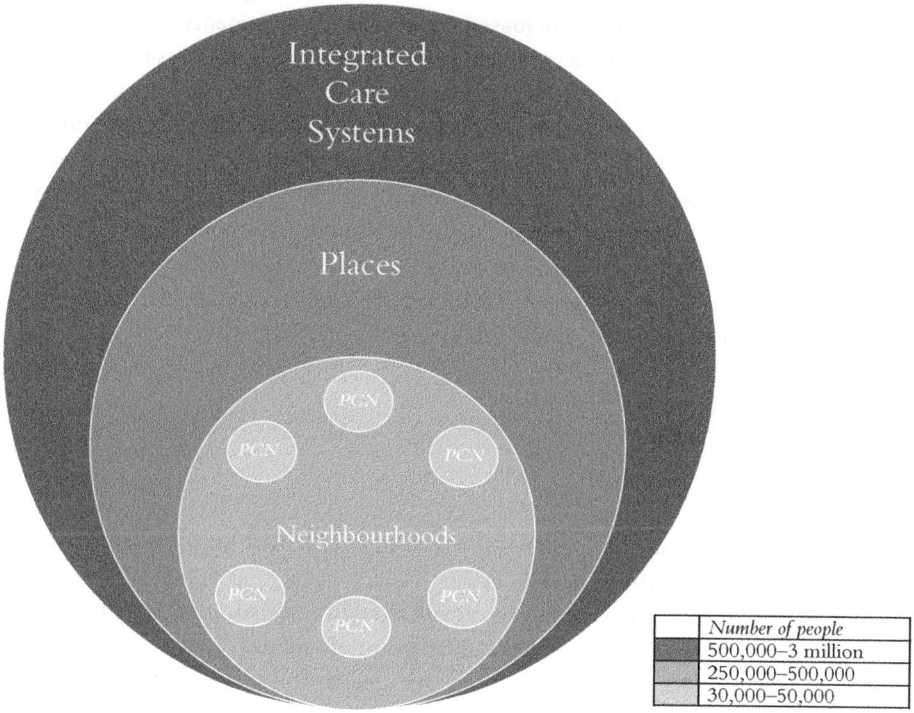

interventions through social prescribing (also known as community referral, this allows GPs, nurses, and other healthcare providers to direct individuals to various local non-medical services to better address their needs).[92] This has improved population health outcomes. This approach, which focuses on identifying and addressing the perceived needs of different communities (e.g., fuel poverty, digital inaccessibility), may (re)build trust in healthcare providers by improving access to the wider socio-economic determinants of health. Thus, taking a more local, community-based approach may be best suited to addressing the needs of marginalised groups.

Box 5.2: Key text: Frimley Health and Care ICB case study: addressing health inequalities in Slough through social prescribing

'69% of Frimley Health and Care ICB's deprived population lives in Slough ... In line with the [national approach] to reducing healthcare inequalities, residents living in

[92] Priya Kumar, 'Addressing Health Inequalities in Slough through Social Prescribing' (2023) https://www.england.nhs.uk/blog/addressing-health-inequalities-in-slough-through-social-prescribing/, accessed 28 August 2023.

the most deprived areas, with multiple chronic conditions including diabetes and hypertension, were identified through a population health management approach, and asked to take part in a questionnaire [based on the wider determinants of health]. This [helped] identify those who were most likely to benefit from a needs assessment and the support as well as identify areas of perceived burden [...] Responses and subsequent targeted interventions were all coded digitally to create a powerful dataset that informed social commissioning offer through richer, deeper insights into patient reported needs [...] Following interventions from [their] social prescribing link workers there has been an increase in the number of completed health checks among [their] diabetic and hypertensive population. There was also a reduction in [emergency department] presentations, NHS 111 and emergency calls and inpatient admissions for those who completed the questionnaire.' (Kumar, 2023)

Summary

- We have examined the historical development and implementation of healthcare policy in the UK.
- Using the analytical framework of intersectionality, we sought to demonstrate that various members of society might be affected differently by the same policy, and those who are already disadvantaged or vulnerable may experience more negative impacts from policy that does not adequately account for their needs.
- We suggest that the future development of healthcare policy and delivery of healthcare services is more hopeful, as ICSs have started to tackle healthcare inequity by addressing the wider social determinants of health.

Questions for reflection

1. Should we take an intersectional approach in the design of healthcare policy, guidance, and laws?
2. Do utilitarian approaches in healthcare law and policy development adequately address challenges around health inequity?
3. Do you agree that equality in healthcare provision is easier to achieve than equity in healthcare?

Recommended resources

- Annabel Sowemimo, *Divided: Racism, Medicine and Why We Need to Decolonise Healthcare* (Wellcome Collection 2023) chapter 9.
- Keisha Ray, 'When Black Health, Intersectionality, and Health Equity Meet a Pandemic' (2023) J Bioeth Inquiry https://link.springer.com/article/10.1007/s11673-023-10299-8, accessed 4 July 2024.

- The Health Foundation, 'The Continuing Impact of COVID-19 on Health and Inequalities' (2022) https://www.health.org.uk/publications/long-reads/the-continuing-impact-of-covid-19-on-health-and-inequalities, accessed 29 November 2023.
- The King's Fund, 'How Does the NHS in England Work and How is it Changing?' (2022) https://www.kingsfund.org.uk/audio-video/how-does-nhs-in-england-work, accessed 29 November 2023.
- Laura Richman, *Relational Health* (CUP 2023), chapter 6.
- Ali Ely Yamin, *When Misfortune Becomes Injustice* (Stanford University Press 2023).

Bibliography

Aftab SA, 'Tackling COVID-19's Effect on BAME Doctors' (2020) https://www.bma.org.uk/news-and-opinion/tackling-covid-19-s-effect-on-bame-doctors, accessed 18 June 2023

Amnesty International UK, 'UK: Government's Coronavirus Bill Explained' (2020) https://www.amnesty.org.uk/coronavirus/uk-coronavirus-bill-explained, accessed 10 July 2023

Anderson M and others, 'United Kingdom: Health System Review 2022' (2022) 24 Health Syst Transit 1

Baum F and Fisher M, 'Why Behavioural Health Promotion Endures Despite its Failure to Reduce Health Inequities' (2014) 36 Soc Health Illn 213

Bevan G, 'The Impacts of Asymmetric Devolution on Health Care in the Four Countries of the UK' (2014) https://www.health.org.uk/sites/default/files/TheImpactsOfAsymmetricDevolutionOnHealthCareInFourCountriesUK.pdf, accessed 29 November 2023

BMA (British Medical Association), 'COVID-19 – Ethical Issues: A Guidance Note' (2020) https://www.bma.org.uk/media/2226/bma-covid-19-ethics-guidance.pdf, accessed 16 July 2023

BMA (British Medical Association), 'A Joint Pledge to End Sexism in Medicine' (2023) https://www.bma.org.uk/end-sexism, accessed 20 August 2023

Bows H and Herring J, 'DNACPR Decisions during COVID-19: An Empirical and Ethical Study' (2022) 30 Med Law Rev 60

Braveman P, 'What are Health Disparities and Health Equity? We Need to Be Clear' (2014) 129 Public Health Rep 5

Charles A, 'Integrated Care Systems Explained: Making Sense of Systems, Places and Neighbourhoods' (2022) https://www.kingsfund.org.uk/publications/integrated-care-systems-explained, accessed 1 September 2023

Crawford R, 'You are Dangerous to Your Health: The Ideology and Politics of Victim Blaming' (1977) 7 Int J Health Serv 663

Crenshaw K, 'Demarginalizating the Intersection of Race and Sex: A Black Feminist Critique of Antidiscrimination Doctrine, Feminist Theory, and Antiracist Politics' (1989) 140 U Chicago Leg F 139

Daniels N, *Just Health Care* (CUP 1985)

DHSC (Department of Health and Social Care), 'Guidance on Implementing the Overseas Visitor Charging Regulations' (2018) https://assets.publishing.service.gov.uk/government/uploads/system/uploads/attachment_data/file/767905/guidance-on-implementing-the-overseas-visitor-charging-regulations.pdf, accessed 29 August 2023

Disability Rights UK, 'Suspension of the Care Act – Act Immediately' (2020) https://www.disabilityrightsuk.org/news/2020/march/suspension-care-act-act-immediately, accessed 18 June 2023

Duffy SW and others, 'The Projected Impact of the COVID-19 Lockdown on Breast Cancer Deaths in England due to the Cessation of Population Screening: A National Estimation' (2022) 126 Brit J Cancer 1355

Dunn P and others, 'Integrated Care Systems: What Do They Look Like?' (2022) https://www.health.org.uk/publications/long-reads/integrated-care-systems-what-do-they-look-like, accessed 29 August 2023

Emanuel EJ and others, 'Fair Allocation of Scarce Medical Resources in the Time of COVID-19' (2020) 382 N Engl J Med 2049

Fawzy A and others, 'Racial and Ethnic Discrepancy in Pulse Oximetry and Delayed Identification of Treatment Eligibility among Patients with COVID-19' (2022) 182 JAMA Int Med 730

Fenney D, 'Tackling Ableism in Health Care: The Role of Primary Care' (2023) https://www.kingsfund.org.uk/blog/2023/06/tackling-ableism-health-care-role-primary-care, accessed 20 August 2023

FitzGerald C and Hurst S, 'Implicit Bias in Healthcare Professionals: A Systematic Review' (2017) 18 BMC Med Ethics 19

Fritz Z and others, 'Ethical Road Map through the COVID-19 Pandemic' (2020) 369 BMJ m2033

Germain S, 'Will COVID-19 Mark the End of an Egalitarian National Health Service?' (2020) 11 Eur J Risk Regul 358

Germain S, 'The Role of Medical Professionals in Shaping Healthcare Law during COVID-19' (2021) 3 Amicus Curiae 33

Germain S and Yong A, *Beyond the Virus: Multidisciplinary and International Perspectives on Inequalities Raised by COVID-19* (Bristol University Press 2023)

Hankivsky O and others, 'An Intersectionality-Based Policy Analysis Framework: Critical Reflections on a Methodology for Advancing Equity' (2014) 13 Int J Equity Health 119

Hodge Jones & Allen, 'NICE Amends COVID-19 Critical Care Guideline after Judicial Review Challenge' (2020) https://www.hja.net/expert-comments/blog/personal-injury/nice-amends-covid-19-critical-care-guideline-after-judicial-review-challenge/, accessed 10 July 2023

Holman D and others, 'Can Intersectionality Help with Understanding and Tackling Health Inequalities? Perspectives of Professional Stakeholders' (2021) 19 Health Res Policy and Syst 97

Hussain-Gambles M, Atkin K, and Leese B, 'Why Ethnic Minority Groups are Under-Represented in Clinical Trials: A Review of the Literature' (2004) 12 Health Soc Care Comm 382

Iacobucci G, 'COVID-19: PHE Review Has Failed Ethnic Minorities, Leaders Tell BMJ' (2020) 369 BMJ m2264

ICNARC (Intensive Care National Audit and Research Centre), 'ICNARC Report on COVID-19 in Critical Care' (2020) https://www.icnarc.org/Our-Audit/Audits/Cmp/Reports, accessed 22 May 2023

Johal HK, Prout R, and Tinkler M, 'Indirect Racial Discrimination in COVID-19 Ethical Guidance' (2020) https://blogs.bmj.com/medical-ethics/2020/08/14/indirect-racial-discrimination-in-covid-19-ethical-guidance/, accessed 12 July 2023

Kittay EF, *Love's Labor: Essays on Women, Equality, and Dependency* (Routledge 2019)

Kumar P, 'Addressing Health Inequalities in Slough through Social Prescribing' (2023) https://www.england.nhs.uk/blog/addressing-health-inequalities-in-slough-through-social-prescribing/, accessed 28 August 2023

Liberty, 'Coronavirus Bill: Liberty Responds to "Drastic Reimagining of State Powers"' (2020) https://www.libertyhumanrights.org.uk/issue/coronavirus-bill-liberty-responds-to-drastic-reimagining-of-state-powers/, accessed 18 June 2023

Liberty, 'Coronavirus: Mental Health and Social Care' (2020) https://www.libertyhumanrights.org.uk/issue/coronavirus-mental-health/, accessed 18 June 2023

Lotta G and others, 'Gender, Race, and Health Workers in the COVID-19 Pandemic' (2021) 397 Lancet 1264

McEntee K, 'What the Coronavirus Bill Could Mean for Mental Health' (2020) https://eachother.org.uk/what-the-coronavirus-bill-could-mean-for-mental-health/, accessed 18 June 2023

Nazroo J and Bhui K, 'New Coronavirus Act May Increase the Mental Health Detention of Ethnic Minority People' (2020) https://legacy.synergicollaborativecentre.co.uk/new-coronavirus-act-may-increase-the-mental-health-detention-of-ethnic-minority-people/, accessed 18 June 2023

Nelson A and Romanis EC, 'The Medicalisation of Childbirth and Access to Homebirth in the UK: COVID-19 and Beyond' (2021) 29 Med Law Rev 661

NHS England, 'Integrating Care: Next Steps to Building Strong and Effective Integrated Care Systems across England' (2021) https://www.england.nhs.uk/wp-content/uploads/2021/01/integrating-care-next-steps-to-building-strong-and-effective-integrated-care-systems.pdf, accessed 1 September 2023

NHS England, 'Integrated Care Systems: Design Framework' (2021) https://www.england.nhs.uk/wp-content/uploads/2021/06/B0642-ics-design-framework-june-2021.pdf, accessed 1 September 2023

NHS England, 'Working Together at Scale: Guidance on Provider Collaboratives' (2021) https://www.england.nhs.uk/wp-content/uploads/2021/06/B0754-working-together-at-scale-guidance-on-provider-collaboratives.pdf, accessed 1 September 2023

NHS England, '2022/23 Priorities and Operational Planning Guidance' (2022) https://www.england.nhs.uk/wp-content/uploads/2022/02/20211223-B1160-2022-23-priorities-and-operational-planning-guidance-v3.2.pdf, accessed 1 September 2023

NHS England, 'What Are Integrated Care Systems?' (nd) (https://www.england.nhs.uk/integratedcare/what-is-integrated-care/, accessed 1 September 2023

NICE (National Institute for Health and Care Excellence), 'COVID-19 Rapid Guideline: Managing COVID-19' (2021) https://www.nice.org.uk/guidance/ng191, accessed 10 July 2023

Oreffice S and Quintana-Domeque C, 'Gender Inequality in COVID-19 Times: Evidence from UK Prolific Participants' (2021) 87 J Dem Econ 261

Parsons JA and Johal HK, 'Best Interests versus Resource Allocation: Could COVID-19 Cloud Decision-Making for the Cognitively Impaired?' (2020) 46 J Med Ethics 447

Paton A, 'Fairness, Ethnicity, and COVID-19 Ethics' (2020) 17 J Bioeth Inq 595

PHE (Public Health England), 'Beyond the Data: Understanding the Impact of COVID-19 on BAME Groups' (2020) https://assets.publishing.service.gov.uk/government/uploads/system/uploads/attachment_data/file/892376/COVID_stakeholder_engagement_synthesis_beyond_the_data.pdf, accessed 1 September 2023

PHE (Public Health England), 'Disparities in the Risk and Outcomes of COVID-19' (2020) https://assets.publishing.service.gov.uk/government/uploads/system/uploads/attachment_data/file/908434/Disparities_in_the_risk_and_outcomes_of_COVID_August_2020_update.pdf, accessed 1 September 2023

Purdie-Vaughns V and Eibach RP, 'Intersectional Invisibility: The Distinctive Advantages and Disadvantages of Multiple Subordinate-Group Identities' (2008) 59 Sex Roles 377

Raleigh V, 'The Health of People from Ethnic Minority Groups in England' (2023) https://www.kingsfund.org.uk/publications/health-people-ethnic-minority-groups-england, accessed 10 July 2023

Rawls J, *A Theory of Justice* (Harvard University Press 1971)

Rockwood K and others, 'A Global Clinical Measure of Fitness and Frailty in Elderly People' (2005) 173 Can Med Assoc J 495

Roth S, 'Intersectionality and Coalitions in Social Movement Research: A Survey and Outlook' (2021) 15 Sociol Compass e12885

Samji H and others, 'Review: Mental Health Impacts of the COVID-19 Pandemic on Children and Youth: A Systematic Review' (2022) 27 Child Adolesc Ment Health 173

Savulescu J, Persson I, and Wilkinson D, 'Utilitarianism and the Pandemic' (2020) 34 Bioeth 620

Sen G, Iyer A, and Mukherjee C, 'A Methodology to Analyse the Intersections of Social Inequalities in Health' (2009) 10 J Hum Dev Cap 397

Shah R and Absoud M, 'The Failure of Provision for Neurodiverse Children during the COVID-19 Pandemic' (2021) 375 BMJ n2711

Strolovitch DZ, *Affirmative Advocacy: Race, Class, and Gender in Interest Group Politics* (University of Chicago Press 2007)

Takeuchi DT and others, 'Equality and Equity: Expanding Opportunities to Remedy Disadvantage' (2018) 42 Generations 13

Tolchin B, Hull S, and Kraschel K, 'Triage and Justice in an Unjust Pandemic: Ethical Allocation of Scarce Medical Resources in the Setting of Racial and Socioeconomic Disparities' (2021) 47 J Med Ethics 200

Tonkin T, 'Racism an Issue in NHS, Finds Survey' (BMA, 2022) https://www.bma.org.uk/news-and-opinion/racism-an-issue-in-nhs-finds-survey, accessed 16 July 2023

UK Government, 'Detentions under the Mental Health Act' (2023) https://www.ethnicity-facts-figures.service.gov.uk/health/mental-health/detentions-under-the-mental-health-act/latest, accessed 18 June 2023

Walker MU, *Moral Contexts* (Rowman & Littlefield 2003)

Washington HA, *Medical Apartheid: The Dark History of Medical Experimentation on Black Americans from Colonial Times to the Present* (Doubleday 2006)

WHO (World Health Organization), 'Coronavirus Disease (COVID-19)' (2023) https://www.who.int/health-topics/coronavirus, accessed 1 June 2023

Yong A and Germain S, 'Ethnic Minority and Migrant Women's Struggles in Accessing Healthcare during COVID-19: An Intersectional Analysis' (2022) 26 J Cult Res 65

Zahuranec DB and others, 'Variability in Physician Prognosis and Recommendations after Intracerebral Hemorrhage' (2016) 86 Neurology 1864

Zayyan S and Frise C, 'COVID-19 in Pregnancy: A UK Perspective' (2022) 15 Obstet Med 216

6

Ethics, Health(care), and Climate Change

Joshua Parker

Modern healthcare systems, marked by their complexity, scale, and reliance on advanced technology, are increasingly recognised as having a substantial environmental footprint.[1] Climate change and environmental degradation pose significant threats to life on earth, including to human health.[2] This creates a tension for modern healthcare: in striving to protect health, healthcare generates emissions and environmental waste which in turn undermine health.

In a speech for the World Health Organization (WHO), its Director-General Tedros Adhanom Ghebreyesus labelled this tension an 'irony':

> The world's health sector facilities churn out CO_2 … this is perhaps ironic – as medical professionals our commitment is to 'first, do no harm'. Places of healing should be leading the way, not contributing to the burden of disease.[3]

I summarise this 'irony' in the following three claims:

(1) Healthcare's primary goal is to protect and promote health.
(2) Modern healthcare systems make a significant contribution to climate change.
(3) Climate change threatens health.

---

1 Manfred Lenzen and others, 'The Environmental Footprint of Health Care: A Global Assessment' (2020) 4 Lancet Planet Health e271.

2 IPCC (Intergovernmental Panel on Climate Change), 'The Physical Science Basis of Climate Change' (2021) https://www.ipcc.ch/report/sixth-assessment-report-working-group-i/, accessed 13 November 2023.

3 WHO (World Health Organization), '72nd World Health Assembly, Geneva, Switzerland' (2019) https://www.pscp.tv/w/1lDGLrerprqxm?t=1h6m38s, accessed 13 November 2023, at minute 39.

A question raised by this 'ironic triad' is: *who* should do *what* to tackle climate change? The relationship between health, healthcare, and climate change raises ethical questions like this one, and in this chapter I aim to explore such ethical questions.

The *who* question refers to healthcare systems and practitioners but may also include patients and wider society. Three main policies to address climate change encompass the 'what' question. Mitigation tackles the causes of climate change by reducing emissions or enhancing carbon sinks. To help individuals cope with climate change that is inevitable, adaptation is required. Compensation is a response to the victims of climate change. Some examples will help illuminate these responses. If we switch inhalers that contain greenhouse gases to those that do not, this would be considered mitigation. Ensuring that hospitals are resilient to flooding or extreme heat is adaptation. Providing healthcare to the victims of climate change might count as part of a compensation package. In this chapter we will think about mitigation.

The chapter is divided into two parts. The first part explores the problem at the heart of the ironic triad. I call this a 'Red Queen problem': it leaves healthcare running to stand still. Mitigation is the main way that healthcare systems can address the Red Queen problem. But mitigation raises three big questions about what healthcare should do in the face of climate change (Box 6.1). I reflect on each of these questions in the second section.

Box 6.1: Three key questions for ethicists and policy makers raised by healthcare systems addressing their emissions through mitigation

1. The burden-sharing question: what is a fair share of the burdens (and benefits) for healthcare systems in adopting policies to tackle climate change?
2. The individual responsibilities question: what responsibilities do healthcare systems, practitioners, patients, and others have to reduce the carbon footprint of healthcare?
3. The promotional duties question: to what extent should healthcare systems and clinicians engage in political means to reduce carbon emissions?

In this chapter, I aim to help readers understand the nature of the problem raised within the ironic triad. The triad raises questions of fairness in how healthcare systems respond to the triad, and so I want to explore how we might go about answering these ethical questions. The bioethical issues that are raised as healthcare systems recognise their role in climate change and the implications for healthcare are emerging and it is important to clarify the issues and lay out potential avenues for responding to these.

The Red Queen problem

In this section I explain the nature of the problem at the heart of the ironic triad. Then I consider some ways healthcare might resolve this problem. First, however, I will say something very brief by way of defence of each of the claims within the ironic triad.

The Intergovernmental Panel on Climate Change (IPCC) states: 'it is unequivocal that human influence has warmed the atmosphere, ocean and land'.[4] In terms of healthcare's contribution to climate change, globally healthcare is thought to account for 4.4 per cent of emissions.[5] Imagine healthcare is a country; then healthcare would rank as the 5th worst emitter on the planet, sitting above Japan but beneath Russia.[6] In 2019, the NHS in England was responsible for 25 megatons of CO_2 equivalent.[7] Some healthcare systems have larger carbon footprints. In the US, healthcare accounts for 10 per cent of all emissions, for instance.[8]

The NHS in England was the first healthcare system to declare ambitions to reduce emissions by 80 per cent and become net zero for emissions under its control by 2040.[9] Various legislation underpins how the NHS in England tackles its emissions.[10] As of 13 November 2023, 69 nations have committed to sustainable low-carbon health systems and 28 have committed to net-zero health systems.[11]

Climate change has been described as 'the biggest global health threat of the 21st century'.[12] Health is damaged by climate change through numerous interacting threats. For instance, climate change is expected to cause 250,000 additional deaths per year, from malnutrition, malaria, diarrhoea, and heat stress.[13]

---

4 IPCC (n2).

5 Health Care Without Harm, 'Health Care's Climate Footprint' (2019) https://noharm-europe.org/ClimateFootprintReport, accessed 13 November 2023. See also Lenzen and others (n1).

6 Health Care Without Harm (n5).

7 Imogen Tennison and others, 'Health Care's Response to Climate Change: A Carbon Footprint Assessment of the NHS in England' (2021) 5 Lancet Planet Health e84.

8 Jeanette Chung and David Meltzer, 'Estimate of the Carbon Footprint of the US Health Care Sector' (2009) 302 JAMA 1970.

9 Greener NHS, 'Delivering a "Net Zero" National Health Service' (2020) https://www.england.nhs.uk/greenernhs/wp-content/uploads/sites/51/2020/10/delivering-a-net-zero-national-health-service.pdf, accessed 13 November 2023.

10 Climate Change Act 2008 and Health and Care Act 2022.

11 WHO (World Health Organization), 'Alliance for Transformative Action on Climate and Health' (2023) https://www.who.int/initiatives/alliance-for-transformative-action-on-climate-and-health/country-commitments, accessed 13 November 2023.

12 Anthony Costello and others, 'Managing the Health Effects of Climate Change: Lancet and University College London institute for Global Health Commission' (2009) 373 Lancet 1693.

13 WHO (World Health Organization), 'Climate Change and Health' (2021) https://www.who.int/news-room/fact-sheets/detail/climate-change-and-health, accessed 13 November 2023.

Moreover, extreme weather events are predicted to undermine the social and environmental determinants of health by threatening air quality, safe drinking water, adequate nutritious food, and secure shelter; not to mention by displacing people and its effects on global poverty.[14]

I assume my first claim – that the goal of healthcare is to protect and promote health – is uncontroversial. But it is worth keeping in mind that climate change is a global phenomenon primarily affecting low- and middle-income countries, and some emissions can assert their effects for hundreds or even thousands of years. When healthcare systems aim to improve health, they aren't typically thinking of the health of people who may be born in the future or in other countries. Though climate change will still pose more local threats, it is worth noting the gap between the clinical encounter and where the effects of emissions from care settings are felt most keenly. What this gap means is that the relatively narrow scope healthcare systems usually take cannot serve as the core guiding reason for addressing their emissions.

Understanding the Red Queen problem

How should we understand the tension raised by this 'ironic triad'? My answer is as a Red Queen problem.

The idea to describe this problem as a Red Queen problem is taken from Lewis Carroll's book *Through the Looking Glass*. Alice is in a race with the Red Queen and despite running as fast as she can, Alice finds she remains in the same place. Eventually, the Red Queen says to Alice: 'Now, here, you see, it takes all the running you can do, to keep in the same place.'[15] Alice must keep running to keep pace with the Red Queen and yet she is also standing still. I think healthcare is in a similar position.

Climate change threatens to undermine health and yet healthcare systems make a contribution to climate change. This situation is perverse as healthcare appears to simultaneously both meet and frustrate its goals. Climate change means healthcare must work harder, and yet healthcare contributes to climate change. Providing healthcare, like running for Alice, is not futile or self-defeating, however. Healthcare can still achieve its goals, but its emissions make it harder.

Framing the challenge that the relationship among health, healthcare, and climate change poses as a Red Queen problem opens numerous ways of tackling it. Each claim of the triad could be addressed individually, or perhaps they should be taken as a whole. I discuss the ethical implications for electing mitigation as the route to solve the Red Queen problem. Though, as the discussion should reveal, addressing claim 2 from the Red Queen problem (p 116) through mitigation has implications for the first and third claims.

---

14 Costello and others (n12); Nick Watts and others, 'Health and Climate Change: Policy Responses to Protect Public Health' (2015) 386 Lancet 1861.

15 Lewis Carroll, *Through the Looking Glass* (Penguin 1871), ch 2.

Mitigation raises normative questions because mitigation in healthcare carries burdens. Resource-intensive health systems are built on emissions. Fundamental changes to what, where, and how healthcare is delivered are necessary to reduce healthcare.[16] For instance, hospital-based healthcare is far more carbon intensive than primary care, and preventative medicine has an even lower carbon footprint than the latter. Some suggest that 'lean [health] service delivery',[17] prevention rather than cure, as well avoiding so-called overdiagnosis and other forms of low-value care are central to low-carbon healthcare.[18] A further burden is the upfront costs associated with low-carbon healthcare transformation through, for example, technologies, innovation, system redesign, and changes in healthcare provision. One example is technologies designed to reduce the carbon footprint of nitrous oxide during childbirth through capture and destruction. These have been quoted at AU$46,000 for a single mobile unit.[19] In some cases, low-carbon alternatives may represent higher ongoing costs. Replacing cheaper inhalers that contain greenhouse gases for more expensive ones that do not contain greenhouse gases when treating respiratory illness provides one pertinent example.[20] Such burdens raise a question about what the fair share of the benefits and burdens of healthcare systems reducing their emissions are. One further question concerns the duty-bearers, given that some decarbonisation efforts will also require behaviour change from patients and professionals alike, such as switching inhalers. Finally, if mitigation in healthcare alone is insufficient to sever the connection between climate change and poor health, should health professionals and institutions rally others to adopt policies to mitigate climate change? I now address each of these questions.

Three normative questions arising from the Red Queen problem

The burden-sharing question

Let us examine the burden-sharing question at the level of institutional responsibilities and healthcare systems.

16 Chris Naylor and John Appleby, 'Environmental Sustainability in Health and Social Care' (2012) https://assets.kingsfund.org.uk/f/256914/x/5087eae6fd/sustainable_health_and_social_care_march_2012.pdf, accessed 13 November 2023.

17 Frances Mortimer, 'The Sustainable Physician' (2010) 10 Clin Med 110.

18 Alexandra Barratt and Forbes McGain, 'Overdiagnosis is Increasing the Carbon Footprint of Healthcare' (2021) 375 BMJ n2407.

19 Alice Gynther and others, 'Nitrous Oxide Use on the Labour Ward: Efficacy and Environmental Impact' (2021) Australasian Anaesthesia 183, 188.

20 Alexander Wilkinson and others, 'Costs of Switching to Low Global Warming Potential Inhalers: An Economic and Carbon Footprint Analysis of NHS Prescription Data in England' (2019) 9 BMJ Open e028763.

The question of a healthcare system doing its fair share when it comes to addressing climate change comes down to an issue of healthcare exceptionalism: to what extent (if any) should the morally valuable goals of healthcare form an exception to mitigation responsibilities? Should healthcare emissions be treated differently compared to other sources of emissions because healthcare serves a socially important purpose? Answering this is about how to balance the goals of healthcare on the one hand, with mitigation responsibilities on the other. Finding the balance can get quite technically and philosophically involved. I simplify things here to give readers a sense both of *how* we can go about resolving this as well as what each of these methods might have to say. Articles that provide greater detail are in the further reading list, for the interested reader.

Broadly, with two competing issues we have two ways to balance them. One method is to treat the issues separately and prioritise one over the other: the goals of healthcare could be put above mitigation responsibilities, or vice versa. Alternatively, we can combine these two issues. This gives three different types of argument we could make. The first two treat mitigation and the goals of healthcare as independent issues. For one we could argue that the goals of healthcare are irrelevant to what healthcare systems should do to reduce its emissions. Alternatively, one could argue that healthcare's role in protecting health means we should exempt healthcare from mitigation responsibilities. A third kind of argument tries to integrate these concerns by limiting what healthcare systems should be expected to do about their emissions in light of its goals.

Here's a simplified way to think about the exceptionalism question. One argument says healthcare emissions should be treated differently – we should give healthcare emissions a free pass and others should pull in the emissions slack to tackle global climate change. Another argument says healthcare emissions are no different to any other, so healthcare should mitigate just the same as everyone else. A final type of argument tries to bring these two perspectives together and argues that sometimes healthcare emissions should be thought of as different but not in other circumstances. Let's go through more detailed examples of these sorts of arguments.

One principle frequently used in debates about climate change is a polluter-pays principle. The idea behind this is straightforward enough: those who make a mess should clean it up.[21] Notice that the criteria for undertaking mitigation is being a polluter, meaning it relies on an ideal of formal equality. Equals are treated equally and the criterion of equality, in this instance, is being a polluter. As a polluter, healthcare is met with neither favour nor discrimination on the basis of its morally valuable role. As the goals and role of healthcare are irrelevant to whether it is a polluter, a polluter-pays principle provides an example of arguments that separate mitigation burdens and the goals of healthcare.

21 Henry Shue, *Climate Justice: Vulnerability and Protection* (OUP 2014) 182–3.

One key difficulty with the polluter-pays principle arises from the fact that healthcare emissions follow a social gradient. The poorest 10 per cent in England use ten times more of their annual CO_2 emissions on healthcare compared to the wealthiest 10 per cent.[22] In other words, as a proportion of their total annual *per capita* emissions, the most disadvantaged in England use around 20 per cent of their annual emissions on healthcare compared to 2 per cent in the wealthiest decile. The worry is that a polluter-pays principle, which is unconcerned with the goals of healthcare, is insensitive to the distribution of mitigation burdens (and healthcare benefits) and so may disproportionately impact socio-economically disadvantaged people and exacerbate existing social inequalities.

If we are worried that a polluter-pays principle treats disadvantaged people unfairly, we could make healthcare exempt from mitigation burdens. Like polluter pays, this kind of argument also treats mitigation burdens and the goals of healthcare separately, but in this case, it is the goals of healthcare that are put first.

Many people think that healthcare is *special*.[23] By 'special', the thought is that because healthcare plays a unique and important role in social justice it should be treated differently compared to other areas of social justice, such as poverty, education, or housing. We could extend this kind of argument to climate change, claiming that as healthcare is special it should be treated differently than other industries such as aviation or fashion.

Norman Daniels provides perhaps the most comprehensive and discussed account of the idea that healthcare is special.[24] Daniels' main argument is that one important goal of justice is to protect opportunity. Daniels sees health as key to protecting opportunity and, as healthcare protects health, then healthcare must also be significant in this chain. Empirical work on the social determinants of health has challenged Daniels' view.[25] If working conditions, poverty, social isolation, and so forth have a greater impact on health than healthcare, how can healthcare be considered special? Daniels responded to this by extending the specialness thesis to cover social determinants, claiming that any 'health need' was special.[26]

Herein lies the problem when we attempt to separate climate justice from health(care) justice. If 'health needs' are special and this justifies treating healthcare separately from mitigation burdens, how do we maintain this distinction in light of the environmental determinants of health, mediated in part by climate change and driven partially by healthcare itself? To simplify, if healthcare is bad for health because it contributes to climate change, how can we justify treating healthcare as special on the basis that it protects health?

---

22 Anand Bhopal and others, 'How Do We Decarbonise Fairly? Emissions, Inequities and the Implications for Net Zero Healthcare' (2022) 115 J R Soc Med 337, 338.

23 Shlomi Segall, 'Is Health Care (Still) Special?' (2007) 15 J Pol Philos 342, 343–7.

24 Norman Daniels, *Just Health: Meeting Health Needs Fairly* (CUP 2007) 29–78.

25 Michael Marmot, 'Social Determinants of Health Inequalities' (2005) 365 Lancet 1099.

26 Daniels (n24) 29–78.

A further point worth noting is that considering healthcare in the mechanisms of producing ill-health through climate change may also inform our view on the justice of those institutions. Rawls, famously, argues that the primary focus of justice should be on the arrangement of the basic institutions of society because they distribute the main benefits (and burdens) in life. For Rawls, injustice provides a decisive reason for reform: 'laws and institutions no matter how efficient and well-arranged must be reformed or abolished if they are unjust'.[27] Climate change is a cause of injustice and to the extent that healthcare is complicit in perpetuating climate injustice, no matter how much good healthcare does, Rawls' view favours reform and this speaks against treating healthcare as special in terms of climate change. If we are to 'reform or abolish' healthcare because of its contribution to climate change, the two cannot be treated as independent.

I've offered some reasons why we should not think about climate change mitigation separately from healthcare's goals and why claiming healthcare is special does not get us far in exempting healthcare from mitigation. We are now left with the issue of how to reconcile the goals of healthcare with mitigation burdens. There are many ways one might go about doing this. I'll discuss one method here for the sake of space.

Start from the assumption that all, especially in wealthy countries, have mitigation duties along the lines of the polluter-pays principle. Everyone has some emissions that they are causally connected to and they are *prima facie* responsible for addressing. From here, we could distinguish a sphere of protected emissions. The distinction between impermissible luxury emissions and permissible subsistence emissions is a useful guide towards which emissions are protected. Subsistence emissions are the minimum necessary emissions to secure a basic need.[28] Basic needs are those needs which, when left unmet, lead to harm; think food, water, shelter, and so forth.[29] The fundamental moral importance of meeting basic needs means that, as long as there are no reasonable alternatives to meet the basic need with fewer emissions, we should accept the costs that meeting basic needs place on others through climate change. In so far as healthcare emissions (1) meet a basic need; and (2) are the minimum necessary to secure the basic need, they are permissible and not liable to mitigation. Many would agree that at least some activities of a healthcare system do indeed meet a basic need, so the further question is whether those emissions are the *minimum* necessary. In this way, we are able to integrate these two concerns of distributive justice. Healthcare is not *absolutely* exempt from mitigation, there are things healthcare can do to reduce

27 John Rawls, *A Theory of Justice* (Harvard University Press 1971) 3.

28 This distinction was first made by Henry Shue who pointed out that it is important not to 'ignore the fact that some sources (of greenhouse gas emissions) are essential and even urgent for the fulfilment of vital needs and other sources are inessential or even frivolous'. Henry Shue, 'Subsistence Emissions and Luxury Emissions' (1993) 15 Law Policy 39.

29 Gillian Brock and David Miller, 'Needs in Moral and Political Philosophy' (2019) https://plato.stanford.edu/archives/sum2019/entries/needs/, accessed 13 November 2023.

its carbon footprint even where this does meet a basic need. But by having a protected sphere of permissible, subsistence emissions, we can integrate mitigation burdens with the morally valuable goals of healthcare.

Individual responsibilities

This section turns from an institution-level to an individual perspective. I mentioned that decarbonising healthcare entails a shift in how, where, and what healthcare is delivered. Behaviour change will be a key component in achieving this pivot. Consider metered-dose inhalers (known as 'puffers').[30] These contain powerful greenhouse gases; hence even small volumes can have a significant impact on the environment.[31] The greenhouse gases in one Ventolin inhaler ('the blue inhaler') amounts to the equivalent of driving 175 miles.[32] Switching inhalers to those with a smaller carbon footprint means revised prescribing patterns, the inconvenience of multiple appointments and learning to use a new inhaler, as well as a worry about a temporary deterioration in asthma control whilst adjustments are made.[33] So, what duties or responsibilities do individual practitioners and patients have to minimise such emissions?

Foundational norms in the doctor–patient relationship are challenged by issues of climate change. Doctors' main concern is the patient in front them. Patients too focus almost exclusively on their own interests when making medical decisions. Considerations of climate change invite a far greater reach in terms of the interests at stake. A second issue is whether reducing *individual* emissions make a difference to global warming. Walter Sinnott-Armstrong argues that individual emissions do not make a difference to a complex phenomenon like climate change and so it would be inappropriate to hold individuals responsible.[34] Sinnott-Armstrong asks us to imagine going for a 'gas-guzzling' drive on a Sunday afternoon just for fun. His point is that the emissions from this do not cause global warming, nor can they be demonstrated to harm somebody, hence individual responsibility is unfair. In Sinnott-Armstrong's view, responsibilities for patients or practitioners to say, change inhalers, would be unfair. The relationship between individual emissions and the harms of global warming is complex and a number of philosophers

---

30 Joshua Parker, 'Barriers to Green Inhaler Prescribing: Ethical Issues in Environmentally Sustainable Clinical Practice' (2023) 49 J Med Ethics 92.

31 Christer Janson and others, 'Carbon Footprint Impact of the Choice of Inhalers for Asthma and COPD' (2020) 75 Thorax 82.

32 Green Inhaler, (nd) https://greeninhaler.org, accessed 13 November 2023.

33 Alexander Wilkinson and Ashley Woodcock, 'The Environmental Impact of Inhalers for Asthma: A Green Challenge and a Golden Opportunity' (2022) 88 Br J Clin Pharmacol 3016.

34 Walter Sinnott-Armstrong, 'It's Not My Fault: Global Warming and Individual Moral Obligations' in Stephen Gardiner and others (eds), *Climate Ethics: Essential Readings* (OUP 2010) 332.

have attempted to clarify this relationship in order to defend conceptions of individual responsibility.[35]

Does climate change mitigation represent a morally justified restriction on patient and professional choice? To approach this, I distinguish between maximum and minimum conceptions of individual responsibilities. The maximum conception tells us when, and to what degree, individuals should be expected to make sacrifices to reduce healthcare emissions. As such, it explains what is owed to individual patients as well as to global and future populations, offering ways of balancing these within the context of healthcare. Clearly, the maximal account raises hard questions: imagine trying to discuss with a patient precisely how few emissions are justified to protect their health whilst also trying to reduce the chance of climate-related flooding in Bangladesh many years from now. Instead, I defend a minimal conception: the minimum that could be morally expected of patients and healthcare professionals where their decisions have implications for global warming.

Certain instances of healthcare are substitutable, and sometimes the substitute has fewer emissions. By substitutable, I mean each option has broadly similar properties: they produce the same kinds of benefits, they have comparable risks and costs, and are similarly efficient in achieving those ends. In effect, substitutability is about replacing the *means* that secure important ends. As emissions are of instrumental value and we care about them only to the degree they bring about important ends, we should be relatively indifferent to a myriad of ways to achieve the same end as long as those means are acceptably similar. Inhaled gases used in anaesthetics to put people to sleep and as pain relief are a useful illustration. As potent greenhouse gases these anaesthetics account for up to 0.1 per cent of all greenhouse gases and 2 per cent of the NHS carbon footprint is inhalation anaesthesia.[36] Alternatives like total intravenous anaesthesia and local and regional anaesthesia have a much lower carbon footprint but oftentimes are just as effective at achieving the goals of anaesthesia.[37] In these examples, we can still achieve certain morally valuable goals (in this case pain relief or effect anaesthesia), but we can do so in a way that has fewer emissions.

In the context of healthcare, where certain options make little or no difference in terms of the ends but the carbon footprint of the means vary, I claim that it is a minimum conception of morality that the option with fewer emissions should be preferred.[38] I summarise this into the following principle:

35 Avram Hiller, 'Climate Change and Individual Responsibility' (2011) 94 The Monist 349; John Broome, 'Against Denialism' (2019) 102 The Monist 110; Garrett Cullity, 'Climate Harms' (2019) 102 The Monist 22.

36 Forbes McGain and others, 'Environmental Sustainability in Anaesthesia and Critical Care' (2020) 125 Br J Anaesth 680.

37 Cliff Shelton and others, 'Towards Zero Carbon Healthcare: Anaesthesia' (2022) 379 BMJ e069030.

38 Joshua Parker and others, 'Green Nudges for Sustainable Anaesthetic Practice: Institutional Support to Make Individual Change Easier' (2023) 78 Anaesthesia 943.

> *Principle of environmental prescribing*: Where two or more treatment options are broadly comparable in terms of effectiveness, efficiency, safety, and so forth, the one with a lesser impact on the environment should be preferred.

This is a minimum requirement of morality because no matter what our precise duties to future individuals and globally are, and regardless of what sacrifices we think patients and doctors should make in securing those distant interests through tackling climate change, where the difference to patients is minimal, they ought to opt for the alternative with the fewest emissions.

A defence of this principle could take a number of forms. One could defend this from a consequentialist perspective whereby we have duties to minimise expected harm.[39] As emissions are thought to increase the risk that people are harmed, then we ought to reduce the risk where we can. Secondly, it could be defended on the basis of a 'duty of easy rescue'. Peter Singer has famously argued that if we can do something good at minimal cost to ourselves then we should.[40] As the costs to individuals here are often zero, or at least tiny, then this principle might be thought of as a principle of *very* easy rescue. A third defence is based on the work of Thomas Scanlon. Scanlon argues,

> [a]n act is wrong if its performance under the circumstances would be disallowed by any set of principles for the general regulation of behaviour that no one could reasonably reject as a basis for informed, unforced, general agreement.[41]

This appeals to a social contract and the idea that moral principles and rules can be derived from forms of mutual agreement. To reasonably reject a principle, according to Scanlon, one must be able to demonstrate that somebody is harmed by putting the principle into action. Moreover, rejecting the principle can't put a greater burden on somebody else. Even if the principle of environmental prescribing, in some instances, places small burdens on individuals, to reasonably reject it they must also show that no greater harms are shifted elsewhere by rejecting it. As the wider harms are those of climate change, it seems unlikely that the inconvenience of changing inhalers, say, is a greater burden than the threats of climate change.

39 Joshua Parker and others, 'How Should Institutions Help Clinicians to Practise Greener Anaesthesia: First-Order and Second-Order Responsibilities to Practice Sustainably' (2023) J Med Ethics https://doi.org/10.1136/jme-2023-109442, accessed 4 July 2024.

40 Peter Singer, 'Famine, Affluence, and Morality' (1972) 1 Philos Public Aff 229.

41 Thomas Scanlon, *What We Owe Each Other* (Harvard University Press 1998) 153.

Promotional responsibilities: a professional duty to resist?

Individual and institutional duties to adopt policies and behaviours to tackle climate change do not exhaust the possibilities for moral inquiry into what healthcare should do regarding climate change. Extensive mitigation by healthcare systems alone will not prevent climate change threatening health given the complexity and scale of climate change. Low-carbon healthcare systems could still find themselves running to stand still if others take inadequate climate action. So what action should healthcare take to ensure that others do their fair share to address climate change?

Elizabeth Cripps calls these 'promotional duties: duties to attempt to bring about necessary *collective* action'.[42] Promotional duties are oftentimes the primary duties that individual citizens have with regards to climate change for Cripps. She defends these on the basis of efficacy, efficiency, and fairness. Cripps lists the following as examples: to campaign and vote for local and national politicians with climate change on their agenda; stand for office if no such candidates exist; lobby and petition politicians; donate to climate-friendly organisations; organise and join summits and marches; write articles; set up websites; and coordinate a 'global citizenship movement'.[43] The political means described by Cripps do not exhaust the options for promotional duties however. This is reflected in actions taken over the past few years by those who do not believe those in power are doing enough regarding climate change. Extinction Rebellion, Insulate Britain, and Just Stop Oil provide a handful of examples from the UK.

I title acts taken by organisations like Extinction Rebellion as 'resistance'. Resistance is an umbrella term describing activism, protest, and forms of civil disobedience amongst other things. Ryan Essex points out resistance entails *active opposition*: acts targeted at certain grievances.[44] Whilst resistance may often be public, forms of 'everyday resistance' occur which are more subversive and not always recognised by those in power. Essex distinguishes two forms of resistance when it comes to health and healthcare. One is resistance as opposition to power where 'resistance can serve as an important means to oppose threats to health, that is, structures, policy, laws, or the multitude of other factors that could negatively impact on health'. The second is 'resistance as constructive', which recognises that 'resistance has a role to play in imagining how society could be better structured to support health and well-being or imagining alternatives to harmful systems and policy'.[45] Within this taxonomy, many acts of organisations like Extinction Rebellion, such as organising marches and non-violent protests,

42 Elizabeth Cripps, *Climate Change and the Moral Agent: Individual Duties in an Interdependent World* (OUP 2013) 116 (emphasis added).

43 Ibid 143.

44 Ryan Essex, 'Resistance in Health and Healthcare' (2021) 35 Bioeth 480.

45 Ryan Essex, 'How Resistance Shapes Health and Well-Being' (2022) 19 J Bioeth Inq 315, 316.

blocking roads, damaging the property of the perpetrators of injustice, lobbying, and campaigning for change are acts of resistance.

Where do healthcare professionals fit into this? Healthcare professionals have already been involved in the forms of resistance listed, such as Doctors for Extinction Rebellion.[46] This raises a question as to whether healthcare professionals' actions are justified? Some respond with criteria by which to assess claims of justifiability.[47] Action must be: against an unjust situation; the last resort; thought to be reasonably effective; and where the local socio-political situation calls for civil disobedience because of the privilege some societies enjoy compared to others. Whilst this framework is useful, it is hard to see how it singles out resistance as being justified amongst *healthcare professionals* rather than simply amongst citizens. Furthermore, just because an act is justified does not mean that it is morally required and what I have in mind is something stronger than a justification for those healthcare professionals who do take to the streets in the name of climate justice.

Four reasons have been offered in favour of a duty to undertake forms of resistance to help mitigate climate change.[48] I've touched upon these already in connection with other duties. One ground is a duty of beneficence.[49] One can see how a duty of easy rescue could, depending on the stakes, be used to argue for a responsibility to become an activist, engage in civil dissidence, and the like. A second is on the basis of averting harm. If resistance helps avert great harm, then individuals can be obligated on this basis.[50] The last two principles are rooted in justice. Iris Marion Young's social connection model of political responsibility offers one such argument.[51] Young's view was that those who take part in social structures that collectively generate harms bear responsibility for challenging and transforming those structures. Where climate change is the product of the day-to-day workings of a society built on burning fossil fuels, no individual can be said to be liable, instead we need to look to the structures that support this regimen and here individuals can be instrumental in dismantling those structures.[52] Finally, for John Rawls, justice is the first virtue of social institutions and where they are unjust then we are obligated to bring about just institutions.[53]

---

46 See Health for Extinction Rebellion https://healthforxr.com, accessed 17 November 2023.

47 Hayley Bennett and others, 'Should Health Professionals Participate in Civil Disobedience in Response to the Climate Change Health Emergency?' (2020) 395 Lancet 304, 305.

48 Francisco Garcia-Gibson, 'The Ethics of Climate Activism' (2023) 14 Wiley Interdis Rev: Climate Change e831.

49 Cripps (n43) 13.

50 Simon Caney, 'Two Kinds of Climate Justice: Avoiding Harm and Sharing Burdens' (2014) 22 J Pol Philos 125.

51 Iris Marion Young, *Responsibility for Justice* (OUP 2010).

52 Robyn Eckersley, 'Responsibility for Climate Change as a Structural Injustice' in Teena Gabrielson and others (eds), *The Oxford Handbook of Environmental Political Theory* (OUP 2016) 346.

53 Rawls (n27) 334.

Each view offers a plausible reason to argue that citizens have certain obligations to engage in resistance in view of climate change. But what does this mean for healthcare professionals in their role as health professionals rather than as citizens? No argument specifically singles out healthcare professionals as being especially obligated to act as compared to other members of the public simply because they are a health professional. We could conclude that healthcare professionals have no such *special* duty and thus share the same responsibilities as their fellow citizens. Indeed, if it is enough to argue that individuals have promotional duties then the appeal to healthcare professionals having special duties is superfluous. Two arguments are potentially relevant, however.

One argument points out that whilst healthcare professionals are of course citizens, they hold a powerful position in society, rooted in trust, and that provides privilege that ought to be utilised for certain ends. As healthcare professionals have trusted voices, they can be powerful for promoting change and so they are obligated to use those voices to sound the alarm on climate change.[54] Furthermore, lending medical authority can provide legitimacy to certain causes. Doctors who marched with Extinction Rebellion in 2019 wore scrubs, 'thinking that the media would find it harder to dismiss medical professional protestors as cranks'.[55]

This argument is insufficient to establish a special responsibility for healthcare professionals to engage in acts of resistance. The mere fact that doctors are trusted does not mean they have a special responsibility to lend their voice to any cause no matter how remote from their work. The argument can be strengthened by framing climate activism as *health* advocacy. Evidence suggests that framing climate change as a threat to health is particularly motiving in bringing about change.[56] Again, however, that 'the climate crisis is a health crisis' is insufficient to ground a special duty of resistance for healthcare workers. This is because many things affect health. As Ruth Faden and Madison Power write, 'everything from crime, war, and natural disasters; to population genetics, environmental hazards, marketing and other corporate practices; to political oppression, income inequality, and individual behaviours has been claimed as a public health problem', leading to a lack of institutional, disciplinary, or social boundaries.[57] The worry is that if clinicians have a special responsibility to speak

---

54 Eric Maibach and others, 'Health Professionals and the Climate Crisis: Trusted Voices, Essential Roles' (2021) 13 World Med Health Policy 137.

55 Shivali Fulchand, 'Could Protesting for Climate Action Damage Doctors' Careers?' (2019) 367 BMJ l6875.

56 Eric Maibach and others, 'Reframing Climate Change as a Public Health Issue: An Exploratory Study of Public Reactions' (2010) 10 BMC Public Health 1; Teresa Myers and others, 'A Public Health Frame Arouses Hopeful Emotions about Climate Change' (2012) 113 Climatic Change 1105

57 Madison Powers and Ruth Faden, *Social Justice: The Moral Foundations of Public Health and Health Policy* (OUP 2006) 10.

out against anything that affects health, this might be overly demanding. What is missing then is a principled reason that draws a boundary around health problems whereby healthcare professionals' trusted voices are such that these create a special promotional duty for practitioners above and beyond that of anyone else. Absent such a boundary, it is difficult to see how a healthcare professional's responsibility is *special* with regards to climate change, or any other problem for that matter, and why we should not simply rely on arguments that apply to all citizens, including healthcare professionals.

Summary

- The relationship between climate change, health, and healthcare raises significant and underexplored ethical questions, making this an important area of study.
- The key tension facing healthcare is the Red Queen problem. One way to resolve this is through mitigation.
- Mitigation raises three important ethical questions for healthcare systems and those who work in them. First there is the question of healthcare's fair share of the burdens of mitigation. Second is which agents have responsibilities to reduce healthcare emissions, in particular patients and professionals. Third is whether healthcare professionals have a special duty of resistance.
- I have explored some of the ways to approach these questions as well as some of the strengths and weaknesses of different positions one could take on these questions.
- A theme for further reflection is whether the answers to the questions I have raised have the same or different foundations? If they are the same, then one moral concept explains all of healthcare's moral obligations to address climate change; for example, a principle of 'do no harm'. On the other hand, perhaps to determine healthcare's mitigation responsibilities, explain why healthcare professionals' practice should be green, and what duties to resist there are requires a handful of different moral concepts specific to each question?

Questions for reflection

1. What medico-legal questions are raised by healthcare systems' emissions?
2. Should healthcare be considered morally special when it comes to addressing climate change?
3. How should we understand the relationship among healthcare, climate change, and health?

Recommended resources

- Simon Caney, 'Climate Change' in Serena Olsaretti (ed), *The Oxford Handbook of Distributive Justice* (OUP 2018).
- Simon Caney, 'Just Emissions' (2012) 40 Philos Public Aff 255.

- Joshua Parker, 'Health Care Exceptionalism and the Burdens of Climate Change Mitigation', forthcoming.
- Anand Bhopal and Ole F Norheim, 'Fair Pathways to Net-Zero Healthcare' (2023) 29 Nature Med 1078.

Bibliography

Barratt A and McGain F, 'Overdiagnosis is Increasing the Carbon Footprint of Healthcare' (2021) 375 BMJ n2407

Bennett H and others, 'Should Health Professionals Participate in Civil Disobedience in Response to the Climate Change Health Emergency?' (2020) 395 Lancet 304

Bhopal A and others, 'How Do We Decarbonise Fairly? Emissions, Inequities and the Implications for Net Zero Healthcare' (2022) 115 J R Soc Med 337

Brock G and Miller D, 'Needs in Moral and Political Philosophy' (2019) https://plato.stanford.edu/archives/sum2019/entries/needs/, accessed 13 November 2023

Broome J, 'Against Denialism' (2019) 102 The Monist 110

Caney S, 'Two Kinds of Climate Justice: Avoiding Harm and Sharing Burdens' (2014) 22 J Pol Philos 125

Carroll L, *Through the Looking Glass* (Penguin 1871)

Chung J and Meltzer D, 'Estimate of the Carbon Footprint of the US Health Care Sector' (2009) 302 JAMA 1970

Costello A and others, 'Managing the Health Effects of Climate Change: Lancet and University College London Institute for Global Health Commission' (2009) 373 Lancet 1693

Cripps E, *Climate Change and the Moral Agent: Individual Duties in an Interdependent World* (OUP 2013)

Cullity G, 'Climate Harms' (2019) 102 The Monist 22

Daniels N, *Just Health: Meeting Health Needs Fairly* (CUP 2007)

Eckersley R, 'Responsibility for Climate Change as a Structural Injustice' in T Gabrielson and others (eds), *The Oxford Handbook of Environmental Political Theory* (OUP 2016)

Essex R, 'Resistance in Health and Healthcare' (2021) 35 Bioeth 480

Essex R, 'How Resistance Shapes Health and Well-Being' (2022) 19 J Bioeth Inq 315

Fulchand S, 'Could Protesting for Climate Action Damage Doctors' Careers?' (2019) 367 BMJ l6875

Garcia-Gibson F, 'The Ethics of Climate Activism' (2023) 14 Wiley Interdis Rev: Climate Change e831

Green Inhaler (nd) https://greeninhaler.org, accessed 13 November 2023

Greener NHS, 'Delivering a "Net Zero" National Health Service' (2020) https://www.england.nhs.uk/greenernhs/wp-content/uploads/sites/51/2020/10/delivering-a-net-zero-national-health-service.pdf, accessed 13 November 2023

Gynther A and others, 'Nitrous Oxide Use on the Labour Ward: Efficacy and Environmental Impact' (2021) Australasian Anaesth 183

Health Care Without Harm, 'Health Care's Climate Footprint' (2019) https://noharm-europe.org/ClimateFootprintReport, accessed 13 November 2023

Health for Extinction Rebellion https://healthforxr.com, accessed 17 November 2023

Hiller A, 'Climate Change and Individual Responsibility' (2011) 94 The Monist 349

IPCC (Intergovernmental Panel on Climate Change), 'The Physical Science Basis of Climate Change' (2021) https://www.ipcc.ch/report/sixth-assessment-report-working-group-i/, accessed 13 November 2023

Janson C and others, 'Carbon Footprint Impact of the Choice of Inhalers for Asthma and COPD' (2020) 75 Thorax 82

Lenzen M and others, 'The Environmental Footprint of Health Care: A Global Assessment' (2020) 4 Lancet Planet Health e271

Maibach E and others, 'Reframing Climate Change as a Public Health Issue: An Exploratory Study of Public Reactions' (2010) 10 BMC Public Health 1

Maibach E and others, 'Health Professionals and the Climate Crisis: Trusted Voices, Essential Roles' (2021) 13 World Med Health Policy 137

Marmot M, 'Social Determinants of Health Inequalities' (2005) 365 Lancet 1099

McGain F and others, 'Environmental Sustainability in Anaesthesia and Critical Care' (2020) 125 Br J Anaesth 680

Mortimer F, 'The Sustainable Physician' (2010) 10 Clin Med 110

Myers T and others, 'A Public Health Frame Arouses Hopeful Emotions about Climate Change' (2012) 113 Climatic Change 1105

Naylor C and Appleby J, 'Environmental Sustainability in Health and Social Care' (2012) https://www.kingsfund.org.uk/sites/default/files/field/field_publication_file/sustainable-health-social-care-appleby-naylor-mar2012.pdf, accessed 13 November 2023

Parker J, 'Barriers to Green Inhaler Prescribing: Ethical Issues in Environmentally Sustainable Clinical Practice' (2023) 49 J Med Ethics 92

Parker J and others, 'Green Nudges for Sustainable Anaesthetic Practice: Institutional Support to Make Individual Change Easier' (2023) 78 Anaesth 943

Parker J and others, 'How Should Institutions Help Clinicians to Practise Greener Anaesthesia: First-Order and Second-Order Responsibilities to Practice Sustainably' (2023) J Med Ethics 10.1136/jme-2023-109442, accessed 21 August 2023

Powers M and Faden R, *Social Justice: The Moral Foundations of Public Health and Health Policy* (OUP 2006)

Rawls J, *A Theory of Justice* (Harvard University Press 1971)

Segall S, 'Is Health Care (Still) Special?' (2007) 15 J Pol Philos 342

Scanlon T, *What We Owe Each Other* (Harvard University Press 1998)

Shelton C and others, 'Towards Zero Carbon Healthcare: Anaesthesia' (2022) 379 BMJ e069030

Shue H, 'Subsistence Emissions and Luxury Emissions' (1993) 15 Law Policy 39
Shue H, *Climate Justice: Vulnerability and Protection* (OUP 2014)
Singer P, 'Famine, Affluence, and Morality' (1972) 1 Philos Public Aff 229
Sinnott-Armstrong W, 'It's Not My Fault: Global Warming and Individual Moral Obligations' in S Gardiner and others (eds), *Climate Ethics: Essential Readings* (OUP 2010)
Tennison I and others, 'Health Care's Response to Climate Change: A Carbon Footprint Assessment of the NHS in England' (2021) 5 Lancet Planet Health e84
Watts N and others, 'Health and Climate Change: Policy Responses to Protect Public Health' (2015) 386 Lancet 1861
WHO (World Health Organization), '72nd World Health Assembly, Geneva, Switzerland' (2019) https://www.pscp.tv/w/1lDGLrerprqxm?t=1h6m38s, accessed 13 November 2023
WHO (World Health Organization), 'Climate Change and Health' (2021) https://www.who.int/news-room/fact-sheets/detail/climate-change-and-health, accessed 13 November 2023
WHO (World Health Organization), 'Alliance for Transformative Action on Climate and Health' (2023) https://www.who.int/initiatives/alliance-for-transformative-action-on-climate-and-health/country-commitments, accessed 13 November 2023
Wilkinson A and Woodcock A, 'The Environmental Impact of Inhalers for Asthma: A Green Challenge and a Golden Opportunity' (2022) 88 Br J Clin Pharmacol 3016
Wilkinson A and others, 'Costs of Switching to Low Global Warming Potential Inhalers: An Economic and Carbon Footprint Analysis of NHS Prescription Data in England' (2019) 9 BMJ Open e028763
Young IM, *Responsibility for Justice* (OUP 2010)

PART II

The Body of Health Law

7

Medical Negligence

Zoe L. Tongue, Elizabeth Chloe Romanis, and Sabrina Germain

When a doctor makes a mistake that causes injury to a patient, there are several avenues for recourse.[1] Patients can go through the NHS complaints procedure, bring an action through a professional regulator (e.g., the General Medical Council), take a negligence claim to the courts, or contact the police so that a prosecution can be brought under criminal law (see Chapter 8). The avenue that patients take depends on what they want to achieve: to trigger an investigation to find out why something happened, to change policy and practice to make sure it does not happen again, to hold a doctor accountable for their injury, or to seek compensation to help them adjust to an injury.

In this chapter, we start by setting out the NHS complaints system to highlight why this may be unsuitable or inadequate for many patients. We then consider what is required to bring a successful medical negligence claim and the gendered impact of litigation.

A significant number of negligence claims are related to pregnancy or birth. Obstetric claims account for 13 per cent of all clinical negligence claims: it is the speciality with the greatest proportion of claims.[2] Successful negligence claims made regarding negligent obstetric care constitute the highest proportion of compensation paid out by the NHS: of the £2.6 billion spent by the NHS in negligence payments in 2022/23, maternity claims accounted for 64 per cent of this.[3] This state of affairs indicates a number of things. Where there is injury during birth that harms the child, a large sum of money is needed to address the adjustments the claimant has to make to their life. That negligence claims are so

---

1 Doctors are not the only healthcare professionals whose errors can have serious consequences. We focus on doctors for reasons of space.

2 NHS Resolution, 'Annual Report and Accounts 2022/23' (2023) https://resolution.nhs.uk/wp-content/uploads/2023/07/NHS-Resolution-Annual-report-and-accounts-2022_23-3.pdf, accessed 27 November 2023, 57.

3 Ibid.

common in this speciality compared to others likely results from the systemic issues in pregnancy and birthing care (explored in Chapter 15) resulting in many women and other people who birth receiving substandard care. These issues will be considered throughout this chapter.

NHS complaints

In England, the NHS Constitution grants patients the right to complain about any aspect of healthcare relating to treatment or services.[4] An effective complaints system helps support victims, providing them with recognition and acknowledgement for the harm they have suffered. It also provides an important learning and feedback opportunity for the NHS, to improve services and treatments delivery.

Since 2002, the Patient Advice and Liaison Services (PALS) have offered independent services in most hospitals to support, advise, and inform patients (or someone acting on their behalf) seeking resolution of a grievance through an informal route.[5] Access to the service is free and conversations with PALS members are confidential.

Patients are advised to speak to clinical staff before approaching PALS. In reality, patients tend to directly approach PALS, feeling disregarded or uncomfortable discussing issues with their care team.[6] This is likely to be especially true for marginalised patients who feel they are not listened to. For example, because they are subject to testimonial injustice: they are not believed because doctors perceive them (because of who they are) as lacking credibility.[7]

Where patients are dissatisfied with the answer provided by the informal process, and no resolution can be reached through PALS, they may engage with the formal process. Patients can do so within 12 months of an incident. Patients can be supported by an NHS complaints advocate.

Formal complaints are accepted in writing, orally, or via email. After the complaint has been acknowledged, a two-stage process may be triggered. First, a local resolution process begins, which results in a report outlining how the complaint was considered and conclusions reached. A way forward may also be provided with a remedial action plan.[8] Most complaints come to an end at

---

4 NHS Constitution, 'Complaint and Redress' (2009) https://www.gov.uk/government/publications/the-nhs-constitution-for-england/the-nhs-constitution-for-england, accessed 21 November 2023.

5 NHS UK, 'What is PALS (Patient Advice and Liaison Service)?' (nd) https://www.nhs.uk/nhs-services/hospitals/what-is-pals-patient-advice-and-liaison-service/, accessed 21 November 2023.

6 J. van Dael and others, 'Do National Politics for Complaint Handling in English Hospitals Support Quality Improvement? Lessons from a Case Study' (2022) 115 J R Soc Med 390.

7 Miranda Fricker, *Epistemic Injustice: Power and the Ethics of Knowing* (OUP 2007) 17.

8 The Local Authority Social Services and National Health Service Complaints (England) Regulations 2009, regulation 14.

this stage. However, if there is no resolution, a complaint can be made to the Parliamentary and Health Service Ombudsman (office responsible for considering complaints made by the public against public authorities including the NHS). The Ombudsman will 'listen to the human stories – to the experiences of individuals and their families'[9] and decide whether to carry out an investigation, to suggest dispute resolution, and to ultimately uphold the cases it determines most deserving.[10]

In 2013, the Ombudsman, examining the system from the patient perspective, published a report acknowledging failures around access and process, communication and responsiveness, and leadership and learning.[11] In 2022, they produced the NHS Complaint Standards. These were intended to offer guidance on how to appropriately action complaints and create a more direct and positive connection between service providers and the public.[12]

However, patients still report dissatisfaction with the complaints system. The 2020 'First Do No Harm' report highlights that women consistently feel disregarded by medical professionals, for example, when reporting serious side effects linked to medicines and medical devices.[13] This dissatisfaction amongst marginalised groups is masked by how data is collected. The government's statistical reporting on who complains about the NHS presents only aggregated data or information by age group.[14]

Where people are frustrated with the long and laborious NHS complaints system, they may turn to the law for recourse in place of complaining (or as well as submitting a complaint).

---

9 Parliamentary and Health Service Ombudsman, 'The NHS Hospital Complaints System: A Case for Urgent Treatment?' (2013) https://www.ombudsman.org.uk/sites/default/files/The_NHS_hospital_complaints_system.%20A_case_for_urgent_treatment_report.pdf, accessed 29 November 2023.

10 Parliamentary and Health Service Ombudsman, 'How We Deal with Complaints' (2022) https://www.ombudsman.org.uk/making-complaint/how-we-deal-complaints#:~:text=We'll%20gather%20all%20the,advice%20to%20inform%20our%20decisions, accessed 6 December 2023.

11 Parliamentary and Health Service Ombudsman (n9).

12 Parliamentary and Health Service Ombudsman, 'NHS Complaint Standards: Summary of Expectations' (2022) https://www.ombudsman.org.uk/sites/default/files/NHS_Complaint_Standards_Summary_of_expectations_December_2022_Final.pdf, accessed 29 November 2023.

13 Baroness Cumberledge, 'First Do No Harm: The Report of the Independent Medicines and Medical Devices Safety Review' (2020) /https://www.immdsreview.org.uk/downloads/IMMDSReview_Web.pdf, accessed 6 December 2023. We are grateful to Professor Emma Cave for pointing us to this report.

14 NHS Digital, 'Data on Written Complaints in the NHS, 2020–23' (2022) https://digital.nhs.uk/data-and-information/publications/statistical/data-on-written-complaints-in-the-nhs/2020-21, accessed 6 December 2023. We are grateful to Emma Cave for pointing us to these statistics.

Figure 7.1: Elements of a negligence claim

The basis of negligence

There are no special rules that differentiate medicine from other contexts: the same elements of the tort of negligence must be established for a claimant to make a successful claim. The claimant must show that they suffered some harm (damage), that the doctor owed them a duty of care, that the actions of the doctor fell below the standard of care they owed (breach), and this breach of their duty caused the harm that they suffered (causation) (see Figure 7.1). Where all these elements are satisfied, the claimant will be entitled to compensation. The basic principle is that funds should be awarded to, *as far as is possible with money*, put the claimant in the position they would have been in had the negligence never occurred.

How these elements have come to be interpreted in the medical context is best understood with consideration of some 'special factors' occurring at the intersection of law and medicine.[15] Law and medicine are both 'two structures of power that carry considerable social legitimacy'.[16] There has historically been a culture of deference, on the part of patients and of the legal profession, towards doctors.[17] With changing societal convention about the status of medicine and of patients as rights holders,[18] and with patients being empowered with information because of resources like the internet,[19] many patients are more willing to use the

15 Margaret Brazier, Emma Cave, and Rob Heywood, *Medicine, Patients, and the Law* (7th edn, Manchester University Press 2023) 211.

16 Elizabeth Chloe Romanis, 'Legal Method and Health Law in Feminist Perspective' in Jean McHale and Atina Krajewska (eds), *Reimagining Health Law: From Medical to Health and Social Care Law* (Edward Elgar, forthcoming).

17 Brazier, Cave, and Heywood (n15) 211.

18 *Montgomery v Lanarkshire Health Board* [2015] UKSC 11, at para [75] per Lady Hale.

19 The internet (where there are some reliable sources) has resulted in patients finding it easier to inform themselves about symptoms, options for treatment, and risks/side-effects: ibid para [76] per Lady Hale.

law to seek recompense after experiencing negligence. Health professionals and policy makers are worried about a potential 'malpractice crisis',[20] with increasing amounts of money paid out to negligence claims.[21] However, the accounts of empowered patients and growing negligence claims ignore those who are consistently marginalised in medicine and law.

Duty of care is established using the usual rules from tort: where it can be shown that it was reasonably foreseeable that the (negligent) actions of the health professional could harm the individual identified as the victim,[22] that there was a sufficiently close relationship between the health professional and the victim,[23] and that there is no public policy reason against recognising a duty of care. When a patient is treated by a health professional working for (or on behalf of) the NHS, establishing that there is a duty of care owed by that health professional to the patient they are treating is straightforward.[24] In the rest of this chapter, we focus on the other elements of negligence.

Understanding damage

There can be no claim for negligence if there is no legally recognisable damage.[25] Injury can be physical or psychiatric (limited to psychiatric conditions recognised by the medical profession).[26] A doctor may behave well below the standard expected but if this does not cause any legally recognisable damage then tort will offer the patient no remedy. Often, damage is not analysed as its own element of establishing negligence, rather it is packaged up with discussion of duty, breach, or causation.[27] Doing this, however, misses the nuances of *what* is considered to be a 'recoverable form of loss', in what circumstances, and *why*. The nature of what is considered loss in medical negligence cases varies vastly. Judges are willing to recognise new 'types' of loss.[28]

---

20 Margaret Brazier, *Law and Healing: A History of a Stormy Marriage* (Manchester University Press 2023) 95.

21 Clare Dyer, 'NHS Negligence Claims: £2.7bn Cost Prompts Renewed Calls for System Reform' (2023) 382 BMJ 1688.

22 *Darnley v Croydon Health Services NHS Trust* [2018] UKSC 50.

23 *Goodwill v British Pregnancy Advisory Service* [1996] 2 All ER 161.

24 DHSC (Department of Health and Social Care), 'The NHS Constitution for England' (2023) https://www.gov.uk/government/publications/the-nhs-constitution-for-england/the-nhs-constitution-for-england#staff-your-responsibilities, accessed 8 November 2023 – see the section on 'Staff: your responsibilities'.

25 *Sidaway v Board of Governors of the Bethlem Royal Hospital and the Maudsley Hospital* [1985] AC 871, 883 per Lord Scarman.

26 E.g., *Oliver v Williams* [2013] EWHC 600.

27 Donal Nolan, 'New Forms of Damage in Negligence' (2007) 70 Med Law Rev 59, 59; Craig Purshouse, 'Judicial Reasoning and the Concept of Damage: Rethinking Medical Negligence Cases' (2015) 15 Med Law Int 155, 156.

28 Purshouse (n27).

Table 7.1: Wrongful pregnancy cases

Case	*McFarlane v Tayside Health Board* [2000] 2 AC 59	*Parkinson v St James and Seacroft University Hospital NHS Trust* [2001] EWCA Civ 530	*Rees v Darlington Memorial Hospital NHS Trust* [2003] UKHL 52
Facts	Negligent vasectomy results in a pregnancy Child is born *healthy*	Negligent sterilisation procedure results in a pregnancy Child is born with a *disability*	Negligent sterilisation procedure results in a pregnancy Parent has a *disability, but the child does not*
Damage recognised	Pain and suffering of pregnancy and birth	Pain and suffering of pregnancy and birth Additional costs associated with disability	Pain and suffering of pregnancy and birth Award of £15,000 in recognition of loss of autonomy (reflecting loss of opportunity to plan their family life)
Damage *not* recognised	Wrongful life (recognition that a child should not have been born) – no compensation awarded for general upbringing of child	Wrongful life (recognition that a child should not have been born) – no compensation awarded for general upbringing of child	Wrongful life – no compensation awarded for general upbringing of child Any additional costs associated with raising a child on the grounds of the parent's disability

Equally, there have been cases where judges have been unwilling to recognise types of loss. Much of what is and is not recognised amounts to policy decision-making by judges. What are termed the 'wrongful pregnancy' cases exemplify the point that some novel legal 'wrongs' are recognised and others are not (see Table 7.1).[29]

In these cases, pregnancy (characterised as personal injury) was recognised as a legal wrong that the claimant had suffered. There has been, however, a consistent unwillingness to recognise the birth of a healthy child as a legal wrong. In *McFarlane*, it was held that the birth of a 'normal, healthy baby' was a 'blessing'. It was stressed that '[t]here is something distasteful, if not morally offensive, in treating the birth of a normal, healthy child as a matter for compensation'.[30] In contrast, in *Parkinson v St James*,[31] a child born following negligent sterilisation had a disability and because of this disability damages were awarded. The court explained that it was a matter of distributive justice. Lord Justice Brooke opined that 'ordinary people would consider that it would be fair for the law to make an award in such a case, provided that it is limited to the extra expenses associated

29 We are grateful to Dr Victoria Adkins for the idea for, and content of, this table.

30 *McFarlane v Tayside Health Board* [2000] 2 AC 59, 111 per Lord Millett.

31 *Parkinson v St James and Seacroft University Hospital NHS Trust* [2001] EWCA Civ 530.

with the child's disability'.[32] It might be argued that these cases raise some big unanswered questions: why is it morally offensive to say that a person has been wronged when they give birth after becoming pregnant because of a doctor's negligence? And if it is offensive to make such a claim, why is it *not* to award compensation where a child is born disabled? Is the implication that a disabled child is less of a blessing than a child without a disability? This moral distinction between disabled and non-disabled fetuses is also one made in relation to abortion law, which some view as problematic (see Chapter 14). It is not clear how the two cases can be distinguished since the negligent act of the doctor did not cause the disability. We raise these points to highlight that the law passes subjective value judgements about what can and cannot be considered legally recognisable damage.

Another issue surrounding damage is that the trauma that can result from negligent medical treatment is often not recognised as actionable harm. Harm that falls short of recognised psychiatric injury is not considered actionable damage in negligence. In *RE v Calderdale*,[33] damages were awarded to a mother and grandmother who experienced post-traumatic stress disorder as a result of negligent care during birth. The decision emphasised that damage will be recognised where there is a psychiatric injury following an experience that was *exceptional in nature* as judged by objective standards by reference to persons of ordinary susceptibility.[34] In the recent case of *Paul v Royal Wolverhampton*, however, the Supreme Court held that doctors do not owe a duty of care to prevent the psychiatric illness of family members caused by the death or medical crisis of an individual owing to the doctor's negligence.[35]

As one High Court decision reiterated '[e]motional responses to unpleasant experiences of even the most serious type do not found a claim for damages'.[36] As such, anger, sadness, grief, shame, and many of the other negative emotions that people can experience after negligent treatment are not, in themselves, actionable. As Mulheron has argued, the requirement that emotional harms amount to recognised psychiatric injury to be actionable will exclude claimants deserving of recognition.[37] This might especially impact on people who are marginalised within healthcare and routinely subject to testimonial injustice.[38] Obstetric negligence, for example, can involve serious violations (touching of

---

32 Ibid [50] per Brooke LJ.

33 *RE (a Minor) and Others v Calderdale & Huddersfield NHS Foundation Trust* [2017] EWHC 824.

34 Ibid [46]–[48].

35 *Paul and Another v Royal Wolverhampton NHS Trust; Polymear v Royal Cornwall Hospitals NHS Trust; Purchase v Ahmed* [2024] UKSC 1.

36 *RK v Oldham NHS Trust* [2003] Lloyd's Rep Med 1 (QB) [20] per Simon J.

37 Rachael Mulheron, 'Rewriting the Requirement for a "Recognised Psychiatric Injury" in Negligence Claims' (2012) 32 OxfJ Leg Stud 77, 102.

38 Fricker (n7) 17.

an intimate area without consent, for example)[39] and in a context where gender norms mean that patients are often treated poorly it is easy to see that there are likely to be serious emotional harms that go unrecognised in negligence.[40]

Standards of care in medicine

The case of *Bolam v Friern Hospital Management Committee* established the leading test for determining whether a doctor had breached their duty of care (see Box 7.1).[41]

Box 7.1: Key case: *Bolam v Friern Hospital Management Committee* [1957] 1 WLR 582

John Bolam was a voluntary patient at a mental health hospital and was advised by his doctors to undergo electro-convulsive therapy (ECT) for his depression. Following the normal practice of the hospital, he was not given a muscle relaxant drug or manual restraints. The treatment resulted in fractures on both sides of his pelvis and other injuries. These were risks which he had not been informed of when he consented to ECT.

Bolam sought damages for negligence for the following three reasons:

1. The doctors had failed to supply him with a relaxant drug to minimise convulsions.
2. The doctors had failed to manually restrain him to limit convulsive movements.
3. The doctors had not informed him of the risks involved in ECT when obtaining consent.

Medical experts highlighted that there was a difference in medical opinion as to whether relaxant drugs and manual restraints should be used during ECT: relaxant drugs carried a risk of mortality and the use of restraints could increase the risk of fractures. Doctors generally avoided warning patients of the risk of fractures unless they explicitly asked about it.

Addressing the jury, McNair J. set out the test for the reasonable standard of care in medical negligence cases: 'In an ordinary case which does not involve any special skill, negligence in law means this: some failure to do some act which a reasonable man in the circumstances would do, or doing some act which in the circumstances a reasonable man would not do [...] How do you test whether this act or failure is negligent? In an ordinary

39 Camilla Pickles and Jonathan Herring, 'Introduction' in Camilla Pickles and Jonathan Herring (eds), *Women's Birthing Bodies and the Law: Unauthorised Intimate Examinations, Power and Vulnerability* (Bloomsbury Publishing 2020) 2.

40 Camilla Pickles and Jonathan Herring (eds), *Childbirth, Vulnerability and Law: Exploring Issues of Violence and Control* (Routledge 2019); see also Chapter 15.

41 [1957] 1 WLR 582.

case it is generally said, that you judge that by the action of the man on the street. He is the ordinary man. In one case it has been said that you judge it by the conduct of the man at the top of the Clapham omnibus [...] But where you get a situation which involves the use of some special skill or competence, then the test whether there has been negligence or not [...] is *the standard of the ordinary skilled man exercising and professing to have that special skill* [...]' [586]

He went on to say that 'a doctor is not guilty of negligence if he has *acted in accordance with a practice accepted as proper by a responsible body of medical men skilled in that particular art* [...] Putting it the other way round, a doctor is not negligent, if he is acting in accordance with such a practice, merely because there is a body of opinion that takes the contrary view.' [587]

Bolam's claim for negligence was unsuccessful: the doctors had acted in accordance with accepted medical opinion, and the mere existence of disagreement within the medical profession was not enough to find that the doctors had breached their duty of care.

The *Bolam* test – that a doctor is not negligent where they 'acted in accordance with a practice accepted as proper by a responsible body of medical men skilled in that particular art' – became a question of whether a doctor could elicit support from their peers. McNair's comments 'de facto handed decisions as to whether the defendant fell below standard of care to the medical professionals who were called as expert witnesses'.[42] While the purpose of a 'reasonable care' test was to establish what *should* have been done in the circumstances,[43] the *Bolam* test meant that medical professionals could simply find peer support for what they did do. The test was skewed towards what was 'ordinary' rather than what was 'reasonable'.[44] The courts therefore deferred to medical expertise when determining whether there had been a breach of duty, instead of scrutinising an 'ordinary' practice to determine its reasonableness.

Sheldon has critiqued the *Bolam* test and the idea of the 'responsible body of medical men' from a feminist perspective, noting that judges and medical professionals 'share the same socio-economic space within society' in the context of class, race, and gender.[45] The legal and medical professions were, and continue to be, largely white, male, and hold an esteemed class position.

42 Brazier (n20) 121.

43 Kenneth Norrie, 'Common Practice and the Standard of Care in Medical Negligence' (1985) Juridical Rev 145; José Miola, 'The Standard of Care in Medical Negligence: Still Reasonably Troublesome?' in Janice Richardson and Ericka Rackley (eds), *Feminist Perspectives on Tort Law* (Routledge 2012), 129.

44 Miola (n43) 129.

45 Sally Sheldon, '"A Responsible Body of Medical Men Skilled in That Particular Art ...": Rethinking the *Bolam* Test' in Sally Sheldon and Michael Thomson (eds), *Feminist Perspectives on Health Care Law* (Routledge 1998) 21.

Sheldon considered how medical paternalism, judicial deference, and the concept of 'accepted' practice have a particular impact on women patients.[46] Medical paternalism refers to the practice of medical professionals dismissing a patient's wishes, needs, or values in favour of their own judgement. For example, in *Sidaway*, a woman undergoing spinal surgery was not informed of the 1–2 per cent chance of spinal column damage.[47] She was left paralysed after surgery. She would not have consented to surgery had she been informed of that risk.[48] Lord Diplock highlighted the undesirableness of 'deterring the patient from undergoing the treatment which in the expert opinion of the doctor it is in the patient's interest to undergo'.[49] The impact of gender stereotypes around women patients being viewed as passive or vulnerable means that women have 'borne a disproportionate brunt of medical paternalism'.[50] Sheldon noted the inability of the medical profession to empathise with someone different to them, including women generally and women such as Ms Sidaway who held a contrary opinion to them.[51] This also applies along the lines of class and race, where medical paternalism and the imbalance of power within the doctor–patient relationship means that some people's wishes, needs, and values go unheard.[52]

This excessive deference to the medical profession was addressed in the later case of *Bolitho v City and Hackney Health Authority* (see Box 7.2).[53]

Box 7.2: Key case: *Bolitho v City and Hackney Health Authority* [1998] AC 232

A two-year-old boy was admitted to hospital with breathing difficulties. He suffered from respiratory failure on two occasions, and a nurse reported these incidents to the doctor leading the boy's care, who did not attend. On both occasions, the boy appeared to have recovered, but subsequently suffered respiratory collapse leading to cardiac arrest. He sustained severe brain damage and died.

The doctor did breach her duty of care by failing to attend to the boy when the first two incidents were reported. However, she argued that even if she had attended, she would not have intubated him given that intubation was a very invasive and risky procedure for a young child. Therefore, the boy would have still died.

---

46 Ibid 19.

47 *Sidaway v Board of Governors of Bethlem Royal Hospital* [1985] 1 All ER 643.

48 Ibid.

49 Ibid 19.

50 Mary Mahowald, 'Sex-Role Stereotypes in Medicine' (1987) 2 Hypatia 21. Miola (n43) 134.

51 Sheldon (n45) 22–4.

52 See Laura D'Anna and others, 'Social Discrimination and Healthcare: A Multidimensional Framework of Experiences among a Low-Income Multi-Ethnic Sample' (2018) 33 Soc. Work Public Health 187.

53 [1998] AC 232.

On the question of whether she should have intubated the boy, the Bolam test was applied. Out of eight medical experts called as witnesses in the case at first instance, five of them stated that they would have intubated the boy at least after the second episode of respiratory failure. As there were experts who would not have intubated the boy, the doctor in question would not have fallen below the proper standard of care if she had attended, not intubated, and the boy had then died. As such, causation for negligence could not be proved.

The House of Lords agreed. However, Lord Browne-Wilkinson took the opportunity to clarify the Bolam test to highlight the scope for court intervention if necessary:

'The court is *not bound* to hold that a defendant doctor escapes liability for negligent treatment or diagnosis *just because he leads evidence from a number of medical experts who are genuinely of the opinion that the defendant's treatment or diagnosis accorded with sound medical practice*. In the *Bolam* case itself, McNair J. [1957] 1 W.L.R. 583, 587 stated that the defendant had to have acted in accordance with the practice accepted as proper by a "*responsible* body of medical men".' [241]

'In particular in cases involving, as they so often do, the weighing of risks against benefits, the judge before accepting a body of opinion as being responsible, reasonable or respectable, will need to be satisfied that, in forming their views, the experts have directed their minds to the question of comparative risks and benefits and have *reached a defensible conclusion* on the matter.' [242]

However, Lord Browne-Wilkinson added: 'I emphasise that in my view it will *very seldom be right* for a judge to reach the conclusion that views genuinely held by a competent medical expert are unreasonable.' [243]

Brazier and Miola note that *Bolitho* was not a 'revolution' for medical negligence law, but simply returned *Bolam* to its proper context.[54] While the test largely weighs in favour of medical opinion, 'blind adherence to *Bolam* in its unrestrained, and much misunderstood, form should no longer be possible'.[55] Instead of 'inappropriate deference', doctors would have to justify their practice as any other professional would.[56] While Lord Browne-Wilkinson noted that it would be only in a rare case that the court would disregard established medical opinion, Mulheron has observed that *Bolitho* has 'certainly changed the outcome of medical negligence lawsuits in more cases than perhaps the label of "rarity" would suggest'.[57] However, despite confirming the court as the final arbiter of

---

54 Margaret Brazier and Jose Miola, 'Bye Bye *Bolam*: A Medical Litigation Revolution?' (2000) 8 Med Law Rev 85.

55 Ibid 113.

56 Ibid 114.

57 Rachael Mulheron, 'Trumping *Bolam*: A Critical Legal Analysis of *Bolitho*'s "Gloss"' (2010) 69 Camb Law J 609, 618.

reasonableness, the *Bolitho* configuration of *Bolam* still largely weighs in favour of medical opinion. For *Bolitho* to be applied, the patient's medical expert must be able to demonstrate that the evidence of the doctor (and their own expert witnesses) lacks a logical basis.[58] It is not enough that their own evidence is logically sound.[59]

The critiques of the *Bolam* test from the perspective of race, gender, and class remain pertinent, despite the *Bolitho* reframing. Miola refers to *Bolam* and medical paternalism as a 'way of thinking' that pervades medical practice in spite of changes to the law.[60] While the representation of women and people of colour within the medical profession has significantly increased,[61] this does not automatically mean that marginalised patients' voices will be listened to.[62] There is a difference between descriptive representation (increasing numbers of people from marginalised groups entering the profession) and substantive representation (in which persons from a marginalised group feel that their interests are represented in decisions/policies).[63] Relying on representation alone to change whose voices are heard in determining standard of care will always be limited. Thinking this way focuses on the *identity* of doctors/health professionals themselves, rather than the *behaviours* and *actions* of doctors (and how these are shaped by the system in which they work) and questioning whether these make sufficient space for the voices of marginalised persons.[64] When marginalised groups enter a long-standing profession, it can be difficult for them to substantively change the ways in which that profession operates.[65]

Paternalism has been a dominant force in modern medicine, and this has especially impacted women and racialised persons.[66] The manner in which doctors are taught (and what is missing from their education),[67] the way in

---

58 Ibid 619.

59 Ibid.

60 Miola (n43) 142.

61 Ibid.

62 Ibid 141–2.

63 We borrow these concepts from political philosophy: Hannah Pitkin, *The Concept of Representation* (University of California Press 1972).

64 Suki Finn, 'Being-from-Birth: Pregnancy and Philosophy' (2023) 19 Euro J Analytic Philos 7–32, 9.

65 On the experiences of a female obstetrician working in the 1980s, see Wendy Savage, *Savage Enquiry* (Virago 1986).

66 Women, racialised people, and, most especially, racialised women are subject to silencing in the healthcare context and not treated as reliable narrators, for example, of their condition or side effects of medications. In such silencing paternalism ('doctor knows best') attitudes are evident. See Rageshiri Dhairyawan, 'The Medical Practice of Silencing' (2021) 398 Lancet 382–3.

67 E.g., there is a pervasive 'lack of emphasis placed on learning how to recognise different clinical presentations in patients from BAME backgrounds': Guan Lim and others, 'Students' Perceptions on Race in Medical Education and Healthcare' (2021) 10 Perspect Med Educ 130, 132. Such an approach reinforces the notion for students that some groups are less important or should be treated as 'atypical'.

which they are taught to respect their peers, and other socially reinforced factors, such as the status of the profession and notions of clinical factors being central in healthcare decisions, mean that what is defended as a reasonable standard of care in medicine can embody institutional racism and androcentrism (male-centred perspectives) regardless of the characteristics of the particular doctor providing care. Doctors practise the behaviours learnt from their training and work in competitive environments embedded within a patriarchal system, which perpetuates sexist and racist practices.[68] For example, obstetrics is an increasingly 'feminised' specialism and yet 'this has not automatically translated into woman-centred care' as obstetric violence and negligence is also perpetuated by women working within a patriarchal system.[69]

In evidencing that a medical opinion is 'responsible', reference is often made to medical guidance.[70] Guidelines, often based on available evidence, do not constitute 'a de facto legal standard of care'[71] but where medical opinion (even if genuinely held) is shown to differ from that in medical guidance it requires explanation. Hurwitz explains that guidance embodies 'a combination of best evidence and judgment', and as such one would assume that recommendations would be 'valid and reliable'.[72] He raises, however, the question of whether too much trustworthiness is invested in medical guidelines. In medical research, there is a lack of diversity,[73] and research is often biased towards certain bodies as the physiological norm – 'male' and 'white' bodies.[74] 'Responsible' opinions are formed on the basis of available evidence and therefore can be based on evidence that has often systematically excluded marginalised populations.

Even where there is evidence relevant to marginalised users of healthcare, specifically around gender and race, there are instances where doctors are not aware of it. In the case of *Blyth v Bloomsbury*, for example, a woman sued her doctor for negligence as he did not inform her of the side effects of the Depo-Provera contraceptive injection.[75] Ms Blyth had explicitly asked her doctor about side effects, but he was unaware of any.[76] Ms Blyth was awarded damages based on the evidence that a female doctor in the same hospital kept a written list of side

---

68 Catarina Barata, Vânia Simões, and Francisca Soromenho, 'Obstetric Violence: A Form of Gender-Based Violence' in Stacy Banwell and others (eds), *The Emerald International Handbook of Feminist Perspectives on Women's Acts of Violence* (Emerald 2023) 203, 211.

69 Ibid.

70 Brazier and Miola (n54).

71 Brian Hurwitz, 'How Does Evidence Based Guidance Influence Determinations of Medical Negligence?' (2004) 329 BMJ 1024.

72 Ibid.

73 E.g., Luther Clark and others, 'Increasing Diversity in Clinical Trials: Overcoming Critical Barriers' (2019) 44 Curr Probl Cardiol 172.

74 Rebecca Dresser, 'Wanted: Single, White Male for Medical Research' (1992) 22 Hastings Cent Rep 24.

75 *Blyth v Bloomsbury Health Authority* (1993) 4 Med LR 15.

76 Ibid.

effects to give to patients.[77] Under current law, this is a clear case of negligence, but there are continuing issues with evidence bias.

There have been some significant social and legal moves towards respecting patient autonomy (see Chapter 9).[78] However, the *Bolam/Bolitho* test remains relevant. Cave and Milo highlight that this test continues to apply in cases concerned with medical diagnosis and treatment, and in relation to the alternative treatments that are offered to patients where they are concerned about certain risks.[79] In *McCulloch*, the Supreme Court found that a doctor was not negligent for failing to offer an alternative treatment on the basis that it would not be medically appropriate, a view which a reasonable body of medical opinion supported.[80] This exemplifies that, in determining standard of care, medical opinion is still prioritised over the values, needs, and wishes of individual patients.

Risk and causation

Once damage and breach have been established, it must be shown that the two are linked: that the breach *caused* the damage (in both fact and law).[81] In medical negligence cases, there are many complicated legal problems around causation: for example, showing that harm would not have come to a patient who was already seriously unwell.[82] More recent case law about complex issues of causation relate to 'counterfactual'-type situations: where doctors do not tell patients about all of the risks of a procedure, did their lack of disclosure *cause* the harm if the risk happens to materialise during the procedure where it was performed adequately?

Doctors have an obligation under their duty of care to disclose the broad or 'material' risks of treatment in order to obtain their patient's informed consent.[83] Failure to do so may result in a breach of this duty, amounting to negligence where a patient suffers a damage that the doctor failed to disclose. The test for when a risk becomes 'material' has evolved within case law over time. Initially, the *Bolam* test would apply, so risk disclosure was construed as an aspect of the doctor's clinical judgement. Thus, in *Sidaway*, the court agreed that the 1–2 per cent chance of spinal column damage and paralysis associated with surgery did not amount to a 'material risk' that the doctor had a duty to disclosure.[84] Ms

77 Ibid.

78 *Montgomery v Lanarkshire* (n18).

79 Emma Cave and Caterina Milo, 'Informing Patients: The Bolam Legacy' (2020) 20 Med Law Int 103, 112.

80 *McCulloch v Forth Valley Health Board* [2023] UKSC 26.

81 The claimant must show that 'but for' the negligence the injury would not have occurred: *Barnett v Chelsea and Kensington Hospital Management Committee* [1969] 1 QB 428. The rules related to remoteness apply – the type of damage (though not necessarily the extent of the damage or the exact way in which it occurred) must be foreseeable: *The Wagon Mound* [1961] AC 388.

82 E.g., *Wilsher v Essex Area Health Authority* [1988] AC 1074.

83 *Chatterton v Gerson* [1981] Q.B. 432.

84 *Sidaway v Board of Governors of Bethlem Royal Hospital* [1985] AC 871.

Sidaway, who had become paralysed following spinal surgery, would not have consented to the treatment if she had been made aware of the risk.[85]

The case of *Chester v Afshar* concerned similar facts to *Sidaway*, where a woman suffered nerve damage during spinal surgery, a risk of which she had not been informed.[86] However, a key difference was that she would have likely consented to surgery even if informed of the risk, although she may have taken a few more days to think about it.[87] Her doctor admitted that he had breached his duty of care, but argued that there was no causation.[88] The House of Lords ruled in favour of Miss Chester by a split of 3–2. While Lords Bingham and Hoffman felt that it would be inappropriate for damages to be awarded where the doctor's breach had not been proven to have increased the risk or worsened the patient's condition, Lords Steyn, Hope, and Walker felt that it would be appropriate to take a 'narrow and modest departure from traditional causation principles' in order to vindicate Miss Chester's right to autonomy and dignity.[89]

In *Montgomery*, the Supreme Court applied the approach to causation established in *Chester*, and set out a test for risk disclosure based upon the subjective needs of the individual patient: 'A risk is material if the reasonable patient in the patient's position would want to be told of it or if the doctor knows or ought to have known that that particular patient would have wanted to have been told of it.'[90] Notably, Lady Hale – in commenting on the importance of the patient's own values – states that the *Bolam* test (determining standard of care) becomes 'quite inapposite' once an issue departs from purely medical considerations.[91] In the context of risk disclosure, where patients' personal values are relevant to their decision to undergo treatment as well as the doctor's medical opinion, the *Bolam* test is inappropriate.

Problems with litigation

Negligent care is often not a singular event, but a pattern of events within the course of care. This can often have more systemic root causes than a negligence action makes space for recognising. Issues such as insufficient ratios of medical staff to patients, insufficient training, and a lack of appropriate equipment can result in negligent care. Excessive stress and overwork, currently a significant issue in the NHS,[92] leads to errors likely to be characterised as negligence.

---

85 Ibid.

86 *Chester v Afshar* [2004] UKHL 41 [5].

87 Ibid [7].

88 Ibid [5].

89 Ibid [24].

90 *Montgomery* (n25) [72]–[73].

91 Ibid [115].

92 Catherine Dominic, Dipesh Gopal, and Sidhu Amandip, '"It's Like Juggling Fire Daily": Well-Being, Workload and Burnout in the British NHS: A Survey of 721 Physicians' (2021) 70 Work 395.

In the context of COVID-19-related negligence claims, Heywood has argued that claims for systemic negligence made directly against hospitals may be more appropriate.[93] Heywood highlights that organisational structures, principles, policies, and protocols adopted by hospitals are necessary to maintain a safe healthcare environment – so where a hospital has failed to maintain this safe system, it may be directly liable for negligence.[94] Bringing an institutional claim against a hospital could go a significant way towards achieving accountability by requiring a more holistic investigation into what went wrong.[95] This could also stimulate systemic changes and improvements to a greater extent than individual claims, by placing the blame at the management level.[96]

Whilst not all instances of negligence are the result of institutional failings, negligence claims around maternity care (the scale of which we outlined in the introduction), for example, is one area where a systemic approach may be most useful.[97] Maternity services are a key area of focus for improvement for the NHS, and independent reviews have identified significant failings and areas for improvement with maternity services across different NHS trusts.[98] The Ockenden review, for example, issued recommendations for improving maternity care across England, including an increased budget for maternity care, maternity training targets, and the ring-fencing of the maternity budget for training purposes.[99] Given the prominence of maternity claims and the fact that these issues speak to the systemic organisation of maternity services, institutional negligence claims may be a more appropriate way of pushing for accountability and improvements in this area.

The structure of negligence litigation itself poses a serious disadvantage to patients who have been injured by poor care and to healthcare professionals who can also be rendered vulnerable by the pressure to provide good care in increasingly hostile conditions (long hours, few resources, workplace culture issues, etc.).[100] In this section, we outline some of the ways in which negligence litigation fails patients, healthcare providers, and the system itself.

---

93 Rob Heywood, 'Systemic Negligence and NHS Hospitals: An Underutilised Argument' (2021) 32 King's Law J 437, 440.

94 Ibid.

95 Ibid 457.

96 Ibid 458–9.

97 NHS Resolution (n2) 56–7.

98 Bill Kirkup, 'Reading the Signals: Maternity and Neonatal Services in East Kent – the Report of the Independent Investigation' (2022) https://assets.publishing.service.gov.uk/media/634fb083e90e0731a5423408/reading-the-signals-maternity-and-neonatal-services-in-east-kent_the-report-of-the-independent-investigation_print-ready.pdf, accessed 10 May 2024; DHSC (Department of Health and Social Care) 'Final Findings, Conclusions and Essential Actions from the Ockenden Review of Maternity Services at Shrewsbury and Telford Hospital NHS' (2022) https://www.gov.uk/government/publications/final-report-of-the-ockenden-review, accessed 17 November 2023.

99 DHSC (n98) 160–1.

100 Dominic and others (n92).

Unfair outcomes

Some elements of negligence are hard to prove – this is especially the case for causation. There are plenty of cases you will come across where your instinct might be that the outcome was unfair, even if the result makes sense as a matter of law. Take for example the case of *Wilsher v Essex Area Health Authority*,[101] in which a premature baby suffered severe damage to his eyes (rendering him blind in one eye and his sight seriously impaired in the other) after a junior doctor negligently administered an excess of oxygen into his bloodstream. While this excess administration of oxygen *could* have caused the damage, there were five factors in total (four related to the baby's prematurity and not to the negligence) that could have caused or contributed to the damage to the baby's eyes. The onus was on the claimant to prove that the negligent act was what 'materially contributed' to the damage.[102] The House of Lords found that 'no one can tell in this case whether excess oxygen did or did not cause or contribute to' the damage since it could have been caused by one of the other completely different potential causes and there was no evidence in the case to establish that the negligence was more likely than any of the other causes.[103] This outcome sits uneasily with our intuitions. At the end of the day, this baby was exposed to some wrongdoing and was injured. It seems sad that he could not obtain some compensation on what seems like a technicality because some other causes could not be ruled out absolutely. Lord Bridge, acknowledging this, concluded his opinion by stating:

> Whether we like it or not, the law ... requires proof of fault causing damage as the basis of liability in tort. We should do society nothing but disservice if we made the forensic process still more unpredictable and hazardous by distorting the law to accommodate the exigencies of what may seem like hard cases.[104]

As this passage acknowledges, the law does result in some outcomes that seem unfair. This might cause us to question whether there is a better way to address injuries in healthcare contexts that involve some negligent care.

Adversarial process

Negligence is an adversarial process: the two sides (claimant and defendant) present their case to the judge(s) who ultimately decide the outcome. The adversarial

101 *Wilsher* (n82).

102 Following *McGhee v National Coal Board* [1973] 1 WLR 1.

103 Wilsher (n82) 1090–1.

104 Ibid 1092.

process can be stressful for an injured claimant.[105] Given that negligence is a technical matter, they will need legal representation. In some instances, the costs associated with pursuing a claim (hiring a lawyer, taking time off work to engage in the process, etc.) can be a barrier to pursuing a negligence claim, especially for persons affected by socio-economic disadvantage. The process is also recognised to be a significant 'source of emotional harm' for health professionals.[106]

Because they are adversarial in nature, proceedings are not structured as a collaborative exercise in uncovering what happened and why. Instead, both sides have incentives to present a packaged version of events that makes it more likely that a claim will (or will not) succeed. Focusing on finding (or avoiding) fault rather than fact-finding can lead to concealment of medical errors because hospitals and doctors have incentives to limit their liability.[107] Consequently, as Tumelty has argued, 'there are often "sharp contrasts" between the goals of plaintiffs [claimants] and the capabilities of litigation' precisely because the process is adversarial.[108] For some people, recognition, explanation,[109] and an apology,[110] and/or some (systemic) change, so that this does not happen to someone else,[111] is more important than damages. Negligence litigation does not help claimants to achieve these outcomes: apologies are not within the power of judges and since cases are dealt with in isolation patterns of negligent care can be easily missed. There is even a case to be made that an adversarial system actively hinders the prevention of medical errors by deterring a culture of transparency and learning from mistakes for improved patient safety.[112]

There are current proposals to move to a 'no fault' system, where negligence would no longer be required for patients to claim damages for injury during medical treatment.[113]

Summary

- Patients can submit form complaints through the NHS complaints system, but this is a lengthy process that could be especially difficult for those in marginalised groups.

105 Mary-Elizabeth Tumelty, 'Exploring the Emotional Burdens and Impact of Medical Negligence Litigation on the Plaintiff and Medical Practitioner: Insights from Ireland' (2021) 41 Leg Stud 633, 641.

106 Ibid 643.

107 Vojko Flis, 'No Fault Compensation for Medical Injuries' (2016) 9 Med Law Soc 73, 75.

108 Mary-Elizabeth Tumelty, 'Plaintiff Aims in Medical Negligence Disputes: Limitations of an Adversarial System' (2023) 31 Med Law Rev 226, 243.

109 Ibid 236.

110 Ibid 238.

111 Ibid 240.

112 Flis (n107) 75.

113 House of Commons Health and Social Care Committee, 'NHS Litigation Reform: Thirteenth Report of Session 2021–22' (2022) https://committees.parliament.uk/publications/22039/documents/163739/default/, accessed 21 November 2023.

- Patients may choose to bring a medical negligence claim in law. There are four elements to a successful medical negligence claim: damage, duty of care, breach of duty, and causation.
- What is legally recognised as damage in law is often a value judgement and some people's perspectives of harm are marginalised in this process.
- The *Bolam* case set out that a doctor had not breached their duty of care if they acted in accordance with agreed medical opinion. This was applied by the courts as excessive deference to the medical profession. This propagated androcentric and racist perceptions about appropriate standards of care.
- The *Bolitho* case clarified the courts' role in properly scrutinising medical opinion, which did introduce some checks on doctors' ability to determine standard of appropriate care.
- In relation to risk disclosure, the law has moved towards a patient-centred approach by acknowledging the importance of informed consent and patients being able to make treatment decisions in line with their own values.
- There are broader issues with medical negligence litigation: it can result in unfair outcomes, it is an adversarial process which can cause stress to both the patient and doctor at the centre of a claim, and it does not adequately account for the institutional or systemic causes of negligence.

Questions for reflection

1. To what extent did *Bolitho* change the *Bolam* test?
2. How does medical negligence law perpetuate gendered and racial injustice?
3. Do you think that the move towards a patient-centred approach in relation to risk disclosure has been a positive change?
4. What would be the benefits of holding institutions accountable for medical negligence instead of individual doctors?

Recommended resources

- Krupa Padhy, 'How Safe is Maternity Care?' (BBC Radio 4, 2023) https://www.bbc.co.uk/programmes/m001ryf6, accessed 29 November 2023.
- NHS Resolution, 'Watch an Introduction to Nadine's Story (Part One)' (2019) https://resolution.nhs.uk/resources/an-introduction-to-nadines-story, accessed 29 November 2023.
- NHS Resolution, 'Watch an Introduction to Nadine's Story (Part Two)' https://resolution.nhs.uk/resources/nadines-story-consent, accessed 29 November 2023.
- TT Arvind and Aisling McMahon, 'Responsiveness and the Role of Rights in Medical Law: Lessons from *Montgomery*' (2020) 28 Med Law Rev 445.
- Taschi Keren-Paz, 'Gender Injustice in Compensating Injury to Autonomy in English and Singaporean Negligence Law' (2019) 27 Fem Leg Stud 33.

- Jonathan Herring and others, 'Elbow Room for Best Practice? Montgomery, Patients' Values, and Balanced Decision-Making in Person-Centred Clinical Care' (2017) 25 Med Law Rev 582.
- Mary-Elizabeth Tumelty, 'Exploring the Emotional Burdens and Impact of Medical Negligence Litigation on the Plaintiff and Medical Practitioner: Insights from Ireland' (2021) 41 Leg Stud 633–56.

Bibliography

Barata C, Simões V and Soromenho F, 'Obstetric Violence: A Form of Gender-Based Violence' in S Banwell and others (eds), *The Emerald International Handbook of Feminist Perspectives on Women's Acts of Violence* (Emerald 2023)

Brazier M and Miola J, 'Bye Bye Bolam: A Medical Litigation Revolution?' (2000) 8 Med Law Rev 85

Brazier M, Cave E and Heywood R, *Medicine, Patients, and the Law* (7th edn, Manchester University Press 2023)

Cave E and Milo C, 'Informing Patients: The Bolam Legacy' (2020) 20 Med Law Int 103

Clark L and others, 'Increasing Diversity in Clinical Trials: Overcoming Critical Barriers' (2019) 44 Curr Probl Cardiol 172

Cumberledge J, 'First Do No Harm: The Report of the Independent Medicines and Medical Devices Safety Review' (2020) /https://www.immdsreview.org.uk/downloads/IMMDSReview_Web.pdf

D'Anna L and others, 'Social Discrimination and Healthcare: A Multidimensional Framework of Experiences among a Low-Income Multi-Ethnic Sample' (2018) 33 Soc Work Public Health 187

Davis A, 'Change, Policy and Practice in Maternity Care since 1948' (2013) https://www.historyandpolicy.org/policy-papers/papers/choice-policy-and-practice-in-maternity-care-since-1948, accessed 27 November 2023

Dhairyawan R, 'The Medical Practice of Silencing' (2021) 398 Lancet 382–3

DHSC (Department of Health and Social Care), 'Final Findings, Conclusions and Essential Actions from the Ockenden Review of Maternity Services at Shrewsbury and Telford Hospital NHS' (2022) https://www.gov.uk/government/publications/final-report-of-the-ockenden-review, accessed 17 November 2023

DHSC (Department of Health and Social Care), 'The NHS Constitution for England' (2023) https://www.gov.uk/government/publications/the-nhs-constitution-for-england/the-nhs-constitution-for-england#staff-your-responsibilities, accessed 8 November 2023

Dominic C, Gopal D and Amandip S, '"It's Like Juggling Fire Daily": Well-Being, Workload and Burnout in the British NHS: A Survey of 721 Physicians' (2021) 70 Work 395

Dresser R, 'Wanted: Single, White Male for Medical Research' (1992) 22 Hastings Cent Rep 24

Dyer C, 'NHS Negligence Claims: £2.7bn Cost Prompts Renewed Calls for System Reform' (2023) 382 BMJ 1688

Finn S, 'Being-from-Birth: Pregnancy and Philosophy' (2023) 19 Euro J Analytic Philos 7

Flis V, 'No Fault Compensation for Medical Injuries' (2016) 9 Med Law Soc 73

Fricker M, *Epistemic Injustice: Power and the Ethics of Knowing* (OUP 2007)

Heywood R, 'Systemic Negligence and NHS Hospitals: An Underutilised Argument' (2021) 32 King's Law J 437

House of Commons Health and Social Care Committee, 'NHS Litigation Reform: Thirteenth Report of Session 2021–22' (2022) https://committees.parliament.uk/publications/22039/documents/163739/default/, accessed 21 November 2023

Hurwitz B, 'How Does Evidence Based Guidance Influence Determinations of Medical Negligence?' (2004) 329 BMJ 1024

Kirkup B, 'Reading the Signals: Maternity and Neonatal Services in East Kent – the Report of the Independent Investigation' (2022) https://assets.publishing.service.gov.uk/media/634fb083e90e0731a5423408/reading-the-signals-maternity-and-neonatal-services-in-east-kent_the-report-of-the-independent-investigation_print-ready.pdf, accessed 10 May 2024

Lim G and others, 'Students' Perceptions on Race in Medical Education and Healthcare' (2021) 10 Perspect Med Educ 130

Mahowald M, 'Sex-Role Stereotypes in Medicine' (1987) 2 Hypatia 21

Miola J, 'The Standard of Care in Medical Negligence: Still Reasonably Troublesome?' in J Richardson and E Rackley (eds), *Feminist Perspectives on Tort Law* (Routledge 2012)

Mulheron R, 'Trumping Bolam: A Critical Legal Analysis of Bolitho's "Gloss"' (2010) 69 Camb Law J 609

Mulheron R, 'Rewriting the Requirement for a "Recognised Psychiatric Injury" in Negligence Claims' (2012) 32 Oxf J Leg Stud 77

NHS Constitution, 'Complaint and Redress' (2009) https://www.gov.uk/government/publications/the-nhs-constitution-for-england/the-nhs-constitution-for-englandhttps://www.gov.uk/government/publications/the-nhs-constitution-for-england/the-nhs-constitution-for-england, accessed 21 November 2023

NHS Digital, 'Data on Written Complaints in the NHS, 2020–23' (2022) https://digital.nhs.uk/data-and-information/publications/statistical/data-on-written-complaints-in-the-nhs/2020-21, accessed 6 December 2023

NHS Resolution, 'Annual Report and Accounts 2022/23' (2023) https://resolution.nhs.uk/wp-content/uploads/2023/07/NHS-Resolution-Annual-report-and-accounts-2022_23-3.pdf, accessed 27 November 2023

NHS UK, 'What is PALS (Patient Advice and Liaison Service)?' (nd) https://www.nhs.uk/nhs-services/hospitals/what-is-pals-patient-advice-and-liaison-service/, accessed 21 November 2023

Nolan D, 'New Forms of Damage in Negligence' (2007) 70 Med Law Rev 59

Norrie K, 'Common Practice and the Standard of Care in Medical Negligence' (1985) Juridical Rev 145

Parliamentary and Health Service Ombudsman, 'How We Deal with Complaints' (nd) https://www.ombudsman.org.uk/making-complaint/how-we-deal-complaints#:~:text=We'll%20gather%20all%20the,advice%20to%20inform%20our%20decisions, accessed 6 December 2023.

Parliamentary and Health Service Ombudsman, 'The NHS Hospital Complaints System: A Case for Urgent Treatment?' (2013) https://www.ombudsman.org.uk/sites/default/files/The_NHS_hospital_complaints_system.%20A_case_for_urgent_treatment_report.pdf, accessed 29 November 2023

Parliamentary and Health Service Ombudsman, 'NHS Complaint Standards: Summary of Expectations' (2022) https://www.ombudsman.org.uk/sites/default/files/NHS_Complaint_Standards_Summary_of_expectations_December_2022_Final.pdf, accessed 29 November 2023.

Pickles C and Herring J (eds), *Childbirth, Vulnerability and Law: Exploring Issues of Violence and Control* (Routledge 2019)

Pickles C and Herring J (eds), 'Introduction' in C Pickles and J Herring (eds), *Women's Birthing Bodies and the Law: Unauthorised Intimate Examinations, Power and Vulnerability* (Bloomsbury Publishing 2020)

Pitkin H, *The Concept of Representation* (University of California Press 1972)

Purshouse C, 'Judicial Reasoning and the Concept of Damage: Rethinking Medical Negligence Cases' (2015) 15 Med Law Int 155

Romanis EC, 'Legal Method and Health Law in Feminist Perspective' in J McHale and A Krajewska (eds), *Reimagining Health Law: From Medical to Health and Social Care Law* (Edward Elgar, forthcoming)

Savage W, *Savage Enquiry* (Virago 1986)

Sheldon S, '"A Responsible Body of Medical Men Skilled in That Particular Art …": Rethinking the Bolam Test' in S Sheldon and M Thomson (eds), *Feminist Perspectives on Health Care Law* (Routledge 1998)

Tumelty ME, 'Exploring the Emotional Burdens and Impact of Medical Negligence Litigation on the Plaintiff and Medical Practitioner: Insights from Ireland' (2021) 41 Leg Stud 633

Tumelty ME, 'Plaintiff Aims in Medical Negligence Disputes: Limitations of an Adversarial System' (2023) 31 Med Law Rev 226

Van Dael J and others, 'Do National Politics for Complaint Handling in English Hospitals Support Quality Improvement? Lessons from a Case Study' (2022) 115 J R Soc Med 390

8

Medical Manslaughter

Amel Alghrani and Hannah Saad

The prosecution of doctors for the offence of gross negligence manslaughter (sometimes referred to as GNM, or 'medical manslaughter') for inadvertently causing the death of a patient has attracted widespread media attention in recent years and has caused much concern. In the UK there are approximately 123,800 NHS doctors, 46 per cent of whom are of Black, Asian, or Minority Ethnic background (BAME).[1] Research indicates that BAME doctors are more than twice as likely to be referred by their employer to the regulator, the General Medical Council (GMC),[2] whilst overseas-qualified doctors are 2.5 times more likely to be referred than UK-qualified doctors.[3] These doctors are also more likely to have harsher regulatory sanctions imposed, such as erasure from the medical register.[4] Whilst much has been written on GNM in recent years, there has been little attention afforded to how the law on manslaughter may impact marginalised healthcare workers. This chapter will explore GNM and consider how the law may impact on diverse groups; namely BAME doctors. In this chapter, we examine whether this documented disparate regulatory treatment by the GMC is replicated at the intersection of healthcare and criminal law in allegations of, and prosecutions for, GNM.

---

1 DHSC (Department of Health and Social Care), 'Record Numbers of NHS Doctors and Nurses in England' (2021) https://www.gov.uk/government/news/record-numbers-of-nhs-doctors-and-nurses, accessed 28 November 2023. We are grateful to Dr Danielle Griffiths and the editors for their useful comments on earlier drafts of this chapter.

2 Doyin Atewologun, Roger Kline, and Margaret Ochieng, 'Fair to Refer? Reducing Disproportionality in Fitness-to-Practice Concerns Reported to the GMC' (2019) https://www.gmc-uk.org/-/media/documents/fair-to-refer-report_pdf-79011677.pdf, accessed 28 November 2023, 21.

3 Ibid.

4 Charlotte Humphrey, Shaista Hickman, and Martin Gulliford, 'Place of Medical Qualification and Outcomes of UK GMC "Fitness-to-Practise" Process: Cohort Study' (2011) 5 BMJ 1817, 1819.

This chapter is split into two parts. Firstly, we set out the law on GNM, highlighting recurring problems with its circular definition and why implementation of this law continues to cause difficulty. Secondly, we highlight how and why the law on medical manslaughter may have a disproportionate impact on BAME doctors.

Evolution of language and semantics in discussions of 'race' and 'ethnicity'

In terms of linguistic considerations, language is continuously evolving, as is the importance of semantics and terminology, when discussing 'race' and 'ethnicity'. 'Race' is a categorisation based mainly on physical attributes or traits, assigning people to a specific race simply by having similar appearances or skin colour (for example Black or white).[5] The term is now widely accepted as a social construct because it is a concept that has been created and defined by society rather than having a basis in biology or genetics. 'Ethnicity' is a common term used to refer to shared cultural experiences, religious practices, traditions, ancestry, language, dialect, or national origins.[6] The Equality Act 2010 defines the protected characteristic of 'race' as including colour, ethnic or national origin, or nationality. Throughout this chapter we use the term BAME, an acronym used to refer to non-white ethnicities who are minoritised in the UK. We note controversy and unease with the term, which stems from the grouping together of diverse ethnicities and the implication that it reflects a singular or homogenous ethnic identity.[7] However, in some contexts it may be appropriate to use this term when making statistical comparisons as the available data has been gathered in such broad terms, adopting the BAME categorisation. This does not detract from, nor negate the need to further subcategorise statistical research to accurately reflect the differential experience of each minority group.

This chapter adopts a critical race theory (CRT) perspective,[8] thereby seeking to highlight experiences, processes, and procedures which, although they may ostensibly appear 'neutral', are far from this.[9] Naturally, the difficulty in proving

5 The Law Society, 'Diversity and Inclusion: A Guide to Race and Ethnicity Terminology and Language' (2023) https://www.lawsociety.org.uk/topics/ethnic-minority-lawyers/a-guide-to-race-and-ethnicity-terminology-and-language, accessed 28 November 2023.

6 Ibid.

7 Adwoa Danso and Yaa Danso, 'The Complexities of Race and Health' (2021) 8 Future Healthc J 22, 24.

8 CRT is an academic field of inquiry, a movement, and/or framework that examines how racism and racial inequality are deeply embedded in society's laws, institutions, and everyday practices. It focuses on the idea that racism is not just an individual problem but is also systemic and structural: Richard Delgado and Jean Stefancic, *Critical Race Theory: An Introduction* (NYU Press 2001).

9 Kimberlé Crenshaw and others (eds), *Critical Race Theory: The Key Writings that Formed the Movement* (The New Press 1995).

causal relationships in the context of racism and bias is confounded by the multilayered, intersecting forms of discrimination experienced by any given social group, which exists 'dynamically across multiple axes of identity'.[10] This chapter touches upon one such intersect – BAME individuals and the overlap with overseas academic qualifications – however, there are other undoubtedly confounding factors, such as class, gender, and religion, which, owing to space constraints, we cannot address here.

Gross negligence manslaughter

The first half of this chapter sets out the law on GNM, highlighting recurring problems with the circular definition and why implementation of this law continues to cause difficulty. This offence, which criminalises inadvertent, unintentional error, has attracted a multitude of criticisms,[11] and has a detrimental mental health and reputational impact upon affected doctors.[12] We differ from other discussions on GNM by highlighting how the law may have a disproportionate impact on BAME doctors, which we elaborate on in 'The BAME doctor' section.[13]

The origins of the law (or lack thereof)

Whilst making mistakes is human, in England and Wales anyone who causes death through gross negligence may face a charge of manslaughter, even where injury may not have been intended. Doctors are no exception. In fatal cases caused by a doctor's inadvertent error, if a jury deems a doctor's conduct to have been grossly negligent, this may result in a conviction for GNM. Thus, the question of whether a doctor's negligence is 'gross' is of central importance. In *R v Bateman*,[14] a doctor faced trial after his patient died in childbirth. Directing the jury, the judge simply advised that they must be satisfied that 'the negligence of the accused went beyond a mere matter of compensation between subjects and

10 Khiara Bridges, 'Introduction: Critical Race Theory and the Health Sciences' (2017) 43 Am J Law Med 179, 180–1.

11 Jo Samanta and Ash Samanta, 'GNM and the Delivery of Healthcare: A Time for Change?' (2019) 26 Eur J Health Law 389; Suzanna Ost, 'Drs Bramhall and Bawa-Garba and the Rightful Domain of the Criminal Law' (2019) 45 J Med Ethics 151; Alun Elias-Jones, 'GNM: Medical Manslaughter or Systems Failure?' (2004) 10 Clin Risk 29; Clare Dyer, 'Manslaughter Convictions for Making Mistakes' (1991) 303 BMJ 1218.

12 Tom Bourne and others, 'The Impact of Complaints Procedures on the Welfare, Health, and Clinical Practice of 7926 Doctors in the UK: A Cross-Sectional Survey' (2015) 5 BMJ 6687, 6692.

13 Oliver Quick, 'Medicine, Mistakes and Manslaughter: A Criminal Combination?' (2010) 69 CLJ 186, 195.

14 *R v Bateman* (1925) 19 Cr App R 8.

showed such disregard for the life and safety of others as to amount to a crime against the state and conduct deserving punishment'.[15]

In the seminal case of *R v Adomako*,[16] Lord Mackay held that negligence is 'gross' when 'the conduct of the defendant was so bad in all the circumstances as to amount … to a criminal act or omission'.[17]

Lord Mackay further set out criteria which purported to provide the 'true legal basis of involuntary manslaughter by breach of duty':[18] This determination depends on the seriousness of the breach, considering the circumstances at the time. The jury must assess whether the doctor's conduct significantly deviated from the proper standard of care, posing a risk of death, to the extent that it should be deemed criminal. Although Lord McKay acknowledged that this assessment involves some circular reasoning, it is a question of degree best decided by the jury, based on whether the conduct was egregiously bad given the risk of death.[19]

Let us delve a little more into the specific facts of the case: John Adomako was an overseas-qualified, Ghanaian-born, locum anaesthetist. During the latter part of an eye operation carried out in Croydon in 1987, Adomako took over the procedure from another anaesthetist, he had had very little sleep after being on call at another hospital and he did not have the assistant he was supposed to have.[20] Whilst in charge of the patient, the breathing tube disconnected and the cessation of the supply of oxygen led to the patient going into cardiac arrest. Adomako panicked,[21] and failed to notice the 'obvious signs' that this disconnect had occurred.[22] Two expert witnesses gave evidence for the prosecution: Professor Payne described the standard of care as 'abysmal' while Professor Adams stated that in his view a competent anaesthetist should have recognised the signs of disconnection within 15 seconds and that the appellant's conduct amounted to 'a gross dereliction of care'.[23] The jury convicted Adomako by a majority of 11 to 1. The Court of Appeal (Criminal Division) and House of Lords dismissed the appellant's appeal. Contrast this to the case of Drs Prentice and Sullman, whose appeals the court heard simultaneously at the same time as Adomako's, and that of Mr

15 Ibid 11–12; Margaret Brazier and Neil Allen, 'Criminalizing Medical Malpractice' in Charles Erin and Suzanne Ost (eds), *The Criminal Justice System and Health Care* (OUP 2007).

16 *R v Adomako* [1995] 1 AC 171.

17 Ibid [187].

18 Ibid [171].

19 Ibid [187].

20 B. Toft and P. Gooderham, 'Involuntary Automaticity: A Potential Legal Defence against an Allegation of Clinical Negligence' (2009) 18 Qual Saf Health Care 69.

21 Adomako stated in evidence that 'after things went wrong I think I did panic a bit': (n16), [182].

22 Ibid [181].

23 Ibid [182].

Holloway, an electrician whose faulty wiring of a residential home resulted in a fatal house fire.[24] Unlike Adomako, their appeals were successful and their convictions were overturned.[25] Prentice and Sullman had committed the errors of injecting a chemotherapy drug (vincristine) into their 16-year-old patient's spine, which led to the patient's painful death.[26] Despite similarities, the judge's condemnation of each doctor varied dramatically. The judge who had initially sentenced Prentice and Sullman had stated that they, two non-Black males, were 'far from being bad men',[27] the inference here being that rather they were good men who, 'contrary to normal behaviour … were guilty of *momentary* recklessness' and 'inadvertence'.[28] This sympathetic language was not extended to Adomako. In contrast, Adomako was berated for his 'failure' to conduct his 'sole duty' by ensuring the patient was breathing satisfactorily[29] – a failure which his Lordship deemed more 'than mere inadvertence', constituting GNM.[30] Arguably, the disparate treatment of different clinicians is evident from the outset. Prentice and Sullman's task of safely injecting the chemotherapy drug might accurately be described as their 'sole duty' to that patient, meanwhile Adomako's failure to notice signs of disconnect in less than four minutes might be considered 'momentary' recklessness. Adomako's case could have been, but was not, seen the same way as his non-Black counterparts.[31] It was from this problematic decision that Lord Mackay's four-step test for GNM, as outlined, emerged.

Many academics have taken issue with the 'circular' logic upon which the fourth element of GNM relies.[32] Namely, that conduct is classified as 'criminal' not by reference to an explicit, objective standard of decision-making, but rather on whether a jury assesses or believes that a crime has been committed.[33] This malleable approach lacks intellectual coherence and generalisable and consistent applicability.[34] The circularity of the definition was unsuccessfully challenged in *R v Misra*.[35] Two junior doctors, Misra and Sirvastava, were convicted of GNM after they failed to notice symptoms

24 *R v Prentice, Sullman, Adomako, Holloway* [1994] QB 302.
25 Ibid.
26 Ibid.
27 The sentencing judge, quoted in Margaret Brazier and Amel Alghrani, 'Fatal Medical Malpractice and Criminal Liability' (2009) 25 J Prof Neg 51, 56
28 *R v Prentice, Sullman, Adomako, Holloway* (n24).
29 *Adomako* (n16).
30 Ibid [183].
31 S. Gardner, 'Manslaughter by Gross Negligence' (1995) 111 LQR 22, 26.
32 See further: Jonathan Herring, *Criminal Law Cases and Materials* (OUP 2010) 291–8; Law Commission, *Involuntary Manslaughter* (1996) https://lawcom.gov.uk/project/criminal-law-involuntary-manslaughter/, accessed 28 November 2023 [3.9].
33 Brazier and Allen (n15) 21.
34 *Adomako* (n16) [183]. R v Misra [2005] 1 Cr App R 21.
35 *R v Misra* [2005] 1 Cr App R 21.

of infection in a patient who had undergone routine knee surgery. The direction had emphasised the importance of there being a serious risk of death, in the light of which the failure to respond appropriately might be characterised as 'truly exceptionally bad'.[36] Their claims that the definition of GNM breached their human rights as it involves retrospective criminalisation (contrary to Article 7) and additionally breached their right to a fair trial (Article 6) failed.

Later cases, such as *R v Rudling* and *R v Sellu*,[37] confirmed the *Misra* approach; that it was a necessary element of GNM that it must be *reasonably foreseeable* that the breach of duty in question gives rise to 'a serious and obvious risk of death'. This foreseeability element was confirmed by the Court of Appeal in *R v Rose*, when they granted the appeal of an optometrist's conviction for GNM.[38] Honey Rose had initially been convicted after failing to sufficiently examine the back of a young patient's eye, which would have shown swelling of the optic nerve and alerted Rose to the possibility of life-threatening papilledema.[39] The young boy later died. Leveson P. stated that there must have been a serious and obvious risk of death.[40] If there is such a risk, but the defendant was unaware of it at the time of the relevant (mis)conduct, regardless of why that might be, the defendant has no case to answer.[41] There are, therefore, now five elements which the prosecution must prove in order for a person to be guilty of an offence of manslaughter by gross negligence (see Box 8.1).

Box 8.1: Key text: Elements of GNM

(a) the defendant owed an existing duty of care to the victim;
(b) the defendant negligently breached that duty of care;
(c) it was reasonably foreseeable that the breach of that duty gave rise to a serious and obvious risk of death (added by *R v Rose*);
(d) the breach of that duty caused the death of the victim; and
(e) the circumstances of the breach were truly exceptionally bad and so reprehensible as to justify the conclusion that it amounted to gross negligence and required criminal sanction.

---

36 *R v Sellu* [2016] EWCA Crim 1716 [151].

37 *R v Rudling* [2016] EWCA Crim 741. Sellu (n 36).

38 *R v Rose* [2018] QB 328.

39 Ibid.

40 Ibid 349.

41 Alexandra Mullock, 'Gross Negligence (Medical) Manslaughter and the Puzzling Implications of Negligent Ignorance: Rose v R [2017] EWCA Crim 1168' (2018) 26 Med LR 346, 352.

Insertion of this additional element of foreseeability has been both welcomed as clarifying the law on GNM, and claimed to have served only to muddy the waters further. As argued by Mullock, 'while the court in Rose asserted that the test remains objective, the objective/subjective dichotomy appears to have become blurred'.[42] Laird further notes how Rose has opened the door to the irrational position that an individual who has assessed risk and subsequently failed to react appropriately, despite being in a position to appreciate the risk, may be culpable, while another, who has completely failed to assess risk, will have no case to answer, thus benefitting from their self-inflicted ignorance.[43] Do you think it is fair that someone who fails to react appropriately to a risk may be held culpable, while someone who remains ignorant of the risk may not?

The BAME doctor

The second half of this chapter explores why BAME doctors may feel particularly at risk of the offence of GNM.[44] To investigate this question, the lifespan of a GNM case is considered. First, we unpack the issue of statistics and why it is difficult to discern how many BAME doctors have been investigated, charged, or prosecuted for GNM.

The prosecution and conviction of doctors for GNM remains comparatively rare. Whilst the Williams Review in 2018 reported a 'marked decline' in *prosecutions* post-*Adomako*,[45] this is in contrast to higher rates of *investigations* since 2013 (151 suspected cases).[46] Statistics on 'medical manslaughter' are not available as a discrete legal category separate from other GNM cases,[47] nor is the ethnicity of those investigated or prosecuted for GNM recorded. Thus, drawing reliable conclusions on how many BAME doctors have been subject to investigation, prosecution, or conviction for GNM is difficult, owing to deficiencies in data collection.[48]

---

42 *Rose* (n38) [77].

43 K. Laird, 'Case Comment: Manslaughter: R v Rose' (2018) 1 Crim LR 76–81; Mullock (n41) 354.

44 DHSC (Department of Health and Social Care), 'Gross Negligence Manslaughter in Healthcare: The Report of a Rapid Policy Review' (2018) https://assets.publishing.service.gov.uk/government/uploads/system/uploads/attachment_data/file/717946/Williams_Report.pdf, accessed 28 November 2023 (hereafter the 'Williams Review').

45 Williams Review (n44).

46 Ibid (emphasis added).

47 Margaret Brazier and others, 'Improving Healthcare through the Use of Medical Manslaughter? Facts, Fears, and the Future (2016) 22 Clin Risk 88.

48 Danielle Griffiths and Andrew Sanders 'The Road to the Dock: Prosecution Decision-Making in Medical Manslaughter Cases' in Andrew Sanders and Danielle Griffiths (eds), *Bioethics, Medicine and the Criminal Law: Medicine, Crime and Society* (CUP 2012).

Griffiths and Quick's research into Crown Prosecution Service (CPS) files in 2019 examined 192 cases relating to 'medical manslaughter'.[49] Those investigations are not representative of the total amount of investigations that will have happened in that time, and the CPS informed them that the table of cases they had provided was compiled manually and relied 'heavily on corporate memory'.[50] The table of 192 cases contained basic factual information about each case: suspect name, date of incident or referral, and the outcome. For some cases, but not all, the table also contained the suspect's medical speciality, a brief description of the failure in question, and the time taken to decide for or against prosecution. The doctor's ethnicity and whether or not they qualified overseas was not recorded by the CPS. Out of the 192 cases referred to the CPS between 2007 and 2018, Griffiths and Quick noted only 12 resulted in prosecutions, thus representing 6 per cent of the total number. Of that 12, not all would have gone to court (in some cases charges may have been dropped), but of those that did, from judgments in the public domain we know that at least six involved BAME doctors.[51]

Notwithstanding the lack of data, the Williams Review acknowledged BAME doctors feel that they are particularly vulnerable to the offence and that this 'was an issue for healthcare services and regulators alike to address'.[52] We now explore why BAME doctors may feel particularly vulnerable to the offence of GNM.

Unexplored ground: why BAME doctors may be more disproportionately impacted

The police and the CPS: institutional racism and unfettered discretion

Criminal investigations into medical deaths, conducted by a subset of the police force, arise from three main sources: familial complaints to police, hospitals contacting police directly, or referral from a coroner regarding suspicious or unnatural death.[53] Since the CPS's establishment in 1986, the responsibilities of investigation and prosecution have been divided between the police and CPS prosecutors, respectively.[54] Nonetheless, the police, given their limited experience

---

49 Danielle Griffiths and Oliver Quick, 'Managing Medical Manslaughter Cases: Improving Efficiency and Transparency' (2019) http://www.bristol.ac.uk/media-library/sites/law/documents/BLRP%20No.%207%202019%20Quick%20et%20al%20-%20merged.pdf, accessed 28 November 2023.

50 Ibid.

51 *Rose* (n38), *Sellu* (n36); *R v Garg* [2012] EWCA Crim 2520; *R v Bawa-Garba* [2016] EWCA Crim 1841; *R v Kovvali* [2013] EWCA Crim 1056, *R v Ramnath* (2009) see BBC News, 'Doctor Guilty of Fatal Injection' (2009) http://news.bbc.co.uk/1/hi/england/staffordshire/7874296.stm, accessed 1 December 2023.

52 Williams Review (n44) 6.

53 Griffiths and Sanders (n48).

54 Ibid.

with such cases,[55] should involve the CPS Special Crime Division (SCD) at an early stage.[56] The SCD, established in 2005, is tasked with handling complex, specialist crimes such as GNM. The Criminal Justice Act 2003 transferred decision-making power, regarding whether to proceed with prosecution, from the police to the CPS.[57] Yet, these regulatory functions are not clearly delineated. Inconsistencies and discrepancies throughout the lifespan of a GNM conviction are evident from the beginning. The Williams Review compiled a range of evidence from medical defence organisations and solicitors attesting to a lack of consistency in which cases coroners 'choose' to report to police.[58]

There may be a fear amongst BAME doctors that they are also more vulnerable to complaint to the police for GNM from families, as well as concerns about how that complaint will be handled by the police. Concern regarding the latter may be influenced by the presence of 'institutional racism' in the police, reported as long ago as 1999.[59] Three decades later, the Casey Report (March 2023), a response to the death of Sarah Everard, who, in March 2021 was abducted, raped, and murdered by a serving Metropolitan police officer, reviewed standards of behaviour and the internal culture of the Metropolitan Police. The report found institutional racism, sexism, and homophobia.[60] The Home Office called for 'urgent action' to address 'deep-rooted ... persistent racial disparities' in policing.[61]

The police have discretion in choosing which doctors to investigate for GNM and will not be immune to the prevalence of institutional racism. Research suggests that the police are habituated to techniques of pre-emptive criminalisation.[62] We know for some offences, BAME individuals remain over twice as likely to

55 Griffiths and Quick (n49).

56 CPS (Crown Prosecution Service), 'Gross Negligence Manslaughter: Legal Guidance' (2019) https://www.cps.gov.uk/legal-guidance/gross-negligence-manslaughter, accessed 28 November 2023.

57 Griffiths and Sanders (n48).

58 Williams Review (n44).

59 William Macpherson, The Stephen Lawrence Inquiry (1999) https://assets.publishing.service.gov.uk/media/5a7c2af540f0b645ba3c7202/4262.pdf, accessed 28 November 2023; see also Lee Bridges, 'The Lawrence Inquiry: Incompetence, Corruption, and Institutional Racism' (1999) 26 J Law Soc 298.

60 Baroness Casey, 'An Independent Review into the Standards of Behaviour and Internal Culture of the Metropolitan Police Service' (2023) https://www.met.police.uk/SysSiteAssets/media/downloads/met/about-us/baroness-casey-review/update-march-2023/baroness-casey-review-march-2023a.pdf, accessed 28 November 2023.

61 Home Affairs Committee, 'Urgent Action Needed to Tackle Deep Rooted and Persistent Racial Disparities in Policing' (2021) https://committees.parliament.uk/work/347/the-macpherson-report-twentytwo-years-on/news/157006/urgent-action-needed-to-tackle-deep-rooted-and-persistent-racial-disparities-in-policing/, accessed 28 November 2023.

62 Diana Fitzgibbon, 'Institutional Racism, Pre-Emptive Criminalisation and Risk Analysis' (2007) 46 Howard J Crime Justice 128.

be arrested.[63] Police decision-making takes an increasingly anticipatory form; decisions are influenced by internalised perceptions that individuals belonging to certain groups are more likely to commit criminal acts.[64] Fitzgibbon observes that in police culture, 'race' is now deployed as shorthand for 'risk'.[65] This may contribute to the disparate application of police discretion.[66] Institutional racism within the police could be a factor that influences whether a BAME doctor will face 'the jackboots of the criminal law',[67] since the process begins with referral to and discretionary investigation by the police. The choice of which cases to pursue for prosecution closely linked with the CPS, thus we now turn our attention to the discretion the CPS hold. We acknowledge that whilst many factors may influence this decision, with regard to the doctors investigated and prosecuted for GNM it is impossible to say how significant a factor ethnicity is as the CPS does not record this information.

The CPS and the prosecutorial approach: unfettered discretion

CPS Guidance is now clear that all CPS areas must refer any medical manslaughter cases to the Special Crime Unit in the Special Crime and Counter-Terrorism Department.[68] However, the prosecutorial stage conducted by the CPS is arguably susceptible to the same pitfalls of institutional racism and subjective discretion. Acknowledging the existence of institutional racism throughout its service,[69] the 'Lammy Review: An Independent Review into the Treatment of, and Outcomes for, Black, Asian and Minority Ethnic Individuals in the Criminal Justice System', published in 2017, reaffirmed its presence, concluding that the CPS's system 'itself [added] some degree of disproportionality'[70] as experienced by BAME individuals. Indeed, the CPS outwardly conceded that prosecutors of GNM

63 Ministry of Justice, 'BAME Disproportionality in the Criminal Justice System in England and Wales' (2016) https://assets.publishing.service.gov.uk/media/5a75928440f0b6360e475224/bame-disproportionality-in-the-cjs.pdf, accessed 28 November 2023, 12; David Lammy, 'An Independent Review into the Treatment of, and Outcomes for, BAME Individuals in the Criminal Justice System' (2017) https://assets.publishing.service.gov.uk/media/5a82009040f0b62305b91f49/lammy-review-final-report.pdf, accessed 28 November 2023 (hereafter the 'Lammy Review').

64 Ibid.

65 Fitzgibbon (n62).

66 Griffiths and Sanders (n48).

67 A phrase borrowed from Ronald Dworkin, see *Life's Dominion: An Argument about Abortion and Euthanasia* (HarperCollins 1993) ch 15.

68 CPS (Crown Prosecution Service), 'Referrals, Approvals and Notifications' (2023) https://www.cps.gov.uk/legal-guidance/referrals-approvals-and-notifications, accessed 28 November 2023.

69 Coretta Phillips, 'Facing Inwards and Outwards? Institutional Racism, Race Inequality and the Role of Black Asian Professional Associations' (2005) 6 Criminol Crim Just 357, 358.

70 Lammy Review (n63) 18.

'find it difficult to judge when to bring a prosecution'.[71] The available guidance on prosecutorial decision-making on GNM sets out guidance; first, there is a two-stage test: (1) evidential sufficiency (realistic prospect of conviction); and (2) public interest considerations.[72] The guidance then sets out the law and details of the GNM offence.[73]

Although the CPS has published guidance as well as a Code for Prosecutors, as Samanta and Samanta note, the guidance presents mainly as a synopsis of current law, and while the Code provides overarching principles for prosecution, it is silent on the exercise of discretion to prosecute.[74] Nevertheless, evidence suggests that the CPS continued to make determinations influenced by evidence of 'bad character' or minimal remorse.[75] Samanta and Samanta warn that legal incoherence has rendered the decision to prosecute dependant 'on chance, luck, or even the defendant's demeanour'.[76] Ultimately, the more coherent and consistent a legal framework is, the less room there is for discriminatory, discretionary application. Ambiguity and inconsistency in prosecutorial decision-making, compounded by the lack of clarity in the law on GNM, may place BAME doctors at a 'particular disadvantage'[77] in comparison to their white counterparts. We acknowledge that of course the CPS could say they often do not know if the suspect is BAME, for instance a BAME doctor may have an Anglo name and the referral may make no reference to the doctor's ethnicity. Notwithstanding this, it is implausible to deny the role ethnicity may play, given the well-documented institutional racism present within the police and CPS and implicit racial biases which individuals may hold.[78]

Juries and expert witnesses: subjective bias as a consequence of legal ambiguity and circularity

The discriminatory chain of discretion and inconsistency stops with neither the police nor the CPS. Rather, the extent of the subjectivity pervading this offence comes to light during trials for GNM, where prosecutions effectively stand or fall on expert medical evidence,[79] and juries are entrusted as subjective gatekeepers of criminality. Juries are responsible for determining whether conduct

71 Law Commission (n32) [3.9].
72 CPS (n56).
73 Ibid.
74 Samanta and Samanta (n11) 401.
75 Ibid.
76 Ibid.
77 Equality Act 2010, s 18(2)(b).
78 Jules Holroyd, 'Implicit Racial Bias and the Anatomy of Institutional Racism' (2015) 101 Crim Justice Matters 30.
79 Oliver Quick, 'Prosecuting "Gross" Medical Negligence: Manslaughter, Discretion, and the Crown Prosecution Service' (2006) 33 J Law Soc 421.

is 'grossly' negligent,[80] with little guidance or clarity beyond answering whether they regarded the doctor's conduct as 'truly exceptionally bad', amounting to a crime.[81] Synonyms such as 'reprehensible',[82] 'wicked', and 'culpable'[83] are used interchangeably and without distinction by the courts. Naturally, juries have thus struggled with this ill-defined concept;[84] there is no indication of where the line between serious mistakes, errors of judgement, and grossly 'bad' negligence ought to be drawn. Yet, the courts continue to stress this distinction – noting the former are 'nowhere near enough' for GNM to be committed[85] – whilst simultaneously failing to clarify it with distinguishable definitions.

The widely publicised case of *Sellu* illustrates the insufficiency of judicial direction regarding GNM. Dr David Sellu, who was born in Sierra Leone and studied medicine at Manchester University, was a senior consultant specialising in gastrointestinal and colorectal surgery. Following an inquest into the death of one of his patients, James Hughes, the coroner focused on the delay in performing surgery and told Sellu's counsel and the court that he believed a crime had been committed. This led to a police investigation into whether or not Sellu had done enough to reduce the delays. The police investigation culminated in the consultant being charged and convicted with GNM for his failure to investigate and operate on the patient with sufficient urgency. Sellu served 15 months (of a two-and-a-half year custodial sentence) when his appeal against conviction was successful.[86] It was held that the trial judge had failed to adequately direct the jury regarding the 'line' separating 'serious mistakes or lapses' from 'truly exceptionally bad' negligence.[87] The extent of the jury's confusion was exemplified by the fact they had to submit a note of question to the court, querying the precise content and remit of their deliberations.[88] Evidently, the imprecise and ambiguous threshold for this offence had led to jury and judicial uncertainty.

A by-product of this uncertainty is that juries' decisions on whether negligence is sufficiently 'gross' are rendered determinative upon the views of expert clinical witnesses.[89] The danger of supplanting decision-making authority from juries to experts was stressed in *Pora*, which concerned a psychologist's evidence on a unreliable confession.[90] The court imposed a duty upon expert witnesses to 'be

80 Anne Lodge, 'GNM on the Cusp: The Unprincipled Privileging of Harm over Culpability' (2017) 81 J Crim Law 125, 127.
81 *Rose* (n38).
82 *Misra* (n35).
83 *Bateman* (n14) [11].
84 Griffiths and Sanders (n48) 117.
85 *Misra* (n35).
86 *Sellu* (n36).
87 Ibid.
88 Ibid 11.
89 Oliver Quick, 'Expert Evidence and Medical Manslaughter: Vagueness in Action' (2011) 38 J Law Soc 496, 502.
90 *R v Pora* [2016] 1 Cr App R3 [24].

careful [and] recognise' the 'need to avoid supplanting the [jury's] role as ultimate decision-maker'.[91] In fact, this was the second ground upon which Dr Sellu's appeal succeeded; the appellate court acknowledged this risk was heightened in the GNM context as the offence consisted of 'a series of descriptions which [were] not expanded upon'.[92] In the face of ambiguity and insufficient legal direction, the jury's decision was predominantly based on 'the opinion of the experts'.[93] The very experts whom the court noted went beyond their remit, offering their conclusions on whether Dr Sellu was guilty of 'gross' negligence;[94] an overextension of function which the lower court failed to remedy.

This reliance upon expert witnesses is of greater concern in the context of GNM given the pool of individuals from which these experts are drawn; the quality of expert witnesses has previously proved critical and problematic.[95] Experts are often retired, practice in unrelated specialities, or are acutely unaware of the realities of current frontline healthcare provision;[96] recent research identified a continual shortage of appropriate experts.[97] Given the degree of deference shown to experts in GNM cases – one prosecutor went as far as saying 'even if I think it's grossly negligent, if I've got an expert who says [it] isn't, I wouldn't be able to prosecute the case … [it] would be doomed to failure'[98] – this shortage is fundamentally problematic.

This diversion of decision-making authority places GNM in a uniquely problematic position. The Lammy Review observed that, overall, jury decision-making appeared to be the only element of the criminal justice process that was not significantly statistically discriminatory.[99] However, this statement was made in reference to the whole criminal justice system; data categorised by offence is not available. Moreover, given the aforementioned deference by juries to expert witnesses, GNM may be uniquely exempt from this one purported aspect of neutrality. The pool of individuals from which these expert witnesses are drawn therefore warrants closer examination. Experts are clinicians drawn from a pool of NHS staff. This is concerning when placed in the wider context where evidence indicates that within the NHS, BAME doctors are excluded, isolated, and harassed at a statistically higher rate than their white colleagues.[100] The disparate blame and scapegoating of BAME doctors within the NHS may be being carried forward into the courtroom in the context of GNM.[101]

---

91 Ibid.
92 *Sellu* (n36) [21].
93 Ibid [23].
94 Ibid [19].
95 *R v Cornish (Errol)* [2016] EWHC 779; *Rudling* (n 37).
96 Williams Review (n44).
97 Griffiths and Quick (n49).
98 Griffiths and Quick (n49) 22.
99 Lammy Review (n63) 31.
100 Danso and Danso (n7).
101 John Launer, 'Ethnic Inequalities in Health: Should we Talk about Implicit White Supremacism' (2019) 96 Postgrad Med J 117.

Individualisation and blame: the wrong approach

Additionally, systemic factors may also put BAME doctors at a greater risk of error and prosecution than their counterparts. In the context of GNM, the criminal law typically seeks an individual to blame,[102] but, by contrast, healthcare professionals work in complex, high-risk environments and when errors occur, it is rarely the result of individual error.[103] Thus, GNM's tendency to '[apportion] blame to individuals' does not sit comfortably when applied to medical errors.[104] Advocates of the 'systems' approach condemn the individualisation of medical error.[105] Systems analysis proffers that errors are 'consequences [not] causes', with their origins not in the perversity of human nature but in 'upstream' systemic factors, for example error traps in organisational processes.[106]

Conversely, GNM's tunnel-vision approach to culpability results in destructive consequences for accused clinicians,[107] whilst simultaneously doing little to remedy contributory systemic failings. The provision of healthcare is indisputably complex;[108] it is built upon 'interdependencies of cognitive decision-making and necessary reliance on optimal functioning of systems'.[109] Yet the courts have persisted in finding evidence of systemic failings to be 'only of peripheral evidence' at trial.[110] This statement was made during the high-profile trial of Dr Hadiza Bawa-Garba and this case illustrates this point well.

Dr Bawa-Garba was a paediatrician of Nigerian descent. In 2015, she was convicted of GNM after the death of six-year-old Jack Adcock from sepsis,[111] and sentenced to two years' imprisonment, suspended. The Court of Appeal unanimously rejected her appeal against conviction.[112] Following Dr Bawa-Garba's GNM conviction, in 2017 the Medical Practitioners Tribunal Service (MPTS), acknowledging that this incident took place amongst wider systemic failings and that the doctor's own failings were not deliberate or reckless, imposed

102 Jenny Vaughan, 'Gross Negligence Manslaughter and the Healthcare Professional' (2016) 98 Bull R Coll Surg Eng 60.

103 Williams Review (n44).

104 Rob Heywood, 'Systemic Negligence and NHS Hospitals: An Underutilised Argument' (2021) 32 Kings Law J 437.

105 James Reason, 'Human Error: Models and Management' (2000) 320 BMJ 768.

106 Ibid.

107 Jenny Vaughan, 'The Case of David Sellu: A Criminal Court is not the Right Place to Determine Blame in Complex Clinical Cases' (2018) BMJ Opinion https://blogs.bmj.com/bmj/2018/03/20/the-case-of-david-sellu-a-criminal-court-is-not-the-right-place-to-determine-blame-in-complex-clinical-cases/, accessed 28 November 2023.

108 Sidney Dekker, *Just Culture: Balancing Safety and Accountability* (Ashgate 2012).

109 Ash Samanta and Jo Samanta, 'Death Caused by Negligent Medical Care: Reconsidering the Role of GNM in the Aftermath of Bawa-Garba' (2021) 21 MLI 293.

110 *Bawa-Garba v GMC* [2018] EWCA Civ 1879 [74].

111 Ibid.

112 *R v Bawa-Garba* (n51).

a sanction of a one-year suspension from practise.[113] The GMC exercised its powers of appeal against MPTS outcomes, arguing that a one-year suspension from practice was insufficient to 'protect the public'.[114] The High Court agreed with the GMC, quashing the suspension and replacing it with the sanction of erasure.[115] The Court of Appeal overturned this ruling, restoring the original suspension order.[116] Subsequently, after a period of 18 months' suspension, Dr Bawa-Garba was cleared by the MPTS to return to practice, subject to conditions.

During the trial of Dr Bawa-Garba it was revealed that the trust's Serious Incident Report following the incident identified 93 failures, only 6 of which were attributable to the doctor herself.[117] The criminal law's narrow focus meant that the abundance of systemic failures – such as inadequate nursing training standards and insufficient rotational staff[118] – were largely ignored and thus at risk of reoccurrence. This is the case despite the historic elucidation of the offence requiring that an assessment of 'seriousness' of the breach is to be conducted 'in all the circumstances in which the defendant was placed'.[119] This general assertion has been largely ignored and individual doctors continue to shoulder the blame for systemic errors and failings. This widely condemned approach led the Royal College of Paediatrics and Child Health to pass a unanimous motion,[120] declaring that 'criminal prosecution … following systemic errors, impairs the advancement of safe healthcare for patients'.[121]

Beyond the patient and clinician-wide issues caused by the individualisation of blame in cases of GNM, narrow application of GNM may disproportionately jeopardise BAME doctors due to the consistently disproportionate impact of the criminal law upon them.[122] This interrelationship was touched upon during the controversy that followed the case of Dr Bawa-Garba, in which the Serious Incident Report following the investigation explicitly concluded that a multitude of systemic and other individual errors took place, yet these were continually

113 MPTS (Medical Practitioners Tribunal Service), MPTS Decision (2017) https://www.mpts-uk.org/-/media/mpts-documents/A11_18_Dr_Bawa_Garba_v_GMC__2018__EWCA_Civ_1879___circular.pdf_75866418.pdf, accessed 29 November 2023.

114 This was done under Medical Act 1983, s 40A.

115 [2018] EWHC 76.

116 [2018] EWCA Civ 1879.

117 When a serious incident has arisen in a hospital, NHS trusts must formally report and investigate serious incidents using a Serious Incident Report, which is deemed an essential part of patient safety and quality improvement efforts in healthcare settings.

118 Ibid.

119 *Adomako* (n16).

120 Nathan Hodson, 'Bawa-Garba Ruling Is Not Good News for Doctors' (2019) 45 J Med Ethics 15.

121 J.S. Bamrah and Ramesh Mehta, 'Back to Blame: Bawa-Garba Could Have Been Any Speciality Trainee' (2018) 11 Sushruta J Health Policy Opin 9, 12.

122 Laura Robertson and John Wainwright, 'Black Boys' and Young Men's Experiences with Criminal Justice and Desistance in England and Wales: A Literature Review' (2020) 4 Genealogy 50.

largely ignored by the court.[123] In response to this, the British Association of Physicians of Indian Origin called for the CPS to bring a charge of corporate manslaughter against the trust, whilst challenging why an investigation into Dr O'Riordan, the white on-call consultant, had not been initiated.[124] Institutional racism and 'outsider' bias within the NHS may have also played roles in the adverse incidents at play in the Bawa-Garba's case. Amidst research that indicates that non-white professionals often receive poorer inductions than their white counterparts,[125] the court was made aware of, but yet disregarded, the fact that Bawa-Garba had recently returned from maternity leave and was not afforded proper induction training.[126] Additionally, she was overstretched, covering the Clinical Assessment Unit, the emergency department, and the 'busy' ward alone.[127] Bawa-Garba was unduly overburdened to an extent that would arguably render any clinician more prone to unintentional error. Moreover, even in her desperate, unsupported position, BAME clinicians are at greater risk of receiving backlash when seeking assistance and are therefore less likely to do so.[128] As Rimmer asserts, 'too often' BAME doctors are not afforded the same 'supportive and compassionate leadership [necessary] to thrive'.[129] This case exemplifies that the systemic nature of issues in healthcare provision are incompatible with the conviction of one individual and offers a familiar example of a BAME doctor bearing the consequences.

Summary

- This chapter has traced the historical development of the offence of GNM in a healthcare context and outlined long-standing criticisms against the offence.
- It explored the potential disproportionate impact on BAME doctors and examined the role of systemic racism and subjective bias in contributing to this impact.
- The chapter identified contributing factors to this disproportionate impact, including institutional racism in the police force, the discretionary role of CPS prosecutors, juries' deference to expert witnesses, and the individualisation of error leading to scapegoating and overcriminalisation of BAME doctors.

---

123 *Bawa-Garba* (n116) [74].

124 Bamrah and Mehta (n121) 12.

125 Jacqui Wise, 'Poor Induction and Lack of Honest Feedback Is Blamed for Higher Rates of GMC Referrals among BAME Doctors' (2019) 365 BMJ 4391.

126 *Bawa-Garba* (n116) [4].

127 Ibid [18].

128 Aisha Majid, 'What Lies Beneath: Getting under the Skin of GMC Referrals' (2020) 368 BMJ 338.

129 Abi Rimmer, 'Ethnic Minority Doctors Are Less Likely than White Colleagues to Report Workplace Improvements during Pandemic' (2020) 371 BMJ 4666.

Questions for reflection

1. How do you think the application of the law of GNM to healthcare professionals strikes a balance between accountability for fatal medical errors and ensuring a culture of continuous learning and improvement in patient safety?
2. Why do you think the issue of disproportionality in the criminal and professional regulation of BAME and overseas-qualified doctors has persisted for decades?
3. What steps do you believe should or could be taken to address these disparities and promote fairness and equity within the regulation of healthcare and the criminal justice system?

Recommended resources

- Anne-Maree Farrell, Amel Alghrani, and Melinee Kazarian, 'Gross Negligence Manslaughter in Healthcare: Time for a Restorative Justice Approach?' (2020) 28 Med Law Rev 536.
- Alexandra Mullock, 'GNM and the Puzzling Implications of Negligent Ignorance: Rose v R [2017] EWCA Crim 1168' (2018) 26 Med Law Rev 346.
- Danielle Griffiths and Oliver Quick, 'Managing Medical Manslaughter Cases: Improving Efficiency and Transparency' (2018) University of Bristol Law Research Paper Series.
- Jo Samanta and Ash Samanta, 'Gross Negligence Manslaughter and the Delivery of Healthcare: A Time for Change?' (2019) 26 Eur J Health Law 389.
- Leslie Hamilton, 'Independent Review of Gross Negligence Manslaughter and Culpable Homicide' (2019) https://www.gmc-uk.org/-/media/documents/independent-review-of-gross-negligence-manslaughter-and-culpable-homicide---final-report_pd-78716610.pdf, accessed 1 December 2023.
- Mustafa Jalal and others, 'Overseas Doctors of the NHS: Migration, Transition, Challenges, and Towards Resolution' (2019) 6 Future Healthc J 76.
- Michelle Robson, Jon Maskill, and Warren Brookbanks, 'Doctors Are Aggrieved – Should They Be? Gross Negligence Manslaughter and the Culpable Doctor' (2020) 84 J Crim Law 312.
- DHSC (Department of Health and Social Care), 'Gross Negligence Manslaughter in Healthcare: The Report of a Rapid Policy Review' (2018) https://assets.publishing.service.gov.uk/government/uploads/system/uploads/attachment_data/file/717946/Williams_Report.pdf, accessed 28 November 2023.

Bibliography

Atewologun D, Kline R, and Ochieng M, 'Fair to Refer: Reducing Disproportionality in Fitness-to-Practice Concerns Reported to the GMC' (2019) https://www.gmc-uk.org/-/media/documents/fair-to-refer-report_pdf-79011677.pdf, accessed 28 November 2023

Bamrah JS and Mehta R, 'Back to Blame: Bawa-Garba Could Have Been Any Speciality Trainee' (2018) 11 Sushruta J Health Policy Opin 9

BBC News, 'Doctor Guilty of Fatal Injection' (2009) http://news.bbc.co.uk/1/hi/england/staffordshire/7874296.stm, accessed 1 December 2023.

Bourne T and others, 'The Impact of Complaints Procedures on the Welfare, Health, and Clinical Practice of 7926 Doctors in the UK: A Cross-Sectional Survey' (2015) 5 BMJ 6687

Brazier M and Alghrani A, 'Fatal Medical Malpractice and Criminal Liability' (2009) 25 J Prof Neg 51

Brazier M and Allen N, 'Criminalizing Medical Malpractice' in C Erin and S Ost (eds), *The Criminal Justice System and Health Care* (OUP 2007)

Brazier M and others, 'Improving Healthcare through the Use of Medical Manslaughter? Facts, Fears, and the Future' (2016) 22 Clin Risk 88

Bridges K, 'Introduction: Critical Race Theory and the Health Sciences' (2017) 43 Am J Law Med 179

Bridges L, 'The Lawrence Inquiry: Incompetence, Corruption, and Institutional Racism' (1999) 26 J Law Soc 298

Baroness Casey, 'An Independent Review into the Standards of Behaviour and Internal Culture of the Metropolitan Police Service' (2023) https://www.met.police.uk/SysSiteAssets/media/downloads/met/about-us/baroness-casey-review/update-march-2023/baroness-casey-review-march-2023a.pdf, accessed 28 November 2023

CPS (Crown Prosecution Service), 'Gross Negligence Manslaughter: Legal Guidance' (2019) https://www.cps.gov.uk/legal-guidance/gross-negligence-manslaughter, accessed 28 November 2023

CPS (Crown Prosecution Service), 'Referrals, Approvals and Notifications' (2023) https://www.cps.gov.uk/legal-guidance/referrals-approvals-and-notifications, accessed 28 November 2023

Crenshaw K and others (eds), *Critical Race Theory: The Key Writings that Formed the Movement* (The New Press 1995)

Danso A and Danso Y, 'The Complexities of Race and Health' (2021) 8 Future Healthc J 22

Dekker S, *Just Culture: Balancing Safety and Accountability* (Ashgate 2012)

Delgado R and Stefancic J, *Critical Race Theory: An Introduction* (NYU Press 2001)

DHSC (Department of Health and Social Care), 'Gross Negligence Manslaughter in Healthcare: The Report of a Rapid Policy Review' (2018) https://assets.publishing.service.gov.uk/government/uploads/system/uploads/attachment_data/file/717946/Williams_Report.pdf, accessed 28 November 2023

DHSC (Department of Health and Social Care), 'Record Numbers of NHS Doctors and Nurses in England' (2021) https://www.gov.uk/government/news/record-numbers-of-nhs-doctors-and-nurses, accessed 28 November 2023

Dworkin R, *Life's Dominion: An Argument about Abortion and Euthanasia* (HarperCollins 1993)

Dyer C, 'Manslaughter Convictions for Making Mistakes' (1991) 303 BMJ 1218.

Elias-Jones A, 'GNM: Medical Manslaughter or Systems Failure?' (2004) 10 Clin Risk 29
Fitzgibbon D, 'Institutional Racism, Pre-Emptive Criminalisation and Risk Analysis' (2007) 46 Howard J. Crime Justice 128
Gardner S, 'Manslaughter by Gross Negligence' (1995) 111 LQR 22
Griffiths D and Sanders A, 'The Road to the Dock: Prosecution Decision-Making in Medical Manslaughter Cases' in A Sanders and D Griffiths (eds), *Bioethics, Medicine and the Criminal Law: Medicine, Crime and Society* (CUP 2012)
Griffiths D and Quick O, 'Managing Medical Manslaughter Cases: Improving Efficiency and Transparency' (2019) http://www.bristol.ac.uk/media-library/sites/law/documents/BLRP%20No.%207%202019%20Quick%20et%20al%20-%20merged.pdf, accessed 28 November 2023
Herring J, *Criminal Law Cases and Materials* (OUP 2010)
Heywood R, 'Systemic Negligence and NHS Hospitals: An Underutilised Argument' (2021) 32 KLJ 437
Hodson N, 'Bawa-Garba Ruling is Not Good News for Doctors' (2019) 45 J Med Ethics 15
Holroyd J, 'Implicit Racial Bias and the Anatomy of Institutional Racism' (2015) 101 Crim Justice Matters 30
Home Affairs Committee, 'Urgent Action Needed to Tackle Deep Rooted and Persistent Racial Disparities in Policing' (2021)https://committees.parliament.uk/work/347/the-macpherson-report-twentytwo-years-on/news/157006/urgent-action-needed-to-tackle-deep-rooted-and-persistent-racial-disparities-in-policing/, accessed 28 November 2023
Humphrey C, Hickman S, and Gulliford M, 'Place of Medical Qualification and Outcomes of UK GMC "Fitness-to-Practise" Process: Cohort Study' (2011) 5 BMJ 1817
Laird K, 'Case Comment: Manslaughter: R v Rose' (2018) 1 Crim LR 76
Lammy D, 'An Independent Review into the Treatment of, and Outcomes for, BAME Individuals in the Criminal Justice System' (2017) https://assets.publishing.service.gov.uk/media/5a82009040f0b62305b91f49/lammy-review-final-report.pdf, accessed 28 November 2023
Launer J, 'Ethnic Inequalities in Health: Should We Talk about Implicit White Supremacism' (2019) 96 Postgrad Med J 117
Law Commission, 'Involuntary Manslaughter' (1996) https://lawcom.gov.uk/project/criminal-law-involuntary-manslaughter/, accessed 28 November 2023
Law Society, 'Diversity and Inclusion: A Guide to Race and Ethnicity Terminology and Language' (2023) https://www.lawsociety.org.uk/topics/ethnic-minority-lawyers/a-guide-to-race-and-ethnicity-terminology-and-language, accessed 28 November 2023
Lodge A, 'GNM on the Cusp: The Unprincipled Privileging of Harm over Culpability' (2017) 81 J Crim Law 125
Macpherson W, The Stephen Lawrence Inquiry (1999) https://assets.publishing.service.gov.uk/media/5a7c2af540f0b645ba3c7202/4262.pdf, accessed 28 November 2023

Majid A, 'What Lies Beneath: Getting Under the Skin of GMC Referrals' (2020) 368 BMJ 338

Ministry of Justice, 'BAME Disproportionality in the Criminal Justice System in England and Wales' (2016) https://assets.publishing.service.gov.uk/media/5a75928440f0b6360e475224/bame-disproportionality-in-the-cjs.pdf, accessed 28 November 2023, 12

MPTS (Medical Practitioners Tribunal Service), MPTS Decision (2017) https://www.mpts-uk.org/-/media/mpts-documents/A11_18_Dr_Bawa_Garba_v_GMC__2018__EWCA_Civ_1879___circular.pdf_75866418.pdf, accessed 29 November 2023

Mullock A, 'Gross Negligence (Medical) Manslaughter and the Puzzling Implications of Negligent Ignorance: Rose v R [2017] EWCA Crim 1168' (2018) 26 Med LR 346

Ost S, 'Drs Bramhall and Bawa-Garba and the Rightful Domain of the Criminal Law' (2019) 45 J Med Ethics 151

Phillips C, 'Facing Inwards and Outwards? Institutional Racism, Race Inequality and the Role of Black Asian Professional Associations' (2005) 6 Criminol Crim Just 357

Quick O, 'Prosecuting "Gross" Medical Negligence: Manslaughter, Discretion, and the Crown Prosecution Service' (2006) 33 J Law Soc 421

Quick O, 'Medicine, Mistakes and Manslaughter: A Criminal Combination?' (2010) 69 CLJ 186

Quick O, 'Expert Evidence and Medical Manslaughter: Vagueness in Action' (2011) 38 J Law Soc 496

Reason J, 'Human Error: Models and Management' (2000) 320 BMJ 768

Rimmer A, 'Ethnic Minority Doctors are Less Likely than White Colleagues to Report Workplace Improvements during Pandemic' (2020) 371 BMJ 4666

Robertson L and Wainwright J, 'Black Boys' and Young Men's Experiences with Criminal Justice and Desistance in England and Wales: A Literature Review' (2020) 4 Genealogy 50

Samanta A and Samanta J, 'GNM and the Delivery of Healthcare: A Time for Change?' (2019) 26 Eur J Health Law 389

Samanta A and Samanta J, 'Death Caused by Negligent Medical Care: Reconsidering the Role of GNM in the Aftermath of Bawa-Garba' (2021) 21 MLI 293

Toft B and Gooderham P, 'Involuntary Automaticity: A Potential Legal Defence against an Allegation of Clinical Negligence' (2009) 18 Qual Saf Health Care 69

Vaughan J, 'Gross Negligence Manslaughter and the Healthcare Professional' (2016) 98 Bull R Coll Surg Eng 60

Vaughan J, 'The Case of David Sellu: A Criminal Court is not the Right Place to Determine Blame in Complex Clinical Cases' (2018) BMJ Opinion https://blogs.bmj.com/bmj/2018/03/20/the-case-of-david-sellu-a-criminal-court-is-not-the-right-place-to-determine-blame-in-complex-clinical-cases/, accessed 28 November 2023

Wise J, 'Poor Induction and Lack of Honest Feedback is Blamed for Higher Rates of GMC Referrals among BAME Doctors' (2019) 365 BMJ 4391

9

Consent to Treatment

Caterina Milo and Thana C. de Campos-Rudinsky

The landmark Supreme Court case *Montgomery v Lanarkshire Health Board* establishes the patient's right to informed consent (IC) and the doctor's duty to disclose information to patients.[1] A breach of such duty may cause a loss and ground a potential claim of medical negligence.[2] IC therefore now frames the relationship between doctors and patients. *Montgomery* marked a legal move away from a 'doctor-knows-best approach' (medical paternalism) where the disclosure of information was determined by doctors alone, towards a patient-centred approach, where patients have a central role in determining which information is disclosed and how medical decisions are made. *Montgomery* gives weight to patients' voices by stressing their right to receive information concerning risks, benefits, and alternatives before undertaking a medical intervention/ treatment. *Montgomery* thus establishes that patients are no longer passive recipients of medical advice but agents and consumers exercising autonomous, informed choices.[3]

This chapter starts by contextualising the evolution of case law as it gradually embraced IC. We also trace how the doctor–patient relationship has evolved over time, moving gradually away from the 'doctor-knows-best approach'. While we

---

1 [2015] UKSC 11.

2 The issue of information disclosure is found in law under both negligence and battery. Negligence, however, sets a different standard of disclosure compared to battery. Whereas avoidance of liability in battery would be achieved via mere 'consent', which is tied to disclosure of 'generic information', negligence requires a higher standard of disclosure, in line with what we now recognise as the 'materiality test'. Though negligence requires 'more' information to be shared in principle, a successful claim is not merely achieved via a failure to disclose such information; this must also be casually connected to the existence of a harm on the side of patients. The latter has been often hard to satisfy in court and has meant that the safeguard of IC may often have a limited reach in practice (e.g., *Diamond v Royal Devon and Exeter NHS Foundation Trust* [2019] EWCA Civ 585). This greatly limits the 'right' to IC in practice.

3 Montgomery (n1) [75].

welcome such a move, we challenge a specific reading of *Montgomery* that sets patients as consumers. We argue that the consumeristic view risks perceiving patients in an overly narrow way, ignoring their whole voice, which includes the physical, the mental, the emotional, the spiritual, and the social components of their humanity. We discuss some of the practical difficulties of the consumeristic view of IC by way of introducing an alternative: the 'ethics of love'. Within the ethics of love approach to IC, patients' voices are defined in a more holistic way as it goes beyond the consumers' expressed desires and includes patients' deepest and most fundamental vulnerabilities and needs.

Gradual recognition of informed consent and its effects on doctor–patient relationships

To speak of IC means to delve into how the doctor–patient relationship unfolds. It is therefore crucial to take a step back and trace the evolution of negligence case law. This will lead us to understand how case law has gradually moved away from a paternalistic 'doctor-knows-best' approach,[4] where only the opinion of doctors mattered, towards a more patient-centred approach to IC, where the voice of patients is central.

From a doctor-centred approach to respect for patients' autonomy: Bolam *to* Chester

Bolam v Friern Hospital Management Committee was the first case to establish both the standard of negligence liability and the standard of information disclosure related to risk assessment and treatment options.[5] These were to be defined by medical expertise and assessment alone. *Bolam* therefore presented a paternalistic approach to IC.[6]

In the subsequent negligence case, *Sidaway v Board of Governors of the Bethlem Royal Hospital*,[7] there is a slight move from paternalism towards a more patient-centred approach to IC. In this case Lord Scarman proposes that the standard of disclosure should be assessed from the reasonable patient perspective: 'the test of materiality is whether in the circumstances of the particular case the court is satisfied that a reasonable person would be likely to attach significance to the risk ...'.[8] However, the majority in this case disagreed with that proposition, holding that a patient was entitled to receive only the

4 See next paragraph for reference to specific pre-Montgomery case law. An overview of these key cases can also be found in Emily Jackson, *Medical Law, Text, Cases and Materials* (OUP 2022), ch 4.

5 [1957] 1 WLR 582.

6 For further reflections on this foundational case refer to Chapter 7 on medical negligence.

7 [1985] AC 871.

8 Ibid [889]–[890].

amount of information that a responsible body of medical opinion considered relevant. For the majority, then, the standard of disclosure was still to be ultimately defined by doctors. The implication of this judgment was that information was considered an aspect of treatment and diagnosis, and thus a matter of clinical judgement.

Later, in *Bolitho v City and Hackney Health Authority*,[9] Lord Browne-Wilkinson questioned the reliability of medical opinion, contending that the mere presence of a number of medical experts sharing an opinion could not in itself be conclusive. This judgment challenged the *Bolam* standard of information disclosure and reassessed the boundaries of disclosure in treatment and diagnosis. Post-*Bolitho*, judges then started to scrutinise the logical foundation of medical opinion. For example, judges started to require doctors pay close attention to the potential evidence both in support of and against their final opinion. The importance of *Bolitho* is that it is the first attempt to limit *Bolam*'s extensive medicalised view of information disclosure. However, the remit of these two cases is different: while in *Bolam* the judgment refers to information disclosure concerning risk, treatment, and diagnosis, in Bolitho the judgment focuses more narrowly on information disclosure of treatment and diagnosis.[10]

The *Pearce v United Bristol Healthcare NHS Trust* case made another relevant step towards a more patient-centred approach.[11] Lord Woolf proposed an adaptation of *Sidaway* to a risk-disclosure context: doctors were to disclose a 'significant risk which would affect the judgment of a reasonable patient'.[12] This would allow the patient to 'determine for him or herself as to what course he or she should adopt'.[13] While this position seems to reflect a more balanced doctor–patient partnership in decision-making, the judgment only went so far. For Lord Woolf, 'significant risk' was only 'significant' if it could indeed affect the judgement of a reasonable patient. Yet, based on the specific facts of *Pearce*, he nevertheless concluded that the 'very small risk' in question was itself not significant. Consequently, in *Pearce*, the patient's individual values and preferences were not actually given consideration. While the language used by the Court of Appeal was suggestive of a movement away from the precedents of medical paternalism and towards a more collaborative, patient-centred approach to decision-making, and while affirming that 'the doctor, in determining what to tell a patient, has to take into account all the relevant considerations', the

---

9 [1997] 3 WLR 1151.

10 See Kathleen Liddell and others, 'Differentiating Negligent Standard of Care in Diagnosis' (2022) 30 Med Law Rev 33; Isabelle Le Gallez, '*Montgomery's* Legal and Practical Impact: A Systematic Review at 6 Years' (2021) 28 J Eval Clin Pract 690. See also *Muller v King's College Hospital NHS Trust* [2017] QB 987.

11 [1999] ECC 167.

12 Ibid [21].

13 Ibid.

judgment ended up reinforcing the status quo: the views of the patient were still rendered insignificant.

An actual step forward occurred, however, in *Wyatt v Curtis*,[14] where Sedley LJ reconsidered Lord Woolf's approach in *Pearce*, explaining that a 'significant risk' should be assessed from the patient's perspective. He acknowledged that the doctor's perspective and the patient's perspective could differ. Doctors could consider a certain risk as irrelevant to merit disclosure, and patients could perceive the same risk as relevant to their decision and therefore worthy of being disclosed. This paved the way for further progress in *Chester v Afshar* (a case that focuses on causation in medical negligence).[15]

In *Chester*, the House of Lords explicitly recognised the need to involve patients in the healthcare decision-making process. It did so by endorsing the patients' right to know any significant risks of a medical intervention. Lord Hope emphasised that the function of the law should be the protection of patients' autonomy and right to choose. In *Chester*, the lack of information disclosure caused the patient to lose the opportunity to consider and perhaps take an alternative course of action. In other words, because doctors failed to disclose relevant information to the patient, the patient was robbed of his right to choose whether to have the surgery, or whether to have it at a different time by the same or another surgeon. Fundamentally, *Chester* rejected the doctor-centred approach and established a more patient-oriented approach to IC, though this theoretical shift was not explicitly stated in the case. Lord Steyn did state, however, that patients have a right to be informed of risks related to a surgery, even if small in magnitude, clearly rejecting a doctor-centred stance.[16] He embraced the language of IC, noting that the court was the final arbiter. He also approved Lord Woolf's remark in *Pearce* that if there was a significant risk affecting the judgement of a reasonable patient, then it is the responsibility of the doctor to inform the patient of that risk.

The Supreme Court judgment in Montgomery *and the explicit shift towards patient-centredness*

A key step towards a patient-oriented approach to IC in the law of negligence was most clearly endorsed by a landmark and transformative Supreme Court case: *Montgomery v Lanarkshire Health Board* (see Box 9.1). This judgment was surely the result of a gradual shift,[17] both within case law (as seen) but also of healthcare practice, which has recognised more and more the centrality of patients and of their diverse voices.

14 [2003] EWCA Civ 1779.

15 [2004] UKHL 41.

16 Ibid [11]–[27].

17 See also *Montgomery* (n1) [81] per Lords Keer and Reed.

Box 9.1: Key case: *Montgomery v Lanarkshire* [2015] UKSC 11

This claim concerns a patient, Mrs Montgomery, who seeks damages on behalf of her son for the injuries which he had suffered during birth. Mrs Montgomery attributes those injuries to negligence on the part of her consultant obstetrician and gynaecologist employed by Lanarkshire Health Board, who was responsible for Mrs Montgomery's care, both during her pregnancy and birth delivery. Most importantly, Mrs Montgomery claims that she was not informed of the risk of shoulder dystocia,[18] connected to her diabetes, and of the possibility of an alternative – safer – delivery through C-section. The latter would have avoided the occurrence of her son's severe disabilities.

In delivering a judgment in favour of Mrs Montgomery, the Supreme Court cemented the move away from paternalism.

First, the *Montgomery* case outlines a new test of information disclosure – the materiality test – which has two limbs.[19] The first limb focuses on the disclosure of what any reasonable person in the patient's position would want to know. This limb has been interpreted as to embody a more 'objective' medical component of the test. The second limb focuses on the needs of the particular patient and their specific circumstances, both of which the doctor should reasonably be expected to be aware of. This second limb can be interpreted to imply a more 'subjective' component. In incorporating both an objective medical element and a more subjective, patient-oriented element, both should be taken into account when deciding what information to disclose. The test serves the purpose of verifying a partnership between doctors' expertise and patients' needs, values, and circumstances.[20] Additionally, information disclosure no longer depends on the magnitude of risks arising,[21] nor on the patient proactively asking questions.[22] In the facts of the case the voice of the patient, Mrs Nadine Montgomery (and her son), was crucially silenced. There is hence, in *Montgomery*, a desire to limit the risk of doctors not sharing information that really matters with their patients. The duty to obtain IC is strictly and clearly tied with a desire to involve patients more, and hear their voices, since it is only when a collaboration between doctors

18 Shoulder dystocia occurs when the baby's shoulder gets stuck in the mother's pelvis during labour. It can cause brain injuries to the baby.

19 *Montgomery* (n1) [87]. For commentary on the materiality test: Michael Dunn and others, 'Between the Reasonable and the Particular: Deflating Autonomy in the Legal Regulation of Informed Consent to Medical Intervention' (2019) 27 Health Care Anal 110.

20 It should be specified that the two components do not carry the same weight. The second limb is relevant only when it is reasonable for doctors to be aware of more subjective circumstances.

21 *Montgomery* (n1) [89].

22 Ibid [73].

and patients is sought that both medical expertise and patients' needs, values, and circumstances can be balanced.[23]

Montgomery, therefore, is innovative in reflecting the view that patients are no longer regarded as mere 'passive recipients' of doctors' advice but are instead conceived as agents and rights-holders.[24]

There are some further nuances of the materiality test that are worth unpacking. Particularly, the test highlights that, while the assessment of risks and benefits is a matter of the doctor's judgement, the way and the amount of information disclosed is calibrated by a patient-centred understanding. For example, while it is the doctor who assesses that there is a risk of shoulder dystocia in Mrs Montgomery's case, the way this information is disclosed varies according to Mrs Montgomery's preferences and values. Now, in determining that the assessment of risks and benefits is a matter of doctor's judgement, *Montgomery* restates the *Bolam* standard of information disclosure,[25] according to which risk assessment and treatment options are to be defined by medical expertise and assessment alone. That is to say, *Montgomery* somewhat still perpetuates a residual *Bolam*'s paternalistic approach to IC,[26] when it reaffirms that the standard of information disclosure belongs to the realm of medical expertise. True, *Montgomery* also tries to balance such paternalism by stressing that information sharing is to be shaped according to patients' values and preferences.[27] In all, however, there remains an internal tension between patient-centredness and paternalism that *Montgomery* does not completely solve.

To be clear, *Montgomery* has marked a crucial legal step forward in the move towards a more patient-centred approach to IC.[28] Case law and professional guidelines on consent pre-*Montgomery* were nothing but expressions of a desire to give more space to patients' views in the medical context.[29] *Montgomery* is the first concrete step towards such desire, clearly expressed via: (1) the provision

23 Ibid [77]–[78], [81], [90]. See also: GMC (General Medical Council), 'Decision Making and Consent, Working with Doctors, Working for Patients' (2020) https://www.gmc-uk.org/-/media/documents/updated-decision-making-and-consent-guidance-english-09_11_20_pdf-84176092.pdf, accessed 14 December 2023

24 *Montgomery* (n1) [75].

25 For an analysis of the existing tension between Bolam and Montgomery see: Emma Cave and Caterina Milo, 'Informing Patients: The Bolam Legacy' (2020) 20 Med Law Int 103.

26 Post-*Montgomery* case law also continues to endorse this *Bolam*-centred approach, see *McCulloch v Forth Valley Health Board* [2023] UKSC 26.

27 *Montgomery* (n1) [82]–[83]; Anne Maree Farrell and Margaret Brazier, 'Not So New Directions in the Law of Consent? Examining Montgomery v Lanarkshire' (2015) 42 J Med Ethics 85, 86.

28 Tracey Elliot, 'Case Comment: A Break with the Past? Or More of the Same?' (2015) 31 Prof Neg 190; Elspeth Reid, 'Montgomery v Lanarkshire Health Board and the Rights of the Reasonable Patient' (2015) 19 Edinb Law Rev 360.

29 See GMC (General Medical Council), 'Consent: Patients and Doctors Making Decision Together' (2008) https://www.gmc-uk.org/-/media/documents/GMC-guidance-for-doctors---Consent---English-2008---2020_pdf-48903482, accessed 14 December 2023.

of a new test of disclosure, which balances the clinical contribution and patient voice;[30] and (2) the acknowledged relevance of dialogue between the parties, to reach a shared decision.[31] Montgomery, in this sense, explicitly establishes the centrality of the patient-oriented approach, even though an internal tension between such approach and paternalism still lingers within the shared-decision-making model.

Subsequent professional guidelines on consent have further sustained and echoed *Montgomery*. For example, the latest General Medical Council (GMC) 2020 guideline on consent (which builds upon the GMC 2008 guideline) emphasises that patients should be supported in their decision-making process through a fruitful and respectful relationship with medical staff; such a relationship takes the form of supported decision-making.[32] This model requires that doctors listen and support patients during their decision-making process, valuing them not merely as decision-makers, but also as people on the path towards making an important personal decision. Doctors, with their medical expertise, should therefore guide patients in making their decision, providing them with relevant information in line with their own medical expertise, yet balanced against the known needs, values, and circumstances of that particular patient. Doctors are not called to reach a mutually agreed decision,[33] but rather to be involved in the decision dynamics as advisors during the decision-making process. They are called, in other words, to be present and accompany their patients in their decision.

A consumeristic view: what is gained and what is lost?

While *Montgomery* advanced the patient-oriented approach to IC, emphasising the key role of patients' voices, one important drawback is the framing in *Montgomery* of patients as consumers of medical goods and services whose desires ought to be considered.[34]

As the judgment in *Montgomery* puts it at [75]:

> Patients are now widely regarded as persons holding rights, rather than as the passive recipients of the care of the medical profession. They are also widely treated as *consumers exercising choices* [emphasis added]: a viewpoint which has underpinned some of the developments in the provision of healthcare services.

30 *Montgomery* (n1) [87]: it should be also clarified that such balance is not uncontested, this particularly in light of the judgment in *McCulloch v Forth Valley* (n26), where the court stressed that the disclosure of what constitutes a reasonable alternative rests on doctors' judgements: [56].

31 *Montgomery* (n1) [90].

32 See particularly: GMC (n29) 5; GMC (n23) 7, 11, 17, 39.

33 This is what the shared-decision-making model might encourage.

34 For critical analysis of the consumeristic approach see also Cave and Milo (n25) 103.

Montgomery defines patients not only as rights-holders but also 'consumers exercising choices'.[35] But what does this expression mean? Consumers are classically those who, in the marketplace, demand a service or a good and receive it through a commercial transaction with the provider who satisfies such a demand.

The idea that patients are consumers is predicated on the understanding that patients are agents responsible for the choices they make and for the resulting consequences. In this sense, there are corresponding duties falling on those who provide goods and services to consumers: not only a duty to hear the consumer's voice, needs, preferences, doubts, but also a duty to try to address them in a satisfactory way. The chief purpose of the provider is to please their clients in an efficient transaction. So, if patients are seen as consumers, the purpose of healthcare providers then also becomes to satisfy the wishes of the patients in a cost-effective, timely transaction.

While this can be seen as a positive outcome for the provision of efficient healthcare services, are there risks connected to embracing the consumeristic approach? We believe there are. The consumerist approach to IC risks reducing *Montgomery*'s positive, dialogical, inclusive approach to IC to a mere transactional account, where information disclosure becomes another automated delivery. If we place too much emphasis on efficiently satisfying the wishes of the patient, whatever those wishes might be, then healthcare professions gradually become mere automatic, expedient provision of medical commodities and consumable items (e.g., a surgery, a treatment, a consultation). To be clear, respecting patients' autonomy is indeed a foundational principle in bioethics.[36] Likewise, efficiency is a key principle for a functioning healthcare governance, especially in a sector overburdened by scarce resources.[37] Yet, an overemphasis on the autonomous choices of the 'consumer' of healthcare services, and on the efficient management of the transactions between consumer and provider, may render the doctor's caring role empty of meaning.

Arvind and McMahon rightly pointed out that the language of consumers in *Montgomery* can risk missing a crucial dimension of the doctor–patient relationship, since it emphasises patients' unilateral decisions at the expense of a collaborative dynamic based on a dialogue between doctors and patients.[38] If brought to an extreme, in narrowly focusing on guaranteeing the autonomous

---

35 This terminology is not new and stems also from the introduction of the internal market in the NHS and Community Care Act 1990.

36 Tom Beauchamp and James Childress, *Principles of Biomedical Ethics* (8th edn OUP 2019) ch 3.

37 Christina Lamb, Daniel Wainstock, and Thana C. de Campos-Rudinsky, 'Ethics of Love for End-of-Life Care: Beyond Autonomy and Efficiency' (2023) 23 Am J Bioeth 76.

38 T.T. Arvind and Aisling McMahon, 'Responsiveness and the Role of Rights in Medical Law: Lessons from Montgomery' (2020) 28 Med Law Rev 445, 462; Sarah Chan and others, 'Montgomery and Informed Consent: Where Are We Now?' (2017) 357 BMJ j2224.

choice of the patient and its efficient delivery, the consumeristic view can risk undermining the doctor–patient *caring* partnership.

One may object to the consumeristic reading of *Montgomery* by claiming that: (1) while access to medical services is of vital importance in a public health system,[39] particularly for the most marginalised groups, at the same time, in a publicly funded healthcare system with scarce resources, patients cannot ask for whatever treatment they wish if it is not medically justified;[40] and (2) *Montgomery*, seen as a whole, does stress the relevance of dialogue and advice.[41] These are correct. However, when the consumeristic approach is interpreted in a more radical way, the upshot is that the role of doctors then naturally becomes extremely limited: presented with the patient's autonomous choice, the doctor would then simply swiftly operationalise the consumer's demands and deliver the requested service in an expedient manner without much thought.[42]

The problem here is that the doctor may risk disregarding the reality that patients face, which is typically more complex than the reality of an average 'consumer'.[43] Patients inevitably face greater difficulties, such as legal and resource limitations, which can greatly constrain their choices, sometimes to the point of completely eliminating options. They can often be in a position of greater vulnerability, discomfort, and distress, compared to the average consumer. Barnes and Prior,[44] for instance, highlight how patients might experience having choice(s) not as an empowering opportunity but as an instance of confusion and uncertainty. Despite having a range of information and options, Barnes and Prior suggest that patients might experience a lack of confidence or decision-making power over the options available – whether because of time constraints or pressing personal circumstances or fears.[45] As a result, many patients feel they

---

39 For a different approach see Sally Sheldon, 'Revisiting the Bolam Test' in Sally Sheldon and Michael Thomson (eds), *Feminist Perspective in Healthcare Ethics* (Routledge 1998).

40 *R (Burke) v General Medical Council* [2005] EWCA 1003.

41 Jonathan Herring and others, 'Elbow Room for Best Practice? Montgomery, Patients' Values, and Balanced Decision-Making in Person-Centred Clinical Care' (2017) 25 Med Law Rev 582.

42 Further evidence of this approach is the case law concerning the assessment of the best interest of patients who lack capacity, which frames it more and more in line with a subjective perspective and less on the relevance of an objective medical component. See: *Aintree University Hospitals Foundation Trust v James* [2013] UKSC 67, *Briggs v Briggs* [2016] EWCOP 48; *Salford Royal NHS Foundation Trust v Mrs P and Q* [2017] EWCOP 23 (Fam).

43 This also finds support in a mixed-methods study on UK patients. See Joanna Goodrich and Jocelyn Cornwell, 'Seeing the Person in the Patient' (2008) https://www.kingsfund.org.uk/publications/seeing-person-patient, accessed 21 October 2020.

44 Marian Barnes and David Prior, 'Spoilt for Choice? How Consumerism Disempowers Public Service Users' (1995) 15 Public Money Manag 53.

45 See also James Marcum, 'The Role of Emotions in Clinical Reasoning and Decision Making' (2013) 38 J Med Philos 501.

are left with no real choice in the end. They may feel more lonely and more uncertain, and less (rather than more) empowered over the choice they are asked to make. This does not entail that patients should not be given choices. On the contrary, we suggest that this should highlight the importance of understanding the complex reality of choices in contexts of higher vulnerability, such as those within healthcare settings, to which the consumerist approach might be oblivious.

The challenges experienced in decision-making processes have also been studied by Jackson.[46] Through a behavioural economic analysis, she reveals how speaking of patients as consumers can create further obstacles to IC. Beyond the issues of rights and the doctor–patient relationship previously discussed, she highlights how patients experience specific vulnerabilities related to the pressure of making a vital decision with major consequences for their life and health. Jackson highlights the power dynamic that exists between the doctor as service provider and the patient as consumer. In view of this power imbalance, service providers have a duty to adequately disclose information in a way that will help patients in their decision-making process.

We ultimately believe that patients' personal and psychological overall situation deserves more than a mere service provision by which a 'tick box' exercise is done. Instead, patients deserve doctors' attentive presence and respectful (and therefore not intrusive) accompaniment throughout their medical journey. This should not be framed as an antagonistic approach between doctors and patients, where the voice of one trumps the voice of the other. Rather, this calls for truly embracing a dialogical relationship between the parties. Again, *Montgomery* is not opposed to a dialogical relationship between the parties; on the contrary, *Montgomery* initiates the patient–doctor partnership model of shared decision-making. However, we do caution that the judgment in *Montgomery*, in framing the patient as a consumer, may lead to an undesirable patient–doctor dynamic.

As mentioned, if the consumeristic view of patients is brought to its extreme, it risks ignoring the broader personal and social reality that patients are facing, and undermining the existence of the dialogical approach with doctors that *Montgomery* supports. It is in the striving towards a better balance between the subjective and the objective, and hence also between the first and the second limbs of the materiality test, that a way needs to be found. Consumerism is problematic insofar as it would advance one (the second limb) with little if any consideration of the other (the first limb). It can risk portraying an antagonistic approach rather than a relational approach where doctor and patients are partners who aim to share a common goal.

46 Emily Jackson, 'Challenging the Comparison in Montgomery between Patients and "Consumers Exercising Choices"' (2021) 29 Med Law Rev 595.

Ethics of love: moving beyond consumerism towards a more holistic account of patient care

The rhetoric used to promote the consumeristic approach to IC revolves mainly around two ideas: autonomous choice and efficient transaction. An over-reliance on autonomy and efficiency as solutions to complex medical questions, such as defining patients' voices, risks, we argue, embracing an overly narrow approach to the doctor–patient relationship in the post-*Montgomery* era. The main risk is the lack of a holistic care ethics approach to IC,[47] which values the patient as a whole person and not merely as a consumer, the doctor as a whole person and not merely as a service provider, and their relationship as a partnership and not merely as a transaction.

To counter the narrow approach of IC offered by the consumeristic view, we propose an alternative approach that seeks to redefine care with love as its central moral value, while still acknowledging both the need to respect the patient's autonomy and the need for efficient, cost-effective healthcare system management.[48] We call this approach the 'ethics of love'. By 'love'[49] in this context, we do not mean romantic emotions, but rather the foundational moral value that should ground all medical encounters.[50] This moral value entails a deliberate choice to be fully attentive and present, offering a respectful (and therefore not intrusive) accompaniment to patients as they navigate their distress and the medical choices they need to make.[51] Neither autonomy nor efficiency rank higher than love for the person, because both autonomy and efficiency are means of loving the patients (in attaining their wellbeing and the common good of all involved in the dynamic of medical care). As means, neither autonomy nor efficiency have value in themselves alone: they should not be implemented in isolation. To be sure, tensions inevitably exist, and yet the ethics of love takes both

47 By care ethics we mean, generally, a normative account that emphasises the moral importance of interpersonal relationships, ascribing ethical value to our interdependence and vulnerabilities in justifying our shared responsibility to care for one another. Here, we put forth an ethical theory of care that centres on love of the whole person, be this person a patient or a doctor, with needs and vulnerabilities that go beyond the material or physical, and include the psychological, mental, social, and even transcendental or spiritual.

48 Lamb, Wainstock, and de Campos-Rudinsky (n37).

49 Some may want to equate love and compassion, a moral value that has been recently incorporated in medical curricula so that medical students can be trained to consider it. Both love and compassion have been defined as practical principles (rather than emotions) guiding choices for the good of the other person. In this sense, they are similar. The difference is that our proposed 'ethics of love' integrate the choice for the good of the other with important questions of the autonomy of the other and the efficiency of the healthcare system.

50 Thana C. de Campos-Rudinsky, 'On Love, Dying Alone, and Community' (2022) 28 New Bioeth 238.

51 Thana C. de Campos-Rudinsky, 'Solidarity and Global Allocation of COVID-19 Vaccines: A Question of Equality?' in Tom Angier, Iain Benson, and Mark Retter (eds), *The Cambridge Handbook on Natural Law and Human Rights* (CUP 2022).

autonomy and efficiency into serious consideration, in an integrated manner. Love never opposes freedom and does not need to be costly or time consuming.

Redefining patients' voices: going beyond (but not against) autonomy and efficiency

Love, as we use it here, aligns with the concept of holistic and compassionate care, which can also be integrated with the principles of autonomy and efficiency. An authentically loving form of care respects the freedom and autonomous decisions of patients, in accordance with principles of justice and an appreciation of the whole person.[52] Also, such care need not be in opposition to efficiency. In fact, there is scientific evidence that love can be offered in simple, non-costly ways. In asking the question of how long it takes and how much it costs to give a suffering patient a loving gaze, attentive and present enough for the patient to feel seen and acknowledged in their suffering, Trzeciak demonstrates that only 40 seconds suffice to attain such a goal.[53]

Integrating autonomy and love

Our proposed ethics of love framework aims to integrate basic care with a more holistic understanding of autonomy and of patients' voices. This redefined care predicated on love comprises the entirety of a person's unique needs (physical, mental, social, and spiritual). This comprehensive view of the patient leads to a more inclusive and diverse conception of patients' voice, encompassing the patients' desires autonomously expressed, but also their deeper vulnerabilities and needs (physical, mental, social, and spiritual), which are often hidden and not explicitly conveyed to the doctor.

While the autonomy of the patient ought to be respected, autonomy is not an unconstrained right. There is no absolute right to choose, as individuals' freedoms are constrained by the common good. For example, my right to autonomously choose a medical treatment can be limited by the public health implications that my individual choice may have upon the health and the common good of my community.

One may want to contend here that our proposed Ethics of Love could justify doctors overruling patients if doctors think it would be for the good of the patient, and especially if such patient is considered particularly marginalised. This is not a trivial point, as medical paternalism has negatively affected the patient–doctor relationship over the past several decades. If 'doctors know best', would this not entail that our Ethics of Love requires that doctors overrule particularly vulnerable patients who don't know what is best for themselves? Again, love

52 Lamb, Wainstock, and de Campos-Rudinsky (n37).

53 Stephen Trzeciak, 'How 40 Seconds of Compassion could Save a Life' (2019) https://www.youtube.com/watch?v=elW69hyPUuI, accessed 23 October 2023.

would never justify overruling patients' autonomy. This would not be love, but an abusive and overbearing form of care. Of course, the tension between autonomy and care is real and we do not pretend it does not exist. Yet, we also believe that good, loving care is possible within the intricate interplay of conflicting values and goals that exist in the reality of healthcare dynamics.

Integrating efficiency and love

Efficiency, like autonomy, is not a principle that can be implemented in isolation. While managing resources efficiently – especially healthcare resources, which are scarce – is a core element of a functional healthcare system, efficiency should not be the number one goal of healthcare providers. Neither autonomy nor efficiency should be overrated values that serve as the solution to all or most bioethical dilemmas. As necessary as autonomy and efficiency are, genuine care emerges from the humbling realisation that particularly during times of vulnerability – such as times of acute illnesses or even ordinary medical needs – when our dependence on one another and the need for companionship become magnified, mere autonomy and efficiency fall short.[54] If it is true that the degree of vulnerability to which one patient is exposed may vary, what remains as a constant is the need for belonging and relationship, beyond a mere consumeristic approach.

Ultimately, we believe that love justifies medical decisions being made not *for* the patient but *with* the patient, respecting the autonomy of the parties involved (patient and doctor alike) and finding reasonable, cost-effective ways of managing such decision.

Practical guidance to operationalising core Ethics of Love elements in the context of informed consent

Attentive presence and respectful accompaniment of patients in their lived experience of vulnerability are at the core of our redefined ethical approach.[55] But how can one be attentively present to patients in distress, and accompany them in a respectful rather than overbearing way, and choose together the best medical option for their specific circumstance? The ethics of love offers practical guidance to implement its core elements of presence and accompaniment throughout the information disclosure process: to communicate truth with love. To explain what this practically entails, one needs to consider the ethical duty of honesty, on the one hand, and the ethical duty of discretion (or prudence), on the other.

Only when honesty is balanced with discretion can truth be communicated in a loving way.[56] Honesty and discretion are, we suggest, integral to the ethics of love approach to IC. The element of honesty relates to doctors' ethical duty

54 Lamb, Wainstock, and de Campos-Rudinsky (n37).

55 de Campos-Rudinsky (n50).

56 Patrick Quinn White, 'Honesty and Discretion' (2021) 50 Philos Public Aff 6.

to disclose truthful, scientifically accurate, evidence-based information to the patient. This seems to be not only uncontroversial but also already supported by *Montgomery*. Unless a 'therapeutic exception'[57] applies, authorising – in very exceptional settings doctors to withdraw information if they consider such disclosure detrimental to the health of the patient[58] – healthcare professionals have an ethical duty of honesty and patients have a correlated right to be informed in a scientifically accurate, evidence-based manner. Honesty therefore is about *truth telling* and *truth receiving*.[59]

The element of discretion further explains how honesty can be more effectively delivered. It relates to doctors' ethical duty to disclose truthful information to the patient using reason and prudence. Reckless communication is antithetical to the ethics of love. While patients have a right to be informed in a scientifically accurate manner, doctors should communicate such evidence-based facts in a way that the truth can be handled, processed, and dealt with. *Montgomery* seems to support this when it stresses the importance of a patient-centred dialogue in doctors' disclosure of information.[60] While this ethical requirement would seem to be straightforward, its operationalisation is not. For example, one may think that communicating with kindness means conveying optimism or even masking the reality with a thin possibility of cure. However, this is not what communicating truth with love and balancing honesty with discretion should look like in reality: communicating the truth in a loving way would never entail nurturing false hope by conveying illusions or lies. Instead, communicating the truth with love empowers the patient with a hopeful – that is, realistic and holistic – perspective. Genuine rather than false hope means presenting a medical condition in light of the patient's unique life circumstances and beyond pure medical statistics.[61]

For truthful information to be disclosed to the patient with reason and prudence, it is imperative that doctors carefully listen to the patient in front of them – to their unique desires, vulnerabilities, and needs. An ethical duty of honesty, which empowers the patient with (genuine) hope, depends on recognising the uniqueness of each patient's voice and going beyond a strictly medical, pragmatic approach to IC that focuses on following mere protocols for most efficiently disclosing data and numerical estimations about cure and prognosis. It seems that *Montgomery* would not in principle oppose what the Ethics of Love proposes in relation to communicating truth with love in the

57 *Montgomery* (n1) [86].

58 Emma Cave, 'The Ill-Informed: Consent to Medical Treatment and the Therapeutic Exception' (2006) 46 Common Law World Rev 140.

59 For a different critical approach, see Jordan Mackenzie, 'Caring by Lying' (2021) 9 Bioeth 877.

60 *Montgomery* (n1) [90].

61 Franco Toscani and Calliope Farsides, 'Deception, Catholicism, and Hope: Understanding Problems in the Communication of Unfavorable Prognoses in Traditionally-Catholic Countries' (2006) 6 Am J Bioeth 6.

balancing of honesty and discretion.[62] However, the consumeristic reading that *Montgomery* allows for could undermine the ethics of love approach to IC: either by turning the doctor–patient relationship into a commercial transaction or, worse, by fostering an antagonistic dynamic between the doctor and the patient, making mutual care and loving support impossible.

Excessively relying on protocols and merely reporting data, numbers, and scientific evidence as efficient ways of proving that the autonomous patient is adequately informed, can easily turn into a tick box exercise of ensuring a 'correct' bedside manner. Love would demand more than these. Love in the medical context requires a commitment to care well for the patient, by being present and accompanying them in their unique journey, without unduly imposing one's care. While this does not entail ditching all protocols, it also entails acknowledging that merely flooding information over the patient for the sake of just sharing data actually leaves the patient alone to deal with a typically overwhelming amount of information.

The ethics of love requires taking the time to be with the patient and accompanying them through their journey of medical care. This is different from service providers being constantly preoccupied with tasks necessary to complete the transaction with the consumer efficiently. Surely this might be perceived as unfeasible in a public healthcare system. True, there is nothing in our argument that claims that love is easy. But the fact that something is not easily accomplished does not mean that it is not ethically required. Interestingly, *Montgomery* itself highlights that time should not be an obstacle to 'good practices', which again shows that the judgement would be in principle supportive of our proposed Ethics of Love – if only the dangers of its consumeristic readings that we have highlighted are addressed.[63]

The ethics of love, ultimately, is less about what providers do (although what they do is extremely important!), and more about *how* they do it. Love forges bonds. Love is about creating a society where all who are ill and vulnerable feel seen, heard, understood, supported, and valued. The ethics of love encourages society to redefine success, shifting the metric from hollow autonomy, independence, efficiency, and productivity to genuine care and loving connections. In the end, the ethics of love is about an entire ethos of belonging, which redefines loving care as a currency of humanity, and fosters also medical environments where the most vulnerable are not abandoned to the storms, but cradled in the warmth of societal empathy and support.

Summary

- The landmark Supreme Court judgment in *Montgomery v Lanarkshire Health Board* emphasises patients' right to IC.

---

62 *Montgomery* (n1) [90].

63 Ibid [58].

- In a move away from medical paternalism, the judgment stresses patients' voices and their right to be informed. Patients are no longer passive recipients of medical advice, but consumers exercising choices.
- While welcoming such a move, we challenge the view of patients as consumers. The consumeristic view risks perceiving patients in an overly narrow way, creating some practical and ethical difficulties around the right to IC.
- We argue for an alternative view, which we call 'ethics of love'. Proposing a holistic care ethics approach to IC, it values the patient as a whole person and not merely as a consumer. It defines patients' voices comprehensively, including their desires, but also their vulnerabilities and needs (physical, mental, social, and spiritual).
- Honesty and discretion are integral elements of the ethics of love approach to IC. When honesty is balanced with discretion, truth can be communicated with love and patients' diverse voices heard.

Questions for reflection

1. What potential and challenges does the consumeristic approach bring to the doctor–patient relationship?
2. How can healthcare professionals better convey information within their medical practice? You may wish to explore this with reference to a specific context of your choice (e.g., COVID-19 vaccinations or abortions, see the 'Recommended resources' section).
3. How can patients better voice their needs and/or concerns in healthcare settings?
4. How can a loving form of care be respectful of autonomy and efficiency?
5. What roles are and/or should honesty and discretion play in the process of information disclosure to patients?

Recommended resources

- Onora O'Neill, *Autonomy and Trust in Bioethics* (CUP 2009).
- Emma Cave, 'Valid Consent to Medical Treatment' (2021) 47 J Med Ethics e31.
- Kings Chambers Podcast, 'Debrief Episode 10: Montgomery v Lanarkshire Health Board (Part I)' https://www.buzzsprout.com/179951/2077788/, accessed 1 September 2023.
- Caterina Milo, 'COVID-19 Vaccination and the Role of Informed Consent: England as a Case Study' 30 Euro J Health Law 428–48.
- Caterina Milo, *Informed Consent to Abortion: Fostering Autonomy and Medical Partnership in Decision-Making Processes* (OUP 2024)
- Uheiro Center for Practical Ethics, 'Waiver or Understanding? A Dilemma for Autonomists about Informed Consent' https://podcasts.ox.ac.uk/waiver-or-understanding-dilemma-autonomists-about-informed-consent, accessed 1 September 2023.
- Uheiro Center for Practical Ethics, 'St Cross Seminar: "I Wouldn't Have Consented If I'd Known That Could Happen": Consenting without

Understanding' https://podcasts.ox.ac.uk/st-cross-seminar-i-wouldnt-have-consented-if-id-known-could-happen-consenting-without-understanding, accessed 1 September 2023.

Bibliography

Arvind TT and McMahon A, 'Responsiveness and the Role of Rights in Medical Law: Lessons from Montgomery' (2020) 28 Med Law Rev 445

Barnes M and Prior D, 'Spoilt for Choice? How Consumerism Disempowers Public Service Users' (1995) 15 Public Money Manag 53

Beauchamp T and Childress J, *Principles of Biomedical Ethics* (8th edn, OUP 2019)

Cave E, 'The Ill-Informed: Consent to Medical Treatment and the Therapeutic Exception' (2006) 46 Common Law World Rev 140

Cave E and Milo C, 'Informing Patients: The Bolam Legacy' (2020) 20 Med Law Int 103

Chan S and others, 'Montgomery and Informed Consent: Where Are We Now?' (2017) 357 BMJ j2224

de Campos-Rudinsky TC, 'On Love, Dying Alone, and Community' (2022) 28 New Bioeth 238

de Campos-Rudinsky TC, 'Solidarity and Global Allocation of COVID-19 Vaccines: A Question of Equality?' in T Angier, I Benson, and M Retter (eds), *The Cambridge Handbook on Natural Law and Human Rights* (CUP 2022)

Dunn M and others, 'Between the Reasonable and the Particular: Deflating Autonomy in the Legal Regulation of Informed Consent to Medical Intervention' (2019) 27 Health Care Anal 110

Elliot T, 'Case Comment: A Break with the Past? Or More of the Same?' (2015) 31 Prof Neg 190

Farrell AM and Brazier M, 'Not So New Directions in the Law of Consent? Examining Montgomery v Lanarkshire' (2015) 42 J Med Ethics 85, 86

GMC (General Medical Council), 'Consent: Patients and Doctors Making Decisions Together' (2008) https://www.gmc-uk.org/-/media/documents/GMC-guidance-for-doctors---Consent---English-2008---2020_pdf-48903482, accessed 14 December 2023

GMC (General Medical Council), 'Decision Making and Consent, Working with Doctors, Working for Patients' (2020) https://www.gmc-uk.org/-/media/documents/updated-decision-making-and-consent-guidance-english-09_11_20_pdf-84176092.pdf, accessed 14 December 2023

Goodrich J and Cornwell J, 'Seeing the Person in the Patient' (2008) https://www.kingsfund.org.uk/publications/seeing-person-patient, accessed 21 October 2020

Herring J and others, 'Elbow Room for Best Practice? Montgomery, Patients' Values, and Balanced Decision-Making in Person-Centred Clinical Care' (2017) 25 Med Law Rev 582

Jackson E, 'Challenging the Comparison in Montgomery between Patients and "Consumers Exercising Choices"' (2021) 29 Med Law Rev 595

Jackson E, *Medical Law, Text, Cases and Materials* (OUP 2022)
Lamb C, Wainstock D and de Campos-Rudinsky TC, 'Ethics of Love for End-of-Life Care: Beyond Autonomy and Efficiency' (2023) 23 Am J Bioeth 76
Le Gallez I, 'Montgomery's Legal and Practical Impact: A Systematic Review at 6 Years' (2021) 28 J Eval Clin Pract 690
Liddell K and others, 'Differentiating Negligent Standard of Care in Diagnosis' (2022) 30 Med Law Rev 33
Mackenzie J, 'Caring by Lying' (2021) 9 Bioethics 877
Marcum J, 'The Role of Emotions in Clinical Reasoning and Decision Making' (2013) 38 J Med Philos 501
Quinn White P, 'Honesty and Discretion' (2021) 50 Philos Public Aff 6
Reid E, 'Montgomery v Lanarkshire Health Board and the Rights of the Reasonable Patient' (2015) 19 Edinb Law Rev 360
Sheldon S, 'Revisiting the Bolam Test' in S Sheldon and Thomson M, *Feminist Perspective in Healthcare Ethics* (Routledge 1998)
Toscani F and Farsides C, 'Deception, Catholicism, and Hope: Understanding Problems in the Communication of Unfavorable Prognoses in Traditionally-Catholic Countries' (2006) 6 Am J Bioeth 6
Trzeciak S, 'How 40 Seconds of Compassion Could Save a Life' (2019) https://www.youtube.com/watch?v=elW69hyPUuI, accessed 23 October 2023

10

Mental Capacity and Decision-Making

Beverley Clough

Disability studies has much to offer healthcare law, given the focus on rethinking central norms and concepts *through* disability, but not just for disabled people. Disability studies is focused on centring disability as part of academic, empirical, and activist work, emphasising the need to be attentive to disability as a starting point rather than an afterthought. The insights generated by reflecting on these core ideas for mental capacity law – particularly around the line between capacity and incapacity and the ways that best-interests assessments are approached – will have broader resonance across the overarching bodies of law considered across this book. One of the cornerstones of healthcare law is patient autonomy. This is reflected in the centrality of consent.[1] Without consent, medical professionals could be liable in the criminal law (battery) or the civil law (trespass to the person, negligence). As Jackson J put it:

> Anyone capable of making decisions has an absolute right to accept or refuse medical treatment, regardless of the wisdom or consequences of the decisions. The decision does not have to be justified to anyone. In the absence of consent any invasion of the body will be a criminal assault. The fact that the intervention is well-meaning or therapeutic makes no difference.[2]

There may be circumstances in which legally this need for consent can be overridden, or when an adult is incapable of deciding for themselves. Central to this is the idea of 'capacity'.

In this chapter, I consider situations where patient autonomy and the right to refuse treatment can be departed from under the Mental Capacity Act 2005

1 And informed consent – see Chapter 9.

2 *Re JB* [2014] EWHC 342 (COP) [2].

(hereafter MCA). The Act covers decision-making in relation to those who have been deemed to lack mental capacity, often individuals with cognitive impairments such as dementia, learning disabilities, autism, or psychiatric disorders. Insights from disability studies are used to draw attention to the ways that this exception to the norm of patient autonomy has been created and maintained through the MCA, and to interrogate the ideas underpinning the law. Cases arising under the legislation can cover a whole range of complex ethical and legal issues including medical treatment, social care, sexual decision-making, and financial matters. This chapter focuses on medical treatment decisions, which are central to the development of the legislation. The MCA has had a somewhat turbulent history, which is unsurprising given that it provides a legal framework for decision-making that often goes against an individual's expressed wishes. The disability lens helps to uncover and challenge the ableist attitudes that shaped the common law prior to the MCA and which have become embedded in the legal framework. The UN Convention on the Rights of Persons with Disabilities (CRPD) poses a key challenge to the MCA and an opportunity to rethink approaches to decision-making in this context.[3]

Introducing a disability perspective

Critical disability scholars highlight the ways that attentiveness to disability can open up ways of rethinking norms and concepts beyond disability, highlighting the ableist foundations of these norms and the ways that they work to marginalise and oppress various groups in society.[4] Much of the early disability studies scholarship was concerned with disability rights and activism. A central tenet of this was the social model of disability. This approach holds that much of the disadvantage experienced by those with impairments is socially imposed rather than pertaining to their bodily or mental state.[5] In its early form, the central ideas of the social model were presented in this statement in the UK by the Union of the Physically Impaired Against Segregation:

> It is society which disables physically impaired people. Disability is something imposed on top of our impairments by the way we are unnecessarily isolated and excluded from full participation in society.[6]

---

3 United Nations Convention on the Rights of Persons with Disabilities (UNCRPD) (adopted 13 December 2006, entered into force 3 May 2008) 2515 UNTS 3.

4 Dan Goodley and others, 'Provocations for Critical Disability Studies' (2019) 34 Disabil Soc 972.

5 Sara Goering, 'Revisiting the Relevance of the Social Model of Disability' (2010) 10 Am J Bioeth 54.

6 The Union of the Physically Impaired Against Segregation and The Disability Alliance, 'Fundamental Principles of Disability' (1975) https://disability-studies.leeds.ac.uk/wp-content/uploads/sites/40/library/UPIAS-fundamental-principles.pdf, accessed 29 November 2023, 4.

Such a view contrasts with the medical or individual model that is often dominant in mental capacity law. The medical model sees 'diagnosis and classification functioning as ends'.[7] Disability, viewed from this perspective, is simply an 'unfortunate state of functioning and being'[8] with a focus on biological cure or management of the condition or person. The core of the social model, in contrast, is that societal structures and institutions, rather than impairments, cause disability and lead to a 'social and moral marginalisation of people with impairments and gives permission to debar them from full participation in society'.[9] The social model separates out disability and impairment, with an impairment being something like an illness or injury, and disability being the disadvantage or loss of opportunities that results from societal barriers. The source of disability is the way that society is organised – through buildings, employment practices, healthcare systems, and so on. A common example is in relation to a wheelchair user being unable to access a building with stairs to the front door. The source of the disability is the lack of ramps or lifts, rather than the impairment. Thinking beyond disability, the social model is a useful tool in making visible the ways in which purportedly 'able bodies' are supported and privileged in society through the design of buildings, education systems, employment practices, and healthcare provision. This is a powerful shift in framing and responding to disability in the law. For health law in particular, it challenges the primacy of diagnosis and a curative approach, instead inviting us to look more carefully at societal and structural issues in shaping lived experience of impairment as well as thinking about different legal responses. Rather than, for example, focusing on curing an impairment such as deafness, the emphasis should be on how society can change to facilitate the inclusion of deaf people.

The CRPD is an important legal development in relation to bringing disability studies and law into conversation. The Convention represented a milestone in international disability rights. It was driven by the participation of disabled people's organisations in the process. There is a social model thread throughout the CRPD. The preamble, for example, stresses the importance of recognising that disability results from the interaction between persons with impairments and attitudinal and environmental barriers to equality and the need to promote and protect human rights for people with disabilities, including those who require more intensive support. The ethos of the CRPD is about taking positive steps to enable rights to be protected.[10] The UK, having ratified the CRPD in 2009, is committed to taking concrete actions to comply with the Convention, which spans legal issues such as equality and discrimination, gender, children with disabilities, the right to life, access to justice, privacy, and liberty.

---

7 Karrie Shogren, 'Considering Context: An Integrative Concept for Promoting Outcomes in the Intellectual Disability Field' (2013) 51 Intellect Dev Disabil 132, 133.

8 Simo Vehmas, 'Ethical Analysis of the Concept of Disability' (2004) 42 Ment Retard 209.

9 Michael Oliver, *Understanding Disability: From Theory to Practice* (Palgrave Macmillan 1996).

10 UNCRPD, Article 4: General Obligations.

Box 10.1: United Nations Convention on the Rights of Persons with Disabilities, Article 12

1. States Parties reaffirm that persons with disabilities have the right to recognition everywhere as persons before the law.
2. States Parties shall recognize that persons with disabilities enjoy legal capacity on an equal basis with others in all aspects of life.
3. States Parties shall take appropriate measures to provide access by persons with disabilities to the support they may require in exercising their legal capacity.

One of the core articles in the CRPD is Article 12; the right to equal recognition before the law for persons with disabilities. It affirms that persons with disabilities should enjoy legal capacity on an equal basis with others in all aspects of life.

In General Comment No 1,[11] the UN Committee on the Rights of Persons with Disabilities affirmed the need for states to holistically examine all areas of the law with a view to ensuring that people with cognitive and psychosocial disabilities have opportunities to express or develop their will and preferences as well as having choice and control over their everyday lives.[12] The General Comment outlines the importance of the concept of legal capacity for the exercise of civil, political, economic, social, and cultural rights and also how, historically, the denial of legal capacity has led to people with disabilities being deprived of such rights through systems of guardianship and substitute decision-making.

The CRPD and Article 12 are particularly important in the context of medical decision-making. The common law and then the MCA have carved out the space for best-interests decision-making on the basis of a *denial* of legal capacity specifically for those with cognitive impairments.

Placing the MCA in context

The story of the MCA really begins in the 1980s. In *F v West Berkshire HA*,[13] the House of Lords considered the situation of a 36-year-old woman (F) with

11 A General Comment is a statement from a treaty body, such as the UN Committee on the Rights of Persons with Disabilities, allowing them to interpret provisions of the Convention or clarify and thematic issues. They are not legally binding but are authoritative.

12 UN Committee on the Rights of Persons with Disabilities, 'General Comment (Number 1) on Art 12: Equal Recognition before the Law' (2014) http://www.ohchr.org/EN/HRBodies/CRPD/Pages/GC.aspx, accessed 14 December 2023.

13 [1989] 2 All ER 545.

learning disabilities who had formed a sexual relationship with another patient in the mental hospital in which she lived. She was said in the judgment to have an intellectual age of five or six years. Expert evidence suggested that it would be a 'disaster' for her if she became pregnant and both health professionals and her mother thought that it was in her best interests to be sterilised. She was seen as unable to consent to this medical treatment and a declaration was sought as to the lawfulness of the operation. It became clear during that there was no clear legal route to authorise the treatment. Unlike the position with children, there was nobody legally authorised to consent to medical treatment on behalf of someone found to lack capacity to consent. This then left medical professionals in a precarious legal position, potentially open to criminal and/or civil prosecution should they provide medical treatment without clear legal authorisation.

In searching for a principle, the House of Lords considered the doctrine of necessity:

> it is the principle of necessity which may render lawful the actions of … the surgeon who amputates the limb of an unconscious passenger [from a railway accident]. It is by virtue of this principle that the doctor who treats him … even the relative who comes to look after him, will commit no wrong when he or she touches his body.[14]

The House of Lords found that the application of the doctrine of necessity could extend beyond emergencies to encompass the situation of the patient who is permanently incapacitated and is never going to be able to give a valid consent.[15] The House of Lords held that

> a doctor can lawfully operate on, or give other treatment to, adult patients who are incapable, for one reason or another, of consenting to his doing so provided that the operation or other treatment concerned is in the best interests of the patient.[16]

There are important disability studies critiques that can be brought to bear on this case. One key issue was the buttressing of the best-interests assessment with the *Bolam* test, such that a person's best interests were framed as those that were not negligent (i.e., in line with a responsible body of medical opinion). This starkly represents a medicalised framing of best interests, in line with the medical model critiqued in disability scholarship, rather than engaging with F's views and the support she might have needed around reproductive choices. Moreover, the language used to describe F and her situation demonstrate further reinforcement of a medicalised model, seeing disability as a deficit and a problematic framing of

14 Ibid [566].
15 Ibid [565].
16 Ibid [551].

mental age and inabilities reinforced F's inherent difference to the non-disabled norm.[17] F's future is similarly seen as one of perpetual disability, necessitating ongoing intervention (F had been residing in the hospital for over 20 years), in contrast to a social model approach that might draw attention to relational and structural changes that might better support F to live in the community. Keywood further notes the problematic focus in the best-interests decision-making on preventing potential pregnancy, rather than 'an examination of how men and women with learning disabilities can best be supported to lead sexually fulfilling lives'.[18]

The Law Lords clearly felt the need to provide a flexible solution to the gap in the law, utilising the common law doctrine of necessity, yet it was clear that this was seen by the judges as not entirely satisfactory. As Lord Bridge opined,

> The issues canvassed in argument before your Lordships revealed the paucity of clearly defined principles in the common law which may be applied to determine the lawfulness of medical or surgical treatment given to a patient who for any reason, temporary or permanent, lacks the capacity to give or to communicate consent to that treatment.[19]

This was still uncertain ground, therefore, and so the Law Commission responded by launching a consultation on a new legal framework to govern this area in 1991. Following this consultation, they set out their recommendations for reform in their report 'Mental Incapacity' in 1995.[20] They outlined a number of problems:

- The law as it stood was 'unsystematic and full of glaring gaps'.[21]
- That it 'failed to keep up with developments in our understanding of the rights and needs of those with mental disability'.[22]
- There was a lack of an effective framework for resolving disputes about the care of people without capacity or for legitimating or regulating the substitute decision-making that regularly took place in practice.
- Societal changes, such as deinstitutionalisation, the ageing population, medical advances, and a rights-focused law and policy agenda were key social and political drivers for change in this area.

---

17 Linda Steele, 'Temporality, Disability and Institutional Violence: Revisiting In Re F' (2017) 26 Griffith L Rev 378.

18 Kirsty Keywood, '"I'd Rather Keep Him Chaste": Retelling the Story of Sterilisation, Learning Disability and (Non)Sexed Embodiment' (2001) 9 Fem Leg Stud 185.

19 *F v West Berkshire* (n13) [548].

20 Law Commission, 'Mental Incapacity' (1995) Law Com No 231.

21 Ibid [1.1].

22 Ibid.

The Law Commission had a number of tensions to navigate in crafting legislation. There was clear recognition of the rights of disabled people in the Law Commission's work, yet this needed to be balanced against a preference for a lack of formality, to ensure that barriers were not placed in the way of the provision of medical treatment by medical professionals and informal carers in their day-to-day care.

The MCA through a disability lens

The process of consultation and then passage through parliament was long and heavily contested. The MCA received Royal Assent in 2005. The Act codified much of the common law but placed it on a statutory footing, providing a clear structure for decision-making. It outlines the approach to assessing mental capacity and mandates that decisions made in relation to someone who lacks capacity must be made in their best interests (unless there is a valid Advance Directive or Lasting Power of Attorney). Section 5 provides a statutory defence to liability that would otherwise arise in relation to battery, meaning that those seeking to use the legislation to provide medical treatment will not be liable for such actions so long as they reasonably believed that the individual lacked capacity and that the action was in their best interests.

Much then hinges on the assessment of capacity. One of the key principles of the legislation, in section 1, is the presumption of mental capacity. Should somebody be assessed as having mental capacity, then their choices will be respected. Should they be found to lack capacity, however, then others may intervene with their decision-making and make decisions in their best interests. The challenge that the CRPD has raised to capacity assessments, and the denial of legal capacity through these, invites us to critically interrogate the assumptions underpinning the MCA.

Capacity

The MCA outlines both a diagnostic and a functional element of capacity. Section 2 outlines the 'diagnostic' requirement for the capacity assessment:

Box 10.2: Mental Capacity Act 2005 s 2

(1) [A] person lacks capacity ... if at the material time he is unable to make a decision for himself ... *because of an impairment of, or a disturbance in the functioning of, the mind or brain.*

(2) It does not matter whether the impairment or disturbance is permanent or temporary.

The Code of Practice, which accompanies the legislation,[23] provides some examples of an impairment or disturbance in the mind or brain, including:

Box 10.3: Mental Capacity Act Code of Practice [4.12]

- Conditions associated with some forms of mental illness.
- Dementia.
- Significant learning disabilities.
- The long-term effects of brain damage.
- Physical or medical conditions that cause confusion, drowsiness, or loss of consciousness.
- Delirium.
- Concussion following a head injury.
- The symptoms of alcohol or drug use.

Section 3 of the MCA then outlines the 'functional' aspect of the capacity assessment:

Box 10.4: Mental Capacity Act 2005 s 3

(1) [A] person is unable to make a decision for himself if he is unable –
  a) to understand the information relevant to the decision,
  b) to retain that information,
  c) to use or weigh that information as part of the process of making the decision, *or*
  d) to communicate his decision ...

(3) The fact that a person is able to retain the information relevant to a decision for a short period only does not prevent him from being regarded as being able to make the decision.

Both the functional and diagnostic elements of the assessment must be established for someone to be deemed to lack capacity. The Court of Protection has been clear that there is 'causal nexus' that needs to be established here – it is not just that the diagnostic and functional aspects must be satisfied, it also must be demonstrated that the functional inability is *caused by* the impairment.[24] It might

23 UK Government, 'Mental Capacity Act Code of Practice' (2007) https://assets.publishing.service.gov.uk/media/5f6cc6138fa8f541f6763295/Mental-capacity-act-code-of-practice.pdf, accessed 29 November 2023.

24 See *PC, NC v City of York Council* [2013] EWCA Civ 478.

be that the functional inability – to understand, or to weigh or communicate information – is caused instead by a quirky personality, or by a language barrier, or lack of education on a particular issue. This can be very hard to disentangle, particularly where there is a lack of clarity as to someone's impairment and the precise impact it has. The case of *Kings College v C* illustrates this.[25] C was a woman who wanted to refuse life-saving renal dialysis following an attempted suicide. There is an interesting discussion in the judgment about the causal link between this functional ability and an impairment of, or disturbance in, the functioning of the mind or brain:

> had I been satisfied that C was unable to use and weigh information in the manner contended for by the Trust, I believe I would have had difficulty in deciding that this inability was, on the balance of probabilities, because of an impairment of, or a disturbance in the functioning of, the mind or brain. … [I]n particular whether what was being seen might be the operation of a personality disorder or simply the thought processes of a strong willed, stubborn individual with unpalatable and highly egocentric views the evidence was likewise somewhat equivocal.[26]

It is worth reflecting here on the importance placed on 'an impairment or disturbance in the functioning of the mind or brain', and indeed why this emphasis on the diagnostic element was thought necessary. This diagnostic or status element to the legislation was not uncontroversial in the consultation and debates leading to the Act. In their consultation paper 'A New Jurisdiction', the Law Commission stated that:

> From the responses received to our consultation paper it appears that more distress is caused by over-extensive use of protective powers than by any stigma found to attach to the term 'mental disorder'. It also seems that the requirement [inclusion of a diagnostic element] goes at least some way towards providing *a safeguard against improper interference in the lives of those whose perceived failure to manage is attributable merely to a lack of inclination or eccentricity*.[27]

In their 1995 report, the Law Commission signalled that the balance fell in favour of including a diagnostic element to ensure that 'the test is stringent

25 [2015] EWCOP 59.

26 Ibid [93].

27 Law Commission, 'Consultation Paper 128 Mentally Incapacitated Adults and Decision Making: A New Jurisdiction' (1992) https://cloud-platform-e218f50a4812967ba1215eaecede923f.s3.amazonaws.com/uploads/sites/30/2016/08/No.130-Mentally-Incapacitated-and-Other-Vulnerable-Adults-Public-Law-Protection.pdf, accessed 29 November 2023 [3.13].

enough *not* to catch large numbers of people who make unusual or unwise decisions'.[28] Recognition was given to the criticisms propounded at the time by Carson, who argued that both a test for capacity and a diagnostic element to this were misconceived:

> Life is not so simple as mental disorder or no mental disorder, capacity or incapacity, though it is regularly portrayed by the law as being such. The Law Commission's interim proposals, if implemented, would continue this dichotomous legal view of the world and avoid meeting the challenge or incorporating and rationalising legal developments such as misrepresentation, consent and undue influence into a more general law about when decisions made by *anyone* are validly made.[29]

The Commission reported Carson's view as being a rejection of a 'medical model' of the assessment of mental capacity, yet gave a number of reasons to reject this 'mainstreaming approach', as they termed it, including that:

- It puts a heavy burden on the test of incapacity.
- Another respondent could not agree that there could be mental incapacity without mental disorder.[30]

The consolidation of the dominance of the medical profession is evident here and in the legislation through the perceived necessity of the diagnostic element. Mental capacity continues to be seen as a medical concern, firmly within the realms of medical expertise. The idea of 'capacity' is accepted as an objective and measurable 'thing' through this discussion by the Law Commission, in contrast to the more recent rejection of this approach by the CRPD Committee. In General Comment No 1, the CRPD Committee noted the conflation of legal capacity (comprised of legal standing and legal agency) with mental capacity (judgements about decision-making skills) which has often been used to justify systems of substitute decision-making or guardianship and the need to abolish these.[31] In particular, and a clear reflection of the social model of disability underpinning the Convention, the Committee stressed that:

> Mental capacity is not, as is commonly presented, an objective, scientific and naturally occurring phenomenon. Mental capacity is contingent on social and political contexts, as are the disciplines,

28 Law Commission (n20) [3.18].

29 David Carson, 'Disabling Progress: The Law Commission's Proposals on Mentally Incapacitated Adults' Decision Making' (1993) 15 J Social Welfare Fam Law 314.

30 Law Commission (n20) [2.15].

31 UNCRPD (n8) [13]–[15].

> professions and practices which play a dominant role in assessing mental capacity.[32]

Instead of relying on such an approach, the Committee stressed the need to provide support to exercise legal capacity, including supported decision-making. This has provoked much debate about what this means in terms of the compatibility of the MCA with the CRPD.[33]

Critiques of the medicalised focus can be developed with insights from disability scholarship and activism stemming from user and survivor movements. As Guidry-Grimes suggests, 'defining illness and disability is a value-laden exercise'[34] and history is replete with examples of the pathologisation of marginalised groups. Potentially discriminatory ideas or presumptions can end up driving diagnosis and definitions of disability. An infamous example of this is the pathologisation and medicalisation of enslaved African-Americans fleeing captivity as 'Drapetomania'.[35] Some groups of users and survivors of psychiatry have contested the dominance of medicalisation and diagnosis, as part of activist efforts to end practices of restraint and forced treatment and to disrupt the power of medical professionals. Bringing these insights to bear on the MCA, particularly given the challenge posed by Article 12 CRPD and the decentring of capacity assessments, offers an opportunity to further scrutinise the role of law in perpetuating medicalised dominance and to better understand the social barriers and factors at play.

Legal commentators have noted that the MCA privileges medicalised conceptions through an assessment of capacity that places a high value on rationality. Taylor draws attention to how assumptions of rationality, independence, and normalcy can produce wrongful and harmful views of disability and humanity of disabled lives.[36] Capacity can be questioned on the 'flimsiest evidence'.[37] This narrow, rational understanding of capacity can lead to a sterile and unsophisticated assessment that does not take adequate account of the relational nature of capacity,

---

32 Ibid [14].

33 Peter Bartlett, 'The United Nations Convention on the Rights of Persons with Disabilities and Mental Health Law' (2012) 75 Med Law Rev 752.

34 Laura Guidry-Grimes, 'Defining Mental Illness and Psychiatric Disability' in Joel Michael Reynolds and Christine Wieseler (eds), *The Disability Bioethics Reader* (Routledge 2022) 273.

35 Bill Bynum, 'Discarded Diagnoses' (2002) 9 Lancet 898.

36 Ashley Taylor, '"Lives Worth Living": Theorizing Moral Status and Expressions of Human Life' (2013) 33 Disability Stud Q https://dsq-sds.org/index.php/dsq/article/view/3875/3404, accessed 29 November 2023.

37 Bartlett (n33) 761. See *An NHS Trust v ST* (2023) EWCOP 40 for a recent example. A 19-year-old girl with a rare mitochondrial disease challenged the decision of the NHS trust to place her on a palliative care pathway. It was not immediately clear what the impairment was that would bring her into the scope of the MCA, with some evidence suggesting the inability to use or weigh information was instead stemming from misplaced hope. However, Roberts J stated that '[t]here is thus no requirement for the court to be able to formulate precisely the underlying condition or conditions which constitute the impairment' [97].

in that people's decision-making abilities are highly context dependent and can be undermined or fostered by situational factors.[38] In the context of sterilisation, there is a long-recognised tendency for professionals and judges to defer to a medicalised understanding of learning disability and 'ignore crucial questions about the importance of men and women with learning disabilities leading socially valued lives and produce a deeply problematic conception of sexed identity'.[39] Furthermore, through this narrow lens, 'patients become understood in terms of physical, mental or emotional frailty and dysfunction',[40] thus situating risks within the person with a cognitive impairment and preventing a broader consideration of the various sources of concerns and the means by which to support the person to meaningfully access their rights and participate fully in society. Such insights resonate with the critiques of the common law and the case of *Re F* discussed earlier.[41]

The opening up of the capacity/incapacity binary catalysed by the CRPD resonates with conceptual debates across other critical theoretical approaches that highlight the white, male, able-bodied norms that underpin liberal legal frameworks. Mental capacity law is explicitly driven by Enlightenment humanist ideals, which place the independent, rational human actor as the central figure against which the incapacitous 'Other' is placed.[42] Disability scholars have long challenged the focus on humanist ideas of rationality and intelligence that are central to social and legal ordering.[43] Joseph, for example, has exposed the entanglement of categorisation of people as 'types' as part of dehumanising colonial and imperial projects to establish human hierarchies.[44] They urge close scrutiny of 'how and why articulations of difference have been inoculated into societies and what historical and contemporary projects they continue to serve',[45] linking back to the earlier point about pathologisation and medicalisation. Mills, in his work on race and the law, highlights how the approaches to justice and equality that are perpetuated in liberal political theory maintain and reinforce white European settler colonial ideas.[46] Pitts, writing on the intersection of disability and race, highlights the processes through which 'white, able-bodied, heterosexual cisgender men become centred as the most

38 Natalie Banner, 'Can Procedural and Substantive Elements of Decision Making be Reconciled with Assessments of Mental Capacity?' (2013) 9 Int J Law Context 71.

39 Kirsty Keywood, 'Sterilising the Woman with Learning Difficulties: In Her Best Interests?' in Jo Bridgeman and Susan Millns (eds), *Law and Body Politics: Regulating the Female Body* (Aldershot 1995).

40 Keywood (n18) 190.

41 n12.

42 See e.g., Vehmas (n8).

43 Ibid.

44 Ameil Joseph, 'The Necessity of an Attention to Eurocentrism and Colonial Technologies: An Addition to Critical Mental Health Literature' (2015) 30 Disabil Soc 1021.

45 Ibid 1037.

46 Charles Mills, *The Racial Contract* (Cornell University Press 1997).

productive (and thereby valuable) citizens within capitalist societies'.[47] This invites us to reflect on the ways that institutions such as healthcare work to protect the interests of certain groups of citizens. These are important insights to consider in a more critical interrogation of the MCA and the assessment of capacity central to it to expose the problematic underpinnings and workings of the capacity/incapacity distinction. We can also see the embeddedness of medicalised and often ableist ideas of cognitive impairment in the best-interests provisions of the MCA.

Best interests

Once it has been established that somebody lacks mental capacity, the legislation states that any decision must be made in their best interests. Section 4 provides guidance on best-interests decision-making:

Box 10.5: Mental Capacity Act 2005 s 4

(1) In determining for the purposes of the Act what is in a person's best interests, the person making the determination must not make it merely on the basis of – the person's age or appearance, or a condition of his, or an aspect of his behaviour, which might lead others to make unjustified assumptions about what might be in his best interests.

(3) He must consider whether it is likely that the person will at some time have capacity in relation to the matter in question, and if it appears likely that he will, when that is likely to be.

(4) He must, so far as is reasonably practicable, *permit and encourage the person to participate, or to improve his ability to participate*, as fully as possible in any act done for him and any decision affecting him.

(5) Where the determination relates to life-sustaining treatment he must not, in considering whether the treatment is in the best interests of the person concerned, be motivated by a desire to bring about his death.

(6) He must consider, so far as is reasonably ascertainable – the person's past and present wishes and feelings and in particular any relevant written statement made by him when he had capacity, the beliefs and values that would be likely to influence his decision if he had capacity, and the other factors that he would be likely to consider if he were able to do so.

(7) He must take into account, if it is practicable and appropriate to consult them, the views of – anyone named by the person as someone to be consulted on the matter in question … anyone engaged in caring for the person or interested in his welfare …

---

47 Andrea Pitts, 'Disability Bioethics and Race' in Joel Michael Reynolds and Christine Wieseler (eds), *The Disability Bioethics Reader* (Routledge 2022); also see Nirmala Erevelles, *Disability and Difference in Global Contexts: Enabling a Transformative Body Politic* (Palgrave Macmillan 2011).

any donee of a lasting power of attorney ... any deputy appointed for the person by the court as to what would be in the person's interests, and in particular, as to the matters mentioned in subsection (6).

Best interests is not a new concept – it was a feature of the common law doctrine of necessity in *Re F*.[48] It is undoubtedly difficult to identify someone's best interests in a given situation, particularly given the many different types of interests that might be pulling in different directions – medical, psychological, relational, financial. Section 4(6) places an emphasis on the individual's 'past and present wishes and feelings', potentially carving a positive space for facilitating their choice, yet this is only one aspect of the broader assessment and the extent to which the individual's wishes will prevail (if ascertained) is variable. The House of Lords Select Committee undertook a Post-Legislative Scrutiny of the MCA in 2014 and noted a number of issues with the application of best-interests decision-making,[49] including:

- 'Staff defined a 'best interests' decision as a 'clinical decision' – and just saw it as a matter of clinical judgment. From the moment of my sister's accident it was as if she belonged to them, they were not interested in what we knew about her and her wishes. I can understand this in the immediate emergency but this went on for months and months, it was a constant battle.' (Evidence submitted by Headway, a charity for brain injury patients).[50]
- Moira Fraser of the Carers Trust reported that families had the impression that 'professionals pick and choose when to involve them'. Furthermore, families who disagreed with the decision being made found they were excluded on the grounds that 'they are not acting in the best interests of the person whom they care for'.[51]

This process of consultation with different organisations and individuals who engage with the MCA on a day-to-day basis is crucial to understanding how the law operates in practice. There was an overarching concern that decisions are driven by clinical and resource decisions, rather than the wishes, beliefs, and feelings of patients. This runs counter to the wording of the legislation and case law, yet perhaps demonstrates the difficulties with seeking to apply this in the medical context where the power of the medical professionals is deeply ingrained.

48 n12.

49 House of Lords Select Committee on the Mental Capacity Act 2005, Report of Session 2013–14 (2014), https://publications.parliament.uk/pa/ld201314/ldselect/ldmentalcap/139/139.pdf, accessed 28 November 2023.

50 Ibid [92].

51 Ibid [93].

Through the lens of disability studies, this medicalisation of best interests that occurs in practice reinforces medical rather than societal and structural responses to disability. These perpetuate an individualised focus on cure, or 'fixing' the individual in the image of the rational, able-bodied, cisgender, white norm. Kafer speaks about this impulse as the 'curative imaginary' – an approach 'that not only expects and assumes intervention but also cannot imagine or comprehend anything other than intervention'.[52] This curative impulse and narrow focus on the individual through a medicalised lens (thus reinforcing clinical interests) prevents structural changes that might better include and facilitate the choices and agency of disabled people.

There have been some cases in which a more patient-centric approach has been emphasised by the judiciary. *Aintree v James* was the first case involving the MCA to reach the Supreme Court.[53] This case, which centred on when it is legally permissible to withhold life-sustaining treatment, signalled a resounding recognition of the centrality of the views of the individual as being 'a component in making the choice which is right for him as an individual human being'[54] as part of the best-interests assessment. However, Lady Hale was keen to stress that nothing in the judgment changed the law as previously understood and that the person's wishes will not always prevail, reaffirming that a patient cannot demand treatment.[55] Thus, whilst signalling the importance and desirability of centring the individual's voice, this is always going to be filtered through clinical judgement and medical dominance.[56] Medico-legal scholarship has often drawn attention to whether prejudicial ideas about the preferences and abilities of disabled people may be masked by supposedly objective assessments of best interests and clinical prognosis.[57] The individual effectively remains a medicalised subject in the best-interests assessment. There is an important power issue facing those deemed to lack capacity under the MCA and it may be difficult to challenge options with which they are not satisfied, except by judicial review.

The case of *Wye Valley NHS Trust v Mr B* has been welcomed by some as demonstrating a more CRPD-compliant way forward for mental capacity law.[58] The case concerned Mr B, a 73-year-old with a history of mental illness together with, in more recent years, poorly controlled Type II diabetes. He developed a chronic foot ulcer due to his poorly controlled diabetes and resistance to medication. The foot became infected, yet he continued to resist treatment other

52 Alison Kafer, *Feminist Queer Crip* (Indiana University Press 2013).

53 [2013] UKSC 67.

54 Ibid [45].

55 Ibid [47].

56 There is here a clear reinforcement of the principles from *R (Burke) v General Medical Council* [2005] EWCA Civ 1003 more recently reiterated in *McCulloch v Forth Valley Health Board* [2023] UKSC 26.

57 Shiela McLean and Laura Williamson, *Impairment and Disability Law and Ethics at the Beginning and End of Life* (Routledge Cavendish 2007).

58 [2015] EWCOP 60.

than dressing changes. The NHS Trust sought declarations that Mr B lacked capacity and that they could treat the ulcer, including by amputation. They brought evidence that without intervention, Mr B would die within a matter of days. Jackson J accepted the clear evidence before the court that Mr B lacked the capacity to make treatment decisions. However, he held that it was not in Mr B's best interests to have the amputation. He was clear that a conclusion that a person lacks decision-making capacity is not an 'off-switch' for his rights and freedoms:

> To state the obvious, the wishes and feelings, beliefs and values of people with a mental disability are as important to them as they are to anyone else, and may even be more important. It would therefore be wrong in principle to apply any automatic discount to their point of view.[59]

This is a clear statement as to the importance of hearing Mr B's wishes, which should influence the approach to best-interests decision-making in other cases. Yet in many ways it leaves the broader structures of best-interests decision-making intact. The case does not unsettle medical dominance in setting the parameters of a decision, or the role of the 'black box' of clinical judgement. Looked at through the lens of the social model of disability, there are no positive obligations to challenge or shift broader disabling dynamics or structures – instead there is simply a recognition of an individual-level right to refuse treatment. Importantly, this is filtered through and reliant upon an assessment of incapacity, reinforcing the problematic power dynamic that maintains the medical control over Mr B and his decision-making. In other words, his right to refuse treatment here is contingent on the medical and judicial agreement as to his best interests. Cases outside of the medical arena further demonstrate the limits of best interests as a vehicle for attending to disabling societal and structural dynamics, and the reinforcement of an individual- and medical-level focus.[60] Such an approach, as Reynolds and Weiseler put it, 'fail[s] to take into account the troubled historical relationship between medical practice and people with disabilities' and 'ignore[s] the larger social, cultural and political forces that oppress people with disabilities and thereby ignore a core component of social determinates of health'.[61]

The Committee on the CRPD have reinforced the need to depart from a best-interests framework, stating that '[t]he "best interests" principle is not a safeguard which complies with article 12 in relation to adults. The "will and preferences" paradigm must replace the "best interests" paradigm to ensure that

59 Ibid [11].

60 See Beverley Clough, 'Choosing the Lesser of Two Evils: The Empty Vessel of Best Interests' (2016) https://thesmallplaces.wordpress.com/2016/10/15/guest-post-by-beverley-clough-choosing-the-lesser-of-two-evils-the-empty-vessel-of-best-interests/, accessed 29 November 2023.

61 Reynolds and Wieseler (n34) 3.

persons with disabilities enjoy the right to legal capacity on an equal basis with others.'[62] This invites further reflection on how the CRPD may open up new ways of approaching decision-making, buttressed by Article 12 and the social model of disability.

The CRPD as a route forward?

The CRPD has been welcomed by disability advocates as a milestone in achieving disability rights. It has been hailed as signalling a 'paradigm shift' in relation to disability rights and demonstrating a more social model approach to disability. The Convention places positive obligations on states to give effect to the rights contained within it, melding civil and political rights with social and economic rights as it does so. This challenges ideas of more negative approaches to rights (e.g., not to have the state or others interfere) that are often seen in other human rights instruments. It contains provisions that directly, and potentially fatally, challenge some of the core suppositions of legal frameworks governing legal responses to disability. A stark example of this is the right contained in Article 12 – that persons with disabilities enjoy legal capacity on an equal basis with others in all aspects of life – which encourages a move away from a binary focus on capacity/incapacity explicitly premised on a cognitive impairment.

However, there has been significant unease about what this may mean in practice, and whether reforming the law in order to be compliant with the CRPD is feasible or desirable.[63]

What is clear is that Article 12 and the CRPD more broadly pose a direct challenge to the MCA, particularly with regard to:

- The diagnostic element of the capacity assessment.
- Substituted decision-making via best interests.
- The lack of legal oversight of decision-making through the MCA (informality).

Whilst there is not space in this chapter to consider or propose routes for legal reform, it is important to reflect from a disability perspective on what the challenges may be. An appropriate response to the CRPD might be to abolish the MCA and do away with challenges to, or interferences in, decision-making. Yet this seems a wrongheaded strategy given the emphasis on support to exercise legal capacity, including supported decision-making, central to the CRPD. Moreover, the vision of the state within and throughout the CRPD emphasises and necessitates positive obligations including with regard to social and economic rights. As such, the idea of law, and the state, taking a step back here seems incongruous with the CRPD.

---

62 UNCRPD (n8) [5].

63 See Mary Donnelly, Rosie Harding, and Ezgi Taşcıoğlu (eds), *Supporting Legal Capacity in Socio-Legal Context* (Hart Publishing 2022).

Alternatively, some might suggest bringing everybody within the potential scope of the MCA by removing the diagnostic threshold. This might entail applying the functional capacity test to everyone, and then taking best-interests decisions for those unable to meet the capacity threshold. This would potentially be less discriminatory, distinguishing people on the basis of their functional capacity rather than being reliant on a diagnosed cognitive impairment. Such a suggestion often invites some unease and discomfort from those without cognitive impairments as to why their decisions might be questioned. It is worth reflecting then on why this should be the case for those with cognitive impairments, bringing us back to the justification proposed by the Law Commission in response to Carson's criticism. It is important then to ask whether this is convincing.

The CRPD invites us to carefully interrogate our legal frameworks and the justifications underpinning them, bringing attention to the ableist assumptions and urging us to rethink these. The thread 'on an equal basis with others' that is central to Article 12 and is woven throughout the CRPD is a reminder of this. Can the law be made disability-neutral? Bickenbach poses the challenge thus:

> Eventually, the folly of this will dawn on people and we shall all joyously realize that we are all abnormal, disabled, impaired, deformed and functionally limited, because, truth be told, that is what it means to be a human being.[64]

Disability scholarship suggests ways that we can disrupt, at a much deeper level, ideals of subjectivity that are based on autonomy, rationality, individualism, and self-determination. As Altermark puts it, 'the politics of intellectual disability is the politics of all of us'.[65] Unseating the norm of the autonomous, rational, individual legal subject and rethinking subjectivity through and with disability, impairment, and difference makes visible the 'sheer diversity of embodied experiences that overwhelm any binary opposition between a normative "able-body" and its disabled other'.[66] In this way, a disability studies perspective helps highlight the ways in which legal and societal processes can reinforce normative hierarchies and relations of power. In being attentive to these processes within the MCA – particularly in the reinforcing of medicalised ideas of capacity/incapacity and best interests – we can begin to challenge their reproduction and effects. It is clear that, following the UNCRPD, and the critiques of the mental capacity framework, 'new, non-discriminatory indicators of support needs are required

64 Jerome Bickenbach, 'Minority Rights or Universal Participation: The Politics of Disablement' in Melinda Jones and Lee Ann Basser Marks (eds), *Disability, Divers-Ability and Legal Change* (Kluwer Law International 1999) 114.

65 Niklas Altermark, *Citizenship Inclusion and Intellectual Disability: Biopolitics Post-Institutionalisation* (Taylor & Francis 2018) 3.

66 Edward Hall and Robert Wilton, 'Towards a Relational Geography of Disability' (2017) 41 Prog Hum Geogr 741.

in the provision of support to exercise legal capacity'[67] if we seek to take the Convention and disability rights seriously.

Summary

- The chapter introduced a disability studies perspective on the MCA 2005.
- It highlighted the importance of social model critiques of the medicalised approach to disability. The social model sees societal barriers and structures, rather than the individual impairment, as the source of disability.
- This perspective can be used to challenge the way that the MCA 2005 approaches cognitive impairments, particularly in terms of assessing capacity and approaching best-interests decision-making.
- The UNCRPD 2006 was presented as offering important challenges to the law in this area and demonstrates the importance of a disability perspective driving legal reform.

Questions for reflection

1. Why does the law distinguish between those with cognitive impairments and those without? Are you convinced by this distinction?
2. Would it be possible to make the law around capacity 'disability neutral'? What might be the problems?
3. What other ways might the social model of disability, or a disability studies perspective, challenge norms in medical law?

Recommended resources

- Peter Bartlett, 'Re-thinking the Mental Capacity Act 2005: Towards the Next Generation of Law' (2023) 86 Med Law Rev 659.
- Fleur Beaupert and Linda Steele, 'Questioning Law's Capacity' (2015) 40 Alt Law J 161.
- Eilionóir Flynn and Anna Arstein-Kerslake, 'State Intervention in the Lives of People with Disabilities: The Case for a Disability Neutral Framework' (2017) 13 Int J Law Context 39.
- Rosemarie Garland-Thomson, 'Misfits: A Feminist Materialist Disability Concept' (2011) 26 Hypatia 591.
- Rosemary Kayess and Phillip French, 'Out of Darkness into Light? Introducing the Convention on the Rights of Persons with Disabilities' (2008) 8 Hum Rights Law Rev 1.

---

67 UN Committee on the Rights of Persons with Disabilities (n8) [29]. See Genevra Richardson, 'Mental Capacity in the Shadow of Suicide: What Can the Law Do?' (2013) 9 Int J Law Context 87.

- Alex Ruck Keene, 'Mental Capacity Law and Policy' https://www.mentalcapacitylawandpolicy.org.uk, accessed 29 November 2023 (webpage with regular blog posts, interviews and legal updates from Alex Ruck Keene KC, a leading barrister in mental capacity law).
- Open Justice Court of Protection project https://openjusticecourtofprotection.org/, accessed 29 November 2023 (blog with useful details about observing Court of Protection cases as well as posts written by observers of previous cases).
- The Small Places https://thesmallplaces.wordpress.com/, accessed 29 November 2023 (blog written by Dr Lucy Series covering issues of mental capacity law).

Bibliography

Altermark N, *Citizenship Inclusion and Intellectual Disability: Biopolitics Post-Institutionalisation* (Taylor & Francis 2018)

Banner N, 'Can Procedural and Substantive Elements of Decision Making be Reconciled with Assessments of Mental Capacity?' (2013) 9 Int J Law Context 71

Bartlett P, 'The United Nations Convention on the Rights of Persons with Disabilities and Mental Health Law' (2012) 75 Med Law Rev 752

Bickenbach J, 'Minority Rights or Universal Participation: The Politics of Disablement' in M Jones and LA Basser Marks (eds) *Disability, Divers-Ability and Legal Change* (Kluwer Law International 1999)

Bynum B, 'Discarded Diagnoses' (2002) 9 Lancet 898

Carson D, 'Disabling Progress: The Law Commission's Proposals on Mentally Incapacitated Adults' Decision Making' (1993) 15 J Social Welfare Fam Law 314

Clough B, 'Choosing the Lesser of Two Evils: The Empty Vessel of Best Interests' (2016) https://thesmallplaces.wordpress.com/2016/10/15/guest-post-by-beverley-clough-choosing-the-lesser-of-two-evils-the-empty-vessel-of-best-interests/, accessed 29 November 2023

Donnelly M, Harding R and Taşcıoğlu E (eds), *Supporting Legal Capacity in Socio-Legal Context* (Hart Publishing 2022).

Erevelles N, *Disability and Difference in Global Contexts: Enabling a Transformative Body Politic* (Palgrave Macmillan 2011)

Goering S, 'Revisiting the Relevance of the Social Model of Disability' (2010) 10 Am J Bioeth 54.

Goodley D and others, 'Provocations for Critical Disability Studies' (2019) 34 Disabil Soc 972

Guidry-Grimes L, 'Defining Mental Illness and Psychiatric Disability' in JM Reynolds and C Wieseler (eds), *The Disability Bioethics Reader* (Routledge 2022)

Hall E and Wilton R, 'Towards a Relational Geography of Disability' (2017) 41 Prog Hum Geogr 741

House of Lords Select Committee on the Mental Capacity Act 2005, Report of Session 2013–14 (2014) https://publications.parliament.uk/pa/ld201314/ldselect/ldmentalcap/139/139.pdf, accessed 28 November 2023

Joseph A, 'The Necessity of an Attention to Eurocentrism and Colonial Technologies: An Addition to Critical Mental Health Literature' (2015) 30 Disabil Soc 1021

Kafer A, *Feminist Queer Crip* (Indiana University Press 2013)

Keywood K, 'Sterilising the Woman with Learning Difficulties: In Her Best Interests?' in J Bridgeman and S Millns (eds), *Law and Body Politics: Regulating the Female Body* (Aldershot 1995)

Keywood K, '"I'd Rather Keep Him Chaste": Retelling the Story of Sterilisation, Learning Disability and (Non)Sexed Embodiment' (2001) 9 Fem Leg Stud 185

Law Commission, 'Consultation Paper 128 Mentally Incapacitated Adults and Decision Making: A New Jurisdiction' (1992) https://cloud-platform-e218f50a4812967ba1215eaecede923f.s3.amazonaws.com/uploads/sites/30/2016/08/No.130-Mentally-Incapacitated-and-Other-Vulnerable-Adults-Public-Law-Protection.pdf, accessed 29 November 2023

Law Commission, 'Mental Incapacity' (1995) Law Com No 231

McLean S and Williamson L, *Impairment and Disability Law and Ethics at the Beginning and End of Life* (Routledge Cavendish 2007)

Mills C, *The Racial Contract* (Cornell University Press 1997)

Oliver M, *Understanding Disability: From Theory to Practice* (Palgrave Macmillan 1996)

Pitts A, 'Disability Bioethics and Race' in JM Reynolds and C Wieseler (eds), *The Disability Bioethics Reader* (Routledge 2022)

Reynolds JM and Wieseler C (eds), *The Disability Bioethics Reader* (Routledge 2022)

Richardson G, 'Mental Capacity in the Shadow of Suicide: What Can the Law Do?' (2013) 9 Int J Law Context 87

Shogren K, 'Considering Context: An Integrative Concept for Promoting Outcomes in the Intellectual Disability Field' (2013) 51 Intellect Dev Disabil 132

Steele L, 'Temporality, Disability and Institutional Violence: Revisiting In Re F' (2017) 26 Griffith L Rev 378

Taylor A, '"Lives Worth Living": Theorizing Moral Status and Expressions of Human Life' (2013) 33 Disability Stud Q https://dsq-sds.org/index.php/dsq/article/view/3875/3404, accessed 29 November 2023

UK Government, 'Mental Capacity Act Code of Practice' (2007) https://assets.publishing.service.gov.uk/media/5f6cc6138fa8f541f6763295/Mental-capacity-act-code-of-practice.pdf, accessed 29 November 2023

UNCRPD (UN Committee on the Rights of Persons with Disabilities), 'General Comment (Number 1) on Art 12: Equal Recognition before the Law' (2014) http://www.ohchr.org/EN/HRBodies/CRPD/Pages/GC.aspx, accessed 14 December 2023

The Union of the Physically Impaired Against Segregation and The Disability Alliance, 'Fundamental Principles of Disability' (1975) https://disability-studies.leeds.ac.uk/wp-content/uploads/sites/40/library/UPIAS-fundamental-principles.pdf, accessed 29 November 2023

Vehmas S, 'Ethical Analysis of the Concept of Disability' (2004) 42 Ment Retard 209

11

Mental Health: Inpatient Care

Magdalena Furgalska

Mental distress touches the lives of many people,[1] with one in four adults experiencing mental ill-health each year.[2] Arguably, the number of people affected by mental illness is much higher; the remainder of the population is likely to have a secondary experience of it through knowing, caring for, or loving someone who experiences a decline in their mental wellbeing. Thus, it is crucial that an array of speedy and appropriate responses to mental distress exist that allow people to flourish and live their lives in the way they wish. The relevance of law in creating such responses cannot be underestimated. Some scholars argue that law on inpatient mental healthcare can be seen as protecting individuals because it provides proper processes for care provision and, arguably, involuntary treatment is better than no treatment.[3] Others argue that the law works to empower the mental health professionals to 'limit bodily integrity, privacy … and capacity to act'.[4] When collecting and examining interview data with people who experience mental distress, I found that inpatient care, which is characterised by coercion, can be seen by people as both helpful and unhelpful. This is because people's experiences vary, and each experience of receiving inpatient care is nuanced and unique. Therefore, existing legal responses to mental distress require

---

1 Note on language: throughout this chapter, I refer to people who find themselves in the mental health system simply as 'people'. I use the term patient when discussing the specific relationship between the person and the law. Participants in my study often referred to themselves as 'patients' when discussing those experiences and were not fond of other terms like mental health service users or clients. When discussing mental ill-health, my participants often described it as an 'illness' or a 'distress'.

2 MIND, 'Mental Health Facts and Statistics' (2020) https://www.mind.org.uk/information-support/types-of-mental-health-problems/mental-health-facts-and-statistics//, accessed 6 August 2023.

3 H. Korosec Jagodic and others, 'Involuntary Treatment is Better Than No Treatment' (2008) 18 Euro Neuropsycho S568.

4 Lawrence Gostin, *Public Health Law and Ethics: A Reader* (University of California Press 2010).

careful scrutiny to account for the diversity of human experience and to ensure that no one is treated in a discriminatory way.[5] Reduction in the use of coercive measures is a central feature of policy developments in recent years.

This chapter provides an overview of the mental health law concerning inpatient care. It challenges various legal provisions in three ways. Firstly, I use empirical data from my study to demonstrate how the law is experienced in real life. This data comprises quotes from 12 people I interviewed about their experiences of mental healthcare. You can find details about the study and participants in my article,[6] which was approved by the University of Birtmingham's Ethics Committee. Secondly, I introduce an account of human rights developments that pose significant challenges for involuntary inpatient care. The chapter then discusses a new perspective, the capabilities approach to mental health.

Medical model of the Mental Health Act 1983

Brief history of the mental health law in England

Advances in psychiatry in the 1950s, specifically new medications, initiated the need for regulatory frameworks for mental health services and for the provision of psychiatric treatment. The 1959 Act, which preceded the current 1983 Act, wholly recognised the medical model in psychiatry, believing that mental health professionals could now cure their patients, just like other medical professionals treating their patients' physical ailments.[7] The medical model views mental illness as a result of some biological shortcoming that is intrinsic to an individual and can be fully remedied by medical responses. Thus, the 1959 Act placed a legal requirement on patients to comply with doctors' advice. However, a decade or so later, with growing general criticism of the medical model, the anti-psychiatry movement emerged, beginning within the psychiatric profession itself.[8] The movement contended that mental illness cannot be classified as an objective scientific fact. Meanwhile, lawmakers were preoccupied with the idea of risk and public protection. At the same time, the MIND charity (which is a mental health

---

5 S. Wessely, 'Independent Review of the Mental Health Act 1983: Modernising the Mental Health Act: Increasing Choice, Reducing Compulsion' (2018) https://assets.publishing.service.gov.uk/media/5c6596a7ed915d045f37798c/Modernising_the_Mental_Health_Act_-_increasing_choice__reducing_compulsion.pdf, accessed 29 November 2023. Here it was noted that people from Black, Asian, and Minority Ethnic (BAME) backgrounds were more likely to be detained under the MHA 1983, and the detention rates for these groups were disproportionately higher.

6 Magdalena Furgalska, '"Informed Consent is a Bit of a Joke To Me": Lived Experiences of Insight, Coercion, and Capabilities in Mental Health Care Settings' (2023) 19 Int J Law Context 456. I would also like to acknowledge the support of the Midlands Graduate School Economic and Social Research Council Doctoral Training Partnership for funding this study.

7 Brenda Hale, *Mental Health Law* (6th edn, Sweet & Maxwell 2017).

8 Thomas Szasz, *Antipsychiatry: Quackery Squared* (Syracuse University Press 2009).

charity in England and Wales founded in 1946 to support and empower people experiencing mental distress) began to scrutinise the 1959 Act, questioning its provisions, heavy reliance on the medical model, and the powers it gave to mental health professionals.[9] MIND strongly advocated for better safeguards and a requirement that people only receive consensual treatment.[10] All of this, against what could be described as a turbulent social background, led to the Mental Health Act (MHA) 1983 being enacted, which regulates the mental health system in England as well as the provision of inpatient psychiatric care, making psychiatric facilities 'both a physical structure and a legal entity; there is little point studying the operation of one without reference to the operation of the other. The same, it must follow, is true of those who enter the system. The patient, or client, is in some sense a product of the legal regime.'[11]

The MHA 1983 appears to survive the test of time. As will be discussed later in this chapter, the lengthy efforts to reform the Act following the Richardson Report 1999 did not translate into substantial reform, but the MHA 2007 amended some of the safeguarding provisions. The MHA 1983 is once again on the law-reform agenda following the Independent Review of the Mental Health Act in 2018,[12] which aimed to modernise the law and minimise coercion. Reform efforts resulted in the Draft Bill,[13] which could potentially change the paternalistic framework of the 1983 Act, but whether it will translate into a law that is enacted remains unknown.

Inpatient care for civil patients: the law

For a patient to come within the remit of the MHA 1983, they must be suffering from what the legislation calls *mental disorder*; this is defined it as 'any disorder or disability of the mind'. The Act has provisions for both civil patients (those admitted to hospital for treatment) and forensic patients (those who have additional criminal offence-related treatment needs whose detention might be subject to different provisions and conditions). In this chapter, I am focusing solely on civil patients.

There are two types of admission to the mental health system. The first type of admission is involuntary or compulsory admission under Part II of the MHA 1983. You may have heard of 'sectioning' before, a fairly well-known colloquialism for compulsory admission to a hospital. The length of each detention is determined by the law, depending on what specific section of the Act the mental health professional relies upon. For instance, under section 2

9 Lawrence O. Gostin, *A Human Condition: The Mental Health Act from 1959 to 1975: Observations, Analysis and Proposals for Reform*, vol 1 (MIND 1975).

10 Ibid.

11 Peter Bartlett and Ralph Sandland, *Mental Health Law, Policy and Practice* (OUP 2014) 37.

12 Wessely (n5).

13 Draft Mental Health Bill, HC Bill (2022–2023) [HC 696].

of the Act, patients are detained for 28 days for assessment and 6 months for treatment under section 3. For admissions under sections 2 or 3 of the Act, the application must be made by either the nearest relative or an Approved Mental Health Professional (usually a social worker). The application must also have the support of two medical professionals, one of which must, under section 12(2) of the Act, have 'special experience in the diagnosis or treatment of mental disorder', with the other having 'previous acquaintance with the patient', however minimal this might be. There are two important justifications for compulsory detention: dangerousness (posing a risk to oneself or others)[14] and the need for treatment. For admission under section 2, the person must be suffering from a mental disorder of 'a nature or degree which warrants admission to the hospital' or the person 'ought to be detained' to protect their own safety or health or for the protection of others. However, for a person to come under section 3, the nature of one's mental disorder 'makes it appropriate for [them] to receive medical treatment in the hospital' or is 'necessary' to protect others or the patient themselves.

Across the chapters in this book, you learn that a person who needs medical treatment for a physical ailment must only receive it when they have consented to it or, in a situation when they are not able to give valid consent, it is deemed to be in their best interests.[15] However, these principles do not apply to patients who are involuntarily detained in mental health hospitals. Perlin and Dorfman have labelled mental health law 'sanist'.[16] This means that the legal system makes assumptions about people who experience mental distress to justify treating them differently to patients in general healthcare. Similar sentiments were shared by some of the participants in my study: Eliza stated that 'under the law, if you are deemed insane it does not really matter what you say when you are sane', alluding to the biases and attitudes the law denotes about people in mental distress (and which the United Nations Convention on the Rights of People with Disabilities (UNCRPD) attempts to address). Thus, it is unsurprising that the law allows for non-consensual treatment in a way which would be deemed unacceptable in general healthcare. Under section 63, patients can be treated without consent. Moreover, in practice, force may be used to administer treatment under section 63, meaning that the treatment may be experienced by people not just as non-consensual but also forced. Section 1(6)(a)(b) of the Mental Health Units (Use of Force) Act 2018 defines force as 'the use of physical, mechanical or chemical

14 Note that this justification survives the test of time despite mental ill-health being a poor predictor of violence and substance abuse is the more likely culprit of violence towards others. People in mental distress are more likely to pose a danger to themselves than others. See J. Monahan, 'Risk Assessment of Violence among the Mentally Disordered: Generating Useful Knowledge' (1988) 11 Int J Law Psychiatry 249.

15 See Chapters 9 and 10 of this book.

16 M.L. Perlin and D.A. Dorman, 'Sanism, Social Science, and the Development of Mental Disability Law Jurisprudence' (1993) 11 Behav Sci Law 47.

restraint of the patient' and may also include 'isolation of the patient'. However, the Act on the whole encourages a reduction in the use of force and a clear recording of the instances when it is used.

Within the involuntary framework, there are a couple of safeguards worth noting. Section 57 states that certain treatments cannot be given without the consent of the patient and the agreement of a Second Opinion Appointed Doctor (also known as a SOAD). These treatments include psychosurgery and chemical castration (to reduce sex drive in men). However, section 57 is rarely used. Arguably, the most important safeguard is provided by section 58, which limits the use of non-consensual treatment to three months. After this time has lapsed, the patient can only be treated with medication with their valid consent, but if the patient lacks mental capacity or if a SOAD confirms the treatment to be appropriate despite the patient's refusal, then the treatment can still be provided. Section 58 has generated significant academic debate, with critics questioning its efficacy.[17] Section 58A provides specific circumstances under which electro-convulsive therapy can be given. Notwithstanding these rules, the treatment may always be provided in emergencies, either by relying on section 62 of the 1983 Act or the common law doctrine of necessity.

Patients may also be voluntarily detained; this is known as 'informal' detention under section 131(1). This means that the patients may leave the hospital whenever they wish to do so, and they may refuse any treatment, in theory. In practice, those who refuse treatment are likely to be sectioned so that the treatment can be provided without consent. A voluntary patient might be prevented from leaving the hospital through the use of section 5, which allows voluntary patients to be sectioned for up to 72 hours but does not allow the use of section 63 (compulsory treatment without consent) at that time. Where deemed necessary, section 5(4) allows for compulsory sectioning of informal patients under sections 2 or 3. Therefore, the framework may leave one questioning whether truly voluntary patients exist or whether voluntary patients are simply those who comply with doctors' advice.[18]

As illustrated in this section, inpatient care is heavily regulated, and it is important to understand how these laws are experienced in practice. In my empirical research, I found that voluntary admission is a mere illusion. This is because as soon as an individual refuses treatment, not only does the law allow for the sectioning of the patient, but mental health professionals will often attempt to persuade or threaten voluntary patients to comply with treatment before they use the law to compel people to do so. This means that the idea of choice that

---

17 Phill Fennel, *Treatment without Consent: Law, Psychiatry, and the Treatment of Mentally Disordered Offenders since 1845* (Routledge 1996); Peter Bartlett, '"The Necessity Must Be Convincingly Shown To Exist": Standards for Compulsory Treatment for Mental Disorder under the Mental Health Act 1983' (2011) 19 Med Law Rev 514.

18 Furgalska (n6); Hale (n7).

is supposed to characterise voluntary admission does not exist in its literal and true meaning. Consider the following stories from Eliza, about the first time she got sectioned as an involuntary patient, and from Lucy, who complied with treatment as a voluntary patient:

> The psychiatrist came [...] and said 'it's like this. Either you think you are ill, so that means you aren't too ill really. You think you're ill and you need to be in the hospital, that means you're not too ill and you don't need to be in the hospital but we will take you there to be on the safe side, or you think you're just ill and don't need to be in the hospital which means you are really ill and we need to take you to the hospital.' So it was a complete Catch 22. I explained I knew I was ill and wanted help but did not want to go to the hospital because I had two small children. So, I got sectioned.
>
> On my way there I had a panic attack, I was so worried about my children. So, the next thing I knew I was being carried by about three men. They got me onto this bed, face down, holding me down, pulled my dress up, pulled my pants down and injected me. [...]
>
> Then following morning, I woke up naked with a sheet over me on a flat mattress on the floor in a small room with white walls and a small window that was barred. That was a lot and that's how I woke up on my 40th birthday.
>
> Eliza

> I didn't refuse treatment in the hospital, but I saw people who did, and it terrified me. And so, I was very much like 'no, thank you very much, I will take my tablets even though they made me feel awful'. So, I was never restrained in the hospital which I am very grateful for. My treatment wasn't consensual, I feel ... I can remember the doctor sort of saying 'you need this, you need this right now' and me being like 'oh okay' and then not remembering anything until the next day. I don't remember ever being asked if I would like a medication. That was never asked of me. It was never a question, it wasn't like 'we can give you some antipsychotics, or you can choose not to have them, this is what they do and this is what they are' they would just go 'we are going to start you on clozapine'. It felt very invasive and abusive ... I felt like my choice was to take the medication and not question it or die.
>
> Lucy

These stories from Eliza and Lucy demonstrate the profound effects that the law, and the medical model that underpins it, have on people's experiences of inpatient care. On the one hand, we have Eliza, who experienced mental distress but did not exhibit dangerous behaviour. In Eliza's case, the focus on the perceived need for treatment and lack of acknowledgement of Eliza's social context resulted in her experiencing sectioning, non-consensual treatment, physical force, and isolation in the hospital. In the study, all of the participants acknowledged that social context is crucial to understanding one's experience and should be considered when deciding on the appropriate course of treatment. Albert shared the following sentiment: 'instead of treating me according to my needs, including social needs and just life needs, they gave me the tablets and said "take that, it will help you"'. As a result of her first experience of inpatient care and the lack of appreciation for her social context and needs, Eliza developed a distrust for the mental health system. Over the years, Eliza was involuntarily detained 17 times. Eventually, Eliza began to comply with doctors' advice – and later *performed* compliance (pretended to comply) without actually complying – to avoid non-consensual interventions.

Then we have the story from Lucy. She stated that she posed a danger both to herself and to her loved ones. However, her compliance meant that she could remain in the hospital as an informal patient. As a voluntary patient, we know that Lucy should have been treated only with her valid consent. However, it does not appear that the consent was actively sought. Instead, Lucy observed what was happening to patients who did not comply with treatment (e.g., restraint, force, isolation) and decided to receive every treatment that was given to her without objecting.

In my research, negative experiences of inpatient care were strongly associated with people feeling that they were not listened to and that they were seen merely as patients and not people whose lives and what is important to them needed to be known or understood. Whereas many of my participants found that inpatient care did help them recover, the medical model, which ignores the social context, meant that the negative experiences overshadowed the good outcomes. It is therefore important to consider other perspectives that can suggest ways for improving experiences of mental healthcare.

Human rights-based approaches and perspectives

The starting point of the rights-based approaches is the perception of mental health law as: (a) inherently discriminatory; and (b) infringing on the human rights of mental health patients compared to patients in general medical care.[19] For this reason, scholars like Donnelly and Laing suggest that mental health law is an anomaly in our legal system, which otherwise values and protects individual

---

19 E.g., Piers Gooding, *A New Era for Mental Health Law and Policy: Supported Decision-Making and the UN Convention on the Rights of Persons with Disabilities* (CUP 2017).

autonomy and upholds the right to refuse any treatment in general healthcare even when it might result in the patient's death.[20] As discussed previously, these values and rights are compromised when one is diagnosed with a mental disorder and receives inpatient care. Coercive care and paternalistic interventions dominate mental healthcare and can be described as commonplace. Thus, unlike general healthcare, which observed a significant shift towards patient autonomy, mental health law may be considered as lagging 50 years behind general medical law and practice. Whereas any restrictions to autonomy in general healthcare are weighted against human rights interests, this default position is not present in everyday mental healthcare.[21]

Nonetheless, the developments in human rights are having a profound effect on mental healthcare. The governments, lawyers, academics, societies at large, and the patients themselves question mental health laws in the context of human rights. For instance, following the growing relevance of human rights in all aspects of law and the introduction of the Human Rights Act 1998, the UK government conducted a lengthy review of the MHA 1983, resulting in a notable Richardson Report proposing a full replacement of the 1983 Act.[22] However, these proposals were met with significant backlash from various stakeholders. Hale states that this was due to the proposal including indefinite detention of those who posed a risk to the public, allowing for treatment of those patients even if there was no apparent benefit to providing such treatment.[23] The MHA 1983 remained in force unchanged until it was amended by the MHA 2007, which, while not resulting in significant changes to the existing legislation, did improve some of the available safeguards, such as introducing section 58A, discussed previously.[24] The incorporation of the European Convention on Human Rights into national law means that it is easier for patients to use human rights law in pursuit of justice where their rights may have been breached.

The introduction of the CRPD,[25] which had been signed and ratified by the UK and under which mental illness is classed as a disability, added significance to a variety of arguments about the discriminatory nature of mental health laws that lead to serious human rights violations. Moreover, it resulted in more concrete questioning of the medical model underpinning mental health legislation

20 Mary Donnelly, 'From Autonomy to Dignity: Treatment for Mental Disorders and the Focus for Patient Rights' in Bernadette Maree McSherry (ed), *International Trends in Mental Health Law* (Federation Press 2008); Judy Laing, 'Coercive Care: Rights, Law and Policy' (2015) 24 Med Law Rev 297.

21 Gooding (n19).

22 Genevra Richardson, 'Report of the Expert Committee: Review of the Mental Health Act 1983' (Cm4480, Department of Health 1999).

23 Hale (n7).

24 For an overview, see Rowena Daw, 'The Mental Health Act 2007: The Defeat of an Ideal' (2007) 16 J Ment Health Law 131.

25 UNCRPD (adopted 13 December 2006, entered into force 3 May 2008) 2515 UNTS 3.

worldwide in favour of the social model of disability.[26] The CRPD recognises mental illness as falling within the scope of the disability. The social model of disability recognises that the main source of disability experienced by people is caused by systemic and societal barriers rather than by an individual's *impairment*.[27] It emphasises the failure of the state to create a society where people do not experience those barriers.

The CRPD has been repeatedly described as a paradigm shift, which means that 'mental health legislation faces an uncertain future'.[28] This is because the Convention represents a shift away from the mindset of detention, compliance, and coercion towards promoting a right to healthcare, supporting individuals, and allowing them active participation at all stages in their mental healthcare.[29] In line with the social model, the CRPD is governed by the principles of legal capacity, equality, and supported decision-making, all of which are contained in Article 12. Legal capacity here, unlike mental capacity, means an ability to hold and exercise rights on an equal basis with others. To achieve said equality, the Convention requires member states to provide mechanisms and support for people with disabilities to fully enjoy their legal capacity. Therefore, it is unsurprising that a vast academic literature adopts the CRPD in thinking about mental health laws.[30]

One of the biggest challenges posed by the CRPD is that the UN treaty bodies have consistently argued that involuntary psychiatric intervention violates the human rights of people with mental ill-health and that it should be abolished.[31] Ultimately, the CRPD requires greater participation of people in their mental health treatment decision-making processes, greater support, and respect for informed consent. Although the values and principles promoted by the CRPD are welcomed, some scholars are concerned about the feasibility of the prohibition of coercion in a psychiatric context.[32] These concerns include worries about the availability of resources, concerns over undue influence by supporters, effective decision-making support measures for people who suffer

---

26 Penelope Weller, *New Law and Ethics in Mental Health Advance Directives* (Routledge 2013).

27 Beverley Clough, '"People Like That": Realising the Social Mode in Mental Capacity Jurisprudence' (2015) 23 Med Law Rev 53.

28 Gooding (n19) 21.

29 Genevra Richardson, 'Involuntary Treatment, Human Dignity and Human Rights' in Marcia Rioux, Lee Ann Basser, and Melinda Jones (eds), *Critical Perspectives on Human Rights and Disability Law* (Martinus Nijhoff Publishers 2011).

30 E.g., Weller (n26); Gooding (n19); Peter Bartlett, 'The United Nations Convention on the Rights of Persons with Disabilities and Mental Health Law' (2012) 75 Med Law Rev 752; George Szmukler, 'The UN Convention on the Rights of Persons with Disabilities: "Rights, Will and Preferences" in Relation to Mental Health Disabilities' (2017) 54 Int J Law Psychiatry 90.

31 See Committee on the Rights of Persons with Disabilities, 'General Comment No. 1, Article 12: Equal Recognition before the Law' (11th session, 2014) [42].

32 See Gooding (n19), particularly ch 7, for an excellent overview of relevant literature.

from severe episodes of psychosis, and patchy evidence for assessing which support mechanisms are actually helping people and truly enable the realisation of human rights. Currently, the major challenge facing mental health services is that, due to resource limitations, these services are inaccessible to many, especially younger people.[33] Thus, the realisation of ambitious human rights goals may not appear to be a priority. Another challenge exists on a more human level – what about people who find involuntary and coercive measures helpful and may not want these fully abolished? I return to this question in the following section.

Inpatient mental healthcare: the capabilities perspective

Capabilities approach: the basics

The capabilities approach originated from economics and philosophy and was founded by Sen and Nussbaum to evaluate human development, wellbeing, and justice.[34] The approach has been developed by others and is gaining popularity among scholars concerned with mental healthcare,[35] health, and disability.[36] The capabilities approach is broadly concerned with two concepts: freedom and social justice. There are two types of freedom that feature in the approach: wellbeing freedom and agency freedom. On the one hand, wellbeing freedom is about promoting wellbeing in general basic terms, such being healthy, well nourished, and having shelter. On the other hand, agency freedom is about the extent to which an individual can pursue the kind of life they want, even at the expense of wellbeing.[37] For example, a person with mental ill-health may exercise their agency freedom by delaying help-seeking in order to pursue other life goals that they might value more at the time. This means that a person exercising agency freedom can be at odds with wellbeing freedom, and recognising this agency freedom allows people to pursue a wide range of *doings* and *beings*. The approach recognises that people's freedoms are constrained by their environments and promotes a culture change within society, moving away from paternalism towards greater autonomy.

---

33 Georgia Punton, Alyson L. Dodd, and Andrew McNeill, '"You're On the Waiting List": An Interpretative Phenomenological Analysis of Young Adults' Experiences of Waiting Lists within Mental Health Services in the UK' (2022) 17 PloS One e0265542. See also Chapters 2 and 4 of this book.

34 Martha C. Nussbaum, *Creating Capabilities: The Human Development Approach* (Harvard University Press 2011); Amartya Sen, *Development as Freedom* (OUP 1999).

35 E.g., Furgalska (n6); Jill Stavert, 'Adapting or Discarding the Status Quo? Supporting the Exercise of Legal Capacity in Scottish Law and Practice' in Mary Donnelly, Rosie Harding, and Ezgi Tassioglou (eds), *Supporting Legal Capacity in Socio-Legal Context* (Hart Publishing 2022).

36 Sridhar Venkatapuram, *Health Justice: An Argument from the Capabilities Approach* (Polity Press 2011); Amita Dhanda, 'Legal Capacity in the Disability Rights Convention: Stranglehold of the Past or Lodestar for the Future?' (2006) 34 Syracuse J Int L Com 429.

37 Sen (n34) 191.

However, in order to have freedom, people need capabilities to secure certain functionings. Capabilities, on the one hand, are real freedoms and opportunities, the doings and beings that people should be and have if they choose to do so. Examples of capabilities include being able to make decisions, having one's bodily integrity respected, being safe, participating in society, feeling justified emotions, and being healthy.[38] Functionings, on the other hand, are the realised or achieved capabilities. Capabilities and functionings translate into freedoms and, thus, social justice.

Social justice in the capabilities approach is not about an ideal and abstract form of justice but, rather, is concerned with practical ways to improve lives, especially those of marginalised groups. Therefore, in evaluating how social justice can be achieved, the capabilities approach considers individual lives as they really are (functionings) along with people's practical opportunities and freedoms (capabilities) to suggest alternatives that will allow people to live better in accordance with who they are and how they wish to live their lives. This leads to the experience of justice. The approach also does not impose any specific account of what a good life is or what good mental health is, but instead recognises that there can be a range of ways of understanding what constitutes a good life or good mental health to individuals. To help individuals experience social justice, the capabilities approach requires an examination of the sources of unfreedom and how these can be remedied.[39] Sources of unfreedom are also sources of injustice. These are made and exist in laws, institutions, policies, and social norms and are experienced individually as freedom-constraining and as injustice. Once these sources of unfreedom are identified, we can use the idea of capabilities to develop opportunities that increase the experience of freedom.

Understanding inpatient care through the capabilities lens

In my empirical study, I found several sources of unfreedom in the lives of my participants. In relation to inpatient care, lack of opportunities to provide informed consent, lack of involvement in decision-making about one's care, not being listened to or believed, and inability to develop meaningful plans for future treatment were all experienced as sources of unfreedom. To eliminate these sources of unfreedom and enhance both agency freedom and social justice, I found that the capabilities for bodily integrity, health, and safety are crucial in improving the experiences of inpatient care.

The capability for bodily integrity is about respecting each person's boundaries.[40] In the context of inpatient care, bodily integrity is about reducing forced and involuntary intervention, respecting people's boundaries,

38 Nussbaum (n34) developed a list of ten central capabilities to which each person is entitled. Sen does not conform to any particular list.

39 Sen (n34).

40 Nussbaum (n34) 37.

and treating them with respect. Returning to the story told by Eliza about her first experience of being sectioned, the force used against her impacted upon her bodily integrity and, as she explained, made her feel violated. One way of improving the capability for bodily integrity would be to develop a new legal framework or amend the current one to contain a number of guiding principles, which would include respect for bodily integrity. Moreover, to understand an individual's boundaries in this context, living wills could be utilised to set out the way in which inpatient care could be provided without violating the person.[41]

Health is clearly an important capability to consider when rethinking mental health treatment. The current mental health law, based on the medical model, focuses on managing symptoms and controlling people's behaviour. On the other hand, Nussbaum, one of the founders of the approach, defines health as meeting basic human needs, 'being adequately nourished, having good health, including reproductive health, and having adequate shelter'.[42] Adapting the capabilities approach in this context requires a wide definition of mental health. Using the approach means accepting that there is no single definition of good mental health and understanding it as being illness or symptom-free would be both reductionist and sanist. Instead, the capability for health in this context means that every person should be able to define what achieving good mental health looks like to them. The minimum level of this achievement would require that people are able to enjoy their life pursuits and are able to exercise their agency, and that not only medical but social and environmental factors are considered in the achievement of this capability. Similarly, changing legal practices through improving people's participation in decision-making processes about them would bring them closer to achieving health.

The capability for safety is also crucial in the context of inpatient care. Using the empirical data, I define the capability for safety as having access to safe space, being free from unnecessary coercion, and having alternatives to coercion but still being able to access the relevant treatment in times of crisis. The capability approach views coercion as a normal part of life but argues that only a subjective level (decided by an individual) of coercion is acceptable and only when it supports an individual's version of a good life or health.[43] This is why Sen, the main founder of the approach, argues that thinking of coercion as something binary – either existing or not existing – is unhelpful as it imposes certain objective standards on everyone's agency freedom, especially as the experience of coercion is something subjective.[44] It is more productive to focus

41 Living wills are also known as advance decisions, a decision made to refuse or consent to treatment in advance for specific circumstances where the person thinks they may not be able to make the decision themselves.

42 Nussbaum (n34) 33.

43 Sen (n34).

44 Ibid 212.

on measures that increase freedom because this will ultimately lead to a reduction of unnecessary coercion. In my empirical research, psychiatric detention itself (without coercive treatments) was seen as cultivating capability for safety despite it being involuntary and thus coercive.

In my study, I found that despite the prevalence of negative experiences of psychiatric care, some forms of involuntary or coercive intervention were not easily dismissed by people with experiences of mental ill-health and treatment. As discussed previously, even though Lucy found non-consensual treatment under the voluntary section abusive, she found the very experience of being in a hospital to be therapeutic:

> It was just such a relief, I felt safe for the first time in months. I felt like … I didn't have the worries of knowing that there was a drawer with all the knives in and sharp objects and just knowing that I was in a safe place. The structure really suited me at the time. I remember going in and actually phoning my mom and saying to her that I was the sanest one in here and my mom being like, 'Ummm, are you sure about that?' and me saying 'yes, definitely, you should see the others'. And I wasn't by a long shot, but I was surrounded by other women who struggled with psychosis and that was a big thing for me. Being surrounded by people with psychosis was strangely comforting for me and we'd sort of sit outside and share with one another about how we were feeling, what was going on in our heads. That was something that was never facilitated by a member of staff, it was always just something that we did for one another.
>
> Lucy

Here, Lucy speaks of the hospital as somewhere that was her safe place in times of crisis. Indeed, she states that this was the first time she had felt safe in a long time. This was not only because she was away from sharp objects, access to which would make her uncomfortable and make harming herself or others easy, but it was also about no longer having to worry about burdening her parents or, in fact, actually harming them. In a candid way, she recounts the value of the friendships she had made with women who, like her, were experiencing psychosis.

However, there is a clear tension between how Lucy talks of her hospital stay and how she talks of receiving treatment whilst under the voluntary section discussed previously. Moreover, these experiences made Lucy feel unable to refuse treatment, fearing what might happen if she did. Therefore, it was the treatment, not the hospitalisation itself, which was experienced as highly problematic. Hence, an important element of a safe place is that it must be free from coercive interventions even when the detention itself remains coercive. Similar to Lucy, Eve, who also experienced involuntary detention and treatment, recognises the value in detention, which she described as involuntary:

> Eventually [...] I was sectioned, they must have held me down and inject me with some sort of drugs. However, I knew that to get off the section was to agree to treatment, so they say it is voluntary, but it isn't voluntary, because they're going to make you. [...] I did need a safe place, not to cry about being sectioned and being put in the hospital, because I was running around the streets, not sleeping and not eating, so I am not going to cry about that. And often people will get better just because they have a safe place and some food. You cannot underestimate how being given a bed, because some people are on the streets, they've got very disturbed life, so being there with a bed and some nutrition can do wonders.
>
> Eve

Just before Eve was involuntarily detained, she was homeless and unable to take care of herself due to the presence of her symptoms. She talked about experiencing mania: running around the town for hours to use up some of her energy and not sleeping for weeks. Eve does not speak fondly of the hospital, as Lucy does, nor does she reflect on the relational aspects of being in a hospital. For Eve, safety was provided because her basic needs like food and shelter were met, and she maintains that the benefits of having those basic needs met cannot be underestimated in helping anyone, especially those experiencing mental health crisis. At the same time, the treatment she received, again, was experienced as non-consensual and abusive.

The capabilities approach offers a different lens through which mental health laws can be evaluated. Scholars like Stavert believe that it may even aid the implementation of the CRPD principles.[45] As I have shown, the capabilities approach offers a more holistic way for understanding human experience of inpatient care and experience of mental ill-health more generally. The approach caters to those who have different preferences for receiving care and it makes those caring for people and those who make and change laws more mindful of the diversity of human experience. The capabilities approach highlights that the process of receiving care is just as important, if not more important, than the outcome itself. Finally, it offers practical ways for thinking about freedom and social justice and this is particularly important to allow people to live the kind of lives they want to live and value, as highlighted by Sophie in her interview: 'social justice [...] In a way, that's what society owes you. But it is about having freedom. At the end of it, it's about having freedom. The most basic right of everybody is to live as they want.'

Conclusion

Mental health laws have achieved a lot of good for some people over the decades. However, although our knowledge and awareness about mental health has

45 Stavert (n35).

improved, the laws have remained largely the same. Inpatient care subjects people to levels of coercion that can be objectively agreed to be unacceptable, especially in light of the developments in general healthcare where patients' autonomy triumphs over what doctors consider to be medically best for them. Therefore, scrutinising, rethinking, and reimagining mental health law is long overdue.

Summary

- This chapter provides an outline of the English mental health law on inpatient care. This includes informal and compulsory detention and the law surrounding inpatient treatment. It discusses the concept of the medical model of disability.
- It offers an account of rights-based approaches to mental health inpatient care in light of significant human rights developments. It discusses the concept of social model of disability.
- It introduces the capabilities approach to inpatient care as a new and alternative perspective through which the relevant laws can be evaluated and reimagined.

Questions for reflection

1. Reflect on what (if anything) surprised you the most when learning about inpatient mental healthcare. You may wish to watch the Bedlam documentary to deepen your reflection (see Recommended resources list).
2. Consider the different perspectives presented in the chapter; that is, the medical model, the rights-based approaches, and the capabilities approach. What do you perceive the advantages/disadvantages of each to be?
3. Is reducing coercion in mental health settings necessary? Why?

Recommended resources

- Alex Ruck-Keene, 'Supporting Decision-Making and Reducing Coercion in Mental Healthcare: In Conversation with Dr Piers Gooding' (2023) https://www.mentalcapacitylawandpolicy.org.uk/supporting-decision-making-and-reducing-coercion-in-mental-health-care-in-conversation-with-dr-piers-gooding/, accessed 10 July 2024.
- Bedlam Case Studies, 'Episode 2: Crisis' (Channel 4, 7 November 2013) https://learningonscreen.ac.uk/ondemand/index.php/prog/05F5E506?bcast=103375763 (this can be accessed by students using their university credentials).
- P. Gooding, B. McSherry, and C. Roper, 'Preventing and Reducing "Coercion" in Mental Health Services: An International Scoping Review of English-Language Studies' (2020) 142 Acta Psychiatr Scand 27.
- Katherine Garratt, 'Reforming the Mental Health Act' (2022) https://researchbriefings.files.parliament.uk/documents/CBP-9132/CBP-9132.pdf, accessed 29 November 2023.

- Magdalena Furgalska, 'Psychiatric Survivors' Views on Advance Consent and Forced Treatment' (2020) https://openjusticecourtofprotection.org/2020/11/05/psychiatric-survivors-views-on-advance-consent-and-forced-treatment/, accessed 29 November 2023.
- Sally Marlow, 'Bound to the Mast' (BBC Radio 4, 27 May 2022) https://www.bbc.co.uk/sounds/play/p0c9b1xp, accessed 10 July 2024.

Bibliography

Bartlett P, '"The Necessity Must Be Convincingly Shown to Exist": Standards for Compulsory Treatment for Mental Disorder under the Mental Health Act 1983' (2011) 19 Med Law Rev 514

Bartlett P, 'The United Nations Convention on the Rights of Persons with Disabilities and Mental Health Law' (2012) 75 Med Law Rev 752

Bartlett P and Sandland R, *Mental Health Law, Policy and Practice* (OUP 2014)

Clough B, '"People Like That": Realising the Social Mode in Mental Capacity Jurisprudence' (2015) 23 Med Law Rev 53

Daw R, 'The Mental Health Act 2007: The Defeat of an Ideal' (2007) 16 J Ment Health Law 131

Dhanda A, 'Legal Capacity in the Disability Rights Convention: Stranglehold of the Past or Lodestar for the Future?' (2006) 34 Syracuse J Int L Com 429

Donnelly M, 'From Autonomy to Dignity: Treatment for Mental Disorders and the Focus for Patient Rights' in B Maree McSherry (ed), *International Trends in Mental Health Law* (Federation Press 2008)

Fennel P, *Treatment without Consent: Law, Psychiatry, and the Treatment of Mentally Disordered Offenders since 1845* (Routledge 1996)

Furgalska M, '"Informed Consent is a Bit of a Joke to Me": Lived Experiences of Insight, Coercion, and Capabilities in Mental Health Care Settings' (2023) 19 Int J Law Context 456

Gooding P, *A New Era for Mental Health Law and Policy: Supported Decision-Making and the UN Convention on the Rights of Persons with Disabilities* (CUP 2017)

Gostin LO, *A Human Condition: The Mental Health Act from 1959 to 1975: Observations, Analysis and Proposals for Reform*, vol 1 (MIND 1975)

Gostin LO, *Public Health Law and Ethics: A Reader* (University of California Press 2010)

Hale B, *Mental Health Law* (6th edn, Sweet & Maxwell 2017)

Jagodic HK and others, 'Involuntary Treatment is Better than No Treatment' (2008) 18 Euro Neuropsycho S568

Laing J, 'Coercive Care: Rights, Law and Policy' (2015) 24 Med Law Rev 297

MIND, 'Mental Health Facts and Statistics' (2020) https://www.mind.org.uk/information-support/types-of-mental-health-problems/mental-health-facts-and-statistics/, accessed 6 August 2023

Monahan J, 'Risk Assessment of Violence among the Mentally Disordered: Generating Useful Knowledge' (1988) 11 Int J Law Psychiatry 249

Nussbaum MC, *Creating Capabilities: The Human Development Approach* (Harvard University Press 2011)

Perlin ML and Dorman DA, 'Sanism, Social Science, and the Development of Mental Disability Law Jurisprudence' (1993) 11 Behav Sci Law 47

Punton G, Dodd AL, and McNeill A, '"You're On the Waiting List": An Interpretative Phenomenological Analysis of Young Adults' Experiences of Waiting Lists within Mental Health Services in the UK' (2022) 17 PloS One e0265542

Richardson G, 'Report of the Expert Committee: Review of the Mental Health Act 1983' (Cm4480, Department of Health 1999)

Richardson G, 'Involuntary Treatment, Human Dignity and Human Rights' in M Rioux, LA Basser and M Jones (eds), *Critical Perspectives on Human Rights and Disability Law* (Martinus Nijhoff Publishers 2011)

Sen A, *Development as Freedom* (OUP 1999)

Stavert J, 'Adapting or Discarding the Status Quo? Supporting the Exercise of Legal Capacity in Scottish Law And Practice' in M Donnelly, R Harding and E Tassioglou (eds), *Supporting Legal Capacity in Socio-Legal Context* (Hart Publishing 2022)

Szasz T, *Antipsychiatry: Quackery Squared* (Syracuse University Press 2009)

Szmukler G, 'The UN Convention on the Rights of Persons with Disabilities: "Rights, Will and Preferences" in Relation to Mental Health Disabilities' (2017) 54 Int J Law Psychiatry 90

Venkatapuram S, *Health Justice: An Argument from the Capabilities Approach* (Polity Press 2011)

Weller P, *New Law and Ethics in Mental Health Advance Directives* (Routledge 2013)

Wessely S, 'Independent Review of the Mental Health Act 1983: Modernising the Mental Health Act: Increasing Choice, Reducing Compulsion' (2018) https://assets.publishing.service.gov.uk/media/5c6596a7ed915d045f37798c/Modernising_the_Mental_Health_Act_-_increasing_choice__reducing_compulsion.pdf, accessed 29 November 2023

12

Confidentiality

Elizabeth Chloe Romanis, Jordan A. Parsons, and Naomi Jones

Confidentiality is the protection of patient information by treating it as sensitive and private. Information can be the subject of protection either by virtue of the relationship between the parties (the person the information is about and the person who receives it) and/or because it is sensitive in nature. In the healthcare context, patient information is protected on both counts – confidentiality is implied and does not need to be explicit. As a matter of law, it 'has always been accepted that information about a person's health and treatment for ill-health is both private and confidential'.[1] The Human Rights Act 1998 stipulates that individuals have a fundamental right to privacy (enforceable against public authorities like the NHS).[2] However, confidentiality is not always absolute. Sometimes disclosing patient information can be necessary in the public interest or (less commonly) the interests of the patient. The law surrounding confidentiality and patient data is complicated and difficult for healthcare professionals to navigate. Unsurprisingly, it is one of the areas in which healthcare professionals seek the most support from professional bodies such as the General Medical Council (GMC).

In this chapter, we start by outlining why confidentiality is important, especially for marginalised groups and/or vulnerable healthcare users. We then explore relevant law and professional guidance governing confidentiality. The duty of confidentiality is not limited to doctors. Anyone who comes into contact with confidential information about/from patients must respect patient confidentiality.[3] However, for reasons of space, we focus on GMC guidance. Finally, we explore two case studies: safeguarding and abortion reporting.

1 [2004] UKHL 22 [145] per Lady Hale.

2 Article 8.

3 Other healthcare professions have their own professional guidance.

Confidentiality matters

Confidentiality is 'critically important to the effective functioning of trusting therapeutic relationships'.[4] The European Court of Human Rights has observed that:

> Respecting the confidentiality of health data is a vital principle … not only to respect the sense of privacy of a patient but also to preserve his or her confidence in the medical profession and in the health services in general.[5]

Without feeling that their privacy will be respected, patients may not feel comfortable to share personal details (or seek support at all), thus impacting the professionals' ability to make the correct diagnosis, offer advice, and commence treatment.[6] This individual good occurs in addition to the societal good from patient confidentiality; in that society can trust its healthcare professionals. There is no such thing as good or effective healthcare without patient privacy.[7] It matters for *all* patients in *all* areas of healthcare but might be especially important for vulnerable people and/or people in difficult circumstances. For example, young people seeking sexual health advice or trans people, nervous about the reaction reaction of their family/people in their social circle, wanting medical support. Confidentiality is particularly determinative for people in these (and similar) circumstances to feel able to access care.

Privacy is also about making sure that people feel respected as individuals in control of their own life and healthcare. Respect for privacy is reflected in the law through Article 8 of the Human Rights Act 1998: the right to a *private* and family life. This may be particularly important in cases where health information is central to the patient's identity. Redfern and Sinclair have emphasised this in the context of healthcare for trans people.[8] It is a crime for a person who has acquired the information in an official capacity to disclose a person's application for a gender recognition certificate with few exceptions.[9] Confidentiality ensures that people are afforded the respect to come out to friends and family at the time and in the manner of their choosing.

---

4 Paul Snelling and Oliver Quick, 'Confidentiality and Public Interest Disclosure: A Framework to Evaluate UK Healthcare Professional Regulatory Guidance' (2022) 22 Med Law Int 3, 31.

5 *Z v Finland* [1997] 25 EHRR 371, [95].

6 GMC (General Medical Council), 'Good Practice in Handling Patient Information' (nd) https://www.gmc-uk.org/-/media/documents/gmc-guidance-for-doctors---confidentiality-good-practice-in-handling-patient-information----70080105.pdf, accessed 23 September 2023.

7 Margaret Brazier, Emma Cave, and Rob Heywood, *Medicine, Patients and the Law* (Manchester University Press 2023) 101.

8 Jan Redfern and Bill Sinclair, 'Improving Health Care Encounters and Communication with Transgender Patients' (2014) 7 J Healthc Commun 25.

9 Gender Recognition Act 2004 s 22.

In practice, many of the problems that arise regarding patient confidentiality are different from those that are talked about as the *big legal issues*. With the NHS increasingly under strain, the potential for day-to-day accidental disclosures is becoming more prominent. Overcrowding in hospitals has led, in some of the worst instances, to healthcare professionals being forced to assess and treat patients in open corridors;[10] otherwise they would not be seen at all. The pretence of privacy in these circumstances is limited. Respecting confidentiality in day-to-day care can be more complex for some marginalised patients; for example, where a patient does not speak English and needs an interpreter. Professionals are guided not to use family members or friends as interpreters because this person would discover confidential information about the patient *before* the patient does, without the patient being able to choose whether that person should know. An informal interpreter might edit the information through lack of understanding or the wish to avoid upsetting the patient. This impacts the patient's autonomy and involvement in their own care, and the professional may not be aware of the full extent of this. Impartial, professional interpreters are therefore considered the gold standard.[11] However, where the language in question is uncommon within the UK, and the local community using it is small and well connected, a professional interpreter may still be peripherally known to the patient. Professional interpreters are bound by the principles of confidentiality, but the patient may feel uncertain about their involvement and may prefer to use a family member to keep healthcare matters within the family only.[12]

Principles of confidentiality

Confidentiality in UK healthcare is, in practice, largely guided by the Caldicott Principles,[13] which arose from a report commissioned by England's Chief Medical Officer (CMO) based on concerns about data transfer within the NHS.[14] The initial six principles have been built upon in 2012 and 2020, bringing us to the current eight principles (see Box 12.1).[15] Each NHS trust has at least one Caldicott Guardian, responsible for ensuring the principles are followed.

10 Ben Ireland, 'At a Glance: "Unsafe and Undignified" – the Nation's Hospitals' (2023) https://www.bma.org.uk/news-and-opinion/at-a-glance-unsafe-and-undignified-the-nation-s-hospitals, accessed 1 September 2023.

11 Sofia Sarfraz and Ian Wacogne, 'Fifteen-Minute Consultation: How to Use an Interpreter in a Medical Consultation' (2019) 104 ADC Ed Prac 231.

12 Ibid 232.

13 Strictly speaking, the Caldicott Principles apply only in England. However, their content in adapted forms is prevalent throughout the UK.

14 Department of Health, 'The Caldicott Committee Report on the Review of Patient-Identifiable Information' (1997) https://webarchive.nationalarchives.gov.uk/ukgwa/20130124064947/http://www.dh.gov.uk/prod_consum_dh/groups/dh_digitalassets/@dh/@en/documents/digitalasset/dh_4068404.pdf, accessed 9 September 2023.

15 National Data Guardian for Health and Social Care, 'The Eight Caldicott Principles' (2020) https://assets.publishing.service.gov.uk/government/uploads/system/uploads/attachment_data/file/942217/Eight_Caldicott_Principles_08.12.20.pdf, accessed 9 September 2023.

Box 12.1: Key text: the Caldicott Principles

1. Justify the purpose(s) for using confidential information.
2. Use confidential information only when it is necessary.
3. Use the minimum necessary confidential information.
4. Access to confidential information should be on a strict need-to-know basis.
5. Everyone with access to confidential information should be aware of their responsibilities.
6. Comply with the law.
7. The duty to share information for individual care is as important as the duty to protect patient confidentiality.
8. Inform patients and service users about how their confidential information is used.

The Caldicott Principles are a higher-level categorisation that healthcare professionals will not ordinarily consult themselves. But they form the basis behind the GMC's guidance on confidentiality for doctors.[16] The GMC guidance enables doctors to comply with good practice surrounding confidentiality. It is not legally binding but is used by the courts as evidence of the profession's view of good practice.[17] Compliance with the guidance is also important because patients can complain to the GMC.[18] Box 12.2 lists the GMC's principles of confidentiality – there is clear similarity with the Caldicott Principles.

Box 12.2: Key text: GMC Confidentiality Principles

1. Use the minimum necessary personal information.
2. Manage and protect information.
3. Be aware of your responsibilities.
4. Comply with the law.
5. Share relevant information for direct care.
6. Ask for explicit consent.
7. Tell patients.
8. Support patients to access their information.

16 E.g., on driving: GMC (General Medical Council), 'Confidentiality: Patients' Fitness to Drive and Reporting Concerns to the DVLA or DVA' (2017) https://www.gmc-uk.org/ethical-guidance/ethical-guidance-for-doctors/confidentiality---patients-fitness-to-drive-and-reporting-concerns-to-the-dvla-or-dva, accessed 9 September 2023.

17 Brazier, Cave, and Heywood (n7) 109.

18 Ibid.

Legal issues around confidentiality tend to fall into two categories. Firstly, *when* information about patients can be disclosed. Healthcare professionals should not reveal private information unless there is legal justification and it is appropriate to do so – the burden is on the health professional to prove disclosure was justified. Secondly, there are additional protections for personal data that can amount to positive obligations on healthcare professionals; that is, positive steps must be taken to protect some medical information. In the rest of this chapter, we examine disclosure and data protection with case studies.

Disclosing personal information

Day to day, health information is shared between healthcare professionals to make routine care possible. Patients are deemed to offer implied consent to the sharing of necessary personal information with all NHS professionals involved in treating them.[19] Stanton explains that healthcare professionals can use the 'surprise test' to consider when they should seek explicit consent:[20] if a patient would be surprised to know how their information was being shared, explicit consent is needed unless impracticable.[21] This is, however, a subjective test: what one patient with one set of values and of one culture believes is highly sensitive personal information might be very different to another.

In what follows we consider the sharing of information between healthcare professionals and *other* bodies/individuals. The right to privacy is not absolute, and the law recognises that sometimes other factors such as public safety or the protection of health outweigh the right to privacy.[22] There are circumstances in which healthcare professionals *must*, as a matter of law, disclose confidential information regardless of whether the patient (with or without capacity) consents. For example:

- Where required by a court.[23]
- Where the patient has an infection that must be reported to the UK Health Security Agency.[24]
- Where the police request information that could lead to the identification of driver who committed a driving offence.[25]
- Where they suspect a patient of involvement with terrorism.[26]

---

19 GMC (n6) [26]–[27].

20 Catherine Stanton, 'Patient Information: To Share or Not to Share?' (2018) 26 Med Law Rev 328, 333.

21 GMC (n6) [29].

22 Human Rights Act 1998 Article 8(2).

23 *General Dental Council v Savery and Others* [2011] EWHC 3011.

24 The Minister for Health and Social Care has the power to pass regulations naming infections/contaminations that must be reported: Public Health (Control of Disease) Act 1984 s 45C(3)(a).

25 Road Traffic Act 1988 s 172(2)(b).

26 Terrorism Act 2000 s 19(1).

- Where there is evidence that the patient is at risk of radicalisation.[27]
- Where there is a legal obligation to make a safeguarding report; for example, where they are concerned that a child may have had, or be at risk of having, female genital mutilation (FGM).[28]

In other cases, there is not an obligation to report, but a healthcare professional *can* do so, without the patient's consent, if there is lawful justification. These cases are more complicated because it requires the healthcare professional to exercise their judgement. It is not only a matter of whether the disclosure is lawful, but also whether disclosure is the right thing to do. The circumstances in which disclosure is lawful and appropriate will differ if the patient has capacity or lacks capacity and is different still where the patient is under 18. What is covered here is not an exhaustive list of *all* the circumstances in which disclosure may be lawful but some of the main guiding legal and ethical principles that healthcare professionals should use when making that determination.

Patients with capacity

Where the patient provides valid informed consent,[29] disclosure of their personal information is 'self-evidently lawful'.[30] There will be circumstances, however, where disclosure may be lawful and justifiable despite patient refusal to consent, or even where a healthcare professional feels it is safer to make a disclosure without discussing it with the patient. A key principle here is that of the *public interest*;[31] where failing to disclose 'may expose others to a risk of death or serious harm', outweighing the public interest in keeping health information confidential.[32] For example:

- where a patient is diagnosed with a medical condition that affects driving,[33] or
- where there is a reasonable belief that a patient might commit a serious crime.[34]

GMC guidance (Box 12.3) outlines several factors that doctors should consider when deciding about disclosure.[35] While these are helpful, applying and balancing them can be complex.

27 The obligation is on NHS trusts, but where a healthcare professional is working for a trust, they will have the obligation to report via the system the trust has established. Counter-Terrorism and Security Act 2015 s 26.

28 Female Genital Mutilation Act 2003 (as amended by the Serious Crime Act 2015).

29 See Chapter 9.

30 Brazier, Cave, and Heywood (n7) 110.

31 *R v Department of Health ex p Source Informatics Ltd* [2000] 1 All ER 786; GMC (n6) [64].

32 Ibid.

33 See n22.

34 *W v Edgell* [1990] 1 All ER 835.

35 GMC (n6) [68].

Box 12.3: Key text: GMC guidance

Relevant factors when deciding about making a disclosure about an adult with capacity:

1. The potential harm or distress to the patient arising from the disclosure – for example, in terms of their future engagement with treatment and their overall health.
2. The potential harm to trust in doctors generally – for example, if it is widely perceived that doctors will readily disclose information about patients without consent.
3. The potential harm to others (whether to a specific person or people, or to the public more broadly) if the information is not disclosed.
4. The potential benefits to an individual or to society arising from the release of the information.
5. The nature of the information to be disclosed and any views expressed by the patient.
6. Whether the harms can be avoided or benefits gained without breaching the patient's privacy or, if not, what is the minimum intrusion.

If a patient refuses to consent to disclosure and there is no risk of harm to others, this refusal should *usually* be respected, even if this places the patient at risk of serious harm.[36] There is a caveat to this statement (provided as an endnote within the GMC guidance), however, which provides that in cases like this, sometimes disclosure without consent could be considered justified if there is clear evidence of the potential for serious harm to the patient and there is no alternative or less intrusive way of preventing the harm. The guidance warns, however, that '[t]his is an uncertain area of law and, if practicable, you should seek independent legal advice'.[37] Guidance from the Department of Health and Social Care (DHSC) suggests that 'serious harm' includes cases of unlawful killing, rape, treason, and child abuse,[38] but not fraud or damage to property.[39] The guidance acknowledges that there is a 'grey area' where healthcare professionals must exercise their judgement considering the wider context. For example, a criminal incident may become more serious if repeated over a period of time.[40]

If a healthcare professional makes the decision that disclosure (against the patient's wishes) is lawful and the right thing to do, this should be handled

36 Ibid [59].

37 Ibid endnote 19.

38 DHSC (Department of Health and Social Care), 'Confidentiality: NHS Code of Practice Supplementary Guidance: Public Interest Disclosures' (2010) https://assets.publishing.service.gov.uk/government/uploads/system/uploads/attachment_data/file/216476/dh_122031.pdf, accessed 9 September 2023, [12].

39 Ibid [13].

40 Ibid [14].

appropriately to ensure that patients' dignity is respected. For example, unless it is unsafe to do so, patients should be told about the disclosure.[41]

Patients lacking capacity

As discussed in Chapter 10, when a patient lacks capacity, all care must be in their best interests.[42] Adults who lack capacity maintain the same right to confidentiality as those who have capacity,[43] but disclosure may be more readily justified for the patient without capacity's protection. The principles of best interests[44] must be applied within the context of confidentiality. A disclosure regarding a patient who lacks capacity must incur 'an overall benefit' to the patient.[45] The patients' privacy and dignity must be the professionals' central concern, and the patient's involvement in deciding whether to disclose must be supported as much as possible (or as much as the patient wishes).[46] Healthcare professionals should consider the patient's previously expressed preferences and anything known about their feelings, beliefs, and values, as well as the views of any person the patient asks to be consulted or who has the legal authority to make decisions on their behalf.[47] If the patient refuses to consent to disclosure, GMC guidance suggests that healthcare professionals should try to persuade them that disclosure is important.[48] However, if the patient still refuses to consent and disclosure is considered to be of overall benefit to them, healthcare professionals can disclose to the appropriate person/ authority.[49] Disclosure should be handled appropriately.[50]

Children and young people

Judgments have emphasised that children and young people have equal rights to confidentiality as adults.[51] Where young people have the capacity to consent, disclosures regarding their medical information should only be made to parents/ persons with parental responsibility (PR) with that child/young person's permission. Where children are young and/or lack the capacity to consent, obtaining consent to treatment requires their parent/carer with PR to be informed of relevant details

---

41 GMC (n6) [63]–[64].

42 MCA (Mental Capacity Act) 2005 s 1(5).

43 The obligations of confidentiality persist after death.

44 MCA 2005 s 4.

45 GMC (n6) [44].

46 Ibid.

47 Ibid [45].

48 Ibid [48].

49 Ibid [49].

50 Ibid [49].

51 *R (Axon) v Secretary of State for Health* [2006] EWHC 37; *Gillick v West Norfolk & Wisbeck Area Health Authority* [1986] AC 112; GMC (General Medical Council), '0–18 Years: Guidance for All Doctors' (nd) https://www.gmc-uk.org/ethical-guidance/ethical-guidance-for-doctors/0-18-years/principles-of-confidentiality, accessed 23 September 2023.

in order to provide valid consent on the child's behalf. In general, parents/persons with PR are key advocates and sources of support for children and young people, and, in day-to-day practice, most information is routinely shared with them, either because that child/young person consents, or because it is in their best interests.[52] However, healthcare professionals may not have to disclose everything a child/young person without capacity confides in them. For example, if a young trans child, who had not come out to their parents, came out to a healthcare professional, the professional may assess it to be in the best interests of that child not to tell their parents/responsible guardians the details of that conversation.

There are circumstances where a professional *may* disclose information to the police and/or children's social care, and circumstances where they are *required* to do so. Healthcare professionals are required to share information with relevant organisations where a child or young person may be at risk of *significant harm*.[53] Significant harm is not strictly defined. GMC guidance states disclosures should be made where *necessary* to protect the child/young person from risk of death or serious harm. This might arise in cases where:

- The child/young person is suffering from, or at risk of, neglect or sexual, physical, or emotional abuse.
- The information would help in the prevention/detention/prosecution of a serious crime committed against the child/young person.
- The child/young person is engaging in behaviour that may put them or others at risk of serious harm.[54]

This is not an exhaustive list. It is good practice to inform the child, young person, or their parent/carer of this disclosure, unless it would put them at additional risk or cause a delay.[55] The next section discusses disclosure in safeguarding for adults and children in more detail.

Disclosure case study: safeguarding

Safeguarding applies to adults and children with or without capacity. There is no universal legal definition of safeguarding. The Department of Health and Social Care describes it as

> protecting an adult's right to live in safety, free from abuse and neglect. It is about people and organisations working together to prevent and

52 GMC (n51).

53 Children Act 1989 s 47. In this context, this is a 'Child Protection'-level referral.

54 GMC (n51) [49].

55 GMC (General Medical Council), 'Protecting Children and Young People: The Responsibilities of All Doctors' (2018) https://www.gmc-uk.org/-/media/documents/protecting-children-and-young-people---english-20200114_pdf-48978248.pdf, accessed 9 September 2023.

> stop both the risks and experience of abuse and neglect, while at the same time making sure that the adult's wellbeing is promoted including, where appropriate, having regard to their views, wishes, feelings and beliefs in deciding on any action.[56]

The Care Act 2014, Social Services and Well-being (Wales) Act 2014, and Adult Support and Protection (Scotland) Act 2007 place safeguarding obligations on healthcare professionals in the NHS in relation to vulnerable adults.[57] The legal duty on local authorities to safeguard children is enshrined within the Children Act 1989. The overarching principle is the welfare of the child is the '*paramount consideration*'.[58] Local authorities have a duty to 'safeguard and promote the welfare'[59] of children and young people in their area, which includes the duty to investigate safeguarding concerns.[60]

Stereotypes can, but should not, permeate snap judgements about who needs an enhanced safeguarding assessment.[61] Recently, for example, abortion providers came under considerable pressure regarding their safeguarding procedures (despite there being processes in place that are more robust than many other health services).[62] Much of this pressure, at its root, was the result of stereotyping that 'reiterates the problematic characterisation of women [and pregnant people] seeking to end unwanted pregnancies as being inherently vulnerable and in need of institutional support'.[63] Evidence also suggests that racism and unconscious bias make families from racialised communities more likely to come to the attention of children's social care, and yet ethnic minority children are simultaneously less likely to receive the support they may need from institutions.[64] The National Society for the Prevention of Cruelty to Children (NSPCC) has important

56 DHSC (Department of Health and Social Care), 'Care and Support Statutory Guidance' (2014) https://assets.publishing.service.gov.uk/government/uploads/system/uploads/attachment_data/file/506202/23902777_Care_Act_Book.pdf, accessed 22 September 2023, [14.7].

57 Ibid [14.5].

58 Children Act 1989 s 1(1) (emphasis added).

59 Ibid, s 17.

60 Ibid s 47.

61 For example, disabled parents are subject to much systemic bias based on a presumed inability to parent. See Mark Higgins, 'The Exam it is Impossible to Pass: How Disabled Parents Are at Risk of Having to Prove the Impossible in Care Proceedings' in Beverley Clough and Jonathan Herring (eds), *Disability, Care and Family Law* (Taylor & Francis 2021).

62 Jordan A. Parsons and Elizabeth Chloe Romanis, 'The Case for Telemedical Early Medical Abortion in England: Dispelling Adult Safeguarding Concerns' (2021) 30 Health Care Anal 73.

63 Elizabeth Chloe Romanis and others, 'Safeguarding and Teleconsultation for Abortion' (2020) 398 Lancet 555.

64 Nuffield Foundation, 'Identifying and Understanding the Link between System Conditions and Welfare Inequalities in Children's Social Care Services' (2019) https://www.nuffieldfoundation.org/wp-content/uploads/2019/11/Final-Report-Identifying-and-understanding-the-link-between-system-conditions-and-welfare-inequalities-in-children%E2%80%99s-social-care-services-March-2020.pdf, accessed 22 September 2023.

anti-racism resources available.[65] We must be cognisant of how stereotypes influence judgements relating to safeguarding, ensuring they do not result in either unnecessarily intrusive agency involvement or missed opportunities to safeguard vulnerable people.

Information sharing is important in safeguarding and is repeatedly raised in safeguarding practice reviews (inquiries conducted when a child or young person has died and there are safeguarding implications).[66] However, it does not mean always sharing confidential information. Healthcare professionals must consider whether breaking confidentiality is justified to keep the person, and/or their children and sometimes others, safe, including whether there is a less intrusive alternative. Maintaining confidentiality to build and uphold the therapeutic relationship is particularly important where the individual is vulnerable or at risk and their engagement with services enhances their safety. A key principle of safeguarding is that it is done *with*, not *to*, the individual, thus highlighting the importance of partnership between the person and professionals.[67] Ideally, information will be shared with the person's consent, thus removing any tension between safeguarding and confidentiality.

If an adult with capacity refuses to consent to disclosure where there are safeguarding concerns, the situation becomes complex. In general, it is unusual that a professional will be permitted to disclose information without a competent patient's consent.[68] However, they may still share concerns if a serious crime has been committed or it is in the public interest.

Some survivors/victims of domestic abuse will not agree to the professional reporting it for many reasons. It is possible, though should not be assumed, that the abuser is pressurising the abuse survivor/victim to refuse to cooperate with any action taken to safeguard them. Where a survivor/victim does not consent to disclosure, they may be more hesitant about the ensuing legal process, and

---

65 NSPCC (National Society for the Prevention of Cruelty to Children), 'Safeguarding Children Who Come from Black, Asian and Minoritised Ethnic Communities' (2022) https://learning.nspcc.org.uk/safeguarding-child-protection/children-from-black-asian-minoritised-ethnic-communities, accessed 22 September 2023.

66 NHS England, 'Safeguarding Adults: Pocket Guide' (nd) https://www.england.nhs.uk/south/wp-content/uploads/sites/6/2016/04/1085-nhs-leaflet-accesible-copy.pdf, accessed 22 September 2023.

67 There are six principles of safeguarding initially created by the Department of Health in 2011, now enshrined within the Care Act (2014). These are: empowerment, prevention, protection, proportionality, partnership, and accountability. Social Care Institute for Excellence, 'Safeguarding Adults' (nd) https://www.scie.org.uk/safeguarding/adults/introduction/six-principles, accessed 22 September 2023.

68 The GMC describes a case of physical abuse of an older adult by her daughter, where, because the patient had capacity, the doctor offered her support, but did not disclose. GMC (General Medical Council), 'Case Study: Should a Doctor Disclose Evidence of Abuse without the Patient's Consent?' (nd) https://www.gmc-uk.org/-/media/gmc-site/ethical-guidance/learning-materials/themes/new---should-a-doctor-disclose-evidence-of-abuse-without-the-patients-consent.pdf, accessed 22 September 2023.

less likely to participate in it, which could not only damage the therapeutic relationship but could also fail to make them safer and even mean that the abuse could escalate. However, the harm they are currently suffering may be significant enough to justify disclosure. Professionals can disclose information to a multi-agency risk assessment conference (MARAC), made up of the local authority, Independent Domestic Violence Advocates, and others, without consent, though consent is preferred.[69] If the professional cannot obtain consent, they must weigh up how much information to disclose and the risk of not reporting.

Another example relates to adults with additional care and/or support needs. The adult safeguarding duty applies when an adult with additional care and/or support needs is at risk of abuse or neglect and their needs preclude them from protecting themselves. The local authority has a duty to undertake a section 42 inquiry if they reasonably believe a person fits this definition.[70] The inquiry can be undertaken without consent if the person lacks capacity and the inquiry is in their best interests, or if an inquiry is in the public interest. Chapter 10 further discusses the interplay between coercion and capacity in adults.

As can be seen, the interpretation and balancing of principles of safeguarding and confidentiality can be challenging; a person's competent refusal should be respected, but abuse should not be ignored. At all times, professionals should support the individual, document concerns, and seek advice from legal and/or safeguarding teams. The right, and legal, course of action will often depend on the individual facts of the case. The previously described principles of information sharing should be followed at all times. Cave has argued that doctors should, in some circumstances, apply to the High Court to exercise its inherent jurisdiction to enable disclosures to protect adults with capacity in vulnerable circumstances.[71]

The tension between confidentiality and safeguarding is complex in cases involving children. We have already introduced children's right to confidentiality,[72] the welfare principle,[73] and the significant harm threshold. Where children and young people lack capacity and there are concerns that they are undergoing, or at risk of, significant harm, the balance tends to shift towards disclosing information to appropriate agencies. Safeguarding practice reviews have repeatedly highlighted the vital importance of information sharing within and between agencies. A key report, 'Every Child Matters',[74] published in 2003 following the murder of

---

69 Safe Lives, 'Sharing Information and MARAC' (2019) https://safelives.org.uk/sites/default/files/resources/Sharing%20Information%20and%20Marac%20GDPR%20FAQs%20-%20England%20%26%20Wales%20version.pdf, accessed 22 September 2023.

70 Care Act 2014 s 42.

71 Emma Cave, 'Disclosure of Confidential Information to Protect the Patient: The Role of Legal Capacity in the Evolution of Professional Guidance' (2015) 3 J Law Med Ethics 7, 22.

72 GMC (n55).

73 Children Act 1989 s 1(1).

74 'Every Child Matters' (2003) https://assets.publishing.service.gov.uk/government/uploads/system/uploads/attachment_data/file/272064/5860.pdf, accessed 21 September 2023.

eight-year-old Victoria Climbié, first emphasised this principle. Multiple agencies (health, police, social care, and charitable/voluntary sectors) had contact with Victoria and were concerned about abuse. However, concerns were not shared, which, had they been, might have highlighted the severity of the abuse and triggered intervention to protect her. A more recent review (2022) following the murders of Star Hobson and Arthur Labinjo-Hughes highlighted that weaknesses in information sharing remain a problem.[75] This review illustrates concerns with the 'significant harm' threshold for disclosure.

Legally, consent from a person with PR is *not* required for social care referrals that meet the 'significant harm' threshold, in order to protect the child. However, if that threshold is not reached,[76] consent is required for referral. Just because that threshold is not reached on one occasion does not mean that there is no risk to the child, as a concern may fit a part of a wider picture, as highlighted by what happened to Star and Arthur. In cases that fall below this threshold, or where there is uncertainty, the GMC suggests professionals discuss with the safeguarding team within their organisation.[77]

Ultimately, when making a safeguarding disclosure about a child, a professional must judge whether the breaking of confidentiality is justified to safeguard the child or young person (applying the welfare principle). In practice, professionals must consider *what* they are disclosing, *who* they are disclosing to, and *why* they are disclosing it.[78] This will depend heavily on context.

Cases involving young people with capacity – with Gillick competence[79] – can be particularly tricky. The young person can consent to treatment (so their parent/carer is not necessarily involved in their healthcare) and, because they have capacity, their insistence that a disclosure is not made may carry more weight. However, if a professional assesses that a young person is undergoing, or at risk of, significant harm, they will still be obliged to disclose information.

Parekh-Hill and others have highlighted the importance of respecting adolescents' privacy within letters following clinic appointments.[80] They suggest clarifying with the young person what they would like to be included in the letter, and the writing of separate letters to GPs and/or other professionals where

75 The Child Safeguarding Practice Review Panel, 'Child Protection in England' (2022) https://assets.publishing.service.gov.uk/government/uploads/system/uploads/attachment_data/file/1078488/ALH_SH_National_Review_26-5-22.pdf, accessed 21 September 2023.

76 E.g., referrals for 'Early Help' or 'Child in Need' interventions.

77 GMC (n55).

78 The government published a statutory framework on information sharing in safeguarding children in 2018: HM Government 'Working Together to Safeguard Children' (2018) https://assets.publishing.service.gov.uk/media/669e7501ab418ab055592a7b/Working_together_to_safeguard_children_2023.pdf, accessed 21 September 2023.

79 *Gillick* (n51). See also Chapter 16.

80 Nathan Alexander Parekh-Hill and others, 'Please Write to Me, Not about Me: Best Practice in Written Communication with Young People' (2023) 108 Arch Dis Child e5.

there are issues that professionals need to know but the young person may not wish their parents to be aware of.

The importance of confidentiality for young people has been emphasised especially in the context of sexual health.[81] In *Axon*, Silber J found that

> the lack of confidentiality would probably or might well deter young people from seeking advice and treatment on contraception, sexually transmitted diseases and abortion, and this would have undesirable and troubled consequences.[82]

Box 12.4: Key text: GMC guidance

Indicators that a young person may be experiencing sexual abuse or exploitation

- The young person is too immature to understand/consent.
- Big differences in age, maturity, and/or power between sexual partners.
- The young person's sexual partner is in a position of trust.
- There was force, a threat of force, emotional/psychological pressure, bribery, or payment to engage in sexual activity or to keep it secret.
- Drugs or alcohol were used to influence the young person to engage in sexual activity.
- The young person's sexual partner is a person known to police/child protection agencies as having had abusive relationships with children/young people.

GMC guidance also acknowledges the importance of a confidential sexual health service for young people, noting that making young people feel safe accessing treatment protects the young person themselves and other young people's health too.[83] They acknowledge, however, that there will be some cases where disclosure is necessary – for example, any cases involving children under 13 (because this is statutory rape)[84] or where there is a clear public interest. The guidance also acknowledges several other indicators that a young person has been subject to abusive or seriously harmful sexual activity and a disclosure may be necessary for safeguarding reasons (see Box 12.4).[85]

While the legal age of consent for sex is 16,[86] it is unlikely that a professional will see a safeguarding or legal need to disclose if two 15-year-olds are in a consensual

81 GMC (n55).
82 *Axon* (n51) [66].
83 GMC (n55) [57].
84 Ibid [60], [58].
85 Ibid [61].
86 Sexual Offences Act 2003 s 9.

sexual relationship. By contrast, if a 15-year-old is in a sexual relationship with a 20-year-old, and/or there is alcohol involved, this would raise significant concerns about child sexual exploitation and would usually warrant disclosure, potentially against the young person's wishes, to safeguard them.

Data protection

Where it is being processed, personal data – even if pseudonymised[87] – is subject to certain special protections in the Data Protection Act 2018 and General Data Protection Regulations.[88] At the time of writing, a new Bill, the Data Protection and Digital Information Bill,[89] is at the House of Lords Committee stage. If passed, this will amend the Data Protection Act 2018.

Health data clearly falls within the parameters of 'personal data'.[90] Health data counts as a 'special category of personal data'.[91] In healthcare, personal data is routinely processed. Processing is described as any operation performed on the data, for example, collection, organisation, storage, use, dissemination, and erasure (among other things).[92] In processing health data, healthcare professionals must abide by some general principles:[93]

- Data must be processed lawfully, fairly, and in a transparent manner in relation to the data subject.
- Data must be collected for specified, explicit, and legitimate purposes and not later used in a manner incompatible with those purposes.
- Data collected must be adequate, relevant, and limited to what is necessary in relation to the purposes for which they are processed.
- Data collected must be accurate and kept up to date, having regard to the purpose for processing.
- Data should be kept in a form that permits identification of the data subject for no longer than necessary for the purpose for which it was processed.
- Data must be processed in a way that best ensures its security.

Healthcare professionals must also abide by principles that govern the use of 'special category data'. Such data can only be processed if one of the

87 Data Protection Act 2018 s 5(1) specifies that terms in the Act (including personal data) have the same meaning as in the European Union General Data Protection Regulation (GDPR). Pseudonymisation is defined in Art 4(5) of the GDPR.

88 While EU law, these regulations have been transposed into UK law following Brexit, in the European Union (Withdrawal) Act 2018.

89 Data Protection and Digital Information Bill https://bills.parliament.uk/bills/3322, accessed 21 September 2023.

90 Personal data is defined in Art 4(1) GDPR.

91 GDPR Art 9(1).

92 Ibid Art 4(2).

93 Ibid Art 5(1).

circumstances outlined in the General Data Protection Regulation is present (see Box 12.5).[94]

Box 12.5: Key text: General Data Protection Regulation Art 5 (2)

Circumstances in which health data (as 'special category data') can be processed (only one of these circumstances must be made out):

- The data subject gives explicit consent for one or more specified purposes.
- Processing the data is necessary to protect vital interests of the data subject or another natural person where the data subject cannot give consent.
- The data are manifestly made public by the data subject.
- Processing the data is necessary for reasons of substantial public interest (in accordance with the law), is proportionate to the aim pursued, and respects 'the essence of the right to data protection'.
- Processing the data is necessary for preventative or occupational health needs, medical diagnosis, or the provision of health or social care or treatment.
- Processing the data is necessary for reasons of public interest in the area of public health in accordance with the law where there are suitable and specific measures to safeguard the rights and freedoms of the data subject.
- Processing the data is necessary for archiving purposes in the public interest, scientific, ... research or statistic purposes in accordance with the law and where there is respect for the essence of the right to data protection and suitable and specific measures to safeguard the data subject's rights and freedoms (e.g., pseudonymisation).*

*Full details of safeguards are outlined in Article 89(1) of the GDPR.

Data case study: abortion-reporting requirements

As explored in Chapter 14, there are various complexities in accessing abortion care in Great Britain. It is a heavily regulated area of healthcare – giving rise to the concept of 'abortion exceptionalism'[95] – and even those who are entitled to care may not be able to access it due to the practical and administrative hurdles involved. Even when an abortion seeker has navigated this legal framework and is to undergo the treatment, there is further regulatory interference. It is here that concerns around patient confidentiality arise.

94 GDPR Art 5(2). There are more provisions in this article, which have been omitted as they are irrelevant in the healthcare context.

95 Jordan A. Parsons and Elizabeth Chloe Romanis, *Early Medical Abortion, Equality of Access, and the Telemedical Imperative* (OUP 2021) 13.

Table 12.1: Information to be included in an abortion notification

Information relating to procedure	Personal information
• Details of the doctor who performed the termination • Details of the two doctors that authorised the termination[a] • Place of termination • Procedure used • Date (of admission, termination, and discharge[b]) • Gestation • Grounds for termination • Complications	• Name • Address • Date of birth • Ethnicity • Marital status • Previous pregnancies[c]

[a] While the doctor performing the termination will ordinarily be one of the two that authorised it, this is not a requirement.

[b] Not all of these fields will be required, depending on the abortion methods used. For example, a medical termination does not ordinarily require admission.

[c] This particular datapoint includes specifying the number of livebirths or stillbirths over 24 weeks, spontaneous miscarriages or ectopic pregnancies, and legal terminations.

The Abortion Act 1967 stipulates that regulations should be made that, amongst other things, require that any registered medical practitioner carrying out an abortion must 'give notice of the termination and such other information relating to the termination as may be so prescribed'.[96] Such notice is to be given to the relevant Chief Medical Officer (CMO), depending on which nation the termination takes place in.[97] The current iteration of these regulations in England and Wales – the Abortion Regulations 1991 – provide full details of the information that a doctor must collect and include in their notification. These are to be found in Schedule 2, where the notification form itself is provided, which requires a significant amount of information. This includes information relating to the procedure, but also detailed personal information (see Table 12.1).

To capture this extensive set of information, the notification form spans six pages. Before 2002, it was required that a hard copy was sent to the CMO 'in a sealed envelope within 7 days of the termination'.[98] However, in 2002, this requirement was relaxed to allow notification within 14 days either in a sealed envelope or digitally.[99] In Scotland, the Abortion (Scotland) Regulations 1991 largely mirrored its counterpart in England and Wales when first made. However, the sealed envelope within seven days requirement remained until a far more recent amendment. In December 2021, the Scottish government

96 Abortion Act 1967 s 2(1)(b).

97 Ibid s 2(2).

98 Abortion Regulations 1991 [as enacted] reg 4(1)(b).

99 Ibid reg 4(a)(ii) and Abortion (Amendment) (Wales) Regulations 2002, reg4(a)(ii). At the time of writing, no amendments to the Abortion Regulations 1991 have been reflected on legislation.gov.uk. As such, we recommend you consult the list of all changes under the 'More Resources' tab if you are citing them.

passed the Abortion (Scotland) Amendment Regulations 2021, coming into force in May 2022. Amongst various amendments, they extended the notification period to 'before the fifteenth day of the calendar month immediately following the calendar month in which the practitioner terminated the pregnancy'.[100] Rather more generous, then, than the 2002 amendments in England and Wales. Further, not only did the Scottish 2021 amendments remove the 'sealed envelope' requirement, permitting electronic notification,[101] but they also limited the data required to only the name of the practitioner and their employer.[102] However, whilst there is no longer a fixed regulatory requirement to report further data directly to the CMO, such data is now reported directly to Public Health Scotland. This administrative change was very much the intention of the Scottish Government, as made clear in its Impact Assessment.[103]

Two things stand out with the reporting requirements on abortion care in England and Wales. Firstly, how detailed the forms are. The information that doctors must collect is extensive, including aspects of the patient's personal life that have no bearing on their treatment. Secondly, that they are *requirements*. They are not guidance or best practice; rather, they are strict, imposed rules on information that the doctor must, by law, collect and report.

Failure to comply with these requirements opens up doctors to legal difficulties. The applicable fields of the form must be completed in full, or else the doctor may be found guilty of a summary offence.[104] As such, there is no professional discretion as to the appropriateness of what to report in a given situation. These regulations effectively imply that there is an appropriate justification for sidelining patient confidentiality in all instances of abortion. This contrasts with the standard approach (as detailed earlier in this chapter) of a careful assessment of whether a breach of patient confidentiality is justifiable on a case-by-case basis. Detailed reporting is no longer a *regulatory* requirement in Scotland, and more recent

100 Abortion (Scotland) Regulations 1991 reg 4(1)(3) as amended by reg 3 Abortion (Scotland) Amendment Regulations 2021.

101 This is not explicitly stated in the Abortion (Scotland) Amendment Regulations 2021. However, the entire substitution of regulation 4 of the Abortion (Scotland) Regulations 1991 to include no sealed envelope stipulation has this effect.

102 Abortion (Scotland) Regulations 1991 reg 4(2) as amended by reg 3 Abortion (Scotland) Amendment Regulations 2021.

103 Scottish Government, 'Abortion (Scotland) Amendment Regulations 2021 – Changes to How Information about Abortions is Provided: Business and Regulatory Impact Assessment' (2021) https://www.gov.scot/binaries/content/documents/govscot/publications/impact-assessment/2021/12/abortion-scotland-amendment-regulations-2021-changes-information-abortions-provided-business-regulatory-impact-assessment/documents/abortion-scotland-amendment-regulations-2021-changes-information-abortions-provided-business-regulatory-impactassessment/abortion-scotland-amendment-regulations-2021-changes-information-abortions-provided-business-regulatory-impact-assessment/govscot%3Adocument/abortion-scotland-amendment-regulations-2021-changes-information-abortions-provided-business-regulatory-impact-assessment.pdf, accessed 21 September 2023.

104 Abortion Act 1967 s 2(3).

data suggest that there are elements of choice as to what information the abortion seeker provides.[105] Nonetheless, detailed reporting remains as the norm.

There is an argument that these reporting requirements do not interfere with confidentiality because the data remain confidential. Once information is reported to the CMO (or, in Scotland, Public Health Scotland), it is kept secure and, when reported in annual statistics, no identifying data are reported. The requirements could be said to satisfy GDPR in de-identifying data. However, this view fails to recognise the invasiveness of collecting the information to report and how sensitive this information may be, even by the standards of medical information. It can reasonably be suggested that the extent of data collected does not 'safeguard the data subject's rights and freedoms'.[106] Further, it does not adequately question whether there is a valid reason for the collection of such data (beyond it being required by law). Véliz argues that

> in order to fully respect and protect privacy, it is not enough to refrain from disclosing information about patients. [...] it is also important to minimize the collection of information, and to use sensitive information only for appropriate purposes (which, in the medical context, is treatment).[107]

We must ask, then, whether such extensive data collection and reporting is for an appropriate purpose. Not least because it is so unique and in the area of sexual and reproductive health, which is widely regarded to necessitate *additional* levels of confidentiality. For example, sexual health clinics operate on a separate computer system to the rest of the NHS, with separate patient identifiers.

The extensive reporting about abortion is evidently not for treatment purposes, as Véliz suggests any data collection ought to be; a pregnancy can be safely and effectively terminated without knowledge of the patient's marital status. The only other possible justification in the context of confidentiality is that it is in the public interest. As a result of the reporting requirements, England and Wales have incredibly detailed statistical data on abortion provision (similarly in Scotland). This is published in an annual report by the DHSC.[108] Having this detailed understanding of abortion care could, if used appropriately, enable improved policy and practice by responding to trends in patient circumstances and needs.

105 Public Health Scotland, 'Termination of pregnancy: Year ending December 2023' (2024) https://publichealthscotland.scot/publications/termination-of-pregnancy-statistics/termination-of-pregnancy-statistics-year-ending-december-2023/, accessed 2 September 2024.

106 GDPR Art 5(2).

107 Carissa Véliz, 'Not the Doctor's Business: Privacy, Personal Responsibility and Data Rights in Medical Settings' (2020) 34 Bioethics 712, 713.

108 Office for Health Improvement and Disparities, 'Abortion Statistics for England and Wales: 2021' (2022) https://www.gov.uk/government/statistics/abortion-statistics-for-england-and-wales-2021, accessed 21 September 2023.

However, while there may be some benefits, abortion care remains an outlier in having such information. The annual statistics are some of the most detailed for a single medical treatment. We must question, then, why we do not think it is important to collect this much information in other areas of healthcare and why abortion care is treated differently.

The balancing act of the public interest test requires us to consider potential harms caused by the reporting requirements. Some abortion seekers may want to keep the fact they are accessing care secret. For example, a victim of domestic abuse may fear repercussions if their abuser finds out. Even if the data are handled correctly and there is minimal risk of a leak, the fear of this may cause some, especially vulnerable people, to reconsider accessing important care. Further, the anxiety that people who do access abortion care may suffer from the recording of personal information that they do not want shared may itself constitute a harm.

In one sense, these reporting requirements do not present a confidentiality challenge to professionals. As we have said, reporting is required by law, and GMC guidance, drawing on the Caldicott Principles, is clear that doctors must comply with the law when handling patient information. However, it may put professionals in difficult situations. If an abortion seeker states they will not go through with the termination if it will be reported, there is a risk that they will instead seek an abortion through unlawful channels. As such, professionals may recognise that in some situations, the reporting requirements may cause harm.

It remains unclear, therefore, how the marginal benefits of the reporting requirements outweigh both the individual and public interest in confidentiality. The rationale provided by the Scottish government in making the amendments speaks directly to the importance of patient confidentiality:

> These changes are needed to improve the security of personal data provided for the abortion statistics and reduce any risks of a data breach.[109]

However, as earlier noted, these changes were largely administrative and did not represent a principled opposition to the practice of abortion reporting in Scotland. England and Wales have made some recent changes to the Abortion Regulations 1991 by way of the Abortion (Amendment) Regulations 2022. However, they merely make minor terminology changes throughout,[110] to reflect the Health and Care Act 2022.[111] There remains an open question as to whether the reporting requirements in England and Wales (or the less strict reporting process of Scotland) are justifiable or, as in Scotland, should be removed. As they stand, the reporting requirements treat abortion care as somehow different to the rest of healthcare, thus marginalising abortion seekers.

109 Scottish Government (n102), [2.2].

110 Abortion (Amendment) Regulations 2022 reg 2.

111 Health and Care Act 2022 s 178.

Summary

- Confidentiality is a critical legal obligation that healthcare professionals owe to patients, but it is not absolute.
- Day-to-day dilemmas about confidentiality can differ from what are considered 'the big legal issues'. Health professionals should be aware of/attentive to this.
- Confidentiality is particularly important for marginalised groups for whom privacy is critical to ensure that they contact healthcare professionals/access healthcare and that they feel that their individuality is respected.
- Decisions about how and when to disclose confidential information to keep patients safe are complex. Healthcare professionals have to balance lots of competing factors – including the importance of respecting confidentiality.
- Health data is 'personal data' and protected by additional legal provisions. There are some instances, however, in which excess personal data is collected in the course of treatment.

Questions for reflection

1. In the following circumstances, can, and should, a healthcare professional lawfully make a disclosure? Would disclosure be the best thing to do? What factors influence your thoughts? What might change your mind?
   a) A 75-year-old who is bedbound following a stroke mentions to their support nurse that their daughter has set up a new credit card for them.
   b) A 30-year-old with a learning disability tests positive for HIV. They say they don't want to tell their partner.
   c) A 14-year-old attends a sexual health clinic walk-in alone and asks for a Chlamydia test. They tell the doctor their sexual partner is 19 years old.
   d) A 15-year-old mentions to their GP that they drink alcohol with friends at parties sometimes. They ask the GP not to tell their parents.
2. Should abortion reporting requirements be relaxed across Great Britain?

Recommended resources

- Carissa Véliz, 'Not the Doctor's Business: Privacy, Personal Responsibility and Data Rights in Medical Settings' (2020) 34 Bioethics 712–18.
- Charles Foster and Roy Gilbar, 'Is There a New Duty to Warn Family Members in English Medical Law? ABC v St George's Healthcare NHS Trust and Others [2020] EWHC 455' (2021) 29 Med Law Rev 359–72.
- Akil Shenoy and Jacob Appel, 'Safeguarding Confidentiality in Electronic Health Records' (2017) 26 Cam Q Healthc Ethics 337–41.

Bibliography

Brazier M, Cave E and Heywood R, *Medicine Patients and the Law* (Manchester University Press 2023)

Cave C, 'Disclosure of Confidential Information to Protect the Patient: The Role of Legal Capacity in the Evolution of Professional Guidance' (2015) 3 J Law Med Ethics 7

Child Safeguarding Practice Review Panel, 'Child Protection in England' (2022) https://assets.publishing.service.gov.uk/government/uploads/system/uploads/attachment_data/file/1078488/ALH_SH_National_Review_26-5-22.pdf, accessed 21 September 2023

Department of Health, 'The Caldicott Committee Report on the Review of Patient-Identifiable Information' (1997) https://webarchive.nationalarchives.gov.uk/ukgwa/20130124064947/ http://www.dh.gov.uk/prod_consum_dh/groups/dh_digitalassets/@dh/@en/documents/digitalasset/dh_4068404.pdf, accessed 9 September 2023

DHSC (Department of Health and Social Care), 'Confidentiality: NHS Code of Practice Supplementary Guidance: Public Interest Disclosures' (2010) https://assets.publishing.service.gov.uk/government/uploads/system/uploads/attachment_data/file/216476/dh_122031.pdf, accessed 9 September 2023

DHSC (Department of Health and Social Care), 'Care and Support Statutory Guidance' (2014) https://assets.publishing.service.gov.uk/government/uploads/system/uploads/attachment_data/file/506202/23902777_Care_Act_Book.pdf, accessed 22 September 2023

'Every Child Matters' (2003) https://assets.publishing.service.gov.uk/government/uploads/system/uploads/attachment_data/file/272064/5860.pdf, accessed 21 September 2023

GMC (General Medical Council), 'Confidentiality: Patients' Fitness to Drive and Reporting Concerns to the DVLA or DVA' (2017) https://www.gmc-uk.org/ethical-guidance/ethical-guidance-for-doctors/confidentiality---patients-fitness-to-drive-and-reporting-concerns-to-the-dvla-or-dva, accessed 9 September 2023

GMC (General Medical Council), 'Protecting Children and Young People: The Responsibilities of All Doctors' (2018) https://www.gmc-uk.org/-/media/documents/protecting-children-and-young-people---english-20200114_pdf-48978248.pdf, accessed 9 September 2023

GMC (General Medical Council), '0–18 Years: Guidance for All Doctors' (nd) https://www.gmc-uk.org/ethical-guidance/ethical-guidance-for-doctors/0-18-years/principles-of-confidentiality, accessed 23 September 2023

GMC (General Medical Council), 'Case Study: Should a Doctor Disclose Evidence of Abuse without the Patient's Consent?' (nd) https://www.gmc-uk.org/-/media/gmc-site/ethical-guidance/learning-materials/themes/new---should-a-doctor-disclose-evidence-of-abuse-without-the-patients-consent.pdf, accessed 22 September 2023

GMC (General Medical Council), 'Good Practice in Handling Patient Information' (nd) https://www.gmc-uk.org/-/media/documents/gmc-guidance-for-doctors---confidentiality-good-practice-in-handling-patient-information----70080105.pdf, accessed 23 September 2023

Higgins M, 'The Exam it is Impossible to Pass: How Disabled Parents Are at Risk of Having to Prove the Impossible in Care Proceedings' in B Clough and J Herring (eds), *Disability, Care and Family Law* (Taylor & Francis 2021)

HM Government 'Working Together to Safeguard Children' (2018) https://assets.publishing.service.gov.uk/media/669e7501ab418ab055592a7b/Working_together_to_safeguard_children_2023.pdf, accessed 21 September 2023

Ireland B, 'At a Glance: "Unsafe and Undignified" – the Nation's Hospitals' (2023) https://www.bma.org.uk/news-and-opinion/at-a-glance-unsafe-and-undignified-the-nation-s-hospitals, accessed 1 September 2023

National Data Guardian for Health and Social Care, 'The Eight Caldicott Principles' (2020) https://assets.publishing.service.gov.uk/government/uploads/system/uploads/attachment_data/file/942217/Eight_Caldicott_Principles_08.12.20.pdf, accessed 9 September 2023

NSPCC (National Society for the Prevention of Cruelty to Children), 'Safeguarding Children Who Come from Black, Asian and Minoritised Ethnic Communities' (2022) https://learning.nspcc.org.uk/safeguarding-child-protection/children-from-black-asian-minoritised-ethnic-communities, accessed 22 September 2023

Nuffield Foundation, 'Identifying and Understanding the Link between System Conditions and Welfare Inequalities in Children's Social Care Services' (2019) https://www.nuffieldfoundation.org/wp-content/uploads/2019/11/Final-Report-Identifying-and-understanding-the-link-between-system-conditions-and-welfare-inequalities-in-children%E2%80%99s-social-care-services-March-2020.pdf, accessed 22 September 2023

Office for Health Improvement and Disparities, 'Abortion Statistics for England and Wales: 2021' (2022) https://www.gov.uk/government/statistics/abortion-statistics-for-england-and-wales-2021, accessed 21 September 2023

Parekh-Hill NA and others, 'Please Write to Me, Not about Me: Best Practice in Written Communication with Young People' (2023) 108 Arch Dis Child e5

Parsons JA and Romanis EC, 'The Case for Telemedical Early Medical Abortion in England: Dispelling Adult Safeguarding Concerns' (2021) 30 Health Care Anal 73

Parsons JA and Romanis EC, *Early Medical Abortion, Equality of Access, and the Telemedical Imperative* (OUP 2021)

Redfern J and Sinclair B, 'Improving Health Care Encounters and Communication with Transgender Patients' (2014) 7 J Healthc Commun 25

Romanis EC and others, 'Safeguarding and Teleconsultation for Abortion' (2020) 398 Lancet 555

Safe Lives, 'Sharing Information and MARAC' (2019) https://safelives.org.uk/sites/default/files/resources/Sharing%20Information%20and%20Marac%20GDPR%20FAQs%20-%20England%20%26%20Wales%20version.pdf, accessed 22 September 2023

Sarfraz S and Wacogne I, 'Fifteen-Minute Consultation: How to Use an Interpreter in a Medical Consultation' (2019) 104 ADC Ed Prac 231

Scottish Government, 'Business and Regulatory Impact Assessment' (2021) https://www.gov.scot/binaries/content/documents/govscot/publications/impact-assessment/2021/12/abortion-scotland-amendment-regulations-2021-changes-information-abortions-provided-business-regulatory-impact-assessment/documents/abortion-scotland-amendment-regulations-2021-changes-information-abortions-provided-business-regulatory-impact-assessment/abortion-scotland-amendment-regulations-2021-changes-information-abortions-provided-business-regulatory-impact-assessment/govscot%3Adocument/abortion-scotland-amendment-regulations-2021-changes-information-abortions-provided-business-regulatory-impact-assessment.pdf, accessed 21 September 2023

Snelling P and Quick O, 'Confidentiality and Public Interest Disclosure: A Framework to Evaluate UK Healthcare Professional Regulatory Guidance' (2022) 22 Med Law Int 3

Social Care Institute for Excellence, 'Safeguarding Adults' (nd) https://www.scie.org.uk/safeguarding/adults/introduction/six-principles, accessed 22 September 2023

Stanton C, 'Patient Information: To Share or Not to Share?' (2018) 26 Med Law Rev 328

Véliz C, 'Not the Doctor's Business: Privacy, Personal Responsibility and Data Rights in Medical Settings' (2020) 34 Bioethics 712

PART III

Applied Health Law and Ethics

13

Assisted Reproduction

Rita D'Alton-Harrison, Philip Bremner, and Cynthia Mbugua

Infertility is defined as 'a disease of the male or female reproductive system defined by the failure to achieve a pregnancy after 12 months or more of regular unprotected sexual intercourse'.[1] Research has shown that there has been a significant reduction in sperm count in men in the Global North, leading to an increase in male infertility,[2] which is likely to be linked to environmental factors.[3] In contrast, research relating to female infertility has largely focused on fertility decline due to age,[4] socio-economic factors,[5] or medical conditions affecting ovulation.[6] Infertility is recognised as a disease or illness that can be treated,[7] and this medicalisation approach has led to the growth of assisted reproduction technologies (ART) and the availability of such treatments through the NHS. However, this chapter will illustrate that access to ART is not equitable. Discrimination can and does occur, based on ethnicity, sexual orientation, and age.

---

1 WHO (World Health Organization), 'Infertility' (2023) https://www.who.int/news-room/fact-sheets/detail/infertility, accessed 7 July 2023.

2 See Hagai Levine and others, 'Temporal Trends in Sperm Count: A Systematic Review and Meta-Regression Analysis' (2023) 23 Hum Reprod Update 646.

3 See Shanna Swan and Stacey Colino, *Count Down: How Our Modern World is Threatening Sperm Counts, Altering Male and Female Reproductive Development, and Imperilling the Future of the Human Race* (Scribner 2021).

4 Female fertility is thought to decline from the age of 35 onwards, although this decline has started to reverse slightly due to the availability of assisted reproduction technology and the ability for women to freeze their eggs.

5 See John Ermisch, 'The Recent Decline in Period Fertility in England and Wales: Differences Associated with Family Background and Intergenerational Educational Mobility' (2023) Popul Stud https://doi.org/10.1080/00324728.2023.2215224, accessed 10 July 2024.

6 A failure to ovulate may be caused by, for example, polycystic ovary syndrome or an overactive or underactive thyroid as well as endometriosis or treatment for cancer.

7 E.g., WHO (World Health Organization), Classification of Diseases ICD-11, code GA31.

The Law Commission defines ART as the placing of an embryo in a woman, or the placing of sperm and eggs in a woman, or the artificial insemination of a woman.[8] ART can involve medical procedures such as in vitro fertilisation (IVF), intrauterine insemination (IUI), intracytoplasmic sperm injection (ICSI), or the use of donor eggs and sperm ('gametes') to produce an embryo. All the procedures involve the collection of gametes and/or fertilisation outside of the body. For example, IVF is the process of fertilising eggs outside of the womb and implanting the resulting embryo into the womb. The first baby was born through IVF in 1978. IUI, however, involves collecting and placing sperm inside the womb. Finally, ICSI involves collecting and placing sperm at the cervix (neck of the womb). These procedures can be used in conjunction with surrogacy, the practice of a woman entering into an agreement with either a couple or single person ('the intended parents') to carry a child for them with a view that the intended parents will be regarded in law as the parents.

Viewing ART as a treatment for infertility alone fails to acknowledge its role in relation to facilitating same-sex parenting. Even the international definition of infertility,[9] fails to recognise that infertility may occur as a result of choosing a same-sex relationship and one questions therefore whether infertility is solely a medical issue. These advanced medical processes come at a cost and decisions have to be made about prioritising limited resources. Such decisions can arguably determine who should be regarded as a deserving patient when it relies on an ability to access free NHS treatment or to have the financial resources to pay privately. Whilst ART is available in England and Wales through the NHS, the decision of allocation is one made using assumptions about 'reproductive age'.[10] The final decisions about prioritising ART treatments in the NHS budget are made at a local level by Integrated Care Boards (ICBs). Availability, therefore, varies depending on geographical area, impacting communities in areas where there are more individuals from a particular ethnic grouping. The most recent available data shows that for NHS funding of IVF cycles in the UK the area with the most funded cycles was Scotland (62 per cent) followed by the north-east of England. The lowest was the east of England.[11] Assistance in reproducing a family is therefore not equitable.

---

8 Law Commission, 'Building Families through Surrogacy: A New Law Volume III: Draft Surrogacy Bill' (2023) Law Com No 262.

9 WHO (n1).

10 The access criteria for NHS-funded IVF are that the woman is under 40 and has not conceived after two years of regular unprotected sex. In such cases three rounds of IVF can be offered: NICE (National Institute of Health and Care Excellence), 'Fertility Problems: Assessment and Treatment (2013) https://www.nice.org.uk/guidance/cg156/chapter/Recommendations#access-criteria-for-ivf, accessed 31 July 2023, [1.11].

11 HFEA (Human Fertilisation and Embryology Authority), 'Fertility Treatment 2021: Preliminary Trends and Figures' (2023) https://www.hfea.gov.uk/about-us/publications/research-and-data/fertility-treatment-2021-preliminary-trends-and-figures/, accessed 27 June 2023.

Ethnicity

The number of individuals from Black and minority ethnic backgrounds in the UK using ART is not conclusive as data and research are complicated by clinics' failure to routinely collect and record this data. However, regulators such as the Human Fertilisation and Embryology Authority (HFEA) and the National Institute for Health and Care Excellence (NICE) as well as the NHS do have mandatory reporting. Mandatory collection and reporting are relatively new requirements and so it is difficult to get a clear picture of trends. The most recent HFEA report data shows that whilst Asian patients represented the largest proportion of users of IVF as compared to the general average, the lowest IVF birth rates were amongst Black patients.[12] Black patients often started IVF at a much later age than other ethnic groups. There were also higher rates of 'tubal infertility' (blockage in the fallopian tubes) reported amongst Black patients. When undergoing fertility treatment using double embryo transfers, Black patients experienced a higher-than-average incidence of multiple births. Sperm from dual heritage or Black donors was more likely to be imported, suggesting there were not enough donors from this ethnic group donating sperm in the UK.

We know from research that, in relation to pregnancy,[13] ethnic minority women often reported poor communication with midwives and health visitors during and post pregnancy due to lack of active listening by healthcare professionals, failure to understand cultural differences, stereotyping, and a lack of respect.[14] Yet the impact of access to ART, advice about ART, and choices of ART treatment are not fully accounted for when treating ethnic minority patients. In spite of the infertility data knowledge, the NICE guideline on the advice to be given about the likelihood of conception and the options fails to include any specific advice for clinics on care for ethnic minority patients.[15] ART carries the risk of multiple births. This risk can be increased based on ethnicity and, as such, some guidance about the risk of multiple births amongst Black patients would be particularly important given that this presents a risk to health during pregnancy.

Armstrong and Plowden conducted a literature review of studies of health disparities and ethnicity in fertility treatment in the US.[16] The differences they found were in terms of reduced access to ART due to the cost of such treatments and disparities in infertility diagnosis. Multiple US studies have linked

---

12 HFEA (Human Fertilisation and Embryology Authority), 'Ethnic Diversity in Fertility Treatment' (2018) https://www.hfea.gov.uk/about-us/publications/research-and-data/ethnic-diversity-in-fertility-treatment-2018/, accessed 31 July 2023.

13 NHS Race and Health Observatory, 'Ethnic Inequalities in Healthcare: A Rapid Evidence Review' (2022) https://www.nhsrho.org/wp-content/uploads/2023/05/RHO-Rapid-Review-Final-Report_.pdf, accessed 14 December 2023, 89.

14 See Chapter 15.

15 NICE (n10).

16 Alicia Armstrong and Torie Plowden, 'Ethnicity and Assisted Reproductive Technologies' (2012) 9 Clin Pract 651.

obesity with infertility, which may be linked to socio-economic factors as well as ethnicity.[17] Whilst studies showed poorer reproductive outcomes for African-American women as well as 'Hispanic' and 'Asian' women when compared to 'Caucasians', none had been able to identify a specific cause. Armstrong and Plowden recommend cultural competency training for all healthcare practitioners,[18] and that a system is put in place for identifying ethnicity when collecting health data as well as advocating for a more accurate system of reporting race and ethnicity in empirical research. Race reporting is often problematic. For example, studies often use 'Asian' to include Indian, Chinese, and Japanese people collectively, when in fact they have different health physiologies. Also, poorer reproductive outcomes might result from a lack of medical knowledge about particular conditions and physiologies. Data shows that Black women have risk factors in terms of achieving a live birth, higher rates of 'tubal factor infertility', and lower implantation rates, whilst Caucasian women's infertility tends, to be caused by endometriosis or infertility due to the fertility health of their male partner.

The NHS '2021/22 Priorities and Operational Planning Guidance' states that in setting operational planning targets health inequalities must be considered, including analysis of waiting times by ethnicity and deprivation.[19] The guidance notes that COVID-19 revealed a link between ethnicity and deprivation, leading to poor health outcomes.[20] Similar planning guidance is needed for fertility clinics and these should be set by HFEA and specifically consider whether when planning fertility decisions, analysis has taken into account ethnicity in order to ensure more positive outcomes for patients. Mandatory record-keeping on ethnicity should also form a part of this planning.

Cases such as *Leeds Teaching Hospital NHS Trust v A* remind us that poor record-keeping by clinics can lead to negative outcomes that impact family formation.[21] In this case, poor record-keeping by a fertility clinic led to issues with the conception and subsequent care of the resulting children. The clinic treated two couples, Mr and Mrs A and Mr and Mrs B. Both couples attended the clinic on the same day and underwent the same ART procedures. Mrs A became pregnant with twins following a successful implantation of the embryo. Mrs B, however, did not become pregnant. It was not until the twins were born that it became clear there had been an error with the collection and transfer of the sperm used to fertilise the eggs. Mr and Mrs A were both Caucasian. Mr and Mrs B were both Black. Mr B's sperm had been used to fertilise Mrs A's eggs

17 Ibid 656.

18 Ibid 653.

19 NHS England, '2021/22 Priorities and Operational Planning Guidance' https://www.england.nhs.uk/wp-content/uploads/2021/03/B0468-nhs-operational-planning-and-contracting-guidance.pdf, accessed 14 December 2023, 8.

20 Ibid 15.

21 [2003] 1 FLR 412.

before embryo transfer took place. This presented a problem with legal parentage as Mr A had only consented to his sperm being used in the treatment. Whilst Mr B had a genetic connection to the child, he had also not consented to being treated with Mrs A, therefore, the necessary fatherhood conditions under the Human Fertilisation and Embryology Act 1990 (the 1990 Act) did not apply.[22] As a result of this case the HFEA imposed conditions on the clinic to improve record-keeping.

Another decision-making area that risks discriminating practices is the approach taken to determine who should access free NHS fertility treatment. There is no consensus about how best to conduct economic evaluations of health interventions relating to infertility. NICE uses a health economics approach to decide on how many IVF cycles the NHS should fund. The quality-adjusted life year (QALY) is a measure of the burden of disease/illness on the quantity and quality of life of patients. QALY is used by NICE to decide how many NHS IVF cycles should be funded. The problem is that the QALY measurement is very subjective and could lead to unintentional discrimination. Fiebert and Brandeau argue that QALY evaluations are often inconsistent when considering current and future childbearing years and infertility and this risks a biased approach to the interventions that are funded.[23] Luyten and others argue that QALYs require comparators and choosing the wrong comparator or less relevant comparators affects the final decision about which medical interventions would be most effective.[24] This is of particular concern given what is known about the differences in reproductive health based on ethnicity. NICE does not publish the specific details of their QALY evaluations for infertility and this lack of transparency further hampers operational planning around ethnicity outcomes.

The practice of surrogacy (often linked with ART) also presents oppositional discourse based on potential exploitation due to the race and class of surrogate mothers, particularly where intended parents enter into agreements with surrogates in the Global South, such as in Africa.

Scholars have argued that such a practice involves an imbalance of power between the dominant group (being Caucasian) and the dominated group (coming from a poor and marginalised group).[25] This has led to Global

22 Human Fertilisation and Embryology Act 1990, s 27. This case pre-dated the Human Fertilisation and Embryology Act 2008.

23 Jeremy Fiebert and Margaret Brandeau, 'Evaluating Cost Effectiveness of Interventions that Affect Fertility and Childbearing: How Health Effects are Measured Matters' (2015) Med Decis Making 818.

24 Jeroen Luyten and others, 'Economic Evaluation of Medically Assisted Reproduction: An Educational Overview of Methods and Applications for Healthcare Professionals' (2022) 85 Best Pract Res Clin Obstet Gynaecol 217, 219.

25 E.g., Laura Harrison, *Brown Bodies, White Babies: The Politics of Cross Racial Surrogacy* (NYU Press 2016); Heather Dillaway, 'Mothers for Others: A Race, Class and Gender Analysis of Surrogacy' (2008) 34 Int J Sociol Fam 301; Andrea Dworkin, *Right Wing Women: The Politics of Domesticated Females* (The Women's Press, 1983), 147.

South jurisdictions such as India, Thailand, and Cambodia curtailing the practice of surrogacy in their regions. However, surrogacy also receives broad support for its ability to economically empower women from marginalised groups. Pande argues that Indian women who took part in a large-scale surrogacy programme in India were capable of making decisions that affected their health and pregnancy,[26] and had 'agency'[27] rather than experiencing victimhood. In addition, surrogacy that uses gamete donation is another way to ensure that couples from dual heritage backgrounds can create children close to their combined ethnicity. Thus, surrogacy can empower family formation based on ethnicity; however, long waiting lists for surrogates and donors and the removal of anonymity for donors in the UK can temper some of this empowerment.[28]

Sexual orientation

In addition to treating medical infertility, ART and surrogacy are important ways of forming families for same-sex parents. Two particular issues arise here, namely access to treatment and recognition as legal parents. The Human Fertilisation and Embryology 2008 (the 2008 Act) made significant reforms in both of these areas compared to its predecessor, the 1990 Act.

Under the 1990 Act, fertility clinics were required to consider the child's need for a father before providing ART treatment.[29] Therefore, single women and female same-sex couples had difficulty accessing ART treatment. This requirement was removed by the 2008 Act and replaced with the requirement to consider the child's need for 'supportive parenting'.[30] Nevertheless, NHS-funded fertility clinics may still require female couples to undergo between 3 and 12 rounds of privately funded IVF treatment before being eligible for free NHS treatment.[31] This contrasts with different-sex couples who are required to try to conceive naturally for two to three years before treatment. Following a judicial review of such a policy applied in a particular fertility clinic,[32] the government

26 Amrita Pande, 'Commercial Surrogacy in India: Manufacturing a Perfect Mother-Worker' (2010) 35 Signs 989.

27 Defined as the power and resources that would help a person fulfil their potential.

28 See Human Fertilisation and Embryology Act (Disclosure of Donor Information) Regulations 2004.

29 HFEA Act 1990 s 13 (5) (as originally enacted).

30 Ibid as amended by HFEA Act 2008, s 14 (2) (b).

31 British Pregnancy Advisory Service, 'Government Pledges to End IVF Policies which Discriminate against Same-Sex Female Couples' (2022) https://bpas-campaigns.org/news/government-pledges-to-end-ivf-policies-which-discriminate-against-same-sex-female-couples/, accessed 28 August 2023.

32 See Baroness Barker's reference to this in Gametes and Embryos Storage Limit Debate. HL Deb 9 November 2021, vol 815, cols 1588–90.

have committed to removing the requirement for female couples to self-fund initial IVF treatment.[33]

In addition to facilitating access to treatment for female couples, the 2008 Act also brought about important changes to legal parenthood following ART that had a particular impact in relation to same-sex couples. Under the 1990 Act it was only possible to recognise a father as the second legal parent. A key policy underpinning the reforms of the 2008 Act was to recognise women-led parenting achieved through ART (see Box 13.1).

Box 13.1: Key legislation: Parenthood in the Human Fertilisation and Embryology Act 2008, Part Two

- The person who gives birth to a child (birth parent) is automatically a legal parent of the child (s 33) and may be the only legal parent.
- The identification of a second legal parent depends on whether or not they are the birth parent's spouse/civil partner.
- The birth parent's spouse/civil partner is presumed to have consented to the ART treatment and is recognised as a legal parent unless they demonstrate that they did not consent to the treatment (ss 35 and 42). These provisions apply regardless of whether or not treatment occurs in a licensed fertility clinic.
- If the birth parent is not married or in a civil partnership and the treatment takes place in a licensed fertility clinic, a second legal parent may be recognised if they meet the agreed fatherhood conditions (s 37) or the agreed female parenthood conditions (s 44). These conditions depend on the ongoing consent of both the birth parent and the second parent.

Historically, recognition of parent–child relationships has been problematic in England and Wales (and internationally)[34] in relation to non-traditional, and in particular same-sex, families. Social attitudes towards same-sex relationships have changed considerably in the period between the enactment of the Civil Partnership Act 2004[35] and the recognition of same-sex marriage in England and Wales and Scotland. Alongside the increasing recognition of same-sex unions

33 See DHSC (Department for Health and Social Care), 'Women's Health Strategy for England' (Cmd 736, 2022), [71].

34 See Katharina Boele-Woelki and Angelika Fuchs (eds), *Legal Recognition of Same-Sex Relationships in Europe: National, Cross-Border and European Perspectives* (Intersentia 2012).

35 See the discussion of the parliamentary debates that led to the passage of the Civil Partnership Act in Carl Stychin, 'Not (Quite) A Horse And Carriage' (2006) 14 Fem Leg Stud 79, 80–1. For England and Wales: Marriage (Same-Sex Couples) Act 2013. For Scotland: Marriage and Civil Partnership (Scotland) Act 2014.

between adults in the UK and other countries around the world, same-sex parenting is becoming more visible and increasingly recognised.[36] Gradually, legislators and courts in various countries are making progress towards facilitating the creation of same-sex families and recognising the parent–child relationships in these families.[37] Despite this progress, there are arguably still gaps between the needs of same-sex families and the rights and responsibilities that UK legislation is willing to confer on them, which still bears the hallmarks of heteronormative assumptions about parenting.[38]

There is a distinction to be drawn between single women and female couples, on the one hand, and single men and male couples, on the other. In some circumstances, it is possible for a single woman or a female couple to be a child's sole legal parent(s) from birth. Although it may be possible for a single man to be one of the child's legal parents at birth, it is never the case that both partners in a male couple will be considered to be the child's legal parents from birth.[39] This distinction in terms of legal parenthood for men and women derives from the common law principle that parturition identifies a child's mother,[40] and it is enshrined in the 2008 Act.[41] Therefore, upon birth, one of the child's, and perhaps his or her only, legal parent(s) will be his or her birth mother.[42] However, section 54 of the 2008 Act allows a male couple (or other intended parents), who are either civil partners or living in an 'enduring family relationship' and one of whom is the child's biological father, to apply for a parental order, between six weeks and six months after birth, making them and not the birth parent (with their consent) the legal parents. This option is now also available to single applicants.[43]

---

36 See e.g., David Hill, 'The Recognition of Homosexual Parents in the United Kingdom', in Katharina Boele-Woelki and Tone Sverdrup (eds), *European Challenges in Contemporary Family Law* (Intersentia 2008).

37 See e.g. Machteld Vonk, *Children and their Parents* (Intersentia 2007); C Grossman and M Herrera, 'Family, Pluralism and Equality: Marriage and Sexual Orientation in Argentine Law' in B Atkin (ed), *International Survey of Family Law* (Jordan Publishing 2011); M Chavez, 'Homoaffective Parentage in Relation to Medically Assisted Reproduction: a Parallel between Brazil and Portugal' in B Atkins (ed), *International Survey of Family Law* (Jordan Publishing 2011).

38 Defined as a world view that promotes heterosexuality rather than other types of unions. See also Julie Wallbank, 'Channeling the Messiness of Diverse Family Lives: Resisting the Calls to Order and De-Centring the Hetero-Normative Family' (2010) 32 J Soc Welf Fam Law 353.

39 See the Law Commission's recommendations for an alternative path to parenthood in surrogacy: 'Building Families through Surrogacy: A New Law (2023) Law Com No 411.

40 *Ampthill Peerage Case* [1977] AC 547, 577.

41 HFEA 2008, s 33(1).

42 Compare the position in France where there is the possibility of having motherless children because women have the right to birth anonymously: Nadine Lefaucheur, 'French Tradition of Anonymous Birth: The Lines of Argument' (2004) 18 Int J Law Policy Fam 319.

43 HEFA 2008, which was enacted following cases such as *B v C (Surrogacy: Adoption)* [2015] EWFC 17.

The 2008 Act makes it clear that a child can only have one other legal parent in addition to the birth mother.[44] However, who this second parent will be depends on the circumstances of conception. If the child is conceived through sexual intercourse, then the common-law presumption of *pater est quem nuptiae demonstrant* will operate, which is rebuttable by DNA evidence.[45] The effect of this is that, at birth, the legal father of a child born through sexual intercourse will be the birth parent's husband, unless the birth parent is unmarried or it has been established that the husband is not the genetic father, in which case it will be the genetic father who is the second legal parent. Even if conception occurs through assisted reproduction the law distinguishes between situations where single women and female couples who are not in a civil partnership/marriage conceive at home. In this situation, the common-law rules apply, whereas female civil partners/married couples are both treated as the child's parents from birth, regardless of whether assisted conception occurs at a clinic or elsewhere, provided no absence of consent can be shown.[46] In addition, where the appropriate consent forms have been signed,[47] female couples who are not in a civil partnership/marriage can be the legal parents on birth provided they are treated at a licensed fertility clinic.[48] In each of these cases, the biological father would not be considered one of the child's legal parents.[49]

By removing the requirement to consider the need for a father, allowing the recognition of a second female parent, and providing a mechanism for male couples to become legal parents following surrogacy, the 2008 Act eliminated key elements of the 1990 Act that discriminated against same-sex parents. Nevertheless, the continuing restriction to two legal parents limits the possibilities for the recognition of collaborative co-parenting arrangements involving more than two parents.[50] If the birth parent is unmarried and no one meets the agreed parenthood conditions then the birth parent will be the sole legal parent. In any event, only one other legal parent may be recognised in addition to the birth parent. In the context of gamete donation, this is achieved by ensuring that gamete donors sign the relevant consent forms so that they are not treated as legal

---

44 HFEA Act 2008, ss 36 and 42.

45 Family Law Reform Act 1969, s 26.

46 HFEA Act 2008, s 42. This distinction has socio-economic implications because individuals with less disposable income to spend on clinical treatment are not being afforded the same legal protection.

47 For an example of where the appropriate consent forms had not been signed see *AB v CD* [2013] EWHC 1418 (Fam).

48 HFEA Act 2008 ss 43 and 44.

49 Ibid s 45(1).

50 See Philip Bremner, 'Collaborative Co-Parenting and Heteronormativity: Recognising the Interests of Gay Fathers' (2017) 29 Child Fam Law Q 293; Nicola Surtees and Philip Bremner, 'Gay and Lesbian Collaborative Co-Parenting in New Zealand and the United Kingdom: "The Law Doesn't Protect the Third Parent"' (2020) 29 Soc Leg Stud 507.

parents. What is more, the various mechanisms in the 2008 Act for recognising a second legal parent are mutually exclusive alternatives.

For the majority of families making use of ART treatment, the recognition of one or two legal parents will accurately reflect their families. However, a variety of parenting arrangements exist, particularly among gay and lesbian families, which challenge the need to limit the number of legal parents to two adults. Gay and lesbian collaborative co-parenting arrangements, for example, might involve a single individual and a same-sex couple or two same-sex couples who seek ART treatment to conceive a child whom they will raise together. Neither these parenting arrangements nor the possibility of adults in a polyamorous relationship conceiving a child through ART are envisaged by the 2008 Act.

Although the parenthood provisions of the 2008 Act recognise a broader range of relationships than the 1990 Act, the existence of a formalised union (i.e., marriage or civil partnership) retains a privileged position. If the birth parent has a husband or civil partner, that person is presumed to be the second legal parent to the exclusion of all others regardless of where conception occurred, provided that some form of ART took place. Any other individual who seeks to be recognised as a second legal parent would need to meet the agreed fatherhood/female parenthood conditions and treatment must take place in a licenced fertility clinic. It is an open question whether this privileging of the existence of a marital relationship is justified in the context of parenthood following ART.

Another example of individuals overlooked in this legislation are trans parents. In the case of *McConnell*,[51] the Court of Appeal held that section 12 of the Gender Recognition Act 2004, which states that '[t]he fact that a person's gender has become the acquired gender under this Act does not affect the status of the person as the father or mother of a child', has both retrospective and prospective effect. In *McConnell* this resulted in the requirement that a trans man who had given birth was registered as the mother (rather than father or parent) of his child. In the context of the 2008 Act, the likely implication is that a trans man would be unable to become a father through the agreed fatherhood conditions and a trans woman would be unable to be recognised under the agreed female parenthood conditions.[52]

It is also worth considering the ways in which the interests of different individuals are given voice in the context of surrogacy. The current position is

---

51 *R (McConnell and YY) v Registrar General and Secretary of State for Health and Social Care and Others* [2020] EWCA Civ 559. See Philip Bremner, 'Birth Registration: "Coherent and Certain" or "an Occasion for Exquisite Embarrassment and Confusion?"' (2020) 42 J Soc Welf Fam Law 524; Alan Brown, 'Trans Parenthood and the Meaning of "Mother", "Father" and "Parent": R (McConnell and YY) v Registrar General for England and Wales [2020] EWCA Civ 559' (2021) 29 Med Law Rev 157.

52 This reinforces the idea that the law seems unable to contemplate two fathers (or two mothers). See Alison Diduck, 'If Only We Can Find the Appropriate Terms to Use the Issue Will Be Solved: Law, Identity and Parenthood' (2007) 19 Child Fam Law Q 458.

that the birth parent and, if married or in a civil partnership, her spouse or civil partner would be the legal parents. The intended parents would then need to apply for a parental order under section 54 of the 2008 Act to become the legal parents. This requires the intended parents to be in an enduring relationship (if they are applying jointly), for one of them to be genetically related to the child, and for the birth parent (and her spouse or civil partner) to consent to the transfer of parenthood. The Law Commission of England and Wales and the Scottish Law Commission have proposed a more streamlined route to legal parenthood (which would apply in situations where certain safeguards had been complied with) where the intended parents can be recognised as legal parents from birth unless the birth parent objects.[53] While this streamlined process would be a welcome development (where it applies), it would not necessarily resolve all the issues that arise. In the case of a dispute, for example, where the birth parent and intended parents each seek recognition as the child's legal parents, it should be possible to recognise multiple legal parents, even though concrete issues relating the exercise of parental responsibility would still remain. To achieve this, the limit of two legal parents would need to be removed. This would facilitate the possibility of recognising multiple parents in different contexts.

Age

The debate regarding age restrictions in ART primarily focuses on women, young people, and people of advanced ages. Different regulations portray the ideal family as one where the parent(s) are healthy, within their reproductive age, mature, financially stable, and can raise the child until they can fend for themselves. Majumdar draws attention to the impact of media in this debate by indicating that the media has portrayed older mothers in a negative light,[54] labelling them as 'desperate' and the doctors who assisted as 'rogue'. These media narratives have also contributed to the numerous ageist assumptions, especially with regard to older parents.

Consequently, cultural shame in relation to infertility can often intensify existing ethnic disparities in seeking help, especially among elderly populations. In some cultures, the ability to conceive and bear children is deeply ingrained in societal norms and expectations. As a result, when someone is involuntarily childless, they may experience a profound sense of shame and inadequacy. This cultural stigma can be particularly pronounced among older generations, who often uphold traditional values and are less inclined to openly discuss sensitive topics like infertility. Accordingly, the intersection of culture and age creates a complex dynamic that hinders individuals from seeking the necessary medical

53 Law Commission of England and Wales and Scottish Law Commission (n8).

54 Anindita Majumdar, 'Outliers and Rogue Doctors: Manufacturing "Anxiety" around Older Mothers in India' (2022) 41 Med Anthropol 616.

or emotional support, perpetuating disparities in access to care and information within these communities and age groups.

In the UK, there are currently no laws that prescribe the maximum or minimum age limit to be a parent other than the requirement that the applicants of a parental order, whose purpose is to transfer legal parentage to the intended parents, must be at least 18 years old.[55] The 2008 Act, therefore, envisages a family where the parent(s) have attained the age of majority. While NICE has made recommendations on the age cut-offs for fertility treatment, the decision largely remains with the NHS local ICBs when the procedure is on the NHS, and with the private fertility clinics in the case of private funding.[56]

The European Convention on Human Rights (ECHR) and the Universal Declaration of Human Rights (UDHR) both recognise the right to found a family.[57] The court in *Briody v St Helens and Knowsley Area Health Authority* contextualised the right to found a family in ART by stating that 'everyone has the right to try to have their own children by natural means, no-one has the right to be provided with a child'.[58] The court in *Evans v Amicus Healthcare Ltd; Hadley v Midland Fertility Services Ltd* further notes that the right to found a family does not extend to IVF,[59] and that the right to IVF is only 'qualified by availability, suitability for treatment and cost'.[60] As a result, regulatory bodies as well as clinics are justified in imposing an age limit, especially in the case of advanced maternal age, which is primarily attributed to diminished ovarian reserve.

While there is no legal age cut-off when accessing ART, there is increased awareness of the impact of age in assessing whether a person is eligible for ART/surrogacy. Countries such as Denmark (46 years old), Belgium (request to be made before the woman is 45 and treatment to be undertaken before she is 48),[61] Netherlands (42 years), and Spain (40 years) have cited age as an element of legal exclusion when accessing state-funded ART. However, as Cavaliere and Fletcher mention, age is only a partial predictor of fertility rates as well as the success rates of ART.[62]

The Welsh Health Specialised Services Committee, which plans and monitors the provision of specialised services in Wales, outlines the criteria for treatment

55 HFEA 2008, s 54(5).

56 NICE is the body that develops recommendations and guides health and care practitioners in England and Wales.

57 ECHR (European Convention on Human Rights), Art 12. UDHR (Universal Declaration of Human Rights) (adopted 10 December 1948) UNGA Res 217 A(III), Art 8.

58 [2001] EWCA Civ 1010 [26].

59 [2003] EWHC 2161.

60 Ibid [264].

61 Guido Pennings, 'Belgian Law on Medically Assisted Reproduction and the Disposition of Supernumerary Embryos and Gametes' (2007) 14 Eur J Health Law 251.

62 Giulia Cavaliere and James Fletcher, 'Age-Discriminated IVF Access and Evidence-Based Ageism: Is There a Better Way?' (2022) 47 Sci Technol Hum Values 986.

and lists age among the factors to be considered. The criteria introduces limitations surrounding age: in people of advanced maternal (40 years or younger) and paternal ages (55 years or younger), as well as imposing a minimum age limit (should be at least 20 years).[63] Since the policy's review date is in 2023, there are proposed plans to reduce the IVF cycles for which women under 40 and between 40 and 42 are eligible, as well as the minimum age being revised to 18.[64] Rationing and the limited access to ART for individuals based on age indicate ways in which the law, hospitals, and different health boards are still adamant about diversifying the family unit.

Per the 2021 Census, an analysis of age-specific fertility rates shows an increase in the fertility rates among older age groups,[65] and this could be primarily attributed to the improved access to different fertility treatments, especially ART. Additionally, in the HFEA's recent statistical release on fertility treatments, the success rates for IVF treatment were lower for women in older age groups, especially when the patient used their own eggs. The proportion of IVF cycles undertaken by women aged 40 and over has also increased. The data also confirms that women above 35 face lower birth rates than younger age groups. The drop in birth rates becomes more pronounced beyond the age of 40, with a significant decrease in success rates for women aged 43–44 and 45–50.[66] The statistics underscore the challenges associated with achieving pregnancy through IVF as women approach and pass their reproductive age.

Much of this analysis reaches for evidence to support the view that our reproductive capabilities are affected by age. However, the Law Commission Surrogacy Report,[67] which reports extensive correspondence from various consultees covering reforms in the law of surrogacy, indicated varied opinions relating to not only the introduction of maximum age restrictions but also the implementation of minimum age limits for both intended parents and surrogates. The debates around initiating a maximum age limit in surrogacy pivoted around several concerns, such as the fertility decline that comes with age, the health of the woman (where the surrogate is past her reproductive age), and the need to have youthful and vibrant parents who could take care of the child until their adulthood. The same reasons have also been cited to justify why

63 Welsh Health Specialised Services Committee, 'Specialist Fertility Services' (2017) https://whssc.nhs.wales/commissioning/whssc-policies/fertility/, accessed 14 November 2023.

64 Fertility Network, 'Fertility Network UK Warns on Proposed Welsh Fertility Policy Changes' (2023) https://fertilitynetworkuk.org/fertility-network-uk-warns-on-proposed-welsh-fertility-policy-changes/, accessed 27 July 2023.

65 ONS (Office for National Statistics), 'Births in England and Wales 2022' (2023) https://www.ons.gov.uk/peoplepopulationandcommunity/birthsdeathsandmarriages/livebirths/bulletins/birthsummarytablesenglandandwales/2022#:~:text=Main%20points,(COVID%2D19)%20pandemic, accessed 27 June 2023.

66 HFEA (n11).

67 Law Commission of England and Wales and Scottish Law Commission (n38).

individuals outside their reproductive age should not be eligible for state-funded assisted conception.

By contrast, other consultees were against introducing a maximum age limit due to the potential for age discrimination, which violates the principles enshrined in the Equality Act 2010. The consultees also argued that age is not an indicator of effective/ineffective parenting. Further, fertility treatment can now take place with donated gametes, averting the risk of age-related anomalies due to using their own gametes during pregnancy. The Law Commission's recommendation concerning the setting of a maximum age was that age is an important factor to be considered, but no limitations should be placed. Age should be considered only when carrying out the welfare assessment of the child in individual cases rather than limiting everyone.

Following the debates portrayed by the Law Commission, some of the voices that have been noticeably marginalised are those of people with advanced maternal/paternal age. Since the law does not expressly provide for an upper age limit concerning surrogacy and assisted conception, clinics can self-regulate and use age as a barrier. As mentioned, the reason behind this is the increased health risks and the ability to care for the child until they transition to adulthood. The World Health Organization (WHO) breaks down the concept of ageing and health, and one of the facts it includes is that age is not an indicator of someone's abilities, as there are older people with the physical/mental capability of a much younger person. Martani and others agree with WHO's analysis of using chronological, biological, and social age as a legal criterion when accessing ART.[68] They argue in favour of a renegotiable and more individualised approach where an individual undertakes a medical examination before utilising assisted conception. This approach would, in turn, promote reproductive autonomy as it allows everyone equal access to fertility treatments when planning to start a family. As acknowledged by Friese and Becker,[69] the constant and consistent use of ART will regularise the idea of parenting at an advanced age.

The law provides that for a parental order to be issued, the intended parents must have attained the age of majority. Regarding a minimum age, the Law Commission noted that retaining the minimum age for a parental order to be granted at 18 is not problematic. However, one of the objections was appertaining to the minimum age limit in adoption cases, which the law sets at 21 for the adoptive parents. However, the view on shifting the minimum age did not spark considerable debate as most people agreed about the minimum age being capped at 18. Additionally, the WHO continues to uphold heteronormativity in creating families by limiting the standard of gauging infertility to one year of unprotected

68 Andrea Martani and others, 'Deconstructing Age(s): An Analysis of the Different Conceptions of Age as a Legal Criterion for Access to Assisted Reproductive Technologies' (2022) 9 J Law Biosci https://doi.org/10.1093/jlb/lsac036, accessed 11 July 2024.

69 Carrie Friese, Gay Becker, and Robert Nachtigall, 'Older Motherhood and the Changing Life Course in the Era of Assisted Reproductive Technologies' (2008) 22 J Aging Stud 65.

sex.[70] This perspective, therefore, makes it difficult for an 18-year-old who identifies as a member of the LGBTQI+ community with the desire to start a family to have access to ART, especially when it is state-funded.

In countries where child marriage is legal, the medical practitioner faces the challenge of providing the required treatment or denying them the opportunity, primarily due to the patient's maturity. Correspondingly, an example of where doctors deliberated on the question of adolescent infertility was raised by Kochman.[71] They were faced with the decision of whether to administer IVF to a married 16-year-old in Israel. Some of the concerns they had were the child's right to education as well as their maturity. They eventually proceeded with the procedure, believing that the patient's right to fertility treatment and the cultural importance of marriage and childbearing must be considered and upheld.[72] He also argues that despite the medical practitioner's conscientious objection to treatment, the decision not to provide fertility treatment would contravene the fundamental right to procreate.[73] Therefore, if the restriction to provide fertility treatment has not been codified, then it would be difficult for a doctor to deny the patient access to fertility treatment, other than in surrogacy cases.

In the African setting, where social security is not well established, children are ordinarily perceived as an investment for the parents.[74] This belief has primarily contributed to the concept of the '*Black Tax*'[75] where once a child can support themselves financially, they are expected to provide and take care of their parents until their demise as payback for parenting. Ordinarily, a child is expected to be financially independent immediately after university, which is typically in the early 20s. Here, we can see how cultural norms encourage prospective parent(s) to have children during their reproductive years in order that the children be financially capable of taking care of the parents in their old age. In this regard, ART and surrogacy can be seen to challenge these cultural values by, firstly, allowing potential parents to circumnavigate the reproductive age hurdle when attempting to start a family. Secondly, as age is not a significant factor to consider when planning for a family, prospective parents will now create a family with the intention of being responsible for them, instead of children being seen as investment vehicles.

Higgs and Gilleard argue that the traditional view of old age is changing and that we need to reconsider the idea that those of advanced ages are dependent.[76]

---

70 WHO (n1).

71 Ronit Haimov-Kochman and others, 'Adolescent Infertility: To Treat or Not to Treat' (2008) 90 Fertil and Steril 2009.

72 Ibid.

73 Ibid.

74 Ruth Evans, 'Children's Caring Roles and Responsibilities within the Family in Africa' (2010) 4 Geog Compass 1477, 1478.

75 Niq Mhlongo (ed), *Black Tax: Burden or Ubuntu?* (Jonathan Ball Publishers 2019).

76 Paul Higgs and Chris Gilleard, 'The Ideology of Ageism versus the Social Imaginary of the Fourth Age: Two Differing Approaches to the Negative Contexts of Old Age' (2020) 40 Ageing Soc 1617.

Different scholars have provided myriad solutions to the legal restrictions based on age. Goold mentions that one of the objections that have been made is that scarce resources should not be available to address this kind of infertility.[77] However, while concerns regarding the health of the mother and the child are valid, restricting people from accessing ART exposes them to further discrimination and imposes limitations on their reproductive rights. Tremellen and others argue in favour of a case-by-case basis since the decision to have a child is an individual choice and no one should be denied this opportunity.[78] Martani and others supported this position by suggesting that an individualised approach is essential as it ensures that access to ART is limited to those who need it and are likely to benefit from it.[79] Using age as a determinant for accessing ART is definitely an issue that lends itself to scrutiny, given the potential of discrimination and the limitation in exercising an individual's reproductive rights. This, in turn, acts as a barrier to family formation.

Summary

- Whilst there has been legislative progress in the UK in terms of age and race equality and the rights of same-sex couples, there are still structural inequalities embedded within the provision of ART and access to treatments, as outlined in this chapter.
- Age and sexual orientation can act as barriers to family formation whereas ethnicity (including class) can affect the type, amount, and quality of fertility treatment that a patient receives.
- Access to ART has improved over the years but these services need to be properly funded to eliminate potential disparities in access to treatment between different groups of service users.
- Despite a number of reforms to legal parenthood following ART treatment, a more thoroughgoing consideration of legal parenthood is required to ensure that diversity in family formation is appropriately recognised.

Questions for reflection

1. What positive steps might the regulator (the HFEA) need to take to ensure that differentials in ethnicity and health are factored into decisions regarding the provision of ART treatment?

---

77 Imogen Goold, 'Should Older and Postmenopausal Women Have Access to Assisted Reproductive Technology?' (2005) 24 Monash Bioeth Rev 27; Imogen Goold, 'Trust Women to Choose: A Response to John A. Robertson's "Egg Freezing and Egg Banking: Empowerment and Alienation in Assisted Reproduction"' (2017) 4 J Law Biosci 507.

78 Kelton Tremellen, Dominic Wilkinson, and Julian Savulescu, 'Should Obese Women's Access to Assisted Fertility Treatment Be Limited? A Scientific and Ethical Analysis' (2017) 57 Aust N Z J Obstet Gynaecol 569.

79 Martani and others (n68).

2. Are there ways to balance societal interests vis-à-vis individual rights when it comes to the consideration of age when accessing ART?
3. To what extent are the most appropriate individuals recognised as the legal parents of a child following ART in a range of contexts?
4. To what extent is it appropriate to consider marriage and civil partnership as pivotal factors in determining parenthood within the context of ART?

Recommended resources

- Thomas Baldwin, 'Reproduction without Sex: Social and Ethical Implications' (2012) 13 EMBO Rep 1049.
- Pedro Brandão, 'European Policies on Same-Sex Relationships, Adoption and Assisted Reproduction' (2022) 11 Int J Reprod Contracept Obstet Gynecol 2306.
- Giulia Cavaliere and James Fletcher, 'Age-Discriminated IVF Access and Evidence-Based Ageism: Is There a Better Way?' (2022) 47 Sci Technol Hum Values 986.
- Rita D'Alton-Harrison, 'Regulating International Surrogacy, "the Elephant in the Room": Some Reflections on Reform from a UK Study' (2019) 31 Child Fam Law Q 47.
- Kirsty Horsey and Emily Jackson, 'The Human Fertilisation and Embryology Act 1990 and Non-Traditional Families' (2023) 86 Med Law Rev 1472.
- Julie McCandless and Sally Sheldon, 'The Human Fertilisation and Embryology Act (2008) and the Tenacity of the Sexual Family' (2010) 73 Med Law Rev 175.
- Anindita Mujamdar, 'Assisted Reproductive Technologies and the Conceptualization of Ageing in India' (2021) 42 Anthropol Ageing 49.
- John Robertson, 'Gay and Lesbian Access to Reproductive Technology' (2004) 44 Case West Reserve Law Rev 323.
- Elizabeth Chloe Romanis, 'Equality-Enhancing Potential of Novel Forms of Assisted Gestation: Perspectives of Reproductive Rights Advocates' (2023) 37 Bioeth 637.

Bibliography

Armstrong A and Plowden T, 'Ethnicity and Assisted Reproductive Technologies' (2012) 9 Clin Pract 651

Atkin B and Banda F, 'Family, Pluralism and Equality: Marriage and Sexual Orientation in Argentine Law' in B Atkin (ed), *International Survey of Family Law* (Jordan Publishing 2011)

Atkin B and Banda F, 'Homoaffective Parentage in Relation to Medically Assisted Reproduction: A Parallel between Brazil and Portugal' in B Atkin (ed), *International Survey of Family Law* (Jordan Publishing 2011)

Boele K-W and Fuchs A (eds), *Legal Recognition of Same-Sex Relationships in Europe: National, Cross-Border and European Perspectives* (Intersentia 2012)

Bremner P, 'Collaborative Co-Parenting and Heteronormativity: Recognising the Interests of Gay Fathers' (2017) 29 Child Fam Law Q 293

Bremner P, 'Birth Registration: "Coherent and Certain" or "an Occasion for Exquisite Embarrassment and Confusion?"' (2020) 42 J Soc Welf Fam Law 524

British Pregnancy Advisory Service, 'Government Pledges to End IVF Policies which Discriminate against Same-Sex Female Couples' (2022) https://bpas-campaigns.org/news/government-pledges-to-end-ivf-policies-which-discriminate-against-same-sex-female-couples/, accessed 28 August 2023

Brown A, 'Trans Parenthood and the Meaning of "Mother", "Father" and "Parent": R (McConnell and YY) v Registrar General for England and Wales [2020] EWCA Civ 559' (2021) 29 Med Law Rev 157

Cavaliere G and Fletcher J, 'Age-Discriminated IVF Access and Evidence-Based Ageism: Is There a Better Way?' (2022) 47 Sci Technol Hum Values 986

DHSC (Department for Health and Social Care), 'Women's Health Strategy for England' (Cmd 736, 2022)

Diduck A, 'If Only We Can Find the Appropriate Terms to Use the Issue Will Be Solved: Law, Identity and Parenthood' (2007) 19 Child Fam Law Q 458

Dillaway H, 'Mothers for Others: A Race, Class and Gender Analysis of Surrogacy' (2008) 34 Int J Sociol Fam 301

Dworkin A, *Right Wing Women: The Politics of Domesticated Females* (The Women's Press, 1983)

Ermisch J, 'The Recent Decline in Period Fertility in England and Wales: Differences Associated with Family Background and Intergenerational Educational Mobility' (2023) Popul Stud https://doi.org/10.1080/00324728.2023.2215224, accessed 10 July 2024.

Evans R, 'Children's Caring Roles and Responsibilities within the Family in Africa' (2010) 4 Geog Compass 1477

Fertility Network, 'Fertility Network UK Warns on Proposed Welsh Fertility Policy Changes' (2023) https://fertilitynetworkuk.org/fertility-network-uk-warns-on-proposed-welsh-fertility-policy-changes/, accessed 27 July 2023

Fiebert J and Brandeau M, 'Evaluating Cost Effectiveness of Interventions that Affect Fertility and Childbearing: How Health Effects are Measured Matters' (2015) Med Decis Making 818

Friese C, Becker G, and Nachtigall R, 'Older Motherhood and the Changing Life Course in the Era of Assisted Reproductive Technologies' (2008) 22 J Aging Stud 65

Goold I, 'Should Older and Postmenopausal Women Have Access to Assisted Reproductive Technology?' (2005) 24 Monash Bioeth Rev 27

Goold I, 'Trust Women to Choose: A Response to John A. Robertson's "Egg Freezing and Egg Banking: Empowerment and Alienation in Assisted Reproduction"' (2017) 4 J Law Biosci 507

Haimov-Kochman R and others, 'Adolescent Infertility: To Treat or Not to Treat' (2008) 90 Fertil and Steril 2009

Harrison L, *Brown Bodies, White Babies: The Politics of Cross Racial Surrogacy* (NYU Press 2016)

HFEA (Human Fertilisation and Embryology Authority), 'Ethnic Diversity in Fertility Treatment' (2018) https://www.hfea.gov.uk/about-us/publications/research-and-data/ethnic-diversity-in-fertility-treatment-2018/, accessed 31 July 2023

HFEA (Human Fertilisation and Embryology Authority), 'Fertility Treatment 2021: Preliminary Trends and Figures' (2023) https://www.hfea.gov.uk/about-us/publications/research-and-data/fertility-treatment-2021-preliminary-trends-and-figures/, accessed 27 June 2023

Higgs P and Gilleard C, 'The Ideology of Ageism versus the Social Imaginary of the Fourth Age: Two Differing Approaches to the Negative Contexts of Old Age' (2020) 40 Ageing Soc 1617

Hill D, 'The Recognition of Homosexual Parents in the United Kingdom' in K Boele-Woelki and T Sverdrup (eds), *European Challenges in Contemporary Family Law* (Intersentia 2008)

Law Commission, 'Building Families through Surrogacy: A New Law Volume III: Draft Surrogacy Bill' (2023) Law Com No 262

Law Commission and Scottish Law Commission, 'Building Families through Surrogacy: A New Law' (2023) Law Com No 411

Lefaucheur N, 'French Tradition of Anonymous Birth: The Lines of Argument' (2004) 18 Int J Law Policy Fam 319

Levine H and others, 'Temporal Trends in Sperm Count: A Systematic Review and Meta-Regression Analysis' (2023) 23 Hum Reprod Update 646

Luyten J and others, 'Economic Evaluation of Medically Assisted Reproduction: An Educational Overview of Methods and Applications for Healthcare Professionals' (2022) 85 Best Pract Res Clin Obstet Gynaecol 217

Majumdar A, 'Outliers and Rogue Doctors: Manufacturing "Anxiety" around Older Mothers in India' (2022) 41 Med Anthropol 616

Martani A and others, 'Deconstructing Age(s): An Analysis of the Different Conceptions of Age as a Legal Criterion for Access to Assisted Reproductive Technologies' (2022) 9 J Law Biosci https://doi.org/doi.org/10.1093/jlb/lsac036, accessed 11 July 2024.

Mhlongo N (ed), *Black Tax: Burden or Ubuntu?* (Jonathan Ball Publishers 2019)

NHS England, '2021/22 Priorities and Operational Planning Guidance' https://www.england.nhs.uk/wp-content/uploads/2021/03/B0468-nhs-operational-planning-and-contracting-guidance.pdf, accessed 14 December 2023

NHS Race and Health Observatory, 'Ethnic Inequalities in Healthcare: A Rapid Evidence Review' (2022) https://www.nhsrho.org/wp-content/uploads/2023/05/RHO-Rapid-Review-Final-Report_.pdf, accessed 14 December 2023

NICE (National Institute of Health and Care Excellence), 'Fertility Problems: Assessment and Treatment' (2013) https://www.nice.org.uk/guidance/cg156/chapter/Recommendations#access-criteria-for-ivf, accessed 31 July 2023

ONS (Office for National Statistics), 'Births in England and Wales 2022' (2023) https://www.ons.gov.uk/peoplepopulationandcommunity/birthsdeathsandmarriages/livebirths/bulletins/birthsummarytablesenglandandwales/2022#:~:text=Main%20points,(COVID%2D19)%20pandemic, accessed 27 June 2023

Pande A, 'Commercial Surrogacy in India: Manufacturing a Perfect Mother-Worker' (2010) 35 Signs 989

Stychin C, 'Not (Quite) A Horse and Carriage' (2006) 14 Fem Leg Stud 79

Surtees N and Bremner P, 'Gay and Lesbian Collaborative Co-Parenting in New Zealand and the United Kingdom: "The Law Doesn't Protect the Third Parent"' (2020) 29 Soc Leg Stud 507

Swan S and Colino S, *Count Down: How Our Modern World is Threatening Sperm Counts, Altering Male and Female Reproductive Development, and Imperilling the Future of the Human Race* (Scribner 2021).

Tremellen K, Wilkinson, D, and Savulescu J, 'Should Obese Women's Access to Assisted Fertility Treatment Be Limited? A Scientific and Ethical Analysis' (2017) 57 Aust N Z J Obstet Gynaecol 569

Vonk M, *Children and their Parents* (Intersentia 2007)

Wallbank J, 'Channeling the Messiness of Diverse Family Lives: Resisting the Calls to Order and De-Centring the Hetero-Normative Family' (2010) 32 J Soc Welf Fam Law 353

Welsh Health Specialised Services Committee, 'Specialist Fertility Services' (2017) https://whssc.nhs.wales/commissioning/whssc-policies/fertility/, accessed 14 November 2023

WHO (World Health Organization), 'Infertility' (2023) https://www.who.int/news-room/fact-sheets/detail/infertility, accessed 7 July 2023

14

Abortion and Contraception

Zoe L. Tongue

In the UK, abortion is legal (in carefully defined circumstances) and contraception is freely available through the NHS. Abortion is both normal and common, with 214,256 legal abortions taking place in England and Wales in 2021.[1] The majority of abortions are medically induced before 12 weeks' gestation using the medication misoprostol and mifepristone, which is a safer drug regimen than penicillin.[2] There are various female-user contraceptives available for free from healthcare providers, including the contraceptive pill, implant, patch, intrauterine device, and injection, and over 450,000 people in England use one of these methods.[3] In 2021, there were over 85,000 prescriptions issued for emergency contraception (the morning-after pill).[4]

There are ongoing ethical debates and issues surrounding the law and healthcare provision in these areas. In the first section of this chapter, 'Feminist ethical perspectives on abortion and contraception', I introduce diverse perspectives on abortion and contraception by setting out feminist approaches to reproductive autonomy. In the second section, 'Access to Abortion and Contraception', I outline the respective law on abortion in Britain and Northern Ireland and the regulation of contraception. In the third section, 'Key Issues in Abortion', I address two key issues surrounding abortion in the UK: decriminalisation

---

1 Office for Health Improvement and Disparities, 'Abortion Statistics, England and Wales: 2021' (2022) https://www.gov.uk/government/statistics/abortion-statistics-for-england-and-wales-2021/abortion-statistics-england-and-wales-2021, accessed 19 October 2023.

2 Patricia Lohr, Jonathan Lord, and Sam Rowlands, 'How Would Decriminalisation Affect Women's Health?' in Sally Sheldon and Kaye Wellings (eds), *Decriminalising Abortion in the UK: What Would It Mean?* (Policy Press 2020) 41.

3 NHS Digital, 'Sexual and Reproductive Health Services, England (Contraception) 2021/2022' (2022) https://digital.nhs.uk/data-and-information/publications/statistical/sexual-and-reproductive-health-services/2021-22, accessed 19 October 2023, ch 2.

4 Ibid ch 3.

and access to abortion on the grounds of fetal impairment. On the latter point, I consider the perspectives of disability rights activists and scholars. Finally, I conclude the chapter by introducing reproductive justice perspectives on access to abortion and contraception, an approach which considers access to reproductive healthcare and reproductive autonomy for those marginalised along the lines of, for example, race, class, and disability. I use the terminology of 'pregnant person' to be inclusive of trans, non-binary, and gender-expansive people who are capable of becoming pregnant and therefore may require access to abortion and contraception.

Feminist ethical perspectives on abortion and contraception

Traditional moral theories have typically approached the issues of abortion and contraception by focusing on whether the fetus has moral status. Feminist scholars have critiqued these approaches, which place the fetus at the centre of moral inquiry, reducing the pregnant person to a mere fetal 'container'.[5] Feminist scholars sought to change this narrative towards one focusing on reproductive and bodily autonomy. Judith Jarvis Thomson published her influential defence of abortion in 1971, which challenged the argument that recognising the fetus as a person from the moment of conception must lead to the conclusion that abortion is immoral.[6] The argument proceeds with a hypothetical scenario in which a famous violinist has a fatal kidney infection, is unconscious, and has been plugged into your circulatory system without your knowledge or consent, so that he can make use of your kidneys.[7] To unplug him would be to kill him. Thomson equated this use of one's body with the use of one's body by the fetus during pregnancy; a right of self-defence, by unplugging yourself from the violinist, equates to a right of self-defence in relation to an unwanted pregnancy.[8] Even if the fetus did have full moral status, this would not override the pregnant person's right to bodily autonomy, as the fetus would not have the right to the use of their body:

> nobody is morally *required* to make large sacrifices, of health, of all other interests and concerns, of all other duties and commitments, for nine years, or even for nine months, in order to keep another person alive.[9]

5 Susan Sherwin, 'Abortion through a Feminist Ethics Lens' (1991) 30 Dialogue 327, 332.

6 Judith Jarvis Thomson, 'A Defense of Abortion' (1971) 1 Philos Pub Aff 47.

7 Ibid 49–50.

8 Ibid 66.

9 Ibid 61–2 (emphasis added).

Relational abortion decisions

Other feminist scholars have highlighted the complex nature of abortion decisions, which point to the need to guarantee reproductive autonomy and permit pregnant people to individually make these moral choices. These choices cannot be determined by declarations on fetal personhood. For example, Susan Sherwin argued that abstract rules about moral status cannot fully capture the range of relevant factors that a pregnant person may consider in deciding whether or not to have an abortion.[10] This includes relational factors – the needs and interests of other family members and the relationship to the fetus, as well as the pregnant person's own needs and interests. Sherwin argued that as abortion decisions are specific to the pregnant person's own experience, pregnant people must be granted the responsibility to make moral decisions about their own pregnancies.[11] Feminist philosophers have emphasised that this is a relational decision: one based on whether the pregnant person is willing to accept a relationship of responsibility to the fetus and their potential future child, not merely whether the pregnant person wishes to refuse the fetus use of their womb.[12]

Gender-based stereotypes

Feminist perspectives on abortion and contraception also connect issues of reproductive autonomy to gender-based stereotypes. Patriarchal ideals assign women's primary biological roles as those of reproduction and motherhood. As those capable of becoming pregnant ought, under this view, to fulfil these roles, they may even be viewed as selfish where pregnancy is seen as a 'tolerable burden'[13] or 'mere event'[14] that they should accept, rather than a process that will have a profound effect on their body and their life. Feminists view this narrative as perpetuating the subordinate status of women and people capable of becoming pregnant. Access to a range of contraceptive methods is an integral aspect of reproductive autonomy, in order to prevent unwanted pregnancies and space out one's pregnancies while allowing for sexual autonomy. In the context of people being denied emergency contraception, Carolyn McLeod has argued that this is harmful to the patient as it perpetuates gender-based stereotypes and stigma over their sexuality and reproductive choices.[15] This can be said to amount to a 'dignitary harm' – a harm affecting the dignity of a group – by perpetuating the

10 Sherwin (n5) 329.

11 Ibid.

12 Catriona Mackenzie, 'Abortion and Embodiment' (1992) 70 Australas J Philos 136, 137.

13 Sherwin (n5) 333.

14 Mackenzie (n12) 155.

15 Carolyn McLeod, 'Harm or Mere Inconvenience? Denying Women Emergency Contraception' (2010) 25 Hypatia 11, 19.

subordinate status of women and people capable of becoming pregnant.[16] Access to methods of pregnancy prevention and termination are important aspects of upholding the dignity of people capable of becoming pregnant.

Access to abortion and contraception in the UK

Abortion in England, Wales, and Scotland

Section 58 of the Offences Against the Person Act (OAPA) 1861 criminalises abortion (or 'procuring a miscarriage' using 'any poison or other noxious thing' or 'any instrument'), an offence that carries a maximum life sentence. In addition to the criminalisation of procuring one's own abortion, the OAPA 1861 also includes an offence under section 59 for procuring or supplying drugs or instruments intended to be used for an abortion, therefore criminalising any third party who knowingly assists in an illegal abortion. This offence also carries a maximum life sentence.

The offence for abortion contained in the OAPA 1861 was modified slightly by the Infant Life (Preservation) Act (ILPA) 1929, which set out the offence of 'child destruction'. Section 1(1) of the ILPA 1929 set out that the offence of child destruction, carrying a maximum life sentence, is committed where any wilful act causes the death of a child capable of being born alive. Section 1(2) took 28-week gestation as the point in which the child is capable of independent existence from the pregnant person. Section 1(1) also contains an exception to the offence, where the death of the fetus was caused in good faith for the purpose of preserving the life of the pregnant person. This narrow exception to the criminal offence of abortion was expanded upon by *Bourne*.[17] Macnaghten J held that if a doctor was of the reasonably held opinion that the consequence of continuing a pregnancy would be to make the pregnant person 'a physical or mental wreck' then this would fall under the preservation of life exception.[18]

Campaigners for abortion law reform post-Second World War highlighted the prevalence of dangerous 'backstreet' abortions, which saw many people hospitalised for associated injuries.[19] Only those that could afford to pay a psychiatrist to certify that they were a 'physical or mental wreck' were able to access legal abortion services, and many pregnant people struggled to afford even a backstreet abortion.[20] The Abortion Act (AA) 1967 was passed as a way of

16 Zoe L. Tongue, 'On Conscientious Objection to Abortion: Questioning Mandatory Referral as Compromise in the International Human Rights Framework' (2022) 22 Med Law Int 349, 363.

17 *R v Bourne* [1938] 3 All ER 615.

18 Ibid.

19 Emma Jones, 'Attitudes to Abortion in the Era of Reform: Evidence from the Abortion Law Reform Association Correspondence' (2011) 20 Women's Hist Rev 283, 294–5.

20 Ibid 285.

addressing this public health problem and avoiding the maternal mortality and morbidity that came from unsafe abortion (see Box 14.1).[21] The AA 1967 did not repeal or replace the above legislation; the criminal offences for abortion contained in the OAPA 1861 and ILPA 1929 remain in force. Instead, it created exceptions to the offences for doctors to perform lawful abortions where they are satisfied that one of four grounds has been met. As the AA 1967 offers these defences only to doctors, any pregnant person who terminates their own pregnancy (for example, by taking abortion medication) without the authorisation of a doctor and outside the circumstances set out by the legislation is committing a criminal offence.

Box 14.1: Key text: Abortion Act 1967

s.1 Medical termination of pregnancy

(1) Subject to the provisions of this section, a person shall not be guilty of an offence under the law relating to abortion when a pregnancy is terminated by a registered medical practitioner if two registered medical practitioners are of the opinion, formed in good faith –
  (a) that the pregnancy has not exceeded its twenty-fourth week and that the continuance of the pregnancy would involve risk, greater than if the pregnancy were terminated, of injury to the physical or mental health of the pregnant woman or any existing children of her family; or
  (b) that the termination is necessary to prevent grave permanent injury to the physical or mental health of the pregnant woman; or
  (c) that the continuance of the pregnancy would involve risk to the life of the pregnant woman, greater than if the pregnancy were terminated; or
  (d) that there is a substantial risk that if the child were born it would suffer from such physical or mental abnormalities as to be seriously handicapped.

(2) In determining whether the continuance of a pregnancy would involve such risk of injury to health as is mentioned in paragraph (a) or (b) of subsection (1) of this section, account may be taken of the pregnant woman's actual or reasonably foreseeable environment.

The Act distinguishes between abortion pre- and post-24-week gestation. Prior to 24 weeks, section 1(1)(a) permits an abortion if two doctors certify in good faith that continuing the pregnancy would pose a greater risk than an abortion to the pregnant person's physical or mental health. Given that modern abortion

[21] Sally Sheldon, *Beyond Control* (Pluto Press 1997) ch 2.

methods are very safe and effective, continuing the pregnancy will always carry more of a risk than an early abortion.[22] This ground is colloquially known as the 'social ground', as it takes into account social factors, as well as medical ones. In effect, anyone can obtain an abortion under section 1(1)(a) provided they fall within the gestational time limit. However, feminist scholars such as Sally Sheldon and Emily Jackson have criticised this section. Sheldon views section 1(1)(a) as reflecting an outdated 'medical paternalism'[23] (particularly in relation to the two-doctor rule) and portraying pregnant people seeking abortions as 'at the end of her tether'.[24] Jackson has argued that despite section 1(1)(a) being broad in practice, it still takes away from the pregnant person's reproductive autonomy by putting the ultimate decision in the hands of doctors.[25]

Following the 24-week limit, access to abortion is restricted to three medical grounds: to prevent grave permanent injury, to prevent a risk to the pregnant person's life, and in cases of fetal impairment.[26] In situations where an abortion is immediately necessary to prevent grave permanent injury or risk to life, only one doctor's authorisation is required (s 1(4) AA 1967). The final ground, fetal impairment, will be discussed in further detail later in this chapter. The requirement of good faith means that a doctor needs to honestly believe that one of the four grounds has been met, so a doctor would be protected from criminalisation even if the ground had not actually been met based on the facts.[27]

For an abortion under any of these grounds to be legal, it must be carried out by a registered practitioner in a premises approved for this purpose, such as a hospital or dedicated abortion clinic.[28] During the COVID-19 pandemic, this was temporarily amended to permit abortion by telemedicine within the first ten weeks of gestation.[29] Registered practitioners could do the consultation and prescribe abortion medication (misoprostol and mifepristone) remotely, which was then posted out to the pregnant person and self-administered at home. The Health Care Act 2022 amended the AA 1967 to make this permanent.[30]

Section 4(1) of the AA 1967 allows doctors to opt out of providing abortion services based on a conscientious objection. Where a doctor has a moral objection to abortion, religious or otherwise, they cannot be compelled by law or contract to 'participate in any treatment' authorised by the Act. The

22 Rosamund Scott, 'Risks, Reasons and Rights: The European Convention on Human Rights and English Abortion Law' (2015) 24 Med Law Rev 1, 13–14.

23 Sheldon (n21) 66.

24 Ibid 38.

25 Emily Jackson, *Regulating Reproduction* (Hart Publishing 2001) 89.

26 AA 1967 s 1(b), (c), and (d).

27 *Jepson v Chief Constable of West Mercia* [2003] EWHC 3318 (Admin).

28 AA 1967 s 1(3).

29 Jordan A. Parsons and Elizabeth Chloe Romanis, *Early Medical Abortion, Equality of Access, and the Telemedical Imperative* (OUP 2021) ch 8.

30 AA 1967 s 1(3A)–(3D).

only exception is in an emergency situation where an abortion is necessary to prevent grave permanent injury or a risk to the pregnant person's life.[31] In *Janaway*, the House of Lords interpreted the word 'participate' to require actual involvement in the abortion procedure itself, so a receptionist could not rely on section 4(1) to refuse to type a letter referring a patient for an abortion.[32] This interpretation was confirmed in *Doogan*, which concerned two midwives objecting to providing one-on-one care to patients who had received abortions on their ward.[33] 'Participate' was taken to mean 'taking part in a "hands-on" capacity'.[34] Reliance on the conscientious objection clause is therefore restricted to direct involvement. General Medical Council (GMC) guidance indicates that objecting doctors should inform patients and refer them to a non-objecting doctor wherever possible,[35] but this is not required by law. Further, although abortions in England and Wales are largely provided through dedicated abortion clinics, there are also concerns that conscientious objection could cause regional variations in access if some areas lacked the requisite number of non-objecting doctors.[36] Some objecting doctors do refuse to refer patients, as they view this as participation (although indirect) in the eventual abortion.[37]

Abortion in Northern Ireland

Prior to 2019, sections 58 and 59 of the OAPA 1861 were also in force in Northern Ireland. The Criminal Justice Act (CJA) (NI) 1945 mirrored the offence of child destruction set out in the ILPA 1929. However, the AA 1967 was not extended to Northern Ireland, meaning that abortion remained largely prohibited in the region until recently. The only exceptions were found across a number of cases. Clarifying (and limiting) the *R v Bourne* exception, the Northern Irish courts set out that the only lawful grounds for an abortion was where there was a risk to the life of the pregnant person, including a risk of suicide, or where continuing the pregnancy would have a 'real and serious adverse effect' on their permanent or long-term health.[38] The uncertainty over when these exceptions would apply, coupled with the 'chilling effect' of the criminal

31 Ibid s 4(2).

32 *Janaway v Salford Health Authority* [1988] UKHL 17.

33 *Greater Glasgow Health Board v Doogan* [2014] UKSC 68.

34 Ibid 38.

35 GMC (General Medical Council), 'Personal Beliefs and Medical Practice' (2013) https://www.gmc-uk.org/ethical-guidance/ethical-guidance-for-doctors/personal-beliefs-and-medical-practice, accessed 19 October 2023, para 12.

36 Sheldon (n21) 56.

37 Tongue (n16) 354–5; Becky Self, Clare Maxwell, and Valerie Fleming, 'The Missing Voices in the Conscientious Objection Debate: British Service Users' Experiences of Conscientious Objection to Abortion' (2023) 24 BMC Med Ethics 1.

38 *Northern Health and Social Services Board v A and Others* [1994] NIJB 1; *Western Health and Social Services Board v CMB and the Official Solicitor* (NI High Ct, 1995).

offences that would apply to doctors performing unlawful abortions, meant that doctors were reluctant to perform abortions even where they would be life-saving.[39] Moreover, an estimated 1,000 Northern Irish pregnant people accessed abortion medication online each year,[40] while up to 1,000 more travelled to England and Wales for legal terminations.[41]

In 2018, the Supreme Court observed that the prohibition on abortion in cases of rape and fatal fetal impairments amounted to a violation of Article 8, the right to private and family life, of the ECHR.[42] In the same year, the United Nations Committee on the Elimination of Discrimination Against Women (CEDAW) issued a report that observed the 'grave and systematic' violation of women's human rights in Northern Ireland resulting from the country's restrictive abortion regime.[43] The Committee recommended that the government repeal sections 58 and 59 of the OAPA 1861 and legislate to provide access to abortion on broader health grounds, as well as in cases of rape and severe fetal impairment.[44]

The following year, the UK government passed the Northern Ireland (Executive Formations) Act 2019, which repealed the relevant sections of the OAPA 1861 in Northern Ireland, so that criminal miscarriage (as it is called in the OAPA 1861) is no longer a criminal offence in the region. The legislation also required new regulations on abortion in Northern Ireland to be passed; the Abortion (Northern Ireland) Regulations 2020 came into effect on 31 March 2020. These regulations are more progressive than the AA 1967, allowing for abortion on request (that is, the pregnant person can simply request an abortion without being required to give a reason or meet any ground) within the first 12 weeks of gestation.[45] From 12 to 24 weeks, the 'social ground' of the AA 1967 is mirrored, with one notable difference: this ground refers only to the

39 Fiona Bloomer and Eileen Fegan, 'Critiquing Recent Abortion Law and Policy in Northern Ireland' (2013) 34 Crit Soc Pol 109, 113.

40 Sally Sheldon, 'How Can a State Control Swallowing? The Home Use of Abortion Pills in Ireland' (2016) 24 RHM 90, 92.

41 DHSC (Department of Health and Social Care), 'Abortion Statistics, England and Wales: 2019' (2020) https://assets.publishing.service.gov.uk/government/uploads/system/uploads/attachment_data/file/891405/abortion-statistics-commentary-2019.pdf, accessed 19 October 2023, para 2.38.

42 Northern Ireland Human Rights Commission, Re Judicial Review [2018] UKSC 27. This case was unsuccessful, however, due to a finding that the Northern Ireland Human Rights Commission did not have standing to bring these proceedings (and thus the court did not have jurisdiction to make a determination about (in)compatibility).

43 CEDAW (Committee on the Elimination of Discrimination Against Women), 'Report of the Inquiry concerning the United Kingdom of Great Britain and Northern Ireland under Article 8 of the Optional Protocol to the Convention on the Elimination of All Forms of Discrimination Against Women' (2018) UN Doc CEDAW/C/OP.8/GBR/1, para 1.

44 Ibid para 85.

45 Abortion (NI) Regulations 2020 reg 3.

physical or mental health of the pregnant woman, and not her existing children.[46] After 24 weeks, abortion is restricted to the same three medical grounds as permitted under the AA 1967.[47] The fetal abnormality ground was updated in the NI Regulations to remove the outdated language of 'handicap'; it instead refers to 'such physical and mental impairment as to be seriously disabled' as well as explicitly mentioning fatal fetal impairments.[48] As in England, Wales, and Scotland, healthcare providers are permitted to conscientiously object to providing abortion services, except in an emergency situation.[49]

As already mentioned, the relevant sections of the OAPA 1861 no longer apply in Northern Ireland. The NI Regulations set out a new offence for terminating a pregnancy outside of the regulations, which does not apply to the pregnant person themselves or where the abortion was performed in good faith to save their life or prevent grave permanent injury to their physical or mental health.[50] The offence of child destruction set out in the CJA (NI) 1945 was also amended to mirror this.[51] Thus, while any pregnant person who terminates their own pregnancy cannot be prosecuted, any healthcare provider or third party who performs an abortion outside of the regulations commits an offence, unless it is an emergency situation. However, while the law in Northern Ireland is now more liberal on paper than in the rest of the UK, there are significant issues with access after ten weeks' gestation, with surgical abortions unavailable from many healthcare providers.[52] In 2021, 161 people from Northern Ireland travelled to England and Wales for their abortions.[53]

Contraception

In 1961, the Family Planning Association approved the use of the contraceptive pill in England.[54] Its prescription was limited to married women, due to the stigma around unmarried women's sexuality. However, the Secretary of State for Health and Social Care at the time confirmed that 'birth control pills' would be made available for both married and single women through the NHS based on medical grounds.[55] Yet this did not happen until the same year that abortion was

46 Ibid reg 4.

47 Ibid regs 5–7.

48 Ibid reg 7.

49 Ibid reg 12.

50 Ibid reg 11.

51 Ibid reg 13.

52 Amnesty International, 'Legal but Not Local: Barriers to Accessing Abortion Services in Northern Ireland' (7 December 2023) https://www.amnesty.org.uk/press-releases/northern-ireland-four-years-decriminalisation-abortion-access-right-not-reality-new, accessed 9 May 2024.

53 Office for Health Improvement and Disparities (n1).

54 Family Planning Association, 'History of Family Planning' https://www.fpa.org.uk/medical-professional/factsheets/, accessed 20 October 2023.

55 HC Deb 4 December 1961, vol 650, cols 922–3 https://api.parliament.uk/historic-hansard/commons/1961/dec/04/birth-control-pills#column_923, accessed 20 Oct 2023.

legalised, with the NHS Family Planning Act 1967 enabling healthcare providers to prescribe the contraceptive pill and give family-planning advice regardless of marital status. This changed in 1974, when all methods of contraception (including long-acting reversible forms such as the intrauterine device) and contraceptive advice became accessible regardless of marital status or age, and at no cost through the NHS.[56]

Emergency contraception was first licensed for use in Britain in the 1980s and became available to purchase from pharmacies without a prescription from 2001. The Society for the Protection of Unborn Children (SPUC) launched a challenge against the over-the-counter sale of the morning-after pill, arguing that the pill was an abortifacient rather than a contraceptive and therefore the sale of it contravened sections 58 and 59 of the OAPA 1861.[57] While the morning-after pill prevents implantation rather than de-implanting a fertilised egg from the uterus lining, the SPUC argued that any interference with a fertilised egg – including the prevention of implantation – amounted to 'miscarriage' within the wording of the OAPA 1861.[58] Justice Munby noted that this argument could call into question the legality of other forms of contraception, including the intrauterine device and the contraceptive pill, which may also prevent implantation.[59] However, Munby J dismissed the case, coming to the conclusion that the term 'miscarriage' presupposed prior carriage – that is, implantation.[60] While in 1861 the term may have included the prevention of implantation, it is left undefined in the OAPA and therefore must be interpreted in line with current understanding and medical knowledge.[61] As such, methods of contraception, including the morning-after pill, do not fall within the criminal offences that cover abortion.

Key issues in abortion

Decriminalisation

While abortion has been partially decriminalised in Northern Ireland, it remains a criminal offence in England, Wales, and Scotland. There are numerous reasons as to why a pregnant person may choose to obtain an abortion outside of the law and formal healthcare system. In one study of people requesting abortion medication from an online provider before telemedicine was authorised in Britain, the most common reasons given were: barriers to accessing in-person care, such as lengthy waiting times and difficulties travelling to a provider; privacy concerns

56 National Health Service Reorganisation Act 1973 s 4.

57 *Smeaton v Secretary of State for Health* [2002] EWHC 610.

58 Ibid [38].

59 Ibid [72].

60 Ibid [353].

61 Ibid [348]–[350].

and a perception of stigma; and fears of experiencing intimate partner violence or control from one's family.[62] Trans, non-binary, and gender-expansive people experiencing an unwanted pregnancy may also feel uncomfortable accessing abortion services through the formal healthcare system, as they can experience misgendering and heightened stigma.[63] Telemedicine can alleviate these issues for many people, but there will remain those who cannot access abortion medication in this way.

The majority of pregnant people who access abortion medication online are at an early gestational stage and generally do not face prosecution in practice. Most of the charges made under sections 58 and 59 OAPA 1861 relate to pregnant people who have terminated their own pregnancies at a late gestational stage, or individuals who terminate (or attempt to) their partner's pregnancy without consent.[64] In 2023, Carla Foster was charged under section 58 for 'procuring a miscarriage' when she was between 32 and 34 weeks' pregnant, using abortion medication she had obtained via telemedicine after telling healthcare providers that she was between 6 and 7 weeks' pregnant.[65] During the first lockdown of the COVID-19 pandemic, Foster and her two existing children had been forced to move back in with her ex-partner, from whom she sought to hide her pregnancy with another man.[66] She was initially sentenced to 28 months' imprisonment, but the Court of Appeal reduced this to a 14-month suspended sentence, and Foster was released after spending 35 days in prison.[67] Dame Victoria Sharp stated the distressing situation that Foster found herself in 'calls for compassion' and held that there was 'no useful purpose' to detaining her.[68] Yet, there have been subsequent cases of people investigated or prosecuted over suspected illegal abortions, including over 'unexplained pregnancy loss'.[69]

Sheldon identifies two historical purposes for the criminalisation of abortion: to prevent or condemn the intentional destruction of the fetus, and to protect pregnant people from harm at a time when illegal abortion was synonymous

---

62 Abigail Aiken and others, 'Barriers to Accessing Abortion Services and Perspectives on Using Mifepristone and Misoprostol at Home in Great Britain' (2018) 97 Contraception 177.

63 Zoe L. Tongue, 'Telemedical and Self-Managed Abortion: A Human Rights Imperative?' (2023) 30 Eur J Health Law 158, 172–3.

64 Sally Sheldon, 'The Decriminalisation of Abortion: An Argument for Modernisation' (2016) 36 OJLS 334, 340; Sally Sheldon and Jonathan Lord, 'Care Not Criminalisation: Reform of British Abortion Law is Long Overdue' (2023) 49 JME 523, 524.

65 *R v Foster* [Sentencing Remarks] (12 June 2023) https://www.judiciary.uk/wp-content/uploads/2023/06/R-v.-Foster-sentencing-remarks-12.6.23.pdf, accessed 20 October 2023.

66 Ibid [19].

67 Ibid [24]; *R v Foster* [Summary of the Decision of the Court of Appeal, Criminal Division] (18 July 2023) https://www.judiciary.uk/wp-content/uploads/2023/07/R-v-Carla-Foster-190723.pdf, accessed 20 October 2023.

68 Ibid.

69 Eleanor Layhe, Anna Meisel, and Divya Talwar, 'More Women Investigated for Illegal Terminations, Says Abortion Provider' (20 February 2024) https://www.bbc.co.uk/news/uk-68305991, accessed 9 May 2024.

with the dangerous 'backstreet' abortion.[70] With abortion medication, the self-management of abortion can be just as safe as an abortion within the formal healthcare system.[71] Sheldon therefore argues that the purpose of criminalisation is therefore condemnation or prevention.[72] In relation to abortions before 24 weeks, which would be permitted by section 1(1)(a) AA 1967, the existence of the criminal offence condemns something that is lawful.

The argument for decriminalisation is, however, more controversial when it comes to the abortion in the later stages of pregnancy. As the Foster case highlights, the criminal law serves a limited purpose as it fails to have a deterrent effect. Pregnant people have abortions in the later stages of pregnancy for a complex range of reasons, for example intimate partner violence, difficult socio-economic circumstances, and where the pregnant person only discovers the pregnancy at a late stage, but the AA 1967 does not permit any flexibility after 24 weeks' gestation. Sheldon and Lord have argued that pregnant people in these situations deserve 'compassion, support and care' rather than criminalisation, as there will always be 'rare cases' of people requiring terminations in the later stages of pregnancy.[73]

The current law is thus viewed as archaic and harmful, and Sheldon has advocated for the wholesale reform of the AA 1967 alongside decriminalisation, to permit abortion on request in the early stages and in a broader range of circumstances in the later stages of pregnancy.[74] Decriminalisation, alongside this expansion of the grounds for later abortions, remains important, as Romanis argues, because the remote prescription of abortion medication increases the likelihood of people falling foul of the criminal law.[75] Herring, Jackson, and Sheldon have also highlighted that non-consensual terminations, such as those by intimate partners, would remain criminalised through other offences.[76] Decriminalisation in Northern Ireland demonstrates that this may similarly be possible in Britain, which would bring all regions of the UK in line with each other in relation to abortion.

Abortion and fetal disability

Section 1(1)(d) of the AA 1967 and section 7 of the NI Regulations create an exception to the general prohibition on later stage abortions based on fetal

70 Sheldon (n64) 347.
71 Tongue (n63) 160–2.
72 Sheldon (n64) 351.
73 Sheldon and Lord (n64) 524.
74 Sheldon (n64) 357–8.
75 Elizabeth Chloe Romanis, '*R v Foster*: Exemplifying the Urgency of the Decriminalisation of Abortion' (2023) 31 Med Law Rev 606, 613.
76 Jonathan Herring, Emily Jackson, and Sally Sheldon, 'Would Decriminalisation Mean Deregulation?' in Sally Sheldon and Kaye Wellings (eds), *Decriminalising Abortion in the UK: What Would It Mean?* (Policy Press 2020).

disability. This means that, aside from where their health or life is seriously at risk, a pregnant person can only decide to have an abortion after 24 weeks *if* the fetus has an impairment. Some scholars view this as perpetuating discriminatory attitudes around disability, through the assumption that having a disabled child should be avoided.[77] In a recent case, Heidi Crowter, a woman with Down's Syndrome, along with Máire Lea-Wilson and her young son, who also has Down's Syndrome, challenged section 1(1)(d) on the basis that it does not distinguish between fatal and non-fatal disabilities.[78] They argued that the ground was in violation of Articles 2 (the right to life), 3 (freedom from torture and cruel, inhuman, and degrading treatment), and 8 (the right to family life) of the European Convention on Human Rights (ECHR).[79] The High Court dismissed the case, given that the rights protected by the ECHR have never been applied to the fetus.[80]

The argument made under Article 8, in relation to the perpetuation of negative attitudes towards living people with disabilities, was taken forward on appeal.[81] However, the Court of Appeal rejected this claim, stating that the section did not promote any negative message about living disabled people, as it was concerned specifically with the unborn fetus.[82] I have critiqued these judgments elsewhere, arguing that while a disability ground for abortion does not constitute discrimination as a matter of law, the stereotypes and attitudes that it perpetuates ought to be addressed.[83] Scholars also emphasise the importance of reproductive autonomy, and Sheldon and Wilkinson argue that nobody 'should be forced to carry to term a disabled, or any other, foetus'.[84] There is also a need to retain access to abortion in cases of fetal impairments, including non-fatal impairments, as these situations are complex and it may be difficult in practice to distinguish between fatal and non-fatal impairments.[85]

Socio-economic disadvantage can also be a reason for having an abortion in cases of fetal impairments, where a pregnant person may be unable to meet the

77 See Sheelagh McGuinness, 'Law, Reproduction, and Disability: Fatally "Handicapped"?' (2013) 21 Med Law Rev 213; Alison Piepmeier, 'The Inadequacy of "Choice": Disability and What's Wrong with Feminist Framings of Reproduction' (2013) 39 Fem Stud 159; Zoe L. Tongue, '*Crowter v Secretary of State for Health and Social Care* [2021] EWHC 2536: Discrimination, Disability, and Access to Abortion' (2022) 30 Med Law Rev 177, 184.

78 *Crowter v Secretary of State for Health and Social Care* [2021] EWHC 2536.

79 Ibid.

80 Ibid.

81 *Crowter v Secretary of State for Health and Social Care* [2022] EWCA Civ 1559.

82 Ibid.

83 Tongue (n77); Zoe L. Tongue, 'Human Rights and Foetal Impairment Grounds for Abortion: *Crowter v Secretary of State for Health and Social Care* [2022] EWCA Civ 1559' (2023) 23 Med Law Int 297.

84 Sally Sheldon and Stephen Wilkinson, 'Termination of Pregnancy for Reason of Foetal Disability: Are There Grounds for a Special Exception in Law?' (2001) 9 Med Law Rev 85, 109.

85 Tongue (n77) 181.

care needs of a disabled child. Yet difficult socio-economic circumstances are also why a pregnant person may require an abortion in the later stages of pregnancy where the fetus does not have an impairment. This distinction is therefore seen as problematic, creating a moral distinction between abortions for disabled and non-disabled fetuses in the later stage of pregnancy. Broadening the grounds for later abortions alongside decriminalisation could go some way to addressing this issue.[86] Some disability rights scholars, who have critiqued disability grounds for abortion, do not conclude that these grounds should be restricted, but rather than efforts must be taken to avoid the routine use of prenatal testing and to address existing socio-cultural attitudes towards disability that may encourage or support abortion where a fetal impairment is discovered.[87] This will also require increased state support for parents of disabled children (financial, social, and educational, and in relation to housing and healthcare needs) and for disabled adults.

Reproductive justice

The framework of 'reproductive justice' refers to a social justice understanding of reproductive rights, addressing the economic, social, and demographic barriers to exercising reproductive autonomy.[88] There are three key tenets of reproductive justice: the ability to have children, to not have children, and to safely parent one's children.[89] For people from already marginalised groups, existing barriers can become compounded and make exercising one's reproductive autonomy in these areas difficult or even impossible. Developed by Black women in the US, this framework has been applied to recognise the impacts of coercive sterilisation, medical racism, and poverty, and broader social issues on reproductive decision-making. For many people, there are more barriers to having children than to not having them. Though developed and applied primarily in the US, this framework also has current relevance in the UK. Scholars have recognised issues such as the hostile environment, the cost-of-living crisis, and the COVID-19 pandemic as reproductive justice issues for constraining individual decisions to have or avoid having children.[90] While access to early abortion was improved during the pandemic due to telemedicine, access to contraception (particularly long-acting

86 Ibid 186.

87 See Adrienne Asch, 'Prenatal Diagnosis and Selective Abortion: A Challenge to Practice and Policy' (1999) 89 Am J Public Health 1649; Tom Shakespeare, 'Choices and Rights: Eugenics, Genetics and Disability Equality' (1998) 13 Disabil Soc 665.

88 Zakiya Luna and Kristin Luker, 'Reproductive Justice' (2013) 9 Annu Rev Law Soc Sci 327.

89 Sister Song, 'About Us' https://www.sistersong.net/about-x2, accessed 20 October 2023.

90 Gwyneth Lonergan, 'Reproductive Justice and Migrant Women in Great Britain' (2012) 23 Women 26; Elizabeth Chloe Romanis, Jordan A. Parsons, and Nathan Hodson, 'COVID-19 and Reproductive Justice in Great Britain and the United States: Ensuring Access to Abortion Care during a Global Pandemic' (2020) 7 J Law Biosci https://doi.org/10.1093/jlb/lsaa027, accessed 11 July 2024; Naomi Delap and Kirsty Kitchen, 'Why the Cost of Living Crisis Is a Reproductive Justice Matter' (2023) 380 BMJ 118.

reversible contraception) and other forms of sexual and reproductive healthcare was limited in some areas due to lockdowns and shortages.[91]

There are also issues with people from marginalised groups being encouraged or even coerced into using contraception or having an abortion. People who are perceived as 'unfit for parenthood', including adolescents, people of colour, and people with physical and intellectual disabilities, are often targeted for long-acting forms of contraception.[92] People with intellectual disabilities are often *required* to use contraception against their wishes. There have been cases in the UK where the courts have ruled to administer long-acting reversible contraception to women with intellectual disabilities without their knowledge,[93] and one in which a woman with intellectual disabilities was to be sterilised,[94] as they lacked mental capacity in relation to pregnancy and sexual intercourse. In 2019, the Court of Protection held that it would be in the best interests of a pregnant woman with an intellectual disability to have an abortion against her wishes.[95] This Declaration was, however, subsequently overturned.[96] Scholars have highlighted the need to support people with intellectual disabilities in making contraceptive and family-planning decisions, rather than making decisions on their behalf.[97] Reproductive justice would require timely access to quality maternity care, contraceptive, and abortion services, as well as other forms of sexual and reproductive healthcare. Alongside this, reproductive justice requires enabling broader social and economic conditions, including addressing discriminatory practices, to support autonomous reproductive decision-making.

Summary

- Feminist scholars have rebutted theories on the moral status of the fetus and argue that access to abortion is necessary for a range of reasons.
- Restrictions on access to abortion and contraception are viewed by feminist scholars as promoting harmful gender-based stereotypes.

91 Neerujah Balachandren and others, 'Impact of the SARS-CoV-2 Pandemic on Access to Contraception and Pregnancy Intentions: A National Prospective Cohort Study of the UK Population' (2022) 48 BMJ Sex Reprod Health 60.

92 Pam Lowe and Sam Rowlands, 'Long-Acting Reversible Contraception: Targeting Those Judged to Be Unfit for Parenthood in the United States and the United Kingdom' (2022) 17 Glob Pub Health 3773.

93 For example, *Re P (Sexual Relations and Contraception)* [2018] EWCOP 10; *Re Z* [2020] EWCOP 20.

94 *Re DD* (No 4) (Sterilisation) [2015] EWCOP 4.

95 *An NHS Foundation Trust v AB & Ors* [2019] EWCOP 26.

96 *Re AB (Termination of Pregnancy)* [2019] EWCA Civ 1215.

97 Sam Rowlands, 'Learning Disability and Contraceptive Decision-Making' (2011) 37 J Fam Plan Reprod Health Care 173; Susan Ledger and others, 'Contraceptive Decision-Making and Women with Learning Disabilities' (2016) 19 Sexualities 698.

- Abortion was legalised in Britain by the AA 1967 but remains a criminal offence outside of the formal healthcare system.
- Abortion remained almost entirely prohibited in Northern Ireland until 2020 and is now partially decriminalised in this region of the UK.
- Contraception, including emergency contraception, is legally distinct from abortion and is not subject to criminal prohibition.
- Arguments for abortion law reform in the UK have recently focused on decriminalisation in Britain and the fetal disability ground.
- The concept of 'reproductive justice' can be applied to consider broader issues with the provision of abortion and contraception in the UK, particularly those concerning people from marginalised groups.

Questions for reflection

1. Why is access to abortion and contraception important?
2. To what extent does the UK's abortion law support pregnant people's reproductive autonomy?
3. Do you agree that abortion should be decriminalised in Britain? Why?
4. 'S.1(1)(d) Abortion Act 1967 discriminates against disabled people.' Critically discuss this statement.
5. How could the provision of contraception in the UK be improved in line with the concept of reproductive justice?

Recommended resources

- Fran Amery, *Beyond Pro-Life and Pro-Choice* (Bristol University Press 2020).
- Sharon Biggs Waller, *Girls on the Verge* (Henry Holt 2019).
- BPAS, Decolonising Contraception, Division of Health Research at Lancaster University, and Shine Aloud UK, 'Long-Acting Reversible Contraception in the UK' (2021) https://www.bpas.org/media/3477/larc-report-final-laid-up.pdf, accessed 20 October 2023.
- Annie Ernaux, *Happening* (Fitzcarraldo Press, 2019).
- Samantha Halliday and others, 'The (Mis)use of Fetal Viability as the Determinant of Non-Criminal Abortion in the Netherlands and England and Wales' (2023) 31 Med Law Rev 538–63.
- Laura Kaplan, *The Story of Jane: The Legendary Underground Feminist Abortion Service* (Vintage, 2022).
- Rishita Nandagiri, Ernestina Coast, and Joe Strong, 'COVID-19 and Abortion: Making Structural Violence Visible' (2020) 46 Int Perspec Sex Reprod Health 83.
- Elizabeth Chloe Romanis, 'Abortion Access and the Benefits and Limitations of Abortion-*Permissive* Legal Frameworks: Lessons from the United Kingdom' (2023) 32 Camb Q Healthc Ethics 378.

Bibliography

Aiken A and others, 'Barriers to Accessing Abortion Services and Perspectives on using Mifepristone and Misoprostol at Home in Great Britain' (2018) 97 Contraception 177

Amnesty International, 'Legal But Not Local: Barriers to Accessing Abortion Services in Northern Ireland' (7 December 2023) https://www.amnesty.org.uk/press-releases/northern-ireland-four-years-decriminalisation-abortion-access-right-not-reality-new, accessed 9 May 2024

Asch A, 'Prenatal Diagnosis and Selective Abortion: A Challenge to Practice and Policy' (1999) 89 Am J Public Health 1649

Balachandren N and others, 'Impact of the SARS-CoV-2 Pandemic on Access to Contraception and Pregnancy Intentions: A National Prospective Cohort Study of the UK Population' (2022) 48 BMJ Sex Reprod Health 60

Bloomer F and Fegan E, 'Critiquing Recent Abortion Law and Policy in Northern Ireland' (2013) 34 Crit Soc Pol 109

Delap N and Kitchen K, 'Why the Cost of Living Crisis is a Reproductive Justice Matter' (2023) 380 BMJ 118

DHSC (Department of Health and Social Care), 'Abortion Statistics, England and Wales: 2019' (2020) https://assets.publishing.service.gov.uk/government/uploads/system/uploads/attachment_data/file/891405/abortion-statistics-commentary-2019.pdf, accessed 19 October 2023

Family Planning Association, 'History of Family Planning' https://www.fpa.org.uk/medical-professional/factsheets/, accessed 20 October 2023

GMC (General Medical Council), 'Personal Beliefs and Medical Practice' (2013) https://www.gmc-uk.org/ethical-guidance/ethical-guidance-for-doctors/personal-beliefs-and-medical-practice, accessed 19 October 2023

Herring J, Jackson E, and Sheldon S, 'Would Decriminalisation Mean Deregulation?' in S Sheldon and K Wellings (eds), *Decriminalising Abortion in the UK: What Would it Mean* (Policy Press 2020)

Jackson E, *Regulating Reproduction* (Hart Publishing 2001)

Jones E, 'Attitudes to Abortion in the Era of Reform: Evidence from the Abortion Law Reform Association Correspondence' (2011) 20 Women's Hist Rev 283

Layhe E, Meisel A, and Talwar D, 'More Women Investigated for Illegal Terminations, Says Abortion Provider' (BBC News, 20 February 2024) https://www.bbc.co.uk/news/uk-68305991, accessed 9 May 2024

Ledger S and others, 'Contraceptive Decision-Making and Women with Learning Disabilities' (2016) 19 Sexualities 698

Lohr P, Lord J, and Rowlands S, 'How Would Decriminalisation Affect Women's Health?' in S Sheldon and K Wellings (eds) *Decriminalising Abortion in the UK: What Would It Mean?* (Policy Press 2020)

Lonergan G, 'Reproductive Justice and Migrant Women in Great Britain' (2012) 23 Women 26

Lowe P and Rowlands S, 'Long-Acting Reversible Contraception: Targeting those Judged to Be Unfit for Parenthood in the United States and the United Kingdom' (2022) 17 Glob Pub Health 3773

Luna Z and Luker K, 'Reproductive Justice' (2013) 9 Annu Rev Law Soc Sci 327

Mackenzie C, 'Abortion and Embodiment' (1992) 70 Australas J Philos 136

McGuinness S, 'Law, Reproduction, and Disability: Fatally "Handicapped"?' (2013) 21 Med Law Rev 213

McLeod C, 'Harm or Mere Inconvenience? Denying Women Emergency Contraception' (2010) 25 Hypatia 11

NHS Digital, 'Sexual and Reproductive Health Services, England (Contraception) 2021/2022' (2022) https://digital.nhs.uk/data-and-information/publications/statistical/sexual-and-reproductive-health-services/2021-22, accessed 19 October 2023

Office for Health Improvement and Disparities, 'Abortion Statistics, England and Wales: 2021' (2022) https://www.gov.uk/government/statistics/abortion-statistics-for-england-and-wales-2021/abortion-statistics-england-and-wales-2021, accessed 19 October 2023

Parsons JA and Romanis EC, *Early Medical Abortion, Equality of Access, and the Telemedical Imperative* (OUP 2021)

Piepmeier A, 'The Inadequacy of "Choice": Disability and What's Wrong with Feminist Framings of Reproduction' (2013) 39 Fem Stud 159

Romanis EC, '*R v Foster*: Exemplifying the Urgency of the Decriminalisation of Abortion' (2023) 31 Med Law Rev 606

Romanis EC, Parsons JA and Hodson N, 'COVID-19 and Reproductive Justice in Great Britain and the United States: Ensuring Access to Abortion Care during a Global Pandemic' (2020) 7 J Law Biosci https://doi.org/10.1093/jlb/lsaa027, accessed 11 July 2024

Rowlands S, 'Learning disability and contraceptive decision-making' (2011) 37 J Fam Plan Reprod Health Care 173

Scott S, 'Risks, Reasons and Rights: The European Convention on Human Rights and English Abortion Law' (2015) 24 Med Law Rev 1

Self B, Maxwell C, and Fleming V, 'The Missing Voices in the Conscientious Objection Debate: British Service Users' Experiences of Conscientious Objection to Abortion' (2023) 24 BMC Med Ethics 1

Shakespeare T, 'Choices and Rights: Eugenics, Genetics and Disability Equality' (1998) 13 Disabil Soc 665

Sheldon S, *Beyond Control* (Pluto Press 1997)

Sheldon S, 'The Decriminalisation of Abortion: An Argument for Modernisation' (2016) 36 OJLS 334

Sheldon S, 'How Can a State Control Swallowing? The Home Use of Abortion Pills in Ireland' (2016) 24 RHM 90

Sheldon S and Lord J, 'Care Not Criminalisation: Reform of British Abortion Law is Long Overdue' (2023) 49 JME 523

Sheldon S and Wilkinson S, 'Termination of Pregnancy for Reason of Foetal Disability: Are There Grounds for a Special Exception in Law?' (2001) 9 Med Law Rev 85

Sherwin S, 'Abortion through a Feminist Ethics Lens' (1991) 30 Dialogue 327

Sister Song, 'About Us' https://www.sistersong.net/about-x2, accessed 20 October 2023

Thomson JJ, 'A Defense of Abortion' (1971) 1 Philos Pub Aff 47

Tongue ZL, '*Crowter v Secretary of State for Health and Social Care* [2021] EWHC 2536: Discrimination, Disability, and Access to Abortion' (2022) 30 Med Law Rev 177

Tongue ZL, 'Human Rights and Foetal Impairment Grounds for Abortion: *Crowter v Secretary of State for Health and Social Care* [2022] EWCA Civ 1559' (2023) 23 Med Law Int 297

Tongue ZL, 'On Conscientious Objection to Abortion: Questioning Mandatory Referral as Compromise in the International Human Rights Framework' (2022) 22 Med Law Int 349

Tongue ZL, 'Telemedical and Self-Managed Abortion: A Human Rights Imperative?' (2023) 30 Eur J Health Law 15

15

Pregnancy and Birth

Elizabeth Chloe Romanis and Zaina Mahmoud

Lady Hale's declaration in *Montgomery v Lanarkshire Health Board*, that 'gone are the days when it was thought that, on becoming pregnant, a woman lost, not only her capacity, but also her right to act as a genuinely autonomous human being',[1] is jarring against the backdrop of pregnancy care in the UK. This was exemplified during the COVID-19 pandemic, in which measures extensively restricted birthing people's rights and many were denied fundamental pregnancy/birth choices, such as where or how to give birth.[2] Long after pubs and restaurants opened, pregnant people had to attend antenatal appointments alone, sometimes to receive difficult news, and/or gave birth alone.[3] In 2024, the All-Party Parliamentary Group on Birth Trauma published their inquiry results, concluding the UK has 'a maternity system where poor care is all-too-frequently tolerated as normal, and women treated as an inconvenience'.[4]

Chapters about pregnancy/birth in health law textbooks are uncommon, notwithstanding the frequency of these issues in discussions on negligence and capacity and the fact that pregnancy/birth affects a lot of people. In this chapter, we consider law and healthcare policy around pregnancy and birth, highlighting how institutional racist and gendered assumptions about pregnant/birthing people preclude them from experiencing their desired birth (and pregnancy) and/or

1 *Montgomery v Lanarkshire Health Board* [2015] UKSC 11 at [16].

2 Elizabeth Chloe Romanis and Anna Nelson, 'Maternal Request Caesareans and COVID-19: The Virus Does Not Diminish the Importance of Choice in Childbirth' (2020) 46 J Med Ethics 726; Anna Nelson and Elizabeth Chloe Romanis, 'Homebirthing in the United Kingdom during COVID-19' (2020) 20 Med Law Int 183.

3 Sophy Ridge, 'Some Hospitals Still Not Allowing Partners to Be Present during Labour' (25 October 2020) https://news.sky.com/story/some-hospitals-still-not-allowing-partners-to-be-present-at-childbirth-12113859, accessed 24 April 2024.

4 AAPG on Birth Trauma, 'Ending the Postcode Lottery on Perinatal Care', https://www.theo-clarke.org.uk/sites/www.theo-clarke.org.uk/files/2024-05/Birth%20Trauma%20Inquiry%20Report%20for%20Publication_May13_2024_0.pdf, accessed 16 May 2024, 9.

seriously impact their health and wellbeing, and, in the most tragic cases, come at the cost of their lives.

Though medico-legal language and culture around pregnancy/birth are hyper-gendered, we describe people physiologically capable of pregnancy/birth in gender-neutral language. Using 'woman' when referring to those capable of pregnancy/birth is too narrow to encompass all physiologically capable,[5] simultaneously it erases the experiences of trans masculine, non-binary, and/or genderqueer birthing people. Reiterating pregnancy is 'something that women do' directly contributes to gender dysphoria experienced by non-women physiologically capable of pregnancy/birth.[6] Moreover, 'woman' is too broad a descriptor of people physiologically capable of pregnancy/birth, as many women (assigned female at birth or not) do not have this capability.[7] Describing pregnant people as 'mothers' – while common – is inappropriate, presupposing their intentions.[8] As people capable of pregnancy were taken as women, pregnant people's treatment remains rooted in socialised and medicalised gender norms,[9] and they face considerable structural discrimination – discrimination by institutions and societal conventions (among other things) that 'legitimises and normalises indirect forms of negative treatment of the "others" and makes it a part of everyday normal life of society'.[10] This chapter shows recognition and exploration of structural discrimination without gender-specific language is possible.

Obstetric violence

Latin American activists coined the term obstetric violence to refer to gender- and race-based injustice 'expressed in the specific techniques and power relations of obstetrics' (healthcare during pregnancy and birth, and after birth).[11] Examples

5 Loretta Ross and Rickie Solinger, *Reproductive Justice: An Introduction* (University of California Press 2017), 7.

6 Gender dysphoria occurs when a person's gender identity does not align with their gender assigned at birth. Kinnon MacKinnon and others, 'Recognizing and Renaming in Obstetrics: How Do We Take Better Care With Language?' (2021) 14 Obstet Med 201.

7 Ross and Solinger (n5).

8 Zaina Mahmoud and Elizabeth Chloe Romanis, 'On Gestation and Motherhood' (2023) 31 Med Law Rev 109.

9 Elizabeth Chloe Romanis and others, 'Reviewing the Womb' (2021) 47 J Med Ethics 820–9; Suki Finn and others, 'Pregnancy: Transformations in Philosophy and Legal Practice' in G. Anthony Bruno and Justin Vlastis (eds), *Rewriting the History of Philosophy: Transformations* (Routledge 2023).

10 Masoud Kamali, *Racial Discrimination: Institutional Patterns and Politics* (Routledge 2009) 6.

11 C.R. Williams and others, 'Obstetric Violence: A Latin American Legal Response to Mistreatment during Childbirth' (2018) 25 BJOG 1208; Rodante van der Waal and Kaveri Mayra, 'Obstetric Violence' in Parveen Ali and Michaela M. Rogers (eds), *Gender-Based Violence: A Comprehensive Guide* (SpringerLink 2023), 415

include 'nonconsensual procedures, neglect, gaslighting, surrogate decision-making, shaming, and discrimination' during obstetric care.[12]

Some argue 'violence' to describe neglect, gaslighting, shaming, and discrimination is too extreme and provocative, or that 'violence' is incorrect as 'neither medicine nor health care staff are violent by nature'.[13] Others characterise such care as 'neglect' or silencing, since 'both staff and patients are victims and both collude with the defensive neglect of silence',[14] objecting to 'violence' where the harm occurring is not physical. However, Chadwick explains how naming it 'violence' precipitates rejection of the normalisation of such treatment and its silencing, diminishing, and erasure of birthing people's experiences.[15] More subtle terminology, like mistreatment or disrespect, discounts how obstetric violence is structural and institutionalised, rather than due to individual healthcare providers' intentions.

Obstetric violence is a global phenomenon[16] – the UK is no exception. NHS organisational failures foster uneven power dynamics and abusive environments; systematic and systemic failures result in denial of pain relief during birth.[17] Government reports reveal how systematic failures of the kind described in the definition of obstetric violence led to a culture of traumatic births and the preventable

12 Rodante van der Waal and others, 'Obstetric Violence: An Intersection Refraction through Abolition Feminism' (2023) 4 Fem Anthropol 91.

13 Ximena Briceño Morales, Laura Victoria Enciso Chaves, and Carlos Enrique Yepes Delgado, 'Neither Medicine Nor Health Care Staff Members Are Violent By Nature: Obstetric Violence from an Interactionist Perspective' (2018) 28 Qual Health Res 1308, 1314; Frank Chervenak and others, 'Obstetric Violence is a Misnomer' (2024) 230 Am J Obstet Gynecol S1138.

14 Maura Lappeman and Leslie Swatz, 'Rethinking Obstetric Violence and the "Neglect of Neglect": The Silence of a Labour Ward Milieu in a South African District Hospital' (2019) 19 BMC Int Health Hum Rights 30, 41; see also Maura Lappeman and Leslie Swatz, 'How Gentle Must Violence Against Women Be in Order to Not Be Violent? Rethinking the Word "Violence" in Obstetric Settings' (2021) 27 Violence Against Women 987.

15 Rachelle Chadwick, 'Breaking the Frame: Obstetric Violence and Epistemic Rupture' (2021) 35 Agenda 104, 109; see also Camilla Pickles, '"Obstetric Violence", "Mistreatment", and "Disrespect and Abuse": Reflections on the Politics of Naming Violations during Facility-Based Childbirth' (2023) 38 Hypatia 628.

16 See Carlos Herrera Vacaflor, 'Obstetric Violence: A New Framework for Identifying Challenges to Maternal Healthcare in Argentina' (2016) 24 Reprod Health Matters 65; Dinusha Perera and others, 'Obstetric Violence is Prevalent in Routine Maternity Care: A Cross-Sectional Study of Obstetric Violence and its Associated Factors among Pregnant Women in Sri Lanka's Colombo District' (2022) 19 Int J Environ Res Public Health 99997.

17 Amelia Hill, '" I Asked Three Times for an Epidural": Why Are Women Being Denied Pain Relief during Childbirth?' (2020) https://www.theguardian.com/lifeandstyle/2020/mar/04/i-asked-three-times-for-an-epidural-why-are-women-being-denied-pain-relief, accessed 3 December 2023.

deaths of birthing people and babies at Shrewsbury and Telford,[18] and in East Kent.[19]

On an individual level, power imbalances between doctors and patients contribute to a culture of silencing and coercion and considerable pressure to comply with healthcare providers. 'Good' patients defer to healthcare providers,[20] who are presumed to be knowledgeable, unbiased, and objective.[21] Though informed consent involves the ability to engage in refusal, patients often report feeling powerless.[22] A recent report found, frequently, consent was not sought during obstetric care, with instances of coercion and obstetric violence.[23] Such failures fall short of legal standards set out in the Human Rights Act 1998 and *Montgomery*.

Herring argues obstetric violence is 'a programme of coercive control against women' embodying the patriarchy, similar to other violence against women.[24] Considering obstetric violence solely through a gender-based approach obscures how gender is entangled with multiple axes of power, marginalisation, and privilege; and, furthermore, that 'woman' is an inadequate term. Chadwick argues obstetric violence is 'shaped by racialised, medicalised and classed norms about "good patients", "good women" and "good birthing bodies"'.[25] Dominant ideologies on motherhood are underpinned by beliefs and experiences of white middle-class women and their families,[26] taken (implicitly) as standard. Research exploring obstetric health inequities reveals treatment as dependent on various factors (e.g., race, gender identity, marriage, income, education), and those without certain social protections (being married, having a high income, and being better educated) face a higher risk of obstetric violence. Only through an intersectional approach,[27] factoring in pregnant people's intersecting

18 Independent Maternity Review, 'Findings, Conclusions and Essential Actions from the Independent Review of Maternity Services at the Shrewsbury and Telford Hospital NHS Trust [Ockenden Report]' (2022) https://assets.publishing.service.gov.uk/media/624332fe8fa8f527744f0615/Final-Ockenden-Report-web-accessible.pdf, accessed 28 November 2023.

19 DHSC (Department of Health and Social Care), 'Reading the Signals: Maternity and Neonatal Services in East Kent: The Report of the Independent Investigation [Kirkup Inquiry]' (HC 681, 2022); AAPG on Birth Trauma (n4).

20 Karin Martin, 'Giving Birth Like a Girl' (2003) 17 Gender & Soc 54.

21 Ruha Benjamin, 'Informed Refusal: Toward a Justice-Based Bioethics' (2016) 41 Sci Tech Hum Values 967, 978

22 Dominick Frosch and others, 'Authoritarian Physicians and Patients' Fear of Being Labeled "Difficult" among Key Obstacles to Shared Decision Making' (2012) 31 Health Aff (Millwood) 1030, 1033.

23 Birthrights, 'Systemic Racism, Not Broken Bodies: An Inquiry into Racial Injustice and Human Rights in UK Maternity Care' (2022) https://www.birthrights.org.uk/wp-content/uploads/2022/05/Birthrights-inquiry-systemic-racism_exec-summary_May-22-web.pdf, accessed 28 November 2023.

24 Jonathan Herring, 'Identifying the Wrong in Obstetric Violence' in Camilla Pickles and Jonathan Herring (eds), *Childbirth, Vulnerability and Law: Exploring Issues of Violence and Control* (Routledge 2019).

25 Rachelle Chadwick, 'Ambiguous Subjects: Obstetric Violence, Assemblage and South African Birth Narratives' (2017) 27 Fem Psychol 489, 504.

26 Sharon Hays, *The Cultural Contradictions of Motherhood* (Yale University Press 1996).

27 For more detail on intersectionality see discussion in Chapter 1.

marginalised identities, like those previously mentioned, can we understand obstetric violence.

Obstetric racism

In the UK, Black pregnant/birthing people are five times more likely, and mixed ethnicity and Asian pregnant/birthing people twice as likely, to die during pregnancy and birth than white pregnant/birthing people.[28] Black pregnant/birthing people experience higher rates of anxiety and immune system responses compared to white pregnant people.[29] Such health outcome disparities have been attributed to 'biological racial differences',[30] with racialised people over-medicalised and deemed high risk.[31] Pathologisation, the unfair or incorrect consideration of something/someone as a medical problem, and devaluation of racialised pregnant/birthing people divert attention from a key factor: medical racism – healthcare providers' perceptions, treatments, and/or diagnostic decisions influenced by a patient's race, placing the patient at risk.[32]

Obstetric violence has been driven by racial capitalism, with modern obstetrics born during the antebellum period through experiments on enslaved Black women[33] perceived as 'much stronger than white women' with 'obstetrical hardiness' or a 'primitive pelvis'.[34] Such beliefs persist, resulting in 'profound disregard' for Black lives:[35] Black pregnant/birthing people are subjected to decreased physical and psychological safety, and are frequently ignored, with their reports of pain disbelieved due to harmful racist misconceptions, for example, being more likely to abuse pain medication or having a higher pain tolerance.[36] Even when socio-economic class and education

28 Marian Knight and others, 'Saving Lives, Improving Mothers' Care Core Report: Lessons Learned to Inform Maternity Care from the UK and Ireland Confidential Enquiries into Maternal Deaths and Morbidity 2018–20' (2022) https://www.npeu.ox.ac.uk/assets/downloads/mbrrace-uk/reports/maternal-report-2022/MBRRACE-UK_Maternal_MAIN_Report_2022_UPDATE.pdf, accessed 28 November 2023.

29 Janet Catov and others, 'The Relationship between Race, Inflammation and Psychosocial Factors among Pregnant Women' (2015) 19 Matern Child Health J 401.

30 Allison Bryant and others, 'Equality in Obstetric Care: Racial and Ethnic Differences in Caesarean Section Delivery Rates' (2009) 23 Paediatr Perinat Epidemiol 454.

31 Khiara M. Bridges, *Reproducing Race: An Ethnography of Pregnancy as a Site of Racialization* (Univeristy of California Press 2011) 111–12.

32 Benjamin (n21).

33 Dorothy Roberts, *Killing the Black Body: Race, Reproduction, and the Meaning of Liberty* (Pantheon Books 1997) ch 1; Rochelle Maurice, 'We Bawl So We Are Heard: The Stories We Must Tell About Obstetric Racism' (2023) 31 Sex Repro Health Matters 1, 3.

34 Bridges (n31) 117–18; Deirdre Cooper Owens, *Medical Bondage: Race, Gender, and the Origins of American Gynecology* (University of Georgia Press 2017) 21.

35 Owens (n34) 77.

36 Dána-Ain Davis, 'Obstetric Racism: The Racial Politics of Pregnancy, Labor, and Birthing' (2019) 38 Med Anthropol Q 560; Vani Mathur, Theresa Morris, and Kelly McNamara, 'Cultural Conceptions of Women's Labor Pain and Labor Pain Management: A Mixed-Method Analysis' (2020) 261 Soc Sci Med 113240.

are considered, Black pregnant/birthing people experience higher rates of morbidity and mortality than white people experiencing socio-economic deprivation.[37]

Birthrights, a charity campaigning for the rights of birthing people, took systematic racism as the starting point for their inquiry into health disparities within maternity care, 'Systematic Racism, Not Broken Bodies'. The report highlighted how Black, Brown, and mixed ethnicity pregnant/birthing people were disproportionately affected by structural barriers to care, regularly dehumanised, ignored, and felt unsafe. Racism and racial discrimination directly impacted on a sense of safety during maternity care.[38] Black, Brown, and mixed ethnicity pregnant/birthing people described how healthcare providers disbelieved and dismissed concerns. They described being seen as less credible due to prejudicial bias about their intersecting marginalised identities (gender, social background, ethnicity, race, sexuality); they experienced testimonial injustice.[39]

Responding to obstetric violence

Combatting racial inequality and obstetric violence requires changes in healthcare delivery.[40] Currently, maternity services struggle to provide healthcare meeting diverse populations' needs. Culturally competent services tailor healthcare provision to meet patients' social, cultural, and linguistic needs, partially – but not entirely – achieved when birthing people feel represented by healthcare providers.[41] However, service delivery changes alone may be insufficient.

Some jurisdictions introduced a specific criminal offence of obstetric violence. In 2007, Venezuela was the first to *legally* define obstetric violence, criminalising:

> the appropriation of the body and reproductive processes of women by health personnel, which is expressed as dehumanized treatment, an abuse of medication, and to convert the natural processes into pathological ones, bringing with it loss of autonomy and the ability to decide freely about their bodies and sexuality, negatively impacting the quality of life of women.[42]

Other Latin American countries, including Argentina and Uruguay, followed suit shortly after. Though some obstetric violence is captured by other broader

37 Emily Petersen and others, 'Racial/Ethnic Disparities in Pregnancy-Related Deaths: United States, 2007–2016' (2019) 68 MMWR 762, 763.

38 Birthrights (n23).

39 Miranda Fricker, *Epistemic Injustice: Power and the Ethics of Knowing* (OUP 2007).

40 Birthrights (n23).

41 Thu T. Nguyen and others, 'Racism during Pregnancy and Birthing: Experiences from Asian and Pacific Islander, Black, Latina, and Middle Eastern Women' (2022) J Racial Ethn Health Disparities 1.

42 Rogelio Pérez D'Gregorio, 'Obstetric Violence: A New Legal Term Introduced in Venezuela' (2010) 111 Int J Gynaecol Obstet 201.

offences,[43] the UK has no specific criminal offence. Pickles argues this is unsurprising: criminal law reflects what society deems the most serious wrongs, with women's experiences often ignored. Writing about unauthorised vaginal examinations in South Africa, she argues for a specific criminal offence of obstetric violence, explaining how the lack of a specific offence signals that these are 'not serious enough to capture the criminal law's attention'.[44] Similarly, Brennan argues for clear identification and labelling of maternity abuse, suggesting reforms informed 'by women's experiences and cognisant of and responsive to the gendered [and racialised] roots of the harm involved'.[45] Criminal law is limited; in the context of institutional abuses and failures, a criminal deterrent emphasising individual responsibility may be ineffective, unintentionally penalising marginalised healthcare professionals.[46]

Obstetric violence and racism are a reality of maternity care, which is why we have started here. The next key issues explored – choice in birth and controlling of pregnant people's behaviour – are manifestations of obstetric violence.

Choice and birth

Acknowledging pregnancy/birth as deeply personal, important, life-changing experiences, the law has long recognised that people must be able to make (some) decisions about birth. Denying 'choices about childbirth forces [people] to relinquish their identity by surrendering to certain life-altering experiences over others'.[47] A series of cases reiterates how pregnant people must be allowed to refuse medical interventions in birth, even where their life or the fetus' life is threatened.[48]

> A competent woman who has the capacity to decide may, for religious reasons, other reasons, for rational or irrational reasons or for no reason at all, choose not to have medical intervention, even though

43 Karen Brennan, 'Reflections on Criminalising Obstetric Violence: A Feminist Perspective' in Camilla Pickles and Jonathan Herring (eds), *Childbirth, Vulnerability and Law* (Routledge 2019) 226.

44 Camilla Pickles, 'When "Battery" is Not Enough: Exposing the Gaps in Unauthorised Vaginal Examinations during Labour as a Crime of Battery' in Camilla Pickles and Jonathan Herring (eds), *Women's Birthing Bodies and the Law: Unauthorised Intimate Examinations, Power and Vulnerability* (Bloomsbury 2020) 127.

45 Brennan (n43) 231–44.

46 See Chapter 8.

47 Elizabeth Chloe Romanis, 'Why the Elective Caesarean Lottery is Ethically Impermissible' (2019) 27 Health Care Anal 249, 255.

48 *St George's Healthcare NHS Trust v S* [1998] 3 All ER 673; *Re MB (Medical Treatment)* [1997] 2 FLR 426 (CA); *Guys and St Thomas NHS Foundation Trust (GSTT) & South London and Maudsley NHS Foundation Trust (SLAM) v R* [2020] EWCOP 4.

> the consequence may be the death or serious handicap of the child she bears, or her own death.[49]

A capacitous pregnant person may refuse medical interventions or disagree with medical advice regarding the management of their birth. A person's incompetence cannot be assumed in any medical context,[50] so they should not be assumed to be incompetent when pregnant and/or giving birth[51] – however, in practice they often are.[52] Ultimately, choice is systematically denied to certain birthing people – particularly, people with serious mental illnesses.[53] That pregnant people can refuse medical interventions in birth does not shed any light on whether positive choices about birth (*asking for* certain forms of support) are respected. Emphasising individual autonomy in birth recognises the very personal nature of birth, while obscuring institutional failures resulting in obstetric violence, including denial of choice.

Limits on choice: capacity

The right to refuse intervention in birth is 'undermined by the courts use of available common law resources in determining capacity,'[54] and legal recognition of implied consent.[55] Forced caesarean section (C/S) cases involve pregnant people seeking to refuse a C/S, but courts find they lack capacity, and thus birth decisions can be made in their best interests. Such cases suggest that 'by virtue of the conditions of labour, birthing people are not sufficiently capable of decision-making'.[56] The extent to which incapacity is assumed is seen in recent comments by Hayden J:

> loss of capacity in the process of labour may crucially inhibit a woman's entitlement to make choices. At this stage the court is required to step in to protect her recognising that this will always require a complex,

49 *Re MB* (n48) at [30].

50 MCA (Mental Capacity Act) 2005 s 1(2).

51 *Re MB* (n48) at [39].

52 Samantha Halliday, *Autonomy and Pregnancy: A Comparative Analysis of Compelled Obstetric Intervention* (Routledge 2016).

53 Samantha Halliday, 'Court-Authorised Obstetric Intervention: Insight and Capacity, a Tale of Loss' in Camilla Pickles and Jonathan Herring (eds), *Childbirth, Vulnerability and Law: Exploring Issues of Violence and Control* (Routledge 2019) 182.

54 John Harrington, 'Privileging the Medical Norm: Liberalism, Self-Determination and Refusal of Treatment' (1996) 16 Leg Stud 348, 358.

55 Jonathan Herring, 'Implied Consent and Vaginal Examination in Pregnancy' in Camilla Pickles and Jonathan Herring (eds), *Women's Birthing Bodies and the Law: Unauthorised Intimate Examinations, Power and Vulnerability* (Bloomsbury 2020).

56 Anna Nelson and Elizabeth Chloe Romanis, 'The Medicalisation of Childbirth and Access to Homebirth in the UK: COVID-19 and Beyond' (2021) 29 Med Law Rev 661, 675.

> delicate and sensitive evaluation of a range of her competing rights and interests.[57]

Such *dicta* imply birthing threatens capacity and undermines birthing people's decisions to the point that doctors can legally challenge their decisions. The notion of the 'good patient' (as described above) means disagreeing with medical advice is taken as evidence of incompetence.[58]

Where a birthing person lacks capacity, courts *always* order the recommended medical intervention (that the person is refusing) in their best interests, often with little analysis explaining *why* such decisions were reached. Deciding an intervention is in a person's best interests is not merely a question of clinical considerations,[59] but with forced C/S, clinical considerations are heavily weighed. Their determinative nature is rooted in assumptions about birthing people's desires, based on gendered assumptions about the pregnant person 'as a mother', prioritising their fetus above all else.

In *DD*, Cobb J declared:'it must be in the best of any woman carrying a full-term child whom she wants to be born alive and healthy that such a result should if possible be achieved'.[60] Notwithstanding this assumption's potential merit applied to wanted pregnancies, its operation as 'universal and automatic'[61] without consideration of individual circumstances is problematic, especially in forced C/S with use of restraints. Why are both traumatic outcomes (forced treatment *and* potentially serious complications) not fully considered?

The Mental Capacity Act (MCA) 2005 emphasises patient participation when making best interests' decisions. Past and present views are recognised, as is the incapacitated person's potential decision, if they had capacity.[62] The MCA Code of Practice introduces a positive obligation to ensure 'all practical means are used to enable and encourage [an incapacitated person] to participate as fully as possible in the decision-making process and any [resulting] action'.[63] Where are the voices of 'incapacitated' people at risk of forced C/S? Often, pregnant people do not have legal representation; sometimes, the Official Solicitor is involved,[64] but – importantly – not to represent the pregnant person, but their

---

57 *GSST & SLAM v R* (n48) at [67].

58 Halliday (n53) 179.

59 MCA 2005, s 4(2); *Aintree University Hospital NHS Foundation Trust v James* [2013] UKSC 67.

60 *The Mental Health Trust, The Acute Trust, The Council v DD* [2014] EWCOP 11, [97].

61 Sara Fovargue, 'In Whose Best Interests? Childbirth Choices and Other Health Decisions' (2021) 137 Law Q Rev 604.

62 MCA 2005, s 4(6).

63 Office of the Public Guardian, 'Mental Capacity Act Code of Practice' (2007) https://assets.publishing.service.gov.uk/media/5f6cc6138fa8f541f6763295/Mental-capacity-act-code-of-practice.pdf, accessed 28 November 2023, [5.23].

64 The Official Solicitor works for the Ministry of Justice and is appointed in cases to help those deemed to lack mental capacity to make decisions.

'best interests'.[65] Halliday notes how judges in cases involving other health needs have been known to meet patients and listen to their motivations for refusing treatment, yet this does not appear to have happened for pregnant people.[66]

Most cases dealing with refusals of birth interventions involve pregnant people with serious mental illnesses,[67] often with complex safety concerns due to medication (e.g., anti-psychotic medication). Particularly troubling is that these cases are often described as 'urgent', either immediately before or as the pregnant person is in labour. 'Urgent' circumstances requiring quick decisions have been criticised: decision-making in emergencies often leads the 'law to abandon its own processes of deliberation'.[68] Pain and stress in pregnancy and birth may seemingly be relied upon to justify medical interventions, without more specific explanation of their effect on the capacity of the pregnant/birthing person or interrogating their best interests. Consequently, Court of Appeal and High Court judgments have stressed that potential issues (such as disagreements where it might be thought the pregnant person lacks capacity or could lack capacity) should be brought to the courts ahead of time.[69] This is particularly important for people with serious mental illnesses who want to be involved in birth decisions earlier in their pregnancy should their health deteriorate.

Recent cases involve doctors seeking 'anticipatory declarations' about what would be lawful if a pregnant person became incapacitated.[70] Though more time to deliberate and the pregnant person's involvement are good, such cases carry risks. Are doctors with court orders 'in their back pockets' less incentivised to pursue a collaborative approach if a pregnant person disagrees with their advice?[71] Fovargue highlights how judges framing anticipatory declarations as 'autonomy protecting' is rather *extraordinary*, as the court is deciding *while the person has capacity* what should happen when/if the pregnant person lacks capacity.[72]

Limits on choice: reasonable alternatives and policy decisions

People's preferences about how and where to give birth are varied and often based on very personal motivations. Some prefer vaginal births, others request C/S (typically defined as a C/S not clinically indicated, though this is a bit of a

65 Halliday (n53) 196–7.

66 Ibid.

67 Ibid 182.

68 John Harrington, 'Time as a Dimension of Medical Law' (2012) 20 Med Law Rev 491, 511.

69 *Re MB* (n48); *NHS Trust & Ors v FG* [2014] EWCOP 30.

70 *United Lincolnshire NHS Hospitals Trust v CD* [2019] EWCOP 24; *GSST & SLAM v R* (n48).

71 Jonathan Herring, *Medical Law and Ethics* (9th edn, OUP 2022) 445.

72 Sara Fovargue, 'Anticipating Issues with Capacitous Pregnant Women: *United Lincolnshire NHS Hospitals Trust v CD* [2019] EWCOP 24 and *Guys and St Thomas' NHS Foundation Trust (GSTT) and South London and Maudsley NHS Foundation Trust (SLAM) v R* [2020] EWCOP 4' (2020) 28 Med Law Rev 781, 792.

misconception).[73] Some feel strongly about hospital births in a midwifery unit with support; others prefer to birth at home (with or without midwives present). Law recognises capacitous patients' refusal of medical interventions, but not an ability to *demand* specific treatment.[74] Patients must be informed of reasonable clinical alternative treatments, including in birth (see Box 15.1).[75]

Box 15.1: Key case: *Montgomery v Lanarkshire Health Board* [2015] UKSC 11

Nadine Montgomery was a small woman and, as a Type I diabetic, was likely to have a larger fetus. There was a risk that she would face labour complications.

There was a 9–10 per cent risk of shoulder dystocia (where the fetus's shoulders become stuck in the birth canal). Nadine asked about any specific risks in delivering vaginally, given her diabetes and small stature, but her doctor did not inform her of the risk of shoulder dystocia.

During childbirth, shoulder dystocia occurred, depriving the fetus of oxygen, and consequently, Nadine's son Sam was born with cerebral palsy.

Nadine pursued an action in negligence, alleging the doctor breached their duty of care by failing to inform her about the risk of shoulder dystocia and that an elective C/S should have been performed.

In the majority judgment delivered by Lord Kerr and Lord Reed, it was held that:

> The doctor is therefore under a duty to take reasonable care to ensure that the patient is aware of any material risks involved in any recommended treatment, and of any reasonable alternative or variant treatments. The test of materiality is whether, in the circumstances of the particular case, a reasonable person in the patient's position would be likely to attach significance to the risk, or the doctor is or should reasonably be aware that the particular patient would be likely to attach significance to it.

The Supreme Court unanimously found in favour of Nadine: her doctor should have informed her of the risk of shoulder dystocia and the possibility of an elective C/S.

(Over)medicalisation of birth and associated policy decisions result in the normalisation of vaginal births in healthcare settings.[76] Request C/S and

---

73 Elizabeth Chloe Romanis, 'Appropriately Framing Maternal Request Caesarean Section' (2022) 48 J Med Ethics 554; Rebecca Brown and Andrea Mulligan, '"Maternal Request" Caesarean Sections and Medical Necessity' (2023) 18 Clin Ethics 312.

74 *R (Burke) v General Medical Council* [2005] EWCA Civ 1003.

75 *Montgomery* (n1); *McCulloch and Others (Appellants) v Forth Valley Health Board (Respondent) (Scotland)* [2023] UKSC 26.

76 Nelson and Romanis (n56) 673.

homebirths are safe, with neither clinically unjustifiable in most circumstances.[77] The National Institute of Health and Clinical Excellence (NICE) recommends healthcare professionals explain the option of homebirths during prenatal care.[78] Prior to 2023, NICE guidelines allowed request C/S, specifying they should not be routinely offered and healthcare professionals should examine the reasons for this preference.[79] These guidelines were criticised: request C/S and vaginal deliveries are comparatively risky, though with different risks, such that request C/S should be routinely discussed during counselling about birth.[80] The 2023 update is more clearly supportive of choice: healthcare professionals should provide accurate and balanced information about C/S, offer to discuss the reasons for the preference, and discuss alternatives, but ultimately:

> If, after an informed discussion about the options for birth (including the offer of perinatal mental health support if appropriate …), the woman or pregnant person requests a caesarean birth, support their choice.[81]

Previous policy allowed hospitals to refer request C/S patients elsewhere,[82] but the updated guidance states request C/S should be offered within the obstetric unit where the pregnant person is receiving care.[83] Importantly, this ensures equal access to request C/S: travelling to a different obstetric unit/hospital may be harder for many (people with disabilities, people from lower socio-economic groups, younger people, people from racialised groups experiencing bias surrounding birthing decisions, and people who do not speak English as a first language).[84] Despite the guidance, in reality, local NHS trusts' policies dictate available birth choices, and access to request C/S and homebirth depends on where an individual lives (a 'postcode lottery'). Increased C/S costs (around £700 more than vaginal births) are cited as a barrier to their provision within an overstretched NHS.[85] However, factoring postpartum mental healthcare costs

77 On request caesarean, see Romanis (n47); on homebirths see Nelson and Romanis (n2).

78 NICE (National Institute for Health and Care Excellence), 'Intrapartum Care for Healthy Women and Babies: CG190' (2014) https://www.nice.org.uk/guidance/cg190, accessed 28 November 2023, [1.1.2].

79 For a summary of what the guidelines *used* to say and critique: see Romanis (n47) 251.

80 Ibid 252. See also Elizabeth Chloe Romanis, 'Addressing Rising Caesarean Rates: Maternal Request Caesareans, Defensive Practice, and the Power of Choice in Childbirth' (2020) 13 Int J Fem Appro Bioethics 1.

81 NICE (National Institute of Health and Care Excellence), 'Caesarean Birth: NG192' (2021) https://www.nice.org.uk/guidance/ng192, accessed 28 November 2023, [1.2.25] and [1.2.29].

82 Romanis (n47).

83 NICE (n78) [1.2.30].

84 Ibid.

85 Birthrights, 'Maternal Request Caesarean Sections' (2018) https://www.birthrights.org.uk/wp-content/uploads/2018/08/Final-Birthrights-MRCS-Report-2108-1.pdf, accessed 28 November 2023.

for those denied choices in birth reveal C/S as cheaper (and less harmful) than denying these requests.[86]

Maternity care during COVID-19 demonstrated how easily institutional structures disregarded the importance of choice in birth.[87] Brione describes how 'at the first sign of pressures, the shutters came down, and restrictions were brought in',[88] as hospital births were the norm; C/S and homebirth availability dramatically and quickly reduced.[89] Many birthing people were alone or accompanied by one person after a certain point in labour (often determined by unnecessary and coerced vaginal examinations).[90] Blanket suspension of request C/S and homebirths were disproportionate and violated human rights:[91] beyond accommodating preferences about often transformative but difficult experiences, choices about and in birth are important, given the stark mental health impact of disregarding such preferences.

Controlling behaviour in pregnancy

Pregnant people are overwhelmed with advice about appropriate behaviour promoting fetal welfare,[92] with intense medical and social scrutiny of diet and activities. Bowden explains how 'there is a growing trend for presenting prenatal harm as a problem of individual behaviour'.[93] What is the law's response when healthcare professionals believe the fetus is harmed by a pregnant person?

Often, public health messaging about pregnancy is contradictory and confusing, supported by limited evidence: for example, a glass of wine while pregnant is *good*, though simultaneously abstinence from any and all alcohol is critical. Importantly, for most substances, only *excessive* use causes fetal harm;[94] the occasional glass of wine does not cause fetal alcohol spectrum disorder (FASD). Pregnant people misusing substances are vulnerable, often due to socio-economic hardship, addiction, and/or violence.[95] Structural factors, including a lack of

86 Nelson and Romanis (n2).

87 Anna Collinson, 'Coronavirus: Uncertainty over Maternity Care Causing Distress' (2020) https://www.bbc.co.uk/news/health-52356067, accessed 24 April 2024.

88 Rebecca Brione, 'Person-Centred Maternity Care: COVID Exposes the Illusion' (2022) 15 Int J Fem Appr Bioethics 131, 143.

89 Nelson and Romanis (n2).

90 Anna Nelson, 'Vaginal Examinations during Childbirth: Consent, Coercion, and COVID-19' (2021) 29 Fem Leg Stud 119.

91 MacKinnon and others (n6).

92 Emily Jackson, *Regulating Reproduction: Law, Technology and Autonomy* (Hart Publishing 2001) 135.

93 Catherine Bowden, 'Is the Unequal Treatment of Maternal and Paternal Liability under the Congenital Disabilities (Civil Liability) Act 1976 Justified?' (2022) 30 Med Law Rev 457.

94 Betsy Thom, Rachel Herring, and Emma Milne, 'Drinking in Pregnancy: Shifting Towards the "Precautionary Principle"' in Susanne MacGregor and Betsy Thom (eds), *Risk and Substance Use: Framing Dangerous People and Dangerous Places* (Routledge 2020).

95 *Paton v British Pregnancy Advisory Service Trustees* [1979] QB 276.

quality prenatal care and poverty, are more likely to contribute to fetal harm than a pregnant person's behaviour.

A fetus is not a legal person and does not have legal rights (though it is subject to some legal protection set out in abortion law). Therefore, a fetus can neither be a murder victim,[96] nor a claimant in a civil action (e.g., negligence).[97] Where a child is born alive but injured by harm caused *in utero*, they may have a claim for negligence.[98] The Congenital Disabilities Act 1976 explicitly excludes the pregnant person from liability for behaviour causing a disability *in utero* (unless the injury resulted from their driving).[99]

Though *AG's Reference (No. 3 of 1994)*[100] was not about the liability of pregnant people, the criminal law does not explicitly exempt pregnant people from criminal liability. In this case, a man attacked his pregnant girlfriend, causing serious injury to the fetus *in utero*. The House of Lords confirmed a person may be guilty of murder or manslaughter (depending on intent) where a fetus *born alive* dies *of* injuries sustained *in utero*.[101] Lord Mustill, *obiter*, noted the possibility of criminal liability for harm short of death.[102] However, *CP (A Child) v Criminal Injuries Compensation Authority* established a fetus could not be the victim of a harm at the time the harm was inflicted, due to the lack of legal personhood.[103] Thus, a pregnant person cannot be guilty of poisoning (and, by the same logic, grievous or actual bodily harm). The difference between these cases hinges on attainment of legal personhood between injury (*in utero*) and death (*ex utero*).[104]

In cases where other elements of homicide are present, proving the death was caused by the negligent or unlawful act would be extremely difficult. For example, would the issue of any criminal negligence (gross negligent manslaughter) arise where a pregnant person's heavy alcohol use resulted in a child with FASD living for only a short while?[105] Would a 17-year-old pregnant person fraudulently purchasing and consuming alcohol on licensed premises be convicted of unlawful

96 *Attorney-General's (AG's) Reference (No. 3 of 1994)* [1997] 3 WLR 421.

97 *Burton v Islington Health Authority* [1993] QB 204; Congenital Disabilities (Civil Liability) Act 1976, s 1(1).

98 Congenital Disabilities (Civil Liability) Act 1976, s 1(1).

99 S.2 This exemption exists because compensation for injury would be obtained from the pregnant person's insurance. The Act actually says 'mother' (rather than pregnant person) — as in law the person who gestates is the mother. We have chosen not to use the word mother, as we described earlier in the chapter; see Mahmoud and Romanis (n8).

100 *AG's Reference (No. 3 of 1994)* (n96).

101 Ibid.

102 Ibid at [949].

103 *CP (A Child) v Criminal Injuries Compensation Authority* [2015] QB 459 per Treacy LJ at [471].

104 Ibid at [472].

105 Margaret Brazier, Emma Cave, and Rob Heywood (eds), *Patients and the Law* (7 edn, Manchester University Press 2023).

act manslaughter if it led to the death of their baby (after it was born alive)?[106] Potentially; the prosecutions have not been tested.

Criminal legal intervention punishing pregnant people, though possible where the fetus dies, should be avoided. If criminalisation was likely to result in better outcomes, then maybe its use is justified, but punishment for punishment's sake is exceptionally unhelpful, ostracising people already structurally disadvantaged due to addiction or poverty. In various US states, criminalisation disproportionately restricts Black women's liberty.[107] Like obstetric violence, surveillance of Black pregnant people here finds its origins in enslavement and white supremacy,[108] and it has led to the problematic belief that Black women are somehow 'less fit mothers, less caring mothers, and less hurt by separation from their children'.[109]

Pregnant people using substances risking fetal harm are more likely to avoid healthcare and/or social care when worried about criminal sanctions.[110] Criminalisation is likely to be ineffective: avoiding healthcare is likely far more harmful to the pregnant person (and the fetus) than getting support (even where substance use continues).

Though pregnant people are neither prosecuted nor detained if they do not comply with medical advice, their behaviour is policed subtly through language used by healthcare professionals, law, and policy. Elsewhere, we argued conflating pregnancy with motherhood enables scrutiny of a pregnant person's decisions, presupposing their intentions and identity, subjecting them to autonomy-limiting regulatory frameworks. Pregnant people failing to act 'maternally' are 'bad mothers', potentially risking their fetus.[111] Treating pregnant people suspiciously and monitoring their behaviour contribute to a culture of surveillance perpetuating pregnant people as untrustworthy, reinforcing institutional cultures of obstetric violence and testimonial injustice.

Summary

- Obstetric violence and obstetric racism are pervasive globally and the UK is no exception. There is active debate about how law could and should respond to obstetric violence.
- While the law consistently reiterates the value of individual choice in birthing, systematically pregnant people are denied the opportunity to have the birth of

106 This was a question raised by a student of one of the authors in an Advanced Issues in Criminal Law class at Durham in 2022–23.

107 Michele Goodwin, *Policing the Womb: Invisible Women and the Criminalization of Motherhood* (CUP 2020).

108 Keisha Ray, *Black Health: The Social, Political, and Cultural Determinants of Black People's Health* (OUP 2023) ch 1; Roberts (n33).

109 Dorothy Roberts, 'The Value of Black Mothers' Work' (1994) 26 Conn L Rev 871, 874.

110 Emma Cave, *The Mother of All Crimes: Human Rights, Criminalization and the Child Born Alive* (Routledge 2004) 113.

111 Mahmoud and Romanis (n8).

their choosing. This happens in the sense that pregnant people, especially those with serious mental illness, are vulnerable to having their refusals of medical intervention overruled and it is hard for pregnant people to practically access services like request C/S and homebirth.

- Pregnant people are subject to intense medical and social monitoring and pressure to always behave in ways that are considered best for the fetus. While civil liability for pregnant people suspected of causing fetal harm is expressly limited, it is not clear that criminal consequences are always precluded.
- Controlling pregnant people's behaviour is a serious interference of their rights, and disproportionality impacts those marginalised in society across a number of axes; for example, gender, race, socio-economics.

Questions for reflection

1. Was Lady Hale right in *Montgomery v Lanarkshire* to say that 'Gone are the days when it was thought that, on becoming pregnant, a woman lost, not only her capacity, but also her right to act as a genuinely autonomous human being'?
2. How should the law respond to obstetric violence and obstetric racism?
3. In *CP (A Child) v Criminal Injuries Compensation Authority*, Lord Dyson MR claimed 'the court should be slow to interpret general criminal legislation as applying' in the context of fetal harm. Why might this be important?

Recommended resources

- Laura Beil, 'Exposed: Cover-Up at Columbia University' https://wondery.com/shows/exposed/ (warning: contains description of sexual assault).
- Dána-Ain Davis, 'Obstetric Racism: The Racial Politics of Pregnancy, Labor, and Birthing' (2019) 38 Med Anthropol 560.
- Samantha Halliday, 'Pregnancy and Severe Mental Illness: Birth Choices, Best Interests and the Untapped Potential of Advance Decisions' (2024) 24 Med Law Int 14–53.
- Zaina Mahmoud and Elizabeth Chloe Romanis, 'On Gestation and Motherhood' (2023) 31 Med Law Rev 109–40.
- Camilla Pickles and Jonathan Herring (eds), *Childbirth, Vulnerability and Law Exploring Issues of Violence and Control* (Routledge 2019).
- Dorothy Roberts, *Killing the Black Body: Race, Reproduction and the Meaning of Liberty* (20th anniversary edn, Vintage Books 2017).

Bibliography

AAPG on Birth Trauma, 'Ending the Postcode Lottery on Perinatal Care' https://www.theo-clarke.org.uk/sites/www.theo-clarke.org.uk/files/2024-05/Birth%20Trauma%20Inquiry%20Report%20for%20Publication_May13_2024_0.pdf, accessed 16 May 2024

Benjamin R, 'Informed Refusal: Toward a Justice-Based Bioethics' (2016) 41 Sci Tech Hum Values 967

Birthrights, 'Maternal Request Caesarean Sections' (2018) https://www.birthrights.org.uk/wp-content/uploads/2018/08/Final-Birthrights-MRCS-Report-2108-1.pdf, accessed 28 November 2023

Birthrights, 'Systemic Racism, Not Broken Bodies: An Inquiry Into Racial Injustice and Human Rights in UK Maternity Care' (2022) https://www.birthrights.org.uk/wp-content/uploads/2022/05/Birthrights-inquiry-systemic-racism_exec-summary_May-22-web.pdf, accessed 28 November 2023

Bowden C, 'Is the Unequal Treatment of Maternal and Paternal Liability under the Congenital Disabilities (Civil Liability) Act 1976 Justified?' (2022) 30 Med Law Rev 457

Brazier M, Cave E, and Heywood R (eds), *Patients and the Law* (7th edn, Manchester University Press 2023)

Brennan K, 'Reflections on Criminalising Obstetric Violence: A Feminist Perspective' in C Pickles and J Herring (eds), *Childbirth, Vulnerability and Law* (Routledge 2019)

Bridges KM, *Reproducing Race: An Ethnography of Pregnancy as a Site of Racialization* (University of California Press 2011)

Brione R, 'Person-Centred Maternity Care: COVID Exposes the Illusion' (2022) 15 Int J Fem Appr Bioethics 131

Brown R and Mulligan A, '"Maternal Request" Caesarean Sections and Medical Necessity' (2023) 18 Clin Ethics 312

Bryant A and others, 'Equality in Obstetric Care: Racial and Ethnic Differences in Caesarean Section Delivery Rates' (2009) 23 Paediatr Perinat Epidemiol 454

Catov J and others, 'The Relationship between Race, Inflammation and Psychosocial Factors among Pregnant Women' (2015) 19 Matern Child Health J 401

Cave E, *The Mother of All Crimes: Human Rights, Criminalization and the Child Born Alive* (Routledge 2004)

Chadwick R, 'Ambiguous Subjects: Obstetric Violence, Assemblage and South African Birth Narratives' (2017) 27 Fem Psychol 489

Chadwick R, 'Breaking the Frame: Obstetric Violence and Epistemic Rupture' (2021) 35 Agenda 104

Chervenak FA and others, 'Obstetric Violence is a Misnomer' (2024) 230 Am J Obstet Gynecol S1138

Collinson A, 'Coronavirus: Uncertainty over Maternity Care Causing Distress' (BBC News, 2020) https://www.bbc.co.uk/news/health-52356067, accessed 24 April 2024

Cooper Owens D, *Medical Bondage: Race, Gender, and the Origins of American Gynecology* (University of Georgia Press 2017)

Davis D-A, 'Obstetric Racism: The Racial Politics of Pregnancy, Labor, and Birthing' (2019) 38 Med Anthropol Q 560

D'Gregorio RP, 'Obstetric Violence: A New Legal Term Introduced in Venezuela' (2010) 111 Int J Gynaecol Obstet 201

DHSC (Department of Health and Social Care), 'Reading the Signals: Maternity and Neonatal Services in East Kent: the Report of the Independent Investigation' [Kirkup Inquiry] (HC 681, 2022)

Finn S and others, 'Pregnancy: Transformations in Philosophy and Legal Practice' in GA Bruno and J Vlastis (eds) *Rewriting the History of Philosophy: Transformations* (Routledge 2023)

Fovargue S, 'Anticipating Issues with Capacitous Pregnant Women: *United Lincolnshire NHS Hospitals Trust v CD* [2019] EWCOP 24 and *Guys and St Thomas' NHS Foundation Trust (GSTT) and South London and Maudsley NHS Foundation Trust (SLAM) v R* [2020] EWCOP 4' (2020) 28 Med Law Rev 781

Fovargue S, 'In Whose Best Interests? Childbirth Choices and Other Health Decisions' (2021) 137 Law Q Rev 604

Fricker M, *Epistemic Injustice: Power and the Ethics of Knowing* (OUP 2007)

Frosch D and others, 'Authoritarian Physicians and Patients' Fear of Being Labeled "Difficult" among Key Obstacles to Shared Decision Making' (2012) 31 Health Aff (Millwood) 1030

Goodwin M, *Policing the Womb: Invisible Women and the Criminalization of Motherhood* (CUP 2020)

Halliday S, *Autonomy and Pregnancy: A Comparative Analysis of Compelled Obstetric Intervention* (Routledge 2016)

Halliday S, 'Court-Authorised Obstetric Intervention: Insight and Capacity, a Tale of Loss' in C Pickles and J Herring (eds), *Childbirth, Vulnerability and Law: Exploring Issues of Violence and Control* (Routledge 2019)

Harrington J, 'Privileging the Medical Nora: Liberalism, Self-Determination and Refusal of Treatment' (1996) 16 Leg Stud 348

Harrington J, 'Time as a Dimension of Medical Law' (2012) 20 Med Law Rev 491

Hays S, *The Cultural Contradictions of Motherhood* (Yale University Press 1996)

Herring J, 'Identifying the Wrong in Obstetric Violence' in C Pickles and J Herring (eds), *Childbirth, Vulnerability and Law: Exploring Issues of Violence and Control* (Routledge 2019)

Herring J, 'Implied Consent and Vaginal Examination in Pregnancy' in C Pickles and J Herring (eds), *Women's Birthing Bodies and the Law: Unauthorised Intimate Examinations, Power and Vulnerability* (Bloomsbury 2020)

Herring J, *Medical Law and Ethics* (9th edn, OUP 2022)

Hill A, '"I Asked Three Times for an Epidural": Why Are Women Being Denied Pain Relief during Childbirth?' (2020) https://www.theguardian.com/lifeandstyle/2020/mar/04/i-asked-three-times-for-an-epidural-why-are-women-being-denied-pain-relief, accessed 3 December 2023

Independent Maternity Review, 'Findings, Conclusions and Essential Actions from the Independent Review of Maternity Services at the Shrewsbury and Telford Hospital NHS Trust [Ockenden Report]' (2022) https://assets.publishing.service.gov.uk/media/624332fe8fa8f527744f0615/Final-Ockenden-Report-web-accessible.pdf, accessed 28 November 2023

Jackson E, *Regulating Reproduction: Law, Technology and Autonomy* (Hart Publishing 2001)

Kamali M, *Racial Discrimination: Institutional Patterns and Politics* (Routledge 2009)

Knight M and others, 'Saving Lives, Improving Mothers' Care Core Report: Lessons Learned to Inform Maternity Care from the UK and Ireland Confidential Enquiries into Maternal Deaths and Morbidity 2018–20' (2022) https://www.npeu.ox.ac.uk/assets/downloads/mbrrace-uk/reports/maternal-report-2022/MBRRACE-UK_Maternal_MAIN_Report_2022_UPDATE.pdf, accessed 28 November 2023.

Lappeman M and Swatz L, 'Rethinking Obstetric Violence and the "Neglect of Neglect": The Silence of a Labour Ward Milieu in a South African District Hospital' (2019) 19 BMC Int Health Hum Rights 30

Lappeman M and Swatz L, 'How Gentle Must Violence against Women Be in Order to Not Be Violent? Rethinking the Word "Violence" in Obstetric Settings' (2021) 27 Violence Against Women 987

MacKinnon K and others, 'Recognizing and Renaming in Obstetrics: How Do We Take Better Care with Language?' (2021) 14 Obstet Med 201

Mahmoud Z and Romanis EC, 'On Gestation and Motherhood' (2023) 31 Med Law Rev 109

Martin K, 'Giving Birth Like a Girl' (2003) 17 Gender & Soc 54

Mathur V, Morris T, and McNamara K, 'Cultural Conceptions of Women's Labor Pain and Labor Pain Management: A Mixed-Method Analysis' (2020) 261 Soc Sci Med 113240

Maurice R, 'We Bawl So We Are Heard: The Stories We Must Tell about Obstetric Racism' (2023) 31 Sex Repro Health Matters 1

Morales XB, Chaves LVE, and Delgado CEY, 'Neither Medicine Nor Health Care Staff Members Are Violent By Nature: Obstetric Violence from an Interactionist Perspective' (2018) 28 Qual Health Res 1308

Nelson A, 'Vaginal Examinations during Childbirth: Consent, Coercion, and COVID-19' (2021) 29 Fem Leg Stud 119

Nelson A and Romanis EC, 'Homebirthing in the United Kingdom during COVID-19' (2020) 20 Med Law Int 183

Nelson A, 'The Medicalisation of Childbirth and Access to Homebirth in the UK: COVID-19 and Beyond' (2021) 29 Med Law Rev 661

Nguyen TT and others, 'Racism during Pregnancy and Birthing: Experiences from Asian and Pacific Islander, Black, Latina, and Middle Eastern Women' (2022) J Racial Ethn Health Disparities 1

NICE (National Institute for Health and Care Excellence), 'Intrapartum Care for Healthy Women and Babies: CG190' (2014) https://www.nice.org.uk/guidance/cg190, accessed 28 November 2023

NICE (National Institute for Health and Care Excellence), 'Caesarean Birth: NG192' (2021) https://www.nice.org.uk/guidance/ng192, accessed 28 November 2023

Office of the Public Guardian, 'Mental Capacity Act Code of Practice' (2007) https://assets.publishing.service.gov.uk/media/5f6cc6138fa8f541f6763295/Mental-capacity-act-code-of-practice.pdf, accessed 28 November 2023

Perera D and others, 'Obstetric Violence is Prevalent in Routine Maternity Care: A Cross-Sectional Study of Obstetric Violence and its Associated Factors among Pregnant Women in Sri Lanka's Colombo District' (2022) 19 Int J Environ Res Public Health 99997

Petersen E and others, 'Racial/Ethnic Disparities in Pregnancy-Related Deaths: United States, 2007–2016' (2019) 68 MMWR 762

Pickles C, 'When "Battery" is Not Enough: Exposing the Gaps in Unauthorised Vaginal Examinations during Labour as a Crime of Battery' in C Pickles and J Herring (eds), *Women's Birthing Bodies and the Law: Unauthorised Intimate Examinations, Power and Vulnerability* (Bloomsbury 2020)

Pickles C, '"Obstetric Violence", "Mistreatment", and "Disrespect and Abuse": Reflections on the Politics of Naming Violations during Facility-Based Childbirth' (2023) 38 Hypatia 628

Ray K, *Black Health: The Social, Political, and Cultural Determinants of Black People's Health* (OUP 2023)

Ridge S, 'Some Hospitals Still Not Allowing Partners to Be Present during Labour' (Sky News, 25 October 2020) https://news.sky.com/story/some-hospitals-still-not-allowing-partners-to-be-present-at-childbirth-12113859, accessed 24 April 2024

Roberts D, 'The Value of Black Mothers' Work' (1994) 26 Conn L Rev 871

Roberts D, *Killing the Black Body: Race, Reproduction, and the Meaning of Liberty* (Pantheon Books 1997)

Romanis EC, 'Why the Elective Caesarean Lottery is Ethically Impermissible' (2019) 27 Health Care Anal 249

Romanis EC, 'Addressing Rising Caesarean Rates: Maternal Request Caesareans, Defensive Practice, and the Power of Choice in Childbirth' (2020) 13 IJFAB 1

Romanis EC, 'Appropriately Framing Maternal Request Caesarean Section' (2022) 48 J Med Ethics 554

Romanis EC and Nelson A, 'Maternal Request Caesareans and COVID-19: The Virus Does Not Diminish the Importance of Choice in Childbirth' (2020) 46 J Med Ethics 726

Romanis EC and others, 'Reviewing the Womb' (2021) 47 J Med Ethics 820–9

Ross L and Solinger R, *Reproductive Justice: An Introduction* (University of California Press 2017)

Thom B, Herring R and Milne E, 'Drinking in Pregnancy: Shifting Towards the "Precautionary Principle"' in S MacGregor and B Thom (eds), *Risk and Substance Use: Framing Dangerous People and Dangerous Places* (Routledge 2020)

Vacaflor CH, 'Obstetric Violence: A New Framework for Identifying Challenges to Maternal Healthcare in Argentina' (2016) 24 Reprod Health Matters 65

Van der Waal R and Mayra K, 'Obstetric Violence' in P Ali and MM Rogers (eds), *Gender-Based Violence: A Comprehensive Guide* (SpringerLink 2023)
Van der Waal R and others, 'Obstetric Violence: An Intersection Refraction through Abolition Feminism' (2023) 4 Fem Anthropol 91
Williams CR and others, 'Obstetric Violence: A Latin American Legal Response to Mistreatment during Childbirth' (2018) 25 BJOG 1208

16

Capable Children's Medical Treatment

Rebecca Limb

In his novel, *The Children Act*,[1] Ian McEwan depicts the fictitious story of Adam Henry, a 17-year-old boy, as he makes decisions regarding his medical treatment for leukaemia. As a capable child, Adam is in the process of 'becoming an adult, becoming a citizen, becoming independent, becoming autonomous, becoming mature and becoming responsible'.[2] Due to the capable child's fluctuating status between childhood and adulthood, their lived experiences are hard to capture and are often neglected in legal literature that has tended to focus on very young children and on parental rights. Drawing on Adam's story, this chapter concentrates on the experiences of the capable child and their legal powers to make healthcare decisions. Using stories to evaluate the law allows us to consider subjective experience and consider the consequences of the law.[3] Adam's story offers valuable insight into the unique ethical and legal dilemmas experienced by capable children when making healthcare decisions. This chapter explores the capable child's power to consent to medical treatment before analysing their power to refuse.

Consenting to medical treatment

Let's dive into the story from *The Children Act*. Sat on her sofa surrounded by handwritten papers, Fiona, an experienced High Court judge in the Family Division, is drafting her judgment for a case involving two children whose parents, due to their differences in faith, are in dispute over their children's place of education. The telephone rings. Her musings are interrupted. Fiona picks up:

---

1 Ian McEwan, *The Children Act* (Vintage 2014).

2 Peter Kelly, 'An Untimely Future for Youth Studies?' (2011) 30 Youth Stud Aust 47, 48.

3 Carrie Menkel-Meadow, 'Telling Stories in School: Using Case Studies and Stories to Teach Legal Ethics' (2000) 69 Fordham L Rev 787, 788.

Box 16.1: Key text: Context

'I'm sorry to disturb you this late, My Lady.'

'It's all right. Go ahead.'

'We've had a call from counsel representing the Edith Cavell hospital, Wandsworth. They urgently need to transfuse a cancer patient, a boy of seventeen years. He and his parents are refusing consent. The hospital would like – '

'Why are they refusing?'

'Jehovah's Witnesses, My Lady.'

'Right.'

'The hospital's looking for an order that it will be lawful to proceed against their wishes.'

She looked at her watch. Just past ten thirty. 'How long have we got?'

'After Wednesday it will be dangerous, they're saying. Extremely dangerous ...'

'... Then list it for hearing on short notice at 2pm on Tuesday ....'[4]

The extract in Box 16.1 depicts an urgent legal challenge from the Edith Cavell hospital regarding their 17-year-old leukaemia patient, Adam, who urgently requires medical intervention. The hospital seeks to administer four therapeutic drugs. Two of the four drugs target cancer cells directly whilst the other two target any cells in its path including healthy cells in the bone marrow. The side effects of this treatment include a weakening of Adam's immune system and will prevent him from creating his own red blood cells. Adam therefore needs blood transfusions. Adam consents to the administration of the four therapeutic drugs but declines the blood transfusion. For medical treatment to be lawfully administered, it is first necessary for doctors to recommend an appropriate medical treatment. Although patients are welcome to propose medical treatments, treatment cannot be demanded and clinicians cannot be compelled to provide treatment that they do not consider to be appropriate.[5] Secondly, effective consent to the appropriate treatment must be obtained.[6] To treat Adam without effective consent may give rise to criminal or tortious liability. The hospital would only be permitted under the common law defence of necessity[7] to administer treatment without effective consent if Adam required emergency medical treatment to save his life or avoid serious harm and so it was not possible to obtain effective consent. In Adam's case, the defence of necessity would not be applicable as the doctors have time, albeit limited, to seek effective consent. For children, effective

4 McEwan (n1) 33–4.

5 *R (Burke) v The General Medical Council* [2005] EWCA 1003. *Manchester University NHS Foundation Trust v Fixsler* [2021] EWHC 1426 (Fam).

6 See Chapter 9.

7 *Glass v UK* [2004] 1 FCR 553.

consent may be provided by a capable child, persons with parental responsibility (PR) for the child, or a court order.[8]

Capable child's power to consent

Consent and capacity are inextricably linked. For patients' consent to be legally valid they must have 'decision-making capacity' (this is decision specific).[9] Obtaining consent can appear to be a simple process of communication, information sharing, and agreement;[10] however, it is more complex as patients' cognition may be impaired by environmental, medical, and social factors, impacting the quality of their consent.[11] Adam comes across as intelligent, well informed, and mature for his age, yet Fiona is concerned that, despite appearances, his cognition may be impaired (see Box 16.2).

Box 16.2: Key text: talking to Adam

'I'll tell you why I'm here, Adam. I want to be sure you know what you're doing. Some people think that you're too young to be taking a decision like this and that you've been influenced by your parents and the elders. And others think you're extremely clever and capable and we should just let you get on with it.'

'Well,' he said eagerly. 'What's your impression so far? How am I doing?'

.... So, how was he doing? 'Pretty well, so far' she said, aware she was taking a risk. 'You give the impression of someone who knows his own mind.'

'Thank you,' he said in a voice derisively sweet.

'But it might just be an impression.'

'I like to make a good impression.'

His manner, his humour, had an element of the silliness that can accompany high intelligence. And it was self-protective. He was surely very frightened.[12]

Adam's age is of importance as the legal regulation differs depending on whether a child is under 16 or aged 16 or 17. Section 8 of the Family Law Reform Act

---

8 *Re R (a Minor)* [1992] Fam 11; *Re W (a Minor) (Medical Treatment: Court's Jurisdiction)* [1993] Fam 64.

9 Paul Appelbaum, 'Assessment of Patients' Competence to Consent to Treatment' (2007) 357 N Engl J Med 1834.

10 Scott Lamont, Cameron Stewart, and Mary Chiarella, 'Capacity and Consent: Knowledge and Practice of Legal and Healthcare Standards' (2019) 26 Nurs Ethics 71, 72.

11 Shamir Cawich and others, 'From the Patient's Perspective: Is There a Need to Improve the Quality of Informed Consent for Surgery in Training Hospitals?' (2013) 17 Perm J 22.

12 McEwan (n1) 103–5.

1969 assumes that children aged 16 and 17 have the capacity to consent to surgical, medical, or dental treatment. The Act limits what medical interventions are considered 'treatment' to interventions that are arguably therapeutic in nature, including ancillary procedures and investigations necessary for a diagnosis and the effective delivery of the treatment (such as anaesthesia prior to an operation).[13] The assumption of capacity does not extend to treatment that is non-therapeutic, such as cosmetic surgery or live organ donation.[14] The Act states that a 16 or 17-year-old's consent is to be 'as effective' as if they are adults. Their consent has the power to authorise or 'effect' the lawful administration of appropriate medical treatment.[15] This presumption is not absolute. If doubt is raised as to the child's capacity, the child will be considered to lack capacity if they are unable to decide for themselves because of an impairment of, or a disturbance in the functioning of, the mind or brain.[16] A patient cannot decide for themselves if they are unable 'to understand the information relevant to the decision, to retain that information, to use or weigh that information as part of the process of making the decision, or to communicate his decision (whether by talking, using sign language or other means)'.[17]

A child under 16 can provide 'effective' consent if they have 'sufficient understanding and intelligence to understand fully what is proposed'.[18] Known as *Gillick* competency, this test has received criticism for its ambiguity. The terms 'sufficient', 'intelligence', and 'to understand fully' are ambiguous, making the application of *Gillick* troublesome for judges and healthcare professionals.[19] Recognising similarities between *Gillick* and the test for incapacity in the Mental Capacity Act (MCA) 2005, and thus an opportunity to ease the application of *Gillick*, Cobb J in *Re S* posited whether the MCA could be used as a tool for interpreting *Gillick*.[20] In *Re X*,[21] this proposition was met with a resounding rejection. Munby J held that Gillick competence is a question of the 'normal development over time of the typical child and teenager'[22] irrespective of any impairment or disturbance of mental functioning, whereas the MCA 'has nothing to do with personal status; it is all to do with impairment or disturbance of mental functioning'.[23]

13 Family Law Reform Act 1969, s 8(b).
14 *Re W* (n8) 70 per Lord Donaldson MR.
15 Family Law Reform Act 1969, s 8.
16 MCA (Mental Capacity Act) 2005, s 2(1).
17 MCA 2005, s 3(1); Chapter 10.
18 *Gillick v West Norfolk and Wisbech AHA* [1986] AC 112, 189 per Lord Scarman.
19 Emma Cave, 'Goodbye Gillick? Identifying and Resolving Problems with the Concept of Child Competence' (2013) 34 Leg Stud 103–22.
20 *Re S (Child as Parent: Adoption: Consent)* [2017] EWHC 2729 (Fam).
21 *Re X (A Child) (No 2)* [2021] EWHC 65 (Fam).
22 Ibid [73].
23 Ibid [56].

Fully understanding the proposed treatment

Fiona considers Adam to know his own mind; however, this is not enough to identify legal capacity. In *Re JA*,[24] the Honourable Mr Justice Baker said of J, a 14-year-old boy refusing treatment for HIV, that

> Although he has an IQ of 105 and is therefore sufficiently intelligent to be capable of making up his own mind, he did not have sufficient understanding of HIV, its aetiology and its potential outcome if medication is not taken.[25]

Adam may know his own mind, but it still needs to be asked – has he understood fully the proposed treatment? During proceedings Fiona asks Adam's doctor how much his patient understands and whether he appreciates what will happen to him if he is not transfused. Mr Carter replies that Adam is informed; however, 'Only in the broadest terms. He knows he could die.'[26] There is some debate as to whether a child consenting to medical treatment is capable if they only understand the proposed treatment in the broadest terms. It is not expected that a child understands 'the detail of the medical science which underpins' the decision,[27] rather a child need only achieve 'sufficient understanding and intelligence to understand fully what is proposed'.[28]

When sharing information with patients, doctors are under a legal duty to 'take reasonable care to ensure that the patient is aware of any material risks involved in any recommended treatment, and of any reasonable alternative or variant treatment'.[29] A material risk, as stated in *Montgomery v Lanarkshire*,[30] is one which:

(i) a reasonable person in the patient's situation would consider significant; and
(ii) the particular patient would consider significant given their unique values and characteristics.[31]

---

24 *Re JA (a Minor) (Medical Treatment Child Diagnosed with HIV)* [2014] EWHC 1135.

25 Ibid [38].

26 McEwan (n1) 67.

27 *NHS Trust v CX (Medical Treatment: Gillick Competence: Consent to Treatment)* [2019] EWHC 3033 (Fam) [22].

28 *University Hospital Plymouth NHS Trust v B (a Minor)* [2019] EWHC 1670 [11].

29 *Montgomery v Lanarkshire Health Board* [2015] UKSC 11, [2]. *McCulloch v Forth Valley Health Board* [2023] UKSC 26 clarified that doctors are under a duty to inform patients of alternative and variant treatments *they* consider to be clinically appropriate even if another body of medical opinion would reach a different conclusion.

30 *McCulloch v Forth Valley Health Board* [2023] UKSC 26.

31 Ibid [82].

Thus, children capable of consenting to medical treatment *should* be informed of risks a reasonable patient would objectively consider significant and any risks the child concerned would consider significant (determined subjectively). The *Montgomery* test does not form part of the capacity test: a child can demonstrate capacity even if they do not understand the material risks. However, whether *Montgomery* applies to children is disputed.[32] If it does not, a doctor's duty is to merely inform children of the risks a responsible body of medical people would consider reasonable to disclose,[33] which makes it easier for doctors to justify withholding information they consider to be distressing.

Harris objects to the claim that a child need only understand broad information and the risks of the proposed treatment.[34] He says, to give informed consent a person needs to 'understand the nature of the course of action to which you are consenting, which, in medical contexts, will include its probable and possible consequences and side-effects and the nature of any alternative measures which might be taken and the consequences of doing nothing'.[35] In *Re M*,[36] M was found to lack capacity because she did not understand the consequences of not having the treatment. In *The Children Act*, Adam understood that he would die; however, concern was raised because Adam lacked an appreciation as to the 'manner of his death'.[37] In *Re E*,[38] it was held that E did not have capacity to consent because he too lacked this appreciation:

> He may have some concept of the fact that he will die, but as to the manner of his death and to the extent of his and his family's suffering I find he has not the ability to turn his mind to it nor the will to do so. Who can blame him for that? If, therefore, this case depended upon my finding of whether or not A is of sufficient understanding and intelligence and maturity to give full and informed consent, I find that he is not.[39]

In addition to being asked to understand the risks associated with not consenting, capable children have been expected to appreciate the wider ramifications of their decision. Lord Scarman, in *Gillick*,[40] stated that a capable child must understand the 'moral and family issues'[41] associated with their decision. Similarly, in

32 Emma Cave and Craig Purshouse, 'Think of the Children: Liability for Non-Disclosure of Information Post-Montgomery' (2020) 28 Med Law Rev 270.

33 *Bolam v Friern Hospital Management Committee* [1957] 1 WLR 582.

34 John Harris, 'Consent and End of Life Decisions' (2003) 29 J Med Ethics 10.

35 Ibid 12.

36 *Re M* (Medical Treatment: Consent) [1999] 2 FLR.

37 McEwan (n1) 67.

38 *Re E (a Minor) (Wardship: Medical Treatment)* [1993] 1 FLR 386, 391 per Ward J.

39 Ibid.

40 *Gillick* (n18).

41 Ibid 165.

Re E,[42] Ward J held that E lacked capacity in part because he did not appreciate the implications of his decision on his family:

> I am quite satisfied that A does not have any sufficient comprehension of the pain he has yet to suffer, of the fear that he will be undergoing, of the distress not only occasioned by that fear but also – and importantly – the distress he will inevitably suffer as he, a loving son, helplessly watches his parents' and his family's distress … I find that he has no realisation of the full implications which lie before him as to the process of dying.[43]

Sufficient maturity is expected of the capable child. Concern was expressed in Adam's case that he does not show sufficient maturity because he is influenced by his parents and religious community. Mr Carter says, 'His views are those of his parents. They're not his own. His objection to being transfused is based on the doctrines of a religious cult for which he may well become a pointless martyr.'[44] Although Adam stresses 'I'm my own man. I'm separate from my parents. Whatever my parents' ideas are, I'm deciding for myself',[45] the counsel for the hospital posed:

> He's frightened of being shunned, isn't that the term you use? Shunned for not doing what you and the elders want. The only world he knows would turn its back on him for preferring life to a terrible death. Is that a free choice for a young lad?[46]

In *Re L*,[47] a case sharing remarkably similar facts to Adam's, L was found to lack decision-making capacity because L's views were a product of a 'sheltered life'. Highly influenced by her parents, L had had limited exposure to a range of beliefs, including views challenging her own, nor was she in possession of all 'the necessary details which it would be appropriate for her to be able to form a view about'.[48] Thus, she was held to lack *Gillick* competency.

What is meant by fully understanding the proposed treatment depends on the nature of the decision. The case law illustrates that where the consent is for a minor medical procedure that carries little risk, such as putting a plaster on a cut, the child need only understand the process of putting a plaster on without

42 *Re E* (n38).
43 Ibid 391.
44 McEwan (n1) 68.
45 Ibid.
46 Ibid 79.
47 *Re L (Medical Treatment: Gillick Competency)* [1998] 2 FLR 810.
48 Ibid 812.

needing to comprehend why they need the plaster, or the risk of severe infection if it isn't used.[49]

In contrast, where the decision carries great risk, such as deciding whether to have a heart transplant, the child may be required to understand the risks involved in having the transplant, such as needing the assistance of a machine providing cardiac support, death, blood clots, stroke, infections and rejection, and the risks associated with not having the transplant, including death. A complex decision has complex information relating to the decision and, therefore, it is more challenging for a child to demonstrate they fully understand the proposed treatment. It is not that the standard for full understanding increases; rather, it is that the information relating to the decision is more difficult to comprehend. As such, a child may have the capacity to consent to certain treatments but not others.[50]

Withholding information from capable children

Although Adam was considered highly intelligent and capable, his doctors were reluctant to inform him of the manner of his death due to its distressing nature. The information Adam was held to be lacking in order to demonstrate his full understanding of the proposed treatment was the information that his medical team had deliberately withheld. There was no attempt made by any adult to disclose the information and give Adam the opportunity to demonstrate his capacity to understand. There are many examples within the case law where doctors and judges have deliberately withheld information from a child. For example, in *Re N*, a child's mother and doctors withheld information about the consequences of refusing treatment, which, in turn, was used as evidence she was incompetent.[51] Mrs Justice Arbuthnot held:

> the parties are agreed that N is not competent in the sense of not merely having an understanding of the nature of the proposed treatment but of having a full understanding of the treatment and also of the consequences of a failure to treat ... the doctor and N's mother explained the possible side effects of the experimental therapy, so far as I am aware, N has not been told by anyone what the consequences are to her of not taking part in the CAR T cell therapy trial: in other words, the certainty of death.[52]

---

49 Jonathan Herring, *Medical Law and Ethics* (9th edn OUP 2023) 237.

50 Stephen Gilmore and Jonathan Herring, '"No" is the Hardest Word: Consent and Children's Autonomy' (2011) 23 Child Fam Law Q 3. NB: Having capacity to consent to some treatment is to be distinguished from fluctuating capacity. In the former, a child's capacity to consent is determined by the nature of the treatment.

51 *Re N (a Child)* [2021] EWHC 2517 (Fam).

52 Ibid [38].

The judge stipulated that this information was 'rightly' withheld.[53] But is it ever right to withhold such information and subsequently use the child's ignorance as evidence that they do not fully understand? As Montgomery explains '[I]t is the refusal of the adults to allow her to be informed that rendered her incompetent, not her ability to comprehend.'[54] Children, by virtue of their social status, are inherently vulnerable and the withholding of information only compounds their vulnerability. Children like N appear to be given a voice; however, in reality they are not.

Studies suggest that healthcare professionals favour open and honest sharing of information with children, informing them of their diagnosis, prognosis, and upcoming treatment; however, information is often withheld at the request of parents.[55] Parents may request this to protect the child from distressing information, reduce anxiety and fear, because they consider the child too young to understand, and/or to maintain hope.[56] Tension arises where parents request non-disclosure but clinicians consider it to be in the child's best interests. Children's desire for information can vary vastly, adding further complexity to the dilemma. Commentators argue that children have a right to know;[57] however, this is not a legal right. Doctors are only under a duty to inform patients consenting to medical treatment; therefore, if the capable child is not the consenting party there is no legal duty to disclose. Moreover, doctors should disclose information that a reasonable doctor would disclose,[58] or, if *Montgomery* is applicable to children,[59] objective *and* subjective material risks. These tests afford clinicians extensive privilege in determining what risks are material, meaning it is easy for information to be lawfully withheld from a child.

Competency cannot be presumed or otherwise from a child's age

A remarkable characteristic of *Gillick* is its focus on *competency* instead of age. *Gillick* recognises that age is a poor indicator of competency and therefore empowers any child under 16 to consent provided they satisfy the *Gillick* competency test. *Bell v Tavistock*[60] threatened the treatment- and person-specific

53 Ibid [29].

54 Martin Woodhead and Heather Montgomery (eds), *Understanding Childhood: An Interdisciplinary Approach* (John Wiley & Son 2003) 292.

55 I. Coyne and others, 'Information-Sharing between Healthcare Professionals, Parents and Children with Cancer: More Than a Matter of Information Exchange' (2016) 25(1) Eur J Cancer Care (Engl) 141.

56 J. Aldridge and others, '"I Can't Tell My Child They Are Dying": Helping Parents Have Conversations with Their Child' (2017) 102 Arch Dis Child Educ Pract Ed 182; Coyne and others (n55).

57 Cristie Cole and Eric Kodish, 'Minors' Right to Know and Therapeutic Privilege' (2013) 15 Virtual Mentor 683.

58 *Bolam v Friern Hospital Management Committee* [1957] 1 WLR 582.

59 [2015] UKSC 11.

60 [2020] EWHC 3274 (Admin).

nature of *Gillick* by presuming a child's competency based on age specifically for children receiving treatment for gender dysphoria. The judges held the risks associated with the administration of puberty blockers would be 'difficult for a child under 16 to understand and weigh up'[61] due to the complexity of the decision and the lack of scientific evidence as to the long-term implications of treatment:

> *Gillick* [1986] AC 112 makes clear that any decision is treatment and person specific. However … we think that it is appropriate in this case to give clear guidance as to the application of the *Gillick* tests to the treatment and cohort of children in question. The conclusion we have reached is that it is highly unlikely that a child aged 13 or under would ever be *Gillick* competent to give consent to being treated with PBs. In respect of children aged 14 and 15, we are also very doubtful that a child of this age could understand the long-term risks and consequences of treatment in such a way as to have sufficient understanding to give consent.[62]

For children with gender dysphoria this decision effectively made it impossible for them to consent to treatment for their condition. By extension, this revision threatened the interpretation of *Gillick* for all medical treatment in its infancy or where there are degrees of uncertainty as to the long-term risks.[63] At appeal it was held the Division Court mistakenly assumed children's competency is based on their age and held that 'nothing about the nature or implications of treatment with puberty blockers allowed for a real distinction from the consideration of contraception in *Gillick* …'[64] *Gillick* remains accessible for all under 16-year-olds.

Concurrent and equal powers to consent

Doctors only require effective consent from one authorised person to administer treatment. Capable children can, therefore, seek their clinicians' advice and provide effective consent to medical treatment without the need for their parents' knowledge and consent.[65] This is important for children who wish to discuss private or personal circumstances, such as their sexual health, gender identity, and/or mental health. Similarly, a child's parents and the court can provide

---

61 Ibid [139].

62 Ibid [145].

63 Kirsty Moreton, 'A Backwards-Step for Gillick: Trans Children's Inability to Consent to Treatment for Gender Dysphoria – Quincy Bell & Mrs A v The Tavistock and Portman NHS Foundation Trust and Ors' (2021) 29 Med Law Rev 699.

64 *Bell v Tavistock and Portman NHS Foundation Trust* [2021] EWCA Civ 1363, [76].

65 *Gillick* (n18).

effective consent without the child's consent. The capable child, their parents, and the court hold concurrent and equal power to consent. Lord Donaldson MR likened consent to a key and those permitted to consent as keyholders.[66] Those with PR (including the court) *automatically* have a key. As a judicial parent the court has inherent jurisdiction to make a 'one-off decision' and wardship power for 'all important decisions' where a child is a ward of court. Children are given a copy of the key when they are *Gillick* competent or presumed to have capacity under section 8 of the Family Law Reform Act 1969. In *The Children Act*, Mr Henry, Mrs Henry, Adam Henry, and the court are all keyholders. Individually any one of their consents will authorise treatment. Consider a situation where Mr Henry consents but his wife and son do not, in the words of Lord Donaldson MR,

> the doctor will be presented with a professional and ethical, but not with a legal, problem because, if he has the consent of one authorised person, treatment will not without more constitute a trespass or a criminal assault.[67]

As keys can both lock and unlock doors, this analogy mistakenly implies that a keyholder also has a legal power to lock the door of consent and prevent the administration of medical treatment. 'Regretful' of this analogy, Lord Donaldson MR has since used the metaphor of a flak jacket – a form of body armour – to describe the protection consent provides doctors:

> [The flak jacket] ... protects the doctor from claims by the litigious whether he acquires it from his patient who may be a minor over the age of 16, or a 'Gillick competent' child under that age or from another person having parental responsibilities which include a right to consent to treatment of the minor. Anyone who gives him a flak jacket (i.e. consent) may take it back, but the doctor only needs one and so long as he continues to have one he has the legal right to proceed.[68]

However, despite the flak jacket of protection that a parent's effective consent affords, doctors are often hesitant to treat an objecting capable child.[69]

---

66 *Re R* (n8) 15.

67 Ibid 15.

68 *Re W* (n8) 69–70.

69 *University Hospitals Plymouth NHS Trust v B* (n28); Rebecca Limb, 'According Appropriate Weight to Children's Wishes and Feelings: University Hospitals Plymouth NHS Trust v B (a Minor) [2019] EWHC 1670 (Fam)' (2021) 29 Med Law Rev 524.

Parent consents and child refuses

In an instance where the child is capable (like that of Adam) is it still legally permissible for the doctor to administer treatment using parental consent? In other words, can a parent's consent override a capable child's objection to medical treatment? During the court proceedings in *The Children Act*, Adam's parents are questioned by the hospital's barrister (Mark Berner QC). The extract of the questions to Mr Henry can be found in Box 16.3.

Box 16.3: Key text: Barrister's questions

Isn't it true that if he agreed to be transfused, he'd be what you'd call disfellowshipped? In other words, cast out of the community?

Dissociated. But it isn't going to happen. He isn't going to change his mind.

He's technically still a child, Mr Henry, in your care. So it's your mind I want to change. He's frightened of being shunned, isn't that the term you use? Shunned for not doing what you and the elders want. The only world he knows would turn its back on him for preferring life to a terrible death. Is that a free choice for a young lad?

If you spend five minutes in his company you'd realise he's someone who knows what he's about and is able to make a decision according to his faith.[70]

The statement 'it's *your* mind I want to change [emphasis added]' is particularly striking as it suggests that if Mr Henry were to change his mind and consent to the blood transfusion, the doctors would be acting lawfully in transfusing blood despite Adam's objection. The law regarding this ethical dilemma is well settled. 'No minor of whatever age has power by refusing consent to treatment to override a consent to treatment by someone who has parental responsibility for the minor …'[71] Adam, like all capable children seeking to refuse medical treatment, is prevented from doing so. Children are thus, by their mere social status, not capabilities, silenced by a best-interest assessment determined by adults.

Although parents can provide effective consent where their child is refusing, it is not easy for them. Whilst the potential benefits to a child's health may make the decision appear simple, to consent means to be responsible for putting their child through a potentially traumatic treatment that carries with it serious side effects, long recovery times, and no certainty of recovery. It can also damage their relationship with their child.

---

70 McEwan (n1).

71 *Re W* (n8) 71.

Capable children's refusals of medical treatment

Are there any instances where Adam, an articulate, highly intelligent 17-year-old has the legal authority to refuse treatment and for this refusal to be respected? Where a capable child refuses treatment, and in the absence of an effective consent, a hospital may seek authorisation to administer treatment from the court under section 8 of the Children Act 1989 or under their powers of inherent jurisdiction. Section 1(1) of the Children Act 1989 states that the welfare of the child is the paramount consideration for the court in all decisions and requires a judge to balance factors relevant to the decision, including, but not limited to, the factors listed in the Children Act 1989 to determine what treatment, if any, is in the child's best interests.[72] When summarising the role of the law in her judgment on Adam, Fiona paraphrased Nolan LJ's infamous reasoning in *Re W*,[73] stating that 'above all' the judiciary have a duty 'to enable the children to come to adulthood and make their own decisions about the sort of life they wanted to lead'.[74] As Ward J held in *Re E*,[75] 'The welfare of the child therefore dominates my decision, and I must decide what E's wellbeing dictates.' Neither legislation nor common law define welfare, which enables judges to weigh and balance the factors they deem appropriate. Fiona considers welfare to be a social concept, involving an 'intricate web of a child's relationships with family and friends [that] was the crucial ingredient. No child is an island', and 'a *mutable* concept, to be evaluated by the standards of the reasonable man or woman of today. What sufficed a generation ago might now fall short.'[76] The social and mutable concepts are present in the judicially created ten-point welfare checklist.[77]

Box 16.4: Judicial welfare checklist

(i) The paramount consideration of the court is the best interests of the child. The role of the court when exercising its jurisdiction is to give or withhold consent to medical treatment in the best interests of the child. It is the role and duty of the court to do so and to exercise its own independent and objective judgment.

(ii) The starting point is to consider the matter from the assumed point of view of the patient. The court must ask itself what the patient's attitude to treatment is or would be likely to be.

---

72 S 1(3)(a)–(g).

73 *Re W* (n8).

74 McEwan (n1) 38.

75 *Re E* (n38) 392.

76 McEwan (n1) 16–17.

77 See *University Hospitals Plymouth NHS Trust v B* (n28) [14]. This checklist is an embellished version (based on judicial decisions) of that in the Children Act 1989.

(iii) The question for the court is whether, in the best interests of the child patient, a particular decision as to medical treatment should be taken.
(iv) The term 'best interests' is used in its widest sense, to include every kind of consideration capable of bearing on the decision, this will include, but is not limited to, medical, emotional, sensory, and instinctive considerations. The test is not a mathematical one; the court must do the best it can to balance all of the conflicting considerations in a particular case with a view to determining where the final balance lies. In reaching its decision the court is not bound to follow the clinical assessment of the doctors but must form its own view as to the child's best interests.
(v) There is a strong presumption in favour of taking all steps to preserve life because the individual human instinct to survive is strong and must be presumed to be strong in the patient. The presumption, however, is not irrebuttable. It may be outweighed if the pleasures and the quality of life are sufficiently small and the pain and suffering and other burdens are sufficiently great.
(vi) Within this context, the court must consider the nature of the medical treatment in question, what it involves, and its prospects of success, including the likely outcome for the patient of that treatment.
(vii) There will be cases where it is not in the best interests of the child to subject him or her to treatment that will cause increased suffering and produce no commensurate benefit, giving the fullest possible weight to the child's and mankind's desire to survive.
(viii) Each case is fact specific and will turn entirely on the facts of the particular case.
(ix) The views and opinions of both the doctors and the parents must be considered. The views of the parents may have particular value in circumstances where they know their own child well. However, the court must also be mindful that the views of the parents may, understandably, be coloured by their own emotion or sentiment.
(x) The views of the child must be considered and be given appropriate weight in light of the child's age and understanding.[78]

The views of children, the Children Act 1989[79] and the judicial welfare checklist make clear, must be 'given appropriate weight in light of the child's age and understanding'. A child's capacity, and their proximity to adulthood, must be taken into consideration when assigning weight to their views. The greater a child's capacity and the closer they are to adulthood, the more influence their views have in the best-interests decision. Their views are not, however, determinative. All factors are balanced against each other to determine the child's

78 Ibid.
79 S 1(3)(a).

best interests. A refusal from a capable child does not act, using Lord Donaldson's metaphor, as a key to lock the door for administration of treatment. Their power to consent is not a power to self-determination; their refusals can be overridden by persons with PR, including the court. Adam had capacity, was aged 17 and 9 months, yet it was still said 'If his eighteenth birthday was tomorrow morning, he would not yet have attained his majority today'.[80] Fiona could not respect his refusal where it was not in his best interests. It appears illogical that a child who tomorrow would be legally permitted to refuse is overruled today by virtue of being under 18. However, to create flexibility would require moving to a system where capacity unlocks autonomy and therefore the inevitable eventuality that a child under 18 – and not necessarily only those 'nearly' 18 – are permitted to refuse life-saving treatment. This eventuality sits uncomfortably with most commenters who prefer a welfare approach for all children.

Although there have been no instances in common law where a judge has accepted a capable child's refusal of treatment to be in their best interest, capable children do refuse treatment in practice. A capable child may refuse a treatment but happily consent to an alternative treatment option. Where the alternative is medically appropriate, clinicians will respect the child's decision. Where a child is seeking to veto all medical treatment, the General Medical Council states a hospital *should* seek legal advice if the treatment is considered to be in the best interests of the capable child.[81] Note the term '*should*' rather than 'must'. A doctor may not seek legal advice because they consider the child's refusal to be reasonable (e.g., where treatment is life-prolonging rather than life-saving or the consequences of refusing are minor). Whilst a doctor may present treatment options, they are not necessarily any more or less in the child's best interests than not receiving the treatment. They are merely *options* for the patient. Lawyers are naturally concerned with only the most exceptional cases that result in judicial intervention. Thousands of decisions are made daily without judicial interference, including refusals of medical treatment. However, due to a lack of empirical evidence these decisions go unnoticed in academic literature.

Beyond the judgment

Unlike in case law where the narrative concludes at the end of the judgment, McEwan's novel continues Adam's story beyond the judgment, focusing on the real-world implications of Fiona's decision to administer treatment. After the blood transfusion, Adam struggled to grapple with his new identity, faced hostility from the religious community as he lost his faith, had arguments with his parents, and received no guidance of how to live post-cancer treatment. As

80 McEwan (n1) 68.

81 GMC (General Medical Council), '0–18 Years: Guidance for All Doctors' (nd) https://www.gmc-uk.org/ethical-guidance/ethical-guidance-for-doctors/0-18-years/principles-of-confidentiality, accessed 9 January 2024, [31].

Fiona reflected, 'without faith, how open and beautiful and terrifying the world must have seemed to him'.[82] When Adam's cancer returned, he refused a blood transfusion and died shortly after. On reflection, was the treatment in Adam's best interests? 'How many pages in how many judgments had she devoted to that term? Welfare, well-being, was social. No child is an island. She thought her responsibilities had ended at the court-room walls. But how could they?'[83] This passage encourages us to question what the term best interests really means and whether it considers the child's life beyond the administration of treatment. Is enough consideration given to the potential ramifications of treatment against a capable child's wishes?

The asymmetry between consent and refusal

Gillick and section 8 of the Family Law Reform Act 1969 were a huge step forward for children's autonomy rights.[84] Capable children now had a legal right to consent to medical treatment and no longer required their parents' knowledge or consent prior to seeking and obtaining advice and treatment. The judgments in *Re R* and *Re W*,[85] as the first cases to address the scope of the power to consent, held that the right to consent does not extend to a right to refuse, which sparked controversy. To argue that a child is competent to consent but not to refuse treatment is an illogical proposition to many commentators. Maclean posits that 'It may be argued that logically the capacity to refuse treatment is co-extensive with the capacity to consent to treatment, and that this should allow the child the same right to refuse treatment as to consent to treatment.'[86] Harris argues that the idea that children agree but not refuse is 'palpable nonsense' – because 'to understand a proposed treatment well enough to consent to it is to understand the consequences of a refusal. And if the consequences of a refusal are understood well enough to consent to the alternative then the refusal must also be competent.'[87]

Herring and Gilmore reject this proposition as 'refusing medical treatment is not always the simple obverse of consenting to a particular treatment'.[88] They argue that there is a substantial difference in what is required in law to be capable to consent as compared to refusing. *Gillick* competency, they suggest, requires a child to merely understand the proposed treatment (not what would happen if they don't have the treatment).[89] The standard required of children to be

82 McEwan (n1) 212.

83 Ibid 212–13.

84 Rachel Taylor, 'Reversing the Retreat from Gillick?' (2007) 19 Child Fam Law Q 81.

85 Ibid.

86 Alasdair Maclean, 'Keyholders and Flak Jackets: The Method in the Madness of Mixed Metaphors' (2008) 3 Clin Ethics 121, 122.

87 Ibid 16.

88 Gilmore and Herring (n50) 5.

89 Ibid.

capable to refuse medical treatment is higher. Lord Donaldson MR explained that 'The more serious the decision, the greater the capacity required'.[90] The information relating to refusing is more complex than consenting and is thus more challenging. Therefore, many children simply do not have the required capacity to make such decisions. Children are expected to understand the implications of refusing treatment, including their death and the manner of their death.[91] As can be seen in these cases most do not meet these high standards. Maclean argues that 'children and young persons, even if intellectually capable of rational decision-making, may not have had the opportunity to reflect on the beliefs and values affected by their education and upbringing'.[92] Children occupy a grey area of borderline capacity where they are not incapable but do not yet have the degree of capacity to make complex decisions. Decision-makers in the grey area are more likely to 'be affected by the risk created by the decision' and thus, according to Maclean, we can say that a child is competent to consent (and refuse to give consent) but not competent to refuse treatment.[93]

If the asymmetry between refusal and consent is due to the difference in the standard of capacity required, then where a child does have capacity to refuse medical treatment their refusal would be respected. However, this has not been the case. Courts have overridden decisions by children considered to understand fully the risks associated with the treatment and the consequences of not receiving it. As MacDonald J said in *University Hospitals Plymouth NHS Trust v B*,[94]

> I have also borne in mind B's stated wishes and feelings. However, the law is clear that the court is not mandated to accept the wishes and feelings of a competent child where to honour those wishes and feelings would result in manifest, and even fatal, harm to that child.[95]

The effect of the law is to say to a child 'You are mature enough to be able to make a decision about your treatment and we will respect your decision if you consent, but if you refuse, we will enable your decision to be readily overridden', or, to it put another way, 'we will respect your right to autonomy, but only if you give the right answer!'[96]

The error of many commentators is to seek to reconcile the statutes and case law through a children's rights lens where capacity unlocks autonomy. *Gillick* and section 8 of the Family Law Reform Act 1969 have been mistakenly hailed as leaps forward in the protection of children's autonomy rights, conferring

---

90 *Re T (Adult: Refusal of Treatment)* [1993] Fam 95 [113].
91 *Re M* (n36), Re E (n38); Re L (n47).
92 Maclean (n86) 126.
93 Ibid 124.
94 *University Hospitals Plymouth NHS Trust v B* (n28).
95 Ibid [18].
96 Herring (n49) 257.

on children the power to make decisions for themselves. However, these laws were never intended to strengthen children's autonomy rights. Rather, their purpose is to protect the welfare of the child, and this is achieved by making it easier for doctors to administer treatment to children. Affording legal parents, capable children, and the court an equal and concurrent power to consent to a child's treatment, and enabling capable children to receive advice and treatment without their parents' knowledge, increases the likelihood that children will receive necessary medical treatment. Moreover, children are also protected from suffering serious harm or death that is a result of: (1) their refusal of medical treatment; (2) their consent to non-therapeutic treatment; and (3) their parent(s) refusing all medical treatment. The defence of necessity also protects against the harm a child would suffer if a doctor were unable to administer medical treatment in an emergency because they lacked the necessary consent.

Children's developmental welfare is also protected. Whilst the power to consent may be considered tokenistic when it is not coupled with the power to veto all treatment, Maclean argues this does not mean the power is not meaningless to the child.[97] Where a child is unaware of the limits of their power to consent, they give their consent freely.[98] Therefore, the power to consent provides children with an opportunity to be the decision-maker, albeit without a level of power that would mean they could feel the consequences of refusing all treatment. As Lord Donaldson MR states 'good parenting involves giving minors as much rope as they can handle without an unacceptable risk that they will hang themselves'.[99]

If welfare is accepted as a unifying ethical principle of children's medical law, then we must refrain from framing the law in terms of an acquisition of rights and empowering children and acknowledge the potentially uncomfortable truth that a child's welfare as objectively perceived is always prioritised above their autonomy. Many capable children's autonomous decisions are overruled by their parents and/or the court if they do not conform with what is generally considered to be a good decision by society/the medical community. As we tend to frame children's medical law through the lens of children's rights under the illusion that child medical law empowers children to be decision-makers, it is perhaps time for the legislator to reconsider whether the ethical principle of welfare is still appropriate for the current and future generation of capable children or whether the law should distinguish its treatment of capable children from all other children.

Summary

- The voices and experiences of capable children making medical decisions are often unrecorded and unheard in court cases and the medical decision-making process.

97 Maclean (n86).

98 Ibid 123.

99 *Re W* (n8) 71.

- The judiciary and legislators are seeking to balance respecting a capable children's developing autonomy, views, and decisions and an understandable social desire to protect all children from unavoidable harms and ensure they survive to adulthood ready and able 'to make their own decisions about the sort of life they wanted to lead'.[100]
- The difficulty in attempting to balance all interests is that it ultimately frustrates the capable child whose voice and capable decision-making is silenced in favour of their welfare as determined by adults.
- This chapter sought to encourage thinking about the decision-making process from the capable child's perspective. Legal narratives, fiction and non-fiction, are a unique way to capture and reflect on the diverse voices of capable children who are making complex medical decisions.

Questions for reflection

1. Listen to the Radio 4 podcast, 'Lung Transplant Teenager' (Inside the Ethics Committee, 31 August 2013). Should John have been informed about the severity of their condition? Is it ever ethically and legally permissible to withhold their prognosis from a capable child? The decision as to whether to withdraw John's life support was made by multiple people, including an ethics committee, his doctors, and family. Did you agree with the decision? To what extent was John involved in this decision-making process?
2. Read Emma Cave and Hannah Cave 'Skeleton Keys to Hospital Doors: Adolescent Adults Who Refuse Life-Sustaining Medical Treatment' (2023) 86 Mod Law Rev 984–1010. Consider the recent evidence that suggests that adolescence can continue until a person's mid-20s. What potential impact does this have on the law of consent?

Recommended resources

- Radio 4, 'Inside the Ethics Committee: Lung Transplant Teenager' (2013) https://www.bbc.co.uk/programmes/b038ym0m, accessed 10 January 2024.
- Emma Cave and Hannah Cave, 'Skeleton Keys to Hospital Doors: Adolescent Adults Who Refuse Life-Sustaining Medical Treatment' (2023) 86 Mod Law Rev 984–1010.
- BBC Three, 'Lilly: A Transgender Story' (2022) (access through Box of Broadcasts using your university credentials or BBC iPlayer).
- Rebecca Limb, 'Realising 16- and 17-Year-Olds' Right to Consent to Deceased Organ Donation' (2023) 35 Child Fam L Q 231.

[100] McEwan (n1) 38.

Bibliography

Aldridge J and others, '"I Can't Tell My Child They Are Dying": Helping Parents Have Conversations with their Child' (2017) 102 Arch Dis Child Educ Pract Ed 182

Appelbaum P, 'Assessment of Patients' Competence to Consent to Treatment' (2007) 357 N Engl J Med 1834

Cave E, 'Goodbye Gillick? Identifying and Resolving Problems with the Concept of Child Competence' (2013) 34 Leg Stud 103–22

Cave E and Purshouse C, 'Think of the Children: Liability for Non-Disclosure of Information Post-Montgomery' (2020) 28 Med Law Rev 270

Cawich S and others, 'From the Patient's Perspective: Is there a Need to Improve the Quality of Informed Consent for Surgery in Training Hospitals?' (2013) 17 Perm J 22

Cole C and Kodish E, 'Minors' Right to Know and Therapeutic Privilege' (2013) 15 Virtual Mentor 683

Coyne I and others, 'Information-Sharing between Healthcare Professionals, Parents and Children with Cancer: More than a Matter of Information Exchange' (2016) 25(1) Eur J Cancer Care (Engl) 141

Drane J, 'Competency to Give an Informed Consent: A Model for Making Clinical Assessments' (1984) 252 JAMA 925

Gilmore S and Herring J, '"No" is the Hardest Word: Consent and Children's Autonomy' (2011) 23 Child Fam Law Q 3

GMC (General Medical Council), '0–18 Years: Guidance for All Doctors' (nd) https://www.gmc-uk.org/ethical-guidance/ethical-guidance-for-doctors/0-18-years/principles-of-confidentiality, accessed 9 January 2024

Harris J, 'Consent and End of Life Decisions' (2003) 29 J Med Ethics 10

Herring J, *Medical Law and Ethics* (9th edn, OUP 2023)

Kelly P, 'An Untimely Future for Youth Studies?' (2011) 30 Youth Stud Aust 47

Lamont S, Stewart C, and Chiarella M, 'Capacity and Consent: Knowledge and Practice of Legal and Healthcare Standards' (2019) 26 Nurs Ethics 71

Limb R, 'According Appropriate Weight to Children's Wishes and Feelings: University Hospitals Plymouth NHS Trust v B (A Minor) [2019] EWHC 1670 (Fam)' (2021) 29 Med Law Rev 524

Maclean A, 'Keyholders and Flak Jackets: The Method in the Madness of Mixed Metaphors' (2008) 3 Clin Ethics 121

McEwan I, *The Children Act* (Vintage 2014)

Menkel-Meadow C, 'Telling Stories in School: Using Case Studies and Stories to Teach Legal Ethics' (2000) 69 Fordham L Rev 787

Moreton K, 'A Backwards-Step for Gillick: Trans Children's Inability to Consent to Treatment for Gender Dysphoria – Quincy Bell & Mrs A v The Tavistock and Portman NHS Foundation Trust and Ors' (2021) 29 Med Law Rev 699

Taylor R, 'Reversing the Retreat from Gillick?' (2007) 19 Child Fam Law Q 81

Woodhead M and Montgomery H (eds), *Understanding Childhood: An Interdisciplinary Approach* (John Wiley & Sons 2003)

17

Organ Donation: Deceased Donation

Aileen Editha

The organ scarcity issue is a long-standing problem that is characterised by a scarcity of organ donors even when there is increasing need for transplantation. In England – and, indeed, many other countries across the UK and globally – the situation is most dire for ethnic minority patients. With exceedingly low organ donation rates but growing representation on waiting lists, ethnic minority patients wait much longer for a transplant match compared to their white counterparts. Until recently, deceased organ donation in England – which is the focus of this chapter – was based on an 'opt-in' framework. This means that an individual would have to 'sign up' to donate their organs in the event of their death. However, to reduce the severity of the organ scarcity issue, England has recently implemented an opt-out framework for deceased organ donations through the Organ Donation (Deemed Consent) Act 2019,[1] which amended, among others, section 3 of the Human Tissue Act 2004.[2] An opt-out system means that, unless an individual has explicitly opted-out, their organs can be donated upon their death. Although this is also referred to as 'deemed consent' or 'presumed consent', there have been several disagreements on whether an opt-out framework can be considered as 'consent' at all.[3]

In this chapter, I will investigate and compare the deceased organ donation rates before and after the implementation of the opt-out framework. Its central aim is to explore whether, how, and why England's new opt-out framework has affected deceased organ donation rates among ethnic minority groups (excluding white minorities). I have chosen to focus on England due to its relatively diverse

1 Organ Donation (Deemed Consent) Act 2019 s 7.

2 Human Tissue Act 2004 s 30.

3 See Pradeep Kumar Prabhu, 'Is Presumed Consent an Ethically Acceptable Way of Obtaining Organs for Transplant?' (2019) 20 J Intensive Care Soc 92, 94: 'the opt-out policy for organ donation agrees that the presumption of consent is a misnomer, as consent as we know it involves an active process with its three well known components'.

population,[4] the availability of data,[5] nuances in the legal framework, and the time at which the change was implemented.[6] Ultimately, I will consider whether existing laws and regulations could help solve the organ scarcity issue that is particularly prominent in ethnic minority communities. I will first provide an overview of why the opt-out framework was enacted and how it operates in practice. I will then focus on organ donation and transplantation among ethnic minority groups. I will show that deceased organ donation rates among ethnic minority patients remain persistently low, even with the implementation of an opt-out framework, and that ultimately alternative and/or additional efforts must be taken to effectively and meaningfully address the organ scarcity issue in ethnic minority communities.

Before the substantive discussions, however, there are important clarifications to be made. Although the only available data include both England *and* Wales, the focus of this chapter is only on England's laws as they have only recently been implemented (in 2019), whereas Wales's opt-out model was enacted in 2013. This is also because of the greater nuances in the law, which we will explore later in the chapter. Additionally, I will only discuss deceased organ donations in relation to adults, since there are additional considerations for organ donation and transplantations involving children. Moreover, I will use the term 'ethnic minority groups (excluding white minorities)' throughout this chapter. This will be used interchangeably with 'ethnic minority patients'. Although the term BAME (Black, Asian, Minority Ethnic or Black, Asian, Mixed Race, and Ethnic Minorities) has conventionally been used by the NHS, its use has recently been discouraged by the UK government following recommendations from the Commission on Race and Ethnic Disparities.[7] In March 2021, the Commission recommended that the term 'BAME' should not be used as it 'emphasise[s] certain ethnic minority groups (Asian and black) and exclude[s] others (mixed, other and white ethnic minority groups) [and] can also mask disparities between different ethnic groups and create misleading interpretations of data'.[8]

4 ONS (Office for National Statistics), 'Ethnic Group, National Identity, Language and Religion' (2021) https://census.gov.uk/census-2021-results/phase-one-topic-summaries/ethnic-group-national-identity-language-and-religion, accessed 3 July 2023.

5 There is more data for analysis, especially regarding ethnic minority groups. Although the NHS Blood and Transplant (NHSBT) data refers to England *and* Wales, the latter only accounts for a small percentage of the data.

6 The change in Wales in 2013 is less recent, while the changes in Northern Ireland and Scotland would be too recent to produce any meaningful changes in relevant data.

7 UK Government, 'Writing about Ethnicity' (2021) https://www.ethnicity-facts-figures.service.gov.uk/style-guide/writing-about-ethnicity, accessed 10 October 2023.

8 Ibid. See also: Commission on Race and Ethnic Disparities, 'Independent Report: Summary of Recommendations' (2021) https://www.gov.uk/government/publications/the-report-of-the-commission-on-race-and-ethnic-disparities/summary-of-recommendations, accessed 10 October 2023.

It is also important to acknowledge the impact of the COVID-19 pandemic on organ donation and transplantation rates in recent years. Throughout the pandemic, the living donation programme was temporarily suspended to lower transmission risks and ensure the safety of donors and recipients. Patients waiting for non-urgent transplants were temporarily removed from waiting lists at the height of the pandemic, and their subsequent reactivation caused a significant increase in numbers from 2021 to 2022.[9] The number of successful transplants performed also decreased since operations were not always possible during the pandemic, especially in light of reduced capacity in intensive care units and safety concerns for immunosuppressed patients. Although these services have now been reopened with increasing 'normalcy', statistics from recent years need to be considered against this backdrop.

The opt-out framework: background and application

Until recently, England's organ donation laws have relied solely on an 'opt-in' system. This means that individuals had to provide explicit consent by 'signing up' to organ donation in the event of their death.[10] However, the law changed in 2020 when the Organ Donation (Deemed Consent) Act 2019 came into effect and implemented an 'opt-out' framework. This means that an individual's organs could be donated in the event of their death, unless they have *explicitly opted-out* either in person or online.[11] This framework was enacted because of the organ scarcity issue, which refers to a high demand for organ donations and transplantations (as reflected by the number of patients on transplant lists) but with a scarce supply of organs and/or organ donors. Organ scarcity is a long-standing issue for the UK more generally. Statistics recorded in the early 1990s showed a consistent disparity in the number of donors, transplants performed, and patients on waiting lists. In 1992, 876 donors made 2,591 transplants possible, but 5,124 patients remained on waiting lists.[12] Despite the long-standing nature of the organ scarcity issue, the opt-out systems have only recently come into force in England (2020), Scotland (2021), and Northern Ireland (2023).[13] These low

9 This change was most significant in 2021 when the height of the pandemic had passed. See NHSBT (NHS Blood and Transplant), 'Organ and Tissue Donation and Transplantation Activity Report 2021/22' (2021) https://nhsbtdbe.blob.core.windows.net/umbraco-assets-corp/27108/activity-report-2021-2022.pdf, accessed 28 November 2023.

10 This was done by registering your 'opt-in' with the Organ Donor Registry. This could be done either in person (e.g., stating preferences when filling out driver's licence forms or obtaining an Organ Donor Card) or online through the NHSBT website. See NHSBT, 'Register your Decision' (2023) https://www.organdonation.nhs.uk/register-to-donate/, accessed 10 October 2023.

11 Ibid.

12 John Fabre, 'Organ Donation and Presumed Consent' (1998) 352 Lancet 150.

13 The Human Tissue (Authorisation) (Scotland) Act 2019 came into effect in 2021, whereas Northern Ireland's Organ and Tissue Donation (Deemed Consent) legislation came into effect on 1 June 2023. For an insightful discussion on this, see Jordan A. Parsons, 'Deemed

numbers persist to this day, even after the change. According to the NHS Blood and Transplant (NHSBT) – the body responsible for blood donation services in England and transplant services across the UK – there was one donor for every five people in the waiting list in 2022/23.[14] This may be caused by several factors, such as resource limitations on hospitals and transplant centres that hold back donation processes, such as tissue matching and transplant procedures. It may also be caused by a lack of suitability; that is, the low turnout of eligible donors following the donor selection process. Additionally, it may also be caused by low consent rates as individuals may be reluctant to donate their organs during their lifetime or even upon their death. Addressing the organ scarcity issue may focus on the former (by reducing the need for transplants), the latter (by increasing the supply of organs and donors), or a combination of both.

The law

Lawful transplantations in England must meet three requirements: (1) the patient must be legally deceased; (2) appropriate consent must be obtained; and (3) the transplantation must concern relevant materials.[15] Although there is no statutory definition for 'death', the judiciary has interpreted this to mean 'brain-stem death' per *Re A*[16] (later confirmed in *Airedale NHS Trust v Bland*),[17] which means 'the death of that part of the brain without which the body cannot function at all without assistance'.[18] The Academy of Royal Colleges sets out additional guidelines for clinicians to determine brain-stem death.[19]

Prior to the change in May 2020, 'appropriate consent' was ranked in order of preference and interpreted to mean: the patient's decision immediately before death (s 6(a)), the decision of the patient's nominated representative (s 6(b)),[20] or

Consent for Organ Donation: A Comparison of the English and Scottish Approaches' (2021) 8 J Law Biosci https://doi.org/10.1093/jlb/lsab003.

14 The 2022/23 Activity Report highlighted that, as of 31 March 2023, there were 1,429 deceased organ donors and 6,959 patients on the active transplant list. See NHSBT, 'Organ and Tissue Donation and Transplantation Activity Report 2022/23' (2023) https://nhsbt dbe.blob.core.windows.net/umbraco-assets-corp/30198/activity-report-2022-2023-final.pdf, accessed 23 December 2023, 4.

15 See Human Tissue Act (HTA) 2004. For adults, appropriate consent can be from the deceased person (s 3) through a nominated representative (s 4) or through a qualifying relationship (s 7). This will be discussed later in this chapter.

16 [1992] 3 Med LR 303.

17 [1993] AC 789 (Fam).

18 Ibid 878. The court also stated that deceased patients are those 'who have suffered "brain death" – whose brain stem has permanently ceased to function and who are dependent on a ventilator to maintain respiration, and whose heart always stops within a week or two at the most' (at 798).

19 Academy of Medical Royal Colleges, 'A Code of Practice for the Diagnosis and Confirmation of Death' (2008) https://www.aomrc.org.uk/wp-content/uploads/2016/04/Code_Practice_Confirmation_Diagnosis_Death_1008.pdf, accessed 28 November 2023, see section 2.

20 'Nominated representative' is further defined in HTA 2004 s 4.

the decision of a person who stood in a 'qualifying relationship' to the patient (s 6(c)).[21] Like 'appropriate consent', 'qualifying relationships' are ranked in a specific hierarchy in case of disagreements. This is ranked in order of spouse/partner, parent/child, brother/sister, grandparent/grandchild, child of a brother/sister, stepfather/stepmother, half-brother/half-sister, and long-standing friend.[22] From its inception, this hierarchy has been criticised for promoting a narrow view of family life and, as David Price noted, may impact a person's right to respect for family life.[23] Sociologist Naomi Gerstel has shown that although white individuals focus on marriage and the nuclear family, racialised persons are more likely to have extended kin ties, especially when they come from less-affluent backgrounds.[24]

However, the Organ Donation (Deemed Consent) Act 2019 amended section 3 of the Act when it came into effect in May 2020.[25] Although 'appropriate consent' is still ranked in order of preference, its hierarchy is now: (1) the patient's decision immediately before death, that is, whether they have opted-in or out (s 6(a)); (2) the decision of the patient's nominated representative (s 6(b)); (3) the deemed consent of the deceased (s 6(ba)); or (4) the decision of a person who stood in 'qualifying relationship' to the patient (s 6(c)).[26] The presumption of consent thus ranks higher than the decisions of friends and families. However, this new provision does not apply to 'excepted adults', which includes those who have resided in England for less than 12 months, or deceased persons who, for a significant period before dying, lacked capacity to understand the effect of the opt-out model. Additionally, the opt-out provision is not applicable to novel transplants.[27]

There are several important aspects to note about the law. Like the framework enforced in Wales, the opt-out *does not replace* the pre-existing opt-in framework; rather, they operate simultaneously. According to the HTA's section 3 hierarchy

21 'Qualifying relationship' is further defined in HTA 2004 s 27(4).

22 Price writes (in a footnote): 'Whilst it was conceded that parents might frequently disagree, as might a person's existing partner and his or her estranged spouse, the existing scheme was justified by the Government on the basis that requiring the consent of all, or a majority, would be unworkable': David Price, 'The Human Tissue Act 2004' (2005) 68 Mod Lang Rev 798, 808.

23 Price (ibid) states that 'it surprised some commentators that spouses and partners (this excludes siblings or other relatives who live together but not "as partners") feature highest despite the absence of any *blood* relationship to the now deceased'.

24 Naomi Gerstel, 'Rethinking Families and Community: The Color, Class, and Centrality of Extended Kin Ties' (2011) 26 Sociol Forum 1.

25 NHSBT, 'Timeline for Max and Keira's Law' (nd) https://www.organdonation.nhs.uk/uk-laws/organ-donation-law-in-england/timeline-for-max-and-keiras-law/, accessed 10 October 2023.

26 The aforementioned hierarchy applies here.

27 HTA 2004 states that the opt-out framework is only applicable to 'permitted materials' as opposed to 'relevant materials', as clarified through the Human Tissue (Permitted Material: Exceptions) (England) Regulations 2020 No 521 regulation 2.

Table 17.1: Reasons behind family refusals to provide consent/authorisation[a]

Reasons for refusal (2018 to 2023)	Asian	Black	Other ethnicity	Mixed*
Family felt it was against their religious or cultural beliefs	29.5%	20.1%	21.6%	10.8%
Patient had previously expressed a wish not to donate	19.7%	23.2%	15.9%	5.4%
Unsure whether the patient would have agreed to donation	9.4%	13.1%	14.8%	8.1%
Family did not want surgery to the body	8.9%	6.4%	13.6%	10.8%

[a] Data from ED Report 2022/23 (n34) 28–9.
* These terms and classifications were used by the NHSBT in the ED Report.

and relevant Codes of Practice, practitioners must first look through the Organ Donor Registry to see if the deceased has *opted-in* or *opted-out* (s 6(a)).[28] If that information is not available, they will consider the presence of a nominated representative (s 6(b)). In their absence, the deemed consent provision will then be considered (s 6(ba)) before finally moving on to the decision of a person who stood in a qualifying relationship (s 6(c)). However, there are some uncertainties on the relationship between and practicalities of the latter two provisions. Throughout the deemed consent process, the patient's family members and/or friends may refuse to provide consent/authorisation – which, as I will explore later, is more prominent among ethnic minority groups. Similarly, those who stood in a qualifying relationship with the patient could also refuse donation, albeit in a specific order. It may be incorrectly assumed that refusals for opt-out donations would *only* centre on the patient's wishes, whereas qualifying persons' refusals would *only* reflect the relatives' views. In practice, the patient's relatives have two opportunities to object to donation and can cite patient-centred or personal reasons (see Table 17.1).[29] Deference to the family is characteristic of a soft opt-out.[30] This is markedly different from a hard opt-out framework, 'where the donor is presumed to have consented for organ donation unless registered to the contrary, and donation proceeds regardless of their families' wishes'.[31]

28 See Human Tissue Authority, 'Code F Part II: Deceased Organ and Tissue Donation' (2023) https://content.hta.gov.uk/sites/default/files/2020-12/Public%20guide%20to%20HTA%20Code%20F%20part%202.pdf, accessed 28 November 2023, [65].

29 Patient-centred reasons would cite objections from what the deceased would have wanted, whereas personal reasons would focus on the relatives' own wishes and views.

30 '[U]nder a soft system there is a presumption in favour of donation, but the family have the final say' (Chris Rudge, 'Organ Donation: Opting In or Opting Out?' (2018) 68 Brit J Gen Pract 62).

31 Gareth Iacobucci, 'Organ Donation: England Will Have an "Opt-Out" System from May 2020' (2020) 368 BMJ m752.

However, the fact that family and friends have *two* opportunities to object suggests that England's law is a *very* soft opt-out system.

Organ scarcity and ethnic minorities

Ethnicity and organ donation

Why and how are transplant success and organ longevity affected by the ethnic backgrounds of donors and recipients? Histocompatibility, also known as tissue compatibility or tissue matching, refers to the degrees of similarity between human leukocyte antigen (HLA) markers or antibodies. HLA markers are present in most cells in the body and are used by the immune system to identify which cells belong in an individual's body and which do not. This is important to protect the body from infections. Each person has numerous types of HLA markers, and some are correlated with ethnicity, geographical origin, and ancestry. However, these biological traits (e.g., ethnic background and ancestry) are often confused with race, which is a purely social construct. I will further explore this issue later in the chapter.

Increased compatibility between the donor and recipient's HLA markers would increase the transplant success rate, as the recipient's immune system will be less likely to reject the transplant material. Increased compatibility also means that the transplanted organ would have more longevity due to the lowered risk of damage from the recipient's immune response. Histocompatibility explains why a transplant is more likely to succeed if the donor and recipient are biologically related, as genetic similarities would lower the risk of the recipient's immune response to the graft or transplant. Although histocompatibility is important for all transplantations, it is more so for certain organs. Renal (kidney) transplants are more successful when donors and recipients match in blood group and tissue type, which is more likely found in families or those of the same ethnic background.[32] Due to the importance of tissue matching, the objective is to obtain a diverse pool of organ donors, as this would 'help serve a growing list of those in need'.[33] In spite of this, the relationship between ethnicity, histocompatibility, and success rates warrants further exploration, as there is a lack of understanding and research for donation and transplantations among ethnic minority groups. I will discuss these problems later in the chapter.

32 Jennifer Kwan and others, 'Donor and Recipient Ethnicity Impacts Renal Graft Adverse Outcomes' (2018) 5 J Racial Ethn Health Dis 1003.

33 Alex Osiadacz, 'Why Diverse Organ Donors Are Needed' (2023) https://newsnetwork.mayoclinic.org/discussion/mayo-clinic-minute-why-diverse-organ-donors-are-needed/, accessed 10 October 2023.

Trends among ethnic minority groups

The organ scarcity issue is amplified among ethnic minority groups. There are low consent rates among deceased organ donations but a steady increase in the number of ethnic minority patients opting out and on waiting lists. To better record this, NHSBT has, since 2016, published the 'Annual Report on Ethnicity Differences in Organ Donation and Transplantation' (ED Report) to supplement the 'Annual Transplant Activity Report'. The ED Report focuses on trends among ethnic minority groups and compares them with more general trends across the Activity Report. The figures I reference are from the 2022/23 ED Report,[34] which is the most recent version available at the time of writing.

Overall, the presence of ethnic minority patients on waiting lists continues to grow. The 2022/23 ED Report shows that, although the number of transplants performed on ethnic minority patients increased by 2.4 per cent, there was a 13 per cent increase in the number of ethnic minority patients waiting for transplants.[35] There were 2,237 ethnic minority patients on the 2022/23 active transplants list, which amounts to a five-year high.[36] The number of living organ donors from ethnic minority groups has increased by 6 per cent, but it is still relatively low compared to pre-pandemic figures.[37] Additionally, the number of deceased organ donors from ethnic minority groups has decreased by 1.9 per cent from 2021/22.[38] This decrease has contributed to much longer wait times for ethnic minority patients. Within one year of being on the waiting list, a white adult has a 48.6 per cent chance of receiving a transplant, while an ethnic minority patient only has a 33.5 per cent chance.[39] While there is only a 14.9 per cent chance that a white adult is still waiting for an organ after three years, that chance is nearly doubled for ethnic minority patients at 28.4 per cent.[40]

The pandemic has undoubtedly prolonged these wait times due to resource limitations (among other things). However, challenges caused by the pandemic – in the field of healthcare or elsewhere – have and continue to disproportionately affect ethnic minority groups.[41] The height of the pandemic saw the temporary suspension of non-urgent transplants, which will have affected many.[42] According

34 NHSBT, 'Annual Report on Ethnicity Differences 2022/23' (2023) https://nhsbtdbe.blob.core.windows.net/umbraco-assets-corp/31332/annual-report-on-ethnicity-differences-final-2022_2023.pdf, accessed 23 December 2023, 3.

35 Ibid 12–15.

36 Ibid 12: 'This is mostly due to increases in the kidney and liver transplant lists, where non-urgent patients have been reactivated after being suspended during the height of the pandemic.'

37 Ibid 31 shows that there are currently 138 living organ donors from ethnic minority groups, whereas in 2018/19 and 2019/20 there were 150 and 159 respectively.

38 Ibid 31: as there were 110 deceased ethnic minority donors in 2021/22 and 108 in 2022/23.

39 Ibid 32.

40 Ibid.

41 See Chapter 5 in this book on health inequity and the pandemic.

42 NHSBT (n34) 5.

to the 2021 Census estimate,[43] ethnic minority groups only account for 18.3 per cent of the entire population in England and Wales. Yet, there is a clear overrepresentation in the number of ethnic minority patients removed from transplant waiting lists: 40.8 per cent (589) of the 1,443 removed were ethnic minorities.[44] This is more than double the 2021 Census estimate for the percentage of ethnic minority groups relative to the entire population.

Longer wait times consequently influence key outcomes, such as transplant success. By the time an ethnic minority patient receives a transplant, their health may have further deteriorated, which may reduce organ longevity and increase chances of donor organ failure. This was confirmed by the NHSBT's new study, stating that '[ethnic minority patients] face significant disadvantages in access to the renal transplant waitlist and may wait twice as long as white recipients for a deceased donor renal transplant.'[45] Consequently, patients end up 'spending longer time on dialysis, so their health may have deteriorated more'.[46] The NHSBT found that, among over 20,000 kidney organs transplanted in over a decade, 'Asian donor and black recipient ethnicities were associated with inferior long-term outcomes, when compared with white counterparts.'[47] Interestingly, these inferior outcomes are also seen among donor ethnicities. Asian and Black donors have the lowest seven-year graft survival rate at 71.9 per cent and 74 per cent respectively, whereas the rate for white donors is 80.5 per cent. These figures remain low even when donor and recipient pairs were of the same ethnicity: 81 per cent of white donor–recipient pairs still had a successful graft, compared to 70.6 per cent of Asian and 69.2 per cent of Black pairs. In the case of renal transplants especially, Black donor–recipient pairs have a 92 per cent increased risk of the donor organ failing compared to white pairs.[48]

As of 2023 there are 2.3 million opt-out registrants and 28.6 million opt-in registrants across all groups and ethnicities in both England and Wales.[49] Although the number of opt-in registrations saw a 1.1 million increase

---

43 ONS (n4).

44 NHSBT, 'Annual Report on Ethnicity Differences 2021/22' (2022) https://nhsbtdbe.blob.core.windows.net/umbraco-assets-corp/28665/annual-report-on-ethnicity-differences-2021_2022.pdf, accessed 23 December 2023, 11–12, compared with (n9) 4. The Activity Report 2021/22 showed that the number of patients on active waiting lists went from 5,699 (2019/20) to 4,256 (2020/21) whereas the ED Report 2021/22 showed a decrease from 1,826 (2019/20) to 1,237 (2020/21) for ethnic minority patients.

45 Abdul Hakeem and others, 'Impact of Asian and Black Donor and Recipient Ethnicity on the Outcomes after Deceased Donor Kidney Transplantation in the United Kingdom' (2021) Lancet Preprint https://doi.org/10.2139/ssrn.3792111, accessed 16 July 2024.

46 Abdul Hakeem and others, 'Asian Donor and Black Recipient Kidney Grafts more Likely to Fail Sooner compared to White Counterparts' (The European Society for Organ Transplantation Congress, Milan, September 2021).

47 Ibid.

48 Ibid.

49 NHSBT (n14) 12–17.

from 2022 to 2023, there was a 4 per cent decrease in the overall consent/authorisation rate for organ donation. These decreasing trends are also reflected among ethnic minority groups as family consent rates are much lower compared to white eligible donors. The 2022/23 ED Report shows that only 40 per cent of ethnic minority patients' families provide consent/authorisation to proceed with deceased organ donation. The rate is almost doubled among white families, at 71 per cent. There is also a rapid decline in the rate at which family members provide consent/authorisation for deceased organ donations. Although the overall consent/authorisation rate has steadily declined from 69 per cent (2021) to 66 per cent (2022) to 62 per cent (2023), this decrease is more significant among ethnic minority groups. The rate among ethnic minority groups has been stable at 41.8 per cent from 2017 to 2019, but this decreased to 34.8 per cent in 2023. The 2022/23 Report shows that family members of deceased ethnic minority patients most commonly cite four reasons for refusing to proceed with organ donation (see Table 17.1). Without the implementation of an opt-out framework, questions surrounding family refusal rates would not have been asked and these reasons would remain unknown. These are valuable considerations to explore; by providing much-needed insight on the root cause(s) of any objections to deceased organ donations, this may aid in ensuring family's refusal and objections can be addressed more effectively.

It is clear that trends among ethnic minority groups show increased severity of the organ scarcity issue and inferior long-term outcomes in regard to transplant success and graft survival. What has been the impact of the recent opt-out framework in England among ethnic minority groups? Thus far, the new framework has had little to no positive impact on deceased organ donation rates among ethnic minority groups. Decreasing trends, even after the opt-out enactment, show, to an extent, that the opt-out model may have *negatively* impacted deceased donation in ethnic minority groups, though this may have been caused by the pandemic. Time will undoubtedly provide further insight into the full extent of the framework's impacts, but it seems clear that relying *solely* on an opt-out framework cannot reduce the organ scarcity issue among ethnic minority groups. While the deemed consent provision may be helpful if individuals forget to take the positive steps necessary to opt-in to organ donation throughout their lifetimes but are otherwise willing, non-donation among ethnic minority groups is premised on more fundamental and deeper objections, which an opt-out model cannot, in and of itself, address.[50]

[50] See Alberto Molina-Pérez, David Rodriguez-Arias, and Janet Delgado, 'Differential Impact of Opt-In, Opt-Out Policies on Deceased Organ Donation Rates: A Mixed Conceptual and Empirical Study' (2022) 12 BMJ Open e057107. See also Aileen Editha, 'Why England's New Opt-Out Won't Help BAME Communities' (2020) https://blogs.bmj.com/medical-ethics/2020/12/04/why-englands-new-opt-out-wont-help-bame-communities/, accessed 10 October 2023.

Looking to the future

What, if any, alternative and/or additional efforts could be made to ensure that organ scarcity among ethnic minority groups is reduced? As shown, consent/authorisation rates among ethnic minority groups remain alarmingly low, especially compared to the growing number of ethnic minority patients on waiting lists. I argue that it will be valuable to implement both patient-centric and community-based approaches to organ donation. A patient-centric approach refers to efforts to raise awareness on the importance of deceased organ donation at the individual level, which includes encouraging people to discuss their decisions with loved ones. This would, at the very least, minimise refusals based on uncertainties as to what the patient would have wanted.

Finally, I will briefly consider two other approaches: effective and equitable allocation of available organs and, crucially, addressing fundamental systemic inequalities.

Revisiting the framework and increasing willingness to donate

The limitations of a soft opt-out system do not necessarily mean that it cannot improve deceased organ donation rates. It is, however, tempting to move towards a hard opt-out system to increase donation rates even further. In a hard opt-out, unless an individual has explicitly opted out, their organs are donated upon their death even when family members object.[51] In addition to potentially being a controversial decision, a hard opt-out system would take several years to implement since it would involve amending existing laws; for example, redefining 'appropriate consent'.[52] Indeed, a soft opt-out framework can and has been shown to improve deceased organ donation rates. It is particularly useful if individuals with no objections, who simply forgot to opt in, and thus had not done so before their death. Additionally, it creates an additional and valuable space for diverse religious and cultural views to be taken into account and respected. Soft opt-out frameworks have shown a great deal of success in other countries. One frequently cited example is Spain since its deceased organ donations rate has become and remains one of the highest in the world at 40.79 per million population (2022) since implementing a soft opt-out system in 1979.[53] However, transplant experts and scholars in Spain, who do not consider the country as an 'opt-out' since it does not retain a list of opt-out registrants,[54] largely attribute Spain's success to a series of policy changes at the hospital and community levels.

---

51 Ibid.

52 Especially s 3(6), which concerns the meaning of appropriate consent for deceased donations.

53 Transplant Observatory, 'Global Observatory on Donation and Transplantation' (nd) https://www.transplant-observatory.org/summary/, accessed 3 July 2023.

54 Rafael Matesanz and Beatriz Domínguez-Gil, 'Opt-Out Legislations: The Mysterious Viability of the False' (2019) 95 Kidney Int 1301.

> The Spanish government established a national transplant network across all hospitals, and invested substantially in facilitating the *early identification* of potential donors by capacitating hospital staff *specifically* for this purpose. A vast transplant coordinator network, specially trained in requesting organ donation, approaches family members.[55]

This raised awareness on the importance of, and helped create positive associations around, organ donation.

In England, family consent/authorisation rates among ethnic minority groups remain relatively low. Increasing this rate is very important, especially since deceased organ donations are at already-low levels. It has been established that family members often refuse to provide consent/authorisation due to various reasons; for example, religious and/or cultural beliefs, uncertainty as to the patient's wishes, the patient expressing a wish not to donate, and because they did not want the body to be subjected to surgery.[56] Some have argued that sole reliance on opt-outs is not enough when there are fundamental objections to organ donation. These concerns and objections cannot be addressed simply through the implementation of the opt-out framework; instead, more targeted and focused efforts should be implemented.

Although there have been efforts to address refusals on the basis of religious and cultural beliefs, more needs to be done. Currently, the NHSBT partners with various local community and religious organisations and has also encouraged religious leaders to show support for organ donation.[57] Moreover, specialist nurses are also trained to communicate with patients' family members about organ donation. This includes answering any questions regarding the process as well as addressing any concerns raised. This is very similar to the system implemented in Spain, which, as we have seen, is considered to be a (if not *the*) reason behind the country's high deceased organ donation rates. With a similar system in place, perhaps England will experience the positive impacts experienced in Spain.

With regard to what the patient would have wanted, whether there is uncertainty or it is known that they would have refused to donate their organs, focus should be directed at raising awareness on the benefits of organ donation and encouraging patients to communicate their decisions to their families. Even though it is important to work and build rapport with families, it is also still imperative to work with potential donors from ethnic minority groups in a community environment or when accessing healthcare services. The NHSBT has been and is currently working with the National BAME Transplant Alliance

55 Harriet Etheredge, 'Assessing Global Organ Donation Policies: Opt-In vs Opt-Out' (2021) 14 Risk Manag Healthc Policy 1985.

56 NHSBT (n44) 28.

57 NHSBT, 'Faith and Donation' (nd) https://www.nhsbt.nhs.uk/how-you-can-help/get-involved/download-digital-materials/faith-and-donation/, accessed 2 July 2023.

(NBTA) to improve organ donation rates (for both living and deceased donations) among ethnic minority groups.[58] The NHSBT Report states that their goal is to 'address these barriers [to organ donation] and give confidence to these communities in not only gaining knowledge of organ donation but how to tackle the topic with their loved ones'.[59]

> Survey results of BAME communities show that not knowing enough about organ donation is also a major barrier to organ donation. NHSBT and the National BAME Transplant Alliance (NBTA) have been working in partnership over a number of years to address these barriers. The Community Investment Scheme and the Living Transplant Initiative are now well-established programmes which empower BAME community groups to promote organ donation in targeted groups.[60]

However, the NBTA's current resources and initiatives focus mainly on improving *living* organ donation rates; there is only limited information and resources on *deceased* organ donations. The most recent – and, according to the website, only – initiative is the Living Transplant Initiative, which aims to 'increase the number of living kidney transplants among BAME communities through a targeted approach'.[61] The NHSBT has outsourced management of this Initiative to the NBTA since 2016, yet there is no mention of a specific scheme to raise such awareness for deceased donations. The Community Grants Programme, previously known as the Community Investment Scheme, simply seeks to award grants to community organisations but there is no uniform approach. Furthermore, the NHSBT only allocates approximately £700,000 annually for the Programme, and this is spread across all types of donations (organ, blood, and stem cell) for all ethnic minority groups. This merely amounts to 3.9 per cent of the total £18 million allocated to help the country effectively transition to an opt-out system.[62] This is a relatively and disproportionately small sum.

It is also imperative to ensure that individuals have an accurate and positive association with organ donation, as was proven to be crucial in Spain. In

58 NHSBT, 'Engagement with Organ Donation in BAME Groups Continues to Grow' (nd) https://www.nhsbt.nhs.uk/news/engagement-with-organ-donation-in-bame-groups-continues-to-grow/, accessed 2 July 2023. See also NBTA (National BAME Transplant Alliance), 'Charities to Celebrate Improved Organ Donation System in England Three Years On' (2023) https://www.nbta-uk.org.uk/news/charities-to-celebrate-improved-organ-donation-system-in-england-three-years-on/, accessed 13 May 2023.

59 NHSBT (n44) 6.

60 NHSBT (n44).

61 Ibid.

62 This amount is to be spent across a period of three to four years: UK Government, 'An Opt-Out System of Organ and Tissue Donation (Impact Assessment)' (2018) https://assets.publishing.service.gov.uk/government/uploads/system/uploads/attachment_data/file/731915/Organ_donation_impact_assessment.pdf, accessed 27 May 2023.

England, such efforts fall within the general management of NHSBT.[63] However, investing in *targeted* initiatives among ethnic minority groups could facilitate more meaningful conversations and permanent changes. Some of the ways these targeted approaches could be actualised is through further equipping the NBTA with appropriate resources to also increase awareness on deceased organ donations. Moreover, specialist nurses responsible for transplant processes must be well versed in issues specific to ethnic minority groups – perhaps with specialist training in cultural competency. In some cases, such difficult conversations may be more comfortable and, as a result, have more positive impacts when conducted with specialist nurses with the same or, at least, similar cultural, religious, and/or ethnic backgrounds.[64] Additionally, paying more attention and due regard to the intersection of individuals' marginalised identities could help form, facilitate, and foster these meaningful connections.[65] Where the possibility of deceased organ donation arises, the approach must be tailored to specific patients and family members.[66] Ultimately, further equipping specialised organisations and personnel with appropriate resources and tools to conduct these tasks could significantly improve awareness and consent/authorisation rates.

Beyond improving consent and authorisation

It is also important to explore efforts that go *beyond* increasing consent/authorisation rates. The 2022/23 ED Report highlights two major barriers in organ donation and transplantation among ethnic minority groups, namely limited organ availability and inefficient referral networks. Although this chapter has thoroughly discussed the former, it is also important to explore how systematic and procedural changes could help reduce the severity of the organ scarcity issue among ethnic minority groups. In particular, further research on histocompatibility needs to be done to ensure effective and equitable allocation and higher transplant success rates. Currently, the allocation of organs to patients on active transplant lists depends largely on compatibility (including ethnicity),

63 Another important criticism is that the framework's introduction was poorly handled, managed, and covered by the media: see Jordan A. Parsons and Greg Moorlock, 'A Global Pandemic is Not a Good Time to Introduce "Opt-Out" for Organ Donation' (2020) 20 Med Law Int 155.

64 See L. Ebony Boulware and others, 'Race and Trust in the Health Care System' (2003) 118 Public Health Rep 358; see also Sandra S. Smith, 'Race and Trust' (2010) 36 Annu Rev Sociol 453.

65 See Kimberlé Crenshaw, 'Mapping the Margins: Intersectionality, Identity Politics, and Violence against Women of Color' (1991) 43 Stan Law Rev 1241. In the context of healthcare, see Daniel Holman and others, 'Can Intersectionality Help with Understanding and Tackling Health Inequalities? Perspectives of Professional Stakeholders' (2021) 19 Health Res Policy Sys https://doi.org/10.1186/s12961-021-00742-w, accessed 16 July 2024.

66 Val Morrison, 'Health Inequalities and Intersectionality' (2015) www.ncchpp.ca/docs/2015_Ineq_Ineq_Intersectionnalite_En.pdf, accessed 27 May 2023.

race, perceived need, and waiting time. For kidney transplants, for instance, this 'need' is assessed by calculating estimated glomerular filtration rate (eGFR), which is one of the most accurate determinants of renal functionality as it measures how well a patient's kidney filters blood. Higher eGFR levels indicate better kidney functioning; a result of 60 or higher is deemed normal functioning.

Prior to late 2021, England – along with most Western high-income jurisdictions – considered a patient's race when calculating eGFR. This is because racially biased studies in the early 1980s suggested that Black patients have higher levels of muscle mass and, consequently, creatinine, which is one of many substances filtered from the blood by the kidney. Although it is not directly taken into account during the testing process, a patient's laboratory result will often indicate two different eGFR results: a lower number for non-Black and a much higher one for Black patients. This is extremely problematic because race is a purely social construct,[67] and assuming predetermined health conditions purely based on a social category is inaccurate and troubling, as it leads to an overestimation of the kidney's functioning. This has resulted in Black adult patients accruing the longest waiting time for kidney transplants (between 605 to 693 days).[68]

The eGFR race adjustment was officially removed from the National Institute of Health and Care Excellence (NICE) Chronic Kidney Disease (CKD) guideline in August 2021,[69] and the 2022/23 ED Report statistics have already shown positive changes. The number of Black patients on renal active transplant lists has increased by 22 per cent from 578 patients (in 2021/22) to 707 in 2022/23 (see Table 17.2), which is double the overall percentage increase and almost double the percentage increase among Asian ethnic minority patients. This suggests that Black adult patients are now more likely to receive the care that they need.

Additionally, efforts to better understand transplant success need to be taken. New studies have shown that solid donor organ failure is much more likely when the donor is from an ethnic minority group, regardless of the recipient's ethnicity. Hannah Valentine, former Chief Scientific Officer for Scientific Workforce Diversity in the US National Institute of Health, stated that this is 'really a complicated and somewhat nuanced situation'.[70]

Perhaps the most challenging yet important change that needs to be implemented is to recognise that, like many other aspects of healthcare, ethnic

---

67 See e.g., Keisha Ray, *Black Health: The Social, Political, and Cultural Determinants of Black People's Health* (OUP 2023); Dorothy Roberts, *Fatal Invention: How Science, Politics, and Big Business Re-create Race in the Twenty-First Century* (2nd edn, The New Press 2021).

68 NHSBT (n14) 39.

69 NICE (National Institute of Clinical Excellence), 'NICE Guideline: Chronic Kidney Disease: Assessment and Management' (24 November 2021) https://www.nice.org.uk/guidance/ng203, accessed 20 December 2023.

70 Hannah Valentine, 'Genetic Diversities as a Paradigm of Inequality Management' (2021) www.esot.org/esot-congress-review, accessed 3 July 2023.

Table 17.2: Number of patients on renal active transplant lists in 2021/22 and 2022/23[a]

Groups	2021/22	2022/23	% change
Asian	989	1121	+ 13%
Black	578	707	+ 22%
Mixed	29	32	+ 10%
Other	159	154	– 3%
White	3,129	3,438	+ 9%
Total	4,884	5,452	+ 11%

[a] NHSBT, 'Annual Report on Ethnicity Differences 2022/23' (n34) 43.

minority patients experience disproportionately negative outcomes. Even with the positive change made to the NICE CKD guidelines, there are misunderstandings on the difference between race and ethnicity persist and these are perpetuated by influential institutions and bodies. The joint statement released by the UK Kidney Association (UKKA), Kidney Care UK, Kidney Research UK, and National Kidney Federation referred to the eGFR race adjustment as 'ethnicity adjustment' and race as 'black ethnicity'.[71] Learned and entrenched factors, such as systemic inequalities and unconscious biases, have perpetuated race-based medicine and resulted in a general lack of trust in healthcare systems and practitioners.[72] To an extent, the first step in addressing the organ scarcity issue among ethnic minority groups is to recognise it as an urgent and serious problem in its own right. This would urge the NHS to enact more tailored solutions that can better address the issue. There needs to be meaningful efforts – indeed, across all sectors of health beyond organ donation – to rebuild meaningful and trusting relationships with ethnic minority communities.

Summary

- In light of increasing needs for transplants and decreasing number of donors (otherwise known as the 'organ scarcity' issue), England has implemented an opt-out framework for deceased organ donations.
- Although this may somewhat improve organ donation rates, it has and will most likely not aid in solving the organ scarcity issue among ethnic minority groups. This issue needs to be recognised, considered, and solved in its own right.

71 UKKA (UK Kidney Association), 'Removal of the Ethnicity Adjustment for Kidney Function Testing and the NICE Chronic Kidney Disease (CKD) Guideline: A Joint Statement from Professional, Patient, and Research Kidney Organisations' (2021) https://ukkidney.org/renal-association/news/2021-nice-ckd-guideline, accessed 20 December 2023.

72 See Sarah Salway and others, 'Obstacles to "Race Equality" in the English National Health Service: Insights from the Healthcare Commissioning Arena' (2016) 152 Soc Sci Med 102. See also Chapter 5.

- Further efforts need to be taken to increase awareness on the importance of organ donation, improve family consent/authorisation rates, ensure equitable and effective allocation, and address systemic inadequacies.

Questions for reflection

- What are your views on applying the opt-out framework to deceased organ donations?
- What roles, if any, can institutions and individuals play to help increase deceased organ donation rates across ethnic minority populations?
- What programmes or efforts can NHSBT implement to increase deceased organ donation rates among members of ethnic minority groups?

Recommended resources

- Dorothy Roberts, 'The Problem with Race-Based Medicine' (2015) https://www.youtube.com/watch?v=KxLMjn4WPBY, accessed 15 June 2023.
- Noor Zurani Md Haris Robson, Azad Hassan Razack, and Norman Dublin, 'Review Paper: Organ Transplants: Ethical, Social, and Religious Issues in a Multicultural Society' (2010) 22 Asia Pac J Public Health 271.
- Harald Schmidt, Dorothy Roberts, and Nwamaka Eneanya, 'Rationing, Racism and Justice: Advancing the Debate around "Colourblind" COVID-19 Ventilator Allocation' (2022) 48 J Med Ethics 126–30.
- Tiffanie Wen, 'Why Don't More People Want to Donate their Organs?' (2014) https://www.theatlantic.com/health/archive/2014/11/why-dont-people-want-to-donate-their-organs/382297/, accessed 3 July 2023.
- Nicola Williams, Laura O'Donovan, and Steve Wilkinson, 'Presumed Dissent? Opt-Out Organ Donation and the Exclusion of Organs and Tissues' (2022) 30 Med Law Rev 268–98.

Bibliography

Academy of Medical Royal Colleges, 'A Code of Practice for the Diagnosis and Confirmation of Death' (2008) https://www.aomrc.org.uk/wp-content/uploads/2016/04/Code_Practice_Confirmation_Diagnosis_Death_1008.pdf, accessed 28 November 2023

Boulware LB and others, 'Race and Trust in the Health Care System' (2003) 118 Public Health Rep 358

Commission on Race and Ethnic Disparities, 'Independent Report: Summary of Recommendations' (2021) https://www.gov.uk/government/publications/the-report-of-the-commission-on-race-and-ethnic-disparities/summary-of-recommendations, accessed 10 October 2023

Crenshaw K, 'Mapping the Margins: Intersectionality, Identity Politics, and Violence against Women of Color' (1991) 43 Stan Law Rev 1241

Etheredge H, 'Assessing Global Organ Donation Policies: Opt-In vs Opt-Out' (2021) 14 Risk Manag Healthc Policy 1985

Fabre J, 'Organ Donation and Presumed Consent' (1998) 352 Lancet 150

Gerstel N, 'Rethinking Families and Community: The Color, Class, and Centrality of Extended Kin Ties' (2011) 26 Sociol Forum 1

Hakeem A and others, 'Asian Donor and Black Recipient Kidney Grafts More Likely to Fail Sooner compared to White Counterparts' (The European Society for Organ Transplantation Congress, Milan, September 2021)

Hakeem A and others, 'Impact of Asian and Black Donor and Recipient Ethnicity on the Outcomes after Deceased Donor Kidney Transplantation in the United Kingdom' (2021) Lancet Preprint https://doi.org/10.2139/ssrn.3792111, accessed 16 July 2023

Holman D and others, 'Can Intersectionality Help with Understanding and Tackling Health Inequalities? Perspectives of Professional Stakeholders' (2021) 19 Health Res Policy Sys https://doi.org/10.1186/s12961-021-00742-w, accessed 16 July 2023

Human Tissue Authority, 'Code F Part II: Deceased Organ and Tissue Donation' (2023) https://content.hta.gov.uk/sites/default/files/2020-12/Public%20guide%20to%20HTA%20Code%20F%20part%202.pdf, accessed 28 November 2023

Iacobucci G, 'Organ Donation: England Will Have an "Opt-Out" System from May 2020' (2020) 368 BMJ m752

Kwan J and others, 'Donor and Recipient Ethnicity Impacts Renal Graft Adverse Outcomes' (2018) 5 J Racial Ethn Health Dis 1003

Matesanz R and Domínguez-Gil B, 'Opt-Out Legislations: The Mysterious Viability of the False' (2019) 95 Kidney Int 1301

Morrison V, 'Health Inequalities and Intersectionality' (2015) www.ncchpp.ca/docs/2015_Ineg_Ineq_Intersectionnalite_En.pdf, accessed 27 May 2023

NHSBT (NHS Blood and Transplant), 'Organ and Tissue Donation and Transplantation Activity Report 2021/22' (2021) https://nhsbtdbe.blob.core.windows.net/umbraco-assets-corp/27108/activity-report-2021-2022.pdf, accessed 28 November 2023

NHSBT (NHS Blood and Transplant), 'Annual Report on Ethnicity Differences 2021/22' (2022) https://nhsbtdbe.blob.core.windows.net/umbraco-assets-corp/28665/annual-report-on-ethnicity-differences-2021_2022.pdf, accessed 23 December 2023

NHSBT (NHS Blood and Transplant), 'Organ and Tissue Donation and Transplantation Activity Report 2021/22' (2022) https://nhsbtdbe.blob.core.windows.net/umbraco-assets-corp/27108/activity-report-2021-2022.pdf, accessed 23 December 2023

NHSBT (NHS Blood and Transplant), 'Annual Report on Ethnicity Differences 2022/23' (2023) https://nhsbtdbe.blob.core.windows.net/umbraco-assets-corp/31332/annual-report-on-ethnicity-differences-final-2022_2023.pdf, accessed 23 December 2023

NHSBT (NHS Blood and Transplant), 'Organ and Tissue Donation and Transplantation Activity Report 2022/23' (2023) https://nhsbtdbe.blob.core.windows.net/umbraco-assets-corp/30198/activity-report-2022-2023-final.pdf, accessed 23 December 2023

NHSBT (NHS Blood and Transplant), 'Timeline for Max and Keira's Law' (nd) https://www.organdonation.nhs.uk/uk-laws/organ-donation-law-in-england/timeline-for-max-and-keiras-law/, accessed 10 October 2023

NICE (National Institute of Clinical Excellence), 'NICE Guideline: Chronic Kidney Disease: Assessment and Management' (24 November 2021) https://www.nice.org.uk/guidance/ng203, accessed 20 December 2023

ONS (Office for National Statistics), 'Ethnic Group, National Identity, Language and Religion' (2021) https://census.gov.uk/census-2021-results/phase-one-topic-summaries/ethnic-group-national-identity-language-and-religion, accessed 3 July 2023

Parsons JA and Moorlock G, 'A Global Pandemic is Not a Good Time to Introduce "Opt-Out" for Organ Donation' (2020) 20 Med Law Int 155

Prabhu PK, 'Is Presumed Consent an Ethically Acceptable Way of Obtaining Organs for Transplant?' (2019) 20 J Intensive Care Soc 92

Price D, 'The Human Tissue Act 2004' (2005) 68 Mod Lang Rev 798

Ray K, *Black Health: The Social, Political, and Cultural Determinants of Black People's Health* (OUP 2023)

Roberts D, *Fatal Invention: How Science, Politics, and Big Business Re-create Race in the Twenty-First Century* (2nd edn, The New Press 2021).

Rudge C, 'Organ Donation: Opting In or Opting Out?' (2018) 68 British J Gen Pract 62

Salway S and others, 'Obstacles to "Race Equality" in the English National Health Service: Insights from the Healthcare Commissioning Arena' (2016) 152 Soc Sci Med 102

Smith SS, 'Race and Trust' (2010) 36 Annu Rev Sociol 453

UK Government, 'An Opt-Out System of Organ and Tissue Donation (Impact Assessment)' (2018) https://assets.publishing.service.gov.uk/government/uploads/system/uploads/attachment_data/file/731915/Organ_donation_impact_assessment.pdf, accessed 27 May 2023

UK Government, 'Writing about Ethnicity' (2021) https://www.ethnicity-facts-figures.service.gov.uk/style-guide/writing-about-ethnicity, accessed 10 October 2023

UKKA (UK Kidney Association), 'Removal of the Ethnicity Adjustment for Kidney Function Testing and the NICE Chronic Kidney Disease (CKD) Guideline: A Joint Statement from Professional, Patient, and Research Kidney Organisations' (2021) https://ukkidney.org/renal-association/news/2021-nice-ckd-guideline, accessed 20 December 2023

Valentine H, 'Genetic Diversities as a Paradigm of Ienequality Management' (2021) www.esot.org/esot-congress-review, accessed 3 July 2023

18

Clinical Research Ethics

Zareen Bheekhun and Silvia Camporesi

Ethical issues emerging from the recruitment[1] of participants in clinical trials can be traced back to the following foundational issue: those who bear the risks and burdens of clinical research are not those who will reap its benefits. In this chapter, we focus on three foundational concepts in clinical research ethics: vulnerability, clinical equipoise, and therapeutic misconception (TM) and unpack them in relation to the context in which they emerged. Through an approach grounded in a historical outlook, we unravel the relationship between these different concepts and their evolution while considering emerging concepts of inclusion and of the shifting nature of clinical research during the pandemic.

Three foundational concepts in clinical research ethics

Pioneer in research ethics, Dr Jay Katz, describes the tension around medicine and clinical research (i.e., experimentation with human beings):

> The history of experimentation with human beings testifies to physicians-scientists' real and caring dedication to the alleviation of mankind's pain and suffering from the ravages of disease. It also testifies to the carelessness with which human beings have been recruited for participation in research, a carelessness that has been too readily obscured by the caring dimension of scientists' work.[2]

---

1 Recruitment or enrolment means: (1) identifying or sourcing potential participants who may be eligible; (2) discussing all aspects of the trial with them, ensuring comprehension and voluntariness, and subsequently obtaining informed consent for participation; (3) conducting a physical examination and screening procedures as mentioned in the protocol; and (4) enrolling the participant based on the eligibility criteria: Nayan Chaudhari and others, 'Recruitment and Retention of the Participants in Clinical Trials: Challenges and Solutions' (2020) 11 Perspect Clin Res 64.

2 Jay Katz, 'Human Experimentation and Human Rights' (1993) 38 St Louis Univ Law J 7.

Here Katz encapsulates the ethical dilemma at the centre of clinical research: those who bear the risks and burdens of clinical research are not those who will benefit from the findings of the research. Although medical treatment often encompasses both research and therapeutic aspects, the research component may not serve the individual therapeutic interests of patients; 'instead their well-being is subordinated to the dictates of a research protocol designed to advance knowledge for the sake of future patients'.[3] Before delving deep into the ethical knot at the centre of clinical research, let's consider the practical elements of clinical research to situate ethical reflection.

A rudimentary explanation of clinical research is a study that involves humans as participants. Experimental research is commonly referred to as clinical research or clinical trials; that is,

> a study where one or more human subjects are prospectively assigned to one or more interventions (which may include placebo or other control) to evaluate the effects of those interventions on health-related biomedical or behavioural outcomes.[4]

At a simple glance, clinical trials/studies are divided into four phases:[5]

- *Phase I*: Studies aim to test and establish tolerability and characterise the pharmacokinetic and pharmacodynamic properties of the experimental drug.[6]
- *Phase II*: Once a dose or a range of safe and tolerable doses of the experimental drug have been determined from Phase I results, Phase II trials aims to evaluate if the drug has any biological activity or effect.[7]
- *Phase III*: Building up on the results from Phases I/II, Phase III is designed to assess the effectiveness of the new intervention compared to existing interventions (already proven and commonly used therapy), that is, discover whether the new intervention has value in clinical practice.[8]
- *Phase IV*: Phase IV trials[9] are also called 'post-inferiority' trials. Phase IV is conducted after the intervention has been licensed and is in use by the

---

3 Ibid.

4 NIH (National Institutes of Health), 'NIH's Definition of a Clinical Trial' (2017) https://grants.nih.gov/policy/clinical-trials/definition.html, accessed 6 December 2023.

5 There are additional phases, such as Phase 1a, Phase 2b, etc. For brevity, these categories are considered under the overall definition of the main phase.

6 Lawrence Friedman, Curt Furberg, and David DeMets, *Fundamentals of Clinical Trials* (5th edn, Springer 2015); NIH (n4); US Food and Drug Administration, 'What Are the Different Types of Clinical Research?' (2018) https://www.fda.gov/patients/clinical-trials-what-patients-need-know/what-are-different-types-clinical-research, accessed 6 December 2023.

7 Friedman, Furberg, and Demets (n6); NIH (n4); US Food & Drug Administration (n6).

8 Friedman, Furberg, and Demets (n6); NIH (n4); US Food & Drug Administration (n6).

9 Phase IV trials are an important part of drug development as their aim is to evaluate the real-world effectiveness of a drug in the general public in a setting outside of the 'controlled trial' situation.

public. Phase IV trials are conducted to determine the long-term safety and effectiveness of the intervention to identify any issues (such as side effects) that may not have been apparent in Phase I, II, or III trials.[10]

Clinical trials assess an intervention's possible effectiveness with key methodologies such as blinding,[11] randomisation,[12] and the use of placebo/control elements.[13] There is also consensus that any clinical trial should begin with an honest null hypothesis.[14] A null hypothesis is when a proposed new intervention (B) and a control intervention (A) (which can be routine care) are equally effective or ineffective. However, applying the concept of a null hypothesis to clinical research is too simplistic. Clinical research is a complex endeavour requiring more careful attention. In the case of a clinical trial (whether the trial is blinded, placebo-controlled, or randomised or not), where Treatment B is compared against established current Therapy A in Population P, the choice between A and B is not arbitrary. The choice of A or B when it comes to a patient is based on a combination of factors such as the effectiveness, the side effects of A and B, and often the comparative costs. The choice of A or B is ethically and practically complex and has an impact on both the clinician and the participant/s.

Vulnerability

Vulnerability as a concept has occupied a key place in research ethics since the publication of the 'Belmont Report: Ethical Principles and Guidelines for the Protection of Human Subjects of Research'.[15] The Belmont

---

10 Viraj Suvarna, 'Phase IV of Drug Development' (2010) 1 Perspect Clin Res 57.

11 Blinding is the commonly used method to reduce human bias. Blinding is where the participants are unaware of which interventions they are receiving. Double blinding is where neither the researchers nor the participants are aware which intervention the participants are receiving.

12 Randomisation refers to a process by which each participant has the same chance of being assigned to either the intervention or control, e.g., toss of a coin. Most often randomisation is done using online resources.

13 Placebo-controlled studies are a way of testing a drug or pharmacological intervention in which, in addition to a group of participants that receives the treatment to be evaluated, a separate control group receives a 'placebo' treatment that is specifically designed to have no real effect.

14 Robert Levine (ed), *Ethics and Regulation of Clinical Research* (2nd edn, Yale University Press 1988); Robert Levine, 'The Nature, Scope, and Justification of Clinical Research: What is Research? Who is a Subject?' in Ezekiel Emanuel and others, *The Oxford Textbook of Clinical Research Ethics* (OUP 2008); Robert Levine, 'The Use of Placebos in Randomized Clinical Trials' (1985) 7 IRB 1.

15 National Commission for the Protection of Human Subjects of Biomedical and Behavioral Research, 'The Belmont Report' (1978) https://www.hhs.gov/ohrp/regulations-and-policy/belmont-report/index.html, accessed 6 December 2023.

Report was published after details of the Tuskegee Study became public in 1972.[16]

Historian of medicine Susan Lederer writes that clinical research ethics was 'born in scandal and reared in protectionism'.[17] By scandal, Lederer refers to the Nuremberg Trials, which were held in Nuremberg, Germany, between 20 November 1945 and 1 October 1946, where, in the aftermath of the Second World War, Nazi doctors and bureaucrats were tried in court for subjecting thousands of concentration camp prisoners to torture under the guise of 'scientific experiments',[18] including subjecting prisoners to extreme rapid changes of high and low pressure, extreme temperatures, malaria infections, mustard gas, sulphanilamide, typhus infections, and forced sterilisation, to name a few.[19] The pillars of clinical research ethics of autonomy of the subject, informed consent, and freedom from coercion were developed as a direct outcome of the Nuremberg Trial and articulated in the Nuremberg Code as essential prerequisites for clinical research.[20] At the time of its publication, however, the Nuremberg Code had limited impact on the regulation of clinical research. Firstly, it had no legal binding authority.[21] Secondly, there was a widespread perception that the atrocities committed in the concentration camps were an anomaly attributable to the totalitarian Nazi regime.[22] Consequently, back then the widespread assumption was that in a democratic country there was no concern regarding the regulation of clinical research, as doctors would 'naturally' behave in an ethical manner towards their patients and the public.[23]

16 James Jones, *Bad Blood: The Tuskegee Syphilis Experiment* (new and exp edn, Free Press; Maxwell Macmillan Canada; Maxwell Macmillan International 1993); Susan Reverby, *Examining Tuskegee: The Infamous Syphilis Study and its Legacy* (University of North Carolina Press 2009).

17 Susan Lederer, *Subjected to Science: Human Experimentation in America before the Second World War* (Johns Hopkins University Press 1997).

18 Drexel Sprecher, *Inside the Nuremberg Trial: A Prosecutor's Comprehensive Account*, vols 1 and 2 (UPA 1999).

19 Paul Weindling, *Victims and Survivors of Nazi Human Experiments: Science and Suffering in the Holocaust* (Bloomsbury Academic 2015).

20 The Nuremberg Code, *Trials of War Criminals before the Nuremberg Military Tribunals*, vol 2, (1949) https://collections.nlm.nih.gov/catalog/nlm:nlmuid-01130400RX2-mvpart, accessed 19 July 2023, 181–2; BMJ, 'The Nuremberg Code (1947)' (1996) 313 BMJ 1448; Evelyne Shuster, 'Fifty Years Later: The Significance of the Nuremberg Code' (1997) 337 New Eng J Med 1436.

21 Shuster (n20).

22 Stephan Kolb and others, 'Apologising for Nazi Medicine: A Constructive Starting Point' (2012) 380 Lancet 722; Susan Miller, 'The Role of Eugenics in Research Misconduct' (2014) 111 Mo Med 386.

23 R.R. Faden, S.E. Lederer, and J.D. Moreno, 'US Medical Researchers, the Nuremberg Doctors Trial, and the Nuremberg Code: A Review of Findings of the Advisory Committee on Human Radiation Experiments' (1996) 276 JAMA 1667.

Although a complex figure not devoid of his own shadows, Harvard Professor of Anaesthesiology, Dr Henry Beecher, is a key figure in clinical research ethics as a whistle-blower who shook the medical community out of their ethical complacency towards their own research practice. In 1966, Beecher published his article 'Ethics and Clinical Research',[24] in which he highlighted 22 examples of research studies conducted within well-known US scientific and medical institutions. Beecher reported the widespread practice of how US researchers and investigators at top institutions were often undertaking serious, and unjustified, risks with the research participants solely for research purposes, failing to safeguard them.[25] The studies included placebo arms,[26] despite the availability of effective treatment (penicillin), leading those in the control arm to develop complications. In a study on immunity, liver cancer cells were injected into patients; the patients were told that they would 'receive some cells', but not told that these would be 'cancer cells'.[27]

Yet, despite his accolades, of which there are many, Beecher's work prior to his involvement in clinical research ethics is controversial, although seldom noted.[28] Beginning in 1951, Beecher collaborated with American intelligence agencies and the US army; he became the principal investigator for research involving hallucinogenic agents to identify a 'truth serum' – which then could be used to make Cold War-era prisoners disclose useful information during interrogation.[29] The research he performed on people who were ostensibly unwilling makes Beecher complicit in and guilty of the type of unethical practices that he later criticised.[30]

The chapter turns now to the Tuskegee Syphilis Study, which ran from 1932 till 1972, and looks at its important legacy for clinical research ethics. The study involved 600 socio-economically deprived African-American men,[31] of which

---

24 Henry Beecher, 'Ethics and Clinical Research' (1966) 274 New Eng J Med 1354.

25 Ibid.

26 A placebo is defined as 'an inert substance usually prepared to look as similar to the active product investigated in a study as possible': Simon Day, *Dictionary for Clinical Trials* (John Wiley 1999), 140–1.

27 Beecher (n24).

28 Jay Katz, '"Ethics and Clinical Research" Revisited: A Tribute to Henry K. Beecher' (1993) 23 Hastings Cent Rep 31; Alfred McCoy, 'Science in Dachau's Shadow: HEBB, Beecher, and the Development of CIA Psychological Torture and Modern Medical Ethics' (2007) 43 J Hist Behav Sci 401; Jonathan Moreno, 'Beecher Reconsidered' (2019) 49 Hastings Cent Rep 3.

29 Jonathan Moreno, *Undue Risk: Secret State Experiments on Humans* (Routledge 2001); Jonathan Moreno, 'Goodbye to All That: The End of Moderate Protectionism in Human Subjects Research' (2001) 31 Hastings Cent Rep 9.

30 See Wikimedia Commons, 'Beecher Reports 1–14' (1959) https://commons.wikimedia.org/wiki/Category:Beecher_Report, accessed 6 December 2023.

31 Most of the African-American men in the study could not read and worked as sharecroppers from the county. They were asked for consent but were intentionally deceived by the researchers, who omitted key information. See Jones (n16).

399 already had syphilis and 301 (the controls) did not, living in Macon County, Alabama. It was designed as a prospective study to document the natural history of syphilis in Black men.[32] Those who were recruited were told they would be examined and treated for '*bad* blood' – a local 'catch-all term' used to refer to several ailments, including syphilis, anaemia, and fatigue – in return for free medical exams, meals, and burial insurance.[33] The men were left untreated for up to 40 years to document the natural evolution and effect of the disease – even when penicillin had become available as an effective treatment for many infections (including syphilis) in the 1950s.[34] Once the details of the Tuskegee Study were published, it became clear that African-American men, and by extension their families, were deliberately harmed for the purpose of observing the effects of untreated syphilis (despite the presence of effective treatments).[35] Shockingly, the study was funded by the US Public Health Department. It led to wide public outcry, and to important changes for the practice as well as the ethics of clinical research. One of these changes was that the US Department of Health, Education and Welfare (HEW) and the US Secretary for Health appointed a nine-member ad hoc advisory panel to investigate whether existing policies to protect the rights of patients participating in health research conducted or supported by the HEW were adequate and/or effective – with the aim of recommending improvements to these existing policies if needed. In 1973, the final report was published; it concluded there was no informed consent in the 600 socio-economically deprived and uneducated African-American men in the Tuskegee Study – in fact, these men were told by officials they were being *treated* for 'bad blood'.[36] In 1973, there was a $10 million settlement of a class action lawsuit by the National Association for the Advancement of Colored People for the survivors of the Tuskegee Syphilis study,[37] of which a few remained.[38] In 1995, years after the start of the Tuskegee Study, then US President, Bill Clinton, delivered a formal apology to the men and the families harmed as a result of the Tuskegee Study.[39]

32 One of the motives for the Tuskegee Study was the firm held belief that diseases, such as syphilis, affected Black people differently to white people. See Jones (n16) and his other works on the subject.

33 Jones (n16).

34 Ibid.

35 Ibid.

36 Ibid.

37 New York Times, 'Blacks in U.S. Syphilis Program Settle Their Suit Out of Court' New York Times (1974) https://www.nytimes.com/1974/12/17/archives/blacks-in-u-s-syphilis-program-settle-their-suit-out-of-court.html, accessed 21 November 2023.

38 Elizabeth Landau, 'Studies Show "Dark Chapter" of Medical Research' (2010) http://www.cnn.com/2010/HEALTH/10/01/guatemala.syphilis.tuskegee/index.html, accessed 6 December 2023

39 Clinton White House Archives, 'Apology for Study Done in Tuskegee' (1997) https://clintonwhitehouse4.archives.gov/textonly/New/Remarks/Fri/19970516-898.html, accessed 6 December 2023.

The Tuskegee Study led to the establishment of the National Commission for the Protection of Human Subjects of Biomedical and Behavioural Research in 1974 (National Commission),[40] which operated between 1974 and 1978 and was tasked with identifying the basic ethical principles and guidelines that should underpin and guide the conduct of acceptable biomedical and behavioural research involving humans.[41] The National Commission published the Belmont Report, which summarised the ethical principles and guidelines for human subject research.[42] The Belmont Report is a key document in clinical research practice and ethics. The Belmont Report articulated three ethical principles for the conduct of clinical research: respect for persons, beneficence, and justice,[43] and it is an essential reference used by institutional review boards (IRBs) and other regulatory bodies to ensure that research fits within ethical requirements.[44]

How are these three principles applied to clinical research practice? Respect for persons refers to the following: informed consent is essential and needs to be meaningful in order to be valid. Safeguards need to be in place for informed consent to be considered valid and therefore the decisional autonomy of the individual is respected. The principle of beneficence refers to: (1) doing no harm to the person; and (2) maximising possible benefit to the person while actively minimising possible harm (non-maleficence).[45] The principle of beneficence (and non-maleficence) also requires an appropriate risk/benefit evaluation of the clinical research project.[46] The principle of justice means that participants need to be selected fairly, not because they are more *readily available for recruitment into research*. Thus, according to the principle of 'justice', there is an implication that there needs to be special protections in place for vulnerable populations, as well as a clear commitment to avoid exploitation.

Despite the importance of vulnerability in clinical research ethics, this concept suffers from considerable conceptual disagreements. These differing points were highlighted in the findings of a 2017 study by Bracken-Roche and colleagues.[47] Their study provided the first in-depth analysis of the discussions, definitions, applications, and justifications of the concept of vulnerability in 11 key policies and guidelines (national and international).[48] The authors described the high degree of inconsistency in national and international policy in the way the term vulnerability is used and argued that this lack of consistency creates challenges for the design and review of research by IRBs and research ethics committees. Perhaps

---

40 National Commission (n15).
41 Ibid.
42 Ibid.
43 Ibid.
44 Ibid.
45 Ibid.
46 Ibid.
47 Dearbhail Bracken-Roche and others, 'The Concept of "Vulnerability" in Research Ethics: An In-Depth Analysis of Policies and Guidelines' (2017) 15 Health Res Policy Syst 8.
48 Ibid.

unsurprisingly, most of the policies and guidelines analysed in the study did not provide a definition for the concept of vulnerability,[49] relying instead on implicit assumptions of a shared understanding of the term.[50] Many of the 11 policies and guidelines still refer to vulnerability in terms of groups who are vulnerable, not individuals; suggesting that the 11 policies and guidelines have not kept up to date with the most recent Council for International Organizations of Medical Sciences (CIOMS) Guidelines, which eliminates the group approach to vulnerability and focuses on characteristics of certain groups that make them vulnerable, such as capacity or competence to consent.[51] Some of these vulnerable groups identified were children, minors, and prisoners, as well as persons with mental health issues, patients in emergency settings, pregnant women, and certain ethnic, cultural, racial, or ethnic minority groups.[52] Bracken-Roche and colleagues also described how the 11 guidelines and policies identified a considerable number of groups as 'vulnerable' – up to a total of 32.[53] When subgroups of those who were considered vulnerable were included, the total increased to 51 groups that would be potentially excluded from participating in research.[54]

What becomes evident in the academic debate on vulnerability is that there is tension between the historical aim to protect individuals from exploitation and harm and a form of paternalism, which in effect excludes individuals from participating in research on the grounds that they have been identified as part of a vulnerable group. This paternalism may in fact potentially limit individual autonomy, one of the principles of the Belmont Report. Overall, the effect of this tension and disagreement leads to poor evidence and worse health outcomes and innovation in these vulnerable groups.[55]

Clinical equipoise

Legal scholar Charles Fried is credited as first to propose the concept of equipoise – in 1974. He explained this concept by saying that clinicians enrolling

49 Ibid.

50 Ibid.

51 CIOMS (Council for International Organizations of Medical Sciences), 'International Ethical Guidelines for Health-Related Research Involving Humans' (2016) https://cioms.ch/publications/product/international-ethical-guidelines-for-health-related-research-involving-humans/, accessed 6 December 2023.

52 Bracken-Roche and others (n47).

53 Ibid.

54 Ibid.

55 Robert Aldridge and others, 'Morbidity and Mortality in Homeless Individuals, Prisoners, Sex Workers, and Individuals with Substance Use Disorders in High-Income Countries: A Systematic Review and Meta-Analysis' (2018) 391 Lancet 241; WHO (World Health Organization), 'WHO World Report on the Health of Refugees and Migrants' (2022) https://www.who.int/news/item/20-07-2022-who-report-shows-poorer-health-outcomes-for-many-vulnerable-refugees-and-migrants, accessed 6 December 2023.

patients into trials should lack preference for either intervention.[56] He did not elaborate further on how equipoise could or should be applied in research. It was respected ethicist,[57] Benjamin Freedman, who, 15 years later, provided an insightful exploration of the complexities surrounding research and its specific ethics.[58] Freedman explained that when a clinical trial proposes to test new treatment B against current accepted treatment A in a defined patient population P, 'it is necessary that the clinical investigator be in a state of genuine uncertainty regarding the comparative merits of treatments A and B for population P'.[59]

Freedman adopted the concept of 'equipoise' to describe the uncertainty between the relative merits of treatment A and B. He recognised that Fried's original version of equipoise was too constraining to meet the needs of research ethics or to hold up to scrutiny from the bioethics and medical community at the time.[60] Freedman explains that equipoise only exists when the evidence of two alternative treatments/arms is exactly balanced; therefore, if there is even a slight accumulation of evidence favouring one arm of the trial, this *necessary* balance is disrupted automatically.[61] In practice, equipoise is a fragile concept, where the exact balancing of evidence between two competing arms of a trial (treatments A and B) is rarely achieved. Freedman goes on to propose an alternative concept called 'clinical equipoise', which he defined as a current or imminent conflict in the peer community over what treatment is preferred for patients for a given condition.[62] This 'split' in the clinical community, explained Freedman, with some clinicians favouring treatment A while others favour treatment B, but with each side recognising that the opposing side has evidence to support its position, represents an 'honest professional disagreement among expert clinicians about a preferred treatment',[63] which then becomes the basic rational for conducting clinical trials.

However, Freedman's expanded concept of clinical equipoise is not without its critics. Bioethicists Franklin Miller and Howard Brody argue that clinical equipoise is not a panacea to the ethical dilemmas it proposes to resolve.[64] Medicine, argue Miller and Brody, is concerned with providing the best care to patients and is essentially governed by principles of therapeutic beneficence/

56 Charles Fried, *Medical Experimentation: Personal Integrity and Social Policy: New Edition* (OUP 1974).

57 Clinical Trials Research Group, 'Tribute to McGill Bioethicist Benjamin Freedman' (nd) https://www.mcgill.ca/ctrg/freedman, accessed 19 July 2023.

58 Benjamin Freedman, 'Equipoise and the Ethics of Clinical Research' (1987) 317 New Eng J Med 141.

59 Ibid.

60 Ibid.

61 Ibid.

62 Ibid.

63 Ibid.

64 Franklin G. Miller and Howard Brody, 'A Critique of Clinical Equipoise: Therapeutic Misconception in the Ethics of Clinical Trials' (2003) 33 Hastings Cent Rep 19.

non-maleficence.[65] Clinical research differs from medical care; its main objective is not concerned with therapeutic motivations towards participants. Clinical trials are dictated by clinical trial protocols,[66] and are simply scientific experiments with the objective of gathering data to prove or disprove a hypothesis; it is hoped that the data obtained will produce generalisable information for the future of society.

When looking at research ethics together with medical ethics, two perspectives become apparent. The first is a *similarity position*, which proposes that the ethics of research is a subsection of medical ethics, and as a result has the same moral considerations as medical ethics.[67] The other perspective is the *difference position*, which argues that medical research and clinical research are two different activities with different end goals; therefore, research must be governed by different ethical principles to that of medical ethics.[68] The border between research and care is not as clear-cut as Miller and Brody portrays it. Both research and care are often performed by physicians and/or healthcare professionals in clinical settings such as hospitals, and both use similar diagnostic interventions. As a result, the prevailing ethical framework is to view clinical research through a therapeutic lens, and the patients who are also participants in research might, understandably, be confused about the aims of the tests they are going through, as they may think they derive a therapeutic benefit from participating in research.[69] An interesting and unexpected phenomenon emerging from the similarity position became apparent in a 1982 study, as discussed in the next section.

Therapeutic misconception

The term therapeutic misconception (TM) was coined by psychiatrist Paul Appelbaum more than 40 years ago.[70] In a 1982 study, Appelbaum and his co-authors interviewed participants enrolled in two psychiatric trials; the first was a comparative clinical trial of two medications for borderline personality disorders, and the second trial assessed the possible effect of social training on chronic schizophrenics.[71] Both trials applied common research techniques, namely

65 Miller and Brody (n64); see critique in Chapter 2

66 Protocols are documents that describe the objectives, design, methodology, statistical considerations (or other methods of data analysis) and organisation of a research study: Health Research Authority, 'Health Research Authority (HRA) Glossary' (2023) https://www.hra.nhs.uk/approvals-amendments/glossary/, accessed 31 August 2023.

67 Michael Bamberg and Nancy Budwig, 'Therapeutic Misconceptions: When the Voices of Caring and Research are Misconstrued as the Voice of Curing' (1992) 2 Ethics Behav 165; Miller and Brody (n64).

68 Ibid.

69 Rebecca Dresser, 'The Ubiquity and Utility of the Therapeutic Misconception' (2002) 19 Soc Philos Policy 271; Miller and Brody (n64).

70 P.S. Appelbaum, L.H. Roth, and C. Lidz, 'The Therapeutic Misconception: Informed Consent in Psychiatric Research' (1982) 5 Int J Law Psychiatry 319.

71 Ibid.

randomisation, blinding, and the use of placebos. Investigators clarified why these techniques were used, as well as their potential impact on the participants if they chose to participate in either trial. Appelbaum and colleagues discovered participants largely expressed inaccurate beliefs about the objective of the trials and its impact on their treatment, including inaccurate beliefs that any decision taken over the course of the trial would be undertaken with their therapeutic benefit in mind.[72] Half of the participants had unrealistic beliefs about the nature or likelihood of benefit to themselves by participating in the study, contrary to prior information provided to them.[73] Equally, some participants believed that, despite acknowledging the use of blinding and placebos, the investigator would act in their best interests; that is, they trusted the investigator would give them the 'active' treatment rather than any placebos.[74] Appelbaum and co-authors emphasised Fried's point that research is distinct from clinical care.[75] Fried argued that the basis of medicine and that of the physician, which he called the '*principle of personal care*', is to ensure the wellbeing of, and prioritise the needs of, the individual patient.[76] For the subject of clinical research, however, there will always be the chance that their interests become secondary to the objectives of research.[77]

The collection of the themes and beliefs voiced by the participants, and Fried's earlier work, led Appelbaum and colleagues to develop their initial concept of TM as a failure to appreciate the distinction between the imperatives of clinical research and of ordinary treatment.[78] Several studies have since subsequently replicated Appelbaum and colleagues' findings across varied types of research outside of psychiatry. TM has been found to be present in research conducted outside of US and Eurocentric environments. The authors of such studies agree that patient-participants have an unrealistic assessment of risks/benefits and/or misunderstand the end objectives of research. Examples of such studies are Mwangi and colleagues' study of TM in a paediatric preventative malaria trial in rural Tanzania,[79] or the case of Nderitul and colleagues' study of TM in HIV/AIDS and clinical research.[80] These studies point to another

72 Ibid.

73 Ibid.

74 Ibid.

75 Ibid.

76 Fried (n56) (emphasis added).

77 Ibid.

78 Appelbaum, Roth, and Lidz (n70); Paul S. Appelbaum and others, 'False Hopes and Best Data: Consent to Research and the Therapeutic Misconception' (1987) 17 Hastings Center Report 20.

79 Rose Mwangi, Paul Ndebele, and Ann Mongoven, 'Understanding, Therapeutic Misconceptions and Perceptions, and Enrollment Decision-Making: A Pediatric Preventive Malaria Trial in Rural Tanzania' (2017) 39 IRB Ethics Hum Res 8.

80 David Nderitul, Naomi Shitemi, and Eunice Kamaara, 'Is There "Therapeutic Misconception" in HIV/AIDS and Clinical Research in Western Kenya?' (2013) 4 J AIDS Clin Res 7.

important aspect of the clinical care and clinical research 'ethical knot', that is, the increasing tendency to run clinical research, such as clinical trials, in low- to middle-income countries, which, backed by an extensive scholarship, represents a way in which 'disadvantaged fractions of populations are trading access for participation' in clinical trials 'to healthcare which they would otherwise not have access to'.[81]

The presence of TM has considerable importance due to its implications on two cornerstones of clinical research: decisional autonomy and IC. A key component of informed consent in the context of medial research is understanding that participation in research is not the same as receiving treatment.[82] Hence, if TM is as widespread as the evidence demonstrates, then there are many individuals who are in fact ill-equipped to evaluate the risks and benefits of clinical research and how the risks and benefits of research could impact them. Due to how TM can impact on the cornerstones of ethical research practice, discussion of TM has shifted towards methods of measuring it. In the first attempt at measuring TM in practice, Appelbaum and co-authors argued that there was a need to develop and validate a 'theoretically grounded measure of TM, assess its diagnostic accuracy, and test previous findings regarding TM's prevalence'.[83]

TM can only be perceived if time and attention is applied to every research encounter. To that point about nuanced assessment of TM, ethicist Jennifer McCormick describes her experiences of working as an observer in the consent process for patients participating in clinical trials.[84] She observes that *both investigators and patients* exhibited TM. McCormick alludes that TM exhibited from investigators was more due to challenges of balancing their dual roles of researcher as well as clinician. TM seems to be especially prevalent in hospital research settings where clinicians wear multiple hats.[85] If there is consensus that TM is present in clinical research at the level of both participants and investigators, what can, and should, we do about it? We will attempt to respond to these questions in the next section, after presenting new types of trials attempting to 'have it both ways' in the next section.

81 Silvia Camporesi and Matteo Mameli, 'Trading Participation for Access to Health-Care: A Morally Relevant Feature of Participation in Clinical Research' (2016) 3 J Sci Hum Arts 1; Rebecca Dresser, *Silent Partners: Human Subjects and Research Ethics* (OUP 2016); Adriana Petryna, 'Clinical Trials Offshored: On Private Sector Science and Public Health' (2007) 2 BioSocieties 21.

82 Appelbaum, Roth, and Lidz (n70); Paul S. Appelbaum, 'Clarifying the Ethics of Clinical Research: A Path toward Avoiding the Therapeutic Misconception' (2002) 2 Am J Bioeth 22.

83 Paul S. Appelbaum and others, 'Therapeutic Misconception in Research Subjects: Development and Validation of a Measure' (2012) 9 Clin Trials 748.

84 Jennifer Cable, 'False Hopes, Informed Consent: The Problem of Therapeutic Misconception and Stage 1 Clinical Trials' (2013) Voices Bioeth https://doi.org/10.7916/vib.vi.6685, accessed 17 July 2024.

85 Ibid.

Adaptive trials: a possible solution to the problem of TM?

New types of clinical trials have emerged in the COVID-19 pandemic, where trials are governed by 'master protocol'.[86] Here we are referring to adaptive[87] and platform trials. Platform and adaptive trials use an overarching protocol designed to answer a number of scientific questions/hypotheses. The advantage of platform protocols is that they allow for experimental therapies to enter or leave the protocol over the course of trial.[88] Other advantages of platform protocols, compared to conventional two-arm trials include a lower recruitment target, shorter time to treatment evaluation (a key timepoint in clinical trials), and greater power to identify effective therapies.[89] Adaptive trials also allow for trial features such as treatment arms' or subject groups' medication dose to be amended during the course of the trial based on pre-specified criteria.[90] However, such trials raise additional complexities in their design, analysis, and logistics of conduct.[91] Platform clinical trials such as adaptive trials existed before the COVID-19 pandemic. However, the pandemic enhanced motivations for using platform and adaptive designs in the search for an effective vaccine against and treatment for the virus. One of the most well-known landmark COVID-19 trials with an adaptive design was the RECOVERY Trial, launched in March 2020.[92] The RECOVERY Trial is a large-scale, multi-arm, open-label, randomised, controlled trial. In the early stages of the COVID-19 pandemic, the RECOVERY Trial

86 Matthieu Roustit and others, 'Platform Trials' (2023) 78 Therapie 29. Master protocols allow one or more interventions to be assessed within the same clinical trial, in one or more patient populations sharing common enrolment, follow-up, and assessment procedures. Platform, basket, and umbrella trials are different examples of trials for which master protocols are developed.

87 Ibid. Adaptive trials cover a heterogeneous group of experimental designs that have in common the possibility to make future amendments to one or more aspects of the experimental design based on accumulated data during the trial. Platform trials are randomised, adaptive trials, potentially without a termination date in order to make it possible to assess several interventions. The trial may change by adding or removing treatment arms according to pre-established rules (in the master protocol).

88 Janet Woodcock and Lisa LaVange, 'Master Protocols to Study Multiple Therapies, Multiple Diseases, or Both' (2017) 377 New Eng J Med 62.

89 Benjamin Saville and Scott Berry, 'Efficiencies of Platform Clinical Trials: A Vision of the Future' (2016) 13 Clin Trials 358.

90 Munyaradzi Dimairo and others, 'The Adaptive Designs CONSORT Extension (ACE) Statement: A Checklist with Explanation and Elaboration Guideline for Reporting Randomised Trials That Use an Adaptive Design' (2020) 369 BMJ m115.

91 Saville and Berry (n89); Francesca Schiavone and others, 'This is a Platform Alteration: A Trial Management Perspective on the Operational Aspects of Adaptive and Platform and Umbrella Protocols' (2019) 20 Trials 264; Dominic Hague and others, 'Changing Platforms without Stopping the Train: Experiences of Data Management and Data Management Systems When Adapting Platform Protocols by Adding and Closing Comparisons' (2019) 20 Trials 294.

92 RECOVERY Trial, 'Randomised Evaluation of COVID-19 Therapy' (2020) https://www.recoverytrial.net/, accessed 6 December 2023.

was set up to identify and simultaneously test available therapies that may be effective against COVID-19 infection.[93] It is important to note that vaccines against COVID-19 were not available until the end of 2020.[94] At its earliest inception, the RECOVERY Trial tested therapies that were at the time being debated among the public, such as hydroxychloroquine and steroids, as well as established therapies, against other conditions.[95] Using the RECOVERY Trial as an example, the advantages of an adaptive design to find effective therapies included the following:

(1) In the early stages of COVID-19, there were many trials testing hydroxychloroquine as a preventative.[96] By June 2020, the RECOVERY Trial, due to its different treatment arms, was able to definitively declare the treatment ineffective, leading the UK Medicines and Healthcare Products Regulatory Agency to instruct the other trials to stop recruitment to hydroxychloroquine arms.[97]
(2) The RECOVERY Trial provided real-time data on what therapies were effective against COVID-19.[98] At the time of writing,[99] the RECOVERY Trial had recruited nearly 49,000 participants across different hospitals internationally; according to the latest cumulative statistics, the RECOVERY Trial reports that the trial is still active at 190 sites.[100] In March 2022, on its second anniversary, the University of Oxford published a summary of astonishing achievements (see Figure 18.1).

By discovering four treatments that effectively reduce deaths from COVID, the RECOVERY Trial has, without a doubt, saved many lives worldwide.[101] It is important to note that low/middle-income countries have shared the benefits of the RECOVERY Trial, particularly since the trial reported that dexamethasone, a relatively inexpensive, easily administered, and readily available drug, was efficient at reducing deaths from COVID-19.[102]

93 RECOVERY Trial, 'Results' (2020) https://www.recoverytrial.net/results, accessed 7 March 2021.

94 BBC News, 'COVID-19 Vaccine: First Person Receives Pfizer Jab in UK' (2021) https://www.bbc.co.uk/news/uk-55227325, accessed 6 December 2023.

95 RECOVERY Trial (n92).

96 Vitória Andrade Palmeira and others, 'Do We Have Enough Evidence to Use Chloroquine/Hydroxychloroquine as a Public Health Panacea for COVID-19?' (2020) 75 Clinics e1928.

97 RECOVERY Trial (n93).

98 Ibid.

99 September 2023.

100 RECOVERY Trial (n92).

101 NHS England, 'COVID Treatment Developed in the NHS Saves a Million Lives' (2021) https://www.england.nhs.uk/2021/03/covid-treatment-developed-in-the-nhs-saves-a-million-lives/, accessed 6 December 2023.

102 RECOVERY Trial (n92); RECOVERY Trial (n93); RECOVERY Trial, 'Low-Cost Dexamethasone Reduces Death by Up to One Third in Hospitalised Patients with Severe

Figure 18.1: RECOVERY Trial results: two years on[a]

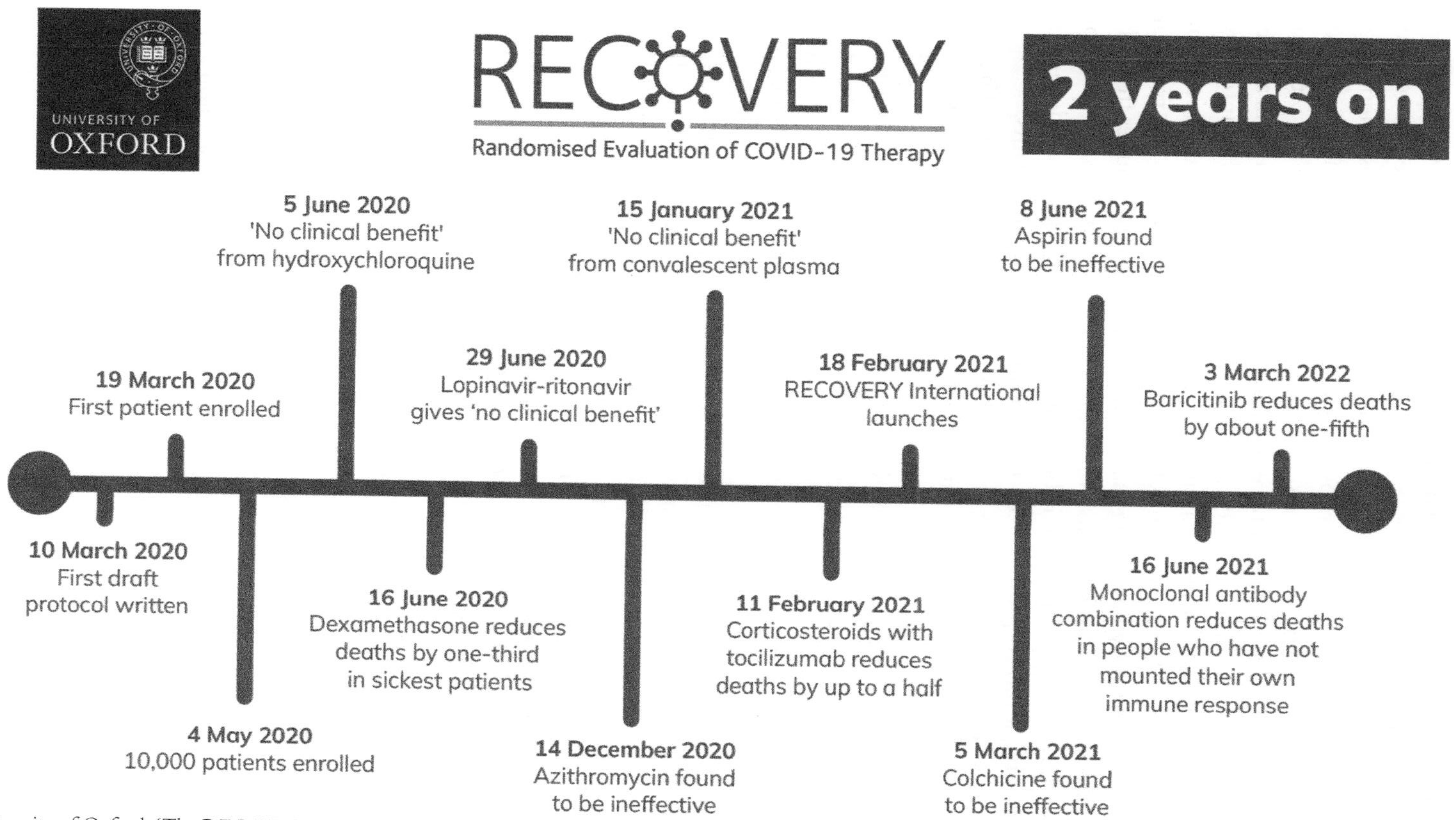

[a] University of Oxford, 'The RECOVERY Trial: Two Years On' (2022) https://www.recoverytrial.net/news/the-recovery-trial-is-two-years-old-today accessed 6 September 2023.

Clinical research ethics has traditionally responded to TM in two ways. First, portraying the issue as a simple communication problem and trying to resolve it on those grounds. That is, researchers and investigators need to ensure that information provided during informed consent, as well as subsequent stages of the clinical trial, details the purpose of the research study and unequivocally differentiates between what is research and what is clinical care/treatment. A rudimentary example of the advice is: 'You are participating in clinical research; the aim of the research or trial to test if this (medication or other intervention) works. Participating in this research is different from receiving clinical care for your benefit.' The second way in which clinical research ethics has traditionally responded to TM is by reiterating that clinicians have different duties from clinical investigators or researchers. This is reiterating the *difference position*: the former is obliged to treat patients in their best clinical interests; the latter do not have a primary obligation to promote the therapeutic care of participants.

However, this way of looking at TM, based on the *difference position*, can be ineffective. Corrigan points out that viewing the informed consent process from a purely medical perspective renders the encounter problematic as it does not acknowledge the many ways in which patients are often dependent on medical expertise and advice.[103] Insights from other disciplines have drawn attention to the nuanced complexities of decision-making. Corrigan also outlines the power dynamics inherent in the medical/research encounter between patients and healthcare professionals, on which anthropology, particularly medical anthropology, has provided considerable scholarship.[104] Sankar argues along similar lines to Corrigan but uses a critique on communication theory in medicine to do so.[105] Sankar calls to attention how information in medicine is usually given (whether in clinical research or routine care), which is through a model/method called 'the transmission model of communication'.[106] This type of communication model proposes that communication is one linear process, meaning that any information given (transmitted) by the sender (e.g., the healthcare staff) will be understood or received as it was intended by the

Respiratory Complications of COVID-19' (2020) https://www.recoverytrial.net/news/low-cost-dexamethasone-reduces-death-by-up-to-one-third-in-hospitalised-patients-with-severe-respiratory-complications-of-covid-19, accessed 6 December 2023; RECOVERY Collaborative Group, 'Dexamethasone in Hospitalized Patients with COVID-19' (2021) 384 New Eng J Med 693.

103 Oonagh Corrigan, 'Empty Ethics: The Problem with Informed Consent' (2003) 25 Soc Health Illn 768; for more studies on informed consent, see Jeremy Sugarman and others, 'What Patients Say about Medical Research' (1998) 20 IRB Ethics Hum Res 1.

104 I. Illich, 'The Medicalization of Life' (1975) J Med Ethics 73; Michel Foucault, 'The Politics of Health in Eighteenth Century' in Paul Rainbow (ed), *The Foucault Reader* (Pantheon Books 1984); Corrigan (n103).

105 Pamela Sankar, 'Communication and Miscommunication in Informed Consent to Research' (2004) 18 Med Anthropol Q 429.

106 Claude Shannon and Warren Weaver, *The Mathematical Theory of Communication* (Urbana 1964); Sankar (n105).

one receiving the information (e.g., the patient).[107] Sankar argues that this model can and has fostered the idea (in healthcare) that improving trial-related information to patients to improve recall and will mitigate any 'misgivings' or 'misconceptions'.[108] But, in fact, if we apply the transmission model of communication to TM, it suggests that the problem lies with the one receiving or interpreting it, that is, the patient – a position that we have argued against in earlier sections, where we have shown that the borders between clinical care and clinical research are often blurred.

Summary

- Clinical research is the controlled experimentation of drugs, devices, and procedures tested on human participants.
- Clinical research historically has caused long-lasting harm to many – as the Nuremberg Trials and Tuskegee Study have shown.
- Vulnerability, clinical equipoise, and TM are three conceptual and practical pillars of clinical research ethics.
- We have argued that a reason for this is the inherent nature of clinical research, where the physician/researcher wears many hats. The borders between clinical research and clinical care are often blurred, which can create TM.
- Vulnerability has traditionally excluded vulnerable groups from research, because of the legacy of the Tuskegee Study and other scandals; however, recently there has been a move away from applying labels of vulnerability to groups and towards finding a way to include participants who can be considered vulnerable in research because of the benefits of accruing data in diverse populations.
- Adaptive and platform trials point to a reconceptualisation of clinical research ethics and offer a promising avenue for the future, potentially minimising the 'ethical knot' by bringing together the participants who bear the risks of research and those who reap the benefits of research.
- Adaptive and platform trials support the *similarity position* by aligning the goals and aims of clinical care and clinical research and enabling these in practice.

Questions for reflection

1. In your own words, how would you explain the ethical knot at the centre of clinical research?
2. What was the one most alarming feature that emerged from Beecher's landmark article?
3. In what ways is therapeutic misconception a problem for the validity of informed consent?

---

107 Shannon and Weaver (n107); Sanker (n105); Richard Ellis and Ann McClintock, *If You Take My Meaning: Theory into Practice in Human Communication* (Bloomsbury Academic 1994).

108 Sanker (n105).

4. What is meant by the statement that clinical equipoise is difficult to achieve in the practice of clinical research?
5. In what ways might adaptive and platform trials solve the problem of clinical equipoise?
6. If given the opportunity, what type of research or clinical trial would you, the reader, consent or decline to participate in, and why?

Recommended resources

- Marci Cottingham and Jill Fisher, 'Gendered Logics of Biomedical Research: Women in US Phase I Clinical Trials' (2022) 69 Soc Probl 492.
- John Gallin, Frederick Ognibene, and Laura Lee Johnson (eds), *Principles and Practice of Clinical Research* (Academic Press 2017).
- Susan Lawrence and Susan Lederer, 'Medical Specimens and the Erasure of Racial Violence: The Case of Harriet Cole' (2023) 49 Med Humanit 457.
- Sandra S.-J. Lee and others, '"I Don't Want to Be Henrietta Lacks": Diverse Patient Perspectives on Donating Biospecimens for Precision Medicine Research' (2019) 21 Genet Med 107.
- Agomoni Ganguli Mitra, 'Off-Shoring Clinical Research: Exploitation and the Reciprocity Constraint' (2012) 13 Dev World Bioeth 111.
- Vicki Xafis and others, 'The Perfect Moral Storm: Diverse Ethical Considerations in the COVID-19 Pandemic' (2020) 12 Asian Bioeth Rev 65.
- Harriet Washington, *Medical Apartheid: The Dark History of Medical Experimentation on Black Americans from Colonial Times to the Present* (Doubleday Books 2006).

Bibliography

Aldridge R and others, 'Morbidity and Mortality in Homeless Individuals, Prisoners, Sex Workers, and Individuals with Substance Use Disorders in High-Income Countries: A Systematic Review and Meta-Analysis' (2018) 391 Lancet 241

Appelbaum PS, 'Clarifying the Ethics of Clinical Research: A Path towards Avoiding the Therapeutic Misconception' (2002) 2 Am J Bioeth 22

Appelbaum PS, Roth LH and Lidz C, 'The Therapeutic Misconception: Informed Consent in Psychiatric Research' (1982) 5 Int J Law Psychiatry 319

Appelbaum PS and others, 'False Hopes and Best Data: Consent to Research and the Therapeutic Misconception' (1987) 17 Hastings Cent Rep 20

Appelbaum PS and others, 'Therapeutic Misconception in Research Subjects: Development and Validation of a Measure' (2012) 9 Clin Trials 748

Bamberg M and Budwig N, 'Therapeutic Misconceptions: When the Voices of Caring and Research Are Misconstrued as the Voice of Curing' (1992) 2 Ethics Behav 165

BBC News, 'COVID-19 Vaccine: First Person Receives Pfizer Jab in UK' (2021) https://www.bbc.co.uk/news/uk-55227325, accessed 6 December 2023

Beecher H, 'Ethics and Clinical Research' (1966) 274 New Eng J Med 1354
BMJ, 'The Nuremberg Code (1947)' (1996) 313 BMJ 1448
Bracken-Roche D and others, 'The Concept of "Vulnerability" in Research Ethics: An In-Depth Analysis of Policies and Guidelines' (2017) 15 Health Res Policy Syst 8
Cable J, 'False Hopes, Informed Consent: The Problem of Therapeutic Misconception and Stage 1 Clinical Trials' (2013) Voices Bioeth https://doi.org/10.7916/vib.vi.6685, accessed 17 July 2024
Camporesi S and Mameli M, 'Trading Participation for Access to Health-Care: A Morally Relevant Feature of Participation in Clinical Research' (2016) 3 J Sci Hum Arts 1
Chaudhari N and others, 'Recruitment and Retention of the Participants in Clinical Trials: Challenges and Solutions' (2020) 11 Perspect Clin Res 64
CIOMS (Council for International Organizations of Medical Sciences), 'International Ethical Guidelines for Health-Related Research Involving Humans' (2016) https://cioms.ch/publications/product/international-ethical-guidelines-for-health-related-research-involving-humans/, accessed 6 December 2023
Clinical Trials Research Group, 'Tribute to McGill Bioethicist Benjamin Freedman' (nd) https://www.mcgill.ca/ctrg/freedman, accessed 19 July 2023
Clinton White House Archives, 'Apology for Study Done in Tuskegee' (1997) https://clintonwhitehouse4.archives.gov/textonly/New/Remarks/Fri/19970516-898.html, accessed 6 December 2023
Corrigan O, 'Empty Ethics: The Problem with Informed Consent' (2003) 25 Soc Health Illn 768
Day S, *Dictionary for Clinical Trials* (John Wiley 1999)
Dimairo M and others, 'The Adaptive Designs CONSORT Extension (ACE) Statement: A Checklist with Explanation and Elaboration Guideline for Reporting Randomised Trials That Use an Adaptive Design' (2020) 369 BMJ m115
Dresser R, *Silent Partners: Human Subjects and Research Ethics* (OUP 2016)
Dresser R, 'The Ubiquity and Utility of the Therapeutic Misconception' (2002) 19 Soc Philos Policy 271
Ellis R and McClintock A, *If You Take My Meaning: Theory into Practice in Human Communication* (Bloomsbury Academic 1994)
Emanuel E, 'The Nazi Medical Experiments' in E Emanuel and others, *The Oxford Textbook of Clinical Research Ethics* (OUP 2008)
Faden RR, Lederer SE, and Moreno JD, 'US Medical Researchers, the Nuremberg Doctors Trial, and the Nuremberg Code: A Review of Findings of the Advisory Committee on Human Radiation Experiments' (1996) 276 JAMA 1667
Fairchild A and Bayer R, 'Uses and Abuses of Tuskegee' (1999) 284 Science 919
Foucault M, 'The Politics of Health in Eighteenth Century' in P Rainbow (ed), *The Foucault Reader* (Pantheon Books 1984)

Freedman B, 'Equipoise and the Ethics of Clinical Research' (1987) 317 New Eng J Med 141

Fried C, *Medical Experimentation: Personal Integrity and Social Policy* (new edn, OUP 1974)

Friedman L, Furberg C, and DeMets D, *Fundamentals of Clinical Trials* (5th edn, Springer 2015)

Hague D and others, 'Changing Platforms without Stopping the Train: Experiences of Data Management and Data Management Systems When Adapting Platform Protocols by Adding and Closing Comparisons' (2019) 20 Trials 294

Health Research Authority, 'Health Research Authority (HRA) Glossary' (2023) https://www.hra.nhs.uk/approvals-amendments/glossary/, accessed 31 August 2023

Illich I, 'The Medicalization of Life' (1975) J Med Ethics 73

Jones J, *Bad Blood: The Tuskegee Syphilis Experiment* (new exp edn, Macmillan International 1993)

Katz J, '"Ethics and Clinical Research" Revisited: A Tribute to Henry K. Beecher' (1993) 23 Hastings Cent Rep 31

Katz J, 'Human Experimentation and Human Rights' (1993) 38 St Louis Univ Law J 7

Kolb S and others, 'Apologising for Nazi Medicine: A Constructive Starting Point' (2012) 380 Lancet 722

Landau E, 'Studies Show "Dark Chapter" of Medical Research' (2010) http://www.cnn.com/2010/HEALTH/10/01/guatemala.syphilis.tuskegee/index.html, accessed 6 December 2023

Lederer S, *Subjected to Science: Human Experimentation in America before the Second World War* (Johns Hopkins University Press 1997)

Levine R, 'The Use of Placebos in Randomized Clinical Trials' (1985) 7 IRB 1

Levine R (ed), *Ethics and Regulation of Clinical Research* (2nd edn, Yale University Press 1988)

Levine R, 'The Nature, Scope, and Justification of Clinical Research: What is Research? Who is a Subject?' in E Emanuel and others, *The Oxford Textbook of Clinical Research Ethics* (OUP 2008)

McCoy A, 'Science in Dachau's Shadow: HEBB, Beecher, and the Development of CIA Psychological Torture and Modern Medical Ethics' (2007) 43 J Hist Behav Sci 401

Miller FG and Brody H, 'A Critique of Clinical Equipoise: Therapeutic Misconception in the Ethics of Clinical Trials' (2003) 33 Hastings Cent Rep 19

Miller S, 'The Role of Eugenics in Research Misconduct' (2014) 111 Mo Med 386

Moreno J, 'Goodbye to All That: The End of Moderate Protectionism in Human Subjects Research' (2001) 31 Hastings Cent Rep 9

Moreno J, *Undue Risk: Secret State Experiments on Humans* (Routledge 2001)

Moreno J, 'Beecher Reconsidered' (2019) 49 Hastings Cent Rep 3

Mwangi R, Ndebele P, and Mongoven A, 'Understanding, Therapeutic Misconceptions and Perceptions, and Enrollment Decision-Making: A Pediatric Preventive Malaria Trial in Rural Tanzania' (2017) 39 IRB Ethics Hum Res 8

National Commission for the Protection of Human Subjects of Biomedical and Behavioral Research, 'The Belmont Report' (1978) https://www.hhs.gov/ohrp/regulations-and-policy/belmont-report/index.html, accessed 6 December 2023

Nderitul D, Shitemi N, and Kamaara E, 'Is There "Therapeutic Misconception" in HIV/AIDS and Clinical Research in Western Kenya?' (2013) 4 J AIDS Clin Res 7

New York Times, 'Blacks in U.S. Syphilis Program Settle Their Suit Out of Court' New York Times (1974) https://www.nytimes.com/1974/12/17/archives/blacks-in-u-s-syphilis-program-settle-their-suit-out-of-court.html, accessed 21 November 2023

NHS England, 'COVID Treatment Developed in the NHS Saves a Million Lives' (2021) https://www.england.nhs.uk/2021/03/covid-treatment-developed-in-the-nhs-saves-a-million-lives/, accessed 6 December 2023

NIH (National Institutes of Health), 'NIH's Definition of a Clinical Trial' (2017) https://grants.nih.gov/policy/clinical-trials/definition.html, accessed 6 December 2023

Nuremberg Code, *Trials of War Criminals before the Nuremberg Military Tribunals*: vol 2 (1949) https://collections.nlm.nih.gov/catalog/nlm:nlmuid-01130400RX2-mvpart, accessed 19 July 2023

Palmeira VA and others, 'Do We Have Enough Evidence to Use Chloroquine/Hydroxychloroquine as a Public Health Panacea for COVID-19?' (2020) 75 Clinics e1928

Petryna A, 'Clinical Trials Offshored: On Private Sector Science and Public Health' (2007) 2 BioSocieties 21

RECOVERY Collaborative Group, 'Dexamethasone in Hospitalized Patients with COVID-19' (2021) 384 New Eng J Med 693

RECOVERY Trial, 'Low-Cost Dexamethasone Reduces Death by Up to One Third in Hospitalised Patients with Severe Respiratory Complications of COVID-19' (2020) https://www.recoverytrial.net/news/low-cost-dexamethasone-reduces-death-by-up-to-one-third-in-hospitalised-patients-with-severe-respiratory-complications-of-covid-19, accessed 6 December 2023

RECOVERY Trial, 'Randomised Evaluation of COVID-19 Therapy' (2020) https://www.recoverytrial.net/, accessed 6 December 2023

RECOVERY Trial, 'Results' (2020) https://www.recoverytrial.net/results, accessed 7 March 2021

Reverby S, *Examining Tuskegee: The Infamous Syphilis Study and Its Legacy* (University of North Carolina Press 2009)

Roustit M and others, 'Platform Trials' (2023) 78 Therapie 29

Sankar P, 'Communication and Miscommunication in Informed Consent to Research' (2004) 18 Med Anthropol Q 429

Saville B and Berry S, 'Efficiencies of Platform Clinical Trials: A Vision of the Future' (2016) 13 Clin Trials 358

Schiavone F and others, 'This is a Platform Alteration: A Trial Management Perspective on the Operational Aspects of Adaptive and Platform and Umbrella Protocols' (2019) 20 Trials 264

Shannon C and Weaver W, *The Mathematical Theory of Communication* (Urbana 1964)

Shuster E, 'Fifty Years Later: The Significance of the Nuremberg Code' (1997) 337 New Eng J Med 1436

Sprecher D, *Inside the Nuremberg Trial: A Prosecutor's Comprehensive Account*, vols 1 and 2 (UPA 1999)

Sugarman J and others, 'What Patients Say about Medical Research' (1998) 20 IRB Ethics Human Res 1

Suvarna V, 'Phase IV of Drug Development' (2010) 1 Perspect Clin Res 57

Teck-Chuan V, 'Therapeutic Misconception' in R Chadwick (ed), *Encyclopedia of Applied Ethics*, vol 4 (Elsevier Science 2012)

University of Oxford, 'The RECOVERY Trial: Two Years On' (2022) https://www.recoverytrial.net/news/the-recovery-trial-is-two-years-old-today, accessed 6 September 2023

US Food and Drug Administration, 'What Are the Different Types of Clinical Research?' (2018) https://www.fda.gov/patients/clinical-trials-what-patients-need-know/what-are-different-types-clinical-research, accessed 6 December 2023

Weindling P, *Victims and Survivors of Nazi Human Experiments: Science and Suffering in the Holocaust* (Bloomsbury Academic 2015)

Weindling P, 'WHO World Report on the Health of Refugees and Migrants' (2022) https://www.who.int/news/item/20-07-2022-who-report-shows-poorer-health-outcomes-for-many-vulnerable-refugees-and-migrants, accessed 6 December 2023

Wikimedia Commons, 'Beecher Reports 1–14' (1959) https://commons.wikimedia.org/wiki/Category:Beecher_Report, accessed 6 December 2023

Woodcock J and LaVange L, 'Master Protocols to Study Multiple Therapies, Multiple Diseases, or Both' (2017) 377 New Eng J Med 62

19

Death and Dying

Dunja Begović, Yakubu Salifu, and Sheila Payne

Debates on death and dying within healthcare law and ethics traditionally focus on euthanasia and physician-assisted suicide. A sometimes overlooked site of potential ethico-legal controversies is the field of palliative care, which is gaining prominence – both as a subject of scholarship and in practice, given changing patterns of ageing, chronic illness, and dying worldwide.[1] We begin this chapter by introducing the issues around death and dying usually prioritised in the ethical and legal literature. We then shed light on some less discussed legal and ethical issues arising from palliative care, especially as they concern equity of access to good-quality care,[2] which can vary depending on resources and socio-economic position.

In the section 'End-of-life issues in health law and ethics', we introduce legal and ethical issues around death and dying. We divide these roughly into issues concerning assisted death (including euthanasia and physician-assisted suicide) and those that have to do with withdrawing life-sustaining care. In the section 'Thinking beyond assisted death and withdrawing treatment', we present the perspective of palliative care and outline the ethical and legal challenges intertwined with this specialised field. We focus on issues related to the inequity of access to palliative care, both globally and within England and Wales.

We will limit our discussion to treatment of adult patients. Palliative care for children introduces a host of other ethical and legal issues that are beyond the scope of this chapter.[3] We focus primarily on the legal framework of England

1 Amani Babgi, 'Legal Issues in End-of-Life Care: Perspectives from Saudi Arabia and United States' (2009) 26 Am J Hospice Palliat Care 119; Chad Kollas and Beth Boyer-Kollas, 'Evolving Medicolegal Issues in Palliative Medicine' (2007) 10 J Palliat Med 1395.

2 For an understanding of the concept of equity in healthcare, and how this relates to (and is different from) equality, please see Chapter 5.

3 See Chapter 16 for discussion of some of these complexities.

and Wales but mention examples from other jurisdictions and the international context where relevant.

End-of-life issues in health law and ethics

End-of-life issues discussed within healthcare law and ethics are often centred on some type of *intervention* into the dying process, and determining whether this would be (legally and/or ethically) justified. Herring notes that 'with technological developments, it has become possible to exercise greater control over our dying'.[4] Brazier, Cave, and Heywood observe that, in recent years, 'the heat of the debate has focused on whether the law should permit some sort of assistance for those who are terminally ill to end their lives'.[5] While these authors acknowledge there are other important issues related to the end of life, they still for the most part adopt this framing, which focuses on certain types of death and may also be based on assumptions about what a 'natural' death looks like.

This focus is not in itself surprising. Scholarship in medical law and ethics will follow (to some extent) developments in public debate, which tends to focus on exceptional and challenging cases. Also, the legal system of England and Wales is (alongside statutory legislation) based on precedents, meaning that outcomes of particular cases – which are, most often, the exceptional cases precisely because some legal intervention is warranted – directly influence the body of law. This does not mean that the issues which traditionally get less attention are not equally important; in fact, the remainder of this chapter illustrates that they are. However, to set the scene, we will highlight the most prominent ethico-legal issues related to the end of life. We discuss two clusters of issues: those related to assisted death (including euthanasia and assisted suicide) and those related to withholding or withdrawing life-sustaining treatment.

Assisted death: legal and ethical issues

While suicide is a varied and complex social phenomenon,[6] people sometimes wish to end their lives to avoid further suffering when faced with pain and discomfort due to a terminal condition.[7] They may also wish to end their lives

4 Jonathan Herring, *Medical Law and Ethics* (9th edn, OUP 2022) 576.

5 Margaret Brazier, Emma Cave, and Rob Heywood, *Medicine, Patients and the Law* (Manchester University Press 2023) 538.

6 For a recent report on suicide statistics in England and Wales, see ONS (Office for National Statistics), 'Suicides in England and Wales: 2020 Registrations' (2021) https://www.ons.gov.uk/peoplepopulationandcommunity/birthsdeathsandmarriages/deaths/bulletins/suicidesintheunitedkingdom/2021registrations, accessed 17 December 2023.

7 Sissel Johansen and others, 'Attitudes towards, and Wishes for, Euthanasia in Advanced Cancer Patients at a Palliative Medicine Unit' (2005) 19 Palliat Med 454.

due to concerns about losing their autonomy and dignity.[8] Depending on the individual's circumstances, assisted death can take the form of (physician-)assisted suicide or euthanasia. Where the person is capable, for example, of taking a lethal dosage of a certain medication, but this needs to be prescribed to them by a health professional, this would be considered assisted suicide. However, in cases where a person is prevented from doing this for various reasons, and the health professional takes a more active role in inducing death, this would be considered euthanasia. These two major types of medically aided death are treated quite differently in the law of England and Wales.

Legal status of assisted death

Suicide itself is not prohibited in the law of England and Wales – however, involving third parties in suicide is. Under the Suicide Act 1961, it is a criminal offence to aid another person in committing suicide, with a possible punishment of up to 14 years' imprisonment.[9] However, according to Crown Prosecution Service (CPS) policy,[10] whether a case will ultimately be prosecuted depends on a number of factors.[11] This includes whether prosecution is deemed to be in the public interest; for example, if there are doubts about whether the accused person acted out of compassion, or whether the deceased person had unequivocally asked for help with ending their life. Very few cases of assisted suicide have been successfully prosecuted since the policy was published in 2009.[12] Nevertheless, assisting in a person's suicide remains illegal, and travelling to access assisted death in another country (as is often done) is only available to individuals with the adequate finances and support.

Euthanasia is defined as the act of deliberately ending a person's life, typically with the goal of relieving suffering.[13] For example, a doctor may give a high dose of lethal medication to a patient that will lead to them dying. The law of England and Wales regards euthanasia as murder or manslaughter,[14] depending

---

8 C. Gamondi and others, 'Family Caregivers' Reflections on Experiences of Assisted Suicide in Switzerland: A Qualitative Interview Study' (2018) 55 J Pain Symptom Manage 1085.

9 S 2(1C).

10 CPS (Crown Prosecution Service), 'Suicide: Policy for Prosecutors in Respect of Cases of Encouraging or Assisting Suicide' (2010) https://www.cps.gov.uk/legal-guidance/suicide-policy-prosecutors-respect-cases-encouraging-or-assisting-suicide, accessed 13 October 2023.

11 These guidelines were introduced because there was ambiguity, see *R (Purdy) v DPP* [2009] UKHL 45.

12 CPS (Crown Prosecution Service), 'Assisted Suicide' (2023) https://www.cps.gov.uk/publication/assisted-suicide, accessed 13 October 2023.

13 Herring (n4).

14 Murder is considered an offence under common law: *Attorney-General's Reference (No 3 of 1994)* [1998] AC 245. Manslaughter is the causing of death without intent (involuntary manslaughter) e.g., gross negligence manslaughter or in cases where there is intent to cause death but a partial defence (voluntary manslaughter) e.g., a suicide pact per the Homicide Act 1957, s 4(1).

on the circumstances. In order for the act to be considered murder, it needs to be shown that the person committing the act both had a clear intention to cause death[15] and made a substantial contribution to causing it. The maximum punishment for this crime is life imprisonment.

It should be stressed that both euthanasia and assisted suicide are currently illegal in England and Wales, despite occasional attempts to change the law. At the time of writing, a recent parliamentary inquiry into assisted dying and assisted suicide involved a variety of experts and advocates presenting evidence for and against retaining the current law on assisted death.[16] However, the law so far remains unchanged.

Ethical debate on assisted death

Discussion about the ethical issues related to assisted death often focuses on the basic bioethical principles of autonomy, beneficence, non-maleficence, and justice.[17] Some authors question if there are circumstances in which the basic ethical duty of the healthcare professional to do no harm (corresponding to the ethical principle of non-maleficence) is actually better promoted by helping a patient to end their life than by trying to keep them alive at any cost.[18] Or it is debated if there is a distinctive moral wrong related to killing someone in order to end their suffering.[19] In addition, two ethical concepts potentially important for this context are dignity and vulnerability.

A recent definition outlines three main dimensions of vulnerability: 'a state of physical, emotional, and cognitive stability that is in danger of being disturbed or destroyed due to being susceptible to destabilizing influences'.[20] Patients in general are considered vulnerable in the medical encounter, as they typically have less knowledge and power than health professionals. Also, advanced disease and the suffering that can come with it can be profoundly destabilising factors. It could be argued that people who want to end their lives due to advanced illness and suffering and require another's assistance (or legal permission) to do

15 Intent can be direct or oblique, see *R v Woollin* (1998) 1 AC 82.

16 House of Commons Health and Social Care Committee, 'Assisted Dying/Assisted Suicide: Inquiry' (2023) https://committees.parliament.uk/work/6906/assisted-dyingassisted-suicide/, accessed 13 October 2023.

17 Tom Beauchamp and James Childress, *Principles of Biomedical Ethics* (OUP 2001). For more detail on these ethical principles see Chapter 2.

18 For an overview of ethical debates on this point, see Fiona Woollard and Frances Howard-Snyder, 'Doing vs. Allowing Harm' in Edward Zalta and Uri Nodelman (eds), *The Stanford Encyclopedia of* Philosophy (2022) https://plato.stanford.edu/archives/win2022/entries/doing-allowing/, accessed 13 October 2023.

19 James Rachels, 'Active and Passive Euthanasia' in James Humber and Robert Almeder (eds), *Biomedical Ethics and the Law* (Springer 1979).

20 Joachim Boldt, 'The Concept of Vulnerability in Medical Ethics and Philosophy' (2019) 14 Philos Ethics Humanit Med 1, 2–3.

so find themselves in a highly vulnerable position, where the vulnerability of suicidal ideation may be compounded by inability to end their pain. This may in particular be an issue for socially marginalised groups such as women.[21]

Dignity is another important concept in thinking about assisted dying. The idea of being able to 'die with dignity' by choosing assisted death when one is no longer able to live as one wishes is pervasive. The importance of this value is apparent in the rhetoric used by advocates of assisted death, including names of particular pieces of legislation (such as Oregon's Death with Dignity Act) or organisations (the Dignitas Right to Die Association in Switzerland). Dignity is an interesting concept in that it also plays an important role in the arguments of those who *oppose* legalising assisted dying.[22]

Although there is a *legal* difference between euthanasia and assisted suicide, there is debate about whether there is a *morally* significant difference between actively killing a person to relieve their suffering or, for instance, stopping life-sustaining treatment and allowing them to die 'naturally' (sometimes also referred to as the act/omission distinction). This question ties into another set of death-related situations treated differently by the law; namely, cases in which there is no active contribution of a health professional (whether by prescribing or giving medication) to a person's death, but life-sustaining treatment is stopped with the awareness that this will allow death to come about. We now turn to outlining these issues.

Withdrawing or withholding life-sustaining treatment: legal and ethical issues

Cases where life-sustaining treatment is stopped typically involve people who are judged to no longer have the capacity to make decisions about their care.[23] Decisions about the care of persons in this situation fall under the Mental Capacity Act 2005, which provides guidance for health professionals on how to determine whether further treatment is in a patient's best interests once they are no longer able to voice their opinion (see Box 19.1). This is also referred to as the 'best-interests test' and encompasses a variety of factors including social and not only medical ones.

Box 19.1: Key case: *Airedale NHS Trust v Bland* [1993] AC 789 (Fam)

A victim of the 1989 Hillsborough disaster, Bland was left in a permanent vegetative state with no prospect of recovery. Ongoing artificial nutrition and hydration was required for

---

21 Hazel Biggs, 'A Pretty Fine Line: Life, Death, Autonomy and Letting it B' (2003) 11 Fem Leg Stud 29.

22 Morten Dige, 'Assisted Death, Dignity, and Respect for Humanity' (2022) 47 J Med Philos 701.

23 For discussion of capacity see Chapter 10.

him to remain alive. After an appeal from his medical team, the House of Lords eventually ruled that it may be lawful to discontinue treatment if this was deemed to be in Bland's best interests. This decision established a legal precedent for withdrawing life-sustaining care from persons in similar circumstances, and thus had significant implications for patients in comparable conditions following the ruling.

A significant and highly publicised case that brought the discussion on stopping life-sustaining treatment to public attention was that of Tony Bland.[24]

In Bland's case, any further treatment was deemed to be futile, which was a central part of the best-interests-based decision made in this case to allow Bland to die.[25] Providing care that is not likely to advance the patient's state was not seen a part of the duty of care normally expected of a medical professional. It should be noted that the application of the best-interests test does not mean asking whether it is in a person's interest to continue living, but, rather, whether the benefits of continuing treatment outweigh the potential negative consequences – as established in another key case, *Aintree University Hospital v James*.[26]

Withdrawing or withholding treatment essential to continuing the life of a patient when there is no viable prospect of recovery or return to normal function might seem in its essence to be not too different from assisted dying as described earlier in this chapter. The similarity is especially stark in cases in which artificial ventilation is removed, where the patient is unable to breathe on their own and so this action will effectively cause them to die. However, the law treats this category of cases very differently to euthanasia and assisted suicide. In cases like *Bland*,[27] the patient will have lost the capacity to make decisions about their treatment, and so the central ethico-legal concern is whether continued treatment or sustaining life is more beneficial than being allowed to die, as the principle of respect for autonomy is no longer invoked.

In cases where people retain capacity, however, but wish to stop or refuse life-saving treatment, there is more controversy. Health professionals may feel unsure what to do,[28] and, due to apparent ethical and legal parallels with assisted dying, it may not be possible for patients with capacity to have their wishes met. Cases like *Re B*[29] have affirmed the respect for the autonomous decision of a patient

24 *Airedale NHS Trust v Bland* [1993] AC 789 (Fam).

25 Sabine Michalowski and Wayne Martin, 'DNACPR Decisions: Aligning Law, Guidance, and Practice' (2022) 30 Med Law Rev 434.

26 [2013] UKSC 67.

27 *Bland* (n24).

28 Kay Phelps and others, 'Withdrawal of Ventilation at the Patient's Request in MND: A Retrospective Exploration of the Ethical and Legal Issues That Have Arisen for Doctors in the UK' (2017) BMJ Support Palliat Care 189.

29 *Re B (Adult Refusal of Medical Treatment)* [2002] EWHC 429 (Fam).

to refuse life-saving medical treatment (such as the use of artificial ventilation), but this can lead to highly uncomfortable scenarios in which persons may need to resort to effectively starving themselves to death by refusing food and water.

This consequence became prominent in *R (Nicklinson) v Ministry of Justice*,[30] in which the applicants argued that their lack of access to assisted dying was incompatible with human rights legislation, specifically because their only option for dying was to effectively starve themselves by refusing life-sustaining nutrition and hydration (see Box 19.2). Particular articles of the European Convention on Human Rights (ECHR) have been used both to argue for and against withholding or withdrawing treatment. Beside Article 8, relevant are also Article 2, the right to life, and Article 3, the prohibition of torture.[31]

Box 19.2: Key case: *R (Nicklinson) v Ministry of Justice* [2014] UKSC 38

Two individuals suffering from locked-in syndrome, Mr Nicklinson and Mr Lamb, argued their lack of access to assisted death (which they both desired) under English law was incompatible with the ECHR. Specifically, they referred to Article 8, or the right to respect for private and family life (European Court of Human Rights). It was ultimately ruled there was no such incompatibility between English law and the ECHR, but further legal challenges followed.

Thinking beyond assisted death and withdrawing treatment

Both assisted death and the stopping of life-sustaining treatment raise critical questions about patient autonomy, the responsibilities of health professionals, and, ultimately, how society views and values life and death. As such, it is not surprising that these questions tend to be at the forefront of legal and ethical debates on death and dying. While important, the kinds of circumstances that lead to ethico-legal dilemmas in this section are fairly rare. However, which kind of deaths we may consider 'ordinary' or 'natural' is not without legally, ethically, and policy-relevant consequences. In the next subsection, 'Legal and ethical issues in palliative care', we explore the legal and ethical issues associated with the type of death that most people around the world tend to experience – namely, death in old age and due to prolonged illness.

Considering the palliative care perspective – where the primary goal is to provide symptom relief and quality of life despite life-threatening illness – is

30 [2014] UKSC 38.
31 Herring (n4).

highly important for having a well-rounded view of the legal and ethical issues related to death and dying. However, dying and illness are not only issues for the law and ethics of healthcare. When assisted dying is discussed in the ethico-legal context, there is often an assumption that, in practice, such deaths would be caused or aided by doctors – however, this is in tension with the wishes of many medical professionals.[32] It has been argued that the way forward in the UK may be to advocate for a de-medicalised approach to regulating assisted dying, modelled after some countries in which it is legal.[33] Besides potential advantages both for patients and health professionals,[34] this model would also give more visibility to palliative care, as it could be required that this option be mentioned explicitly before a request to access assisted dying is approved.[35] Some argue that the ethical values underpinning assisted dying advocacy and the palliative care approach are not that dissimilar.[36] We have shown some parallels but in what follows we highlight issues unique to palliative care. If the law reformed around death and dying in the future, legislation may also bring these two seemingly disparate areas (palliative care and assisted death) closer together, and so it is important to discuss the legal and ethical implications of both.

Legal and ethical issues in palliative care

People in most parts of the world tend to live longer and die at an older age than in the past, giving them more time to consider their preferences about the end of life. People in some countries also die in hospitals or other healthcare settings more often than they did in the past, so are more likely to be under the care of medical professionals at the end of their lives. Taking care of the terminally ill and dying has developed into a distinct medical specialty – palliative medicine – but palliative care, as an area of practice and research, is broader than this specialty.

Palliative care is defined by the World Health Organization (WHO) as 'an approach that improves the quality of life of patients (adults and children) and their families who are facing problems associated with life-threatening illness or serious health-related suffering' and which 'prevents and relieves suffering through the early identification, correct assessment and treatment of pain and

32 BMA (British Medical Association), 'Physician-Assisted Dying Survey' (2021) https://www.bma.org.uk/advice-and-support/ethics/end-of-life/physician-assisted-dying/physician-assisted-dying-survey, accessed 13 October 2023.

33 Nancy Preston, Sheila Payne, and Suzanne Ost, 'Breaching the Stalemate on Assisted Dying: It's Time to Move beyond a Medicalised Approach' (2023) 382 BMJ 1968.

34 Suzanne Ost, 'The De-medicalisation of Assisted Dying: Is a Less Medicalised Model the Way Forward?' (2010) 18 Med Law Rev 497.

35 Preston, Payne, and Ost (n33).

36 Samia Hurst and Alex Mauron, 'The Ethics of Palliative Care and Euthanasia: Exploring Common Values' (2006) 20 Palliat Med 107.

other problems, whether physical, psychosocial or spiritual'.[37] Some of the main features visible from this definition are the focus on symptoms, the goal of relieving pain and suffering, and a multifaceted approach to health (considering its spiritual, psychological, and social dimensions), leading to an interdisciplinary approach. Another key word to note here is 'life-threatening'; although it is not exclusively provided at the end of life,[38] palliative care is often associated with the goal of providing the patient with a more comfortable experience during dying.

In the next subsection, we outline some of the legal and ethical issues associated with the provision of palliative care. Then, in the following section we focus on the issue of (both global and local) disparities in access to palliative care, which we identify as a major ethical and policy issue in this area.

Palliative care: legal and ethical status

Palliative care is practised and regulated differently throughout the world. It is important to note that palliative care can be general or specialist. General palliative care can be delivered by all health professionals, while specialist palliative care is delivered by people with additional training on the topic. In the UK, the majority of specialist palliative care is delivered by hospices, which are largely independent charitable organisations. They are not regulated in the same way as state-funded healthcare provision.[39] However, the UK does have national plans and policies in place regarding the provision of palliative care.[40]

Legislation in some countries (like Germany, France, and Belgium) explicitly recognises a right to palliative care, treating it as a service that patients are entitled to in specific circumstances. In the context of legal debate in England and Wales, the existence of palliative care is often used as a counterargument to proposals for legalising assisted dying, especially euthanasia.[41] This seems to put palliative care in an antagonistic role to other end-of-life options. Yet in some countries

---

37 WHO (World Health Organization), 'Quality Health Services and Palliative Care: Practical Approaches and Resources to Support Policy, Strategy and Practice' (2021) https://www.who.int/publications/i/item/9789240035164, accessed 17 December 2023, 9.

38 The term 'end-of-life care' can have different meanings in different contexts. In the UK, this is used to refer to approximately the last two years of life – so 'end of life' and 'palliative care' are used synonymously. In most other countries it means the last few weeks, days, or hours of life. See Sheila Payne and others, 'Revised Recommendations on Standards and Norms for Palliative Care in Europe from the European Association for Palliative Care (EAPC): A Delphi Study' (2022) 36 Palliat Med 680–97.

39 Although such organisations will still be subject to the reporting from the Care Quality Commission (CQC; established by the Health and Social Care Act 2008). Hospice care is specified as falling under the purview of the CQC in the Health and Social Care Act 2008 (Regulated Activities) Regulations 2014.

40 Karen Van Beek and others, 'Comparison of Legislation, Regulations and National Health Strategies for Palliative Care in Seven European Countries (Results from the Europall Research Group): A Descriptive Study' (2013) 13 BMC Health Serv Res 1–11.

41 Herring (n4).

such as Belgium and the Netherlands, palliative care and assisted dying (including euthanasia) coexist as legal options at the end of life.

There are several ethical issues that arise for the provision of palliative care. These include, but are not limited to, the application of the 'standard' ethical principles such as informed consent, autonomous and patient-centred decision-making, equity, justice, doing good, and doing no harm, among others. Specific to the area of palliative care is the emphasis on alleviation of pain and suffering, as opposed to seeking treatment or a cure for disease (although, of course, the goal of reducing suffering is very much central to all of medicine). In this sense, beneficence and non-maleficence could be seen as central principles.

The concepts of vulnerability and dignity, which we introduced in the previous section, are also highly relevant for palliative care. It could be argued that the vulnerability of persons receiving palliative care may be even higher than of the 'ordinary' patient, due to the physical as well as existential suffering that can occur at the end of life. In the social sense, we could also speak of the institutional vulnerability of people at the end of life insofar as they may not be receiving the adequate level of care dependent on their living situation.

Ideas of 'dignity-conserving care'[42] and 'dignity therapy'[43] have been advocated in recent years. These approaches have to do with ensuring that the patient feels valued and sees their life as meaningful even as it comes to an end, which is often achieved through psychotherapeutic interventions. As we have seen in the previous section, dignity is often invoked in arguments about assisted dying, but it also has a significant place in palliative care debates – especially as research on what patients consider important for a good death has shown that maintaining dignity is highly valued in this context.[44]

One of the basic bioethical principles is justice, which entails having a right to fair treatment in healthcare. This principle is not only applied to individuals, but also entire populations. An agreement signed by the World Health Assembly in 2014 determined that it was an ethical obligation of all countries to ensure palliative care was an integral component of their healthcare systems, and that palliative care should sit alongside active treatments for disease, where appropriate.[45] Later, at the Global Conference on Primary Health Care in 2018, WHO's Astana Declaration also highlighted the need for palliative care to

---

42 Harvey Chochinov, 'Dignity-Conserving Care – a New Model for Palliative Care: Helping the Patient Feel Valued' (2002) 287 JAMA 2253.

43 Marina Martínez and others, '"Dignity Therapy", a Promising Intervention in Palliative Care: A Comprehensive Systematic Literature Review' (2017) 31 Palliat Med 492.

44 Sheila Payne and others, 'Perceptions of a "Good" Death: A Comparative Study of the Views of Hospice Staff and Patients' (1996) 10 Palliat Med 307.

45 WHO (World Health Organization), 'Monitoring the Achievement of the Health-Related Millennium Development Goals' (2014) https://apps.who.int/gb/ebwha/pdf_files/WHA67/A67_19-en.pdf, accessed 13 October 2023.

be included as part of the Universal Health Coverage goals.[46] The worldwide development and delivery of palliative care appears to be an important goal of global health policy – but what is this ethical obligation based on?

Research suggests important benefits come from access to palliative care services. Olyuase and others undertook a systematic review of 42 randomised controlled trials on behalf of the National Institute of Health Research, to consider the benefits of specialised hospital palliative care in contrast to non-specialist palliative care.[47] Focused on cancer patients, the study demonstrates significant improvements in patient satisfaction, self-reported quality-of-life indicators, improvements in symptom control, reduced levels of depression, and a significant increase in patients dying in their chosen place.[48]

Returning to the central goal of palliative care – to relieve pain and suffering at the end of life – it could be argued that its inadequate or unequal provision may well be the major ethical issue for this field or the source of such major issues. Inequity can, however, also be seen as a human rights and legal issue – for example, it has been argued that lack of access to essential pain relief constitutes 'torture' and degrading treatment under the ECHR.[49] The next subsection addresses inequity specifically, highlighting its important legal and ethical dimensions.

Disparities in access to palliative care

Palliative care is in different stages of development throughout the world. The WHO indicates that, out of the approximately 40 million people who need palliative care, only about one eighth get access to it. It is also estimated that two thirds of all people who need palliative care live in low- and middle-income countries.[50] The need for palliative care is expected to continue rising due to the world's ageing population, as well as a rise in the prevalence of non-communicable diseases, especially cancer.[51] Therefore, existing issues may only be exacerbated in the future, as more people will need palliative care but may not be in an equal position to receive it.

Several ethico-legal issues surface in particular for access to opioid medicines, which are used to relieve pain.[52] Countries are encouraged by the WHO to have

---

46 WHO (World Health Organization), 'Astana Declaration' (2018) https://www.who.int/publications/i/item/WHO-HIS-SDS-2018.61, accessed 13 October 2023.

47 Adejoke Oluyase and others, 'Hospital-Based Specialist Palliative Care Compared with Usual Care for Adults with Advanced Illness and their Caregivers: A Systematic Review' (2021) https://www.journalslibrary.nihr.ac.uk/hsdr/hsdr09120#/full-report, accessed 17 December 2023.

48 Ibid.

49 Natasa Mavronicola, *Torture, Inhumanity and Degradation under Article 3 of the ECHR: Absolute Rights and Absolute Wrongs* (Bloomsbury Academic 2021).

50 WHO (n37).

51 S. Etkind and others, 'How Many People Will Need Palliative Care in 2040? Past Trends, Future Projections and Implications for Services' (2017) 15 BMC Med 102.

52 WHO (n46).

opioid painkillers such as morphine, codeine, and fentanyl as part of their lists of essential medicines. High-income countries consume up to 93 per cent of the world's morphine, yet 70 per cent of deaths from cancer occur in low- and middle-income countries. A recent study highlights that at least 80 per cent of people globally do not have access to pain medicines (especially opioids) used in palliative care, predominantly in low- and middle-income countries.[53] This raises serious ethical issues about justice, fairness, and equity. Apart from the lack of availability of palliative and pain medication, cost and patient behaviour are important barriers that need to be looked at if universal health coverage is to be ensured, as these barriers could especially worsen the plight of patients in lower middle-income countries.[54]

An example of addressing this important issue comes from Uganda, which approached the lack of morphine in two main ways: firstly, by importing cheaper morphine powder and reconstituting it to make it affordable and accessible to those who need it; and secondly, by making changes to the legal framework allowing specially trained nurses, and not just doctors, to prescribe morphine.[55]

As with other nations that have made progress in palliative care, Uganda, using the WHO public health palliative model as a guide, has a national policy that directs all palliative care activities. Palliative care is included in the curricula for health training, and this has served as a hub for training palliative care professionals throughout Africa. Therefore, with an increased force of health professionals trained in palliative care, Uganda has been able to incorporate palliative care into its Univeral Health Coverage, with 90 per cent of its district heath facilities having access to palliative care services.[56]

This example clearly shows the contribution that laws and policy can make to realising broad ethical obligations. However, approaches such as the one described in Uganda should go hand in hand with a global commitment to ensuring equality in basic resources such as essential medications. Also, as much as services must be non-discriminatory to ensure equality, some groups of people may

53 Diederik Lohman and others, 'Advancing Global Palliative Care over Two Decades: Health System Integration, Access to Essential Medicines, and Pediatrics' (2022) 64 J Pain Symptom Manage 58.

54 Anne Merriman and Richard Harding, 'Pain Control in the African Context: The Ugandan Introduction of Affordable Morphine to Relieve Suffering at the End of Life' (2010) 5 Philos Ethics Humanit Med 10.

55 In England and Wales, prescribing strong painkillers ('product[s] subject to special medical prescription') is regulated by the Human Medicines Regulations 2012, s 214. This regulation states that such prescription-only medicines can only be prescribed by doctors, dentists, supplementary prescribers, nurse independent prescribers, or pharmacist independent prescribers.

56 Julia Downing and others, 'Cancer and Palliative Care in COVID-19 and Other Challenging Situations – Highlights from the Uganda Cancer Institute – Palliative Care Association of Uganda 3rd Uganda Conference on Cancer and Palliative Care, 23–24 September 2021, Held in Kampala, Uganda and Virtually' (2021) 15 ecancermedicalscience 1333.

need special treatment to satisfy requirements of fairness. For example, some people needing palliative and end-of-life care may be disadvantaged based on their geographic location and socio-economic status, and their access to care services may be less supported by health professionals. This is due to either lack of institutional palliative care facilities or lack of resources to support those requiring management at home.

The evolution of palliative care is far from uniform. This is the case even among resource-rich nations where challenges in provision remain,[57] which is made especially visible in pandemics, with devastating impacts on the most vulnerable members of the population.[58] Although the UK is considered a world leader in the provision of palliative care, the resources and access to palliative care are not equal within the country.[59] A review of studies on this topic from the last few decades suggests that palliative care needs, as well as their availability and perception of their quality, may vary depending on a person's socio-economic position.[60] Regional differences in provision were also noted, such as people living in more deprived areas experiencing longer referral times to hospices and specialist palliative care. This is in line with scholarship on the social determinants of health,[61] showing the growing inequities in access to all healthcare.[62] More targeted research is needed to identify the exact impacts of socio-economic position on access to palliative care. Nevertheless, current findings suggest there are issues with disparity that need to be addressed by practice and policy.

Palliative care matters: addressing disparities

The importance of palliative care as an end-of-life option is well supported by insights from research and practice. The palliative care approach is globally gaining recognition, as evidenced by its inclusion in major policy documents, and is increasingly seen as a basic part of good-quality healthcare or even treated as a right in some jurisdictions. However, there is great variety worldwide in both

---

57 Barbara Reville and Anessa Foxwell, 'The Global State of Palliative Care: Progress and Challenges in Cancer Care' (2014) 3 Ann Palliat Med 129.

58 Meghan de Boer and others, 'The Underrepresentation of Palliative Care in Global Guidelines for Responding to Infectious Disease Outbreaks: A Systematic Narrative Review' (2022) 14 Int Health 453.

59 Kathrin Woitha and others, 'Ranking of Palliative Care Development in the Countries of the European Union' (2016) 52 J Pain Symptom Manage 370.

60 Maddy French and others, 'Exploring Socioeconomic Inequities in Access to Palliative and End-Of-Life Care in the UK: A Narrative Synthesis' (2021) 20 BMC Palliat Care 1.

61 For discussion of the social determinants of health see Chapter 4.

62 Michael Marmot, 'Fair Society, Healthy Lives' (2013) https://www.instituteofhealthequity.org/resources-reports/fair-society-healthy-lives-the-marmot-review/fair-society-healthy-lives-full-report-pdf.pdf, accessed 17 December 2023; Michael Marmot, 'Health Equity in England: The Marmot Review 10 Years On' (2020) 368 BMJ m693.

regulation and provision.[63] The unequal distribution of access to palliative care, both globally and within resource-rich countries such as the UK, raises ethical and human rights issues about equity and fairness. To help achieve *health for all* as per the Universal Health Coverage goals, including for people from lower socio-economic backgrounds, it is pertinent to aim to reduce this disparity through adequate policies.

Summary

- Palliative care typically focuses on symptom relief rather than treatment and is often applied where illness is incurable. Therefore, distinct ethico-legal issues are likely to arise that are not covered by 'mainstream' ethico-legal discussions of death and dying, which tend to centre euthanasia and assisted dying.
- Nevertheless, some ethical issues do overlap (respect for autonomy, vulnerability, balancing between respecting patient wishes and beneficence, etc.) and some notable legal cases in England and Wales also have implications for the palliative context, which is why it is important to consider both areas together.
- Differing regulation of palliative and end-of-life care in different countries, as well as varying levels of palliative care development, lead to uneven access to care. Disparities in provision arise not only globally, but also within particular countries (even wealthy ones like England and Wales), often tracking socio-economic divisions within populations.
- Disparities in the provision of palliative care are likely to become even more prominent as the global population is on average living longer and people are increasingly dying from progressive, chronic conditions such as dementia.
- If there is a moral imperative for the global provision of good-quality palliative care, then there may be a case for treating it as a healthcare-related right, as done by some countries, and adopting adequate legislation and policies to ensure equity of access.

Questions for reflection

- How are options for care near the end of life determined by legislation in England and Wales?
- How is the practice of palliative care experienced by patients, families, and healthcare professionals?
- How can legal and ethical frameworks be adapted to better address the evolving needs and challenges of palliative care in the context of death and dying?
- In what ways can a palliative care perspective influence and inform the development of legal and ethical guidelines surrounding death and dying to ensure compassionate, patient-centred end-of-life care?

63 Felicia Knaul and others, 'Alleviating the Access Abyss in Palliative Care and Pain Relief – an Imperative of Universal Health Coverage: The Lancet Commission Report' (2018) 391 Lancet 1391.

Recommended resources

- Julian Abel, 'Compassionate Communities and End-of-Life Care' (2018) 18 Clin Med 6.
- Frank Brennan, 'Dignity: A Unifying Concept for Palliative Care and Human Rights' (2014) 22 Prog Palliat Care 88.
- Nathan Cherny and others (eds), *Oxford Textbook of Palliative Medicine* (OUP 2021).
- Charles Foster, 'What is Man, that the Judges are Mindful of Him? Lessons from the PVS Cases' (2005) 5 J Philos Sci Law 1.
- Pauline Kouwenhoven and others, 'Developments in Euthanasia Practice in the Netherlands: Balancing Professional Responsibility and the Patient's Autonomy' (2019) 25 Eur J Gen Pract 44.
- Lukas Radbruch and others, 'Redefining Palliative Care: A New Consensus-Based Definition' (2020) 60 J Pain Symptom Manage 754.
- Yakubu Salifu and others, '"My Wife is My Doctor at Home": A Qualitative Study Exploring the Challenges of Home-Based Palliative Care in a Resource-Poor Setting' (2021) 35 Palliat Med 97.
- Libby Sallnow and others, 'Report of the Lancet Commission on the Value of Death: Bringing Death Back into Life' (2022) 399 Lancet 837.
- Henk Ten Have and Jos Welie, 'Palliative Sedation versus Euthanasia: An Ethical Assessment' (2014) 47 J Pain Symptom Manage 123.

Bibliography

Babgi A, 'Legal Issues in End-of-Life Care: Perspectives from Saudi Arabia and United States' (2009) 26 Am J Hospice Palliat Care 119

Beauchamp T and Childress J, *Principles of Biomedical Ethics* (OUP 2001)

Biggs H, 'A Pretty Fine Line: Life, Death, Autonomy and Letting it B' (2003) 11 Fem Leg Stud 29

BMA (British Medical Association), 'Physician-Assisted Dying Survey' (2021) https://www.bma.org.uk/advice-and-support/ethics/end-of-life/physician-assisted-dying/physician-assisted-dying-survey, accessed 13 October 2023

Boldt J, 'The Concept of Vulnerability in Medical Ethics and Philosophy' (2019) 14 Philos Ethics Humanit Med 1

Brazier M, Cave E, and Heywood R, *Medicine, Patients and the Law* (Manchester University Press 2023)

Chochinov H, 'Dignity-Conserving Care – a New Model for Palliative Care: Helping the Patient Feel Valued' (2002) 287 JAMA 2253

CPS (Crown Prosecution Service), 'Suicide: Policy for Prosecutors in Respect of Cases of Encouraging or Assisting Suicide' (2010) https://www.cps.gov.uk/legal-guidance/suicide-policy-prosecutors-respect-cases-encouraging-or-assisting-suicide, accessed 13 October 2023

CPS (Crown Prosecution Service), 'Assisted Suicide' (2023) https://www.cps.gov.uk/publication/assisted-suicide, accessed 13 October 2023

de Boer M and others, 'The Underrepresentation of Palliative Care in Global Guidelines for Responding to Infectious Disease Outbreaks: A Systematic Narrative Review' (2022) 14 Int Health 453

Dige M, 'Assisted Death, Dignity, and Respect for Humanity' (2022) 47 J Med Philos 701

Downing J and others, 'Cancer and Palliative Care in COVID-19 and Other Challenging Situations – Highlights from the Uganda Cancer Institute – Palliative Care Association of Uganda 3rd Uganda Conference on Cancer and Palliative Care, 23–24 September 2021, Held in Kampala, Uganda and Virtually' (2021) 15 ecancermedicalscience 1333

Etkind S and others, 'How Many People Will Need Palliative Care in 2040? Past Trends, Future Projections and Implications for Services' (2017) 15 BMC Med 102

French M and others, 'Exploring Socioeconomic Inequities in Access to Palliative and End-Of-Life Care in the UK: A Narrative Synthesis' (2021) 20 BMC Palliat Care 1

Gamondi C and others, 'Family Caregivers' Reflections on Experiences of Assisted Suicide in Switzerland: A Qualitative Interview Study' (2018) 55 J Pain Symptom Manage 1085

Herring J, *Medical Law and Ethics* (9th edn, OUP 2022)

House of Commons Health and Social Care Committee, 'Assisted Dying/Assisted Suicide: Inquiry' (2023) https://committees.parliament.uk/work/6906/assisted-dyingassisted-suicide/, accessed 13 October 2023

Hurst S and Mauron A, 'The Ethics of Palliative Care and Euthanasia: Exploring Common Values' (2006) 20 Palliat Med 107

Johansen S and others, 'Attitudes towards, and Wishes For, Euthanasia in Advanced Cancer Patients at a Palliative Medicine Unit' (2005) 19 Palliat Med 454

Knaul FM and others 'Alleviating the Access Abyss in Palliative Care and Pain Relief – an Imperative of Universal Health Coverage: The Lancet Commission Report' (2018) 391 Lancet 1391

Kollas C and Boyer-Kollas B, 'Evolving Medicolegal Issues in Palliative Medicine' (2007) 10 J Palliat Med 1395

Lohman D and others, 'Advancing Global Palliative Care over Two Decades: Health System Integration, Access to Essential Medicines, and Pediatrics' (2022) 64 J Pain Symptom Manage 58

Marmot M, 'Fair Society, Healthy Lives' (2013) https://www.instituteofhealthequity.org/resources-reports/fair-society-healthy-lives-the-marmot-review/fair-society-healthy-lives-full-report-pdf.pdf, accessed 17 December 2023

Marmot M, 'Health Equity in England: The Marmot Review 10 Years On' (2020) 368 BMJ m693

Martínez M and others, '"Dignity Therapy", a Promising Intervention in Palliative Care: A Comprehensive Systematic Literature Review' (2017) 31 Palliat Med 492

Mavronicola N, *Torture, Inhumanity and Degradation under Article 3 of the ECHR: Absolute Rights and Absolute Wrongs* (Bloomsbury Academic 2021)

Merriman A, 'Going the Extra Mile with the Bare Essentials: Home Care in Uganda' (2010) 18 Prog Palliat Care 18–22

Merriman A and Harding R, 'Pain Control in the African Context: The Ugandan Introduction of Affordable Morphine to Relieve Suffering at the End of Life' (2010) 5 Philos Ethics Humanit Med 10

Michalowski S and Martin W, 'DNACPR Decisions: Aligning Law, Guidance, and Practice' (2022) 30 Med Law Rev 434

Oluyase A and others, 'Hospital-Based Specialist Palliative Care Compared with Usual Care for Adults with Advanced Illness and their Caregivers: A Systematic Review' (2021) https://www.journalslibrary.nihr.ac.uk/hsdr/hsdr09120#/full-report, accessed 17 December 2023

ONS (Office for National Statistics), 'Suicides in England and Wales: 2020 Registrations (2021) https://www.ons.gov.uk/peoplepopulationandcommunity/birthsdeathsandmarriages/deaths/bulletins/suicidesintheunitedkingdom/2021registrations, accessed 17 December 2023

Ost S, 'The De-medicalisation of Assisted Dying: Is a Less Medicalised Model the Way Forward?' (2010) 18 Med Law Rev 497

Payne SA, Langley-Evans A, and Hillier R, 'Perceptions of a "Good" Death: A Comparative Study of the Views of Hospice Staff and Patients' (1996) 10 Palliat Med 307

Payne SA, and others, 'Revised Recommendations on Standards and Norms for Palliative Care in Europe from the European Association for Palliative Care (EAPC): A Delphi Study' (2022) 36 Palliat Med 680–97

Phelps K and others, 'Withdrawal of Ventilation at the Patient's Request in MND: A Retrospective Exploration of the Ethical and Legal Issues That Have Arisen for Doctors in the UK' (2017) BMJ Support Palliat Care 189

Preston N, Payne S, and Ost S, 'Breaching the Stalemate on Assisted Dying: It's Time to Move beyond a Medicalised Approach' (2023) 382 BMJ 1968

Rachels J, 'Active and Passive Euthanasia' in J Humber and R Almeder (eds), *Biomedical Ethics and the Law* (Springer 1979)

Reville B and Foxwell A, 'The Global State of Palliative Care: Progress and Challenges in Cancer Care' (2014) 3 Ann Palliat Med 129

Van Beek K and others, 'Comparison of Legislation, Regulations and National Health Strategies for Palliative Care in Seven European Countries (Results from the Europall Research Group): A Descriptive Study' (2013) 13 BMC Health Serv Res 1

WHO (World Health Organization), 'Monitoring the Achievement of the Health-Related Millennium Development Goals' (2014) https://apps.who.int/gb/ebwha/pdf_files/WHA67/A67_19-en.pdf, accessed 13 October 2023

WHO (World Health Organization), 'Astana Declaration' (2018) https://www.who.int/publications/i/item/WHO-HIS-SDS-2018.61, accessed 13 October 2023

WHO (World Health Organization), 'Quality Health Services and Palliative Care: Practical Approaches and Resources to Support Policy, Strategy and Practice' (2021) https://www.who.int/publications/i/item/9789240035164, accessed 17 December 2023

Woitha K and others, 'Ranking of Palliative Care Development in the Countries of the European Union' (2016) 52 J Pain Symptom Manage 370

Woollard F and Howard-Snyder F, 'Doing vs. Allowing Harm' in E Zalta and U Nodelman (eds), *The Stanford Encyclopedia of Philosophy* (2022) https://plato.stanford.edu/archives/win2022/entries/doing-allowing/, accessed 13 October 2023

Index

Note: References to figures appear in *italic* type; those in **bold** type refer to tables. References to footnotes show both the page number and the note number (146n66).

T

U

V

W

Y

Printed and bound by CPI Group (UK) Ltd, Croydon, CR0 4YY
15/09/2026
14962389-0001